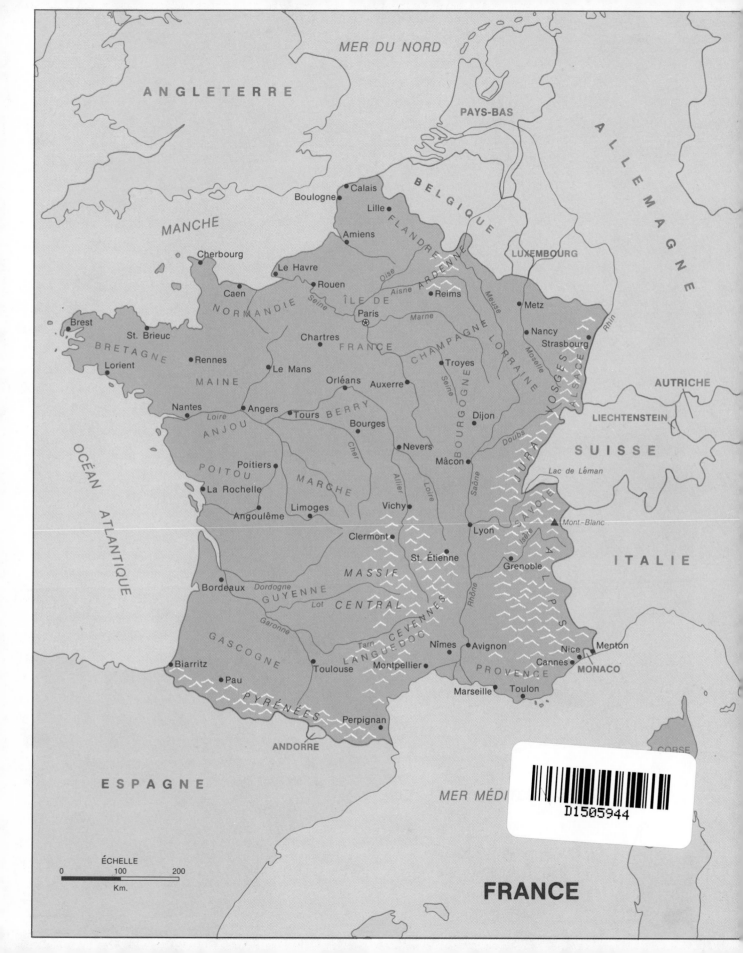

MER DU NORD

ANGLETERRE

PAYS-BAS

ALLEMAGNE

MANCHE

BELGIQUE

LUXEMBOURG

• Calais
Boulogne •
Lille •
Amiens •

FLANDRE

ARDENNE

Metz •

Cherbourg •
Le Havre •
• Rouen
Caen •

Oise

Aisne

Reims •

Nancy •
Strasbourg •

Seine

ÎLE DE

Marne

Meuse

Moselle

VOSGES

ALSACE

Rhin

Brest •
St. Brieuc •

NORMANDIE

Paris ⊛

FRANCE

CHAMPAGNE

LORRAINE

AUTRICHE

Chartres •

BRETAGNE

• Rennes

Troyes •

LIECHTENSTEIN

Lorient •

MAINE

• Le Mans

Orléans •
Auxerre •

Seine

BOURGOGNE

SUISSE

Nantes •

Angers •

Loire

• Tours

BERRY

Bourges •

Dijon •

Doubs

JURA

Lac de Léman

ANJOU

Cher

Nevers •

Mâcon •

Saône

OCÉAN

Poitiers •

POITOU

MARCHE

Allier

Loire

▲ Mont-Blanc

La Rochelle •

SAVOIE

Isère

Limoges •

Vichy •

ATLANTIQUE

Angoulême •

Lyon •

ITALIE

Clermont •

ALPES

St. Étienne •

Grenoble •

Bordeaux •

Dordogne

GUYENNE

MASSIF

Rhône

Lot

CENTRAL

GASCOGNE

Garonne

CÉVENNES

LANGUEDOC

Nîmes •

Avignon •

Nice •

Menton •

Cannes •

MONACO

Biarritz •

Tarn

Toulouse •

Montpellier •

PROVENCE

• Pau

PYRÉNÉES

Perpignan •

Marseille •

Toulon •

ANDORRE

CORSE

ESPAGNE

MER MÉDI

ÉCHELLE

0   100   200

Km.

FRANCE

Thème et Variations
An Introduction to French Language and Culture

Fourth Edition

M. Peter Hagiwara
University of Michigan

Françoise de Rocher
University of Alabama

WILEY

John Wiley & Sons
New York Chichester Brisbane Toronto Singapore

Cover Art: Henri Matisse Composition (les velours)
 (Colorphoto Hans Hinz)
Cover: Designed by Ann Marie Renzi
Interior Illustrations: Hal Barnell
Production Supervisor: Marion Forbes
Photo Editor: Stella Kupferberg
Photo Researcher: Linda Gutierrez

Library of Congress Cataloging in Publication Data:

Hagiwara, Michio P.
  Thème et variations.

  Includes index.
  1. French language—Textbooks for foreign speakers—
English. 2. French language—Grammar—1950—
I. Rocher, Françoise de. II. Title.

PC2129.E5H34 1989   448.2′421   88-27815
ISBN 0-471-63133-7

Printed in the United States of America

10 9 8 7 6 5 4 3 2 1

Preface

Thème et Variations is a beginning-level French program, designed to introduce students to basic French structures and vocabulary as well as contemporary French culture and civilization. It consists of a textbook, including an *Annotated Instructor's Edition*, a student workbook (**Cahier d'exercices**), and a laboratory tape program which comprises recorded tapes and a complete script (*Tape Program for Laboratory Directors*). The tapes are available for purchase or on loan for local duplication. Ancillary materials, new in the fourth edition, are composed of a *Test Bank* for each lesson, transparencies for overhead projectors, and computer-assisted instruction.

The fourth edition of *Thème et Variations* is based on enthusiastic reviews and suggestions from the many users of the third edition, as well as our own classroom experience with it. We have concentrated our revision on improving aspects suggested by the users and reviewers and on making numerous refinements of our own, and have retained the features that contributed to the strength of the earlier editions. Thus the basic format has not been changed: Each lesson revolves around a topic, which is developed and expanded through a wide variety of learning activities, much as a theme is varied in musical compositions. All exercise directions are in French, in order to create an all-French classroom atmosphere. New patterns and vocabulary are practiced in situational contexts, which encourage students to learn the vocabulary and express themselves creatively and spontaneously. The main components have also been retained: **Conversations**, **Structures** (formerly **Explications et Exercices oraux**), **Applications**, *Compréhension auditive*, *Exercices écrits* (including expanded review exercises), and **Exercices de prononciation**.

1. CONVERSATIONS

Mini-dialogues and/or a series of questions about a drawing serve as a point of departure for the main topic or key structures of each lesson. They are designed to be used in warm-up activities for each class meeting; the *Annotated Instructor's Edition* offers comments as well as suggestions for variations and expansion. English equivalents of these mini-dialogues appear in each corresponding lesson of the **Cahier d'exercices**. At the end of **Conversations** is a short section in English entitled *Différences*. Expanded to Lessons 1–20 in the fourth edition, it discusses a fundamental aspect of contemporary French civilization related to the topic of the lesson. Pertinent vocabulary is presented in both English and French, and is frequently employed in the subsequent sections of the same lesson. As students progress, *Différences* is supplemented by reading passages in French, which appear in **Applications**.

2. STRUCTURES

Explanations of structures and oral exercises form a single unit. They are distinguished from each other by use of two different type styles. The explanations are succinct and explicit, provide comparison with English when necessary, and include a definition of all pertinent grammatical terms. There are abundant examples, charts, diagrams, and drawings that promote effective and efficient assimilation of structures. The explanations are in English so that beginning students can read them on their own without falling into the trap of gross oversimplification or incorrect generalization of rules. We continue to provide French grammatical terms so that the instructor may briefly summarize the day's grammar in class using simple French.

The *Annotated Instructor's Edition* provides helpful hints for grammar explanation and exercises, as well as suggestions for the use of related pronunciation exercises. It also suggests possible abridgement or deletion of certain items in the light of active and passive control of structures by students.

Each grammar point is followed by a series of oral exercises, progressing rapidly from simple structural manipulation to open-ended questions that invite students to express their opinions and describe daily activities. In order to encourage greater student participation, the fourth edition contains more exercises that involve two student responses to a single cue or exercises that constitute task-oriented activities. The instructor need not do all the oral exercises in any given lesson. Approximately sixty percent of the oral exercises are included in the tape program, so that students can practice them in the language laboratory or at home with their own recorders. The tape program also includes a few supplementary oral exercises, for which the script is provided in both the **Cahier d'exercices** and the *Annotated Instructor's Edition*.

3. APPLICATIONS

In **Applications**, the grammatical patterns and vocabulary students have already acquired in **Conversations** and **Structures** are grouped together in more natural contexts. In a series of activities, beginning with *Situations*, students now apply what they have learned. There is a wide variety of activities, and the instructor may select those most suited to his or her class and schedule.

The first activity in **Applications** is *Situations*, which in the fourth edition involves three to four students in a series of vignettes, allowing more students to participate and encouraging improvisation. The vocabulary and phrases in these dialogues are selected in order to encourage students to talk about their own environments, activities, and plans: family, home, friends, course work, sports, travel, past experiences, future plans, and so on. Several dialogues incorporate the *niveau-seuil* approach with a description of specific situations in which students learn how to make requests, how to give, accept, or decline invitations, how to apologize, how to express appreciation, feelings, opinions, and so on. Such dialogues are followed by *Projets*, which encourage students to create and reenact similar situations.

The *Expressions utiles* summarize words and phrases pertinent to the theme of the lesson; most have already occurred in **Conversations**, **Structures**, and *Situations*. They are put to immediate use through a series of projects and questions under *Pratique*, and through other activities such as *Mini-compositions*, *Questions*, role-play, personalized questions for short conversations, composition topics, and others. All these activities provide a review and reinforcement of the basic vocabulary and structures of the lesson. From Lesson 8 on, except for Lesson 12 (about the mid-point in the book), there is also *lecture*—reading passages with special exercises for comprehension and vocabulary, focusing on a specific aspect of French culture and tradition introduced by the lesson. English equivalents of the *Situations* and *Expressions utiles* are provided in the corresponding lessons of the **Cahier d'exercices**.

4. VOCABULAIRE

The lesson vocabulary lists lexical items, with English equivalents, occurring in **Conversations**, the oral exercises of **Structures**, and *Situations*—a minimum vocabulary for each lesson. Words and idioms appearing exclusively in **Conversations** and the oral exercises are printed in boldface, for the benefit of accelerated or review courses that may wish to concentrate on mini-dialogues and oral grammar exercises.

5. COMPRÉHENSION AUDITIVE

Each lesson is accompanied by a wide variety of listening comprehension exercises on tape. The answer sheets are in the **Cahier d'exercices**, which also contains answer keys to help students check their performance. The *Annotated Instructor's Edition* has the tapescript and answer keys as well.

6. EXERCICES ÉCRITS

The **Cahier d'exercices** contains writing exercises corresponding to each grammar point of the lesson. Many call for individualized answers and thus prepare students gradually to produce original sentences. Students evaluate their work by checking the answer keys or sample answers at the end of each workbook lesson. In the fourth edition, the amount of written exercises has been increased, with an expanded review exercise (without answer keys) at the end of every three lessons. We continue to give simple word games in *Jeux* (with answer keys), designed to review some of the structures and vocabulary of the lesson.

7. EXERCICES DE PRONONCIATION

These twenty-four mini-lessons focus on the basic pronunciation problems encountered by speakers of American English. Many have been completely rewritten to make them an integral part of **Conversations** and **Structures**. We continue to separate them from the rest of the text because this arrangement not only makes lesson planning more flexible but also facilitates locating and frequently reviewing specific phonological items. All the exercises are available on tape. Brief contrastive explanations of French and English pronunciation are included in the **Cahier d'exercices**, in which the exercises are also duplicated.

Acknowledgements

Since the publication of the first edition in 1977, we have received many comments and suggestions from users throughout the United States and Canada. We appreciate their contribution to the preparation of the fourth edition. For their review of the third edition and suggestions for this edition we are grateful to Jean-Phillippe Aubert, McGill University; Judy Aydt, Southern Illinois University–Carbondale; Eric Hollingsworth Deudon, Radford University; Weber D. Donaldson, Jr., Tulane University; Nicole Fouletier-Smith, University of Nebraska; Joe Evans, Colorado State University; Françoise Giraudet-Lay, University of North Carolina–Greensboro; Julie Herschensohn, University of Washington; Nelle Hutter, Iowa State University; Donald H. Kellander, Duquesne University; Elizabeth Lapeyre, University of Idaho; Venne-Richard Londré, University of Missouri; Daniel Moors, University of Florida; Carol Murphy, University of Florida; Deborah Nelson, Rice University; Robert D. Peckham, University of Tennessee–Martin; J. Eric Swenson, Portland State University; Katalin Volker, Shepherd College; and William Wrage, Ohio University.

We would also like to express our special thanks to Professor Gregory de Rocher of the University of Alabama and Anne Lindell of Eastern Michigan University for their many helpful suggestions and corrections during the preparation of the manuscript for this edition.

m.p.h.
f.de r.

Contents

Thème et Variations
Fourth Edition

LES ÉTUDIANTS

« À bientôt. Bon voyage ! »

« Alors, comment ça va ? »

À Paris.

À Grenoble.

LES FRANÇAIS

Un marchand de poisson et de fruits de mer.

Ce sont des artistes.

Il fait la vendange.

Il récolte des artichauts.

Ils travaillent
dans une usine automobile.

Il vient de trouver une truffe.

Un boulanger.

Un marchand de journaux.

Un couturier et son mannequin.

Ils sont sportifs.

Ils travaillent dans un studio de télévision.

« J'espère que ce tableau
sera un succès ! »

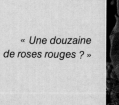

« Je vous donne
des cerises ? »

« Une douzaine
de roses rouges ? »

Un laboratoire
à l'Institut Pasteur.

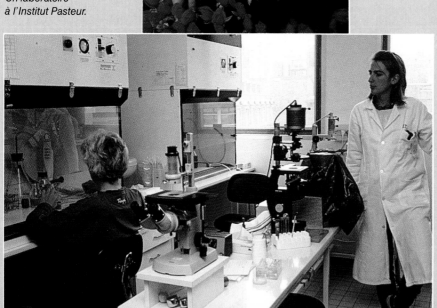

La France est célèbre
pour la haute couture.

Exercices de prononciation[1]

NOTATION PHONÉTIQUE

Voyelles

/a/	**la**	/la/		/ə/	premier	/prəmje/
/ɑ/	**pâte**	/pɑt/		/y/	sur	/syr/
/e/	**clé**	/kle/		/ø/	deux	/dø/
/ɛ/	**père**	/pɛr/		/œ/	jeune	/ʒœn/
/i/	**ici**	/isi/		/ɑ̃/	enfant	/ɑ̃fɑ̃/
/o/	b**eau**	/bo/		/ɛ̃/	vin	/vɛ̃/
/ɔ/	p**o**rte	/pɔrt/		/õ/	bon	/bõ/
/u/	**où**	/u/		/œ̃/(/ɛ̃/)	un	/œ̃/(/ɛ̃/)

Semi-consonnes

/j/	**fille**	/fij/		/ɥ/	suis	/sɥi/
/w/	**ou**i	/wi/				

Consonnes

/b/	**bien**	/bjɛ̃/		/ɲ/	ligne	/liɲ/
/d/	**d**ans	/dɑ̃/		/p/	page	/paʒ/
/f/	font	/fõ/		/r/	rose	/roz/
/g/	**g**auche	/goʃ/		/s/	sont	/sõ/
/ʒ/	joli	/ʒɔli/		/ʃ/	chaise	/ʃɛz/
/k/	café	/kafe/		/t/	tu	/ty/
/l/	livre	/livr/		/v/	vous	/vu/
/m/	**m**adame	/madam/		/z/	zéro	/zero/
/n/	**n**on	/nõ/				

1 ORTHOGRAPHE FRANÇAISE ET PRONONCIATION[2]

/i/	tax**i**, cr**i**t**i**que, d**i**ff**i**c**i**le, **y**, st**y**lo, **Y**ves
/e/ ; /ɛ/	André, clé, et, cahier ; derrière, chaise, être, Seine
/a/	madame, à la carte, table, façade, garage, Canada
/u/	b**ou**tique, dét**ou**r, r**ou**te, t**ou**ché, s**ou**pe, bonj**ou**r, v**ou**s, **où**
/o/ ; /ɔ/	s**au**ce, b**eau**, tabl**eau**, styl**o** ; m**o**de, n**o**te, p**o**rte, al**o**rs, s**o**l
/y/	men**u**, déb**u**t, v**u**e, ét**u**de, **u**ne, m**u**r, s**u**r, b**u**reau, Deb**u**ssy
/ø/ ; /œ/	mili**eu**, p**eu**, bl**eu**, d**eu**x ; chauff**eu**r, prof**e**ss**eu**r, j**eu**ne, s**eu**l
/ɛ̃/	Chop**in**, Gaugu**in**, v**in**, médec**in**, b**ien**, ma**in**tenant, tra**in**, **un**
/ɑ̃/	dét**en**te, nu**an**ce, **en**semble, d**an**s, fr**an**çais, **en**fant
/õ/	cray**on**, b**on**, b**on**jour, Dij**on**, m**on**tre, rép**on**se, garç**on**
/wa/	réserv**oir**, répert**oir**e, cr**oi**ssant, v**oi**là, Ren**oir**, coul**oir**
/k/	bou**qu**et, li**qu**eur, co**qu**ette, **qu**estion, **qu**atre, **qu**and, **qu**i

---

[1]Detailed explanations of French pronunciation are in the **Cahier d'exercices**. Note: Some of the words used for pronunciation practice are selected because they illustrate certain sounds and are not listed in the end vocabulary (*Lexique Français-Anglais*).

[2]Only the basic sound-spelling relationships are presented here. Note that many final consonant letters (except **-r**) and the letter **-e** are silent.

/ɲ/	filet mignon, cognac, vignette, peigne, ligne, agneau
/ʃ/	chauffeur, chef, champagne, attaché, Charlotte, chaise
/j/	Versailles, Marseille, bouillon, famille, jeune fille

2 RYTHME ET ACCENT

a) a→about→aboutir→aboutissons
mode→module→moduler→modulation
fil→philo→philosophe→philosophie
barre→barrique→barricade→barricader
prof→prophète→prophétique→prophétiser
orgue→organe→organique→organiser→organisateur
centre→central→centralise→centraliser→centralisation

b) **Deux syllabes** (˘ –)

photo, auto, musique, visite, touriste, beauté, bonjour, monsieur, parlez, encore, question

Trois syllabes (˘ ˘ –)

monument, animal, téléphone, liberté, écoutez, répétez, après moi, s'il vous plaît, vous parlez

Quatre syllabes (˘ ˘ ˘ –)

académie, démocratique, économie, c'est un cahier, voilà la table, écoutez bien, comment ça va ?

Cinq syllabes (˘ ˘ ˘ ˘ –)

université, possibilité, organisation, répétez la phrase, c'est la salle de classe, où sont les cahiers ?

3 ALPHABET FRANÇAIS

a	/a/	**h**	/aʃ/	**o**	/o/	**v**	/ve/
b	/be/	**i**	/i/	**p**	/pe/	**w**	/dubləve/
c	/se/	**j**	/ʒi/	**q**	/ky/	**x**	/iks/
d	/de/	**k**	/ka/	**r**	/ɛʀ/	**y**	/igʀɛk/
e	/ə/	**l**	/ɛl/	**s**	/ɛs/	**z**	/zɛd/
f	/ɛf/	**m**	/ɛm/	**t**	/te/		
g	/ʒe/	**n**	/ɛn/	**u**	/y/		

é	« e » accent aigu	**ç**	« cé » cédille
è	« e » accent grave	**e**	« e » minuscule
ê	« e » accent circonflexe	**E**	« e » majuscule
ë	« e » tréma	**-**	trait d'union

stylo : **s-t-y-l-o**
journal : **j-o-u-r-n-a-l**
lettre : **l-e**-*deux* **t-r-e**[1]
été : **e** *accent aigu*-**t-e** *accent aigu*

[1]Note that the equivalent of *double* in French is **deux**: **deux t**, **deux l**, etc.

là-bas : **l-a** *accent grave-trait d'union-***b-a-s**
Noël : **n** *majuscule-***o-e** *tréma-***l**
français : **f-r-a-n-c** *cédille-***a-i-s**

Signes de ponctuation

,	virgule	!	point d'exclamation
.	point	?	point d'interrogation
;	point-virgule	...	points de suspension
:	deux points	—	tiret

4 VOYELLES /i/, /e/, /ɛ/

a) /i/ livre, disque, lit, ici, midi, difficile, il finit, il arrive, six livres ; île ; **y**, stylo, Maryse

b) /e/[1] été, clé, télévision ; parler, entrer, penser ; répétez, écoutez, répondez ; maison, aimer, j'ai ; des, les, mes, tes, ces ; et

c) /ɛ/[1] père, mère, frère ; être, fenêtre ; avec, fer, sel, serviette, elle accepte ; chaise, aide, j'aime ; treize, pleine

d) /e-ɛ/[1] ces-seize, et-elle, fée-faire, j'ai-j'aime, né-neige, thé-thème, clé-claire ; élève, sévère, Hélène, les pères, les mères, des frères, ces chaises ; cédez-cède, espérer-espère, répété-répète, préféré-préfère

e) /ɛ-e/[1] fermez, servez, cherchez, perdez, rester, percer, dernier, verger, versé, berger, bercé, Hervé, pester, resté

f) /e-ɛ/ ces-sais, des-dais, fée-fait, thé-tait, les-lait, mes-mais, aller-allais, mangé-mangeaient, parlez-parlait, finissez-finissait, irai-irais, finirai-finirais, vendrai-vendrais

5 VOYELLES /u/, /o/, /ɔ/

a) /u/ **ou**, s**ou**s, n**ou**s, v**ou**s, j**ou**rnal, t**ou**s·les j**ou**rs, n**ou**s tr**ou**vons ; **où** ; g**oû**ter, c**oû**ter

b) /o/[2] métr**o**, styl**o**, m**o**t, n**o**s, v**o**s, r**o**se, ch**o**se, p**o**se, pr**o**se ; rôle, pôle, bientôt ; anim**aux**, chev**aux**, journ**aux** ; **eau**, b**eau**coup, tabl**eau**, chât**eaux**

c) /ɔ/[2] p**o**rte, n**o**te, p**o**ste, h**o**mme, d**o**nne, D**o**rd**o**gne, s**o**l, j**o**li, phil**o**s**o**phe, **o**béir, fr**o**mage ; m**au**vais, **au**t**o**mobile

d) /o-ɔ/[2] b**eau**-b**o**l, s**o**t-s**o**tte, d**o**s-d**o**rt, f**au**t-f**o**lle, m**o**t-m**o**lle, n**o**s-n**o**tre, v**o**s-v**o**tre, t**ô**t-t**o**rt, p**o**t-p**o**ste, n**ô**tre-n**o**tre, v**ô**tre-v**o**tre

e) /ɔ-o/ d**o**d**o**, m**o**t**o**, ph**o**t**o**, c**o**t**eau**, chr**o**n**o**, p**o**mm**eau**, r**o**b**o**t, p**o**t**eau**, t**o**nn**eau**, L**o**t**o**, G**o**d**o**t, M**o**r**eau**

6 VOYELLES /y/, /ø/, /œ/

a) /i-u-y/ **y-où-eu**, si-sous-su, dit-doux-du, fit-fou-fut, gît-joue-jus, lit-loup-lu, mis-mou-mu, ni-nous-nu, pis-pou-pu, ri-roue-rue, t'**y**-tout-tu, vie-vous-vu

---

[1]Basically, /e/ occurs in a syllable that does not end with a consonant sound; /ɛ/ occurs in a syllable that ends in a consonant sound. The only exception is (*f*).

[2]At the end of a word, /o/ occurs when the word does not end in a consonant sound (except /z/) or when the spelling is **ô**; /ɔ/ occurs when the word ends with a consonant sound other than /z/ or when the spelling is not **ô**.

b) /y/   d**u**, **u**ne, s**u**r, m**u**r, min**u**te, ét**u**de, m**u**sique, b**u**reau, f**u**tur, s**u**cre, c**u**lture, de l**u**xe, **u**ne r**u**e, **u**ne min**u**te ; d**û**, s**û**r, m**û**r

c) /e-o-ø/   **et-eau-eux, ces-sot-ceux, des-dos-d'eux, fée-faut-feu, mes-mot-meut, né-nos-nœud, vé-veau-veut**

d) /ø/[1]   d**eu**x, bl**eu**, q**ue**ue, p**eu**, v**eu**t, f**eu**, j**eu**, chev**eu**x, curi**eu**x, danger**eu**x ; cr**eu**ser, vend**eu**se, séri**eu**se

e) /ɛ-ɔ-œ/   **air-or-heure, Berre-bord-beurre, sert-sort-sœur, l'air-lors-leur, sel-sol-seul, mer-mort-meurt, père-port-peur, flaire-flore-fleur**

f) /œ/[1]   **œuf, sœur, cœur** ; b**eu**rre, l**eu**r, fl**eu**r, h**eu**re, s**eu**l, j**eu**ne, profess**eu**r, vend**eu**r, amat**eu**r, ils v**eu**lent, ils p**eu**vent, pl**eu**rer, déj**eu**ner

g) /y-ø-œ/   **su-ceux-sœur, du-deux-d'heure, mur-meut-meurt, pu-peut-peuvent, vu-veut-veulent, plu-pleut-pleure**

h) /u-y-ø/   **ou-eu-eux, bout-bu-beurre, doux-du-deux, fou-fut-feu, joue-jus-jeux, mou-mu-meut, nous-nu-nœud, pou-pu-peu, vous-vu-veux** ; d**ou**zième-d**eu**xième, d**ou**ze heures-d**eu**x heures, d**ou**ze enfants-d**eu**x enfants, d**ou**ze ans-d**eu**x ans[2]

i) /u-ø-œ/   **ou-eux-heure, bout-bœufs-beurre, d'où-deux-d'heure, sous-ceux-seul, pou-peu-peur, voulons-veux-veulent, pouvez-peux-peuvent, mouvoir-meut-meuvent**

7 VOYELLES /a/, /ɑ/

a) /a/   **la, ma, ta, sa, ça, chat, mal, madame, cinéma, patte, garçon, quatre, quart, Canada, ça va mal ; à, là ; femme, solennel**

b) /ɑ/   **pâte, tâche, mâle ; bas, classe, tasse, phrase, gaz**

c) /i-e-ɛ-a/   **y-et-êtes-a, si-ces-cette-sa, mis-mes-mette-ma, fit-fée-fête-femme, qui-quai-quel-car, dit-des-dette-dame, lit-les-laine-là, t'y-tes-tête-ta**

d) /u-o-ɔ-ɑ/   **bout-beau-bol-bas, poule-pôle-Paul-pâle, loup-l'eau-lors-las, tout-tôt-tonne-tâche, mou-mot-molle-mâle**

8 VOYELLES NASALES /ɛ̃/, /ɑ̃/

a) /ɛ-ɛ̃/   **belle-bain, sel-sain, faites-faim, mettent-main, pelle-pain, plaire-plein, frère-frein, grêle-grain**

b) /ɛ̃/   cous**in**, jard**in**, médec**in**, s**im**ple, t**im**bre ; s**yn**dicat, s**ym**pathique ; p**ain**, tr**ain**, f**aim** ; pl**ein**, att**ein**t, R**eim**s ; b**ien**, r**ien**, v**ien**t, comb**ien** ; exam**en**, lycé**en**, europé**en** ; **un**, l**un**di, br**un**, parf**um**, h**um**ble[3]

c) /ɛ̃-ɛn/   **améric**ain**-améric**aine**, s**ain**-s**aine**, v**ain**-v**aine**, m**ain**-m**ène**, mexic**ain**-mexic**aine**, l**in**-l**aine**, r**ein**-r**eine**, tr**ain**-tr**aîne**, pl**ein**-pl**eine**, fr**ein**-fr**eine**, gr**ain**-gr**aine****

d) /jɛ̃-jɛn/   anc**ien**-anc**ienne**, ital**ien**-ital**ienne**, canad**ien**-canad**ienne**, v**ien**t-v**ienne**nt, t**ien**t-t**ienne**nt, dev**ien**t-dev**ienne**nt, maint**ien**t-maint**ienne**nt, m**ien**-m**ienne**, t**ien**-t**ienne**, s**ien**-s**ienne**

---

[1]Basically, /ø/ occurs in syllables that have no pronounced consonant after it (except /z/) ; /œ/ occurs in syllables that have a pronounced consonant other than /z/.

[2]The last four pairs contrast /u-ø/ only.

[3]Both **un** and **um** could be pronounced /œ̃/ (see the explanation in the **Cahier d'exercices**).

e) /ɑ-ɑ̃/[1]　bas-**banc**, las-l'**an**, mât-**ment**, pas-**pan**, pâte-**pente**, tâche-**tant** cas-**quand**, passer-**penser**, attendre-**entendre**, j'apprends/j'**en** prends, on attend/on **entend**, ils attendent/ils **entendent**

f) /ɑ̃/　**dans**, **grand**, **quand**, **Jean**, **blanc**, **champ**, **chambre** ; par**ent**, **entendre**, présid**ent**, t**emps**, **exemple**, **ensemble**, nov**embre**

g) /ɑ̃-an/　**plan**-plane, **an**-Anne, **Jean**-Jeanne, **pan**-panne, **Caen**-Cannes, **ment**-manne, pays**an**-paysanne, artis**an**-artisane, catal**an**-catalane, partis**an**-partisane

h) /ɑ̃-amɑ̃/　élég**ant**-élég**amment**, brill**ant**-brill**amment**, cour**ant**-cour**amment**, puiss**ant**-puiss**amment** ; réc**ent**-réc**emment**, innoc**ent**-innoc**emment**, évid**ent**-évid**emment**, pati**ent**-pati**emment**, prud**ent**-prud**emment**, intellig**ent**-intellig**emment**, viol**ent**-viol**emment**

i) /ɛ̃-ɑ̃/　**bain**-banc, **lin**-lent, **main**-ment, **pain**-pan, **teint**-tant, **vingt**-vent, **rein**-rend, **plein**-plan, **grain**-grand, **éteint**-étang, **faim**-fend, **mainte**-menthe, **atteindre**-attendre

j) /ɑ̃-ɛn/　**cent**-saine, **pan**-peine, **vent**-vaine, **plan**-pleine, **ment**-mène, prend-**prennent**, apprend-**apprennent**, compr**end**-compr**ennent**, entrepr**end**-entrepr**ennent**, surpr**end**-surpr**ennent**

9　VOYELLE NASALE /ɔ̃/

a) /o-ɔ̃/, /ɔ̃/　**eau**-on, beau-**bon**, faut-**font** ; **vont**, **mont**, **non**, **long**, **longue**, **oncle**, **montre**, garç**on**, rép**ond**, fr**onton**, gr**ondons**, m**ontons** ; t**omber**, c**ompter**, c**ombien**, c**omposition**

b) /ɔ̃-ɔn/　**bon**-bonne, **non**-nonne, **son**-sonne, **dont**-donne, pard**on**-pard**onne**, men**tion**-men**tionne**, sta**tion**-sta**tionne**, rais**on**-rais**onne**, aband**on**-aband**onne**

c) /ɛ̃-ɑ̃-ɔ̃/　**saint**-sans-sont, **vain**-vent-vont, **lin**-l'an-long, **pain**-pan-pont, **bain**-banc-b**on**, **rein**-rend-rond, **frein**-franc-front, **mainte**-menthe-monte

d) /ɛ̃-ɑ̃-ɔ̃/[2]　**un** pantalon, **on** invente, **un** long temps, cent cinq ponts, **cinquante** maisons, **un** menton, **un** bon temps, **empruntons**, **invention**, **implantons**, **inconscient**, **inconvénient**, **un** mensonge, **intention**, **convaincant**, **on** prend du v**in** blanc

10　CONSONNE /ʀ/[3]

a) /ʀ/　gris-**rit**, gré-**ré**, grève-**rêve**, gras-**rat**, grouille-**rouille**, gros-**rôt**, grue-**rue**, grince-**rince**, gronde-**ronde** ; **rit**, **ride**, **réponse**, **récent**, **rêve**, **règle**, **rat**, **ravi**, **roue**, **rouge**, **rôt**, **rose**, **robe**, **Rome**, **rue**, **rhume**, **rang**, **rentre**, **rein**, **rince**, **rond**, **ronron**, **repas**, **revenir**

b) /ʀ/　p**r**ix, t**r**i, f**r**it, p**r**é, g**r**é, p**r**ès, c**r**aie, f**r**ais, p**r**oue, t**r**ou, f**r**ouf**r**ou, g**r**os, t**r**op, p**r**of, p**r**op**r**e, g**r**as, g**r**asse, t**r**uc, b**r**ut, f**r**uste, p**r**end**r**e, c**r**aind**r**e, t**r**omperie

c) /ʀ/　ci**re**, li**re**, di**re**, fini**r**, parti**r**, pè**re**, mè**re**, frè**re**, fai**re**, ra**re**, pa**rt**, reta**rd**, ga**re**, qua**rt**, lou**rd**, cou**rs**, sou**rd**, fo**rt**, mo**rt**, so**rt**, to**rt**, po**rt**, su**r**, mu**r**, pu**r**, du**r**, sœu**r**, peu**r**, heu**re**, beu**rre**, pleu**re**

---

[1]**Attendre** and **apprendre** contain /a/ rather than /ɑ/. A slash (/) rather than a hyphen (-) will be used when the items in each contrasting pair consist of two or more words.

[2]Unlike the preceding exercise, all the nasal vowels are mixed.

[3]The consonant /ʀ/ is practiced in five positions: (*a*) word-initial (after a brief practice on /gʀ/ → /ʀ/); (*b*) after a consonant; (*c*) word-final; (*d*) before a consonant; (*e*) word-final vs. before a word-final consonant. These exercises also review many vowels.

d) /R/ firme, myrte, cirque, ferme, Berne, servent, cherche, parle, arme, larme, carte, arbre, parc, courbe, lourde, courte, sourde, porte, forte, morte, sortent, dorment, mordent, corde

e) /R/ char-Charles, port-porte, part-partent, pars-parle, sort-sortent, car-carte, sert-servent, dort-dorment, mer-merle, père-perle, fer-ferme, perds-perdre

11 SEMI-CONSONNES /j/, /w/, /ɥ/

a) /i-j/ **y**-hier, si-c**i**el, dit-d**i**eu, fie-f**i**ère, lit-l**i**er, mie-m**i**eux, nie-n**i**er, pie-p**i**ège, rit-r**i**en, tire-t**i**ers, vit-v**i**eux

b) /j/ lieu, premier, dernier, janvier ; payer, essayer, employer, voyage, voyons ; travail, soleil, sommeil, pareil ; billet, travailler, famille, corbeille, fille, fouille, nouille

c) /u-w/ **ou**-oui, dou**x**-doué, fou-fouet, loup-louer, nous-nouer, sous-souhait, chou-chouette, mou-mouette, avoue-avouer

d) /w/ Louis, Louise, ouest, Rouen ; mois, oiseau, toi, voix, soir, loi, emploi, boîte ; voyage, doyen, moyen, Royan ; moins, coin, loin, soin, besoin

e) /wa-wɛ̃/ oie-oint, coi-coin, loi-loin, foi-foin, joie-joint, moi-moins, poix-point, soi-soin

f) /y-ɥ/ bu-buée, du-duel, fut-fuite, lu-lueur, mu-muet, nu-nuage, pu-puer, rue-ruine, sue-sueur, tu-tuer, continue-continuez

g) /ɥ/ huit, lui, cuit, cuire, cuisine, cuillère, suite, ensuite, nuit, minuit, aujourd'hui, je suis, huile, tuile, ruine, ennui, puis, depuis, fuir, conduit, produire, traduisons, nuage, nuée, nuance

h) /w-ɥ/ oui-huit, bouée-buée, souhait-suer, fouir-fuir, Louis-lui, nouer-nuée, mouette-muette, roué-rué, joint-juin

i) /y-ø-jø/ eu-eux-yeux, du-deux-dieu, mu-meut-mieux, pu-peu-pieux, vu-veux-vieux, su-ceux-cieux

12 CONSONNE /l/[1]

a) /l/ lit, les, l'air, la, loup, l'eau, lors, las, lu, leur, lampe, linge, longe

b) /l/ il, mil, elle, sel, mal, bal, poule, moule, pôle, saule, Paul, col, pâle, pull, nul, seul, l'animal, l'école, l'échelle

c) /l/ table, capable, probable, possible, lisible, meuble, oncle, socle, simple, temple, ongle, angle

d) /l/ film, filtre, calme, palme, halte, salve, calque, palpe, les Alpes, Malte, soldat, le golfe, Adolphe, résulter, insulter

e) /al-o/ journal-journaux, animal-animaux, général-généraux, cheval-chevaux, hôpital-hôpitaux, métal-métaux ; oral-oraux, rural-ruraux, national-nationaux, régional-régionaux, capital-capitaux, principal-principaux

---

[1]The clear release of /l/ is practiced in four positions: (*a*) word-initial; (*b*) word-final; (*c*) word-final after a consonant; (*d*) before a consonant.

13 LIAISONS OBLIGATOIRES

a) après **être**[1]
je suis étudiant, je suis étudiante, tu es américain, tu es américaine, il est américain, elle est à côté de Jean, nous sommes en classe, ils sont à la maison, elles sont à la maison

b) pronom sujet + verbe
j'arrive/vous arrivez, j'écoute/vous écoutez, j'aime/vous aimez, j'ai/nous avons, j'essaie/nous essayons, il étudie/ils étudient, elle entre/elles entrent, il obéit/ils obéissent, elle attend/elles attendent

c) déterminant + nom
un étudiant/des étudiants, un avion/des avions, une enveloppe/des enveloppes, l'arbre/les arbres, l'idée/les idées, à l'agent/aux agents, mon oncle/mes oncles, ton examen/tes examens, son ami/ses amis, notre étude/nos études, votre école/vos écoles, leur étudiant/leurs étudiants

d) nombre + nom
un enfant, deux enfants, trois enfants, dix élèves, vingt élèves, vingt-trois armoires, quarante-deux arbres ; premier étage, premier arrêt, dernier étage, dernier enfant[2]

e) verbe + pronom sujet
il est/est-il ?, elles sont/sont-elles ?, ils ont/ont-ils ?, il finit/finit-il ?, elle fait/fait-elle ?, ils obéissent/obéissent-ils ?, elle attend/attend-elle ?, elles vendent/vendent-elles ?, il a/a-t-il ?, elle va/va-t-elle ?, il arrive/arrive-t-il ?, elle mange/mange-t-elle ?

f) adjectif + nom
le petit enfant/les petits enfants, l'autre élève/les autres élèves, le grand hôtel/les grands hôtels, la grande armoire/les grandes armoires, le vieil arbre/les vieux arbres, le bel oiseau/les beaux oiseaux

g) pronom objet + verbe
je l'ai/je les ai, tu l'attends/tu les attends, il nous écoute, elle vous entend, elles l'aiment/elles les aiment ; j'en ai/je n'en ai pas, ils en ont/ils n'en ont pas ; j'y suis/vous y êtes, j'y arrive/nous y arrivons

h) après **dans/sous/en**[3]
dans un cours, dans une classe, dans un jardin ; sous un arbre, sous une table, sous un cahier ; en avion, en été, en hiver, en automne

i) après **très/bien/plus**[4]
très important, très intelligent, très utile ; bien entendu, bien exprimé, bien aimé ; plus ennuyeux, plus intéressant, plus agréable

14 LIAISONS INTERDITES ET LIAISONS FACULTATIVES

a) après le nom singulier[5]
l'avocat est là/l'avocate est là, l'étudiant américain/l'étudiante américaine, le client impatient/la cliente impatiente, le président impulsif/la présidente impulsive, l'Américain énergique/l'Américaine énergique, Jean est ici/Jeanne est ici, Raymond est là/Raymonde est là, Robert arrive/Roberte arrive

[1]Liaison is optional after **vous êtes**: **vous êtes // étudiante** or **vous êtes étudiante**.

[2]The last four phrases practice the liaison of **premier** and **dernier** (in liaison, they are pronounced like their feminine form: **première**, **dernière**).

[3]And after other monosyllabic prepositions (such as **sans**)

[4]And after other monosyllabic adverbs (such as **moins**)

[5]In the first expression of each pair, there is *liaison interdite* after the subject noun, whereas in the second, there is a linking (**enchaînement**) of the *pronounced* consonant with the following vowel.

b) après **et**   Jean est un bon élève/Jean et un bon élève, Michel est ingénieur/Michel et un ingénieur, Pierre est un enfant/Pierre et un enfant, Jacques et Anne, lui et elle

c) devant le **h aspiré**[1]   les ordres/les hors-d'œuvre, les autres échelles/les hautes échelles, les huîtres/les huit enfants, les zéros/les héros, il est en eau/il est en haut, les ondes/les onze, les ondulations/les onze nations

d) après **quand**/**comment**[2]   Quand arrive-t-il ?/Quand est-ce qu'il arrive ?/Je ne sors pas quand il pleut ; Quand arrive le train ?/Quand est-ce que le train arrive ?/Je reste à la maison quand elle vient ; Comment allons-nous à Paris ?/Comment allez-vous ?/ Comment aller chez lui ?

15 SYLLABATION ET ENCHAÎNEMENT CONSONANTIQUE

Lisez chaque phrase lentement, ensuite rapidement.[3]

1. Que—lle heu—re es—t-il ?
   I—l est di—x heu—res et demie.
2. Que—l â—ge a—vez-vous ?
   J'ai ving—t et u—n ans.
3. Que—l â—ge a Ma—rianne ?
   Ma—rianne a sei—ze ans.
4. Mi—chè—le es—t en retard ?
   Non, e—lle a—rri—vé à l'heure.
5. Vo—tre on—cle es—t e—n I—ta—lie ?
   Oui, i—l ha—bi—te à Rome.
6. Qu'est-ce que vous fai—tes au—jour—d'hui ?
   Nou—s é—tu—dions jus—qu'à troi—s heures.
7. Quan—d est-ce que tu vas chez to—n a—mie ?
   Je vais che—z e-lle e—n a—vril.
8. Est-ce que vou—s ê—tes é—tu—diants ?
9. Ro—be—rt es—t-i—l en—co—re en classe ?
10. Se—s en—fants sont dan—s u—ne é—cole ma—ter—nelle.
11. Nou—s a—llons co—mman—der un repas dan—s un res—tau—rant.
12. Vo—tre a—mie es—pa—gnole vou—s a—ttend che—z elle.
13. Vou—s a—llez vi—si—ter Qué—be—c et Mont—ré—a—l e—n au—tomne.
14. Pie—rre et Thé—rèse von—t é—tu—dier au—x É—ta—ts-U—nis.

16 INTONATION DESCENDANTE[4]

a) imperatives   Parlez. ↘ Parlez français. ↘
Écoutez. ↘ Écoutez la phrase. ↘
Lisez. ↘ Lisez cette phrase. ↘
Un moment. ↘ Un moment ↗ s'il vous plaît. ↘
Répondez. ↘ Répondez ↗ à la question. ↘
Déjeunons. ↘ Déjeunons ↗ à midi et demi. ↘

---

[1]And before the word **onze** (last two pairs)

[2]Exceptions, as shown here are: **Quand est-ce que**, **Comment allez-vous** (referring to health), and **quand** used as a conjunction.

[3]Ties ‿ indicate both liaison and linking, and dashes show the syllabic division of words in spoken French.

[4]In Lessons 16–18, the arrows indicate general intonation patterns (↗ rising; ↘ falling).

b) interrogatives   Où est le cahier ? ↘ Où est le cahier ↗ de Jean-Paul ? ↘
Comment allez-vous ? ↘ Comment allez-vous ↗ aujourd'hui ? ↘
Quelle est la date ? ↘ Quelle est la date ↗ de son anniversaire ? ↘
Qui parle ? ↘ Qui parle français ? ↘ Qui parle français ↗ avec vous ? ↘
Que voulez-vous ? ↘ Que voulez-vous faire ↗ demain soir ? ↘

c) exclamatives   Quel professeur ! ↘ Quelle question ! ↘ Quel beau temps ! ↘ Quel beau tableau ! ↘ Comme il fait beau ! ↘ Comme vous êtes gentils ! ↘ Comme il travaille ! ↘ Quelle belle chambre ↗ vous avez ! ↘ Comme la sœur d'Yves ↗ est intelligente ! ↘

17   INTONATION MONTANTE

1. Vous arrivez ? ↗ Vous arrivez ↗ à neuf heures ? ↗
2. Vous travaillez ? ↗ Vous travaillez ↗ à deux heures ? ↗ Vous travaillez ↗ à deux heures ↗ avec vos amis ? ↗
3. Voulez-vous ? ↗ Voulez-vous ↗ aller au cinéma ? ↗ Voulez-vous ↗ aller au cinéma ↗ avec nous ? ↗
4. Tu comprends ? ↗ Tu comprends ↗ la question ? ↗ Tu comprends ↗ la question ↗ de ce monsieur ? ↗
5. Jean-Pierre ? ↗ Jean-Pierre ↗ parle-t-il français ? ↗ Jean-Pierre ↗ parle-t-il français ↗ tous les jours ? ↗ Jean-Pierre ↗ parle-t-il français ↗ tous les jours ↗ avec vous ? ↗
6. Voyage-t-elle ? ↗ Voyage-t-elle ↗ avec ses parents ? ↗ Voyage-t-elle ↗ avec ses parents ↗ en Allemagne ? ↗
7. Sort-il souvent ? ↗ Sort-il souvent ↗ avec ses copains ? ↗ Sort-il souvent ↗ avec ses copains ↗ le samedi soir ? ↗
8. Allons-nous manger ? ↗ Allons-nous manger ↗ quelque chose ? ↗ Allons-nous manger ↗ quelque chose ↗ dans ce café ? ↗ Allons-nous manger ↗ quelque chose ↗ dans ce café ↗ avant notre départ ? ↗

18   INTONATION MONTANTE-DESCENDANTE ET GROUPES RYTHMIQUES

1. Il arrive. ↘ Il arrive ↗ de Marseille. ↘ Il arrive ↗ de Marseille ↗ à trois heures. ↘
2. Mes parents. ↘ Mes parents ↗ voyagent ensemble. ↘ Mes parents ↗ voyagent ensemble ↗ en Espagne. ↘
3. Je ne sais pas. ↘ Je ne sais pas ↗ s'il pleut. ↘ Je ne sais pas ↗ s'il pleut souvent. ↘ Je ne sais pas ↗ s'il pleut souvent ↗ à Paris. ↘ Je ne sais pas ↗ s'il pleut souvent ↗ à Paris ↗ en hiver. ↘
4. Nous parlons. ↘ Nous parlons ↗ français. ↘ Nous parlons français ↗ tous les jours. ↘ Nous parlons français ↗ tous les jours ↗ dans ce cours. ↘
5. C'est lui. ↘ C'est lui ↗ qui m'a téléphoné. ↘ C'est lui ↗ qui m'a téléphoné ↗ hier soir. ↘ C'est lui ↗ qui m'a téléphoné ↗ hier soir ↗ vers dix heures. ↘
6. C'est moi. ↘ C'est moi ↗ qui l'ai trouvé. ↘ C'est moi ↗ qui l'ai trouvé ↗ dans la salle à manger. ↘ C'est moi ↗ qui l'ai trouvé ↗ dans la salle à manger ↗ de la maison. ↘
7. C'est un hôtel. ↘ C'est un hôtel ↗ qui est vieux. ↘ C'est un hôtel ↗ qui est vieux ↗ mais qui est confortable. ↘
8. Voilà le livre. ↘ Voilà le livre ↗ que j'ai acheté. ↘ Voilà le livre ↗ que j'ai acheté ↗ à la librairie. ↘ Voilà le livre ↗ que j'ai acheté ↗ à la librairie ↗ près de la gare. ↘

19   VOYELLE /ə/[1]

a) premi**e**r, pr**e**nez, cr**e**vaison, s**e**cret, gr**e**din, d**e**gré, pauvr**e**té, Gr**e**noble, at**e**lier, Montp**e**llier, nous app**e**lions ; c**e** soir, c**e**ci, j**e** joue

[1]The letter **e** represents the **e caduc** that is not pronounced.

b) samédi, médécin, proménadé, envéloppé, céla, mainténant, lentément, rapidément, améner, dévéloppément, la sémainé ; Où est lé médécin ?, Voilà lé cahier, C'est lé stylo dé Marié, Il est dans lé cahier, Jé n'ai pas dé sœurs, Jé n'achèté pas dé pommés, Je né comprends pas céla

c) léçon-laissons, lé cahier/les cahiers, cé livre/ces livres, jé lèvé/j'élèvé, jé fais/j'ai fait, jé finis/j'ai fini, jé choisis/j'ai choisi, jé dis/j'ai dit, jé mangeais/j'ai mangé, jé dansais/j'ai dansé

d) je jetté/nous jétons/vous jétez, jé mèné/nous ménons/vous ménez, j'apellé/vous appélez, je lèvé/vous lévez, je rappellé/vous rappélez, j'amèné/vous aménez, j'achèté/vous achétez ; tu enlèvés/tu enlévais, tu achèvés/tu achévais, ellé jetté/ellé jétait ; j'emmèné/vous emménez/vous emmènérez, j'épellé/vous épélez/vous épellérez, j'achèté/vous achétez/vous achètérez, je préféré/vous préférez/vous préférérez, je répété/vous répétez/vous répétérez

e)[1] le poste/la poste/les postes, le livre/la livre/les livres, le page/la page/les pages, le mode/la mode/les modes, le tour/la tour/les tours, le somme/la somme/les sommes ; j'avais/je vais, j'apprends/je prends, j'amène/je mène, j'avoue/je voue, j'apporte/je porte

20   CONSONNE NASALE /ɲ/

a) /ɲ/   li**gn**e, si**gn**e, pei**gn**e, sai**gn**e, campa**gn**e, champa**gn**e, Espa**gn**e, Allema**gn**e, monta**gn**e, espa**gn**ol, Polo**gn**e, sei**gn**eur, ensei**gn**er, soi**gn**é, ma**gn**ifique, si**gn**al, a**gn**eau

b) /n-ɲ/   pei**n**e-pei**gn**e, a**nn**eau-a**gn**eau, rei**n**e-rè**gn**e, dî**n**e-di**gn**e, plai**n**e-plai**gn**e, peinait-pei**gn**ait, en scè**n**e-ensei**gn**e

c) /ɛ̃-ɲ/   ba**in**-bai**gn**e, sa**in**-sai**gn**e, re**in**-rè**gn**e, cra**int**-crai**gn**ent, pla**int**-plai**gn**ent, pe**int**-pei**gn**ent, att**eint**-attei**gn**ent, f**eint**-fei**gn**ent, j**oint**-joi**gn**ent

21   CONSONNES /s/, /z/, /ʃ/, /ʒ/

a) /s/   **s**i, **s**es, **s**ait, **s**a, **s**ourd, **s**ot, **s**ort, **s**ur, mon**s**ieur ; de**ss**in, lai**ss**er, pa**ss**er, choisi**ss**ez, re**ss**embler ; **sc**ience, **sc**ène, niè**c**e, piè**c**e, commen**c**er ; **ç**a, fran**ç**ais, re**ç**u, gar**ç**on, commen**ç**ons ; e**x**pliquer, e**x**primer, e**x**press ; nata**t**ion, pa**t**ience

b) /z/   zig**z**ag, **z**éro, a**z**ur ; mu**s**ique, cho**s**e, voi**s**in, mai**s**on, sai**s**on, choi**s**issent ; e**x**ercice, e**x**amen, e**x**emple, e**x**act, e**x**écutif

c) /s-z/   poi**ss**on-poi**s**on, ce**ss**e-sei**z**e, ru**ss**e-ru**s**e, dou**c**e-dou**z**e, bai**ss**er-bai**s**er, ba**ss**e-ba**s**e, les Cau**ss**es/les cau**s**es, ils **s**ont/ils‿ont, vous **s**avez/vous‿avez, nous **s**avons/nous‿avons, ils **s**'aiment/ils‿aiment

d) /sj-zj/   situa**t**ion, addi**t**ion, pen**s**ion, condi**t**ion, na**t**ion, na**t**ional, sensa**t**ion, sensa**t**ionnel, pa**t**ience, con**sc**ience ; occa**s**ion, divi**s**ion, télévi**s**ion, éli**s**ion, vi**s**ion, préci**s**ion, infu**s**ion, confu**s**ion, déci**s**ion

e) /s-ʃ/   ses-**ch**ez, seize-**ch**aise, sa-**ch**at, sous-**ch**ou, sien-**ch**ien, cent-**ch**ant, casse-**c**ache, russe-ru**ch**e, France-fran**ch**e, casser-ca**ch**er, masser-mâ**ch**er, penser-pen**ch**er, sauce-**ch**ausse

---

[1]The nouns listed here have two genders with different meanings: **le poste** *the post/position/***la poste** *the post office;* **le livre** *the book/***la livre** *the pound* (weight), etc.

f) /ʒ/   j'ai, **j**ambe, **j**our, **j**amais, **j**oli, **j**upe, dé**j**à, **J**ean ; nei**g**e, gara**g**e, **j**u**g**e, rou**g**e, collè**g**e, baga**g**e, a**g**ir, ma**g**ie, â**g**é ; **G**eor**g**es, man**g**eons, Peu**g**eot, plon**g**eons, corri**g**eons, son**g**eais, corri**g**eait

22 CONSONNES /p/, /t/, /k/ et /b/, /d/, /g/

a) /p-t-k/   **p**ire, **p**ère, **p**art, **p**our, **p**ôle, **p**orte, **p**u, **p**eu, **p**eur, **p**ain, **p**an, **p**ont ; **t**ire, **t**aire, **t**ard, **t**out, **t**ôt, **t**ort, **t**u, **t**hé, **t**héâtre, **t**hème, **t**héorie ; **qu**i, **qu**ai, **qu**el, **c**ar, **c**ourt, **c**orps, **qu**eue, **c**œur, **k**ilo, **k**iosque, **ch**rétien, **ch**romatique

b) /p-t-k/   ty**p**e, tuli**p**e, crê**p**e, Die**pp**e, na**pp**e, fra**pp**e, grou**p**e, sou**p**e, envelo**pp**e, ju**p**e, occu**p**e ; vi**t**e, me**tt**ent, pa**tt**e, dou**t**e, bo**tt**e, chu**t**e, pein**t**e ; typi**qu**e, publi**c**, chè**qu**e, blo**c**, tru**c**, cin**q**, ban**qu**e

c) /b-d-g/   **b**illet, **b**é**b**é, **B**erne, **b**at, **b**out, **b**ol, **b**as, **b**u, **b**œuf, **b**eurre, **b**ain, **b**anc, **b**on ; **d**it, **d**es, **d**ette, **d**ate, **d**oute, **d**onne, **d**u, **d**'eux, **d**'heure, **d**'un, **d**ans, **d**ont ; **G**uy, **g**ai, **g**uerre, **g**are, **g**oût, **g**orge, **g**az, **g**ueule, **g**ain, **g**ant, **g**onfle

d) /b-d-g/   ton-tom**b**e, bon-bom**b**e, bas-bar**b**e, vers-ver**b**e, cou-cour**b**e ; vend-ven**d**ent, attend-atten**d**ent, entend-enten**d**ent, répond-répon**d**ent, second-secon**d**e, profond-profon**d**e, blond-blon**d**e, mont-mon**d**e, gare-gar**d**e, regard-regar**d**e, perd-per**d**ent, lourd-lour**d**e, sourd-sour**d**e ; bas-ba**gu**e, long-lon**gu**e, or-or**gu**e, lent-lan**gu**e

23 CONSONNES /m/, /f/, /v/

a) /m/   main-mê**m**e, sain-sè**m**e, thym-thè**m**e, point-poè**m**e, flanc-fla**mm**e, grand-gra**mm**e, fend-fe**mm**e, on-ho**mm**e, nom-no**mm**e, pont-po**mm**e, son-so**mm**e, dont-dô**m**e, bon-bau**m**e

b) /f-v/   neuf-neu**v**e, sauf-sau**v**e, juif-jui**v**e, actif-acti**v**e, affirmatif-affirmati**v**e, négatif-négati**v**e, auditif-auditi**v**e, passif-passi**v**e, relatif-relati**v**e, sportif-sporti**v**e, locatif-locati**v**e

c) /v/   écrit-écri**v**ent, décrit-décri**v**ent, suit-sui**v**ent, vit-vi**v**ent, boit-boi**v**ent, doit-doi**v**ent, reçoit-reçoi**v**ent, déçoit-déçoi**v**ent, peut-peu**v**ent, gré-grè**v**e, gras-gra**v**e, très-trê**v**e

24 EXERCICES SUPPLÉMENTAIRES

a)[1]   à la mode, ambiance, au contraire, ballet, bon voyage, bouillon, bourgeois, carte blanche, cherchez la femme, coup d'état, critique, croissant, début, débutante, ensemble, entrée, esprit de corps, hors-d'œuvre, lingerie, liqueur, matinée, menu, milieu, nuance, première, rapport, réservoir, de rigueur, soupe du jour, suite

b)[2]   Alain, Albert, André, Antoine, Charles, Daniel, Denis, Étienne, François, Frédéric, Georges, Gérard, Guy, Henri, Jacques, Jean, Jules, Julien, Laurent, Louis, Marc, Marcel, Michel, Paul, Philippe, Pierre, René, Yves, Jean-Pierre, Jean-Jacques, Jean-Claude, Pierre-Yves

Andrée, Anne, Brigitte, Caroline, Catherine, Cécile, Chantal, Christine, Claire, Danielle, Denise, Françoise, Frédérique, Gilberte, Gisèle, Hélène, Isabelle, Jacqueline, Janine, Jeanne, Laurence, Marcelle, Margot, Marie, Martine, Michèle, Mireille, Monique, Nicole, Renée, Sylvie, Yvette, Anne-Marie, Marie-Catherine, Marie-Claire

---

[1]These are French expressions used in English. Compare the French and typical American pronunciation.

[2]These are typical male and female names. Pronounce the vowels as accurately as you can.

c)[1] André Ampère, Brigitte Bardot, Simone de Beauvoir, Georges Bizet, Albert Camus, Paul Cézanne, Maurice Chevalier, Frédéric Chopin, Pierre et Marie Curie, Claude Debussy, Alain Delon, Gustave Flaubert, Paul Gauguin, Charles Gounod, Victor Hugo, Édouard Manet, Marcel Marceau, Paul Matisse, François Mitterrand, Yves Montand, Louis Pasteur, Maurice Ravel, Jean-Paul Sartre, François Truffaut

d)[2] Bâton Rouge, Bellefontaine, Belle Fourche, Bellevue, Boisé, Butte, Cœur d'Alène, Crève-Cœur, Des Moines, Des Plaines, Détroit, Du Bois, Dubuque, Eau Claire, Fond du Lac, Grosse Pointe, Lac qui Parle, La Grange, Montclair, Paris, Pierre, Pontchartrain, Racine, Saint-Cloud, Saint-Louis, Terre Ḥaute, Versailles

---

[1] These are well-known names in France. How many can you identify?

[2] These are names of American cities. Do you know in what states they are? Compare the French and typical American pronunciation.

1 Bonjour !

LESSON OBJECTIVES

Theme and Culture

1. Greeting and leave-taking
2. Classroom objects and classmates

Communication Skills

1. Polite and informal expressions of greeting and leave-taking
2. Identifying an object or a person (*What is this?*; *Who is this?*; *It's...*)
3. Changing statements into questions (*This is a cassette*; *Is this a cassette?*)
4. Making statements using the indefinite and definite articles (*a book*, *the book*)
5. Expressing location of an object or a person with regard to another object or person (*Where is the book?*; *It's on the table*; *Where is Marie?*; *She's behind Paul*)
6. Following routine classroom directions

Structures

1.1 The noun and the indefinite article
1.2 Questions using **Est-ce que**; negations using **ne ... pas**
1.3 The definite article
1.4 Locative prepositions
1.5 Use of **il**, **elle**, **ils**, **elles**
1.6 Personal subject pronouns and **être**

CONVERSATIONS[1]

TABLEAU 1

BIENVENUE !
WELCOME !
HERZLICH WILLKOMMEN !
BENVENUTO !

BIENVENUE EN FRANCE

A. Bonjour !

MONIQUE	Bonjour, Monsieur (Madame, Mademoiselle).
PROFESSEUR	Bonjour, Mademoiselle. Comment allez-vous ?
MONIQUE	Très bien, merci. Et vous ?
PROFESSEUR	Bien, merci.

B. Au revoir !

MONIQUE	Excusez-moi, je suis en retard.
PROFESSEUR	Au revoir, Mademoiselle.
MONIQUE	À demain, Monsieur.

TABLEAU 2

[1]Conversations A and B represent formal speech, while C and D are more typical of informal speech among friends. All the mini-dialogues in **Conversations** are recorded on tape (but not the questions concerning a picture, for example A of Lesson 3), and their English equivalents are in the **Cahier d'exercices** (in Part Three, **Clés**, of each lesson). Note: indicates that the given material is recorded on tape.

📼 C. Salut !

JEAN	Salut, Philippe.
PHILIPPE	Tiens, salut, Jean. Ça va ?
JEAN	Oui, ça va. Et toi ?
PHILIPPE	Comme ci comme ça.

📼 D. À tout à l'heure !

BERNARD	Excuse-moi, je suis en retard.
MARTINE	À tout à l'heure, Bernard.
BERNARD	Oui, à tout à l'heure.

« Au revoir ; à demain. »

DIFFÉRENCES[1]

Les salutations

French people shake hands much more often than North Americans do. A brief but fairly firm handshake accompanies every **Bonjour** (*Hello*) and **Au revoir** (*Good-bye*) to friends and colleagues alike, whether they are meeting for the first time or the five hundredth. With relatives and close friends it is customary to kiss each other lightly on both cheeks. This occurs most commonly between female friends and among members of the opposite sex. Men usually do not embrace other males except during certain official ceremonies.

[1]The section *Différences* will give you a glimpse of contemporary French culture and civilization.

The words **Monsieur** /məsjø/, **Mademoiselle** /madmwazɛl/, and **Madame** /madam/ are used in French as a sign of politeness. Their meaning is similar to English *sir*, *Miss*, and *ma'am*. Although the use of these terms is optional in English, the French terms are often obligatory in formal speech. As titles, they are abbreviated in writing as **M.**, **Mlle**, and **Mme** (for example, **M. Moreau**, **Mlle Lacombe**, **Mme Georget**), and correspond to English *Mr.*, *Miss*, and *Mrs.* (French has no equivalent for English *Ms.*). Family names are usually omitted in greeting people after **Monsieur**, **Mademoiselle**, and **Madame**: you say **Bonjour, Madame**, and **Au revoir, Monsieur** rather than **Bonjour, Madame Georget**, **Au revoir, Monsieur Moreau**.

Comment allez-vous ? is a polite way of saying *How are you?*, while **(Comment) Ça va ?** is more informal. **Bonjour** *Hello* can be either formal or informal, but **Salut** *Hi* is always informal. The distinction between the formal and informal levels of speech is very important, and you will learn to make it as you progress further in your study of French.

STRUCTURES

1.1 NOM (SINGULIER ET PLURIEL) ; ARTICLE INDÉFINI UN, UNE, DES

1. Nouns are words that designate persons, animals, things, places, or ideas. All French nouns have a gender (**genre**): either masculine (**masculin**) or feminine (**féminin**). The gender of each noun must be learned thoroughly.[1] The indefinite article, corresponding to English *a* or *an*, is **un** /ɛ̃/ (or œ̃/)[2] before a masculine noun, and **une** /yn/ before a feminine noun.

MASCULINE			FEMININE		
un livre	/ɛ̃livʀ/	*a book*	**une** chaise	/ynʃɛz/	*a chair*
un stylo	/ɛ̃stilo/	*a pen*	**une** table	/yntabl/	*a table*
un cahier	/ɛ̃kaje/	*a notebook*	**une** clé	/ynkle/	*a key*

Before a word beginning with a vowel sound, **un** is pronounced /ɛ̃n‿/ because of *liaison*.[3] All liaisons will be marked with a tie ‿ in the grammar explanations of Lessons 1–8 (the tie ‿ is not a part of written French). The feminine article **une** is pronounced /yn/, but the /n/ is pronounced as the first sound of the following word.

un‿étudiant	/ɛ̃netydjɑ̃/	*a (male) student*
une étudiante	/ynetydjɑ̃t/	*a (female) student*

2. The plural of nouns is usually formed by adding **-s** to the singular, as in English. But the **-s**, like most other word-final consonants, is not pronounced in French. As a result, you cannot tell, simply by listening to a noun alone, whether it is singular or plural.

---

[1] You can tell the gender of certain nouns from their endings (suffixes). See Appendix A (p. A1) for typical masculine and feminine endings of nouns.

[2] Both pronunciations are possible, but /ɛ̃/ is more common in Parisian French. See Pronunciation Lesson 8 of your **Cahier d'exercices**.

[3] The final consonant letter of most French words is silent, but it is pronounced in *liaison* when followed by a word beginning with a *vowel sound*. Liaison is explained in Pronunciation Lesson 13 of your **Cahier d'exercices**.

Qu'est-ce c'est ?

livre	/livʀ/,	**livres**	/livʀ/	*book, books*
table	/tabl/,	**tables**	/tabl/	*table, tables*

The singular indefinite articles **un** and **une** become **des** before a plural noun; **des** is pronounced /de/ before a consonant sound and /dez‿/ before a vowel sound because of liaison. So in spoken French it is the *article* that shows whether the noun is singular or plural. English has no equivalent for **des**; its closest counterpart is *some*.

un crayon	→ **des** crayons	*a pencil* → *(some) pencils*
une montre	→ **des** montres	*a watch* → *(some) watches*
un‿étudiant	→ **des‿**étudiants	*a student* → *(some) students*
une étudiante	→ **des‿**étudiantes	*a student* → *(some) students*

3. Some nouns do not form their plural by adding **-s** to the singular. For instance, singular nouns that already end in **-s** do not change their form in the plural. *All* such nouns are masculine; again, in spoken French you listen to the *article* to tell whether the noun is in the singular or plural.

un cours, des **cours**	*a course, (some) courses*
un campus, des **campus**	*a campus, (some) campuses*

4. The expression **Qu'est-ce que c'est ?** *What is it/this/that?* (or *What are they/these/those?*) asks for identification of an object or objects. In the answer, **c'est** corresponds to *It is, this is, that is.* It is pronounced /sɛ/ before a consonant and /sɛt‿/ in liaison.

Qu'est-ce que c'est ? /kɛskəsɛ/	*What is it/this/that?*
C'est‿un livre.	*It/This/That is a book.*
C'est‿une montre.	*It/This/That is a watch.*

The plural of **c'est** is **ce sont** /səsõ/; it corresponds to *they are, these are, those are.*

Qu'est-ce que c'est ?	*What are they/these/those?*
Ce sont des livres.	*They/These/Those are books.*
Ce sont des clés.	*They/These/Those are keys.*

1 un cahier
2 un crayon
3 un livre
4 un mur
5 un stylo
6 une chaise
7 une clé
8 une montre
9 une porte
10 une table
11 un étudiant
12 une étudiante

TABLEAU 3

A *Écoutez bien et répétez après moi.*[1]

1. un cahier
2. un crayon
3. un livre
4. un mur

5. un stylo
6. une chaise
7. une clé
8. une montre

9. une porte
10. une table
11. un étudiant
12. une étudiante

B *Maintenant, répétez après moi.*[2]

1. C'est un cahier.
2. C'est un crayon.
3. C'est un livre.
4. C'est un mur.

5. C'est un stylo.
6. C'est une chaise.
7. C'est une clé.
8. C'est une montre.

9. C'est une porte.
10. C'est une table.
11. C'est un étudiant.
12. C'est une étudiante.

C *Écoutez les questions et les réponses.*[3]

Qu'est-ce que c'est ? (crayon) — C'est un crayon.
Qu'est-ce que c'est ? (table) — C'est une table.
Qu'est-ce que c'est ? (chaise) — C'est une chaise.

[1]*Listen carefully and repeat after me.*

[2]*Now, repeat after me.*

[3]*Listen to the questions and answers.* The words in parentheses indicate the objects pointed out by the instructor.

Maintenant, répondez aux questions.[1]

1. Qu'est-ce que c'est ?   (stylo)
2. Qu'est-ce que c'est ?   (montre)
3. Qu'est-ce que c'est ?   (table)
4. Qu'est-ce que c'est ?   (mur)

5. Qu'est-ce que c'est ?   (porte)
6. Qu'est-ce que c'est ?   (crayon)
7. Qu'est-ce que c'est ?   (livre)
8. Qu'est-ce que c'est ?   (clé)

D *Regardez et écoutez bien.*[2]

C'est un stylo ; ce sont des stylos.
C'est une chaise ; ce sont des chaises.
Cest un étudiant ; ce sont des étudiants.
C'est une étudiante ; ce sont des étudiantes.

Continuez.[3]

1. C'est un cahier.
2. C'est un mur.
3. C'est une clé.
4. C'est un livre.

5. C'est une porte.
6. C'est un étudiant.
7. C'est une étudiante.
8. C'est un crayon.

E *Regardez bien et répondez aux questions.*[4]

Modèle :   Qu'est-ce que c'est ?   (crayon)
C'est un crayon.
Qu'est-ce que c'est ?   (clés)
Ce sont des clés.

1. Qu'est-ce que c'est ?   (cahier)
2. Qu'est-ce que c'est ?   (cahiers)
3. Qu'est-ce que c'est ?   (stylos)
4. Qu'est-ce que c'est ?   (clés)

5. Qu'est-ce que c'est ?   (murs)
6. Qu'est-ce que c'est ?   (clé)
7. Qu'est-ce que c'est ?   (stylo)
8. Qu'est-ce que c'est ?   (chaises)

Compréhension auditive[5]

1.2   FORME INTERROGATIVE **EST-CE QUE... ?** ; FORME NÉGATIVE **NE ... PAS**

1. To change a statement into a question, just add **Est-ce que** /ɛskə/ to the beginning of the statement. This type of question is usually accompanied by a rising intonation.

STATEMENT

C'est un livre.
It is a book.
Ce sont des étudiants.
They are students.

QUESTION

→ **Est-ce que** c'est un livre ?
→ *Is it a book?*
→ **Est-ce que** ce sont des étudiants ?
→ *Are they students?*

---

[1]*Now, answer the questions.*

[2]*Look and listen carefully.*

[3]*Continue.* Continue with the pattern by putting the sentences in the singular (**C'est un cahier**) into the plural (**Ce sont des cahiers**).

[4]*Look carefully and answer the questions.* The words in parentheses indicate the objects used. If there are two objects (**clés** as against **clé**), answer in the plural (**Ce sont des clés**).

[5]*Listening comprehension*: In addition to structural exercises, the tape program also contains listening comprehension exercises, as indicated here.

2. To form a negative sentence, add **ne** /n(ə)/[1] (**n'** before a vowel sound) before the verb (**est**/**sont**), and **pas** /pɑ/ (/pɑz/ in liaison) immediately after it. **C'est** /sɛ/ becomes **Ce n'est pas** /snɛpɑ/, and **Ce sont** /səsõ/ becomes **Ce ne sont pas** /sənsõpɑ/.

C'est un cahier.	It is a notebook.
→ Ce **n'est pas** un cahier.	→ It is not a notebook.
C'est une porte.	It is a door.
→ Ce **n'est pas** une porte.	→ It is not a door.
Ce sont des stylos.	They are pens.
→ Ce **ne** sont **pas** des stylos.	→ They are not pens.
Ce sont des clés.	They are keys.
→ Ce **ne** sont **pas** des clés.	→ They are not keys.

AFFIRMATIVE	NEGATIVE
C'est un.../C'est une...	Ce n'est pas un.../Ce n'est pas une...
Ce sont des...	Ce ne sont pas des...

A *Écoutez bien.*

Est-ce que c'est un livre ?   — Oui, c'est un livre.
Est-ce que c'est un stylo ?   — Oui, c'est un stylo.
Est-ce que ce sont des clés ?   — Oui, ce sont des clés.

Répétez après moi.

Est-ce que, Est-ce que, Est-ce que, Est-ce que

Maintenant, posez des questions.[2]

> *Modèle :*   C'est une étudiante.
> **Est-ce que c'est une étudiante ?**

1. C'est une table.	5. C'est un cahier.
2. Ce sont des stylos.	6. Ce sont des murs.
3. Ce sont des chaises.	7. Ce sont des crayons.
4. C'est une porte.	8. Ce sont des clés.

B *Regardez et répétez.*

Ce n'est pas un crayon. Ce n'est pas une clé. C'est un stylo.
Ce ne sont pas des clés. Ce ne sont pas des stylos. Ce sont des crayons.

Maintenant, répétez après moi.

C'est, Ce n'est pas ; C'est, Ce n'est pas ; C'est, Ce n'est pas
Ce sont, Ce ne sont pas ; Ce sont, Ce ne sont pas ; Ce sont, Ce ne sont pas

Mettez chaque phrase au négatif.[3]

> *Modèle :*   C'est une table.   Ce sont des clés.
> **Ce n'est pas une table.**   **Ce ne sont pas des clés.**

1. C'est un crayon.	5. C'est une chaise.
2. Ce sont des montres.	6. Ce sont des étudiantes.
3. C'est un cahier.	7. Ce sont des livres.
4. Ce sont des portes.	8. C'est une clé.

[1]The vowel /ə/ is pronounced in some cases, and omitted in others. See Pronunciation Lesson 19 of your **Cahier d'exercices**.

[2]*Now, ask questions.* You change each statement you hear into a question by putting **Est-ce que** in front and by changing the intonation to a rising one.

[3]*Put each sentence into the negative.*

C *Maintenant, posez des questions à votre partenaire.*[1]

> *Modèle :* (stylo/crayon)
> (Mireille) **Qu'est-ce que c'est ? Est-ce que c'est un stylo ?**
> (Daniel) **Non, ce n'est pas un stylo, c'est un crayon !**

1. (crayon/stylo)
2. (crayons/stylos)
3. (porte/mur)
4. (cahier/livre)

5. (montre/clé)
6. (tables/chaises)
7. (clés/stylos)
8. (portes/murs)

1.3 ARTICLE DÉFINI LE, LA, L', LES

1. The definite article, corresponding to English *the*, is **le** /l(ə)/ before a masculine singular noun, and **la** /la/ before a feminine singular noun. In the examples below, **voilà** is an expression used in pointing out a person or a thing; it corresponds to English *there is* or *there are*, as in *There's the book!* and *There it is!*.

Voilà **un** cahier.	*There's a notebook!*
→ Voilà **le** cahier.	*→ There's the notebook!*
Voilà **une** porte.	*There's a door!*
→ Voilà **la** porte.	*→ There's the door!*

If the word following the definite article begins with a vowel sound, both **le** and **la** become **l'**.

Voilà **un** étudiant.	*There's a (male) student!*
→ Voilà **l'**étudiant.	*→ There's the (male) student!*
Voilà **une** étudiante.	*There's a (female) student!*
→ Voilà **l'**étudiante.	*→ There's the (female) student!*

2. The plural form of the definite article, used before both masculine and feminine nouns, is **les** /le/ (/lez/ in liaison).

Voilà **des** clés.	*There are (some) keys!*
→ Voilà **les** clés.	*→ There are the keys!*
Voilà **des** étudiants.	*There are (some) students!*
→ Voilà **les** étudiants.	*→ There are the students!*

The chart below is a summary of the forms of the indefinite and definite articles. The abbreviations *m* and *f* stand for *masculine* and *feminine* (or **masculin** and **féminin** in French), and *s* and *pl* for *singular* and *plural* (or **singulier** and **pluriel**). These abbreviations will be used throughout our text.

		BEFORE A CONSONANT	BEFORE A VOWEL	
s	*m*	**un** ↔ **le**	**un** ↔ **l'**	*a/an* ↔ *the*
	f	**une** ↔ **la**	**une** ↔ **l'**	
pl	*m, f*	**des** ↔ **les**	**des** ↔ **les**	*(some)* ↔ *the*

---

[1]*Now, ask your partner questions.*

A *Répétez après moi.*

un livre, le livre
une montre, la montre
des stylos, les stylos
des chaises, les chaises

un étudiant, l'étudiant
une étudiante, l'étudiante
des étudiants, les étudiants
des étudiantes, les étudiantes

B *Maintenant, modifiez les phrases suivantes.*[1]

Modèle : Voilà un livre.
Voilà le livre.

Voilà des cahiers.
Voilà les cahiers.

1. Voilà un cahier.
2. Voilà une montre.
3. Voilà un étudiant.
4. Voilà une porte.
5. Voilà des livres.

6. Voilà des clés.
7. Voilà des étudiants.
8. Voilà une clé et un stylo.
9. Voilà un professeur et un étudiant.
10. Voilà une table et une chaise.

Compréhension auditive

1.4 PRÉPOSITIONS LOCATIVES **DEVANT**, **DANS**, **SUR**, ETC.

1. The five prepositions below are used to indicate the location of people or things in relation to others. The interrogative expression **Où est... ?** (*pl* **Où sont... ?**) corresponds to English *Where is/are...?*.

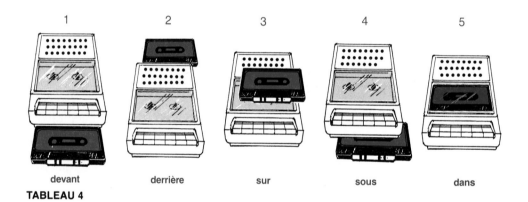

1	2	3	4	5
devant	derrière	sur	sous	dans

TABLEAU 4

Où est la cassette ?   *Where is the cassette?*
1. La cassette est **devant** le magnétophone.   *in front of*
2. La cassette est **derrière** le magnétophone.   *behind*
3. La cassette est **sur** le magnétophone.   *on, on top of*
4. La cassette est **sous** le magnétophone.   *under*
5. La cassette est **dans** le magnétophone.   *in, inside*

2. Study the following expressions. **À côté de** (**d'** before a vowel sound) is another expression of location, meaning *next to* or *beside*.

---

[1]*Now, change the following sentences.* Repeat each sentence you hear, while replacing **un/une/des** with **le/la/l'/les**.

Les étudiants ne sont pas dans la classe.

Qui[1] **est-ce** ? /kiεs/	*Who is this/that/it?*
— **C'est** Robert.	*This/That/It is Robert.*
Est-ce que c'est Monique ?	*Is this/that/it Monique?*
— Non, **ce n'est pas** Monique.	*No, this/that/it is not Monique.*
Où est Monique, alors ?	*Where is Monique, then?*
— Monique **est à côté de** Jacques.	*Monique is next to Jacques.*

TABLEAU 5

Marie est derrière Paul.
Paul est devant Marie.

Jeanne est à côté de Michel.
Michel est à côté de Jeanne.

Monique est devant Robert.
Robert est derrière Monique.

A *Regardez bien et répétez après moi.*

La cassette est devant le magnétophone.
La cassette est derrière le magnétophone.
La cassette est sur le magnétophone.
La cassette est sous le magnétophone.
La cassette est dans le magnétophone.

[1]*Who;* note the difference between **Qu'est-ce que c'est ?** /kεskəsε/, used for things, and **Qui est-ce ?** /kiεs/, used for persons.

Répétez.

devant le magnétophone
derrière le magnétophone
dans le magnétophone

sur le magnétophone
sous le magnétophone

Maintenant, répondez aux questions.

1. Où est la cassette ?   (dans)
2. Où est la cassette ?   (devant)
3. Où est la cassette ?   (derrière)

4. Où est la cassette ?   (sur)
5. Où est la cassette ?   (sous)
6. Où est le magnétophone ?   (sur)

TABLEAU 6

B *Regardez le Tableau 6. C'est une salle de classe. Répondez aux questions.*

1. Regardez le tableau et le professeur. Où est le professeur ? Où est le tableau ?
2. Regardez la montre et le livre. Où est la montre ? Où est le livre ?
3. Regardez la table. Où est la montre ? Où est le livre ? Où est le magnétophone ?
4. Regardez le magnétophone et la corbeille. Où est le magnétophone ?
5. Est-ce que le professeur est dans la classe[1] ? Est-ce que la chaise et la table sont dans le couloir ?

C *Regardez et écoutez.*

Qui est-ce ? C'est (Marie).
Est-ce que c'est (Paul) ? Non, ce n'est pas (Paul).
Où est (Paul), alors ? (Paul) est à côté de (Robert).
Où est (Jeanne) ? (Jeanne) est devant (Jacques).
Et où est (Michel) ? (Michel) est derrière (Marie).

Maintenant, répondez aux questions.

1. Qui est-ce ?
2. Est-ce que c'est (Jean) ?
3. Où est (Jean) ?
4. Est-ce que (Marie) est devant (Jacqueline) ?

5. Est-ce que c'est (Michel) ?
6. Où est Michel ?
7. Qui est-ce ?
8. Est-ce que (Paul) est derrière (Jean-Paul) ?

---

[1]**dans la classe**   *in the classroom*; **la classe** is a shortened form for **la salle de classe** *classroom*.

Est-ce que le livre est sur la table ?

1.5 PRONOMS PERSONNELS SUJETS IL, ELLE, ILS, ELLES

1. **Il** *and* **elle**. The subject pronoun **il** can replace any masculine singular noun, and **elle** can replace any feminine singular noun. **Il** corresponds to *he* or *it*, and **elle** to *she* or *it*.

Où est **Paul** ?	
—**Il** est dans la classe.	*He is in the classroom.*
Où est **Marie** ?	
—**Elle** est dans le couloir.	*She is in the hallway.*
Où est **le crayon** ?	
—**Il** est dans le livre.	*It is in the book.*
Où est **la cassette** ?	
—**Elle** est sur la table.	*It is on the table.*

2. **Ils** *and* **elles**. These pronouns correspond to English *they*. **Elles** is used *exclusively* for feminine plural nouns. **Ils** is used for masculine plural nouns as well as for a *combination* of masculine and feminine nouns.

Où sont **Robert** et **Paul** ? (*m + m*)	Où sont **le cahier** et **le stylo** ? (*m + m*)
—**Ils** sont dans la classe.	—**Ils** sont sur la table.
Où sont **Marie** et **Anne** ? (*f + f*)	Où sont **les clés** ? (*f pl*)
—**Elles** sont dans le couloir.	—**Elles** sont sur le livre.
Où sont **Robert** et **Marie** ? (*m + f*)	Où sont **le crayon** et **la clé** ? (*m + f*)
—**Ils** sont dans la maison.	—**Ils** sont sur le cahier.

A *Regardez et répétez après moi.*[1]

Voilà un livre ; il est sur la table.
Voilà un stylo ; il est sous le livre.
Voilà une montre ; elle est devant le livre.
Voilà des crayons ; ils sont dans le livre.
Voilà des clés ; elles sont derrière le cahier.

[1]Recorded in a substantially modified form.

Maintenant, répondez aux questions.

1. Où est le livre ?
2. Où est le stylo ?
3. Où est la montre ?

4. Où sont les crayons ?
5. Où sont les clés ?
6. Où est la table ?

B *Regardez et répondez aux questions.*

1. Est-ce que (Jeanne) est devant ou derrière (Marc) ?
2. Est-ce que (Michel) est à côté de (Laure) ?
3. (Yves), où est (Thierry) ?
4. Est-ce que (France) et (Isabelle) sont dans la classe ?
5. Est-ce que (Jacques) et (Marie) sont dans le couloir ?
6. Est-ce que (Marie) et (Michel) sont devant (le professeur) ?
7. Est-ce que (Paul) et (Daniel) sont derrière (Jeanne) ?
8. Où sont (Monique) et (Charles) ?

 Compréhension auditive

« Est-ce que vous êtes journaliste —Non, je ne suis pas journaliste, je suis étudiante. »

1.6 PRONOMS PERSONNELS SUJETS ; ÊTRE

1. Study the personal pronouns used as the *subject* of a sentence listed in the chart below, along with their English equivalents.

		SINGULAR		PLURAL	
First Person		**je**	*I*	**nous**	*we*
Second Person		**tu**	*you*	**vous**	*you*
Third Person	*m*	**il**	*he, it*	**ils**	*they*
	f	**elle**	*she, it*	**elles**	*they*

2. **Tu** and **vous**. These two pronouns correspond to English *you*. **Tu** is known as the "familiar" form. It is used among close friends, family members, and when address-

ing children and animals. **Vous** is the plural form of **tu**, used when addressing more than one person you call **tu**. In addition, **vous** is known as the "polite" form, used in addressing people you do not call **tu**. As a polite form, **vous** is used both as the singular and as the plural. In many language classes, students call each other **tu** but address the instructor as **vous**.

3. *Conjugation.* Verbs must agree in *person* (first, second, third person) and *number* (singular, plural) with the subject. For example, in English the verb *to be* is conjugated *I am, you are, she is,* etc. (rather than **I is[1], *you am, *she are*). The different verb forms that go with different subjects make up the *conjugation* (**la conjugaison**) of the verb. The verb **être** *to be* is conjugated in the following way. Note that in negative sentences **ne** (**n'** before a vowel sound) comes before the verb, and **pas**, after the verb. The small box in the margin summarizes the conjugation of **être**.

AFFIRMATIVE				NEGATIVE		
je **suis**	/ʒəsɥi/	*I am*		je **ne suis pas**	*I am not*
tu **es**	/tɥɛ/	*you are*		tu **n'es pas**	*you are not*
il **est**	/ilɛ/	*he/it is*		il **n'est pas**	*he/it is not*
elle **est**	/ɛlɛ/	*she/it is*		elle **n'est pas**	*she/it is not*
nous **sommes**	/nusɔm/	*we are*		nous **ne sommes pas**	*we are not*
vous_**êtes**	/vuzɛt/	*you are*		vous **n'êtes pas**	*you are not*
ils **sont**	/ilsõ/	*they are*		ils **ne sont pas**	*they are not*
elles **sont**	/ɛlsõ/	*they are*		elles **ne sont pas**	*they are not*

4. **Est-ce que/qu'**. The interrogative expression **Est-ce que**, which you learned in Lesson 1.2, becomes **Est-ce qu'** before a word beginning with a vowel sound (such as **il**, **elle**, **ils**, **elles**, and names of persons, like **Anne**).

BEFORE A CONSONANT SOUND	BEFORE A VOWEL SOUND
Est-ce que je suis dans_une classe ?	**Est-ce qu'**il est derrière la maison ?
Est-ce que tu es dans le couloir ?	**Est-ce qu'**elle est sous la table ?
Est-ce que nous sommes dans la classe ?	**Est-ce qu'**ils sont dans_un restaurant ?
Est-ce que vous_êtes devant la maison ?	**Est-ce qu'**elles sont devant la maison ?
Est-ce que Paul est dans le couloir ?	**Est-ce qu'**Anne est devant la porte ?

5. In French, the indefinite article **un**, **une**, **des** is omitted when a noun denoting *profession* follows **être**. Note that in English, *a* or *an* must be used before singular nouns.

Je suis_**étudiant**.	*I am a student.*
Vous n'êtes pas **médecin**.	*You are not a doctor.*
Ils ne sont pas **professeurs**.	*They are not professors.*
Elle n'est pas_**étudiante**.	*She is not a student.*

6. In French, the adjectives agree in gender (*m/f*) and number (*s/pl*) with the noun or pronoun which they describe. Note below that adjectives denoting nationality do not begin with a capital letter (**la majuscule**). Adjectives such as **français**, below, that end in **-s** in the masculine singular do not add another **s** in the masculine plural form.

Bill est_**américain**. (*m s*)	*Bill is American.*
Jenny est_**américaine**. (*f s*)	*Jenny is American.*

---

[1]The asterisk (*) is used to point out incorrect words and phrases.

Les professeurs sont **américains**. (*m pl*)   *The professors are American.*
Les étudiantes sont **américaines**. (*f pl*)   *The students are American.*

Jean-Paul est **français**. (*m s*)   *Jean-Paul is French.*
Monique est **française**. (*f s*)   *Monique is French.*
Les professeurs sont **français**. (*m pl*)   *The professors are French.*
Monique et Marie sont **françaises**. (*f pl*)   *Monique and Marie are French.*

When the adjective modifies a combination of masculine and feminine nouns, the masculine plural form is used.

Bill et Jenny sont **américains**. (*m + f*)   *Bill and Jenny are American.*
Monique et Michel sont **français**. (*f + m*)   *Monique and Michel are French.*

A   *Exercice de contrôle*[1]

Je suis dans la classe.
1. Vous   2. Tu   3. Les étudiants   4. Nous

Je ne suis pas dans le couloir.
1. Le professeur   2. Les étudiants   3. Nous   4. Vous

Nous ne sommes pas médecins.
1. (Janine)   2. Vous   3. (Paul et Cécile)   4. Je

(Robert) est étudiant[2].
1. (Marie)   2. (Marie et Paul)   3. (Marie et Jeanne)   4. (Monique)

B   *Parlons de nous.*[3] *Répondez aux questions.*

Modèle :   Est-ce que vous êtes professeur ?
Non, je ne suis pas professeur, je suis étudiant(e).

1. Est-ce que vous êtes médecin ?
2. Est-ce que vous êtes français(e) ?
3. Est-ce que je suis étudiant(e) ?
4. Est-ce que je suis médecin ?
5. Est-ce que (Michel) est journaliste ?
6. Est-ce que (Jeanne) est française ?
7. Est-ce que (Pauline) et (Marie) sont médecins ?
8. Est-ce que (Jacqueline) et (Robert) sont français ?

C   *Où est-ce que nous sommes ? Répondez aux questions.*

1. Est-ce que nous sommes dans une classe ? Est-ce que nous sommes dans le couloir ?
2. Est-ce que vous êtes dans un restaurant ? Où est-ce que vous êtes ?
3. Regardez (Caroline). Est-ce qu'elle est dans la classe ? Qui[4] est devant (derrière/à côté de) (Caroline) ?
4. Regardez (Michel). Est-ce qu'il est devant ou derrière (Marie) ? Qui est devant (derrière) (Michel) ?
5. (Charles), où est-ce que vous êtes ? Est-ce que vous êtes devant (Jeanne) ?

---

[1]**Contrôle** means *check* or *verification*. An exercise of this kind is designed to see if you have learned the conjugation of a verb. First, repeat the entire model sentence after the instructor. Then, as you hear each cue word, use it in the appropriate place (subject position) and say the sentence again, making any other necessary changes (in this case, the appropriate verb form for the subject).

[2]If the subject is feminine singular or plural, **étudiant** must be changed to **étudiante** or **étudiantes**.

[3]*Let's talk about ourselves.*

[4]*Who*

D   *Maintenant, faites des dialogues avec votre partenaire, d'après ce modèle.*[1]

Monsieur (Mademoiselle) Raymond est dans la classe.
(Jacques) **Pardon, Monsieur (Mademoiselle). Est-ce que vous êtes Monsieur (Mademoiselle) Raymond ?**
(Sylvie) **Ah non, Monsieur (Mademoiselle).**
(Jacques) **Où est Monsieur (Mademoiselle) Raymond, alors ?**
(Sylvie) **Il (Elle) est dans la classe.**

1. Monsieur (Mademoiselle) Raymond est dans le bureau.
2. Monsieur (Mademoiselle) Chabrier est derrière la maison.
3. Monsieur (Madame) Durand est devant la maison.
4. Monsieur (Madame) Bosquet est dans la maison.

 Compréhension auditive

APPLICATIONS

 A   **Situations**[2]

Bonjour !

Christine Johnson est américaine. Elle est en France. Elle est étudiante en français[3]*. Le cours de français*[4] *est terminé. Christine est maintenant devant la porte de la classe. Voilà Jean-Paul Chabrier, un ami de Christine, dans le couloir. Il est français. Il est étudiant en anglais.*

JEAN-PAUL	Bonjour, Christine.	
CHRISTINE	Tiens, bonjour, Jean-Paul. Ça va ?	5
JEAN-PAUL	Oui, ça va. Et toi ?	
CHRISTINE	Pas mal, merci.	

Elle est maintenant dans le couloir. Elle est avec Jean-Paul.

JEAN-PAUL	Qu'est-ce que c'est ? Est-ce que c'est le livre de français ?	10
CHRISTINE	Oui, et voilà le cahier d'exercices.	
JEAN-PAUL	Comment est le cours de français ?	
CHRISTINE	Il est très intéressant.	

Voilà une dame. Elle cherche le bureau.[5]

deux cent deux /døsɑ̃dø/
/**s'il vous plaît** *please*/
là-bas *over there* *Fine.*
You are welcome./to
Jean-Paul

LA DAME	Excusez-moi, Mademoiselle. Où est la salle 202°, s'il vous plaît° ?	15
CHRISTINE	La salle 202 ? Elle est là-bas°.	
LA DAME	Ah bon.° Merci, Mademoiselle.	
CHRISTINE	De rien°, Madame. (*à Jean-Paul*°) Excuse-moi, Jean-Paul. Je suis en retard.	
JEAN-PAUL	Au revoir, Christine.	
CHRISTINE	Au revoir, et à tout à l'heure.	

---

[1]*Now, make up dialogues with your partner, according to this model.*

[2]*English equivalents of the dialogue portion (but not the narrative passage in italics at the beginning or the questions at the end) are in your* **Cahier d'exercices** *(in Part Three,* **Clés***, of each lesson).*

[3]*She is studying French (literally, She is a student in French).*

[4]*The French class. Note that* **de français** *means of the French language:* **un cours de français** *a French course,* **un livre de français** *a French (text)book,* **un professeur de français** *a French teacher (a teacher who teaches French).*

[5]*She is looking for the office.*

Le cours est terminé. Les étudiants sont dans le couloir.

Répondez aux questions. (lignes 1–3)

1. Est-ce que Christine est française ?
2. Est-ce qu'elle est en France ?
3. Est-ce que le cours de français est terminé ?
4. Est-ce que Christine est derrière la porte de la classe ?
5. Est-ce que Jean-Paul est américain ?
6. Est-ce qu'il est étudiant en français ?

(lignes 4–19)

7. Où sont Christine et Jean-Paul maintenant ?
8. Où est la dame ?
9. Où est la salle 202 ?
10. Est-ce que Christine est en retard ?

B   Expressions utiles[1]

Les salutations

Bonjour, { Monsieur. / Mademoiselle. / Madame. }   Salut, { Robert. / Martine. }

[1]English equivalents of *Expressions utiles* are in your **Cahier d'exercices** (in **Clés** of each lesson). Your instructor will tell you which expressions you need to learn.

Comment allez-vous ? } ⎫ (Très) bien, merci. ⎫ ⎧ Et vous ?
Comment ça va ? } ⎬ Pas mal, merci. ⎬ ⎨ Et toi ?
                               Comme ci comme ça.
                               Pas très bien.

Au revoir.
À demain.
À tout à l'heure.

En classe

Écoutez bien,
Regardez (le tableau),
Répétez (après moi),
Lisez (la phrase),
Écrivez (le mot),   } s'il vous plaît.
Répondez (en français),
Répondez à la question,
Encore une fois,
Plus fort,

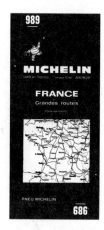

C **Mini-composition :** *Nous sommes dans la classe. Écrivez un paragraphe en employant les mots indiqués.*[1]

(1) Je/être/dans/cours de français. (2) Nous/être/dans/salle de classe. (3) Voilà/livre de français. (4) Cahier d'exercices/être/sous/chaise. (5) Voilà Anne/et/professeur. (6) Ils/être/ dans/couloir,/devant/porte. (7) Anne/être/américaine,/mais/professeur/ne pas/être/amé- ricain. (8) Il/être/français. (9) Ils/être/dans/classe/maintenant. (10) Je/être/à côté de/Anne.

D **Renseignements et opinions**

1. Comment allez-vous ?
2. Est-ce que vous êtes étudiant(e) ? Est-ce que vous êtes américain(e) ? Est-ce que je suis étudiant(e) ?
3. Où est-ce que nous sommes maintenant ? Où est le livre de français ? Où est le cahier d'exercices ?
4. Regardez. Est-ce que je suis devant ou derrière la table ? Et où est-ce que je suis mainte- nant ?
5. Est-ce que le cours de français est terminé ? Est-ce que la leçon est terminée ?

Compréhension auditive (basée sur[2] l'Application A)

Dictée : « Nous sommes dans la classe. » (basée sur l'Application C)

---

[1]*Write a paragraph by using the indicated words.* In order to make complete sentences out of these "dehydrated" ones, select the verb form that goes with the subject, and add the appropriate articles and prepositions where they are needed. For example, the first sentence would become **Je suis dans un cours de français**.

[2]**basée sur** *based on*

VOCABULAIRE[1]

Noms[2]

un ami	*friend* (male)	la dame	*lady*	le **médecin**	*doctor*
l'anglais *m*	*English language*	un **étudiant**	*(male) student*	**Monsieur** *m*	*Mr., sir*
le **bureau**	*office*	une **étudiante**	*(female) student*	la **montre**	*watch*
le **cahier**	*notebook*	un exercice	*exercise*	le **mur**	*wall*
la **cassette**	*cassette, tape*	le français	*French language*	la **porte**	*door*
la **chaise**	*chair*	la France	*France*	le **professeur**	*professor*
la **classe**	*class, classroom*	le(la) **journaliste**	*journalist*	le **restaurant**	*restaurant*
la **clé**	*key*	le **livre**	*book*	la **salle (de classe)**	*(class)room*
la **corbeille**	*wastebasket*	**Madame** *f*	*Mrs., ma'am*	le **stylo**	*pen*
le **couloir**	*hall, hallway*	**Mademoiselle** *f*	*Miss*	la **table**	*table*
le **cours**	*course; class*	le **magnétophone**	*tape recorder*	le **tableau**	*blackboard*
le **crayon**	*pencil*	la **maison**	*house*		

Verbes

être *irrég*[3] *to be*

Adjectifs

américain(e)	*American*	intéressant(e)	*interesting*
français(e)	*French*	terminé(e)	*finished*

Adverbes

alors	*then*	**là-bas**	*over there*	**très**	*very*
bien	*well, fine*	maintenant	*now*		
comment	*how*	**où**	*where*		

Prépositions

à côté de	*next to*	**derrière**	*behind*	**sous**	*under*
dans	*in*	**devant**	*in front of*	**sur**	*on, on top of*
de	*of*	en	*in*		

Autres expressions

À demain.	*See you tomorrow.*	De rien.	*You're welcome.*
Ah bon !	*Really!, I see.*	elle cherche	*she is looking for*
Ah non !	*Oh, no!*	**en retard**	*late*
À tout à l'heure.	*See you soon.*	**est-ce que... ?**	*(question marker)*
au revoir	*good-bye*	**et**	*and*
bonjour	*hello, good morning (afternoon)*	**et toi ?**	*and you?, what about you?*
(Comment) ça va ?	*How are you?*	**et vous ?**	*and you?, what about you?*
comme ci comme ça	*so-so*	**excuse-moi**	*excuse me*
Comment allez-vous ?	*How are you?*	**excusez-moi**	*excuse me*

[1]Each lesson ends with a list of new words and phrases occurring in **Conversations**, the oral exercises of **Structures** (but excluding those occurring in the directions and footnotes), and *Situations* of **Applications**. New words and phrases occurring in **Conversations** and the oral exercises of **Structures** are in boldface, while those appearing only in *Situations* are not. Verbs that are not fully presented in their entire conjugation patterns are shown, under *Autres expressions*, in the exact forms in which they appear in the text (for example, **elle cherche**). The vocabulary of Lesson 1 excludes articles and subject pronouns. Vocabulary in **Applications**, beyond *Situations*, is listed in the end vocabulary (*Lexique Français-Anglais*).

[2]The gender of nouns is shown by the definite article **le** or **la**. If the noun begins with a vowel sound, the indefinite article **un** or **une** is used. If neither article can occur with the noun, the gender will be indicated by *m* or *f*.

[3]This designation (abbreviation of *irrégulier*) refers to verbs whose conjugation patterns cannot be predicted from the infinitive form.

merci	*thank you*	**qui**	*who*
ne ... pas	*not*	**Qui est-ce ?**	*Who is it?, Who are they?*
non	*no*	**regardez**	*look (at)*
ou	*or*	**Salut !**	*Hi!*
oui	*yes*	s'il vous plaît	*please*
pardon	*excuse me*	**Tiens !**	*Well!*
pas mal	*not bad*	**voilà**	*there is, there are*
Qu'est-ce que c'est ?	*What is it?, What are they?*		

2 Est-ce que vous aimez le cours ?

LESSON OBJECTIVES

Theme and Culture

1. Daily activities and schedules
2. The French university system

Communication Skills

1. Asking about/Describing simple daily activities and schedules
2. Asking/Answering questions about general location (*At the library*) and possession (*Marie's book*)
3. Asking/Answering questions using numbers (1–60)
4. Using expressions equivalent to *there is/are*, *there aren't*
5. Asking/Answering questions about the time of day
6. Asking/Answering questions about one's preferences (likes and dislikes)

Structures

2.1 First-conjugation verbs (**-er**) (1)
2.2 **À** + the definite article
2.3 **De** + the definite article
2.4 Cardinal numbers (0–60); **il y a**; **combien de... ?**
2.5 Time expressions (1)
2.6 **Avoir** and **pas de**

CONVERSATIONS

TABLEAU 7

34

A. Le cours de chimie et le cours d'histoire

AHMED   J'aime le cours de chimie. Et toi ?

CLAUDINE   Moi[1], je déteste le cours de chimie. Il est très difficile.

AHMED   Ah bon ?[2] Est-ce que tu détestes aussi le cours d'histoire ?

CLAUDINE   Non, au contraire[3]. J'aime beaucoup le cours d'histoire.

TABLEAU 8

B. La pendule avance de cinq minutes.

CHRISTINE   Oh ! là ! là ! Regardez la pendule. Je suis en retard !

MME PINEAU   Non, non, vous n'êtes pas en retard.

CHRISTINE   Comment cela ?[4] Il est presque une heure !

MME PINEAU   Mais non[5], la pendule avance de cinq minutes[6]. À ma montre[7], il est seulement une heure moins dix.

C. J'ai seulement un cours aujourd'hui.

DANIEL   Tu travailles au labo[8] aujourd'hui ?

MARYSE   Non, aujourd'hui je travaille à la bibliothèque.

DANIEL   Tu n'as pas de cours ?

MARYSE   J'ai seulement un cours à dix heures.

[1]*I, Me*; a stressed form of **je**.

[2]*Really?*

[3]*on the contrary*

[4]*How's that?*

[5]*Oh, no* (more emphatic than **Non**)

[6]**avancer de ... minutes**   *to be . . . minutes fast*

[7]*By/According to my watch*

[8]**labo** = laboratoire

Le cours de chimie est difficile.

DIFFÉRENCES

Les études universitaires

The system of higher education in France has undergone a series of reforms since the famous political upheaval of May 68, a massive combined student and labor strike in 1968 that paralyzed the entire nation for several weeks. Today there are many more universities and branch campuses, and students participate in university administration. Each course carries a specific number of **Unités de Valeur**, comparable to the credit system, and the traditional large lecture courses (**cours magistraux**), characterized by difficult single end-of-year examinations and little personal contact with professors, are mostly supplemented by small recitation sections (**travaux pratiques**), with more papers and specific assignments, and more frequent feedback regarding student progress (**contrôle continu**).

Specialization begins early in the French school system. While still in the **lycée** (equivalent of our high school and the first year of college), students are to select their field, according to their preferences and past records, from several disciplines, such as humanities (**philosophie-lettres**), social sciences (**économie-sciences sociales**), physical science (**mathématiques-sciences physiques**), natural science (**mathématiques-sciences naturelles**), and several others. In order to enter the university, they must not only finish the **lycée** but also pass a written and oral examination called **le baccalauréat**, administered nationally by the Ministry of Education. About two-thirds of the students pass the test.

The university begins in mid- to late October, and the academic year lasts until late June. Many courses run for the entire year, meeting only once or twice a week. The first two years of study, called **le premier cycle**, lead to the **DEUG (Diplôme d'Études Universitaires Générales)**. Two more years, or **le deuxième cycle**, lead to **la Licence** and then to **la Maîtrise**, generally considered to be a little more advanced than the American master's degree. Beyond begins **le troisième cycle**, leading to **le Doctorat**. Tuition is virtually free at French universities, the majority of which are government-financed. Food at university cafeterias (**les restaurants universitaires**), also financed by the government, costs very little. In addition, many students receive scholarships or a modest stipend (**les bourses**) from the government to defray part of their study and living expenses.

STRUCTURES

2.1 VERBES DU PREMIER GROUPE (-ER) (1)[1]

1. Verbs whose infinitive (**infinitif** *m*), or unconjugated form as listed in dictionaries, ends in **-er** /e/ are known as first-conjugation verbs (**verbes** *m* **du premier groupe**). The conjugated forms consist of a stem (**la racine**) and endings (**les terminaisons** *f*) attached to the stem. In a verb like **parler** *to speak*, **parl-** is the stem, and it remains the same throughout the conjugation. In the list below, the endings are shown in blue. Note that four out of six forms (for **je**, **tu**, **il/elle**, **ils/elles**) are pronounced alike, and that the **vous** form is pronounced like the infinitive.

parler /paʀle/   *to speak*

je **parle**	/paʀl/		nous **parlons**	/paʀlõ/
tu **parles**	/paʀl/		vous **parlez**	/paʀle/
il/elle **parle**	/paʀl/		ils/elles **parlent**	/paʀl/

parler

parle	parlons
parles	parlez
parle	parlent

Alice et une amie préparent l'examen d'histoire.

The subject pronoun **je** (first-person singular) becomes **j'** before a verb that begins with a vowel sound.

je parle	**je** cherche	**je** regarde
j'arrive	j'entre	j'aime

2. The present-indicative tense (**le présent de l'indicatif**) expresses an action or event that takes place in the present. We will be using this tense until Lesson 9. The present indicative corresponds to three different constructions in English.

je parle
{ *I speak*
  I am speaking
  I do speak }

vous regardez
{ *you look*
  you are looking
  you do look }

---

[1]There are several subclasses of first-conjugation verbs. They will be discussed fully in Lesson 7.3 (p. 148).

Of the three English equivalents above, the first two are the most common. As for the distinction between these two, the context will tell you which is more appropriate.

Je **parle** français dans le cours de français.	*I speak French in the French class.*
Écoutez Monique. Elle **parle** !	*Listen to Monique. She is speaking!*
Je **travaille** deux heures pour le cours de chimie.	*I study two hours for the chemistry course.*
Je ne suis pas libre ; je **travaille** maintenant.	*I am not free; I am working now.*

3. In spoken French, the third-person plural ending **-ent** is silent. The difference between the third-person singular (**il**, **elle**) and plural (**ils**, **elles**) can be heard only if there is liaison in the plural form between the subject pronoun and the verb.

DIFFERENCE CANNOT BE HEARD		DIFFERENCE CAN BE HEARD[1]	
il **cherche**	/ilʃɛrʃ/	il **arrive**	/ilaʀiv/
ils **cherchent**	/ilʃɛrʃ/	ils **arrivent**	/ilzaʀiv/
elle **parle**	/ɛlpaʀl/	elle **aime**	/ɛlɛm/
elles **parlent**	/ɛlpaʀl/	elles **aiment**	/ɛlzɛm/

4. *Question and negation.* A statement can be changed to a question by adding **est-ce que** (**qu'** before a vowel sound) at the beginning.

Vous parlez français.	*You speak French.*
→ **Est-ce que** vous parlez français ?	→ *Do you speak French?*
J'écoute une cassette.	*I am listening to a cassette.*
→ **Est-ce que** j'écoute une cassette ?	→ *Am I listening to a cassette?*
Elle cherche le médecin.	*She is looking for the doctor.*
→ **Est-ce qu'**elle cherche le médecin ?	→ *Is she looking for the doctor?*

A negative sentence is formed by adding **ne** (**n'** before a vowel sound) before the verb, and **pas** after.

Ils parlent japonais.	*They speak Japanese.*
→ Ils **ne** parlent **pas** japonais.	→ *They do not speak Japanese.*
J'écoute l'étudiant.	*I am listening to the student.*
→ Je **n'**écoute **pas** l'étudiant.	→ *I am not listening to the student.*

🔊 **A** *Exercice de contrôle*

Je regarde le tableau.

1. Le professeur	2. Nous	3. Les étudiants	4. Vous

Vous entrez dans la classe.

1. Je	2. (Michel)	3. Tu	4. Les étudiants

Je n'arrive pas en retard.

1. Le professeur	2. Vous	3. Nous	4. (Marianne)

Nous ne cherchons pas le professeur.

1. Vous	2. Tu	3. Je	4. Les étudiants

---

[1]The difference cannot be heard if these sentences are in the negative, because **n'** will block liaison: **il n'arrive pas** sounds like **ils n'arrivent pas**, and **elle n'aime pas** like **elles n'aiment pas**.

1. arriver
2. trouver
3. entrer
4. regarder
5. écouter
6. aimer
7. parler
8. quitter

TABLEAU 9

🎞 **B** *Regardez le Tableau 9 et répétez après moi.*

1. L'étudiant arrive au[1] bâtiment.
2. Il trouve la classe.
3. Il entre dans la classe.
4. Il regarde la montre.

5. Il écoute le professeur.
6. Il aime le cours.
7. Il parle au[1] professeur.
8. Il quitte la classe.

Maintenant, répondez aux questions d'après ce modèle.

Est-ce qu'il arrive à la maison ?
(Marianne) **Non, il n'arrive pas à la maison.**
(Robert)   **Il arrive au bâtiment.**

1. Est-ce qu'il arrive à la résidence[2] ?
2. Est-ce qu'il trouve le couloir ?
3. Est-ce qu'il entre dans le restaurant ?
4. Est-ce qu'il regarde la pendule ?

5. Est-ce qu'il écoute les étudiants ?
6. Est-ce qu'il aime le livre ?
7. Est-ce qu'il parle au médecin ?
8. Est-ce qu'il quitte la maison ?

🎞 **C** *Maintenant, répondez d'après ce modèle.*

Est-ce que vous arrivez à la maison ?
(Charles) **Non, nous n'arrivons pas à la maison.**
(Monique) **Nous arrivons au bâtiment.**

1. Est-ce que vous arrivez à la résidence ?
2. Est-ce que vous trouvez la maison ?
3. Est-ce que vous entrez dans la maison ?
4. Est-ce que vous regardez la pendule ?

5. Est-ce que vous écoutez les étudiants ?
6. Est-ce que vous aimez le livre ?
7. Est-ce que vous parlez au médecin ?
8. Est-ce que vous quittez la maison ?

[1]**Au** is a combined form of **à** and **le** (discussed in Lesson 2.2).
[2]**résidence** *dormitory*

D *Répondez aux questions.*

1. Est-ce que vous parlez français ? Est-ce que (Jeanne) parle français ? Est-ce je parle (japonais) ?
2. Est-ce que vous regardez la montre ? Est-ce que je regarde la porte ? Est-ce que (Jacques) regarde le tableau ?
3. Est-ce que vous aimez le cours de français ? Est-ce que (Marie) aime le cours de français ? Est-ce que j'aime les étudiants dans le cours ?
4. Est-ce que vous quittez la classe maintenant ? Est-ce que je quitte la classe maintenant ? Est-ce que (Paul) quitte la résidence maintenant ?
5. Est-ce vous êtes dans un cours de français ? Est-ce que vous arrivez en retard ? Est-ce que j'arrive en retard ?
6. Qui est dans un cours de (chimie) ? Est-ce que vous aimez le cours ? Est-ce que le cours est facile ou difficile ?

🔲 *Compréhension auditive*

🔲 *Compréhension auditive*

2.2 CONTRACTION DE L'ARTICLE DÉFINI AVEC À

The preposition **à** means *to*, *in*, or *at*. When it precedes the definite article, **à** + **le** becomes **au**, and **à** + **les** becomes **aux**. Both forms are pronounced /o/ (in liaison, **aux** ‿ is pronounced /oz/). No change in form occurs in the combination **à** + **la** and **à** + **l'**. In exercise A, **à** corresponds to English *to*. In exercise B, it corresponds to *at* or *in*, indicating location.[1]

Voilà **le** vendeur.	Je parle **au** vendeur.
Voilà **la** vendeuse.	Je parle **à la** vendeuse.
Voilà **l'**étudiant.	Je parle **à l'**étudiant.
Voilà **les** médecins.	Je parle **aux** médecins.
Voilà **les** ‿ étudiants.	Je parle **aux** ‿ étudiants.

à + le		
à + le	→	au
à + les		aux

à + la		
à + la	→	NO CHANGE
à + l'		

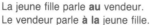

La jeune fille parle **au** vendeur.
Le vendeur parle **à la** jeune fille.

TABLEAU 10

Les jeunes filles parlent **à l'**enfant.
L'enfant parle **aux** jeunes filles.

[1]The preposition **dans**, which you learned in Lesson 1.4, means specifically *inside* something, whereas **à** simply refers to a general location.

Les étudiants travaillent à la bibliothèque.

A *Répétez après moi.*

Voilà le vendeur. Nous parlons au vendeur.
Voilà la vendeuse. Nous parlons à la vendeuse.
Voilà l'étudiant. Nous parlons à l'étudiant.
Voilà l'étudiante. Nous parlons à l'étudiante.
Voilà les professeurs. Nous parlons aux professeurs.
Voilà les étudiants. Nous parlons aux étudiants.

Continuez de la même façon.[1]

1. Voilà le professeur.
2. Voilà les étudiantes.
3. Voilà les journalistes.
4. Voilà les vendeuses.
5. Voilà le médecin.
6. Voilà l'étudiante.

B *Indiquez où sont les gens.*[2]

Modèle : Voilà la bibliothèque. Nous.
Nous sommes à la bibliothèque.

1. Voilà le restaurant. Nous.
2. Voilà le cinéma. Les étudiants.
3. Voilà l'université. Nous.
4. Voilà le laboratoire. Vous.
5. Voilà la bibliothèque. Tu.
6. Voilà l'hôpital. Le professeur.
7. Voilà la résidence. Nous.
8. Voilà le stade. Les étudiants.

2.3 CONTRACTION DE L'ARTICLE DÉFINI AVEC **DE**

1. The preposition **de** (pronounced often simply as /d/) has several meanings, one of which is *of*. It occurs commonly in the construction noun + **de** + noun, in which the second noun (excluding proper names[3]), without any article, describes or modifies the first noun. Note that English places two nouns next to each other, the first one describing the second.

un cours **de** psychologie	*a psychology class (course)*
un livre **de** français	*a French (text)book*
un cahier **d'**exercices	*a workbook (exercise book)*
une salle **de** classe	*a classroom*

---

[1]*Continue in the same way.*

[2]*Indicate where the people are.* Make up sentences using the locations and the subjects you hear.

[3]A proper name represents names of people and places: Jean-Paul, Christine, Mlle Moreau, Paris, New York.

2. **De** is also used to indicate *possession*. In this construction, the second noun is the possessor and is preceded by an article, unless it is a proper name: noun + **de** + article + noun (or noun + **de** + proper name). Note that English often uses noun + 's + noun, the first one indicating the possessor.

la montre **de** Michel	*Michel's watch* [the watch of Michel]
le livre **de l'**étudiant	*the student's book* [the book of the student]
la porte **de la** maison	*the door of the house*
les clés **de** Monique	*Monique's keys* [the keys of Monique]

3. The preposition **de** combines with the definite articles **le** and **les** to form **du** /dy/ and **des** /de/ (/dez/ in liaison). No change occurs in the combination **de + la** and **de + l'**. In the sentences below, **parler de** corresponds to English *to speak/talk about/of* (**parler à**, in Lesson 2.2, corresponds to *to speak to*).

Voilà **le** vendeur.	Je parle **du** vendeur.
Voilà **la** vendeuse.	Je parle **de la** vendeuse.
Voilà **l'**étudiant.	Je parle **de l'**étudiant.
Voilà **les** médecins.	Je parle **des** médecins.
Voilà **les** étudiantes.	Je parle **des** étudiantes.

4. Do not confuse the combined form **des** (**de + les**) and the plural indefinite article **des** *some* (singular: **un, une**), presented in Lesson 1.1.

Ce sont les clés **des** vendeurs.	*of the* (**de + les**)
Nous parlons **des** médecins.	*of/about the* (**de + les**)
Voilà **des** vendeurs.	*some* (plural of **Voilà un vendeur.**)
Nous cherchons **des** vendeuses.	*some* (plural of **Nous cherchons une vendeuse.**)

de + le		
de + les	→	du
		des

de + la		
de + l'	→	NO CHANGE

Est-ce qu'ils parlent des cours ? Non, ils parlent du professeur.

TABLEAU 11   Il parle **du** professeur.   Elle parle **de la** montre.   Il parle **des** livres.

 A   *Répétez après moi.*

Voilà le professeur. Je parle du professeur.
Voilà la maison. Je parle de la maison.
Voilà l'étudiant. Je parle de l'étudiant.
Voilà les étudiants. Je parle des étudiants.

Continuez de la même façon.

1. Voilà le jardin.
2. Voilà l'université.
3. Voilà le laboratoire.

4. Voilà le restaurant.
5. Voilà l'étudiant.
6. Voilà les professeurs.

 B   *Faites des phrases d'après ce modèle.[1]*

le stylo ; le professeur
C'est le stylo du professeur.

les cassettes ; les étudiants
Ce sont les cassettes des étudiants.

1. le livre ; l'étudiante
2. la montre ; le professeur
3. les clés ; les vendeuses
4. le cahier ; le journaliste

5. les chaises ; les étudiants
6. la porte ; la classe
7. la bibliothèque ; l'université
8. l'hôpital ; les médecins

C   *Maintenant, faites des dialogues avec votre partenaire, d'après ce modèle.*

Le professeur est à la bibliothèque.
(Philippe)   **De qui[2] est-ce que tu parles ?**
(Sophie)   **Je parle du professeur.**
(Philippe)   **Où est le professeur ?**
(Sophie)   **Il est à la bibliothèque.**

1. Le professeur est au laboratoire.
2. Le médecin est à l'hôpital.
3. Les jeunes filles[3] sont à la piscine.
4. Les étudiants sont à la maison[4].

   Compréhension auditive

[1]*Make up sentences according to this model.*

[2]*About/Of whom*

[3]**jeune(s) fille(s)**   *girl(s)*

[4]**La maison** by itself means *the house,* but **être à la maison** means *to be (at) home.*

2.4 NOMBRES CARDINAUX (DE 0 À 60) ; Il Y A ; COMBIEN DE

1. Study the cardinal numbers 0 to 20 below.

0	**zéro**	/zeʀo/	7	**sept**	/sɛt/	14	**quatorze**	/katɔʀz/
1	**un (une)**	/ɛ̃/ (/yn/)	8	**ḥuit**	/ɥit/	15	**quinze**	/kɛ̃z/
2	**deux**	/dø/	9	**neuf**	/nœf/	16	**seize**	/sɛz/
3	**trois**	/tʀwɑ/	10	**dix**	/dis/	17	**dix-sept**	/dissɛt/
4	**quatre**	/katʀ/	11	**onze**	/õz/	18	**dix-huit**	/dizɥit/
5	**cinq**	/sɛ̃k/	12	**douze**	/duz/	19	**dix-neuf**	/diznœf/
6	**six**	/sis/	13	**treize**	/tʀɛz/	20	**vingt**	/vɛ̃/

Numbers 21 to 59 are a combination of **vingt, trente, quarante, cinquante** plus 1 to 9. Note the use of the hyphen in all numbers except in **et un** /eɛ̃/.

21	**vingt et un**	/vɛ̃teɛ̃/	30	**trente**	/tʀɑ̃t/	43	**quarante-trois**
22	**vingt-deux**	/vɛ̃tdø/[1]	31	**trente et un**		44	**quarante-quatre**
23	**vingt-trois**		32	**trente-deux**		45	**quarante-cinq**
24	**vingt-quatre**		33	**trente-trois**		50	**cinquante** /sɛ̃kɑ̃t/
25	**vingt-cinq**		34	**trente-quatre**		51	**cinquante et un**
26	**vingt-six**		39	**trente-neuf**		52	**cinquante-deux**
27	**vingt-sept**		40	**quarante** /kaʀɑ̃t/		55	**cinquante-cinq**
28	**vingt-huit**		41	**quarante et un**		56	**cinquante-six**
29	**vingt-neuf**		42	**quarante-deux**		60	**soixante** /swasɑ̃t/

2. Change in the pronunciation of the final consonants occurs in some of the numbers when they *precede* a noun. The final consonant of **cinq, six, ḥuit, dix** as well as their related numbers (**vingt-cinq, trente-six, quarante-huit,** etc.) becomes silent before a word beginning with a consonant sound; conversely, all final consonants are pronounced when there is liaison.

BY ITSELF		BEFORE A CONSONANT		BEFORE A VOWEL	
1	/ɛ̃/	**un** livre	/ɛ̃/	**un** enfant	/ɛ̃n/
2	/dø/	**deux** livres	/dø/	**deux** enfants	/døz/
3	/tʀwɑ/	**trois** livres	/tʀwɑ/	**trois** enfants	/tʀwɑz/
5	/sɛ̃k/	**cinq** livres	/sɛ̃/	**cinq** enfants	/sɛ̃k/
6	/sis/	**six** livres	/si/	**six** enfants	/siz/
8	/ɥit/	**ḥuit** livres	/ɥi/	**ḥuit** enfants	/ɥit/
10	/dis/	**dix** livres	/di/	**dix** enfants	/diz/
20	/vɛ̃/	**vingt** livres	/vɛ̃/	**vingt** enfants	/vɛ̃t/

Un and other numbers ending in **un** must be changed to **une** before a feminine noun.

un crayon, **vingt et un** crayons	*one pencil, twenty-one pencils*
une chaise, **vingt et une** chaises	*one chair, twenty-one chairs*
une minute, **trente et une** minutes	*one minute, thirty-one minutes*

3. *The **h** muet and **h** aspiré.* The letter **h** is never pronounced in French. However, there are two kinds of **h** in French. One is known as **h** muet *mute h* and allows both liaison and elision, as if it did not exist at all: **les hôtels** /lezɔtɛl/, **l'hôtel** /lɔtɛl/.

---

[1]The **-t** of **vingt** is silent in 20, but is pronounced in 21 through 29.

The other, known as **h aspiré** *aspirate h*, blocks both liaison and elision as if it were an invisible consonant: **les ḥaches** /leaʃ/, **la ḥache** /laaʃ/. All instances of **h aspiré** in our text will be marked with a dot under it: **ḥ**. The word **ḥuit** begins with an **h aspiré**. Although the word **onze** does not, it too behaves as if it did.

Je regarde les//ḥuit livres.   Où sont les//**onze** cahiers ?

4. **Il y a**. The expression **il y a** corresponds to English *there is*, *there are*, in the general sense of *there exist(s)*.

Est-ce qu'**il y a** des chaises dans la classe ?
Are there any chairs in the classroom?

— Oui, **il y a** vingt-deux chaises dans la classe.
Yes, there are twenty-one chairs in the classroom.

Do not confuse **il y a** and **voilà**, both of which correspond to *there is/are* in English. **Voilà**, which you learned in Lesson 1.3, is used specifically to *point out* someone or something (in English, *There it is!*, *There's the book!*, *There's Paul!*). **Il y a** does not refer to a location and is usually followed by an expression of location.

Il y a un jardin derrière la maison.
There is a garden behind the house.

Est-ce qu'**il y a** des étudiants à la résidence ?
Are there students at the dormitory?

Voilà une salle de classe.
There's a classroom!

Voilà la maison du professeur.
There is the professor's house!

5. **Combien de... ?** The interrogative expression **combien de** (**d'** before a vowel sound) + noun is an equivalent of English *how many/how much* + noun. It can be used with **est-ce que** to form questions.

Combien de chaises est-ce qu'il y a dans la classe ?
How many chairs are there in the classroom?

Combien d'étudiants est-ce que vous cherchez ?
How many students are you looking for?

Combien de livres est-ce qu'elle a ?
How many books does she have?

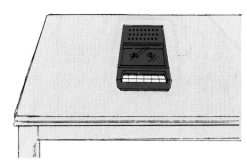

TABLEAU 12   « **Voilà** le magnétophone ! »   **Il y a** un magnétophone **sur** la table.

 A *Répétez après moi.*[1]

0, 1, 2, 3, 4 ... 10 ; 10, 9, 8, 7 ... 0.
11, 12, 13 ... 20 ; 20, 19, 18 ... 0.
21, 22, 23, 29, 30, 31, 32, 33, 40, 41, 42, 43, 44, 50, 51, 52, 53, 54, 55, 60.

[1]Recorded in a substantially modified form.

📼 **B** *Comptez maintenant.*[1]

1. Comptez par deux de 0 à 30.[2]
2. Comptez par trois de 0 à 30.
3. Comptez par trois de 30 à 60.
4. Comptez par cinq de 0 à 60.

📼 **C** *Répétez après moi.*

Un : un professeur et un étudiant
Deux : deux professeurs et deux étudiants
Trois : trois professeurs et trois étudiants

On continue de la même façon.

a. quatre	d. sept	g. dix
b. cinq	e. huit	h. vingt
c. six	f. neuf	i. vingt et un

D *Posez des questions d'après ce modèle.*

combien/chaises/dans la classe
Combien de chaises est-ce qu'il y a dans la classe ?

1. combien/étudiants/dans la classe	4. combien/étudiants/à l'université
2. combien/médecins/à l'hôpital	5. combien/pages/dans le livre
3. combien/bâtiments/sur le campus	6. combien/minutes/dans une heure

E *Répondez aux questions.*

1. Regardez la classe. Combien de chaises est-ce qu'il y a dans la classe ? Combien d'étudiants est-ce qu'il y a ? Et combien de jeunes filles ?
2. Regardez le livre de français. À quelle page[3] est-ce que la leçon 1 commence ? Et la leçon 2 ?
3. Combien de lettres est-ce qu'il y a dans le mot *professeur* ? Et dans le mot *livre* ? Et dans le mot *français* ?
4. Combien d'heures est-ce qu'il y a dans un jour ? Et combien de jours est-ce qu'il y a dans une semaine ?
5. Combien de secondes /səgõd/ est-ce qu'il y a dans une minute ? Combien de minutes est-ce qu'il y a dans une heure ?

📼 *Dictée*

2.5 L'HEURE (1)

1. Study the time expressions below; they go with Tableau 14 (p. 48) used in oral exercise A.

Quelle heure est-il ?	*What time is it?*
Il est neuf heures du matin.	*It is nine in the morning.*
Il est dix heures et quart.	*It is a quarter past ten.*
Il est onze heures vingt.	*It is twenty past eleven.*
Il est midi et demi.	*It is half past twelve (noon).*
Il est deux heures moins vingt de l'après-midi.	*It is twenty to two in the afternoon.*

---

[1]*Now, count.* Recorded in a substantially modified form.
[2]*Count by two's from 0 to 30.*
[3]*On what page*

Il est cinq heures moins le quart.	*It is a quarter to five.*
Il est six heures et demie du soir.	*It is half past six in the evening.*
Il est minuit et demi.	*It is half past twelve (midnight).*

a) The word **heures** *o'clock*[1] (**heure** in the case of **une heure**) must always be used for time expressions, except for **midi** *noon* and **minuit** *midnight*. The **f** of **neuf heures** is pronounced /v/: /nœvœʀ/. The phrase **est-il** is an inverted form of **il est**, used in questions.

b) The phrase **et demie** is used after the feminine noun **heure(s)**, and **et demi** (without the **e**) after the masculine nouns **midi** and **minuit**.

c) In French, fifteen minutes past the hour is expressed by **et quart**, and a quarter to the hour by **moins** /mwɛ̃/ **le quart** (note the definite article **le**). **Moins** *to, of* (literally, *less, minus*) is used to indicate time remaining to the hour in the second half of the hour. **Et** occurs only with **et demi(e)** and **et quart**.

d) Use of the phrases **du matin** *in the morning*, **de l'après-midi** *in the afternoon*, and **du soir** *in the evening* is optional in French, just as in English. They are used only for emphasis or clarification.

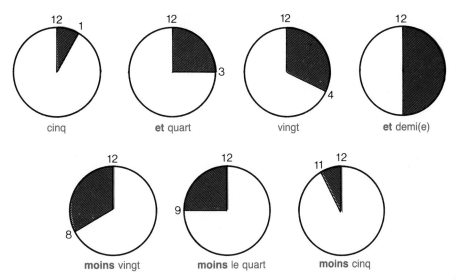

TABLEAU 13

2. Be careful to distinguish between **Quelle heure...** and **À quelle heure....** The first is used only in asking what time it is. The second, with the preposition **à**, asks for the time when *something takes place*, and the answer must also contain **à** + time.

Quelle heure est-il ?	*What time is it?*
— Il est dix heures dix.	*It's ten past ten.*
À quelle heure est-ce que vous déjeunez ?	*What time do you eat lunch?*
— Je déjeune **à** une heure.	*I eat lunch at one.*
À quelle heure commence le cours ?	*What time does the class begin?*
— Il commence **à** onze heures.	*It begins at eleven.*

[1]literally, *hours*

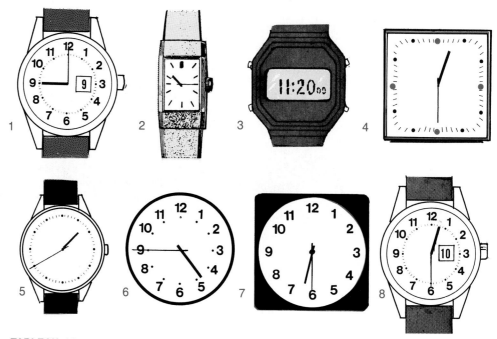

TABLEAU 14

A *Quelle heure est-il ? Regardez le Tableau 14 et répétez après moi.*

1. Il est neuf heures du matin.
2. Il est dix heures et quart.
3. Il est onze heures vingt.
4. Il est midi et demi.
5. Il est deux heures moins vingt de l'après-midi.
6. Il est cinq heures moins le quart.
7. Il est six heures et demie du soir.
8. Il est minuit et demi.

Maintenant, répondez à ces questions.

1. Regardez le numéro 3. Quelle heure est-il ?
2. Regardez le numéro 6. Quelle heure est-il ?
3. Regardez le numéro 7. Quelle heure est-il ?

On continue de la même façon.

B *Regardez le Tableau 14. Chaque montre avance de cinq minutes.*

1. Regardez le numéro 4. Quelle heure est-il ?
2. Regardez le numéro 1. Quelle heure est-il ?
3. Regardez le numéro 7. Quelle heure est-il ?

On continue de la même façon.

9. Regardez les photos à la page 49. Quelle heure est-il ?

C *Répondez aux questions.*

1. Est-ce qu'il y a une bibliothèque à l'université ? À quelle heure est-ce qu'elle est ouverte[1] ?
2. Est-ce qu'il y a un restaurant universitaire ? À quelle heure est-ce qu'il est ouvert[1] ?

[1]**Ouverte** *open* is used with **bibliothèque**, a feminine noun, while **ouvert** is used with **restaurant**, a masculine noun. The agreement of adjectives with nouns will be fully presented in Lesson 8.2.

3. Est-ce que nous étudions le français ? Où est le cours ? À quelle heure est-ce qu'il commence ?
4. Qui étudie (la chimie) ? Où est le cours ? À quelle heure est-ce qu'il commence ?
5. À quelle heure est-ce que vous déjeunez ? À quelle heure est-ce que vous rentrez à la maison ?
6. Où êtes-vous à dix heures du matin ? Et à onze heures du soir ? Demandez-moi[1] où je suis à midi et demi.

 Compréhension auditive

2.6 AVOIR ; PAS DE

avoir	
ai	avons
as	avez
a	ont

1. Study the conjugation of **avoir** /avwaʀ/ *to have* below. Note that the **tu** and **il/elle** forms are pronounced alike, though spelled differently. The third-person plural **ils ont** and **elles ont** are pronounced /ilzõ/, /ɛlzõ/ in liaison. Be careful to distinguish between these forms and the corresponding forms of **être**: **ils sont**, **elles sont** /ilsõ/, /ɛlsõ/, which you learned in Lesson 1.5.

j'**ai**	/ʒe/	nous **avons**	/nuzavõ/
tu **as**	/tɥa/	vous **avez**	/vuzave/
il/elle **a**	/ila/, /ɛla/	ils/elles **ont**	/ilzõ/, /ɛlzõ/

2. **Pas de** /pɑd/. In negative sentences, **un/une/des** + noun after the verb becomes **de** + noun (**d'** before a vowel sound).

Avez-vous **un** stylo ?	*Do you have a pen?*
— Non, je n'ai pas **de** stylo.	*No, I don't have a pen.*
Avez-vous **une** montre ?	*Do you have a watch?*
— Non, je n'ai pas **de** montre.	*No, I don't have a watch.*
Est-ce que M. Savin a **des** enfants ?	*Does Mr. Savin have any children?*
— Non, il n'a pas **d'**enfants.	*No, he doesn't have any children.*
Est-ce que vous posez **des** questions ?	*Do you ask any questions?*
— Non, je ne pose pas **de** questions.	*No, I don't ask any questions.*

[1]*Ask me*

Ils n'ont pas de cours à midi.

The negative form of **il y a** + **un/une/des** is **il n'y a pas de**.

Est-ce qu'**il y a des** chats dans la classe ?	*Are there any cats in the classroom?*
— Non, **il n'y a pas de** chats.	*No, there are no cats.*

The only exception is with **être**. After **être**, the indefinite articles **un/une/des** do not change to **de**. You learned the following constructions in Lesson 1.2.

Est-ce que c'est un livre ?	*Is it a book?*
— Non, ce **n'**est **pas** un livre.	*No, it isn't a book.*
Est-ce que ce sont des cahiers ?	*Are they notebooks?*
— Non, ce **ne** sont **pas des** cahiers.	*No, they aren't notebooks.*

Elle a une montre.
Il n'a **pas de** montre.

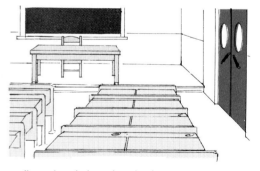

Il y a des chaises dans la classe.
Il n'y a **pas d'**étudiants dans la classe.

TABLEAU 15

A *Exercice de contrôle*

J'ai des cours aujourd'hui.

1. Nous 2. Vous 3. Les étudiants 4. Le professeur

Nous n'avons pas d'examens demain.

1. Je 2. Les étudiants 3. Le professeur 4. Vous

Est-ce que vous avez le livre de français ?

1. nous 2. (Laurence) 3. tu 4. les étudiants

B *Mettez les phrases suivantes au négatif d'après le modèle.*

> J'ai un examen demain.
> **Je n'ai pas d'examen demain.**

1. J'ai un cours à midi.
2. Elle a des examens demain.
3. Vous avez un vélomoteur.

4. Nous avons une bonne idée[1].
5. Il y a un livre sur la table.
6. Il y a des chaises dans le couloir.

C *Répondez aux questions.*

1. Est-ce que vous avez un cours à midi ? Demandez-moi si[2] j'ai un cours à midi. Est-ce que nous avons un examen demain ?
2. Est-ce que vous avez une montre ? Demandez-moi si j'ai une montre. Demandez à (Daniel) s'il[3] a une montre.
3. Est-ce que vous avez un chat ? Demandez-moi si j'ai un chien. Est-ce qu'il y a des chiens dans la classe ?
4. Est-ce que vous avez des livres à la maison[4] ? Demandez-moi si j'ai des livres à la maison. Est-ce qu'il y a des livres dans le couloir ?

Compréhension auditive

APPLICATIONS

Ils ont rendez-vous à trois heures devant la statue.

A Situations

Tu n'as pas d'idée ?

Michel Leroux a rendez-vous[5] à trois heures avec Ignès Lacombe devant la bibliothèque de l'université. Il est déjà trois heures cinq. Michel est en retard et il marche vite. À trois heures dix il arrive à la bibliothèque. Ignès est là[6] avec son° amie Christine.

her

---

[1]**bonne idée** *good idea*
[2]*Ask me if*
[3]**Si** *if* and **il** or **ils** combine to form **s'il** or **s'ils**. (**Elle** and **elles** do not combine: **si elle, si elles**.)
[4]**à la maison** *at home*
[5]**avoir rendez-vous** *to have an appointment, a date* (no article is used in this expression)
[6]**là** *there* (Do not confuse this word with the definite article **la**, pronounced the same way.)

my	MICHEL	Excuse-moi, Ignès. Je suis un peu en retard. Je n'ai pas de montre, et mon° vélomoteur est en panne[1].

                              5

You don't have any luck./
my
    IGNÈS   Salut, Michel. Tu n'as pas de chance.° Voici[2] mon° amie Christine. Elle est aussi dans le cours de journalisme.

    MICHEL   Bonjour, Christine. Ça va ?

  CHRISTINE   Bonjour, Michel.

*So/**jusqu'à** until*   MICHEL   Alors°, nous travaillons ensemble pour le cours jusqu'à° sept heures ?   10

OK, fine   IGNÈS   Oui, d'accord°. Christine a une très bonne idée pour un article sur Gorbatchev.

  CHRISTINE   J'ai aussi une bibliographie de deux pages.

    MICHEL   Formidable ! Moi, justement, je n'ai pas d'idée.

    IGNÈS   Tu n'as pas de montre. Tu n'a pas de vélomoteur. Tu n'as pas d'idée. Tu as le livre de journalisme au moins° ?   15

au moins *at least*
Shucks!   MICHEL   Le livre de journalisme ? Zut alors !° il est à la maison.

Répondez aux questions. (lignes 1–3)

  1. À quelle heure est-ce que Michel a rendez-vous ?
  2. Où est-ce qu'il a rendez-vous ?
  3. Quelle heure est-il ?
  4. Pourquoi[3] est-ce qu'il marche vite ?
  5. À quelle heure est-ce qu'il arrive à la bibliothèque ?

(lignes 4–16)

  6. Qu'est-ce que[4] Michel n'a pas ?
  7. Qui est avec Ignès ?
  8. Jusqu'à quelle heure[5] est-ce que les étudiants travaillent ?
  9. Qui n'a pas d'idée ?
  10. Où est le livre de journalisme de Michel ?

« Patrick a une idée formidable ! »

[1]**être en panne** *to be broken, not to be working*

[2]*Here is* (opposite of **Voilà** *There is*)

[3]*Why.* The answer begins with **Parce que** *because* (**Parce qu'** before a vowel sound).

[4]*What*

[5]*Until what time*

B Expressions utiles

Les cours[1]

l'anthropologie
l'architecture
les beaux-arts *m*
la biologie
la botanique
la chimie
le commerce
le droit

la géographie
l'histoire
l'informatique
le journalisme
les mathématiques *f*
la médecine
la musique
la photographie

la physique
la psychologie

les sciences *f* { humaines / naturelles / physiques / politiques

la sociologie
la zoologie

Les langues vivantes[2]

le français
l'allemand
l'anglais
l'arabe

le chinois
l'espagnol
l'hébreu
l'italien

le japonais
le polonais
le portugais
le russe

Les études

être étudiant(e) en { chimie / histoire }   étudier { la chimie / l'histoire }

étudier / travailler { très peu / un peu / beaucoup / trop }

J'aime (beaucoup) / Je n'aime pas / Je déteste } { le cours. / le professeur. / le manuel[3] / le livre. }

Le cours (n')est (pas) { (très) facile / difficile. / utile / intéressant. / comme ci comme ça. / facultatif / obligatoire. }

C Pratique

1. Quelles langues[4] est-ce que vous parlez ? Quelle langue est-ce que je parle ?
2. Comment est le cours de français ? Est-ce qu'il est facile ou difficile ? Est-ce que vous travaillez un peu, beaucoup, ou trop ?
3. Quel cours[5] est-ce que vous aimez ? Quel cours est-ce que vous détestez ? Complétez les phrases suivantes.[6]

   J'aime (beaucoup) _____.   Je déteste _____.

4. Donnez votre opinion sur quelques cours.[7]

   Le cours de _____ est facile.
   Le cours de _____ est difficile.
   Le cours de _____ est utile.
   Le cours de _____ n'est pas utile.
   Le cours de _____ est comme ci comme ça.
   Le cours de _____ est intéressant.
   Le cours de _____ est ennuyeux.

UNIVERSITÉ DE DROIT, D'ÉCONOMIE ET DES SCIENCES D'AIX-MARSEILLE
FRANCE

INSTITUT D'ÉTUDES FRANÇAISES POUR ÉTUDIANTS ÉTRANGERS

15, Rue Gaston-de-Saporta
13625 AIX-EN-PROVENCE
FRANCE

[1]All nouns in this list are feminine, except **beaux-arts**, **commerce**, **droit**, and **journalisme**.

[2]*Modern* (literally, *living*) *languages.* The gender of languages in French is masculine. The definite article is omitted only with the verb **parler** and in expressions like **en français** and **de français**. In all other cases, the article must be used: **J'étudie le français ; Le français n'est pas difficile**. (See Lesson 8.1.)

[3]*textbook*

[4]*What languages*

[5]*What course*

[6]*Complete the following sentences.*

[7]*Give your opinion on a few courses.*

Mini-composition : *Trois étudiants travaillent ensemble. Écrivez un paragraphe en employant les mots indiqués.*

(1) Je/quitter/cours/français. (2) Je/regarder/pendule. (3) Il/être/déjà/4 h[1]/demie. (4) Monique/être/là,/devant/porte/bâtiment. (5) Nous/avoir/rendez-vous/avec/Robert/à/bibliothèque. (6) Nous/marcher/vite/parce que/nous/être/en retard. (7) Nous/arriver/à/bibliothèque/à/5 h/moins/quart. (8) Nous/parler/de/projet/pour/cours/journalisme. (9) Cours/être/très/intéressant/et/professeur/être/amusant. (10) Je/avoir/très bonne idée/pour/article/sur/Gorbatchev. (11) Monique/avoir/bibliographie/de/2/pages. (12) Nous/travailler/ensemble/jusqu'à/7 h.

En général[2], à quelle heure commence ou commencent :

la première séance de cinéma[3] ?
la dernière[4] séance de cinéma ?
la première émission[5] à la télévision ?
les premiers cours à l'université ?
les concerts de musique classique ?

Renseignements et opinions

1. Où est-ce que nous sommes ? Quelle heure est-il ? À quelle heure est-ce que le cours commence ?
2. Combien d'étudiants est-ce qu'il y a dans la classe ? Combien d'étudiantes est-ce qu'il y a ? Combien de chaises est-ce qu'il y a ?
3. Demandez-moi[6] où je suis à dix heures du matin. Demandez-moi où je déjeune et à quelle heure.
4. Où est-ce que vous êtes à midi ? Demandez à (Jacques) où il est à six heures du soir.
5. Est-ce qu'il y a un restaurant universitaire sur le campus ? À quelle heure est-ce qu'il est ouvert ? À quelle heure est-ce qu'il est fermé ?
6. Qui[7] étudie (la botanique) ? À quelle heure est le cours ? Où est le cours ?

Compréhension auditive (basée sur l'Application A)

Dictée : « Le cours de français »

[1]Spell out all time expressions fully (e.g., **4 h** as **quatre heures**).
[2]*In general*
[3]*the first movie show*
[4]*last*
[5]*TV program*
[6]*Ask me*
[7]*Who*

VOCABULAIRE[1]

Noms

une **amie**	friend (female)	une **idée**	idea	la **page**	page
un **après-midi**	afternoon	le **japonais**	Japanese language	la **pendule**	clock
un **article**	article	le **jardin**	garden	la **piscine**	swimming pool
le **bâtiment**	building	la **jeune fille**	girl	le **quart**	quarter
la **bibliographie**	bibliography	le **jour**	day	le **rendez-vous**	appointment, date
la **bibliothèque**	library	le **journalisme**	journalism	la **résidence**	dormitory
le **campus**	campus	le **labo**	lab	la **seconde**	second
la **chance**	luck	le **laboratoire**	laboratory	la **semaine**	week
le **chat**	cat	la **leçon**	lesson	le **soir**	evening
le **chien**	dog	la **lettre**	letter	le **stade**	stadium
la **chimie**	chemistry	le **matin**	morning	une **université**	university
le **cinéma**	movie theater; movies	**midi** m	noon	le **vélomoteur**	moped
un **examen**	exam	**minuit** m	midnight	le **vendeur**	salesman
une **heure**	hour; o'clock	la **minute**	minute	la **vendeuse**	saleslady
l'**histoire** f	history	le **mot**	word		
un **hôpital**	hospital	le **numéro**	number		

Verbes

aimer	to like, love	**compter**	to count	marcher	to walk
arriver	to arrive	**déjeuner**	to eat lunch	**parler**	to speak
avancer (de ... minutes)	to be (... minutes) fast (clock)	**demander**	to ask (for)	**quitter**	to leave
		détester	to hate	**regarder**	to look at; to watch
avoir irrég	to have	**écouter**	to listen (to)	**rentrer**	to go (come) home
chercher	to look for	**entrer (dans)**	to enter	**travailler**	to work; to study
commencer	to begin	**étudier**	to study	**trouver**	to find

Adjectifs

bon (bonne)	good	**facile**	easy	**quelle... ?**	what ... ?
demi(e)	half	formidable	great	**universitaire**	(of) university
difficile	difficult	**ouvert(e)**	open		

Adverbes

aujourd'hui	today	**demain**	tomorrow	**presque**	almost
aussi	also, too	ensemble	together	**seulement**	only
beaucoup	a lot	justement	as a mater of fact; exactly	un peu	a little
déjà	already	là	there	vite	quickly

Prépositions

à at, to, in   avec with   pour for

Autres expressions

à la maison	at home	jusqu'à	until
à ma montre	by (according to) my watch	**mais**	but
à quelle heure	at what time	**mais non**	oh, no
à quelle page	on what page	**moi**	me
au contraire	on the contrary	**moins**	minus
au moins	at least	**Oh! là ! là !**	Oh my!
avoir de la chance	to be lucky	**par**	by
avoir rendez-vous	to have an appointment, a date	**pas de**	not any
combien de	how much, how many	pourquoi	why
Comment cela ?	How so?	**Quelle heure est-il ?**	What time is it?
d'accord	OK, fine; agreed	qu'est-ce que	what
de ... à	from ... to	**si**	if
être à la maison	to be (at) home	voici	here is, here are
être en panne	to be broken, not to be working	Zut (alors) !	Shucks!
il y a	there is (are)		

[1]Cardinal numbers from 0–60 are on p. 44.

3 Bonne fête !

Theme and Culture
1. Expressions of calendar dates
2. Holidays and school vacations

Communication Skills
1. Expressing events and schedules in terms of days of the week and dates
2. Expressing possession (*my, your*)
3. Making requests through commands
4. Requesting information about objects and persons (*What book? Which person?*)
5. Asking/Answering questions using numbers (1–100)
6. Expressing the time of day in the twenty-four hour system.

Structures
3.1 Ordinal numbers; names of months
3.2 Days of the week; use of **oui/si**
3.3 First-conjugation verbs (2): **essayer** type; inversion; imperative
3.4 Possessive adjectives: **mon, ton, votre**
3.5 Interrogative adjective **quel**
3.6 Cardinal numbers (61–100); official time expressions

CONVERSATIONS

A. Le calendrier

Regardez la photo à la page 57. C'est un calendrier. Il y a sept jours dans une semaine et douze mois dans une année. Répétez les mois de l'année après moi.

Janvier, février, mars, avril, mai, juin, juillet, août, septembre, octobre, novembre, décembre.

Combien de mois est-ce qu'il y a dans une année ?

Quels sont les mois de l'année ?

Quels sont les mois d'automne /ɔtɔn/ ?

Quels sont les mois d'été ?

Quel est le premier mois de l'année ? Et le dernier mois ?

Maintenant, répétez les jours de la semaine après moi.

Lundi, mardi, mercredi, jeudi, vendredi, samedi, dimanche.

JANV	FEVR	MARS	AVRIL	MAI	JUIN
1 V JOUR de l'AN	1 L Ella	1 M Aubin	1 V Hugues	1 D FÊTE du TRAV.	1 M Justin
2 S Basile	2 M Présentation	2 M Charles le Bon	2 S Sandrine	2 L Boris	2 J Blandine
3 D Epiphanie	3 M Blaise	3 J Guénolé	3 D PÂQUES	3 M Phil., Jacq.	3 V Kévin
4 L Odilon	4 J Véronique	4 V Casimir	4 L Isidore	4 M Sylvain	4 S Clotilde
5 M Edouard	5 V Agathe	5 S Olive	5 M Irène	5 J Judith	5 D Fête-Dieu
6 M Melaine	6 S Gaston	6 D Colette	6 M Marcellin	6 V Prudence	6 L Norbert
7 J Raymond	7 D Eugénie		7 J J.-B. de la S.	7 S Gisèle	7 M Gilbert
8 V Lucien	8 L Jacqueline	7 L Félicité	8 V Julie	8 D VIC. 45/F. J.-d'Arc	8 M Médard
9 S Alix	9 M Apolline	8 M Jean de D.	9 S Gautier	9 L Pacôme	9 J Diane
10 D Guillaume	10 M Arnaud	9 M Françoise	10 D Fulbert	10 M Solange	10 V Landry
11 L Paulin	11 J N.-D. Lourdes	10 J Vivien	11 L Stanislas	11 M Estelle	11 S Barnabé
12 M Tatiana	12 V Félix	11 V Rosine	12 M Jules	12 J ASCENSION	12 D Guy
13 M Yvette	13 S Béatrice	12 S Justine	13 M Ida	13 V Rolande	13 L Antoine de P.
14 J Nina	14 D Valentin	13 D Rodrigue	14 J Maxime	14 S Matthias	14 M Elisée
15 V Rémi	15 L Claude	14 L Mathilde	15 V Paterne	15 D Denise	15 M Germaine
16 S Marcel	16 M Mardi-Gras	15 M Louise de M.	16 S Benoît-J.	16 L Honoré	16 J J.F. Régis
17 D Roseline	17 M Cendres	16 M Bénédicte	17 D Anicet	17 M Pascal	17 V Hervé
18 L Prisca	18 J Bernadette	17 J Patrice	18 L Parfait	18 M Eric	18 S Léonce
19 M Marius	19 V Gabin	18 V Cyrille	19 M Emma	19 J Yves	19 D Romuald
20 M Sébastien	20 S Aimée	19 S Joseph	20 M Odette	20 V Bernardin	20 L Silvère
21 J Agnès	21 D Carême	20 D PRINTEMPS	21 J Anselme	21 S Constantin	21 M ÉTÉ
22 V Vincent	22 L Isabelle	21 L Clémence	22 V Alexandre	22 D PENTECÔTE	22 M Alban
23 S Barnard	23 M Lazare	22 M Léa	23 S Georges	23 L Didier	23 J Audrey
24 D Fr. de Sales	24 M Modeste	23 M Victorien	24 D Jour du Souvenir	24 M Donatien	24 V Jean-Bapt.
25 L Conv.S.Paul	25 J Roméo	24 J Cath. de Su.	25 L Marc	25 M Sophie	25 S Prosper
26 M Paule	26 V Nestor	25 V Annonciation	26 M Alida	26 J Bérenger	26 D Anthelme
27 M Angèle	27 S Honorine	26 S Larissa	27 M Zita	27 V Augustin	27 L Fernand
28 J Th. d'Aquin	28 D Romain	27 D Rameaux	28 J Valérie	28 S Germain	28 M Irénée
29 V Gildas	29 L Auguste	28 L Gontran	29 V Catherine S.	29 D Fête des Mères	29 M Pierre, Paul
30 S Martine		29 M Gwladys	30 S Robert	30 L Ferdinand	30 J Martial
31 D Marcelle		30 M Amédée		31 M Visitation	
		31 J Benjamin			

JUIL	AOUT	SEPT	OCT	NOV	DEC
1 V Thierry	1 L Alphonse	1 J Gilles	1 S Th. de l'E.J.	1 M TOUSSAINT	1 J Florence
2 S Martinien	2 M Julien-Ey.	2 V Ingrid	2 D Léger	2 M Défunts	2 V Viviane
3 D Thomas	3 M Lydie	3 S Grégoire	3 L Gérard	3 J Hubert	3 S Xavier
4 L Florent	4 J J.M.Vian.	4 D Rosalie	4 M Fr. d'Assise	4 V Charles	4 D Barbara
5 M Antoine	5 V Abel	5 L Raïssa	5 M Fleur	5 S Sylvie	5 L Gérald
6 M Mariette	6 S Transfiguration	6 M Bertrand	6 J Bruno	6 D Bertille	6 M Nicolas
7 J Raoul	7 D Gaëtan	7 M Reine	7 V Serge	7 L Carine	7 M Ambroise
8 V Thibault	8 L Dominique	8 J Nativité N.D.	8 S Pélagie	8 M Geoffroy	8 J Imm. Concept.
9 S Amandine	9 M Amour	9 V Alain	9 D Denis	9 M Théodore	9 V P. Fourier
10 D Ulrich	10 M Laurent	10 S Inès	10 L Ghislain	10 J Léon	10 S Romaric
11 L Benoît	11 J Claire	11 D Adelphe	11 M Firmin	11 V ARMISTICE 1918	11 D Daniel
12 M Olivier	12 V Clarisse	12 L Apollinaire	12 M Wilfried	12 S Christian	12 L Jeanne F.C.
13 M Henri, Joël	13 S Hippolyte	13 M Aimé	13 J Géraud	13 D Brice	13 M Lucie
14 J FÊTE NATIONALE	14 D Evrard	14 M La Sainte-Croix	14 V Juste	14 L Sidoine	14 M Odile
15 V Donald	15 L ASSOMPTION	15 J Roland	15 S Th. d'Avila	15 M Albert	15 J Ninon
16 S N.D. Mt-Carmel	16 M Armel	16 V Edith	16 D Edwige	16 M Marguerite	16 V Alice
17 D Charlotte	17 M Hyacinthe	17 S Renaud	17 L Baudouin	17 J Elisabeth	17 S Gaël
18 L Frédéric	18 J Hélène	18 D Nadège	18 M Luc	18 V Aude	18 D Gatien
19 M Arsène	19 V Jean Eudes	19 L Emilie	19 M René	19 S Tanguy	19 L Urbain
20 M Marina	20 S Bernard	20 M Davy	20 J Adeline	20 D Edmond	20 M Abraham
21 J Victor	21 D Christophe	21 M Matthieu	21 V Céline	21 L Près. Marie	21 M HIVER
22 V Marie-M.	22 L Fabrice	22 J AUTOMNE	22 S Elodie	22 M Cécile	22 J Fr.-Xavière
23 S Brigitte	23 M Rose de L.	23 V Constant	23 D Jean de C.	23 M Clément	23 V Armand
24 D Christine	24 M Barthélemy	24 S Thècle	24 L Florentin	24 J Flora	24 S Adèle
25 L Jacques	25 J Louis	25 D Hermann	25 M Crépin	25 V Catherine L.	25 D NOËL
26 M Anne, Joa.	26 V Natacha	26 L Côme, Dam.	26 M Dimitri	26 S Delphine	26 L Etienne
27 M Nathalie	27 S Monique	27 M Vinc. de Paul	27 J Emeline	27 D Avent	27 M Jean
28 J Samson	28 D Augustin	28 M Venceslas	28 V Sim., Jude	28 L Jacques d. I.M.	28 M Innocents
29 V Marthe	29 L Sabine	29 J Michel	29 S Narcisse	29 M Saturnin	29 J David
30 S Juliette	30 M Fiacre	30 V Jérôme	30 D Bienvenue	30 M André	30 V Roger
31 D Ignace de L.	31 M Aristide		31 L Quentin		31 S Sylvestre

Combien de jours est-ce qu'il y a dans une semaine ?

Quels sont les jours de la semaine ?

Quel est le premier jour de la semaine ? Et le dernier jour ?

Quels sont les jours de congé ?

B. C'est le vingt et un septembre.

ROBERT	Quelle est la date aujourd'hui ?
JACQUELINE	C'est jeudi.
ROBERT	Non, non, je demande la date. Est-ce le vingt septembre ?
JACQUELINE	Non, c'est le vingt et un septembre.

« C'est pour l'anniversaire de ma sœur. »

C. C'est l'anniversaire de mon frère.

MME GEORGET	Est-ce que votre anniversaire est le 21 mars ?
CÉCILE	Non, le 21 mars, c'est l'anniversaire de mon frère.
MME GEORGET	Tiens[1], c'est drôle. C'est aussi l'anniversaire de mon mari.
CÉCILE	Et c'est le premier jour du printemps.

DIFFÉRENCES

Les jours fériés[2]

Holidays in France are a time for festivities, family get-togethers, traditional food and drink, and joyous celebrations. Many French holidays are religious in origin, dating back to the early Middle Ages, even though many French avoid too much display on religious days, even at Christmas and Easter. Other holidays commemorate historic events. **La Fête Nationale**, Bastille Day (July 14) commemorates the Revolution of 1789. On that day, the revolutionaries stormed the Bastille fortress in Paris, long used as a prison and regarded as a symbol of despotism and oppression. People celebrate the day with a great deal of enthusiasm by singing *La Marseillaise*, the French national anthem, organizing parades, dancing in the streets, and watching fireworks.

All French workers receive five weeks of paid vacation during the year (most of them take four weeks in August) in addition to the holidays listed below. When a holiday falls on a Thursday (which is always the case for Ascension), many employers make a

[1]*Well!*
[2]*Holidays*

Le quatorze juillet est le jour de la Fête Nationale en France.

long, four-day weekend by closing their businesses on Friday; this custom is known as **faire le pont** (literally, *to make the bridge* or *to bridge over*).

Le Jour de l'An (1ᵉʳ janvier)	*New Year's Day*
Le Lundi de Pâques (mars ou avril)	*Easter Monday*
La Fête du Travail (1ᵉʳ mai)	*May Day (Labor Day)*
La Fête de la Victoire (8 mai)	*Victory Day (end of World War II)*
L'Ascension (mai, un jeudi)	*Ascension Day (40 days after Easter)*
Le Lundi de Pentecôte (mai ou juin)	*Whit Monday (10 days after Ascension)*
La Fête Nationale (14 juillet)	*Bastille Day*
L'Assomption (15 août)	*Assumption Day*
La Toussaint (1ᵉʳ novembre)	*All Saints' Day (French Memorial Day)*
La Fête de la Victoire (11 novembre)	*Armistice Day (end of World War I)*
Noël (25 décembre)	*Christmas*

 BELIER *(21 mars- 20 avril.)*

 TAUREAU *(21 avril- 20 mai.)*

 GEMEAUX *(21 mai- 21 juin.)*

 CANCER *(22 juin- 22 juillet.)*

 LION *(23 juillet- 23 août.)*

VIERGE *(24 août- 22 septembre.)*

 BALANCE *(23 septembre- 23 octobre.)*

 SCORPION *(24 octobre- 22 novembre.)*

 SAGITTAIRE *(23 novembre- 21 décembre.)*

 CAPRICORNE *(22 décembre- 20 janvier.)*

 VERSEAU *(21 janvier- 19 février.)*

 POISSONS *(20 février- 20 mars.)*

Les congés scolaires[1]
In public schools, classes are held all day (until four or five in the afternoon) on Monday, Tuesday, Thursday, and Friday, and until noon on Saturday (primary school children have no classes on Wednesday, and **lycée** students have morning classes). There are several vacation periods. Most universities also follow similar schedules, but with shorter periods except for summer vacation.

vacances[2] **de février (vacances d'hiver)**	Ten days in February
vacances de printemps (vacances de Pâques)	Close to two weeks from late March to early April
vacances d'été (grandes vacances)	About ten weeks, beginning in late June and ending in early September
vacances de Toussaint	Ten days from the end of October to early November
vacances de Noël	Two weeks, from December to January

STRUCTURES

3.1 NOMBRES ORDINAUX ; LES MOIS DE L'ANNÉE

1. The ordinal numbers (*first*, *second*, *third*, etc., in English) are formed by adding **-ième** to the corresponding cardinal numbers, except for **premier** *m* and **première** *f*. If the cardinal number ends in **-e**, the **e** is dropped before adding **-ième**: **quatre → quatrième**, **onze → onzième**. Note also the irregular formation in the case of **cinq → cinquième** and **neuf → neuvième**. (Note that the ordinal numbers are used as a header on the left-side page of our book to identify the lessons.)

un, une	→ **premier, première**[3]		dix	→ **dixième** /dizjɛm/
deux	→ **deuxième**[4]		onze	→ **onzième**[5]
trois	→ **troisième**		dix-neuf	→ **dix-neuvième**
quatre	→ **quatrième**		vingt	→ **vingtième**
cinq	→ **cinquième**		vingt et un	→ **vingt et unième**
six	→ **sixième** /sizjɛm/			/vɛ̃teynjɛm/
sept	→ **septième** /sɛtjɛm/		vingt-sept	→ **vingt-septième**
ḥuit	→ **ḥuitième**[5]		trente	→ **trentième**
neuf	→ **neuvième**			

2. Ordinal numbers are often represented by Roman or Arabic numerals followed by **e** or **ème**.

premier, première	Ier, Ière ; 1er, 1ère
deuxième	IIe/IIème ; 2e/2ème
cinquième	V^e/Vème ; 5e/5ème
dixième	X^e/Xème ; 10e/10ème
vingtième	XXe/XXème ; 20e/20ème

---

[1]*School holidays* (**congés** literally, *days off*)

[2]*vacation.* In this meaning the word **vacances** is always in the plural.

[3]Note that the **accent grave** (`) occurs only in the feminine form.

[4]**Second** and **seconde** /sgɔ̃/, /sgɔ̃d/ also occur, but usually to denote the second item in a series of two.

[5]There is no elision before these words: **C'est le ḥuitième mois, C'est la onzième leçon** (see Lesson 2.4).

3. Names of months were presented in **Conversation A**. Review them again here, paying careful attention to pronunciation. Note that they do not begin with capital letters in French.

janvier	/ʒɑ̃vje/	*January*	**juillet**	/ʒɥijɛ/	*July*
février		*February*	**août**	/u, ut/	*August*
mars	/maʀs/	*March*	**septembre**	/sɛptɑ̃bʀ/	*September*
avril	/avʀil/	*April*	**octobre**		*October*
mai		*May*	**novembre**		*November*
juin	/ʒɥɛ̃/	*June*	**décembre**		*December*

A *Donnez le nombre ordinal qui correspond à chaque nombre cardinal.*[1]

Modèle : un
        premier

a. deux	d. cinq	g. vingt-trois	j. quarante-quatre
b. trois	e. dix	h. vingt-cinq	k. cinquante et un
c. neuf	f. vingt	i. trente et un	l. soixante

B *Changez les expressions suivantes d'après le modèle.*

Modèle : La leçon numéro deux
        La deuxième leçon

1. La leçon numéro six
2. La leçon numéro neuf
3. La leçon numéro dix
4. La leçon numéro vingt et un
5. La leçon numéro vingt-deux
6. La leçon numéro vingt-cinq

C *Répondez aux questions.*

1. Quel est le premier mois de l'année ? Et le septième ? Et le dixième ? Et le onzième ?
2. Est-ce que mai est le sixième mois de l'année ? Est-ce que mars est le cinquième mois de l'année ?
3. Combien de mois est-ce qu'il y a dans une année ? Quel est le dernier mois de l'année ?

Dictée

3.2 LES JOURS DE LA SEMAINE ; EMPLOI DE **OUI**/**SI**

1. Names of the days of the week were presented in **Conversations**. Review the pronunciation as shown below. In France, as in most European countries, Monday is the first day of the week. Unlike English, in French days of the week, like names of the months, are not capitalized.

lundi	/lɛ̃di/	*Monday*	**vendredi**	/vɑ̃dʀədi/	*Friday*
mardi	/maʀdi/	*Tuesday*	**samedi**	/samdi/	*Saturday*
mercredi	/mɛʀkʀədi/	*Wednesday*	**dimanche**	/dimɑ̃ʃ/	*Sunday*
jeudi	/ʒødi/	*Thursday*			

2. Dates are always preceded by the definite article **le** when they occur in a sentence, followed by the month. The ordinal number is used only for the *first* of the month: **premier**.

Quelle est la date aujourd'hui ?   *What is today's date?*
— C'est **le premier** octobre.   *It's the first of October.*
Quelle est la date de Noël ?   *What is the date of Christmas?*
— C'est **le vingt-cinq** décembre.   *It's December 25th.*

[1]*Give the ordinal number that corresponds to each cardinal number.*

3. The phrase **c'est** *it is* is used to express dates in French. **Aujourd'hui** *today* cannot be the subject of a sentence. The phrase **est-ce** is an inverted form of **c'est**, used in questions.[1] Note that **Quel jour** usually refers to the day of the week, while **Quelle est la date** refers to the day of the month.

Quel jour **est-ce** aujourd'hui ?	*What day is it today?*
— **C'est** (aujourd'hui) jeudi.	*It's Thursday (today).*

You will recall from Lesson 2.5 that **il est** *it is* and **est-il ?** are used to express clock time in French.

Quelle heure **est-il** ?	*What time is it?*
— **Il est** dix heures et quart.	*It's quarter past ten.*

4. Unlike English, dates and days of the week in French are not preceded by a preposition.

Nous arrivons à Paris **samedi**.	*We arrive in Paris **on** Saturday.*
L'hiver commence **le 22 décembre**.	*Winter begins **on** December 22nd.*

When the definite article **le** is used before a day of the week, it usually corresponds to English *every*.

Le mardi je déjeune à midi.	*On Tuesday**s** (Every Tuesday) I eat lunch at noon.*
Êtes-vous libre **le vendredi** ?	*Are you free on Friday**s** (every Friday)?*

5. **Oui** *versus* **Si**. French has two words meaning *yes*, and they are not used interchangeably. **Oui** is used for all affirmative answers to *affirmative* questions or statements. But **Si** must be used for all affirmative answers to *negative* questions or statements.

AFFIRMATIVE QUESTIONS/STATEMENTS	NEGATIVE QUESTIONS/STATEMENTS
Est-ce que Paul a des frères ?	Est-ce que Paul n'a pas de frères ?
— **Oui**, il a deux frères.	— **Si**, il a deux frères.
Est-ce que c'est mardi aujourd'hui ?	Est-ce que ce n'est pas mardi ?
— **Oui**, c'est mardi.	— **Si**, c'est mardi.

A *Répondez aux questions.*

1. Quel jour est-ce aujourd'hui ? Quelle est la date ? Quelle est la date demain ? Quelle heure est-il ?
2. Quel est le premier jour de la semaine ? Et le dernier jour de la semaine ? Quel est le dernier mois de l'année ?
3. Quels sont les mois d'été ? Et les mois d'automne /ɔtɔn/ ? Et les mois de printemps /prɛ̃tɑ̃/ ? Et les mois d'hiver /ivɛʀ/ ?

B *Répondez aux questions.*

1. Est-ce que samedi est le sixième jour de la semaine ? Est-ce que jeudi n'est pas le cinquième jour ?
2. Est-ce qu'il n'y a pas trente jours en septembre ? Est-ce qu'il y a trente jours en juin ?
3. Avez-vous des cours le samedi ? Est-ce que vous n'avez pas de cours le lundi ? Quels jours n'avez-vous pas de cours ?

C *Parlons du calendrier et des jours fériés.*

1. Quelle est la date de Noël ? Et la date de la Fête Nationale en France ? Et la date de la Déclaration de l'Indépendance américaine ?

---

[1]**Est-ce** and **c'est** can be replaced by **est-ce que nous sommes** and **nous sommes**: Quel jour est-ce que nous sommes (aujourd'hui) ? — Nous sommes jeudi.

2. Quelle est la date de la Fête du Travail en France ? Et aux États-Unis[1] ?
3. Quelle est la date de *Thanksgiving* aux États-Unis ? Et la date de la Saint-Valentin ?
4. Quelle est la date de la Toussaint ? Et la date de *Halloween* ? Et la date du Nouvel An[2] ?
5. En quel mois est-ce que les vacances d'été commencent ? Quelle est la date de la rentrée ?

 Compréhension auditive

3.3 VERBES DU PREMIER GROUPE (-ER) (2) ; ESSAYER ; INVERSION ; IMPÉRATIF

1. Verbs ending in **-ayer**, such as **essayer** *to try (on)* and **payer** *to pay for,* change the **y** in the stem to **i**, except for the **nous** and **vous** forms.

essayer

essaie	essayons
essaies	essayez
essaie	essaient

j' **essaie**	/esɛ/		je **paie**	/pɛ/
tu **essaies**			tu **paies**	
il/elle **essaie**			ill/elle **paie**	
nous_**essayons**	/esɛjõ/		nous **payons**	/pɛjõ/
vous_**essayez**			vous **payez**	
ils/elles_**essaient**	/esɛ/		ils/elles **paient**	/pɛ/

2. *Question by inversion.* In most cases, a statement can be changed into a question by one of three different ways. The first is to place **Est-ce que** in front of the statement and use rising intonation, as you learned in Lesson 1.2. The second is to use rising intonation alone, with no other change in the statement. This type occurs frequently in colloquial French, but almost never in written French. A third way is to *invert* (reverse the order of) the subject pronoun and the verb, using rising intonation. In written language, a hyphen connects the verb and the inverted subject pronoun. For the moment, we will use inversion only for the **vous** form.[3]

Vous cherchez la vendeuse. →
- **Est-ce que vous cherchez** la vendeuse ?
- **Vous cherchez** la vendeuse ?
- **Cherchez-vous** la vendeuse ?

In inversion, **ne/n'** comes before the verb, and **pas** after the inverted subject pronoun.

Parlez-vous français ?   Aimez-vous le cours ?
→ **Ne** parlez-vous **pas** français ?   → N'aimez-vous **pas** le cours ?

3. *Imperative forms.* Imperative sentences—commands, such as *Do (something), Don't do (something)*—are formed by deleting the subject pronouns **vous, tu,** or **nous.** They are pronounced with a descending intonation. Note that imperative sentences are often shown with the exclamation mark (!). It does not mean that the speaker is angry or shouting.

INDICATIVE	IMPERATIVE
Vous **regardez** les blousons.	→ **Regardez** les blousons !
Vous **n'essayez pas** le blouson.	→ **N'essayez pas** le blouson !

The **tu** form command drops the **s** of the ending **-es** (no difference in pronunciation).

Tu **entres** dans la boutique.	→ **Entre** dans la boutique !
Tu ne **cherches** pas la boutique.	→ Ne **cherche** pas la boutique !

---

[1]**aux États-Unis** *in the United States*
[2]**Nouvel An** *New Year's Day*
[3]Inversion with other subject pronouns will be presented in Lesson 5.4.

The **nous** form command corresponds to English *Let's (do something)*, *Let's not*.

Parlons français en classe[1] !   *Let's speak French in class!*

Ne **parlons** pas anglais !   *Let's not speak English!*

4. **S'il te/vous plaît.** Commands are often followed by **s'il te plaît** or **s'il vous plaît** *please*. **S'il te plaît** is used when you are addressing someone with **tu**, and **s'il vous plaît** when you are addressing someone with **vous**. These formulas of politeness are usually attached to the *end* of the sentence, unless you want to attract someone's attention (for example, in a store), in which case it is placed at the beginning.

Écoute la cassette, **s'il te plaît**.   *Please listen to the cassette.*

Parlez français, **s'il vous plaît**.   *Please speak French.*

S'il vous plaît, Madame. Combien est-ce que cela coûte ?   *Please (Excuse me), ma'am. How much does that cost?*

1	2	3	4
arriver	regarder	entrer	chercher

5	6	7	8
parler	essayer	payer	quitter

TABLEAU 16

 A   *Regardez le Tableau 16 et répétez après moi.*

La jeune fille arrive à la boutique.
Elle regarde les blousons.
Elle entre dans la boutique.
Elle cherche la vendeuse.
Elle parle à la vendeuse.
Elle essaie les blousons.
Elle paie le blouson à la vendeuse.[2]
Elle quitte la boutique.

[1]**en classe** *in class* (cf. **dans la [salle de] classe** *in the classroom*)
[2]*She pays the salesperson (saleslady) for the jacket.*

Il cherche un blouson.

Maintenant, posez des questions d'après ce modèle.

J'arrive à la boutique.
Arrivez-vous à la boutique ?

1. J'arrive à la boutique.
2. Je regarde les blousons.
3. J'entre dans la boutique.
4. Je cherche la vendeuse.

5. Je parle à la vendeuse.
6. J'essaie les blousons.
7. Je paie le blouson à la vendeuse.
8. Je quitte la boutique.

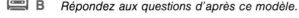 **B** *Répondez aux questions d'après ce modèle.*

Je regarde les blousons ?[1]
(Maryse) **Oui, regardez les blousons, s'il vous plaît.**
(Patrick) **Mais non[2], ne regardez pas les blousons !**

1. J'entre dans la boutique ?
2. Je cherche la vendeuse ?
3. Je parle à la vendeuse ?

4. J'essaie les blousons ?
5. Je paie le blouson à la vendeuse ?
6. Je quitte la boutique ?

C *Il y a deux étudiants maintenant. Ajoutez des phrases d'après ce modèle.*

Nous regardons les blousons.
(Michel) **Ne regardons pas les blousons !**
(Sylvie) **Si, regardons les blousons !**

1. Nous entrons dans la boutique.
2. Nous cherchons la vendeuse.
3. Nous parlons à la vendeuse.
4. Nous essayons les blousons.

5. Nous payons les blousons à la vendeuse.
6. Nous quittons la boutique.

---

[1]The meaning here is *Shall I look at . . . ?* rather than *Do I look at . . . ?*

[2]**Mais non** *Oh, no* (more emphatic than **non** alone)

D *Posez des questions à votre partenaire, d'après ce modèle.*

chercher la montre
(Anne-Marie) **Je cherche la montre ?**
(Pierre-Yves) **Oui, cherche la montre, s'il te plaît.**

1. poser une question au vendeur
2. regarder le livre
3. écouter la cassette

4. parler à la vendeuse
5. étudier la leçon
6. entrer dans le bureau

 Compréhension auditive

3.4 ADJECTIFS POSSESSIFS (1) : **MON, TON, VOTRE**

Words corresponding to English *my, your, his, her, its, our,* and *their* are known as possessive adjectives. In French, the possessive adjective agrees in gender (*m/f*) and number (*s/pl*) with the noun that follows it. You may first want to take a look at the summary of all the forms in Lesson 4.4 (p. 91).

1. The possessive adjective for the first-person singular (**je**) is **mon** /mõ/ before a masculine singular noun, and **ma** /ma/ before a feminine singular noun.

   Où est **mon** cahier ?   Where is my notebook?
   Où est **ma** montre ?   Where is my watch?

   If the word following the possessive adjective begins with a vowel sound, **mon‿** /mõn/ is used for *both* masculine and feminine nouns.

   Voilà **mon‿**appartement (*m*).   There's my apartment.
   Voilà **mon‿**adresse (*f*).   There's my address.

   Mes is used before both masculine and feminine plural nouns.

   Où sont **mes** livres (*m*) ?   Where are my books?
   Où sont **mes** clés (*f*) ?   Where are my keys?
   Où sont **mes‿**amis (*m*) ?   Where are my friends?

2. The forms of the possessive adjective for **tu** are **ton** /tõ/ before a masculine singular noun, and **ta** /ta/ before a feminine singular noun: **ton‿** /tõn/ is used before both masculine and feminine singular nouns that begin with a vowel sound.

   Où est **mon** frère ?   — Voilà **ton** frère.
   Où est **ma** sœur ?   — Voilà **ta** sœur.

   Où est **mon‿**ami (*m*) ?   — Voilà **ton‿**ami (*m*).
   Où est **mon‿**amie (*f*) ?   — Voilà **ton‿**amie (*f*).

   Before a plural noun, **tes** /te/ (/tez‿/ in liaison) is used.

   Où sont **mes** frères ?   — Voilà **tes** frères.
   Où sont **mes** sœurs ?   — Voilà **tes** sœurs.
   Où sont **mes‿**amis ?   — Voilà **tes‿**amis.

3. The possessive adjective for the **vous** form is **votre** before a masculine or feminine noun. It is pronounced /vɔtʀə/ before a consonant,[1] and /vɔtʀ/ before a word beginning with a vowel sound.

   Où est **mon** stylo ?   — Voilà **votre** stylo.   /vɔtʀə/
   Où est **ma** chaise ?   — Voilà **votre** chaise.   /vɔtʀə/

[1]In fast colloquial French, **votre** /vɔtʀə/ is often shortened to /vɔt/ before a consonant sound.

Où est **mon** appartement ?   — Voilà **votre** appartement. /vɔtʀ/

Où est **mon** adresse ?   — Voilà **votre** adresse. /vɔtʀ/

Before a plural noun, **votre** becomes **vos** /vo/, /voz/ .

Où sont **mes** frères ?   — Voilà **vos** frères.

Où sont **mes** sœurs ?   — Voilà **vos** sœurs.

Où sont **mes** amis?   — Voilà **vos** amis.

Est-ce que c'est **ton** livre ?   Est-ce que c'est **votre** chaise ?
— Ah oui, c'est **mon** livre.   — Oui, c'est **ma** chaise.

TABLEAU 17

A   *Remplacez*[1] ***un**, **une**, **des** par **mon**, **ma**, **mes** d'après les modèles.*

Voilà un cahier.   C'est une table.
Voilà mon cahier.   **C'est ma table.**

1. Voilà une montre.
2. Voilà des clés.
3. Voilà une enveloppe.
4. Voilà un voisin[2].
5. Voilà des crayons.
6. Voilà un appartement.
7. Ce sont des amis.
8. C'est un ami.
9. C'est une amie.
10. Ce sont des voisines[2].
11. C'est une adresse.
12. C'est un professeur.

B   *Répétez l'exercice précédent. Remplacez **un**, **une**, **des** par **votre** ou **vos**, d'après les modèles.*

Voilà un cahier.   C'est une table.
Voilà votre cahier.   **C'est votre table.**

C   *Regardez bien et répondez d'après les modèles.*

Est-ce que c'est mon cahier ? (livre)
Mais non, ce n'est pas votre cahier. C'est votre livre !
Est-ce que c'est votre cahier ? (livre)
Mais non, ce n'est pas mon cahier. C'est mon livre !

1. Est-ce que c'est mon livre ? (cahier)
2. Est-ce que c'est ma montre ? (stylo)
3. Est-ce que ce sont mes crayons ? (clés)
4. Est-ce que c'est votre cahier ? (livre)
5. Est-ce que c'est votre stylo ? (montre)
6. Est-ce que ce sont vos parents ? (camarades)

---

[1]*Replace*
[2]**voisin** /vwazɛ̃/, **voisine** /vwazin/ *neighbor*

D *Maintenant, répondez aux questions.*

1. Voilà mon livre de français. Avez-vous votre livre de français ? Où est votre cahier d'exercices ?
2. Le (23 novembre) est la date de mon anniversaire. Quelle est la date de votre anniversaire ?
3. (Jeanne), qui[1] est votre voisin(e) de gauche[2] ? (Jacques), qui est votre voisin(e) de droite ?
4. Est-ce que je ne suis pas votre professeur ? Est-ce que vous n'êtes pas mes étudiants ? Est-ce que je suis votre père (mère) ?
5. Regardez-vous ma montre ? Est-ce que je regarde votre montre ? Est-ce que (Janine) regarde votre livre ?
6. Est-ce que j'ai votre adresse ? Avez-vous mon adresse ? Est-ce que (Jacques) a votre adresse ?

E *Posez des questions à votre partenaire. Prenez des notes.[3]*

1. Où est ton père ?   (Mon père est à New York/Mon père est mort[4]/etc.[5])
2. Où est ta mère ?   (Ma mère est aussi à New York/Ma mère est morte[4]/etc.)
3. Est-ce que tu as des frères ?   (J'ai un frère/J'ai deux frères/Je n'ai pas de frères/etc.)
4. Comment s'appelle ton frère ? (Comment s'appellent tes frères ?)[6]   (Mes frères s'appellent Bill et Mike/Mon frère s'appelle Bob/etc.)
5. Est-ce que tu as des sœurs ?
6. Comment s'appelle ta sœur ? (Comment s'appellent tes sœurs ?)
7. Est-ce que tu as une stéréo ?
8. Où est ta stéréo ?   (Ma stéréo est dans mon appartement/dans ma chambre/etc.)

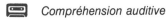 *Compréhension auditive*

3.5 ADJECTIF INTERROGATIF **QUEL**

1. The interrogative adjective **quel** + noun corresponds to English *Which/What* + noun. **Quel** is always used with a noun, and asks for more information about it. There are four different forms (**quel, quelle, quels, quelles**) to agree in gender (*m/f*) and number (*s/pl*) with the noun it modifies. All these forms are pronounced /kɛl/, except when there is liaison in the plural forms: (/kɛlz/).

Quel livre est sur la table ?	*What/Which book is on the table?*
— Mon livre est sur la table.	*My book is on the table.*
Quelles clés sont ici ?	*What keys are here?*
— Les clés de la maison sont ici.	*The house keys are here.*
Quels étudiants cherchez-vous ?	*What/Which students are you looking for?*
— Je cherche vos étudiants.	*I am looking for your students.*

2. If **quel** + noun is used with a verb that takes a preposition, then the preposition must be moved to the beginning of the question. Note that in English the preposition is normally left at the end of the question.

Vous parlez **de la maison à côté de la boutique**.	*You are talking **about** the house next to the shop.*
→ **De quelle maison** parlez-vous ?	→ *What/Which house are you talking **about**?*

---

[1]*who*

[2]**voisin(e) de gauche/de droite** *neighbor on the left/right*

[3]*Take notes.* If this exercise is done, you may be asked to report the results of your interview when you study more possessive adjectives in Lesson 4.4.

[4]**mort** /mɔʀ/, **morte** /mɔʀt/ *dead, deceased*

[5]**et caetera** /etseteʀa/

[6]**Comment s'appelle(nt)... ?** *What is (are) the name(s) of . . . ?*

« Voyons... quelle est l'adresse exacte de l'avocat ? »

Ils sont **dans** le bureau là-bas.	*They are **in** the office over there.*
→ **Dans** quel bureau est-ce qu'ils sont ?	*→ What/Which office are they **in**?*

3. When used with **être**, **quel** is sometimes separated from the noun it modifies. But it still agrees in gender and number with the noun, which comes after **être**. This construction corresponds to English *What is . . .* + noun.

Quel est votre **nom** ?	*What is your name?*
— Marie-Claire Pouleur.	
Quelle est votre **nationalité** ?	*What is your nationality?*
— Je suis belge.	
Quelle est votre **profession** ?	*What is your profession?*
— Je suis professeur.	
Quelle est votre **adresse** ?	*What is your address?*
— C'est 28, chaussée de Waterloo.[1]	
Quel est votre **sport** préféré ?	*What is your favorite sport?*
— C'est le tennis /tɛnis/.	

4. *Cognates.* Words that are spelled more or less alike in two languages and have the same meaning are called "cognates." Many French nouns ending in **-ité** (feminine) have English cognates ending in *-ity.* Likewise, many French nouns ending in **-sion**, **-ssion**, or **-tion** (all feminine) usually have English cognates with the same endings. You can recognize many more French words by learning to identify cognates. Appendix A (p. A1) gives you a list of easily recognizable cognate endings.

---

[1]Note that a comma is used after the house number.

ité /ite/	**-sion** /zjõ/, sjõ/[1]	**-ssion** /sjõ/	**-tion** /sjõ/
capacité	conclusion	expression	éducation
générosité	décision	mission	option
liberté	dimension	possession	nation
nationalité	inversion	profession	négation

TABLEAU 18   Je pense **à un livre**.   **À quel livre** est-ce que tu penses ?

A *Regardez le Tableau 16 à la page 64. Posez des questions d'après ce modèle.*

Vous arrivez à la boutique.
À quelle boutique est-ce que j'arrive ?

1. Vous arrivez à la boutique.
2. Vous regardez les blousons.
3. Vous entrez dans la boutique.
4. Vous cherchez la vendeuse.
5. Vous parlez à la vendeuse.
6. Vous essayez les blousons.
7. Vous payez le blouson à la vendeuse.
8. Vous quittez la boutique.

B *Regardez maintenant le Tableau 9 à la page 39. Posez des questions d'après ce modèle.*

J'arrive au bâtiment.
À quel bâtiment arrivez-vous ?

1. J'arrive au bâtiment.
2. Je trouve la classe.
3. J'entre dans la classe.
4. Je regarde la montre.
5. J'écoute le professeur.
6. J'aime le cours.
7. Je parle au professeur.
8. Je quitte la classe.

C *Nous posons des questions à une Française. Répétez après moi.*

Quel est votre nom ? — Monique Georget.
Quelle est votre nationalité ? — Je suis française.
Quelle est votre profession ? — Je suis institutrice[2].
Quelle est votre adresse ? — 27, rue de Craponne.
Quel est votre sport préféré ? — C'est le tennis.

Maintenant, posez des questions.

1. Jacqueline Chaumière.
2. Je suis canadienne.
3. Je suis infirmière.
4. 17, avenue Victor-Hugo.
5. C'est le camping /kãpiŋ/.
6. Je suis dentiste.
7. Je suis américain.
8. C'est le football[3].
9. C'est 45, rue du Commerce.
10. Jim Wilson.

[1]The pronunciation /zjõ/ always occurs when the **s** is between two vowel sounds, as in the first two examples. If it is preceded by a consonant letter, it is pronounced /sjõ/, as in the last two examples.

[2]schoolteacher

[3]**Le football** in French always means *soccer*, a very popular sport in Europe. **Le football américain** *American-style football* is rarely played in Europe.

D *Comment est-ce que vous demandez les renseignements suivants ?[1]*

1. l'heure
2. la date
3. le nom d'une personne
4. la nationalité de la personne
5. la date de l'anniversaire de la personne
6. la profession de la personne
7. l'adresse de la personne
8. le sport préféré de la personne
9. l'adresse des parents de la personne

Maintenant, faites une interview d'un de vos camarades en utilisant ces expressions.[2]

3.6 NOMBRES CARDINAUX (DE 61 À 100) ; L'HEURE (2)

1. Numbers between 61 and 99 are counted *in sets of twenty*. First try to associate any number in the 60s and 70s with **soixante**, and any number in the 80s and 90s with **quatre-vingt**. Then add 1–9 for those in the 60s and 80s, and 10–19 for those in the 70s and 90s.[3] Note also that **et** occurs in 21, 31, 41, 51, 61, and 71, but not in 81 and 91. The plural marker appears only in **quatre-vingts** *eighty*.

60	**soixante**	80	**quatre-vingts**
61	soixante **et un**	81	quatre-vingt-**un** /katʀəvɛ̃ɛ̃/
62	soixante-**deux**	82	quatre-vingt-**deux**
63	soixante-**trois**	83	quatre-vingt-**trois**
64	soixante-**quatre**	84	quatre-vingt-**quatre**
65	soixante-**cinq**	85	quatre-vingt-**cinq**
66	soixante-**six**	86	quatre-vingt-**six**
69	soixante-**neuf**	89	quatre-vingt-**neuf**
70	soixante-**dix**	90	quatre-vingt-**dix**
71	soixante **et onze**	91	quatre-vingt-**onze** /katʀəvɛ̃ɔ̃z/
72	soixante-**douze**	92	quatre-vingt-**douze**
73	soixante-**treize**	93	quatre-vingt-**treize**
74	soixante-**quatorze**	94	quatre-vingt-**quatorze**
75	soixante-**quinze**	95	quatre-vingt-**quinze**
76	soixante-**seize**	96	quatre-vingt-**seize**
77	soixante-**dix-sept**	97	quatre-vingt-**dix-sept**
78	soixante-**dix-huit**	98	quatre-vingt-**dix-huit**
79	soixante-**dix-neuf**	99	quatre-vingt-**dix-neuf**
		100	**cent** /sɑ̃/

2. **Un** in 61 and 81 must be changed to **et une** before a feminine noun.

soixante **et un** livres   quatre-vingt-**un** étudiants
soixante **et une** tables   quatre-vingt-**une** chaises

[1]*How do you ask for the following information?* **Renseignements** *information* is usually used in the plural as in *Renseignements et opinions* of our **Applications**.

[2]*Now do an interview of one of your classmates by using those expressions.* The person selected pretends to be a famous person so that the **vous** and **votre** forms are used in the questions.

[3]In Switzerland, people often say **septante** (70), **octante** (80), **nonante** (90), and in Belgium, **septante** (70), **quatre-vingts** (80), and **nonante** (90).

3. *Time.* In France as well as in the rest of Europe, the twenty-four hour clock is used to indicate office and store business hours, transportation schedules, and the starting times for public events such as concerts, plays, movies, and lectures. This eliminates the necessity of having to specify A.M. and P.M. The word **heure(s)** is normally abbreviated as **h**.

10 h 10 dix heures dix
12 h 35 douze heures trente-cinq (= une heure moins vingt-cinq)
20 h 30 vingt heures trente (= huit heures et demie du soir)
23 h 45 vingt-trois heures quarante-cinq (= minuit moins le quart)

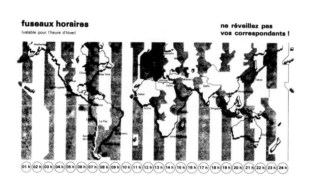

horaires d'ouverture

le lundi de 13h à 19h
et du mardi au samedi
de 10h à 19h

 A *Lisez à haute voix les nombres suivants.*[1]

60, 61, 62, 63, 70, 71, 72, 75, 76, 77, 79, 80, 81, 82, 84, 89, 90, 91, 92, 93, 94, 95, 96, 97, 98, 99.

B *Comptons maintenant.*[2]

1. Comptez par dix de 10 à 100.
2. Comptez par cinq de 50 à 100.
3. Comptez par deux de 60 à 80.
4. Comptez par deux de 80 à 100.

C *Répondez aux questions.*

1. Combien d'heures est-ce qu'il y a dans un jour ? Et dans deux jours ? Et dans trois jours ?
2. Regardez notre livre de français. À quelle page commencent les leçons suivantes ?

   a. la première leçon   c. la troisième leçon
   b. la deuxième leçon   d. la quatrième leçon

3. Lisez les adresses suivantes.

   a. 72, rue de Rivoli   d. 86, boulevard Saint-Michel
   b. 95, rue Saint-Jacques   e. 91, rue Saint-Martin
   c. 79, avenue Victor Hugo   f. 68, rue de Seine

4. Lisez les phrases suivantes, puis redites l'heure d'une autre façon.[3]

   a. Le train arrive à 9 h 50.   d. Le concert commence à 20 h 40.
   b. Le film commence à 21 h 45.   e. Le restaurant est ouvert à 19 h 30.
   c. Le musée est fermé à 19 h 30.   f. Le monument est fermé après 20 h.

Dictée

[1]*Read the following numbers out loud.* Recorded in a substantially modified form.

[2]Recorded in a substantially modified form.

[3]*Read the following sentences, then say the time again in another way.* Use the twelve-hour system: **neuf heures cinquante** becomes **dix heures moins dix du matin**.

APPLICATIONS

« *Voici une carte pour mon copain Jules.* »

🔊 **A** **Situations**

Bonne fête ![1]
C'est vendredi soir. Il est 20 heures. Christine est dans l'appartement d'Ignès. Elles regardent la télévision. Julien Reynaud frappe à[2] *la porte.*

I'm coming	CHRISTINE	Oui, j'arrive° !

à la main *in his hand*   *Elle ouvre*[3] *la porte. Julien entre avec un bouquet à la main°.*

	CHRISTINE	Tiens, salut, Julien. Ça va ?	5
TV program	JULIEN	Bonsoir, Christine. Bonsoir, Ignès. Ah, vous regardez la télévision ? Quelle émission° est-ce que c'est ?	
	IGNÈS	C'est un film de Cocteau : *La Belle et la Bête.*	
	JULIEN	Ah oui ? Justement, c'est un de mes films préférés.	
Good, Fine.	CHRISTINE	Ah bon.° Regarde le film avec nous, alors.	10
	IGNÈS	Mais qu'est-ce que c'est ? Tu as des fleurs ?	
	JULIEN	Oui, c'est pour toi[4].	
How nice of you!	IGNÈS	Pour moi ? Comme tu es gentil !° Mais pourquoi est-ce que tu apportes des fleurs ? Ce n'est pas mon anniversaire.	
	JULIEN	Pourquoi ? Parce que c'est aujourd'hui le 10 septembre. Et c'est la Sainte Ignès[5]. Bonne fête !	15

[1]*Happy saint's day!* (literally, *Happy celebration!*; for the saint's day, see footnote 5 below)

[2]**frapper à** *to knock on* (a door)

[3]From **ouvrir** *to open* (presented in Lesson 14.1); it is conjugated like a first-conjugation verb (**-er**) in the present tense.

[4]**pour toi** *for you*; **toi** is a form of **tu** used after a preposition (like **moi**).

[5]**la [fête de] Sainte Ignès**: The religious calendar has a saint for each day. If a person is named after one of the saints, then that saint's day is celebrated. For adults, this custom is more prevalent than celebrating birthdays.

Julien donne le bouquet de fleurs à Ignès.

petits gâteaux *cookies*

certainly

IGNÈS C'est vrai ! C'est ma fête aujourd'hui. Christine, est-ce que nous avons des petits gâteaux° ?

CHRISTINE Oui, sûrement°. Fêtons la Sainte Ignès.[1]

La Belle et la Bête *de Cocteau*.

Répondez aux questions. (*lignes 1–2*)

1. Quel jour est-ce ?
2. Quelle heure est-il ?
3. Où est Christine ?
4. Qui frappe à la porte ?
5. Qui ouvre la porte ?

(*lignes 3–20*)

6. Quelle émission est-ce que les jeunes filles regardent ?
7. Qu'est-ce que Julien apporte ?
8. Pour qui sont les fleurs ?
9. Pourquoi est-ce que Julien apporte un bouquet ?
10. Qu'est-ce qu'Ignès demande ?

[1]*Let's celebrate Saint Ignès' Day.*

B **Expressions utiles**

Le campus

Les étudiants sont
{
au bâtiment de langues modernes.
au laboratoire (de langues).
au restaurant universitaire.
au stade.
à l'université.
à la piscine.
à la cité (universitaire)[1].
à la bibliothèque.
à la résidence.
à la librairie[2].
}

Le bâtiment
La (salle) de classe
L'amphi(théâtre) *m*
Le bureau
}
est
{
près d'ici / loin d'ici[3]
à gauche / à droite.
au rez-de-chaussée[4].
au premier (étage) / au deuxième (étage)[5].
}

C **Pratique**

1. Dans quel bâtiment est la classe de français ? À quel étage ? Où est le laboratoire de langues ? Où est mon bureau ?
2. Combien de fois par semaine[6] êtes-vous à la bibliothèque ? Combien de fois par semaine déjeunez-vous au restaurant universitaire ?
3. Est-ce qu'il y a une bibliothèque sur le campus ? À quelle heure est-ce qu'elle est ouverte ? À quelle heure est-elle fermée ?
4. Est-ce qu'il y a un stade sur le campus ? Est-ce qu'il est loin ou près d'ici ? Est-ce que la cité est loin d'ici ?
5. Habitez-vous à la résidence ? Comment s'appelle[7] votre résidence ? Est-ce qu'il y a un restaurant universitaire à la résidence ?

D **Mini-composition :** *Nous célébrons la fête. Écrivez un paragraphe en employant les mots indiqués.*

(1) Ce/être/aujourd'hui/8 octobre. (2) Ce/être/vendredi/et/nous/ne pas/avoir/cours. (3) Il/être/cinq/heure/après-midi. (4) Nous/chercher/le numéro/de/appartement/de/Brigitte. (5) Brigitte/être/une/de/mon camarades. (6) Nous/trouver/appartement/et/frapper/à/porte. (7) Je/avoir/fleurs/et/Jacques/apporter/petits gâteaux,/car[8]/ce/être/la Sainte Brigitte. (8) Nous/entrer/dans/appartement. (9) Nous/fêter/la Sainte Brigitte/et/regarder/télévision. (10) Nous/rentrer/à/résidence/à/7 h.

[1]**cité** *student dormitory area* (not *city*, which is **ville**)
[2]**librairie** *bookstore* (not *library*, which is **bibliothèque**)
[3]*near/far from here*
[4]*on the first floor (ground floor)*
[5]*on the second/third floor*; note the difference in counting floors in the French and American systems.
[6]*How many times a week*
[7]*What is the name of*
[8]*because*

E Dialogue : *Mme Georget pose des questions. Complétez le dialogue.*

MME GEORGET ... ?
CÉCILE La date de mon anniversaire, c'est le 23 octobre.
MME GEORGET ... ?
CÉCILE Oui, j'ai un frère. Il s'appelle[1] Pierre.
MME GEORGET ... ?
CÉCILE Si, j'ai une sœur. Elle s'appelle Isabelle.
MME GEORGET ... ?
CÉCILE Mes parents habitent[2] à Dijon.
MME GEORGET ... ?
CÉCILE Mon père est ingénieur.
MME GEORGET ... ?
CÉCILE Je cherche un appartement parce que je n'aime pas la résidence.

	9–10	11–12	12–1	1–2	2–3
LUNDI	français	biologie	anglais	(déjeuner)	histoire
MARDI	français	biologie (labo)	(déjeuner)	français (labo)	histoire
MERCREDI	français	biologie	anglais	(déjeuner)	histoire
JEUDI	français	biologie (labo)	biologie (labo)	(déjeuner)	histoire
VENDREDI		biologie	anglais	(déjeuner)	

F *Bill Broussard est un étudiant américain. Voici son emploi du temps[3]. Posez des questions à Bill.*

1. À quelle heure/avoir/cours de français ?
2. Combien de fois par semaine[4]/avoir/cours de biologie ?
3. À quelle heure/déjeuner ?
4. Combien de fois par semaine/avoir/cours d'histoire ?
5. Quel est/premier cours ?
6. Combien de fois par semaine/avoir/cours d'anglais ?
7. Combien de cours/avoir/le vendredi ?
8. Quand[5]/être/au labo de langues[6] ?

[1]**Il s'appelle** *His name is* (literally, *He calls himself*)
[2]**habiter** *to live*
[3]**un emploi du temps** *schedule*
[4]*How often, How many times a week*
[5]*When*
[6]**labo(ratoire) de langues** *language lab(oratory)*

« Est-ce que tu es libre à trois heures ? »

G Renseignements et opinions

1. Quelle est la date aujourd'hui ? Quelle heure est-il ? Est-ce que le cours est terminé ? Êtes-vous libre[1] à trois heures ?
2. Quel est votre premier cours demain ? À quelle heure ? Quel est votre dernier cours demain ? À quelle heure êtes-vous libre demain ?
3. Quels jours êtes-vous dans la classe de français ? Est-ce que vous êtes là le samedi ? Et le lundi ?
4. Quelle est la date de votre anniversaire ? Demandez-moi la date de mon anniversaire.
5. Quelle est la date de la Fête de la Victoire aux États-Unis ? Et en France ? Quelle est la date de la Fête du Travail en France ? Et aux États-Unis ?
6. Quelle est la date du dernier jour de cours ? Quand est-ce que les vacances de Noël (de printemps) commencent ?

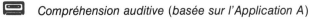 *Compréhension auditive (basée sur l'Application A)*

Dictée : « Nous fêtons la Sainte Christine. » (basée sur l'Application D)

[1]*free*

VOCABULAIRE[1]

Noms

une **adresse**	address	la **façon**	way	le **Nouvel An**	New Year's Day
une **année**	year	la **fête**	holiday; saint's day	**novembre** m	November
un **anniversaire**	birthday	**février** m	February	**octobre** m	October
août m	August	le **film**	movie, film	les **parents** m	parents
un **appartement**	apartment	la **fleur**	flower	le **père**	father
l'**automne** m	autumn	le **football**	soccer	le **petit gâteau**	cookie
une **avenue**	avenue	le **frère**	brother	la **phrase**	sentence
avril m	April	l'**hiver** m	winter	le **printemps**	spring
le **blouson**	jacket, windbreaker	l'**indépendance** f	independence	la **profession**	profession
		une **infirmière**	nurse	la **question**	question
le **boulevard**	boulevard	une **institutrice**	schoolteacher	la **rentrée**	return to school (after vacation)
le **bouquet**	bouquet	**janvier** m	January		
la **boutique**	boutique, shop	le **jeudi**	Thursday	la **rue**	street
le **calendrier**	calendar	**juillet** m	July	la **Saint(e)** ...	Saint . . .'s Day
le(la) **camarade**	friend	**juin** m	June	la **Saint-Valentin**	Valentine's Day
le **camping**	camping	le **lundi**	Monday	le **samedi**	Saturday
cent	one hundred	**mai** m	May	**septembre** m	September
la **chambre**	bedroom	la **main**	hand	la **sœur**	sister
le **concert**	concert	le **mardi**	Tuesday	le **sport**	sport; sports
le **congé**	leave, day off	le **mari**	husband	la **stéréo**	stereo
la **date**	date	**mars** m	March	la **télévision**	television
décembre m	December	le **mercredi**	Wednesday	le **tennis**	tennis
la **déclaration**	declaration	la **mère**	mother	la **Toussaint**	All Saints' Day
le(la) **dentiste**	dentist	le **mois**	month	le **train**	train
le **dimanche**	Sunday	le **monument**	monument	le **travail**	work, labor
une **émission**	TV program	le **musée**	museum	les **vacances** f	vacation
une **enveloppe**	envelope	la **nationalité**	nationality	le **vendredi**	Friday
les **États-Unis** m	the United States	**Noël** m	Christmas	le(la) **voisin(e)**	neighbor
l'**été** m	summer	le **nom**	name		

Verbes

apporter	to bring	**essayer**	to try (on)	frapper à	to knock on (a door)
donner	to give	fêter	to celebrate	**payer**	to pay (for)

Adjectifs

autre	other	gentil(le)	nice	**quel(le)**	what, which
canadien(ne)	Canadian	**mort(e)**	dead, deceased	**suivant(e)**	following; next
dernier(ière)	last	**national(e)**	national	vrai(e)	true
drôle	funny	**préféré(e)**	favorite		
fermé(e)	closed	**premier(ière)**	first		

Adverbes

puis	then	sûrement	certainly, surely	**Préposition**	
				après	after

Autres expressions

Ah !	Oh!	La Belle et la Bête	Beauty and the Beast
Au oui ?	Really?	**lisez**	read
aux États-Unis	in the United States	(elle) ouvre	(she) opens
Bonne fête !	Happy saint's day!	parce que	because
Bonsoir	Good evening	**poser une question**	to ask a question
comme	how	pour moi	for me
comment s'appelle(nt)... ?	what is (are) the name(s) of . . . ?	pour toi	for you
de droite	(on the) right	**redites**	say again
de gauche	(on the) left	**si**	yes
d'une autre façon	in another way	**s'il te plaît**	please

[1]Possessive adjectives, ordinal numbers, and cardinal numbers are excluded.

4 Qu'est-ce que vous faites ?

LESSON OBJECTIVES

Theme and Culture

1. Climate and weather
2. Sports activities and events

Communication Skills

1. Talking about sports and other activities
2. Talking about weather and climate
3. Expressing how frequently one does certain activities
4. Expressing actions and events in the immediate future
5. Expressing possession (*his/her/its, our, their*)
6. Asking/Answering questions using numbers (1–1000)

Structures

4.1 **Faire**; expressions of frequency
4.2 Weather expressions
4.3 **Aller**; expressions of future time
4.4 Possessive adjectives (2): **son**, **notre**, **leur**; summary
4.5 Second-conjugation verbs (**-ir**)
4.6 Cardinal numbers (100–1000)

CONVERSATIONS

TABLEAU 19

🔲 A. Un champion de tennis

GILBERTE   Regarde le jeune homme là-bas[1]. Est-il français ?
CHANTAL   Non, il est américain.
GILBERTE   Ah bon[2]. Est-ce qu'il fait du sport ? Il est bien[3] musclé.
CHANTAL   Du sport ? C'est Greg Wilson, le champion de tennis !

[1]**là-bas**   *over there* (cf. **là** *there*)
[2]*I see*
[3]*très*

79

TABLEAU 20

SPORTS DE GLACE ET NATATION
SPECTACLES - MANIFESTATIONS
CONGRÈS ET SÉMINAIRES

le palais des sports et des congrès

☆ PATINOIRE ARTIFICIELLE
☆ PISTES DE CURLING
☆ PISCINE 25 x 12,5
☆ BASSIN POUR ENFANTS
☆ TENNIS
☆ SNACK-BARS
☆ CLUB LOISIRS - VACANCES

Tél. (50) 21.15.71

B. Il pleut encore.

CLAUDE   Quel temps fait-il ?[1]
DOMINIQUE   Il fait froid et il pleut.[2]
CLAUDE   Ah non ! Il pleut encore ?
DOMINIQUE   Oui. N'oublie pas ton parapluie.

C. Où sont vos parents ?

DANIEL   Où sont vos parents ?
SOPHIE   Nos parents sont au cinéma avec leurs amis.
DANIEL   Et leur voiture ?
SOPHIE   Leur voiture est dans le garage.

DIFFÉRENCES

Les sports

The French are much more sports-minded nowadays than they were in the past, when the majority in fact did little in the way of organized athletics. Today young people readily participate and compete in team sports such as tennis, basketball, and soccer, while individual sports such as swimming, hiking, bicycling, skiing, and sailing are also popular. Hockey, baseball, and North American football remain uncommon, although there are rugby teams in the country. At the university level, there are many sport clubs for students to join, but since the universities are organized around academic work, there are no official teams or intercollegiate games as in North America. For each sport in France, there is a **Fédération** that supplies all information regarding affiliated clubs and associations and sponsors regional and national public events. The modern Olympic Games (**Les Jeux Olympiques**) were revived in the late nineteenth century by a Frenchman, Pierre de Coubertin.

Among the so-called **sports-spectacles** (*spectator sports*), the most popular are soccer, horse racing, and automobile and bicycle racing. As for soccer (**le football**)[3], teams are organized by city and regional sport clubs. **La Fédération française de football** sponsors **les Championnats de France** every year for both amateurs and professionals, and **la Coupe de France** for professional teams. Horse racing (**les courses de chevaux**) is also a well-attended event; the best known is **le Grand Prix de Longchamp** in Paris. As for **les courses automobiles**, you may have heard of the grueling **24 heures du Mans** and **le Rallye de Monte-Carlo**.

[1]*What's the weather like?*

[2]*It's cold and it's raining.*

[3]**Le football américain**, or American football, is hardly played in Europe.

C'est le Tour de France. Les cyclistes arrivent enfin à Paris !

One event that has no real equivalent in North America is **le Tour de France**. This international cross-country bicycle race by professional cyclists takes place in July, and was first held in 1903. It covers 4,000 km in a little over 20 days, winding through mountains and plains, and ending in Paris. The race is divided into **étapes**, or daily stages, each 150–250 km long, depending on the terrain. Each day's progress is treated as a major sports event by radio, TV, and newspapers, and despite heavy commercialization in recent years, many watch it with avid interest.

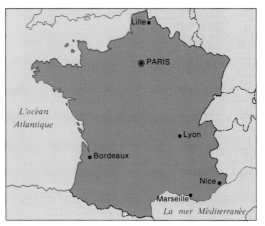

Le climat en France

France is a relatively small country, though it is the second largest in Europe after the Soviet Union. In terms of the United States, it is about the same size as Kansas, Missouri, and Iowa put together. Its northern latitude corresponds to that of Winnipeg, Canada, and its southern latitude to that of Detroit. Although France is situated farther north than much of the United States, its climate is among the most temperate, yet varied, in Western Europe. The Atlantic regions enjoy mild winters—the temperature rarely goes below freezing, and the summer is cool and humid. In the Mediterranean areas, which include the French Riviera, winter is relatively warm, while summer is quite hot and generally dry. The mountainous areas, especially the Alps, the Pyrenees, and the central part of France known as **le Massif Central**, have long, harsh winters and short, cool summers.

STRUCTURES

4.1 **FAIRE** ; EXPRESSIONS DE FRÉQUENCE

1. The basic meaning of **faire** is *to do* or *to make*, as in the examples below. The **-ai-** of **faisons** is pronounced /ə/, dropped in rapid speech. The **vous** and **ils/elles** forms do not end in **-ez** and **-ent**.[1] Note that the singular forms are pronounced alike.

faire	
fais	faisons
fais	faites
fait	font

Je **fais** mes devoirs.[2]	/fɛ/	*I do my homework.*
Tu **fais** ton devoir d'anglais.		*You do your English homework.*
Il **fait** son lit.		*He makes his bed.*
Nous **faisons** notre travail.	/f(ə)zõ/	*We do our work.*
Vous **faites** des fautes.	/fɛt/	*You make mistakes.*
Ils **font** les exercices.	/fõ/	*They do the exercises.*

2. **Faire** also means *to study*, *to play* (sports, music, etc.), *to go* (and do some kind of sport activity). In this usage, the name of the activity must be preceded by **de** + definite article

En hiver, ils font du ski dans les Alpes.

Nous **faisons du** tennis.	*We play tennis.*
Vous **faites du** ski.	*You ski (go skiing).*
Ils **font du** football.	*They play soccer.*
Je **fais de la** musique.	*I play (study) music.*
Tu **fais du** français.	*You study French.*
Elle **fait de la** natation.	*She swims (goes swimming).*

[1]Since **il/elle** and **ils/elles** take the same verb forms, respectively, we will usually alternate between the masculine and feminine subject pronouns in verb conjugation lists beginning with this lesson.

[2]**Devoir** *homework* is usually in the plural, unless it is modified by an adjective or a phrase, as in **mon devoir de français, c'est un devoir difficile**.

In a negative sentence, only **de** or **d'** is used.

Je fais **du** tennis.

→ Je **ne** fais **pas de** tennis.

Elle fait **de la** musique.

→ Elle **ne** fait **pas de** musique.

Nous faisons **de l'**aérobique.

→ Nous **ne** faisons **pas d'**aérobique.

Vous faites **de l'**anglais ?

→ Vous **ne** faites **pas d'**anglais ?

3. Although **faire** means *to do*, in a question like **Qu'est-ce que vous faites ?** *What do you do (are you doing)?*, the answer does not necessarily contain **faire** unless the expression used in the answer calls for it.

Qu'est-ce que vous **faites** ?

— Je **fais** mes devoirs.

Qu'est-ce que tu **fais** ?

— Je **regarde** la télé[1].

Qu'est-ce qu'elles **font** le lundi ?

— Elles **déjeunent** ensemble.

What are you doing?

I'm doing my homework.

What are you doing?

I'm watching TV.

What do they do on Mondays?

They eat lunch together.

4. Study the following expressions of frequency.

tout le temps	*all the time*
tous les jours	*every day*
toujours	*always*
(très) souvent	*(very) often*
de temps en temps /d(ə)tãzãtã/	*from time to time*
(trois) fois *f* **par** { **jour** / **semaine** / **mois** }	*(three) times a* { *day* / *week* / *month* }
rarement	*rarely*
Combien de fois par semaine... ?	*How many times a week . . . ?*

Toujours, **souvent**, and **rarement** usually follow the verb directly.

Je **fais toujours** mon lit.

Nous **parlons souvent** de Marie.

Elle **écoute rarement** la radio.

I always make my bed.

We often talk about Marie.

She rarely listens to the radio.

TABLEAU 21   Il **fait** de la musculation.   Il **fait** du ski.   Elle **fait** de la natation.   Ils **font** du tennis.

 A   *Exercice de contrôle*

Je fais le devoir de français.

1. Nous   2. Tu   3. Vous   4. Les étudiants

---
[1]**télé** = télévision

Je ne fais pas de fautes.

1. (Paul)   2. (Paul et Marie)   3. Nous   4. Vous

Est-ce que vous faites de la musculation¹ ?

1. tu   2. (Jeanne)   3. vos camarades   4. nous

B *Faites des phrases avec les expressions suivantes.*

1. Je fais mon lit
2. Je fais des fautes de grammaire   ⎫   rarement².
3. Je fais (du ski)   ⎬   de temps en temps.
4. Je déjeune dans un restaurant   ⎪   tous les jours.
5. Je fais mon devoir de français   ⎬   (deux) fois par semaine.
6. Je suis dans le cours de français   ⎪   souvent².
7. J'étudie à la bibliothèque   ⎪   toujours².
8. Je mange des pommes   ⎭

C *Répondez aux questions.*

1. Est-ce que vous faites toujours vos devoirs ? Demandez-moi³ si je fais toujours mon travail.
2. Est-ce que vous faites toujours votre lit ? Demandez-moi si je fais toujours mon lit.
3. Qu'est-ce que vous faites comme sport ? Demandez à (Michel) s'il fait de la natation.
   Demandez à (Jeanne) si elle fait du camping.
4. Qu'est-ce que vous faites à midi ? Qu'est-ce que vous faites dans le cours de français ?
5. Qu'est-ce que je fais dans mon bureau ? Qu'est-ce que vous faites à la bibliothèque ?

D *Aimez-vous les sports ? Qu'est-ce que les gens suivants font comme sport ?⁴*

1. Mark Spitz   6. Larry Bird
2. Jack Nicklaus   7. Joe Montana et Joe Morris
3. Scott Hamilton   8. Chris Evert et John McEnroe
4. Nancy Lopez   9. George Brett et Fernando Valenzuela
5. Magic Johnson   10. Mary Lou Retton

E *Complétez les phrases suivantes avec votre partenaire. Employez les expressions de fréquence.*

1. Nous parlons français...   4. Nous mangeons...
2. Nous regardons la télé...   5. Nous faisons le devoir de français...
3. Nous sommes à la bibliothèque...

🔲 *Exercice supplémentaire*

Ils font du football le samedi.

¹*bodybuilding*
²Put these adverbs immediately after the verb: **Je fais rarement du tennis**.
³*Ask me*
⁴*What sport do these people play?*

4.2 LE TEMPS QU'IL FAIT

1. Study the expressions below. The verb **faire** is used to express many weather conditions, except in the case of **neiger** *to snow* and **pleuvoir** (an irregular verb) *to rain*.

Quel temps fait-il ?	*What is the weather like?*
Il fait beau.	*It is nice (weather).*
Il fait du soleil.	*It is sunny.*
Il fait chaud.	*It is hot/warm.*
Il fait frais.	*It is cool.*
Il fait froid.	*It is cold.*
Il fait (très) mauvais.	*It is (very) bad weather.*
Il fait du vent.	*It is windy.*
Il neige.	*It snows/It is snowing.*
Il pleut.	*It rains/It is raining.*

In a negative sentence, **du soleil** and **du vent** become **de soleil** and **de vent**.

Il fait **du soleil**.	→ Il ne fait pas **de soleil**.
Il fait **du vent**.	→ Il ne fait pas **de vent**.

2. As an equivalent of English *in (the)* + season, the preposition **en** is used with **été** *summer*, **automne** /ɔtɔn/ *autumn, fall*, and **hiver** *winter* (all with liaison), but **au** is used with **printemps** /pʀɛ̃tɑ̃/ *spring*. They are all masculine nouns.

Il fait très chaud **en été**.	*It is very hot in summer.*
Il fait frais **en automne**.	*It is cool in autumn.*
Il fait très froid **en hiver**.	*It is very cold in winter.*
Il pleut souvent **au printemps**.	*It often rains in spring.*

When the name of a season modifies a noun, the preposition used is **de/d'**.

Juillet est un mois **d'été**.	*July is a summer month.*
Quels sont les mois **d'hiver** ?	*What are the winter months?*
J'aime les vacances **de printemps**.	*I like spring vacation.*

Nous sommes **en été**.	Nous sommes **en hiver**.	Nous sommes **en automne**.	Nous sommes **au printemps**.
Il fait **beau**.	Il fait **froid**.	Il fait **frais**.	Il fait très **mauvais**.
Il fait **du soleil**.	Il **neige**.		Il fait **du vent**.
Il fait **chaud**.			Il **pleut**.

TABLEAU 22

 A *Regardez le Tableau 22. Répétez toutes les phrases*[1] *après moi... Maintenant, parlons un peu des saisons et du climat de notre région. Répondez aux questions.*

---

[1]**toutes les phrases** *all the sentences*

1. Quelle saison vient[1] après l'été ? Et quelle saison vient après l'automne ? Et quelle saison vient après l'hiver ?
2. En quelle saison est-ce qu'il neige ? En quelle saison est-ce qu'il fait très chaud ? En quelle saison est-ce qu'il pleut souvent ?
3. Quels sont les mois d'hiver ? Quels sont les mois d'été ? Et quels sont les mois de printemps ?
4. Dans notre région, quel temps fait-il en été ? Et en hiver ? Et au printemps ?
5. Quel temps fait-il aujourd'hui ? Quelle heure est-il ? Quelle est la date aujourd'hui ?

TABLEAU 23

B   *Regardez le Tableau 23. Quelle saison est-ce dans chaque dessin[2] ? Faites une description du temps qu'il fait.[3]*

C   *Regardez les photos à cette page. Quel temps fait-il ?*

🔲   *Compréhension auditive*

---

[1]**vient**   *comes* (du verbe **venir**, Leçon 6.6)
[2]**chaque dessin**   *each drawing*
[3]*Make a description of the weather.*

4.3 **ALLER** ; EXPRESSIONS DU FUTUR

aller

1. Study the conjugation of **aller** *to go, to be going*. It is always followed by a mention of where one is going. Note that the **tu** and **il/elle** forms are pronounced alike, though spelled differently. Be careful to distinguish the conjugated forms of **aller** from **avoir** (presented in Lesson 2.6).

Je **vais** à Paris.	/vɛ/	Nous_**allons** au restaurant.	/alō/
Tu **vas** à Marseille.	/va/	Vous_**allez** à l'université.	/ale/
Elle **va** à Chicago.	/va/	Elles **vont** au cinéma.	/vō/

Note also that you have learned four verbs whose **ils/elles** form ends in **-ont**.

être : ils/elles **sont**	**aller** : ils/elles **vont**
avoir : ils/elles_**ont**	**faire** : ils/elles **font**

The **tu** form of **aller** drops the **-s** in imperative sentences.

Tu **vas** à la bibliothèque.	Tu ne **vas** pas au cinéma.
→ **Va** à la bibliothèque !	→ Ne **va** pas au cinéma !

2. As you saw in the **Conversations** of Lesson 1, **aller** is also used in reference to health.

Comment_**allez**-vous aujourd'hui ?	*How are you today?*
— (Je **vais**) Bien, merci.	*(I'm) Fine, thank you.*
Comment **va** votre mère ?	*How is your mother?*
— (Elle **va**) Comme ci comme ça.	*(She's) So-so.*

3. **Aller** + infinitive is used to express actions or events in the near future (**le futur proche**). It corresponds to the English construction *to be going* + infinitive. In negative sentences, **ne** and **pas** come around the conjugated form of **aller** and before the infinitive.

Je **parle** français.	*I speak French.*
→ Je **vais parler** anglais aussi.	*→ I'm going to speak English also.*
Ils ne **déjeunent** pas à midi.	*They don't eat lunch at noon.*
→ Ils **vont déjeuner** à une heure.	*→ They're going to eat lunch at one.*
Travaillez-vous maintenant ?	*Are you working now?*
→ **Allez**-vous **travailler** plus tard ?	*→ Are you going to work later?*
Paul ne **fait** pas son lit.	*Paul doesn't make his bed.*
→ Paul ne **va** pas **faire** son lit.	*→ Paul isn't going to make his bed.*

4. Here are some expressions of future time.

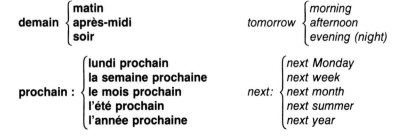

demain {	**matin**	*tomorrow* {	*morning*
	après-midi		*afternoon*
	soir		*evening (night)*

prochain : {	**lundi prochain**	*next:* {	*next Monday*
	la semaine prochaine		*next week*
	le mois prochain		*next month*
	l'été prochain		*next summer*
	l'année prochaine		*next year*

TABLEAU 24   Elle **va** très bien.   Ils **vont à** l'école.   Ils **vont regarder** la télévision.

A *Exercice de contrôle*

Je vais au labo demain après-midi.
1. Vous   2. Tu   3. Le professeur   4. Les étudiants

Je vais en Europe l'été prochain.
1. Nous   2. (Paul)   3. Les étudiants   4. Vous

Je ne vais pas regarder la télé ce soir[1].
1. Les étudiants   2. Vous   3. Tu   4. Nous

B *Mieux vaut tard que jamais.[2] Ajoutez des phrases d'après ce modèle.*

Vous ne déjeunez pas maintenant ?   Il ne travaille pas maintenant ?
Non, mais je vais déjeuner plus tard[3].   **Non, mais il va travailler plus tard.**

1. Vous ne mangez pas maintenant ?
2. Vous ne travaillez pas au labo maintenant ?
3. (Paul) ne parle pas anglais maintenant ?
4. Nous ne quittons pas la classe maintenant ?
5. (Pierre et Marie) ne font pas leurs devoirs maintenant ?

C *Répondez aux questions.*

1. Comment allez-vous aujourd'hui ? Demandez à (Françoise) comment elle va. Demandez-moi[4] comment je vais.
2. Allez-vous être à l'université l'année prochaine ? Où allez-vous être demain matin ? Demandez à (Paul) où il va être lundi prochain.
3. Où allez-vous après le cours de français ? Demandez à (Mireille) où elle va après le cours. Demandez-moi où je vais après le cours.
4. Allez-vous en France l'été prochain ? Demandez-moi où je vais l'été prochain. Demandez à (Jeanne) où elle va samedi prochain.
5. À quelle heure allez-vous dîner ? Demandez-moi où je vais dîner. Demandez à (Charles) où il va dîner.
6. Quelle leçon est-ce que nous allons étudier la semaine prochaine ? Qu'est-ce que vous allez faire l'été prochain ?

---

[1]**ce soir** *this evening, tonight*
[2]*Better late than never* (un proverbe)
[3]**plus tard** *later*
[4]*Ask me*

D *Révision de la contraction de l'article défini avec* **à** *et* **de**. *Faites des phrases d'après ce modèle.*

> Je vais ... laboratoire ... classe.
> **Je vais du laboratoire à la classe.**

1. Je vais ... classe ... bibliothèque.
2. Nous allons ... restaurant ... cinéma.
3. Est-ce qu'ils vont ... cinéma ... résidence ?
4. Est-ce qu'elle va ... classe ... laboratoire ?
5. Allez-vous ... classe ... bureau ?
6. Tu vas ... laboratoire ... restaurant.

4.4 ADJECTIFS POSSESSIFS (2) : **SON, NOTRE, LEUR** ; RÉVISION

1. The possessive adjective for the third-person singular (**il**, **elle**) is **son** before a masculine singular noun, **sa** before a feminine singular noun, and **son** /sōn/ before any singular noun that begins with a vowel sound. Note below that all these forms correspond to English *his*, *her*, and *its*. In French, unlike English, possessive adjectives agree in gender and number with the *noun possessed*, not with the *possessor*.

le frère **de Jean**	→ **son** frère	*his* brother
le frère **de Marianne**	→ **son** frère	*her* brother
le président **du groupe**	→ **son** président	*its* president
la sœur **de Jean**	→ **sa** sœur	*his* sister
la sœur **de Marianne**	→ **sa** sœur	*her* sister
la capitale **de la France**	→ **sa** capitale	*its* capital
l'adresse (*f*) **de Jean**	→ **son** adresse	*his* address
l'ami (*m*) **de Marianne**	→ **son** ami	*her* friend
l'horloge (*f*) **de l'église**	→ **son** horloge	*its* clock

« Voilà ma sœur avec son mari et leurs deux enfants. »

Ses is used before a masculine or feminine plural noun. Again, it corresponds to *his, her,* or *its.*

les sœurs **de Jean**	→ **ses** sœurs	*his sisters*
les_amis **de Marianne**	→ **ses**_amis	*her friends*
les régions **de la France**	→ **ses** régions	*its regions*

2. The possessive adjective for **nous** is **notre** /nɔtRə/[1] before a singular noun (the final vowel /ə/ is dropped before a vowel sound). **Nos** is used before a plural noun. Both **notre** and **nos** correspond to *our* in English.

Cherchez-vous **votre** journal ?	— Oui, nous cherchons **notre** journal.
Où est **votre** maison ?	— Voilà **notre** maison.
Est-ce que c'est **votre** enfant ?	— Oui, c'est **notre** enfant.
Aimez-vous **vos** cours ?	— Oui, nous_aimons **nos** cours.
Où sont **vos**_amis ?	— Voilà **nos**_amis.

3. The possessive adjectives for **ils** and **elles** are **leur** /lœR/ before a singular noun and **leurs** before a plural noun. Both forms correspond to *their* in English.

Ils regardent **leur** photo.	Elles_apportent **leur** livre.
→ Ils regardent **leurs** photos.	→ Elles_apportent **leurs** livres.
Ils_aiment **leur** enfant.	Elles cherchent **leur** ami.
→ Ils_aiment **leurs**_enfants.	→ Elles cherchent **leurs**_amis.

4. The chart below summarizes the forms of all the possessive adjectives. Remember, they agree in gender (*m/f*) and number (*s/pl*) with the *following noun*, and not with the possessor.

SINGULAR			PLURAL		
Before a Consonant		Before a Vowel	Before a Consonant	Before a Vowel	
m	*f*	*m* and *f*	*m* and *f*		
mon	**ma**	**mon**_	**mes**	**mes**_	*my*
ton	**ta**	**ton**_	**tes**	**tes**_	*your*
son	**sa**	**son**_	**ses**	**ses**_	*his, her, its*
notre			**nos**	**nos**_	*our*
votre			**vos**	**vos**_	*your*
leur			**leurs**	**leurs**_	*their*

A *Modifiez les phrases suivantes d'après ces modèles.*

Voilà le cahier de (Paul). 　　　C'est le cahier de (Marie).
Voilà son cahier. 　　　**C'est son cahier.**

1. Voilà le livre de (Marc).
2. Voilà la montre de (Jeanne).
3. Voilà la chaise de (Martine).
4. Voilà les stylos de (Cécile).
5. C'est la camarade de (Jacques).
6. C'est l'adresse du professeur.
7. C'est la table du professeur.
8. Ce sont les étudiants du professeur.

[1]In fast colloquial French, **notre** is often pronounced /nɔt/ before a consonant sound.

B *Répondez aux questions.*

1. Regardez-vous le livre de (Marie) ?
2. Avez-vous l'adresse de (Cécile) ?
3. Êtes-vous la sœur de (Paul) ?
4. Avez-vous les clés de (Sylvie) ?
5. Faites-vous les devoirs de (Paul) ?
6. Aimez-vous la montre de (Jean) ?

C *Faites un compte rendu de l'interview de votre partenaire.*[1]

Exemple : Je parle de (Jacqueline). Son père est à Miami. Sa mère est aussi à Miami. Jacqueline n'a pas de frère. Mais elle a une sœur. Sa sœur s'appelle (Cindy). Jacqueline a une stéréo dans sa chambre. Sa camarade de chambre[2] s'appelle (Maria)...

D *Répondez aux questions. Utilisez des adjectifs possessifs dans vos réponses.*

1. Est-ce que c'est notre classe ? Est-ce que ce sont nos chaises ? Où est notre tableau ?[3]
2. Regardez-vous le livre de (Sophie) ? Regardez-vous la montre de (Daniel) ? Est-ce que (Michel) regarde le livre de (Marie) ?
3. Où sont les chaises de (Jacques) et (Mireille) ?[3] Où sont leurs livres ?[3] Est-ce qu'ils ont leurs cahiers d'exercices ?
4. Où habitent vos parents ? Est-ce que leurs voisins sont français ? Est-ce que leur voiture est américaine ?
5. Est-ce que les Français[4] ont une Fête du Travail ? Quelle est la date de leur Fête du Travail ?

E *Révision.*[5] *Exercice de contrôle*

Nous cherchons notre frère et notre sœur.

1. Tu	2. Vous	3. Les enfants	4. L'étudiant

J'aime ma chambre et mon lit.

1. Tu	2. Vous	3. (Robert)	4. (Marie)

Vous téléphonez à vos parents.

1. Les étudiants	2. Je	3. Ma camarade	4. Nous

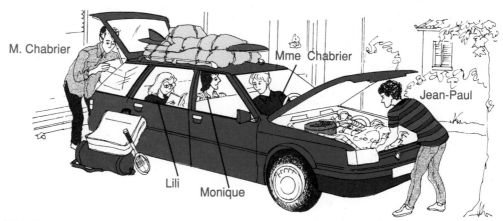

M. Chabrier   Mme Chabrier   Jean-Paul   Lili   Monique

TABLEAU 25

[1]Continuation of Exercise E of Lesson 3.4.
[2]**un/une camarade de chambre** *roommate* (*pl* **camarades de chambre**)
[3]Commencez votre réponse par **Voilà**...
[4]*the French (people)*; nouns (but not adjectives) denoting nationality always begin with a capital letter.
[5]*Review*. In this exercise, make the possessive adjective agree with the subject (for example: **Tu cherches ton frère et ta sœur**).

F *Révision. Regardez le Tableau 25.*[1] *C'est la famille Chabrier. La famille habite à Tours. Il y a M. et Mme Chabrier et leurs trois enfants, Jean-Paul, Monique et Lili. Répétez les phrases après moi.*

Le frère est devant la voiture.
Le père est derrière la voiture.
La mère est dans la voiture.
Les sœurs sont dans la voiture, derrière la mère.
La famille habite à Tours.

Vous êtes Jean-Paul. Répétez après moi.

Je suis devant la voiture.
Mon père est derrière la voiture.
Ma mère est dans la voiture.

Mes sœurs sont dans la voiture, derrière ma mère.
Ma famille habite à Tours.

1. Vous êtes Monique et Lili. Décrivez la scène.[2] (*Notre frère est devant la voiture*, etc.)
2. Vous êtes un(e) camarade de Jean-Paul. Vous parlez à Jean-Paul. Décrivez la scène. (*Je suis un(e) camarade de Jean-Paul. Je parle à Jean-Paul. Tu es devant la voiture*, etc.)
3. Vous parlez à Monique et à Lili. Décrivez la scène. (*Je parle à Monique et à Lili. Votre frère est devant la voiture*, etc.)
4. Vous êtes un(e) camarade de Jean-Paul. Mais vous ne parlez pas à Jean-Paul. Décrivez la scène. (*Je suis un(e) camarade de Jean-Paul. Jean-Paul est devant la voiture. Son père est derrière la voiture*, etc.)
5. Vous êtes un(e) camarade de Monique et de Lili. Décrivez la scène. (*Leur frère est devant la voiture*, etc.)

Compréhension auditive

Compréhension auditive

4.5   VERBES DU DEUXIÈME GROUPE (-**IR**)

1. The infinitives of second-conjugation verbs end in -**ir**. Note that the singular forms are pronounced alike, and the plural forms all contain -**ss**- /s/ between the stem and the ending.

finir /finiʀ/   *to finish*

je **fin**is /fini/	nous **fin**issons /finisõ/
tu **fin**is	vous **fin**issez /finise/
il **fin**it	ils **fin**issent /finis/

finir

finis	finissons
finis	finissez
finit	finissent

2. Compare the conjugation of the third-person singular and plural forms. The difference lies in the presence of /s/ in the plural. Liaison, when it occurs, also indicates that the verb is in the plural.

il choi**sit**	/ʃwazi/	elle ob**éit**	/ɔbei/
ils choi**sissent**[3]	/ʃwazis/	elles ob**éissent**	/ɔbeis/
elle rem**plit**	/ʀãpli/	il applau**dit**	/aplodi/
elles rem**plissent**	/ʀãplis/	ils applau**dissent**	/aplodis/

[1]In this exercise, you review various forms of all the possessive adjectives.
[2]*Describe the scene.*
[3]Note that -**s**- between vowels is pronounced /z/ (**choisis**, **maison**, **faisons**), while -**ss**- is pronounced /s/ (**finissons**, **obéissez**, **passer**).

Le chauffeur obéit à l'agent de police.

TABLEAU 26   Ils **applaudissent** après le discours.   Elle **choisit** un blouson.   Il **remplit** la fiche.

A   *Exercice de contrôle*[1]

Je finis mes devoirs.
1. Nous   2. Tu   3. Vous   4. Les étudiants

Nous choisissons nos cours.
1. Je   2. Les étudiants   3. Tu   4. L'étudiant

Je remplis ma fiche.
1. Vous   2. Tu   3. Le professeur   4. Les enfants

Ils applaudissent la championne.
1. Je   2. Vous   3. Tu   4. Nous

B   *Répondez aux questions.*

1. Choisissez-vous vos cours ? Est-ce que vos parents choisissent vos cours ? Est-ce que je choisis mes étudiants ?
2. Finissez-vous toujours vos devoirs ? Demandez à (Mireille) si elle finit toujours ses devoirs. Demandez-moi si je finis toujours mon travail.

---

[1]Make the possessive adjective agree with the subject (for example: **Nous finissons nos devoirs.**).

3. Obéissez-vous toujours aux agents de police[1] ? Demandez-moi si j'obéis toujours aux agents de police. Demandez à (Robert) s'il obéit toujours à ses parents.
4. Applaudissez-vous après un bon concert ? Et après un mauvais concert ? Applaudissez-vous quand le cours est terminé ?

Compréhension auditive

4.6 NOMBRES CARDINAUX (DE 100 À 1.000)

For numbers between 100 and 1000, **et** does not appear in 101, 201, 301, 401, and so on. The plural marker **-s** appears only when **cents** is not followed by another numeral (for example, **deux cents**, but not in **deux cent dix**).

100	**cent** /sɑ̃/	500	**cinq cents** /sɛ̃sɑ̃/
101	**cent un** /sɑ̃ɛ̃/	555	**cinq cent cinquante-cinq**
102	**cent deux**	600	**six cents** /sisɑ̃/
111	**cent onze** /sɑ̃ɔ̃z/	666	**six cent soixante-six**
199	**cent quatre-vingt-dix-neuf**	700	**sept cents**
200	**deux cents**	777	**sept cent soixante-dix-sept**
201	**deux cent un** /døsɑ̃ɛ̃/	800	**huit cents**
300	**trois cents**	888	**huit cent quatre-vingt-huit**
333	**trois cent trente-trois**	900	**neuf cents**
400	**quatre cents**	999	**neuf cent quatre-vingt-dix-neuf**
444	**quatre cent quarante-quatre**	1.000	**mil, mille**[2]

A *Lisez à haute voix les nombres suivants.*

188, 197, 224, 241, 269, 283, 313, 373, 393, 488, 555, 595, 616, 674, 824, 848, 888, 926, 979, 999, 1.000.

B *Comptons maintenant.*

1. Comptez par cent de 100 à 1.000.
2. Comptez par cinquante de 50 à 1.000.

C *Maintenant, répondez à ces questions.*

1. Combien de jours est-ce qu'il y a dans une année ? Combien de minutes est-ce qu'il y a dans deux heures ? Et dans trois heures ?
2. Regardez votre livre de français. Quelles leçons est-ce qu'il y a :

   a. à la page 101 ?
   b. à la page 284 ?
   c. à la page 333 ?

   d. à la page 376 ?
   e. à la page 399 ?
   f. à la page 483 ?

3. Lisez les adresses suivantes.

   a. 107, rue de Rivoli
   b. 292, rue Saint-Martin
   c. 293, avenue Daumesnil /domenil/

   d. 296, rue Saint-Honoré
   e. 277, rue Saint-Jacques
   f. 185, rue de la Harpe

Dictée

---

[1]**un agent de police** (or **un agent**) *policeman*. Note that **obéir** takes **à** + noun.
[2]Both are pronounced /mil/. Note that French uses a period rather than a comma for 1,000.
[3]Recorded in a substantially modified form.

APPLICATIONS

Ils font du jogging. C'est bon pour la santé.

A Situations

Jouons au tennis !
Il est trois heures. Christine est dans sa chambre. Elle finit son travail, elle bâille et regarde par la fenêtre. Il fait beau et le soleil brille. Il n'y a pas de nuages dans le ciel. Les feuilles des arbres sont magnifiques, car c'est l'automne. Le téléphone sonne.

JEAN-PAUL	Allô[1]... c'est toi, Christine ?	
CHRISTINE	Ah, bonjour, Jean-Paul. Comment ça va ?	5
JEAN-PAUL	Ça va bien, merci. Écoute, est-ce que tu es libre à quatre heures aujourd'hui ?	
CHRISTINE	Oui. Pourquoi ?	
JEAN-PAUL	Je suis chez Julien[2]. Nous allons jouer au[3] tennis à quatre heures. Tu viens[4] avec nous ?	
CHRISTINE	Avec plaisir. Mais je n'ai pas de raquette.	10
JEAN-PAUL	Je vais apporter la raquette de Michel. Il va faire du footing avec son frère.	
CHRISTINE	Ah bon.° Mais qui est notre quatrième partenaire ?	
JEAN-PAUL	Ma sœur va jouer avec nous. Son cours de chimie finit à trois heures. Alors, c'est d'accord° ?	
CHRISTINE	Oui, c'est d'accord. Rendez-vous à quatre heures devant le court[5] de tennis. À bientôt.	15
JEAN-PAUL	Oui, à tout à l'heure.	

Fine. (margin note for **Ah bon.°**)

d'accord *agreed, OK*

[1]*Hello* (used only in telephone calls)

[2]**chez Julien** *at Julien's;* **chez** means *at the home of*

[3]**jouer** *to play* takes **à** + definite article before the name of a game or sport.

[4]*Are you coming;* from **venir** *to come* (see Lesson 6.6 for conjugation).

[5]**Un court** /kuʀ/ **de tennis**, or simply **un court**, is *a tennis court;* **un cours** /kuʀ/ is *a course.*

Répondez aux questions. (*lignes 1–3*)

1. Quelle heure est-il ?
2. Où est Christine ?
3. Quel temps fait-il ?
4. Comment sont les feuilles des arbres ?

(*lignes 4–17*)

5. Qui téléphone à Christine ?
6. Comment va Jean-Paul ?
7. À quelle heure est-ce que Christine est libre aujourd'hui ?
8. Où est Jean-Paul ?
9. Quelle raquette est-ce que Christine va utiliser ?
10. Où est-ce que Christine a rendez-vous avec ses copains ?

« Je joue aux boules tous les week-ends. »

B Expressions utiles

Le temps et les saisons

Il fait beau (temps).
Il fait mauvais (temps). } J'aime le beau temps.

Il fait froid.
Il fait chaud. } Je déteste { le froid.
Il fait du vent. } { la chaleur.
{ le vent.

Il pleut.
Il pleut à verse. } Je n'aime pas { la pluie.
Il neige. } { la neige.

Au printemps } il fait frais.
En automne }

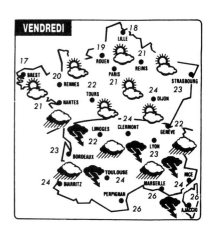

Les sports

faire
{
de l'aérobique *m*
du cyclisme
du patin (à glace / à roulettes)
du ski / du ski nautique
du tennis
du yachting
de la gymnastique
du footing (jogging)
de la natation
}

jouer[1]
{
au basket(-ball)
au golf
au hockey
au foot(ball)
au tennis
au base-ball
}

regarder (à la télévision)
aller à
assister à[2]
}
un match
{
de tennis
de foot(ball)
de basket(-ball)
}

L'équipe
{
est bonne.
est médiocre / moyenne.
est mauvaise / n'est pas bonne.
}

L'équipe (ne) gagne (pas)
{
souvent.
toujours.
de temps en temps.
}

C **Pratique**

1. Quelle est votre saison préférée ? Pourquoi ?
2. Comment sont les hivers dans notre région ?
3. En quel mois est-ce que « l'heure d'été » commence ? En quel mois est-ce qu'elle finit ?
4. Nommez des sports d'été typiques. Nommez des sports d'hiver typiques. Nommez des sports de plein air[3].
5. Dans un match de football, combien de joueurs est-ce qu'il y a dans chaque équipe ? Et dans un match de base-ball ? Et dans un match de basket ?
6. Est-ce qu'il y a une équipe de football à notre université ? Comment est notre équipe ? Est-ce qu'elle gagne souvent ?
7. Est-ce qu'il y a une équipe de basket-ball professionnel dans notre ville ? Quelle est votre équipe préférée ?
8. Qu'est-ce que vous faites souvent ? Qu'est-ce que vous ne faites pas souvent ? Utilisez les expressions dans les deux colonnes suivantes.

ACTIVITÉ	FRÉQUENCE
faire/tennis	tout le temps
assister/à/matchs/football	(presque) tous les jours
faire/natation	(très) souvent
faire/footing	de temps en temps
faire/gymnastique	(une) fois par jour/semaine/mois
en/été/regarder/matchs/base-ball	rarement
faire/patin à glace	ne ... pas

---

[1]**jouer** *to play* takes **à** + definite article before the name of a game or sport.

[2]*to attend*

[3]/dəplɛnɛʀ/ *outdoor*. Sample answer: **Le ski et le golf sont des sports de plein air**. Use of **des** rather than **les** in this answer will be explained in Lesson 8.1.

D **Mini-composition :** *Une promenade dans un jardin. Écrivez un paragraphe en employant les mots indiqués.*

(1) Il/faire/un peu/frais/mais/très beau/aujourd'hui. (2) Jeanne/et/Maryse/finir/leur/travail. (3) Elle/faire/deux/sandwich[1]/dans/leur/cuisine. (4) Elles/aller/à/jardin botanique/de/université. (5) Elles/ne pas/avoir/cours/parce que/ce/être/samedi. (6) Elles/arriver/à/entrée/de/jardin/à/2 h. (7) Elles/choisir/banc/et/elles/regarder/arbres. (8) Soleil/briller/et/il y a/ne pas/nuages/dans/ciel. (9) Les/feuilles/de/les/arbre/être/magnifique. (10) Mais/bientôt/hiver/aller/arriver. (11) Jeanne/aimer/hiver/car/elle/faire/ski/et/patin. (12) Maryse/ne pas/aimer/hiver/car/elle/ne pas/faire/sport.

E **Questions :**[2] *Je vais au match de basket. Posez des questions sur les parties soulignées.*[3]

C'est aujourd'hui (1) samedi. Je suis (2) dans ma chambre. Je fais (3) mon devoir d'anglais. Il est (4) onze heures. Je vais finir mon devoir (5) avant le déjeuner. Je vais au match de basket (6) à deux heures. (7) Notre équipe est très bonne. Le match va être intéressant (8) parce que l'équipe adverse[4] est bonne aussi.

Clé : (1) Quel jour (2) Où (3) Qu'est-ce que (4) Quelle heure (5) Quand (6) À quelle heure (7) Quelle (8) Pourquoi

F **Renseignements et opinions**

1. Quelle est la date aujourd'hui ? En quelle saison est-ce que nous sommes ? Qu'est-ce que nous faisons maintenant ?
2. Quel temps fait-il aujourd'hui ? Quel temps est-ce qu'il va faire ce soir[5] ? Et demain matin ?
3. Qu'est-ce que vous allez faire ce soir ? Et qu'est-ce vous allez faire demain matin ?
4. À quelle heure déjeunez-vous ? À quelle heure finissez-vous votre déjeuner ? À quelle heure finissez-vous votre dîner ?
5. Quel est votre sport préféré à la télévision ? Regardez-vous souvent les matchs ?
6. Qu'est-ce que vous faites comme sport en été ? Qu'est-ce que vous faites comme sport en hiver ?

Compréhension auditive (basée sur l'Application A)

Compréhension auditive (basée sur les Applications A et B)

Dictée : « Nous faisons une promenade. » (basée sur l'Application D)

---

[1]*pl* **sandwichs, sandwiches**

[2]Beginning with this lesson, you will be reviewing the use of various question words. You ask a question about the underlined part of each sentence. For example, the first question would be **Quel jour est-ce aujourd'hui ?** and the second, **Où est-ce que vous êtes ?** or **Où êtes-vous ?** The key (**Clé**) will be provided only for Lessons 4 and 5.

[3]*Ask questions about the underlined parts.*

[4]**adverse** *opponent*

[5]**ce soir** *tonight, this evening*

VOCABULAIRE[1]

Noms

un **agent (de police)**	policeman	la feuille	leaf	le(la) partenaire	partner
un arbre	tree	la **fiche**	slip, card	le **patin (à glace)**	(ice) skate
le **base-ball**	baseball	la **fois**	time	le plaisir	pleasure
le **basket(-ball)**	basketball	le footing	jogging	la **police**	police
le **cahier d'exercices**	workbook	le **Français**	Frenchman	la **pomme**	apple
le(la) **camarade de chambre**	roommate	le **garage**	garage	la raquette	racket
le(la) **champion(ne)**	champion	le **golf**	golf	la **région**	region
le ciel	sky	la **grammaire**	grammar	la **saison**	season
le copain	friend, pal	la **gymnastique**	gymnastics	la **scène**	scene
le court	court	un **homme**	man	le **ski**	ski
le **devoir**	homework	le **lit**	bed	le **soleil**	sun
un **enfant**	child	mil (**mille**)	one thousand	la **télé**	TV
l'**Europe** f	Europe	la **musculation**	bodybuilding	le **téléphone**	telephone
la **famille**	family	la **natation**	swimming	le **temps**	weather
la **faute**	mistake	le nuage	cloud	le **vent**	wind
la fenêtre	window	le **parapluie**	umbrella	la **voiture**	car

Verbes

aller irrég	to go	**finir**	to finish	**pleuvoir** irrég	to rain
applaudir	to applaud	**habiter**	to live	**remplir**	to fill out
bâiller	to yawn	jouer (à)	to play	sonner	to ring
briller	to shine	**manger**	to eat	**téléphoner (à)**	to telephone
choisir	to choose	**neiger**	to snow	utiliser	to use
dîner	to have dinner	**obéir (à)**	to obey		
faire irrég	to do; to make; to be (weather)	**oublier**	to forget		

Adjectifs

beau (bel, belle)	beautiful	**jeune**	young	**musclé(e)**	muscular
chaud(e)	warm	libre	free	**prochain(e)**	next
frais (fraîche)	cool	magnifique	magnificent, splendid		
froid(e)	cold	**mauvais(e)**	bad		

Adverbes

encore	still; again	**quand**	when	**souvent**	often
plus	more	**tard**	late	**toujours**	always; still
plus tard	later	**rarement**	rarely		

Préposition

chez at the house of

Autres expressions

À bientôt.	See you soon.	**il fait beau, chaud, du soleil, du vent, frais, froid, mauvais**	the weather is nice, warm, sunny, windy, cool, cold, bad
allô	hello (telephone)		
avec plaisir	with pleasure, gladly	**il pleut**	it's raining
car	because, for	**lisez**	read
combien de fois	how many times, how often	**par semaine**	per week
comme	as	**Quel temps fait-il ?**	What's the weather like?
décrivez	describe	**tous les jours**	every day
de temps en temps	from time to time	**tout le temps**	all the time
faire du patin (à glace)	to ice-skate, go ice-skating	tu viens ?	are you coming?
faire du ski	to ski, go skiing		
faire du sport	to practice sports		

[1]Possessive adjectives and cardinal numbers are excluded.

5 Allons au café !

LESSON OBJECTIVES

Theme and Culture

1. Food and drinks in cafés
2. The role of cafés in French society

Communication Skills

1. Ordering drinks in cafés
2. Expressing needs (*I want the book, I want to do*)
3. Asking *yes-no* questions in more varied ways
4. Expressing ability or inability to do things
5. Expressions such as to *be cold, hot, hungry*, etc.

Structures

5.1 **Vouloir**
5.2 Demonstrative adjective **ce**; determiners
5.3 Third-conjugation verbs (**-re**)
5.4 Interrogative patterns: **n'est-ce pas** and inversion
5.5 **Pouvoir**
5.6 Expressions with **avoir**

CONVERSATIONS

TABLEAU 27

 A. Au café

ALAIN Moi[1] je vais commander un citron pressé[2]. Et toi, Ahmed, qu'est-ce que tu veux ?
AHMED Cette jolie boisson rose, qu'est-ce que c'est ?

[1]Stressed pronouns such as **moi, toi,** and **lui** are often used along with subject pronouns to emphasize the subject (for **je, tu,** and **il,** respectively), or by themselves when there is no verb to go with the subject, or after **être: Moi, je parle anglais, et toi ?** *I speak English, what about you?* (literally, *and you?*). **Qui est-ce ? — C'est lui.** *Who is it? It's he/ him.* They will be presented in Lesson 12.2 (p. 261)).

[2]*Fresh lemon juice*; the customer adds ice, water and sugar to taste.

ALAIN C'est un lait fraise[1]. C'est délicieux.
AHMED Ah non, je déteste le lait. Je veux un Coca-Cola.

TABLEAU 28

B. C'est probablement Daniel.

MARYSE J'entends la sonnette.
JACQUELINE J'attends Daniel. C'est probablement lui[2].
MARYSE Tu ne vas pas répondre ?
JACQUELINE Si, je descends tout de suite.

C. Voilà un café.

MONIQUE Comme il fait chaud ![3]
JACQUES Tu as raison. J'ai chaud et je suis fatigué.
MONIQUE Tiens, voilà un café. Tu veux boire quelque chose ?
JACQUES Bonne idée ! Je veux quelque chose de frais[4].

DIFFÉRENCES

Les cafés

The ever-popular French cafés breathe old-world nostalgia into today's fast-paced, modern society. **Le café Procope** in Paris, dating back to 1686, is said to be the oldest and one of the most famous cafés in the world. Early in the 18th century, it became the favorite haunt of intellectuals and writers, who discovered the joy of tasting coffee (something new then) while reading newspapers (also new) and exchanging ideas. The commemorative plaque of Procope mentions some of its renowned customers, including Voltaire, Benjamin Franklin, Balzac, Victor Hugo, Verlaine, and others. It was so successful that by 1720 there were more than 300 cafés in Paris alone.

[1]*Cold milk with strawberry syrup*
[2]*he/him* (stressed form of **il**)
[3]*How warm/hot it is!*
[4]*something cold* (literally, *something cool*)

The cafés in different districts of a large city reflect their usual clientele. In modest-income residential areas, small cafés come alive after work and in the evening as customers order drinks, read the newspaper, play cards, watch TV, and talk with one another about politics, cars, the younger generation, pet peeves, and so on. Cafés near a university or **lycée** attract students who drop by with friends for lunch or after classes. In business and shopping areas, some customers drop by in the morning for breakfast and order **croissants** with **café** (*coffee*), **café au lait** (strong coffee mixed with hot

À la terrasse d'un café.

milk and sugar), or **chocolat** (*hot chocolate*). These cafés are crowded at noon with people having a light lunch. They may order a **sandwich jambon-beurre** (ham in buttered French bread), pizza, or a **croque-monsieur** (a grilled ham and cheese sandwich). The choice of beverage ranges from coffee and tea to mineral water and soft drinks to beer and wine. In the afternoon, business people meet at cafés for a relaxed discussion, while tourists and shoppers stop by to rest. In the evening, movie- and theatergoers enjoy **un pot** (*a drink*) at a nearby café before returning home.

Cafés open onto the sidewalk (**la terrasse**), where most people prefer to sit in good weather, seemingly oblivious to the noisy traffic in the street just beyond, and enjoy watching the passers-by. Drinks generally cost more served at a sidewalk table than inside. By law, the prices of drinks are posted on both the outside and inside of the café. You need not worry about tipping the waiter, as the service charge of about 12 to 15% is automatically included in **l'addition** (*the check*), though some people leave small loose change (up to 50 **centimes**, or a half franc). In some ways cafés are less lively than in days gone by, especially because of home entertainment provided by television and other hobbies. But cafés are resilient and still remain one of France's venerable social institutions.

STRUCTURES

5.1 VOULOIR

1. Study the conjugation of **vouloir** *to want*. Note that the stem vowel alternates between **-eu-** /ø/, /œ/[1] and **-ou-** /u/. The consonant /l/ occurs in the plural forms and in the infinitive, but not in the singular forms. **Vouloir** may be followed by a noun (*to want something*) or an infinitive (*to want to do something*).

vouloir	
veux	voulons
veux	voulez
veut	veulent

Je **veux** trois oranges.	/vø/
Tu **veux** ton cahier ?	
Elle ne **veut** pas de café.	
Nous **voulons** téléphoner à nos parents.	/vulõ/
Vous ne **voulez** pas déjeuner maintenant ?	/vule/
Elles **veulent** parler à leur voisin.	/vœl/

[1]The alternation of /ø/ and /œ/ is automatic here: /ø/ occurs when the verb form ends in /ø/ (an open syllable) as in **veux** and **veut**, and /œ/ occurs when it ends in a consonant sound (a closed syllable), as in **veulent**.

2. **Vouloir dire**. The expression **vouloir dire** (literally, *to want to say*) corresponds to the English verb *to mean*.

Qu'est-ce que cela (ça)[1] **veut dire** ?	*What does that mean?*
Qu'est-ce que le mot « chocolat » **veut dire** en anglais ?	*What does the word "chocolat" mean in English?*
Qu'est-ce que vous **voulez dire** ?	*What do you mean?*

In reply to questions like the above, **vouloir dire** is followed either by a quotation (definition), or by **que** (**qu'** before a vowel sound) *that* and a sentence (known as a "dependent" or a "subordinate" clause). The use of **que** is obligatory in French before a dependent clause, whereas use of *that* is optional in English.

Cela **veut dire** « hot chocolate ».	*That means "hot chocolate."*
« Un café » **veut dire** « une tasse de café ».	*"A coffee" means "a cup of coffee."*
Ça **veut dire qu'**elle ne va pas travailler ce soir.	*That means (that) she isn't going to work tonight.*
Ça **veut dire que** le café n'est pas ouvert.	*That means (that) the café isn't open.*

A *Exercice de contrôle*

Je veux un chocolat.
1. Nous 2. Vous 3. Tu 4. Les clients

Je ne veux pas de café.
1. La cliente 2. Tu 3. Vous 4. Les enfants

Je veux téléphoner à mes parents.[2]
1. Vous 2. Tu 3. Nous 4. Les étudiants

Je ne veux pas faire mon travail.[3]
1. Nous 2. Tu 3. Les étudiants 4. Vous

B *Vous êtes dans un café. Regardez la liste de boissons dans les* Expressions utiles *à la page 115. Je suis le garçon (la serveuse). Faites un dialogue d'après ce modèle.*

(Michel) **Je veux un thé. Tu veux un thé ?**
(Cécile) **Moi, je ne veux pas de thé. Je veux un café.**
(Michel) (*au professeur*) **Nous voulons un café et un thé.**
(Cécile) **Oui, apportez un café et un thé.**

C *Répondez aux questions.*

1. Voulez-vous aller en France ? Demandez-moi si je veux aller en France. Demandez à (Sylvie) si elle veut aller en France.
2. Voulez-vous aller dans un café ? Qu'est-ce que vous voulez commander ? Qu'est-ce que « croque-monsieur » veut dire ?[4]
3. Qu'est-ce que vous voulez faire demain ? Posez la même question[5] à votre voisin(e) de gauche.
4. Qu'est-ce que le mot « infusion » veut dire en anglais ? Qu'est-ce que le mot « chocolat » veut dire ?

Exercice supplémentaire

[1]**Qu'est-ce que** *What*; Both **cela** and **ça** mean *that* (**ça** is more informal).
[2]Change **mes** to make it agree with the subject.
[3]Change **mon** to make it agree with the subject.
[4]Consultez les *Différences* de cette leçon.
[5]**la même question** *the same question*; use the **tu** form.

5.2 ADJECTIF DÉMONSTRATIF **CE** ; LES DÉTERMINANTS

1. The demonstrative adjective is used to point out a noun being mentioned: *this book, that man, these rooms, those people.* In French, the demonstrative adjective has four written forms to agree in gender (*m/f*) and number (*s/pl*) with the noun it modifies: **ce**, **cette**, **cet**, **ces**. **Ce** is used before a masculine singular noun, and **cette** before a feminine singular noun. If the masculine singular noun begins with a vowel sound, **cet** /sɛt/ is used. As a result, the forms of the demonstrative adjective are pronounced the same before a singular noun that begins with a vowel sound: /sɛt/ (for **cet**, **cette**). **Ce**, **cet**, and **cette** correspond to English *this* or *that*.[1]

Ce garçon[2] parle anglais.	*This/That waiter . . .*
Cette serveuse est française.	*This/That waitress . . .*
Cet étudiant cherche son livre.	*This/That (male) student . . .*
Cette étudiante est américaine.	*This/That (female) student . . .*

    Ces, used before a plural noun, corresponds to *these* or *those.*

Ces clients parlent anglais.	*These/Those customers . . .*
Ces étudiants travaillent beaucoup.	*These/Those students . . .*
Ces étudiantes sont américaines.	*These/Those students . . .*

2. *Determiners.* Determiners (**les déterminants** *m*) always occur before a noun and identify what kind of noun it is: definite, indefinite, something possessed by someone, something being pointed out, and so on. Only one determiner can be used before each noun. The chart below summarizes the various forms of the determiners: for the possessive adjectives, only the forms for **je** and **vous** are given (a complete list was presented in Lesson 4.4). For the nouns following these determiners and beginning with a consonant sound, think of words like **livre(s)** and **chaise(s)**; for those beginning with a vowel sound, think of **étudiant(s)** and **étudiante(s)**. Note that before a vowel sound, you cannot tell the gender of the noun, except with **un** /ɛ̃n/ and **une** /yn/.

	SINGULAR				PLURAL				LESSON
	BEFORE CONSONANT		BEFORE VOWEL		BEFORE CONSONANT		BEFORE VOWEL		
	m	*f*	*m*	*f*	*m*	*f*	*m*	*f*	
INDEFINITE ARTICLE	un	une	un‿	une	des		des‿		1.1
DEFINITE ARTICLE	le	la	l'		les		les‿		1.3
INTERROGATIVE ADJECTIVE	quel	quelle	quel	quelle	quels	quelles	quels‿	quelles‿	3.5
POSSESSIVE ADJECTIVE	mon / votre	ma	mon‿ / votre		mes / vos		mes‿ / vos‿		3.4
DEMONSTRATIVE ADJECTIVE	ce	cette	cet	cette	ces		ces‿		5.2

[1]French normally does not differentiate between *this* (*these*) and *that* (*those*). For cases where such distinctions must be made, see Lesson 22.1.

[2]**Garçon** can mean either *boy* or *waiter*, depending on the context.

A *Remplacez chaque[1] article défini par l'adjectif démonstratif, d'après ce modèle.*

Écoutez la cassette.
Écoutez cette cassette.

Ne regardez pas le tableau.
Ne regardez pas ce tableau.

1. Regardez la table.
2. Ne regardez pas le livre.
3. Écoutez les cassettes.
4. N'écoutez pas l'étudiant.

5. Copiez les phrases.
6. Ne parlez pas à l'étudiante.
7. Répétez la réponse.
8. Faites les exercices.

B *Regardez le Tableau 16 à la page 64. Répondez aux questions d'après ce modèle.*

À quelle boutique arrivez-vous ?
J'arrive à cette boutique.

C *Maintenant, regardez le Tableau 9 à la page 39. Posez des questions à votre partenaire, d'après ce modèle.*

À quel bâtiment est-ce que tu arrives ?
J'arrive à ce bâtiment.

Compréhension auditive

Ils attendent l'autobus.

5.3 VERBES DU TROISIÈME GROUPE (-RE)

1. The infinitives of third-conjugation verbs end in **-re**. As with first (**-er**) and second (**-ir**) conjugation verbs, the singular forms are all pronounced alike. The sound /d/ is heard only in the plural forms.

vendre

vends	vendons
vends	vendez
vend	vendent

vendre /vãdʀ/ *to sell*

Je ne **vends** pas mon livre. /vã/
Tu ne **vends** pas ta montre.
   Il **vend** des fleurs.

Nous ne **vendons** pas de fleurs. /vãdõ/
Vous **vendez** votre voiture. /vãde/
Ils **vendent** leur maison. /vãd/

2. The difference in spoken French between the third-person singular and plural forms is that the consonant /d/ is heard only in the plural (the verb ending **-ent**, silent, indicates like **-e** that the preceding consonant is pronounced). Presence of liaison also indicates that the verb is in the plural.

[1]*each*

il descend	/desɑ̃/			elle entend	/ɑ̃tɑ̃/		
ils descen**dent**	/desɑ̃d/			elles_enten**dent**	/ɑ̃tɑ̃d/		
elle répond	/ʀepɔ̃/			il attend	/atɑ̃/		
elles répon**dent**	/ʀepɔ̃d/			ils_atten**dent**	/atɑ̃d/		

3. Here is a summary of the three regular conjugation patterns in written and spoken French. Note that the plural forms of both second- and third-conjugation patterns have a stem consonant not heard in the singular forms (/s/ and /d/, respectively), and that *all* the singular forms of each group sound alike.

FIRST CONJUGATION				SECOND CONJUGATION				THIRD CONJUGATION			
parler				**finir**				**vendre**			
parle	**parlons**	/paʀl/	/paʀlɔ̃/	**finis**	**finissons**	/fini/	/finisɔ̃/	**vends**	**vendons**	/vɑ̃/	/vɑ̃dɔ̃/
parles	**parlez**	/paʀl/	/paʀle/	**finis**	**finissez**	/fini/	/finise/	**vends**	**vendez**	/vɑ̃/	/vɑ̃de/
parle	**parlent**	/paʀl/	/paʀl/	**finit**	**finissent**	/fini/	/finis/	**vend**	**vendent**	/vɑ̃/	/vɑ̃d/

A *Exercice de contrôle*

Je réponds à la question.[1]
1. Vous   2. L'étudiant   3. Nous   4. Les étudiants

Je n'entends pas la question.
1. Les étudiants   2. Tu   3. Vous   4. L'étudiant

J'attends le train et j'entends le train.
1. Nous   2. Le touriste   3. Les touristes   4. Vous

B *Répondez aux questions.*

1. Je pose des questions, n'est-ce pas ? Entendez-vous mes questions ? Répondez-vous à mes questions ?
2. Regardez. C'est ma montre. Est-ce que je vends ma montre ? Vendez-vous votre montre ?
3. Où est-ce que nous sommes ? Est-ce que j'attends mes étudiants ? Attendez-vous le professeur ? Pourquoi pas ?[2]
4. Répondez-vous aux lettres de vos parents ? Et vos parents répondent-ils à vos lettres ?

C *Révision des verbes. Répondez aux questions.*[3]

1. Avez-vous des cours le samedi ?
2. Allez-vous au cinéma demain soir ?
3. Où êtes-vous maintenant ?
4. Répondez-vous à mes questions ?
5. Posez-vous des questions ?
6. Arrivez-vous en retard ?
7. Voulez-vous mon crayon ?
8. Attendez-vous un taxi ?
9. Obéissez-vous aux agents ?
10. Avez-vous un chat ?
11. Choisissez-vous vos cours ?
12. Faites-vous toujours vos devoirs ?
13. Vendez-vous votre montre ?
14. Voulez-vous aller au cinéma ?

Exercice supplémentaire

---

[1]**répondre à**   *to answer* (something/someone)

[2]*Why not?*

[3]When you reply negatively to affirmative questions containing **un**, **une**, or **des**, you must change it to **pas de**, except after **être**.

« Est-ce que tu téléphones souvent à Ahmed ? — Oui, et toi, parles-tu souvent à John ? »

5.4 FORME INTERROGATIVE **N'EST-CE PAS ?** ; INVERSION

There are four ways of forming a question: (1) by intonation alone, (2) with **Est-ce que... ?**, (3) with **..., n'est-ce pas ?**, and (4) by inversion. In Lesson 3.3 we briefly discussed three of these.

1. The most informal way to change a statement into a question is to keep the declarative sentence and simply change the intonation from that of a normal statement (usually rising and falling) to a rising one. This is very common in spoken French, but *not* in written language.

   STATEMENT   QUESTION
   Vous cherchez un café.   → Vous cherchez un café ?

2. Another way to change a statement into a question is to add **Est-ce que** in front of the statement and use a rising intonation. You learned this in Lesson 1.2.

   STATEMENT   QUESTION
   Vous cherchez un café.   → Est-ce que vous cherchez un café ?

3. A third way is to add **n'est-ce pas ?** at the end of the statement. This type of question usually implies that the speaker is expecting agreement or confirmation from the listener. It can be added to both affirmative and negative sentences.

   STATEMENT   QUESTION
   Vous cherchez un café.   → Vous cherchez un café, **n'est-ce pas ?**

   Michel parle anglais, **n'est-ce pas ?**   *Michel speaks English, doesn't he?*
   Vous téléphonez à Jean, **n'est-ce pas ?**   *You are phoning Jean, aren't you?*
   Il n'a pas de frères, **n'est-ce pas ?**   *He doesn't have any brothers, does he?*

4. A fourth and final way to form a question is to *invert* the subject and the verb, except in the case of the **je** form.[1] Inversion is considered more formal than (1) or (2) above.

STATEMENT	QUESTION
Vous cherchez un café.	→ **Cherchez-vous** un café?
Nous allons au cinéma.	→ **Allons-nous** au cinéma ?
Tu veux ce livre.	→ **Veux-tu** ce livre ?

In negative sentences, **ne** (**n'** before a vowel sound) still precedes the verb, but **pas** comes after the subject, which is connected to the verb with a hyphen and cannot be separated from it.

Tu **ne** vas **pas** manger maintenant.	→ **Ne** vas-tu **pas** manger maintenant ?
Vous **ne** faites **pas** de tennis.	→ **Ne** faites-vous **pas** de tennis ?
Nous **n'**avons **pas** de devoirs.	→ **N'**avons-nous **pas** de devoirs ?

5. The third-person singular and plural forms involve a change in pronunciation. When inverted, the subject pronouns **il**, **elle**, **ils**, **elles** are *always* pronounced /til/ or /tɛl/ after the verb. The source of this /t/ is explained below.

   a) The plural forms always end in **-ent** or, in a few cases, in **-ont**. The final letter **-t** is pronounced in liaison with the following **ils** or **elles**.

Ils finissent leurs devoirs.	→ **Finissent-ils** leurs devoirs ?
Elles téléphonent à leurs parents.	→ **Téléphonent-elles** à leurs parents ?
Ils ne **vont** pas au restaurant.	→ Ne **vont-ils** pas au restaurant ?
Elles ne **font** pas de natation.	→ Ne **font-elles** pas de natation ?

   b) The singular form of some verbs ends in **-t** or **-d**. In liaison, these letters are pronounced /t/.

Il est à la maison.	→ **Est-il** à la maison ?
Elle ne **fait** pas de ski.	→ Ne **fait-elle** pas de ski ?
Il ne **finit** pas son travail.	→ Ne **finit-il** pas son travail ?
Elle répond à la question.	→ **Répond-elle** à la question ?

   c) If the verb form does not end in **-t** or **-d**, then **-t-** must be inserted between the verb and **il** or **elle** so that the spelling can reflect the pronunciation /til/ or /tɛl/. This applies to all verb forms that end in a vowel letter, including *all* first-conjugation verbs.

Il a des frères.	→ **A-t-il** des frères ?
Elle va au café.	→ **Va-t-elle** au café ?
Il y **a** un stylo sur la table.	→ Y **a-t-il** un stylo sur la table ?
Il n'y **a** pas de crayons.	→ **N'**y **a-t-il** pas de crayons ?
Elle entre dans le café.	→ **Entre-t-elle** dans le café ?
Il ne **regarde** pas le menu.	→ Ne **regarde-t-il** pas le menu ?

[1]Inversion with **je** is possible with a few verbs. You may hear, for example: **Suis-je en retard ?**; **Ai-je votre réponse ?** Normally, however, **Est-ce que ... ?** is preferred whenever the subject is **je**.

d) If the subject of the sentence is a noun, the inversion occurs with a corresponding third-person pronoun (**il**, **elle**, **ils**, **elles**). It is as though there were two subjects in such a sentence: the real subject (noun) and the inverted subject (pronoun).

Robert mange-t-**il** des fruits ?   **Vos parents** sont-**ils** à la maison ?

Marie ne fait-**elle** pas de tennis ?   **Marie et Paul** ne font-**ils** pas de ski ?

Le train est-**il** ici ?   **Les étudiants** vont-**ils** travailler ?

TABLEAU 29

A   *Posez des questions d'après ces modèles.*[1]

Nous allons déjeuner dans ce café.

> (Jacques) **Nous allons déjeuner dans ce café ?**
> (Marie)   **Est-ce que nous allons déjeuner dans ce café ?**
> (Daniel)   **Nous allons déjeuner dans ce café, n'est-ce pas ?**
> (Pascale) **Allons-nous déjeuner dans ce café ?**

1. Nous choisissons la terrasse[2].
2. Il y a une table libre[3].
3. Vous voulez un croque-monsieur.
4. Nous commandons une boisson.
5. Nous demandons l'addition[4].
6. Vous allez payer l'addition.

B   *Posez des questions en employant l'inversion.*

1. (Jacques) parle bien français.
2. (Sylvie) adore Robert Redford.
3. (Jean) ne vend pas ses livres.
4. (Jacques et Paul) ont sommeil.
5. (Michel et Marie) n'ont pas faim.
6. (Jeanne et Sophie) sont en classe.

C   *Répondez aux questions.*[5]

1. Sommes-nous dans la classe ? (Marianne) n'est-elle pas ici ? (Jean et Monique) ne sont-ils pas ici ?
2. Je fais (du ski). Ne faites-vous pas (de ski) ? Qu'est-ce que vous faites comme sport ? Posez la même question à (Mireille).
3. Je parle français, n'est-ce pas ? Est-ce que je ne parle pas anglais ? Est-ce que vous ne parlez pas anglais ?

Exercice supplémentaire

Compréhension auditive

[1] Only the inversion is practiced on the tape.
[2] *sidewalk* (of a café)
[3] *unoccupied* (literally, *free*) *table*
[4] *bill* (in a café or restaurant)
[5] Use **si** to reply affirmatively to *negative* questions (Lesson 3.2).

5.5 POUVOIR

Pouvoir *to be able, can* is conjugated like **vouloir**. The stem vowel alternates between **-eu-** /ø/, /œ/ and **-ou-** /u/. The consonant /v/ occurs only in the plural forms and in the infinitive. **Pouvoir** is usually followed by an infinitive.

pouvoir	
peux	pouvons
peux	pouvez
peut	peuvent

Je **peux** parler au professeur.	/pø/
Tu ne **peux** pas aller au cinéma ?	
Elle **peut** rester[1] à la maison.	
Nous **pouvons** déjeuner à une heure.	/puvõ/
Vous ne **pouvez** pas manger en classe.	/puve/
Elles ne **peuvent** pas téléphoner à Jacques.	/pœv/

A *Exercice de contrôle*[2]

Je peux finir mon travail.

1. Vous   2. Tu   3. Nous   4. Cet étudiant

Vous pouvez téléphoner à vos parents.

1. Tu   2. Ces étudiants   3. Cette étudiante   4. Je

Je ne peux pas attendre mon professeur.

1. Nous   2. Tu   3. Ces étudiants   4. Vous

B *Répondez aux questions.*

1. Regardez le plafond. Est-ce que je peux toucher le plafond ? Pouvez-vous toucher le plafond ?
2. Est-ce que nous pouvons déjeuner en classe ? Est-ce que je peux déjeuner au resto-U[3] ?
3. Qu'est-ce que vous pouvez faire ce soir ? Qu'est-ce que vous ne voulez pas faire ce soir ?
4. Qu'est-ce que vous pouvez faire ce week-end ? Qu'est-ce que vous ne voulez pas faire ce week-end ?

C *Interprétation. Ajoutez des phrases d'après ce modèle.*

Je ne vais pas déjeuner à midi.
(Charles) **Ça veut dire que vous ne pouvez pas déjeuner à midi.**
(Cécile) **Non, ça veut dire que vous ne voulez pas déjeuner à midi.**

1. Je ne vais pas déjeuner au resto-U.
2. Je ne vais pas attendre l'autobus.
3. Vous n'allez pas parler anglais en classe.
4. (Mireille) ne va pas à la bibliothèque aujourd'hui.
5. (Nicole et Sophie) ne vont pas au cinéma ce soir.

Dictée

5.6 EXPRESSIONS AVEC AVOIR

1. **Avoir** means *to have* (Lesson 2.6); but it is used in a number of expressions in which it is an equivalent of English *to be* rather than *to have*. The subject in such expressions usually denotes human beings or animals. The words **faim**, **soif**, **sommeil**, **chaud**, and **froid** may be preceded by modifiers such as **très** and **un peu**.

Nous_avons (très) **faim**.	*We're (very) hungry.*
Avez-vous **soif** ?	*Are you thirsty?*

---

[1]**rester** *to stay, to remain*
[2]Make the possessive adjectives agree with the subject.
[3]**resto-U** (ou **Resto-U**) = restaurant universitaire

Ce garçon a soif. *Ce monsieur a sommeil.* *Ce chien a froid.*

J'**ai** (un peu) **sommeil**.	*I'm (a little) sleepy.*
Regarde le chien ; il **a chaud**.	*Look at the dog; he is hot.*
Ferme la fenêtre ; j'**ai** un peu **froid**.	*Close the window; I'm a little cold.*
Elle **a** toujours **raison**.	*She is always right.*
Vous_**avez tort**.	*You are wrong.*
Quel âge avez-vous ?	*How old are you?*
J'**ai dix-neuf ans**.	*I'm nineteen (years old).*

2. With regard to **chaud** and **froid**, note that they can be used with **faire**, **avoir**, and **être** with three different meanings.

  a) Weather expressions

Il **fait chaud** aujourd'hui.	*It's hot today.*
Il va **faire froid** ce soir.	*It's going to be cold tonight.*

  b) Human beings and animals

Nous_**avons chaud**.	*We are hot.*
Ce chat **a froid**.	*This cat is cold.*

  c) Objects

Ce chocolat **est** très **chaud**.	*This chocolate is very hot.*
Mon lait n'**est** pas **froid**.	*My milk is not cold.*

TABLEAU 30 Il **a chaud** et il **a soif**. Il **fait froid** et elle **a froid**. A-t-elle **tort** ?
— Non, elle **a raison**.

A *Interprétation. Ajoutez des phrases d'après ce modèle.*

> Je veux manger quelque chose[1].
> **Vous avez faim.**

1. Je veux boire quelque chose.
2. Je veux faire la sieste[2].
3. Il fait chaud dans la classe.
4. Il fait froid ici.
5. Deux et trois font[3] cinq.
6. Cinq et six font dix.

B *Posez des questions d'après ce modèle.*

> (Marie), demandez à (Jacques) quel âge il a.
> (Marie)   **Quel âge as-tu ?**
> (Jacques)   **J'ai dix-neuf ans.**
> (Marie)   **Il a dix-neuf ans.**

1. (Mireille), demandez à (Daniel) quel âge il a. Demandez quel âge a son père.
2. (Robert), demandez à (Renée) quel âge elle a. Demandez quel âge a sa mère.
3. (Jean), demandez à (Monique) quel âge elle a. Demandez quel âge a (son frère).
4. (Jeanne), demandez-moi quel âge a le président des États-Unis.

C *Répondez aux questions.*

1. Avez-vous faim ? Demandez à (Jean) s'il a faim. Qu'est-ce que nous voulons faire quand nous avons faim ?
2. Avez-vous soif ? Demandez à (Frédérique) si elle a soif. Qu'est-ce que nous voulons faire quand nous avons soif ?[4]
3. Avez-vous sommeil ? Demandez à (Michel) s'il a sommeil. Qu'est-ce que nous voulons faire quand nous avons sommeil ?[5]
4. En quelle saison est-ce qu'il fait chaud ? Avez-vous chaud ? Quand est-ce que nous avons chaud ?
5. En quelle saison est-ce qu'il fait froid ? Avez-vous froid ? Quand est-ce que nous avons froid ?
6. Est-ce que j'ai toujours raison ? Est-ce que j'ai toujours tort ? Demandez à (Isabelle) si elle a toujours raison.

Compréhension auditive

APPLICATIONS

A Situations

Au café
Après leurs cours, Jean-Paul, Christine et Ahmed Fakhri ont rendez-vous au café près de l'université. Ahmed est un étudiant marocain. Aujourd'hui, Christine amène une nouvelle camarade[6]. Elle s'appelle Mayoumi Okada. Elle est japonaise et fait du français à l'Institut pour étudiants étrangers. Christine présente Mayoumi à ses amis.

---

[1]*something*

[2]**faire la sieste**   *to take a nap*

[3]**font**   *equals*

[4]Utilisez **boire** *to drink.*

[5]Utilisez **faire la sieste**.

[6]Several words designate different kinds of friends. **Copain** *m* (**copine** *f*) denotes a fairly close friend (*a buddy*); **camarade** *m, f* indicates a more casual and less close friend; **ami(e)**, used especially in the plural, can mean *friends* in a general sense, but used in the singular, it can imply a very close friend (like a *boyfriend* or *girlfriend*).

« Alors, qu'est-ce que tu veux boire ? »

JEAN-PAUL	Alors, comment trouves-tu[1] l'institut ?	5
MAYOUMI	Ne parle pas trop vite, s'il te plaît. Mon français n'est pas très bon.	
JEAN-PAUL	Bon, d'accord. Est-ce que tu aimes tes cours à l'institut ?	

MAYOUMI Ah oui, beaucoup. Les cours sont intéressants et les professeurs sont très sym-
nice, friendly pathiques°.

AHMED	Alors, qu'est-ce que tu veux boire ?	10
CHRISTINE	Moi, j'ai très soif. Je vais prendre un citron pressé. Et toi, Mayoumi ?	
MAYOUMI	Euh[2]... Qu'est-ce que c'est, un citron pressé ?	
CHRISTINE	C'est un mélange de jus de citron et d'eau sucrée. C'est très rafraîchissant.	
MAYOUMI	Rafraîchissant ? Qu'est-ce que cela veut dire ?	
JEAN-PAUL	Ça veut dire que c'est délicieux quand il fait chaud et quand tu as très soif.	15
MAYOUMI	Oui, j'ai soif. Alors, un citron pressé pour moi.	
AHMED	Pour moi, un café. J'ai sommeil et je vais travailler tard ce soir. Et toi, Jean-Paul, qu'est-ce que tu veux boire ?	

beer on tap JEAN-PAUL Pour moi, une bière pression°.

AHMED	D'accord. Garçon, s'il vous plaît !	20

« Cette boisson est très rafraîchissante. »

[1]*How do you like;* **trouver** *to find* is often used to elicit or express an opinion.
[2]signe d'hésitation (*Well. . ., Er. . .*)

Répondez aux questions. (*lignes 1–4*)

1. Où les jeunes gens ont-ils rendez-vous ?
2. Comment s'appelle la nouvelle camarade de Christine ?
3. Quelle est la nationalité de Mayoumi ?
4. Qu'est-ce qu'elle étudie ?

(*lignes 5–20*)

5. Comment trouve-t-elle l'institut ?[1]
6. Qu'est-ce que Christine veut boire ?
7. Qu'est-ce que c'est, un citron pressé ?
8. Pourquoi Ahmed commande-t-il un café ?
9. Qu'est-ce que Jean-Paul veut boire ?
10. Continuez la conversation entre Ahmed et le garçon.[2]

B

Au café

Aller dans un café
Chercher une table libre[3] à la terrasse[4]

Commander
- une boisson chaude (un café, un chocolat)
- un apéritif / un digestif[5]
- une boisson rafraîchissante
- un croissant / une brioche

au garçon
à la serveuse

Commander
Manger
Prendre[7]
- un sandwich au jambon (un sandwich jambon-beurre)
- un croque-monsieur / un croque-madame[6]
- une quiche / une pizza

Boissons typiques[8]

Café et thé

un café nature / un café noir
un crème
un café au lait
un chocolat

un thé
- (nature)
- au lait
- (au) citron

une infusion[9]

Alcools[10]

un Cinzano
un cognac
un Cointreau

un petit blanc[11]
un porto
un whisky[12]

---

[1]Réponse : **Elle trouve que... et que...**

[2]La réponse n'est pas enregistrée sur la bande magnétique.

[3]**libre** *free (unoccupied)*

[4]**à la terrasse** *on the sidewalk*

[5]**apéritif** *before-dinner drink*; **digestif** *after-dinner drink*

[6]a **croque-monsieur** (see the *Différences* of this lesson) with a fried egg on top

[7]verbe irrégulier (Leçon 6.1)

[8]Reminder: English equivalents or explanations are in your **Cahier d'exercices** (Part Three, **Clés**, of each lesson).

[9]*herbal tea*

[10]/alkɔl/ = **boissons alcoolisées** *alcoholic beverages*

[11]un petit verre de vin blanc

[12]usually Scotch whisky

Boissons rafraîchissantes

une bière (à la) pression[1]	un panaché[7]
une bouteille de bière	un Schweppes
un citron pressé[2]	un quart d'eau minérale[8]
un Coca(-Cola) / un Pepsi(-Cola)[3]	un Perrier
un jus de fruit	un Évian
un lait fraise[4]	un Vittel
une limonade[5]	un Vichy
une orangeade[6]	un diabolo-menthe[9]
un Orangina[6]	un Perrier-menthe[10]

C Pratique

1. Il est sept heures et demie. Vous voulez prendre le petit déjeuner[11] dans un café. Qu'est-ce que vous allez commander ?[12]
2. Il est presque une heure. Vous avez faim. Vous allez déjeuner dans un café. Qu'est-ce que vous voulez commander ?[12]
3. Il fait chaud et vous avez chaud. Vous trouvez un café. Qu'est-ce que vous allez commander ?
4. Vous voulez goûter quelque chose de nouveau. Qu'est-ce que vous allez commander ? Pourquoi choisissez-vous cette boisson ?
5. Indiquez le mot qui n'appartient pas à[13] chaque série. Dites pourquoi.[14]

   un crème—un Perrier—une infusion—une brioche
   une bière—un lait fraise—un cognac—un petit blanc
   un chocolat—une pizza—une quiche—un croissant
   un Pepsi-Cola—un Orangina—un Cinzano—un Schweppes

D

Voici une série de situations et d'actions. Mettez ces actions dans l'ordre logique[15] et ajoutez un sujet à chaque verbe. N'oubliez pas de faire accorder les verbes avec le sujet.[16]

1. *Le cours*
   a) quitter la classe
   b) trouver une chaise
   c) écouter le professeur
   d) entrer dans la classe
   e) faire les devoirs
   f) rentrer à la résidence

2. *Ma journée*
   a) quitter le dernier cours
   b) aller au premier cours
   c) déjeuner à midi et demi
   d) regarder la télévision
   e) rentrer à la maison
   f) dîner à six heures et demie

[1]*beer on tap*

[2]*fresh lemon juice, served separately with water and sugar to suit taste*

[3]*Very often both are simply called* **un Coca**.

[4]*cold milk with strawberry syrup*

[5]*soft drink, somewhat like 7-Up*

[6]*orange-flavored soda*

[7]*half* **limonade** *and half beer*

[8]**Un quart** *is 250 cc (about half a pint). Perrier is strongly carbonated, Évian and Vittel are not, and Vichy is slightly carbonated.*

[9]*a mixture of mint-flavored syrup and* **limonade**

[10]*a mixture of mint-flavored syrup and Perrier*

[11]*breakfast*

[12]Consultez les *Différences* de cette leçon (p. 102).

[13]**qui n'appartient pas à** *which does not belong to*

[14]*Say why.* Par exemple : **Un croissant n'est pas une boisson ; un citron pressé n'est pas une boisson alcoolisée.**

[15]*Put these actions in the logical order*

[16]*Don't forget to make the verbs agree with the subject.*

3. *Dans une boutique*
   a) essayer un blouson
   b) entrer dans la boutique
   c) payer le blouson
   d) choisir un blouson
   e) arriver à une boutique
   f) regarder la vitrine

4. *Dans un café*
   a) trouver une table libre
   b) payer l'addition[1]
   c) finir le repas
   d) commander un croque-monsieur
   e) regarder l'addition
   f) aller dans un café

E **Questions :** *Une Américaine et son camarade français sont dans un café. Lisez d'abord le paragraphe, ensuite posez des questions sur les parties soulignées.*

J'ai rendez-vous (1) avec Michel cet après-midi. (2) Il est déjà là quand j'arrive au café. Il fait (3) chaud cet après-midi. J'ai chaud et très soif. Je veux boire (4) quelque chose de frais. (5) Michel veut commander une bière pression. Je commande (6) un Coca-Cola. (7) Le garçon apporte la boisson. Il n'y a pas de glaçons dans mon verre[2]. J'appelle le garçon. Je demande des glaçons (8) au garçon. Nous parlons (9) de nos cours. Nous quittons le café (10) à quatre heures.

Clé : 1. Avec qui   2. Qui   3. Quel temps   4. Qu'est-ce que   5. Qui   6. Qu'est-ce que   7. Qui   8. À qui   9. De quoi[3]   10. À quelle heure

F **Renseignements et opinions**

1. Qu'est-ce que vous voulez faire ce week-end ? Et qu'est-ce que vous ne pouvez pas faire ce week-end ?
2. Est-ce qu'il fait chaud ou froid dans cette classe ? Avez-vous chaud ou froid en ce moment ?
3. Combien de jours est-ce qu'il y a dans une année ? Combien de secondes y a-t-il dans une heure ? Combien de minutes y a-t-il dans un jour ?
4. Est-ce que vous attendez la fin du cours avec impatience ? À quelle heure finit-il ? Où voulez-vous aller après le cours ?
5. Est-ce que vous entendez ma question ? Voulez-vous répondre à ma question ? Mes questions sont-elles faciles ou difficiles ?
6. Préparez une question à poser à votre professeur au sujet des[4] cafés en France.

Compréhension auditive (basée sur l'Application A)

Compréhension auditive (basée sur l'Application B)

Dictée : « Commandons quelque chose. »

---

[1]**addition** *bill* (in a café or restaurant)

[2]**un glaçon** *an ice cube*; **un verre** *a glass*: In many cafés in France, ice cubes for drinks are often furnished only upon request, since the drinks are kept cold before serving.

[3]*About what*

[4]**au sujet de** *concerning*

VOCABULAIRE

Noms

une **addition**	check, bill (café or restaurant)	
un **âge**	age	
un **an**	year	
un **autobus**	bus	
la **bière (pression)**	beer (on tap)	
la **boisson**	drink	
le **café**	café; coffee	
le **chinois**	Chinese language	
le **chocolat**	chocolate	
le **citron**	lemon	
le **citron pressé**	fresh lemonade	
le(la) **client(e)**	customer	
le **Coca-Cola**	Coca-Cola	
la conversation	conversation
le **croque-monsieur**	grilled ham and cheese sandwich
l' eau f	water
la **faim**	hunger
la **fraise**	strawberry
le garçon	waiter; boy
une **infusion**	herbal tea
un institut	institute
les jeunes gens m	young people
le jus	juice
le **lait**	milk
le mélange	mixture
le **plafond**	ceiling
le **président**	president
la **réponse**	answer
le **resto-U**	university cafeteria
la **sieste**	nap
la **soif**	thirst
le **sommeil**	sleep
la **sonnette**	doorbell
le **taxi**	taxi
le **thé**	tea
la **terrasse**	sidewalk (of a café)
le(la) **touriste**	tourist
le **week-end**	weekend

Verbes

adorer	to love	
amener	to bring	
attendre	to wait for	
commander	to order	
continuer	to continue; to go on	
copier	to copy	
descendre (de)	to go down; to get off
entendre	to hear
pouvoir irrég	to be able, can
présenter (à)	to introduce
répéter	to repeat
répondre (à)	to answer
toucher	to touch
vendre	to sell
vouloir irrég	to want, wish
vouloir dire	to mean

Adjectifs

délicieux(euse)	delicious	
étranger(ère)	foreign	
fatigué(e)	tired	
japonais(e)	Japanese	
joli(e)	pretty	
marocain(e)	Moroccan
même	same
nouveau (nouvel, nouvelle)	new
pressé(e)	squeezed
rafraîchissant(e)	refreshing
rose	pink
sucré(e)	sweet
sympathique	nice, likeable

Adverbes

ici here	**probablement** probably	trop too, too much

Prépositions

entre between	près de near, next to

Autres expressions

avoir chaud	to be warm		cela	that
avoir faim	to be hungry		**faire la sieste**	to take a nap
avoir froid	to be cold		**n'est-ce pas ?**	isn't it so?
avoir raison	to be right		**Pourquoi pas ?**	Why not?
avoir soif	to be thirsty		**prendre** irrég	to take
avoir sommeil	to be sleepy		**que**	that
avoir tort	to be wrong		**Quel âge avez-vous ?**	How old are you?
avoir x ans	to be x years old		**quelque chose**	something
boire irrég	to drink		**tout de suite**	right away
ça	that			

6 À table et bon appétit !

LESSON OBJECTIVES

Theme and Culture

1. Names of foods and meals
2. Meals in homes and restaurants

Communication Skills

1. Understanding basic sentence patterns, especially those that conflict with English
2. Getting information through open-ended questions (*Who, Whom, What*)
3. Expressing indefinite or unspecified quantity with noncount nouns (*some, any*)
4. Expressing actions/events in the immediate past (*I have just done*)
5. Expressing origin (*Where do you come from?, I come from . . .*)
6. Ordering food from menus
7. Asking/Answering questions about eating habits

Structures

6.1 **Prendre, apprendre, comprendre**
6.2 Basic sentence patterns
6.3 Interrogative subject pronouns: **qui... ?, qu'est-ce qui... ?**
6.4 Interrogative object pronouns: **qui est-ce que... ?, qu'est-ce que... ?**
6.5 Partitive article
6.6 **Venir, tenir**

CONVERSATIONS

A. Dans un restaurant

Hors-d'œuvre

LE GARÇON Bonjour, Monsieur. Voulez-vous des hors-d'œuvre ?
LE CLIENT Oui. Voyons[1]... apportez-moi des huîtres.

Viande

LE GARÇON Bien, Monsieur. Que voulez-vous comme viande ?
LE CLIENT Voyons... j'ai très faim aujourd'hui. Apportez-moi un bifteck avec des frites.

[1]*Let's (Let me) see*

119

TABLEAU 31

Légumes

LE GARÇON   Très bien, Monsieur. Que voulez-vous comme légumes ?

LE CLIENT   Voyons... apportez-moi des asperges.

Boisson

LE GARÇON   Bien, Monsieur. Et comme boisson ?

LE CLIENT   Voyons... j'ai très soif aujourd'hui. Apportez-moi une demi-bouteille de Bordeaux et un quart d'eau minérale.

(plus tard) *Addition*

LE CLIENT   Garçon, l'addition, s'il vous plaît.

LE GARÇON   Oui, Monsieur. Voilà, Monsieur.

LE CLIENT   Oh ! là ! là ! 320 F[1] ! Vous plaisantez, j'espère !

LE GARÇON   Ah non, Monsieur. Et le service n'est pas compris.[2]

TABLEAU 32

[1]**F** = francs

[2]When the service charge is not included in the price of the meal, it is automatically added to the food bill (generally 12–15%). If the menu says **service compris** or **prix nets** /nɛt/, then the charge is included.

B. Le concierge¹ est un peu dur d'oreille².

ANNE-MARIE	Bonjour, Monsieur. Je cherche M. Bernard.
LE CONCIERGE	Pardon, Mademoiselle. Qu'est-ce que vous cherchez ?
ANNE-MARIE	Je cherche M. Bernard. Est-ce qu'il est ici ?
LE CONCIERGE	Pardon, qui est-ce que vous cherchez ?
ANNE-MARIE	MONSIEUR BERNARD ! Est-il ici ?
LE CONCIERGE	Ah, vous cherchez M. Bernard ? Non, il n'est pas ici.

Un déjeuner en famille.

DIFFÉRENCES

Les repas

In France **le petit déjeuner** (*breakfast*) is usually much lighter than in the United States and is at the origin of what is popularly called a "continental breakfast." Typically, it consists of slices of French bread with butter and jam, and sometimes **brioches** (*light, round rolls*) or **croissants**, usually served on Sundays and special occasions since they are expensive. The drink usually served with breakfast is **café au lait**, tea, or hot chocolate.

The French traditionally eat their main meal at noon—hence they take a long lunch break, normally lasting two hours. This custom is still prevalent in the provinces, though in large cities like Paris some working people are beginning to take a shorter lunch break. The traditional **déjeuner** (*lunch*) consists of several courses, starting

¹See *Differences* of Lesson 10 (p. 211) for an explanation of this word.

²**être dur(e) d'oreille** *to be hard of hearing* (Le concierge n'entend pas très bien.)

with **ḥors-d'œuvre** (*appetizers*) such as **des crudités** (*raw vegetables*) or **charcu-terie** (*cold cuts*), followed by a meat or fish dish, vegetables, and potatoes, rice or pasta. After that comes a lettuce salad, cheese, and a dessert of fresh fruit, pastry, or ice cream. Slices of hard-crusted French bread are served throughout the meal, except with dessert.

Children usually have a **goûter** (*snack*) after school, around 4 or 5 P.M., of hot chocolate with bread and jam, or, for a treat, a **pain au chocolat** (round roll with chocolate inside). **Le dîner** (*dinner*) is usually a light meal. It is served later than in the United States, typically around eight o'clock. It often includes soup, which replaces the **ḥors-d'œuvre**, omelette or cold meat, vegetables, cheese and bread, and fresh fruit or pudding. **Le souper** (*late supper*), eaten after a movie, theater, concert, or party, is nowadays a rare event. The French generally drink wine or mineral water with lunch and dinner. Coffee is served in a **demi-tasse** after dessert. Preparation as well as enjoyment of good meals has always been considered one of the most important daily activities in France, where the average family is said to spend close to 40% of its budget on food.

STRUCTURES

6.1 PRENDRE, APPRENDRE, COMPRENDRE

1. The conjugation of **prendre** *to take* has three distinct stem vowels, as shown in the transcription below: /ɑ̃/ in the singular, /ən/ in the **nous** and **vous** forms, and /ɛn/ for the **ils** and **elles** forms. Note that the singular forms are identical in pattern to the third-conjugation verbs (**-re**). **Prendre** is also used in the general sense of *to eat* and *to drink*. Nouns designating meals, such as **le petit déjeuner** *breakfast*, **le déjeuner** *lunch*, **le dîner** *dinner*, and **le repas** *meal* cannot be used with **manger** *to eat*.

« Voulez-vous prendre un bain de neige, vous aussi ? » (Carnaval d'Hiver, Québec)

prendre	
prends	prenons
prends	prenez
prend	prennent

Je ne **prends** pas de bain le lundi.   /pʀɑ̃/
          Tu **prends** une douche maintenant ?
      Elle ne **prend** pas de café.
      Nous **prenons** un bain après le dîner.   /pʀənɔ̃/
Vous ne **prenez** pas de bière ?   /pʀəne/
      Elles **prennent** leur dîner à la maison.   /pʀɛn/

2. **Apprendre** *to learn* and **comprendre** *to understand* are conjugated like **prendre**. Note that **apprendre** can be followed by a noun or **à** + infinitive

J'**apprends** le français.	Je **comprends** le français.
Tu **apprends** l'espagnol.	Tu **comprends** l'espagnol.
Il **apprend** cette leçon.	Elle **comprend** cette leçon.
Nous **apprenons** à faire du ski.	Nous **comprenons** ce sport.
Vous **apprenez** à compter en français.	Vous **comprenez** la leçon.
Ils **apprennent** à faire du tennis.	Elles **comprennent** la question.

A *Exercice de contrôle*

Je prends mon petit déjeuner.
1. Vous   2. Les étudiants   3. Tu   4. Nous

J'apprends à parler français.
1. Vous   2. Tu   3. Les étudiants   4. (Jeanne)

Je n'apprends pas à faire du ski.
1. Tu   2. Vous   3. Cet enfant   4. Ces enfants

J'apprends et comprends le français.
1. Nous   2. Tu   3. (Michel)   4. Les étudiants

B *Maintenant, posez-moi¹ des questions.*

1. Demandez-moi à quelle heure je prends mon petit déjeuner.
2. Demandez-moi où je prends mon déjeuner.
3. Demandez-moi à quelle heure je prends mon dîner.
4. Demandez-moi si j'apprends à faire du ski.
5. Demandez-moi si je comprends mes étudiants.
6. Demandez-moi quelles langues je comprends.

C *Répondez aux questions.*

1. À quelle heure prenez-vous votre petit déjeuner ? Qu'est-ce que vous prenez comme boisson ?
2. Je prends trois repas par jour. Et vous, est-ce que vous ne prenez pas trois repas par jour ? Demandez à (Rose) combien de repas elle prend par semaine.
3. Quelle langue apprenons-nous dans ce cours ? Quelle leçon apprenons-nous cette semaine ? Quelle langue n'apprenons-nous pas ?
4. En général, prenez-vous une douche ou un bain ? Qui ne prend pas de bain ? Qui ne prend pas de douche ?
5. Quel sport comprenez-vous bien ? Demandez à (Paul) quel sport il comprend très bien.
6. Apprenez-vous à parler espagnol ? Qu'est-ce que vous apprenez à faire dans ce cours ?

Exercice supplémentaire

Compréhension auditive

¹**posez-moi** *ask me*

6.2 STRUCTURE DES PHRASES

Ils traversent la rue.

1. As you make more progress in French, it will become increasingly important for you to understand the basic patterns of French—especially the patterns involving verbs—and know how they differ from those of English. In this lesson we will discuss the concept of *objects*.

   a) A complete sentence in French consists of at least two elements: a *subject* (**le sujet**) and a *verb* (**le verbe**). The verb describes what the subject does.

SUJET	VERBE
Je	travaille.
Marie	arrive.
Nous	déjeunons.

   b) Some verbs, like **aimer** *to like*, **finir** *to finish*, and **entendre** *to hear*, are called *transitive verbs* and usually require the presence of a *direct object* (**le complément d'objet direct**, or simply **l'objet direct** *m*). The direct object "receives" the action of the verb performed by the subject, and it is not preceded by any preposition.

SUJET	VERBE	OBJET DIRECT
Anne	aime	le dessert.
Tu	finis	ton repas.
Vous	entendez	l'autobus.

   c) Other verbs, like **parler** *to speak*, **obéir** *to obey*, and **répondre** *to answer* take an *indirect object* (**le complément d'objet indirect**, or simply **l'objet indirect**). The indirect object is *always* preceded by the preposition **à**; but expressions of time or place with **à** (**à midi**, **à deux heures**, **à Paris**, **au restaurant**) are not indirect objects.

SUJET	VERBE	OBJET INDIRECT
Je	parle	**au** garçon.
Nous	obéissons	**à** l'agent.
Vous	répondez	**aux** questions.

d) Some verbs, like **montrer** *to show*, **donner** *to give*, and **payer** *to pay* (*for*), can take both direct and indirect objects. The direct object usually precedes the indirect object.

SUJET	VERBE	OBJET DIRECT	OBJET INDIRECT
Je	montre	la photo	**à** mon camarade.
Jacques	donne	la réponse	**au** professeur.
Vous	payez	l'addition	**à** la serveuse.

e) Nouns that are preceded by a preposition other than **à** are called *objects of a preposition* or *a prepositional phrase* (**le groupe prépositionnel**).

SUJET	VERBE	GROUPE PRÉPOSITIONNEL
Michel	travaille	**pour** le professeur.
Sylvie	danse	**avec** son ami.
Nous	parlons	**de** nos cours.

2. French verbs do not always take the same types of objects as their English counterparts: **J'écoute la radio** (direct) but *I listen to the radio* (indirect); **Je réponds à la question** (indirect) but *I answer the question* (direct); **Je paie le livre au vendeur** (direct and indirect) but *I pay the salesperson for the book* (direct and a prepositional phrase with *for*). You will need to learn the following verbs thoroughly because they show conflicting patterns between French and English.

attendre	J'**attends** l'autobus.	*I **wait for** the bus.*
chercher	Je **cherche** un taxi.	*I **look for** a taxi.*
écouter	J'**écoute** la radio.	*I **listen to** the radio.*
regarder	Je **regarde** la maison.	*I **look at** the house.*
obéir à	J'**obéis aux** ordres.	*I **obey** the orders.*
répondre à	Je **réponds à** la question.	*I **answer** the question.*
téléphoner à	Je **téléphone à** Marie.	*I **phone** Marie.*
penser à	Je **pense à** mes parents.	*I **think of** my parents.*
demander	Je **demande** le livre à Paul.	*I **ask** Paul **for** the book.*
payer	Je **paie** le livre à Jeanne.	*I **pay** Jeanne **for** the book.*
entrer dans	J'**entre dans** la classe.	*I **enter** the classroom.*
monter dans	Je **monte dans** l'autobus.	*I **get on** the bus.*
descendre de	Je **descends de** l'autobus.	*I **get off** the bus.*

3. In dictionaries, the objects are sometimes abbreviated as **qqn** (for **quelqu'un** *some-one*) and **qqch** (for **quelque chose** *something*). This abbreviation is also used in our end vocabulary.

demander **qqch à qqn**	to ask someone for something
→ Je demande **le livre à Suzanne**.	→ I ask Suzanne for the book.
téléphoner **à qqn**	to telephone someone
→ Vous téléphonez **à vos parents**.	→ You telephone your parents.

1 traverser

2 regarder

3 entrer

4 choisir

5 commander

6 finir

7 demander

8 aller

9 attendre

10 monter

11 descendre

12 rentrer

TABLEAU 33

A *Regardez le Tableau 33. C'est Jean-Paul, un étudiant français. Il prend son dîner. Répétez après moi.*

1. Il traverse la rue.
2. Il regarde le menu.
3. Il entre dans le restaurant.
4. Il choisit la table.
5. Il commande le dîner.
6. Il finit le dîner.
7. Il demande l'addition à la serveuse.
8. Il va à l'arrêt d'autobus.
9. Il attend l'autobus.
10. Il monte dans l'autobus.
11. Il descend de l'autobus.
12. Il rentre à la maison.

B *Maintenant, ajoutez des phrases d'après ces modèles.*

Il traverse la rue.
Nous aussi, nous traversons la rue.

Il regarde le menu.
Nous aussi, nous regardons le menu.

On continue avec les phrases basées sur l'exercice A.

C *Maintenant, répondez aux questions d'après ces modèles.*

Traversez-vous la rue ?
Non, je ne traverse pas la rue.

Regardez-vous le menu ?
Non, je ne regarde pas le menu.

On continue avec les phrases basées sur l'exercice A.

D *Posez des questions à votre partenaire, d'après ces modèles.*

À quelle heure/avoir/premier cours ?
(Marie) **À quelle heure est-ce que tu as ton premier cours ?**
(Jean) **J'ai mon premier cours à (neuf heures).**

Où/aller/après/dernier cours ?
(Marie) **Où est-ce que tu vas après ton dernier cours ?**
(Jean) **Après mon dernier cours je vais (à la bibliothèque).**

1. Qu'est-ce que/faire/comme sport ?
2. Combien/fois/par semaine/aller/laboratoire de langues ?
3. Combien/cours/avoir/aujourd'hui ?
4. À quelle heure/avoir/premier cours ?
5. Où/aller/après/dernier/cours ?
6. Qu'est-ce que/vouloir/faire/ce soir ?

Maintenant, faites un compte rendu[1] de votre interview d'après ce modèle.

Je vais parler de (Jean).
Il fait (de la natation) comme sport.
Il va au laboratoire de langues (deux) fois par semaine.
Il a (quatre) cours aujourd'hui.
...

Exercice supplémentaire

6.3 PRONOM INTERROGATIF SUJET **QUI... ?, QU'EST-CE QUI... ?**

Interrogative pronouns (in English *who* and *what*) occur quite frequently in all kinds of conversations. Both French and English make distinctions between pronouns designating human beings (English *who*) and those referring to animals, things, and ideas (English *what*). In addition, however, it is very important to distinguish in French between interrogative pronouns used as subject, direct object, or object of a preposition in all questions.

[1]**compte rendu** *report*

1. A pronoun stands for a noun. The interrogative pronoun used as the *subject* of a sentence is **qui** /ki/ *who* when the subject is a human being,[1] and **qu'est-ce qui** /kɛski/ *what* in all other cases.

Marie parle anglais.	***Marie*** *speaks English.*
→ **Qui** parle anglais ?	→ ***Who*** *speaks English?*
Votre dessert est délicieux.	***Your dessert*** *is delicious.*
→ **Qu'est-ce qui** est délicieux ?	→ ***What*** *is delicious?*

2. Grammatically, both **qui** and **qu'est-ce qui** are in the third-person singular and masculine (like the subject pronoun **il**), since it is totally unspecified as to the number and gender. As a result, the verb following it is also in the third-person singular (same rules in English). Note in the last question below that the adjective **ouvert**, modifying **Qu'est-ce qui**, is in the masculine.

Mes amis parlent français.	*My friends speak French.*
→ **Qui parle** français ?	→ *Who speaks French?*
Nous pouvons quitter la classe.	*We can leave the classroom.*
→ **Qui peut** quitter la classe ?	→ *Who can leave the classroom?*
La bibliothèque n'**est** pas ouverte.	*The library is not open.*
→ **Qu'est-ce qui** n'**est** pas ouvert ?	→ *What is not open?*

3. Be careful to distinguish between the interrogative pronoun **qu'est-ce qui** *what* and the interrogative adjective **quel(le)(s)** *what*, which you learned in Lesson 3.5. Both correspond to English *what*, but **quel(le)(s)** is an adjective and it *must* have a noun in the same sentence with which it agrees in both gender and number. **Quel(le)(s)** also implies *which*, suggesting that there are several alternative answers to the question.

ADJECTIVE

Quel livre est sur la table ?	*What/Which book is on the table?*
Quel enfant fait ce bruit ?	*What/Which child is making that noise?*
Quelle est votre **nationalité** ?	*What is your nationality?*

PRONOUN

Qu'est-ce qui est sur la table ?	*What is on the table?*
Qu'est-ce qui fait ce bruit ?	*What is making that noise?*
Qu'est-ce qui est difficile ?	*What is difficult?*

TABLEAU 34   **Qui** tombe de l'arbre ?   **Qu'est-ce qui** tombe du bureau ?

---

[1]An alternate form **Qui est-ce qui** exists, but it is more emphatic than **Qui**, and less often used.

A *Vous êtes dur(e) d'oreille.*[1] *Vous n'entendez pas très bien. Alors, vous allez poser des questions sur le sujet de chaque phrase.*

> *Modèle :* Quelqu'un[2] regarde le tableau.
> **Pardon ?**[3] **Qui regarde le tableau ?**

1. Quelqu'un regarde la pendule.
2. Quelqu'un est à la porte.
3. Je peux regarder le livre.
4. Mes étudiants parlent français.
5. Nous travaillons beaucoup.
6. Vous êtes intelligents.

B *Posez des questions sur le sujet de chaque phrase, d'après ce modèle.*

> Notre cours commence à (dix) heures.
> **Pardon ? Qu'est-ce qui commence à (dix) heures ?**

1. Notre cours finit à (onze) heures.
2. Mon chat n'est pas dans la classe.
3. Cet exercice n'est pas difficile.
4. La bibliothèque est ouverte.
5. Mes questions sont faciles.
6. Notre cours finit dans (dix) minutes.

C *Maintenant, posez des questions en employant* **qui** *ou* **qu'est-ce qui** *selon le cas.*[4]

1. Nous parlons bien français.
2. Notre cours n'est pas difficile.
3. (Mireille) est dans la classe.
4. Vous ne pouvez pas rester ici.
5. Mes clés sont sur la table.
6. J'aime faire (du ski).
7. Vous comprenez mes questions.
8. (Marie) et (Paul) sont américains.

6.4   PRONOM INTERROGATIF OBJET DIRECT **QUI EST-CE QUE... ?, QU'EST-CE QUE... ?**

1. The interrogative pronoun used as the *direct object* of a verb is **qui est-ce que** /kiɛskə/ *who(m)* for human beings, and **qu'est-ce que** /kɛskə/ *what* in all other cases. The basic process involves replacing the direct object noun with an interrogative pronoun and placing it at the beginning of the sentence. Note that the **que** of **est-ce que** is reduced to **qu'** before a word beginning with a vowel sound (second and fourth examples below).

Vous cherchez **un médecin**.	*You are looking for **a doctor**.*
→ **Qui est-ce que** vous cherchez ?	→ ***Who(m)*** *are you looking for?*
Elle comprend **le professeur**.	*She understands **the professor**.*
→ **Qui est-ce qu'**elle comprend ?	→ ***Who(m)*** *does she understand?*
Vous traversez **la rue**.	*You cross **the street**.*
→ **Qu'est-ce que** vous traversez ?	→ ***What*** *do you cross?*
Ils écoutent **la cassette**.	*They are listening to **the cassette**.*
→ **Qu'est-ce qu'**ils écoutent ?	→ ***What*** *are they listening to?*

---

[1]**être dur(e) d'oreille**   *to be hard of hearing*

[2]*Someone*

[3]*Pardon me?*: You pretend you did not hear the statement completely and ask a question about it.

[4]*Now, ask questions using* **qui** *or* **qu'est-ce qui** *as the case may be.*

Qu'est-ce qui intéresse ce couple ? Qu'est-ce qu'ils regardent ?

2. The verb that takes **qui est-ce que** or **qu'est-ce que** can be in the infinitive form, preceded by a conjugated verb such as **aimer**, **aller**, and **vouloir**.

Michel **aime parler français**.	*Michel likes to speak French.*
→ **Qu'est-ce que** Michel **aime faire** ?	*→ What does Michel like to do?*
Vous_**allez faire vos devoirs**.	*You are going to do your homework.*
→ **Qu'est-ce que** vous_**allez faire** ?	*→ What are you going to do?*
Elle ne **veut** pas **manger la pomme**.	*She doesn't want to eat the apple.*
→ **Qu'est-ce qu'**elle ne **veut** pas **man-ger/faire** ?	*→ What doesn't she want to eat/do?*

3. The **est-ce que** of **qui est-ce que** and **qu'est-ce que** can be replaced by an inversion of the subject pronoun and the verb (except for the **je** form).

Qui **est-ce que nous_écoutons** ?	Qu'**est-ce que tu veux** ?
→ Qui **écoutons-nous** ?	→ Que **veux-tu** ?
Qui **est-ce que vous cherchez** ?	Qu'**est-ce qu'elles regardent** ?
→ Qui **cherchez-vous** ?	→ Que **regardent-elles** ?

TABLEAU 35   Qui **est-ce qu'**elle cherche ?   **Qu'est-ce qu'**elle cherche ?

 A *Posez des questions en employant* **qui est-ce que**.

> *Modèle :*   Je cherche mon ami.
> **Pardon ? Qui est-ce que vous cherchez ?**

1. Je cherche (Jean-Paul).
2. J'aime mes étudiants.
3. Je n'attends pas mes parents.

4. Nous aimons nos parents.
5. (Marie) écoute le professeur.
6. Je vais regarder un étudiant.

B *Posez des questions en employant* **qu'est ce que** *d'après ce modèle.*

> Je cherche un restaurant.
> **Pardon ? Qu'est-ce que vous cherchez ?**

1. Je cherche un café.
2. Je ne veux pas regarder le menu.
3. Je ne choisis pas la table.

4. Nous commandons notre repas.
5. Nous allons manger des pizzas.
6. Mon ami veut manger un steak /stɛk/.

C *Maintenant, posez des questions en employant* **qui est-ce que** *ou* **qu'est-ce que**, *selon le cas.*

1. Je n'ai pas mon cahier.
2. Je cherche mon stylo.
3. Je n'aime pas le football.
4. Nous allons regarder la télé.

5. Nous étudions cette leçon.
6. Nous voulons attendre nos amis.
7. (Cécile) aime la musique.
8. (Gilbert) écoute le professeur.

D *Maintenant, répondez aux questions.*

1. Qui est-ce ?
2. Qu'est-ce que je fais ?
3. Qu'est-ce qui est sur la table ?
4. Qu'est-ce qu'il y a sous la table ?

5. Qui êtes-vous ?
6. Que regardez-vous ?
7. Que faites-vous dans ce cours ?
8. Qui apprend le français ?

 Compréhension auditive

6.5 ARTICLE PARTITIF **DU, DE LA, DE L'**

1. French, like English, has two kinds of nouns: "count" and "noncount" (or "mass"). A count noun refers to objects you can count, and has singular and plural forms (*a book, two books; a spoon, three spoons*). You already know that in French an indefinite or unspecific count noun is usually preceded by **un**, **une** in the singular, and **des** in the plural (Lesson 1.1).

Je cherche **un** couteau.	*I'm looking for a knife.*
Apportez-moi **une** fourchette.	*Bring me a fork.*
Il y a **des** tables à la terrasse.	*There are tables on the sidewalk.*

2. A noncount or mass noun refers to an object that you usually do not count (*sugar, water, bread, paper*). In French, an indefinite or unspecific noncount noun is usually preceded by the *partitive article*: **du, de la**, or, before a vowel sound, **de l'**.[1] In many cases, the partitive article corresponds to English *some* or *any*. But note that the use of *some* and *any* is optional in English, whereas use of the partitive article is obligatory in French to express any undetermined or indefinite quantity.

Avez-vous **de l'**eau ?	Do you have { *some* / *any* / ___ } water?
Nous avons **du** vin et **de la** bière.	We have (some) wine and beer.
Voilà **du** pain et **de la** viande.	There's (some) bread and meat.
Apportez-moi **de l'**eau.	Bring me (some) water.
Avez-vous **du** café ?	Do you have (any) coffee?

3. Do not confuse the partitive article (which often corresponds to *some* or *any*) with the preposition **de** + **le/la/l'** meaning *of the* or *about the* (Lesson 2.3). The context will usually clear up any ambiguity.

Apportez **du** vin rouge. (*partitive*)	Bring some red wine.
Voilà le prix **du** vin. (*preposition* **de** + **le**)	There's the price of the wine.
Je commande **de la** viande. (*partitive*)	I order some meat.
Je parle **de la** viande. (**parler de** + **la**)	I'm speaking of (about) the meat.

4. **Pas de.** In Lesson 2.6.2 you learned that the indefinite article (**un, une, des**) becomes **de** or **d'** in negative sentences before a direct object. Likewise, the partitive article (**du, de la, de l'**) becomes **de** or **d'**.

Je veux **un** crayon.	Je veux **du** sucre.
→ Je ne veux pas **de** crayon.	→ Je ne veux pas **de** sucre.
Vous faites **une** faute.	Elle mange **de la** viande.
→ Vous ne faites pas **de** faute.	→ Elle ne mange pas **de** viande.
Ont-elles **des** cassettes ?	Voulez-vous **de l'**eau ?
→ N'ont-elles pas **de** cassettes ?	→ Ne voulez-vous pas **d'**eau ?

The only exception is after **être**: **être** always requires **un, une, des**, or **du, de la, de l'** in both affirmative and negative sentences.

C'est **un** cahier.	C'est **du** café.
→ Ce n'est pas **un** cahier.	→ Ce n'est pas **du** café.
C'est **une** montre.	C'est **de la** crème.
→ Ce n'est pas **une** montre.	→ Ce n'est pas **de la** crème.
Ce sont **des** crayons.	C'est **de l'**eau minérale.
→ Ce ne sont pas **des** crayons.	→ Ce n'est pas **de l'**eau minérale.

5. Use of the partitive article is not limited to food and drink. It occurs with any noncount noun.

Nous avons **du** travail.	We have (some) work.
Apportez-moi **du** papier.	Bring me (some) paper.

---

[1]The names of beverages you learned in Lesson 5 (*Expressions utiles*) are preceded by **un/une** or numerals because they indicate a *specific portion* or *serving* in a restaurant or café: **Apportez-moi** *un* **café ; Voulez-vous** *deux* **thés ?**

Avez-vous **de l'**argent ?	*Do you have (any) money?*
Elles_ont **de l'**imagination.	*They have (some) imagination.*

Two of the weather expressions (Lesson 4.2) and **faire** + activity (Lesson 4.1) also use the partitive article. In these expressions, the negative partitive article is also **de**.

Il fait **du** vent.	Je fais **du** tennis.
→ Il **ne** fait **pas de** vent.	→ Je **ne** fais **pas de** tennis.
Il fait **du** soleil.	Vous faites **de la** natation.
→ Il **ne** fait **pas de** soleil.	→ Vous **ne** faites **pas de** natation.

TABLEAU 36

A   *Regardez le Tableau 36. C'est une salle à manger¹. Répétez après moi.*

1. une assiette	7. des légumes *m*	10. du poivre
2. une bouteille	des carottes *f*	11. du sel
3. un couteau	des petits pois *m*	12. du sucre
4. une cuillère	des haricots verts *m*	13. de la viande
5. une fourchette	8. du beurre	14. un buffet
6. un verre	9. du pain	15. une nappe
		16. une serviette

B   *Continuez à regarder le Tableau. Répondez à ces questions.*

1. Y a-t-il des bouteilles sur la table ?
2. Et des couteaux² ?
3. Et des assiettes ?
4. Y a-t-il des montres sur la table ?
5. Et des cahiers ?
6. Et des légumes ?
7. Y a-t-il du café sur la table ?
8. Et de la viande ?
9. Et du pain ?
10. N'y a-t-il pas de sel sur la table ?
11. N'y a-t-il pas de beurre ?
12. N'y a-t-il pas de buffet dans la salle à manger ?

¹**salle à manger** *dining room*

²Singular nouns ending in **-eau** add **-x** to form the plural: **couteau** → **couteaux**, **tableau** → **tableaux**. This point will be taken up in Lesson 8.4 (p. 174).

C *Répondez aux questions.*

1. Mangez-vous de la viande ? Est-ce que les végétariens mangent de la viande ? Qu'est-ce qu'ils mangent ?
2. Avez-vous du travail aujourd'hui ? Demandez-moi si j'ai du travail. Demandez à (Paul) s'il a du travail.
3. Avez-vous du papier ? Demandez-moi si j'ai du papier. Voici quelque chose. Qu'est-ce que c'est ?
4. Avez-vous de l'argent dans votre poche ? Demandez-moi si j'ai de l'argent. Demandez à (Jeanne) si elle a de l'argent.
5. Faites-vous de la gymnastique ? Qu'est-ce que vous faites comme sport ? Qui ne fait pas de tennis ?
6. Est-ce qu'il fait du soleil aujourd'hui ? Fait-il du vent ? Fait-il froid ? Quel temps fait-il aujourd'hui ?
7. Regardez la photo à cette page. Que fait le couple ? Qu'est-ce qu'il y a sur la table ? Et derrière le couple ?

Compréhension auditive

6.6 VENIR, TENIR

1. Study the conjugation of **venir** *to come*. Note that the consonant sound /n/ is heard only in the plural forms, and that only the **nous** and **vous** forms have the same stem as the infinitive.[1]

venir

viens	venons
viens	venez
vient	viennent

Je **viens** de Montréal. /vjɛ̃/
Tu **viens** de Québec.
Marie **vient** au labo ce matin.

Nous **venons** à Québec en avril. /v(ə)nõ/
Vous **venez** au cours demain ? /v(ə)ne/
Elles **viennent** de Paris. /vjɛn/

2. **Venir de** + infinitive expresses an action that has just taken place in the immediate past. Literally, it means *to come from doing* (something) and is the equivalent of English *to have just done* (something).

Allez-vous déjeuner ?
— Non, je **viens de manger**.

Qu'est-ce qu'elle **vient de faire** ?
— Elle **vient de téléphoner** à Jacques.

Are you going to eat lunch?
  No, I have just eaten.

What has she just done?
  She has just telephoned Jacques.

[1]Several verbs derived from **venir** are also conjugated like **venir**, although none are used in this lesson.

devenir	to become	**parvenir à**	to succeed	**revenir**	to come back
intervenir	to intervene	**prévenir**	to warn		

3. **Tenir**, conjugated just like **venir**, basically means *to hold* or *to keep*.[1]

tenir	
tiens	tenons
tiens	tenez
tient	tiennent

Je **tiens** la main de cet enfant.	*I am holding this child's hand.*
Tiens le livre près de cette lampe.	*Hold the book near this lamp.*
Il **tient** une boutique en ville.	*He has/manages a store in town.*
Nous **tenons** toujours nos promesses.	*We always keep our promises.*
Vous **tenez** ma clé dans votre main.	*You are holding my key in your hand.*
Ils **tiennent** ce magasin.	*They have/manage this store.*

4. **Tiens** and **Tenez** correspond to English *Here, Look here, Listen*, and are used to attract the listener's attention to something. **Tiens !** *Well!* (and sometimes **Tiens, tiens !** *Well, well!*) indicates surprise.

Je ne comprends pas vos difficultés.	*I don't understand your difficulties.*
— **Tenez**, voici un exemple.	*Listen, here is an example.*
Bonjour, Jean-Jacques.	*Hello, Jean-Jacques.*
— Boujour, Marie. **Tiens**, voici un petit cadeau pour toi.	*Hello, Marie. Here, here's a little gift for you.*
Regardez par la fenêtre.	*Look out the window.*
— **Tiens**, il neige !	*Well, it's snowing!*

TABLEAU 37   Elle **vient de déjeuner**.   Le professeur **vient d'arriver**.   Il **vient de prendre** une douche

 **A**   *Exercice de contrôle*

Je viens au cours de français.

1. Nous   2. Le professeur   3. Vous   4. Les étudiants

Je ne viens pas du resto-U.

1. Vous   2. Tu   3. Les étudiants   4. Nous

Je viens d'arriver au cours.

1. Vous   2. Tu   3. Les étudiants   4. Le professeur

Je ne tiens pas toujours mes promesses.

1. Nous   2. Tu   3. Vous   4. Mes copains

---

[1]There are other verbs conjugated like **tenir**, which are not included in the structural exercises of this lesson. Many have cognates in English ending in *-tain*.

appartenir à	*to belong to*	**entretenir**	*to entertain*	**retenir**	*to retain*
contenir	*to contain*	**maintenir**	*to maintain*	**soutenir**	*to sustain*
détenir	*to detain*	**obtenir**	*to obtain*		

B *Répondez aux questions.*

1. De quelle ville venez-vous ? Demandez à (Danielle) d'où elle vient. Demandez-moi d'où je viens.
2. Qui vient à l'université à pied[1] ? Qui vient en voiture[2] ? Qui vient en autobus ? Et qui vient à bicyclette[3] ?
3. À quelle heure venez-vous à ce cours ? D'où est-ce que vous venez ? Où allez-vous après ce cours ?
4. Tenez-vous toujours vos promesses ? Peut-on toujours tenir ses promesses ? Que veut dire ce proverbe : « Promettre et tenir sont deux » ?
5. Quand vous mangez, tenez-vous votre fourchette dans la main gauche ? Dans quelle main est-ce que les Français tiennent leur fourchette ?

C *Répondez aux questions.*

1. Regardez bien. Je vais fermer mon livre. Qu'est-ce que je viens de faire ? Je vais regarder ma montre. Qu'est-ce que je viens de faire ?
2. (Paul), regardez le plafond. Très bien. Qu'est-ce que vous venez de faire ? (Jeanne), regardez votre montre. Qu'est-ce que vous venez de faire ?
3. Conjuguons[4] le verbe **venir**. Qu'est-ce que nous venons de faire ? Conjuguons le verbe **tenir**. Qu'est-ce que nous venons de faire ?
4. (Mireille), allez au tableau. Qu'est-ce qu'elle vient de faire ? Épelez le mot **viande**. Qu'est-ce qu'elle vient de faire ? Merci, (Mireille). Vous pouvez retourner à votre place. Qu'est-ce qu'elle vient de faire ?

APPLICATIONS

🔲 A **Situations**

À table et bon appétit ![5]

Ignès invite Christine à dîner[6] chez elle. Elle invite aussi Ahmed, un copain marocain. Le repas va être très simple, car Ignès a une cuisine minuscule et elle n'a pas beaucoup de *a lot of time* *temps°. Il est sept heures et demie, et les invités viennent d'arriver. Ils apportent des fleurs à Ignès.[7]*

everyone	IGNÈS	Bonsoir, tout le monde°. Entrez.	5
Here	AHMED	Tiens°, Ignès, voici un petit bouquet.	
(Please) sit down.	IGNÈS	Oh, merci. Asseyez-vous.° Qu'est-ce que vous prenez comme apéritif, du porto ou du jus de tomate ?	
	CHRISTINE	Du porto pour moi.	
	AHMED	Et pour moi, du jus de tomate. Je ne prends pas d'alcool.	10

Ignès apporte les boissons.

	CHRISTINE	Qu'est ce que tu prépares, Ignès ?	
Well	IGNÈS	Eh bien°, pour commencer nous avons une soupe aux légumes. C'est une vieille	
old recipe		recette°. J'ouvre[8] ce paquet avec des ciseaux. Maintenant, je vais mélanger le contenu avec de l'eau... comme ça.	15

[1]**à pied** *on foot*

[2]**en voiture** *by car*

[3]**à bicyclette** *on a bicycle*

[4]**conjuguer** *to conjugate*

[5]**à table** *let's sit down (at the table)*; **bon appétit** *I hope you have a good meal* or *Enjoy your meal*, customarily said when serving a meal, especially to guests.

[6]**inviter qqn à** + infinitif *to invite someone to do (something)*

[7]Dinner guests often bring a bouquet of flowers, candy, or a bottle of wine.

[8]**ouvre** du verbe **ouvrir** *to open* (Leçon 14.1)

« À table ! »

	CHRISTINE Bravo ! C'est de la cuisine moderne. Et qu'est-ce que nous allons manger après ?
	IGNÈS Alors après, nous avons des saucisses et des haricots verts.
musulman(e) *Moslem*	AHMED Des saucisses... mais je ne peux pas manger de porc. Je suis musulman°.
goodness	CHRISTINE Ah, Mon Dieu°, c'est vrai. Qu'est-ce que tu vas faire ? 20
	AHMED Ce n'est pas grave. Je peux manger du fromage.
	IGNÈS Tu as raison. Je vais faire une omelette au fromage[1].
	AHMED Tu es très gentille. D'accord.
	IGNÈS Bon, après la viande, nous avons une salade, et comme dessert, un énorme bol de mousse au chocolat[2]. 25
	CHRISTINE Ah bon ! J'adore ça.
	IGNÈS Veux-tu couper le pain, s'il te plaît ?
of course	CHRISTINE Oui, bien sûr°.
	IGNÈS Bon alors, la soupe est prête. À table et bon appétit !

Répondez aux questions. (*lignes 1–4*)

1. Qui est-ce qu'Ignès invite à dîner ?
2. Comment est sa cuisine ?
3. À quelle heure arrivent les invités ?
4. Qu'est-ce qu'ils apportent à Ignès ?

(*lignes 5–29*)

5. Qu'est-ce qu'ils prennent comme apéritif ?
6. Comment est-ce qu'Ignès prépare la soupe ?
7. Qu'est-ce qu'il y a comme viande ?
8. Qu'est-ce que les musulmans ne peuvent pas manger ?
9. Qu'est-ce qu'Ignès va préparer pour Ahmed ?
10. Qu'est-ce qu'il y a comme dessert ?

[1]*cheese omelette* (literally, *omelette with cheese*)

[2]**un énorme bol de mousse au chocolat** *a huge bowl of chocolate mousse* (light dessert made with chocolate and egg whites)

B   Expressions utiles[1]

Les repas

commander ⎱
prendre ⎰ ⎰ un repas
finir ⎰ ⎱ le petit déjeuner   demander ⎱
payer ⎰ ⎱ le déjeuner   payer ⎰ l'addition
⎱ le dîner

Viande, volailles (f), etc.

un biftek / un steak   /stɛk/   du poulet
une saucisse[2]   une omelette
du rosbif   du saucisson[3]
du jambon   un sandwich (au jambon / au fromage)
du poisson   un hamburger   /ãbuʀgœʀ/
de la dinde   un hot-dog

Légumes m

des asperges *f*   du riz
des carottes *f*   des pommes de terres frites / des frites
des petits pois *m*   une salade composée
des haricots verts *m*   une salade de tomates / concombres

Fruits m

une banane   un pamplemousse
une pomme   des cerises *f*
une poire   des fraises *f*
une orange   du raisin[4]

Boissons f[5]

du café   du jus de tomate
du thé   du Coca-Cola
du chocolat   de l'eau (minérale)
du lait   du vin
du jus /ʒy/ d'orange   de la bière

cafétéria

la cafétéria est une formule de restauration ; saine, rapide, économique ; elle vous propose un choix de menus variés.

BAR RESTAURANT EN LIBRE SERVICE

zup sud – rennes

C   Pratique

1. Vous êtes au restaurant universitaire. Qu'est-ce que vous voulez comme viande ? Et comme légumes ? Et comme fruit ? Et comme boisson ?
2. Vous êtes au restaurant universitaire. Vous êtes pressé(e)[6]. Vous avez seulement quinze minutes pour manger. Qu'est-ce que vous allez choisir ?
3. Où prenez-vous votre déjeuner ? Qu'est-ce que vous prenez d'habitude[7] comme viande ? Et comme légumes ? Et comme boisson ?

---

[1] Only basic food items are presented here. Complete restaurant menus with cultural notes will be found in Lesson 20.
[2] **saucisse** *sausage*
[3] **saucisson** (slices of) hard sausage such as salami
[4] **Raisin** *grape, grapes* is a noncount noun in French.
[5] Consultez aussi les *Expressions utiles* de la leçon 5 (p. 115).
[6] **être pressé(e)** *to be in a hurry*
[7] **d'habitude** *usually*

4. Indiquez le mot qui n'appartient pas à chaque série.

   a) du café—du chocolat—du riz—de l'eau
   b) une orange—une saucisse—une pomme—une banane
   c) des carottes—des haricots verts—des asperges—des cerises
   d) de la bière—de la dinde—du poulet—du rosbif
   e) du thé—du raisin—des pommes de terre—des nappes

D Mini-composition : *Ignès et Julien sont au resto-U. Complétez le passage suivant. N'oubliez pas l'article partitif quand il est nécessaire.*

(1) Il/être/1 h/demi. (2) Ignès/et/Julien/aller/déjeuner/ensemble. (3) Ils/prendre/poulet,/riz/et/haricots verts. (4) Ils/ne pas/vouloir/frites. (5) Comme/boisson,/Ignès/prendre/jus de tomate/et/Julien/prendre/eau minérale. (6) Pourquoi/ils/ne pas/manger/beaucoup ? (7) Ce/être/parce que/ils/être/au régime[1]. (8) Le/resto-U/être/bondé,/mais/ils/trouver/table libre[2]/près de/porte. (9) Ils/ne pas/pouvoir/rester longtemps[3]/car/ils/avoir/cours/à/2 h. (10) Ils/venir/prendre/leur/déjeuner/et/ils/aller/quitter/restaurant.

E Questions : *Deux étudiantes américaines déjeunent sur l'herbe. Lisez d'abord le paragraphe, ensuite posez des questions sur les parties soulignées.*

C'est aujourd'hui (1) jeudi. Il fait (2) très beau et chaud. Cindy rencontre (3) Anne. Anne est (4) sa camarade de chambre[4]. (5) Elles veulent manger sur l'herbe. Elles vont (6) au resto-U ensemble. Elles veulent emporter[5] (7) des sandwichs et des boissons. (8) Le restaurant est bondé. Elles trouvent un bon endroit (9) sous un arbre. Elles mangent les sandwichs (10) de bon appétit[6].

DES RESTAURANTS OUVERTS 24 h SUR 24		
AU PIED DE COCHON "Le fameux restaurant des Halles" Fruits de mer - Grillades 6, r. Coquillère - 236. 11.75 +	**LE GRAND CAFE** 742.75.77 "Crustacé de vermeil" Banc d'huîtres réfrigéré - Poissons 4, bd des Capucines	**LA MAISON D'ALSACE** Foie gras - choucroutes Banc d'huîtres - Boutiques 39, Champs-Elysées - 359.44.24

F Composition : *Choisissez un des sujets suivants et écrivez une composition d'à peu près 100 mots.[7]*

1. Faites une interview d'un(e) de vos camarades dans le cours de français. Ensuite, préparez une description de cette personne.
2. Quelles sont vos activités préférées en été (ou en hiver) ? Où allez-vous ? Que faites-vous ? Faites-vous ces choses seul(e)[8] ou avec quelqu'un ?
3. Quels sont vos projets pour ce week-end ? Qu'est-ce que vous allez faire ? Pourquoi ? Qu'est-ce que vous voulez faire ? Qu'est-ce que vous ne pouvez pas faire ?

[1]**être au régime** *to be on a diet*
[2]*empty* (literally, *free*) *table*
[3]*stay (for a) long (time)*
[4]**camarade de chambre** *roommate*
[5]**emporter** *to take out*
[6]**de bon appétit** *with a good appetite*
[7]*write a composition of about 100 words* (about the same length as the dehydrated paragraph of **Application D**)
[8]**seul** (*f* **seule**) *alone*

4. Qu'est-ce que vous faites le vendredi (ou un autre jour de la semaine) ? Décrivez vos activités de dix heures du matin à dix heures du soir.

5. Quel est votre restaurant préféré ? Quand prenez-vous vos repas dans ce restaurant ? Qu'est-ce que vous commandez souvent ? Pourquoi aimez-vous ce restaurant ?

G   Renseignements et opinions

1. À quelle heure prenez-vous votre petit déjeuner ? Qu'est-ce que vous prenez d'habitude[1] comme boisson ?

2. À quelle heure déjeunez-vous ? Où ? Qu'est-ce que vous prenez d'habitude comme légumes ?

3. Combien de langues parlez-vous ? Quelle langue apprenez-vous en ce moment ? Quelle langue voulez-vous apprendre ?

4. Qui comprenez-vous bien ? Qui est-ce que vous ne comprenez pas très bien ? Pourquoi pas ?

5. Qu'est-ce que vous pouvez faire dans ce cours ? Qu'est-ce que vous ne pouvez pas faire ? Mentionnez deux choses.

6. De quelle ville venez-vous ? De quelle ville vient votre voisin(e) de gauche (droite) ?

📟 *Compréhension auditive (basée sur l'Application A)*

📟 *Compréhension auditive (basée sur les Applications B et C)*

[1]**d'habitude**   *usually*

VOCABULAIRE

Noms

l'alcool *m*	alcohol	l'**espagnol** *m*	Spanish language	la **poche**	pocket
un apéritif	before-dinner drink	la **fourchette**	fork	le **poivre**	pepper
l'**argent** *m*	money	le **franc (F)**	franc	le porc	pork
un **arrêt**	stop	les **frites** *f*	french fries	le porto	port wine
une **asperge**	asparagus	le fromage	cheese	la **promesse**	promise
une **assiette**	plate	les **haricots verts** *m*	green beans	le **proverbe**	proverb
le **bain**	bath			la recette	recipe
le beurre	butter	le **hors-d'œuvre**	hors d'oeuvre	le **repas**	meal
la **bicyclette**	bicycle	une **huître**	oyster	la salade	salad
le **bifteck**	steak	un(e) invité(e)	guest	la **salle à manger**	dining room
le bol	bowl	la **langue**	language	la saucisse	sausage
le **Bordeaux**	Bordeaux wine	le **légume**	vegetable	le **sel**	salt
la **bouteille**	bottle	le **menu**	menu	la **serveuse**	waitress
le buffet	buffet	la mousse au	chocolate mousse	le **service**	service; service charge
la **carotte**	carrot	chocolat			
les ciseaux *m*	scissors	la **musique**	music	la **serviette**	napkin
le(la) **concierge**	building superintendent	le(la) musulman(e)	Moslem	la soupe	soup
le contenu	contents	la **nappe**	tablecloth	le **steak**	steak
le **couple**	couple	une omelette	omelette	le **sucre**	sugar
le **couteau**	knife	une **oreille**	ear	le temps	time
la **cuillère**	spoon	le **pain**	bread	la tomate	tomato
la cuisine	kitchen	le **papier**	paper	le(la) **végétarien(ne)**	vegetarian
le **déjeuner**	lunch	le paquet	package	le **verbe**	verb
la **demi-bouteille**	half-bottle	le **petit déjeuner**	breakfast	le **verre**	glass
		les **petits pois** *m*	peas	la **viande**	meat
le dessert	dessert	le **pied**	foot	la **ville**	town
le **dîner**	dinner	la **pizza**	pizza		
la **douche**	shower	la **place**	seat		

Verbes

apprendre (à) *irrég*	to learn (to)	**espérer**	to hope	préparer	to prepare
comprendre *irrég*	to understand	**fermer**	to close	**rester**	to stay
		inviter (à)	to invite (to)	**retourner**	to go back, return
conjuguer	to conjugate	mélanger	to mix	**tenir** *irrég*	to hold; to keep
couper	to cut	**monter (dans)**	to go up; to get on	**traverser**	to cross
épeler	to spell	plaisanter	to joke	**venir** *irrég*	to come
		prendre *irrég*	to take; to eat; to drink	**venir de** + *inf*	to have just + past part

Adjectifs

compris(e)	included	**intelligent(e)**	intelligent	**petit(e)**	small
dur(e)	hard	**minéral(e)**	mineral	prêt(e)	ready
énorme	enormous, huge	minuscule	tiny	simple	simple
gauche	left	moderne	modern	**vert(e)**	green
grave	serious	musulman(e)	Moslem	vieux (vieil, vieille)	old

Autres expressions

à bicyclette	on a bicycle	**être dur(e) d'oreille**	to be hard of hearing
à pied	on foot	Mon Dieu !	Goodness !
Asseyez-vous.	(Please) sit down.	Oh !	Oh !
À table !	Let's sit down (at the table)!	ouvrir *irrég*	to open
bien sûr	of course	**promettre** *irrég*	to promise
Bon appétit !	Enjoy your meal.	**que**	what
Bravo !	Bravo!	**quelqu'un**	someone
comme ça	this way	**qui est-ce que**	who(m)
Eh bien...	Well . . .	tout le monde	everybody
en général	generally	**Voyons...**	Let's see . . .
en voiture	by car		

7 Faisons des courses !

LESSON OBJECTIVES

Theme and Culture

1. Shopping in various stores
2. Specialty stores

Communication Skills

1. Getting information through open-ended questions (*for whom*, *about what*, *where*, *how*, etc.)
2. Expressing generalities (*One does/does not*)
3. Expressing relative quantities (*too little/few*, *enough*, *a lot*) and specific quantities (*a kilogram of*, *two pieces of*)
4. Drinking various beverages
5. Expressing one's needs for things and activities
6. Shopping at various specialty stores

Structures

7.1 Interrogative pronouns: **À qui/quoi est-ce que**, **De qui/quoi est-ce que**; review of other interrogative expressions (**Où**, **Comment**, **Combien de**, etc.)
7.2 Indefinite pronoun **on**
7.3 First-conjugation verbs (**-er**) (3): stem-changing verbs
7.4 Expressions of quantity: **beaucoup de**, **un kilo de**, etc.
7.5 **Boire**
7.6 **Avoir besoin de**

CONVERSATIONS

🔲 A. Au supermarché

MAYOUMI Excusez-moi, Madame. Je cherche de l'aspirine.

L'EMPLOYÉE On[1] ne vend pas d'aspirine au supermarché,[2] Mademoiselle.

MAYOUMI Ah non ? Où vend-on de l'aspirine, alors ?

L'EMPLOYÉE À la pharmacie.

🔲 B. Allez à la boucherie.

CINDY Madame, où est-ce qu'on achète de la viande ?

MME SAVIN Quelle sorte de[3] viande voulez-vous ?

CINDY Un kilo de veau.

MME SAVIN Allez à la boucherie près du bureau de tabac.

---

[1]*one, they* (discussed in Lesson 7.2)

[2]On ne vend pas certaines choses au supermarché : par exemple, des médicaments *medicine* et des cigarettes.

[3]*What kind of* (expression invariable)

142

TABLEAU 38

🔲 C. J'ai besoin de quelque chose.

BOB	J'ai besoin de café.
MME GEORGET	Vous pouvez acheter du café à l'épicerie du coin.
BOB	Ah bon. J'ai aussi besoin d'eau minérale.
MME GEORGET	Vous allez trouver ça aussi à l'épicerie.

Primeurs
Épicerie Fine
Charcuterie
Crémerie
Vins Fins
Dépôt de Pain
Fleurs

Au supermarché.

DIFFÉRENCES

Les magasins

When French people go shopping, they take along a basket, a mesh bag (**filet** *m*) or a small folding shopping cart with two wheels (**le caddy**). Large brown bags are not available in most stores. In fact, people think nothing of carrying home those long, hard-crusted thin loaves of bread (**baguettes** *f*) without any wrapping. Although chains of supermarkets (**supermarchés** *m*) and combinations of supermarkets and discount stores (**hypermarchés** *m* or **grandes surfaces** *f*) have sprung up in every French city, especially in the outskirts, most people still prefer the open market and their favorite individual neighborhood specialty stores for fresher food, more personal attention, and greater convenience. Except in very large cities, those who have a car often combine shopping in local stores with a once-a-week visit to a supermarket for bulk items. In contrast to the rather impersonal nature of the **supermarché** and **hypermarché**, where you have to bag your own purchased items in a hurry, the merchants of specialty shops routinely greet each customer who enters with a hearty « **Bonjour, Madame** » or « **Bonjour, Monsieur** », and an equally warm « **Merci, Madame** » and « **Au revoir, Monsieur** » upon leaving—to which the customer always replies in turn. You will find a list of typical stores and their merchandise in the *Expressions utiles* of this lesson.

« Regardez mes baguettes ! »

STRUCTURES

7.1 PRONOM INTERROGATIF OBJET À QUI EST-CE QUE... ?, DE QUOI EST-CE QUE... ? ; AUTRES EXPRESSIONS INTERROGATIVES

1. The interrogative pronoun used for the indirect object is **à qui est-ce que** for human beings, and **à quoi est-ce que** in all other cases.

Vous répondez **au pharmacien**.	*You answer **the pharmacist**.*
À qui est-ce que vous répondez ?	***Who(m)** do you answer?*
Vous répondez **à sa question**.	*You answer **his question**.*
À quoi est-ce que vous répondez ?	***What** do you answer?*

2. Other constructions involving preposition + noun (except for expressions of time and place) can be replaced by preposition + **qui/quoi est-ce que**, with **qui** used for human beings, and **quoi** in all other cases. You learned in Lesson 3.5 that in French, unlike English, the preposition cannot be left at the end of a question.

Vous parlez **de vos parents**.	*You are speaking of your parents.*
→ **De qui est-ce que** vous parlez ?	*→ **Who(m)** are you speaking **of**?*
Vous parlez **de vos examens**.	*You are speaking of your exams.*
→ **De quoi est-ce que** vous parlez ?	*→ What are you speaking **of**?*
Elle travaille **pour mon oncle**.	*She works for my uncle.*
→ **Pour qui est-ce qu**'elle travaille ?	*→ **Who(m)** does she work **for**?*
→ Elle travaille **avec un ordinateur**.	*She works with a computer.*
→ **Avec quoi est-ce qu**'elle travaille ?	*→ What does she work **with**?*

3. Again, except for the **je** form, **est-ce que** can be replaced by an inversion of the subject pronoun and the verb.

À qui **est-ce que tu penses** ?   De qui **est-ce que nous parlons** ?
→ À qui **penses-tu** ?   → De qui **parlons-nous** ?
À quoi **est-ce que Michel pense** ?   Avec quoi **est-ce que vous travaillez** ?
→ À quoi **Michel pense-t-il** ?   → Avec quoi **travaillez-vous** ?

4. Here is a summary of the interrogative pronouns you have studied.

	PERSONNES	AUTRES	LEÇON
Sujet	**qui**	**qu'est-ce qui**	6.3
Objet direct	**qui est-ce que** **qui** + *inversion*	**qu'est-ce que** **que** + *inversion*	6.4
Objet indirect	**à qui est-ce que** **à qui** + *inversion*	**à quoi est-ce que** **à quoi** + *inversion*	7.1
Après d'autres prépositions (par exemple, **de**)	**de qui est-ce que** **de qui** + *inversion*	**de quoi est-ce que** **de quoi** + *inversion*	7.1

5. *Other interrogative expressions.* You have been using interrogative expressions other than pronouns, such as **quand**, **comment**, **combien de**, and **où**. The following is a summary of these expressions.

TIME: **quand/à quelle heure**
Jean-Pierre arrive ce soir à sept heures.
    Quand est-ce que Jean-Pierre arrive ?   *When . . . ?*
    À quelle heure arrive-t-il ?   *What time . . . ?*

PLACE: **où**
Nous allons au restaurant.
    Où est-ce que nous allons ?   *Where . . . ?*

Note that **de** + place is replaced by **d'où**.

Vous arrivez de Rome.
    D'où est-ce que vous arrivez ?   *Where . . . from?*

MANNER: **comment**
Elle va très bien.
    Comment va-t-elle ?   *How . . . ?*

QUANTITY: **combien de** (+ noun)
Il a deux sœurs.
    Combien de sœurs a-t-il ?   *How many . . . ?*
Elle achète un litre de lait.
    Combien de lait achète-t-elle ?   *How much . . . ?*

REASON: **pourquoi**
Elle va à la boucherie parce qu'elle veut acheter du veau.
    Pourquoi va-t-elle à boucherie ?   *Why . . . ?*

À qui est-ce qu'il pense ?   À quoi est-ce qu'elle pense ?

TABLEAU 39

A *Posez des questions sur la dernière partie de chaque phrase, d'après ces modèles.*

Je déjeune avec un ami.   (Marie) travaille avec quelqu'un.
Avec qui déjeunez-vous ?   **Avec qui Marie travaille-t-elle ?**

1. Je parle à un étudiant.   4. (Jean) travaille avec quelqu'un.
2. Je compte sur[1] quelqu'un.   5. (Marie) pense à quelqu'un.
3. Je réponds à quelqu'un.   6. (Monique) travaille pour quelqu'un.

B *Posez des questions en employant* **à quoi**, **avec quoi** *ou* **de quoi**.

1. Je pense à mes vacances.   4. (Paul) compte sur son ordinateur.
2. Je parle d'un restaurant.   5. (Cécile) téléphone à un bureau.
3. Je travaille avec un ordinateur.   6. (André) répond à ma question.

C *Maintenant, posez des questions en employant* **à qui**, **à quoi**, **de qui**, **de quoi**, *etc.*

1. Je parle d'un étudiant.   6. Je parle à un ami.
2. Je pense à mon travail.   7. Je réponds à une étudiante.
3. Je réponds à vos questions.   8. Je pense à quelqu'un.
4. Je téléphone au bureau de poste.   9. Je compte sur mon ordinateur.
5. Je compte sur quelqu'un.   10. Je travaille avec des livres.

D *Posez des questions sur la dernière partie de chaque phrase. Employez* **que**, **où**, **à quelle heure**, **quand**, **comment**, **combien** *et* **pourquoi**.

Modèles :   Je suis dans la classe.   Je déjeune à midi.
              Où êtes-vous ?   **À quelle heure déjeunez-vous ?**

1. Je vais très bien aujourd'hui.   7. Je comprends vos conseils[2].
2. Je vais à mon cours.   8. Le cours est intéressant.
3. Je prends un parapluie.   9. Je déjeune après mon cours.
4. Je prends un parapluie parce qu'il pleut.   10. Après le déjeuner, je prends un café.
5. J'attends l'autobus.   11. Je travaille deux heures.
6. Je descends de l'autobus.   12. Mon premier cours est à dix heures.

Compréhension auditive

---

[1]**compter sur**   *to count on*
[2]**conseils** *m*   *advice (on emploie souvent ce mot au pluriel)*

7.2 PRONOM INDÉFINI **ON**

1. **On** is a subject pronoun corresponding to *one*, *they*, *we*, or *you* in a very general sense. It is used in all situations where the subject is an *indefinite* or *unspecified* human being. Grammatically, **on** is a third-person singular masculine pronoun, just like **il**. In inversion, **on** is pronounced /tõ/; if the verb ends in a vowel letter, **-t-** must be inserted to show this pronunciation.

On ne fait pas cela.
> *One does not do that.*
> *We/You don't do that.*
> *That is not done.*[1]

Parle-t-on français au Canada ?
> *Does one speak French in Canada?*
> *Do you/they speak French in Canada?*
> *Is French spoken in Canada?*[1]

Où vend-on du veau ?
> *Where does one sell veal?*
> *Where do they/you sell veal?*
> *Where is veal sold?*[1]

2. In colloquial French, **on** often replaces the **nous** form.[2]

Nous allons manger à midi.
→ **On va** manger à midi.
Qu'est-ce que **nous allons** faire ?
→ Qu'est-ce qu'**on va** faire ?

Allons-nous faire cela ?
→ **Va-t-on** faire cela ?
Nous apprenons le français.
→ **On apprend** le français.

[1]**On** + active voice can be used as a substitute for the English passive voice. The passive voice is discussed in Lesson 16.5.

[2]In very colloquial French, you may hear **Nous, on** /nuõ/, such as **Nous, on va manger à midi** ; **Nous, on va à la boulangerie**.

A *Répétez après moi.*

On vend du pain à la boulangerie.
On vend du bœuf à la boucherie.
On vend du jambon à la charcuterie.
Pour[1] acheter du sel et du poivre, on va à l'épicerie.
Pour acheter de l'aspirine, on va à la pharmacie.
Pour acheter du beurre et du fromage, on va à la crémerie.

Nous allons faire des courses[2]. Répondez aux questions.

1. Où vend-on du pain ?
2. Où vend-on du poivre ?
3. Où vend-on de l'aspirine ?
4. Où vend-on du fromage ?

5. Où va-t-on pour acheter du sel ?
6. Où va-t-on pour acheter du beurre ?
7. Où va-t-on pour acheter du jambon ?
8. Où va-t-on pour acheter du bœuf ?

B *Nous ne voulons pas travailler. Je vais proposer certaines choses. Vous êtes d'accord avec moi[3]. Ajoutez des phrases d'après ces modèles.*

Parlons anglais !
D'accord, on va parler anglais.

N'allons pas au cours !
D'accord, on ne va pas aller au cours.

1. N'allons pas au cours de français !
2. Regardons la télé !
3. Jouons aux cartes[4] !
4. Ne faisons pas les devoirs !

5. Allons au cinéma !
6. Prenons un taxi !
7. Dansons après le cinéma !
8. Rentrons à minuit !

C *Répondez aux questions.*

1. Quelle langue parle-t-on dans ce cours ? Quelle langue parle-t-on en France ? Quelles langues parle-t-on au Canada ?
2. Quelle langue est-ce qu'on apprend dans ce cours ? Quelle leçon étudie-t-on en ce moment[5] ?
3. En quelle saison fait-on du camping ? En quelle saison fait-on du ski ? Et en quelle saison fait-on du base-ball ?
4. En général, à quelle heure dîne-t-on aux États-Unis ? En France, à quelle heure dîne-t-on ?[6]
5. Regardez la photo à la page 147. Quelle sorte de magasin est-ce ? Que vend-on dans ce magasin ? Qui est la dame ?

7.3 VERBES DU PREMIER GROUPE (-ER) (3)

All first-conjugation verbs, which you learned in Lesson 2.1, have the same ending: **-e**, **-es**, **-e** in the singular, and **-ons**, **-ez**, **-ent** in the plural. But several subclasses of verbs in this group show slight irregularities either in spelling or in the last vowel of the stem (before the endings are attached).

1. **Manger** and **commencer** type
   In spoken French, verbs of this type are completely regular. But their written forms change so that orthography corresponds to pronunciation. In order to represent the /ʒ/ and /s/ sounds of the stem before **-ons**, an **e** is inserted in verbs like **manger**, and **c** becomes **ç** in verbs like **commencer**.

[1]**Pour** + infinitif est un équivalent de *(in order) to* + verbe en anglais.
[2]**faire des courses** *to do (some) errands*
[3]**être d'accord avec** *to agree with*
[4]**jouer aux cartes** *to play cards*
[5]**en ce moment** = maintenant
[6]Consultez les *Différences* de la Leçon 6 (p. 121).

manger

mange	mangeons
manges	mangez
mange	mangent

commencer

commence	commençons
commences	commencez
commence	commencent

manger /mɑ̃ʒe/ *to eat*

je **mange**	/mɑ̃ʒ/
tu **manges**	
elle **mange**	
nous **mangeons**	/mɑ̃ʒõ/
vous **mangez**	/mɑ̃ʒe/
elles **mangent**	/mɑ̃ʒ/

commencer /kɔmɑ̃se/ *to begin*

je **commence**	/kɔmɑ̃s/
tu **commences**	
il **commence**	
nous **commençons**	/kɔmɑ̃sõ/
vous **commencez**	/kɔmɑ̃se/
ils **commencent**	/kɔmɑ̃s/

Other verbs conjugated like **manger** and **commencer**:

corriger	*to correct*	**effacer**	*to erase*
nager	*to swim*	**prononcer**	*to pronounce*

2. **Payer**, **employer**, and **essuyer** type

These verbs share the common feature of having **y** in the infinitive form. The **y** is retained in the **nous** and **vous** forms (pronounced /j/), but in all other forms it becomes **i**. (**Payer** type was presented in Lesson 3.3.)

payer /pɛje/ *to pay for*

je **paie**	/pɛ/
tu **paies**	
il **paie**	
nous **payons**	/pɛjõ/
vous **payez**	/pɛje/
ils **paient**	/pɛ/

employer /ɑ̃plwaje/ *to use*

j'**emploie**	/ɑ̃plwa/
tu **emploies**	
elle **emploie**	
nous **employons**	/ɑ̃plwajõ/
vous **employez**	/ɑ̃plwaje/
elles **emploient**	/ɑ̃plwa/

essuyer /esɥije/ *to wipe*

j'**essuie**	/esɥi/
tu **essuies**	
il **essuie**	
nous **essuyons**	/esɥijõ/
vous **essuyez**	/esɥije/
ils **essuient**	/esɥi/

payer

paie	payons
paies	payez
paie	paient

employer

emploie	employons
emploies	employez
emploie	emploient

essuyer

essuie	essuyons
essuies	essuyez
essuie	essuient

Other verbs conjugated like **payer**, **employer**, and **essuyer**:

essayer	*to try (on)*	**envoyer**	*to send*	**appuyer sur**	*to press*
		nettoyer	*to clean*	**ennuyer**	*to annoy, bore*

3. **Répéter** type

Verbs whose infinitive ends in **é** + consonant + **er** change the **é** /e/ to **è** /ɛ/ in all but the **nous** and **vous** forms.

répéter /ʀepete/ *to repeat*

je **répète**	/ʀepɛt/	nous **répétons**	/ʀepetõ/
tu **répètes**		vous **répétez**	/ʀepete/
elle **répète**		elles **répètent**	/ʀepɛt/

répéter

répète	répétons
répètes	répétez
répète	répètent

Other verbs conjugated like **répéter**:

compléter	*to complete*	**espérer**	*to hope*	**préférer**	*to prefer*

4. **Acheter** and **appeler** type

Verbs whose infinitive ends in **e** + consonant + **er** either change **e** (not pronounced) to **è** /ɛ/, or double the following consonant. The vowel sound /ɛ/ occurs in all forms that undergo this change.

acheter /aʃte/ *to buy*

j'**achète**	/aʃɛt/
tu **achètes**	
il **achète**	
nous **achetons**	/aʃtõ/
vous **achetez**	/aʃte/
ils **achètent**	/aʃɛt/

appeler /aple/ *to call*

j'**appelle**	/apɛl/
tu **appelles**	
elle **appelle**	
nous **appelons**	/aplõ/
vous **appelez**	/aple/
elles **appellent**	/apɛl/

acheter

achète	achetons
achètes	achetez
achète	achètent

appeler

appelle	appelons
appelles	appelez
appelle	appellent

Other verbs conjugated like **acheter** and **appeler**:

amener (j'**amène**)	*to bring*	**épeler** (j'**épelle**)	*to spell*
lever (je **lève**)	*to raise*	**jeter** (je **jette**)	*to throw*

La cliente achète des légumes et paie les légumes.

A *Donnez la forme* **je** *et la forme* **nous** *de chaque verbe d'après ce modèle.*

corriger
je corrige, nous corrigeons

1. payer	4. employer	7. espérer	10. amener
2. essayer	5. envoyer	8. préférer	11. jeter
3. essuyer	6. répéter	9. acheter	12. appeler

B *Mettez tous les éléments de chaque phrase au singulier,[1] d'après ces modèles.*

Vous payez vos additions.
Tu paies ton addition.
Nous préférons nos amis.
Je préfère mon ami.

Ils achètent des livres.
Il achète un livre.

1. Vous amenez vos frères.
2. Nous répétons les phrases.
3. Ils emploient leurs ordinateurs.
4. Elles achètent des disquettes.
5. Vous appelez les étudiants.
6. Ils essaient des blousons.
7. Nous nettoyons nos chambres.
8. Vous complétez ces phrases.

[1]*Put all the elements of each sentence into the singular*

C *Répondez aux questions.*

1. Nettoyez-vous votre chambre ? Combien de fois par mois ?
2. Quelle saison préférez-vous ? Quel sport préférez-vous ?
3. Qu'est-ce que vous répétez en classe ? Après qui ?
4. En France, quand on a une question à poser[1], on lève le doigt, comme ça. Aux États-Unis, qu'est-ce qu'on fait quand on a une question à poser ?[2]
5. Épelez le mot **préfère**, comme dans l'expression « je préfère ». Où est-ce qu'il y a un accent aigu[3] ? Y a-t-il un accent grave[4] dans ce mot ?
6. Regardez. Qu'est-ce que je fais ?[5] Maintenant, qu'est-ce que je fais ?[6] Et qu'est-ce que je fais ?[7]

Exercice supplémentaire

Exercice supplémentaire

7.4 EXPRESSIONS DE QUANTITÉ : BEAUCOUP DE, UN KILO DE, ETC.

1. Adverbs that express quantity (such as **beaucoup** *much, a lot,* and **trop** *too much*) can occur with the construction **de/d'** + noun. In this pattern, count nouns are in the plural, and noncount nouns are in the singular.

(très) peu de   *(very) few, little*
Roland a **(très) peu d'**amis.   *Roland has (very) few friends.*
Mireille a **(très) peu d'**argent.   *Mireille has (very) little money.*

assez de   *enough*
Elle n'achète pas **assez de** pommes.   *She doesn't buy enough apples.*
Elle n'achète pas **assez de** viande.   *She doesn't buy enough meat.*

beaucoup de   *much, many, a lot of*
Nous faisons **beaucoup d'**exercices.   *We do a lot of exercises.*
Nous avons **beaucoup de** patience.   *We have a lot of patience.*

trop de   *too many, too much*
Il y a **trop de** chaises.   *There are too many chairs.*
Il y a **trop de** lait.   *There is too much milk.*

combien de   *how many, how much*
Combien de livres avez-vous ?   *How many books do you have?*
Combien de café veulent-ils ?   *How much coffee do they want?*

Un peu de *a little* can only be used with noncount nouns. For count nouns, **quelques** (without **de**) must be used.

J'ai **un peu d'**argent sur moi.   *I have a little money on me.*
J'ai **quelques** amis à Paris.   *I have a few friends in Paris.*

[1] *a question to ask*
[2] Employez l'expression **lever la main**.
[3] *acute accent* (´)
[4] *grave accent* (`)
[5] Employez **épeler un mot**.
[6] Employez **effacer**.
[7] Employez **essuyer**.

| TABLEAU 40 | **peu de** livres | **assez de** livres | **beaucoup de** livres | **trop de** livres |

2. In order to express a definite or specific quantity of a noncount noun, use the construction number + measuring unit + **de** + noun. Note that English has similar constructions.

(a)	**du** papier	→ **un morceau (une feuille) de** papier	*a piece (a sheet) of paper*
(b)	**du** pain	→ **trois morceaux**[1] **de** pain	*three pieces of bread*
(c)	**du** vin	→ **une bouteille de** vin	*a bottle of wine*
(d)	**du** lait	→ **deux verres de** lait	*two glasses of milk*
(e)	**du** café	→ **cinq tasses de** café	*five cups of coffee*
(f)	**de la** viande	→ **deux kilos de** viande	*two kilograms of meat*[2]

TABLEAU 41

« *Donnez-moi un kilo d'oignons et un kilo de carottes, s'il vous plaît.* »

[1]**morceau** *s*, **morceaux** *pl*
[2]1 kilogram = 2.2 pounds

A *Modifiez les phrases suivantes d'après ce modèle.*

> Il y a du jambon et du rosbif.
> (Daniel) **Il y a beaucoup de jambon.**
> (Maryse) **Mais il n'y a pas assez de rosbif.**

1. Il y a des légumes et de la viande.
2. Il y a des étudiants et des chaises.
3. On a du lait et de la crème.

4. On a du papier et des crayons.
5. J'ai des amis et de l'argent.
6. Vous avez de l'eau et du vin.

Deux bols de café et des tartines de beurre et de confiture.

B *Parlons de notre cours. Modifiez les phrases suivantes en employant les expressions suivantes, d'après le modèle.*

> **pas de → très peu de → peu de → un peu de/quelques → assez de → beaucoup de → trop de**

> Les étudiants ont de l'énergie.
> **Les étudiants ont beaucoup d'énergie.**

1. Les étudiants ont des examens.
2. Les étudiants font des fautes.
3. Les étudiants prennent de la bière.
4. Les étudiants ont du travail.
5. Nous avons des vacances.

6. J'ai de l'imagination.
7. J'ai des amis au Canada.
8. Le professeur prend du vin.
9. Le professeur a de l'argent.
10. Le professeur a des livres.

C *Maintenant, répondez à ces questions.*

1. Avez-vous de l'argent ? Et vos parents ? Et le président des États-Unis ?
2. Prenez-vous du lait ? Et vos parents ? Et les enfants ?
3. Mangez-vous de la viande ? Et vos parents ? Et les végétariens ?
4. Avez-vous des devoirs ce soir ? Et votre camarade de chambre[1] ?

[1]**camarade** *m, f* **de chambre** *roommate*

TABLEAU 42

D *En France, on ne mange pas beaucoup au petit déjeuner. On prend une grande tasse ou un bol de café au lait ou de chocolat. On mange des tartines de beurre et de confiture[1] ou parfois[2] des croissants ou des brioches.[3] Aux États-Unis, le petit déjeuner est plus varié[4]. Regardez le Tableau 42 et répétez le vocabulaire après moi.*

1. du bacon[5]	5. de la crème	9. des saucisses *f*
2. du beurre	6. du jus /ʒy/ d'orange	10. un bol de céréales[7] *f*
3. du café ou du chocolat	7. du lait	11. du sucre
4. de la confiture	8. un œuf[6]	12. un toast /tost/

Maintenant, parlons de notre petit déjeuner.

1. Qui prend du jus d'orange ? Combien de verres de jus d'orange prenez-vous ?
2. Qui prend du café ? Combien de tasses de café prenez-vous ?
3. Qui prend des céréales ? Combien de bols de céréales ?
4. Qui prend des saucisses ou du bacon ? Combien de (saucisses/bacon) mangez-vous ?
5. Qui prend des œufs ? Combien d'œufs mangez-vous ?
6. Qui prend du pain ? Combien de morceaux de pain prenez-vous ?
7. Qu'est-ce que je mange au petit déjeuner ? Devinez.
8. Qu'est-ce que les Français prennent au petit déjeuner ?

Dictée

7.5 BOIRE

The conjugation of **boire** *to drink* is somewhat like **pouvoir**: the stem-final consonant /v/ is heard only in the plural forms, and the **nous** and **vous** forms have a stem vowel that is different from all the other forms.

boire

bois	buvons
bois	buvez
boit	boivent

Je **bois** du champagne.   Nous **buvons** de la bière.
Tu **bois** de l'eau minérale.   Vous **buvez** du lait.
Elle **boit** du chocolat.   Ils **boivent** du vin français.

A *Exercice de contrôle*

Je bois du lait au petit déjeuner.

1. Nous   2. Tu   3. Vous   4. Les enfants

Je ne bois pas de vin au déjeuner.

2. Les étudiants   2. Nous   3. (Marie)   4. Vous

[1] *slices of bread with butter and jam*
[2] **parfois** *sometimes*
[3] Consultez les *Différences* de la Leçon 6 (p. 121).
[4] *more varied*
[5] /bakõ/ ou /bekɔn/
[6] /œf/ au singulier, /ø/ au pluriel : **un œuf** /ɛ̃nœf/, **deux œufs** /døzø/.
[7] On emploie le mot **céréales** *cereal* au pluriel.

B *Répondez aux questions.*

1. Qu'est-ce que vous buvez au petit déjeuner ? Qu'est-ce que vous ne buvez pas au petit déjeuner ? Buvez-vous du champagne au petit déjeuner ?

2. Qu'est-ce que vous buvez au dîner ? Demandez-moi si je bois du vin au dîner. Demandez à (Frédérique) si elle boit de la bière au dîner.

3. Qu'est-ce que les enfants boivent souvent quand ils sont petits ? Qu'est-ce que les enfants ne boivent pas ?

4. Demandez-moi ce que[1] je bois au petit déjeuner. Demandez-moi ce que je bois au dîner. Demandez-moi ce que je bois de temps en temps.

7.6 AVOIR BESOIN DE

1. **Avoir besoin de** means *to need* (literally, *to have need of*). Note in the last two examples below that when it is followed by **le/les** + noun, **de** combines with the article to form **du** and **des**, respectively.

J'**ai besoin de** ton livre.	*I need your book.*
As-tu **besoin de** ce verre ?	*Do you need this glass?*
Michel **a besoin d'**une montre.	*Michel needs a watch.*
Nous avons **besoin de** la table.	*We need the table.*
Avez-vous **besoin du** journal ?	*Do you need the newspaper?*
Elles ont **besoin des** clés.	*They need the keys.*

2. If **avoir besoin de** occurs with nouns of *unspecified* or *indefinite* quantity, then it is used like **beaucoup de**, with no article after it.

Voilà **des** crayons. J'ai beaucoup **de** crayons.
Voilà **du** sucre. On a beaucoup **de** sucre.

Voilà **des** crayons. J'ai besoin **de** crayons.	*I need (some) pencils.*
Voilà **du** sucre. As-tu besoin **de** sucre ?	*Do you need (any) sugar?*
Y a-t-il **de la** crème ? On a besoin **de** crème.	*We need (some) cream.*
As-tu **de l'**argent ? J'ai besoin **d'**argent.	*I need (some) money.*

Elle a besoin d'argent.

---

[1]**ce que** *what* (literally, *that which*). In questions, it will become **Qu'est-ce que... ?**

3. **Avoir besoin de** may be followed by an infinitive.

Il **a besoin de faire** des courses.	*He needs to do (some) errands.*
Elles **ont besoin d'aller** au magasin.	*They need to go to the store.*
Qu'est-ce que vous **avez besoin de faire** ?	*What do you need to do?*

 A *Répondez aux questions.*

1. Je vais à la boulangerie. Je vais acheter du pain. Où est-ce que je vais ? De quoi est-ce que j'ai besoin ?
2. Je vais à la charcuterie. Je vais acheter du porc. De quoi est-ce que j'ai besoin ? Où est-ce que je vais ?
3. (Michel) va à la boucherie. Il va acheter du bœuf. Où va Michel ? De quoi a-t-il besoin ?
4. (Jacques) et (Marie) vont à l'épicerie. Ils vont acheter du café et du thé. De quoi ont-ils besoin ? Où vont-ils ?
5. Nous allons à la papeterie /papɛtʀi/. Nous allons acheter du papier et des stylos. De quoi avons-nous besoin ? Où allons-nous ?
6. (Jeanne), vous allez à la charcuterie. Vous allez acheter du jambon. Où allez-vous ? De quoi avez-vous besoin ?

B *Répondez aux questions.*

1. De quoi avez-vous besoin quand vous allez au laboratoire ? Et quand vous allez au supermarché ?
2. De quoi a-t-on besoin pour manger ? Et pour manger de la soupe ? Et pour boire quelque chose ?
3. Avez-vous besoin du livre de français ? Demandez à (Chantal) si elle a besoin de son cahier d'exercices.
4. Qu'est-ce que nous avons besoin de faire dans ce cours ? Qu'est-ce que vous avez besoin de faire ce soir ?
5. Où avez-vous besoin d'aller chaque jour ? À quelle heure avez-vous besoin de rentrer à la maison ?

 Exercice supplémentaire

APPLICATIONS

 A **Situations**

Faisons un pique-nique !
Jean-Paul, sa sœur Monique et deux copains visitent la vallée de la Dordogne, une très belle
southwest *région dans le sud-ouest° de la France. Aujourd'hui, ils louent des bicyclettes et voyagent*
le long de along *le long de° la Dordogne. Il fait chaud et ils commencent à[1] être fatigués. Ils arrivent près*
d'un village.

Say | JEAN-PAUL | Dites donc°, moi, je commence à avoir faim. Pas vous ? | 5
| JULIEN | Moi aussi, j'ai faim. Quelle heure as-tu, Monique ? |
| MONIQUE | Il est onze heures et demie. Nous pouvons aller dans ce village pour faire des courses[2]. |

[1]When followed by an infinitive, **commencer** *to begin* requires the preposition **à** before the infinitive.
[2]**faire des courses** /kuʀs/ *f   to do/run (some) errands* (cf. **un cours** /kuʀ/   *a course*)

IGNÈS	Bonne idée ! De quoi a-t-on besoin exactement ?
JEAN-PAUL	Pour faire des sandwichs on a besoin de baguettes et de tranches de jambon. 10
JULIEN	Moi, je veux du pâté de campagne¹.
JEAN-PAUL	Bon, on achète aussi un peu de pâté. Allons à la boulangerie et ensuite à la charcuterie.
IGNÈS	Moi, je mange beaucoup de fruits. Achetons des fraises et des cerises.
JEAN-PAUL	D'accord. Et qu'est-ce qu'on achète comme boisson ? 15
JULIEN	Un litre d'Orangina et une bouteille d'eau minérale.
JEAN-PAUL	Oui, bonne idée. Allons aussi à l'épicerie.
IGNÈS	Nous avons besoin d'un couteau pour faire les sandwichs. Qui a un couteau ?
MONIQUE	Moi, j'ai mon couteau suisse° dans mon sac à dos°. J'ai aussi des verres en plastique° et des serviettes en papier°. 20
JEAN-PAUL	Tu penses à tout ! Bon, faisons nos courses.
MONIQUE	Et après, faisons un pique-nique au bord de° la rivière.

Swiss army knife/back-pack/plastic glasses/paper napkins

at the edge of

Répondez aux questions. (*lignes 1–4*)

1. Où est la vallée de la Dordogne ?
2. Qu'est-ce que les quatre jeunes gens louent ?
3. Que font-ils le long de la rivière ?
4. Où arrivent-ils ?

(*lignes 5–22*)

5. Quelle heure est-il ?
6. Qu'est-ce qu'ils vont acheter à la boulangerie ?
7. Où vont-ils pour acheter du jambon et du pâté ?
8. Quelle sorte de fruits achètent-ils ?
9. Où est le couteau suisse de Monique ?
10. Où vont-ils faire un pique-nique ?

FRANCE
DORDOGNE
PÉRIGORD

Ils vont faire une promenade à bicyclette.

Ils font un pique-nique.

¹*country-style pâté* (**Pâté** *is like a soft meat loaf, to be spread over bread.*)

B Expressions utiles

Les magasins

ON VA :	POUR ACHETER :
à la boucherie chez le boucher[1]	du bœuf, du veau, de l'agneau, de la volaille (des poulets, des dindes)
à la boulangerie chez le boulanger	du pain, des croissants, des brioches
à la charcuterie chez le charcutier	du porc, de la volaille, des plats cuisinés[2], du jambon, du saucisson, des saucisses, du pâté
à la crémerie chez le crémier	du lait, de la crème, du beurre, des œufs, du fromage
à l'épicerie chez l'épicier	du thé, du café, du chocolat, du vin, de l'eau minérale, du sel, du sucre, du poivre, des œufs, des conserves (des boîtes de conserves[3])
à la librairie chez le libraire	des livres
à la papeterie /papɛtʀi/ chez le papetier /paptje/	des articles scolaires, des articles de bureau
à la pharmacie chez le pharmacien	des médicaments[4], des produits d'hygiène
au bureau de tabac /taba/ chez le buraliste	des cigarettes, des timbres-poste[5], des journaux[6]
à la maison de la presse	des journaux, des revues, des hebdomadaires, des livres de poche[7], des bandes dessinées[8]
chez le marchand de vin	du vin, des apéritifs, des digestifs, de l'eau minérale
chez le marchand de primeurs	des fruits, des légumes

Certains magasins combinent deux spécialités.

la boucherie-charcuterie	la boulangerie-pâtisserie
l'épicerie-alimentation[9]	la librairie-papeterie

C Pratique

1. Voici les ingrédients pour une omelette au jambon. Où peut-on acheter ces aliments ?

des œufs	du sel	des fines herbes[10]
du jambon	du poivre	du lait

[1]*to the butcher's*; **chez** *to/at the home of* can be extended to apply to stores and offices: **chez le boulanger, chez le médecin.**

[2]*prepared food*

[3]**boîte** *can*, **boîte de conserves** *canned food*: **une boîte de sardines, une boîte de tomates,** etc.

[4]On emploie le mot **médicaments** *medicine* au pluriel.

[5]*postage stamps*

[6]pluriel de **journal** *newspaper*

[7]*pocketbooks (paperbacks)*

[8]*comic books*

[9]At the **épicerie-alimentation**, one can buy, in addition to the products mentioned under **épicerie**, other items such as fresh produce and fruit, milk, and a limited selection of cold cuts, cheeses, and wine.

[10]*combination of several herbs for seasoning*

2. Où vend-on les produits suivants ?

un dictionnaire	des crayons	des huîtres
des poulets	des journaux	de la moutarde
des asperges	des bananes	des saucisses
des croissants	de l'aspirine	une boîte de sardines
de la crème	des cahiers	une bouteille d'huile

3. Regardez les photos de magasins à cette page. Qu'est-ce qu'on peut acheter dans ces magasins ?

4. Il fait beau et chaud. Plusieurs étudiants décident de faire un pique-nique au lieu de[1] déjeuner au restaurant universitaire. De quoi ont-ils besoin ? Où vont-ils acheter ces aliments ?

5. Aux États-Unis, qu'est-ce qu'on peut acheter au « *delicatessen* » ? Est-ce que le « *deli* » est la même chose que[2] la charcuterie en France ?

D **Mini-composition :** *Je vais préparer un dîner. Complétez le passage en employant les mots indiqués.*

(1) Je/inviter/trois/copain/à/dîner/chez moi. (2) Je/aller/préparer/un/repas/simple,/car/je/ ne pas/avoir/beaucoup/argent. (3) Je/être/maintenant/à/supermarché/près de/mon/appartement. (4) Il y a/encore/beaucoup/pommes de terre[3]/et/assez/haricots verts/à/maison. (5) Je/avoir besoin de/viande. (6) Je/vouloir/acheter/steaks,/mais/je/ne pas/pouvoir/ parce que/ils/coûter/trop cher[4]. (7) Je/choisir/jambon,/et/je/acheter/aussi/légumes/pour/ salade. (8) Je/ne pas/acheter/dessert,/car/Anne/aller/apporter/une tarte aux pommes[5]. (9) Après/courses/je/nettoyer/le/appartement. (10) Les/invité/aller/arriver/vers[6] 6 h. (11) Je/ espérer/que/mon/copains/avoir/faim.

Voilà un nouveau magasin d'informatique.

E **Questions :** *On va faire des courses. Posez des questions sur les parties soulignées.*

Nous allons faire (1) des courses ce matin. D'abord[7] nous allons (2) à la librairie, car nous avons besoin (3) d'un livre de linguistique. Nous avons aussi besoin d'un dictionnaire (4) français-espagnol.[8] Ensuite nous allons au magasin d'informatique' (5) pour acheter des dis-

[1]**au lieu de** *instead of*

[2]**la même chose que** *the same thing as*

[3]**pommes de terre** *potatoes*

[4]**coûter trop cher** *to cost too much*

[5]*an apple pie* (pies in France are open-faced)

[6]*around* (literally, *toward*)

[7]*First*

[8]Commencez la question par **De quelle sorte de**.

quettes. (6) Ce nouveau magasin est près de la librairie. Le propriétaire de ce magasin est (7) un ami de mon père. Il est (8) très sympathique. Nous avons besoin d'acheter (9) quatre revues[1]. Pour cela, nous allons à la maison de la presse. Nous pouvons aller à la charcuterie (10) avant de[2] rentrer. Nous voulons acheter des plats (11) cuisinés, (12) parce que nous ne voulons pas faire la cuisine[3].

F Renseignements et opinions

1. Qu'est-ce qu'on peut acheter au supermarché aux États-Unis, mais pas en France ?
2. Y a-t-il des boulangeries dans notre ville ? Y a-t-il des papeteries ? et des pharmacies ?
3. Quand vous avez très soif, qu'est-ce que vous voulez boire ? Est-ce que c'est votre boisson préférée ?
4. Quelle est votre librairie préférée ? Pourquoi ?
5. Y a-t-il un marché en plein air[4] dans notre ville ? Dans quelle sorte de ville peut-on trouver un marché en plein air ?
6. À quoi pensez-vous souvent ? À qui pensez-vous souvent ? De quoi parlez-vous souvent ? De qui parlez-vous souvent ?

Compréhension auditive (basée sur l'Application A)

Compréhension auditive (basée sur l'Application B)

Dictée : « Je fais des courses. » (basée sur l'Application D)

[1]*magazines*

[2]**avant de** + infinitif *before doing (something)*

[3]**faire la cuisine** = préparer un repas

[4]**en plein air** *outdoor*

VOCABULAIRE

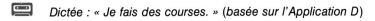

Noms

un **accent**	accent	la **crème**	cream	le pâté de campagne	country-style
une **aspirine**	aspirin	la **crémerie**	cheese and milk		pâté
le **bacon**	bacon		shop	la **pharmacie**	pharmacy
la baguette	long, thin loaf of	la **disquette**	floppy disk(ette)	le pique-nique	picnic
	bread	le **doigt**	finger	le plastique	plastic
le **bœuf**	beef	la Dordogne	Dordogne River	la rivière	river
le bord	edge, bank	un(e) **employé(e)**	employee	le **rosbif**	roast beef
la **boucherie**	butcher shop	l'**énergie** f	energy	le sac à dos	backpack
le(la) **boulanger(ère)**	baker	une **épicerie**	grocery store	le **sandwich**	sandwich
la **boulangerie**	bakery	le fruit	fruit	la **sorte**	kind
le **bureau de poste**	post office	l'**imagination** f	imagination	le sud-ouest	southwest
le **bureau de tabac**	tobacco shop	le **jambon**	ham	le **supermarché**	supermarket
le **Canada**	Canada	le **kilo**	kilo	le **tabac**	tobacco
la **carte**	(playing) card	le litre	liter	la **tasse**	cup
les **céréales** f	cereal	le **magasin**	store	le **toast**	toast
la cerise	cherry	le **moment**	moment	la tranche	slice
le **champagne**	champagne	le **morceau**	piece	la vallée	valley
la **charcuterie**	pork butcher shop	un **œuf**	egg	le **veau**	veal
le **coin**	corner	une **orange**	orange	le village	village
la **confiture**	jam	un Orangina	orange-flavored	le **vin**	wine
le **conseil**	advice		soda		
la course	errand	un **ordinateur**	computer		
le couteau suisse	Swiss army knife	la **papeterie**	stationery shop		

Verbes

acheter	*to buy*	**deviner**	*to guess*	louer	*to rent*
appeler	*to call*	**effacer**	*to erase*	**nettoyer**	*to clean*
boire *irrég*	*to drink*	**employer**	*to use*	**penser (à)**	*to think (of)*
compléter	*to complete*	**envoyer**	*to send*	**préférer**	*to prefer*
compter sur	*to count on*	**essuyer**	*to wipe*	visiter	*to visit*
corriger	*to correct*	**jeter**	*to throw*	voyager	*to travel*
danser	*to dance*	**lever**	*to raise*		

Adjectifs

aigu(ë)	*acute* (accent)	**grave**	*grave* (accent)	suisse	*Swiss*
chaque	*each, every*	**quelques**	*a few*		

Adverbes

ensuite	*then*	exactement	*exactly*

Autres expressions

au bord de	*on the bank of, at the edge of*	faire un pique-nique	*to have a picnic*
assez de	*enough*	**jouer aux cartes**	*to play cards*
avoir besoin de	*to need*	le long de	*along*
beaucoup de	*much, many, a lot of*	**peu de**	*few, little*
ce que	*what, that which*	**pour** + *inf*	*in order to* + inf
Dites donc	*Say*	**quelle sorte de**	*what kind of*
d'où	*from where*	**quoi**	*what*
en ce moment	*right now*	**trop de**	*too much, too many*
faire des courses	*to do/run errands*	**un peu de**	*a little*

8 Voilà notre famille.

LESSON OBJECTIVES

Theme and Culture

1. Kinship terms
2. Family relations

Communication Skills

     general preferences (*to like*, *to love*, *to dislike*)
2. Describing people and objects using adjectives (*he is smart, they are smart*)
3. Describing one's family
4. Asking/Answering questions regarding one's knowledge or familiarity (*to know, not to know*)
5. Recognizing cognates of French adjectives
6. Expressing directions (*I leave for…, I leave…to go to…*)
7. Regions and cities of France

Structures

8.1 Use of the definite article
8.2 Adjectives used with subject: singular
8.3 **Connaître, savoir**
8.4 Adjectives: plural; the plural of nouns in **-aux** and **-eaux**
8.5 **Partir, sortir**

CONVERSATIONS

🔊 **A.   La famille de Jean-Paul et les Brunot**[1]

Regardez le Tableau 43 à la page 164. La famille de Jean-Paul est à gauche et les Brunot sont à droite. Ils sont cinq dans la famille Chabrier. Ils sont quatre dans la famille Brunot. Regardez les Chabrier[1] *et dites après moi.*

Voici Jean-Paul. Jean-Paul est le **frère** de Monique.
Voici Monique. Monique est la **sœur** de Jean-Paul.

Voici les parents de Jean-Paul et de Monique.
Jean-Paul est le **fils** /fis/ de M. et Mme Chabrier.
Monique est leur **fille** /fij/.

[1]*the Brunots; the Chabriers*: note that in French no **-s** is added to proper names.

163

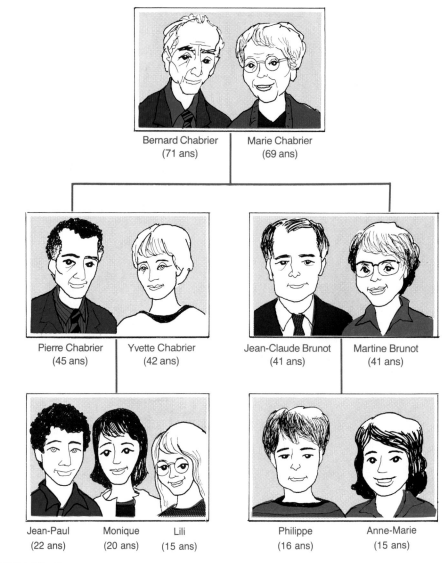

Bernard Chabrier
(71 ans)

Marie Chabrier
(69 ans)

Pierre Chabrier
(45 ans)

Yvette Chabrier
(42 ans)

Jean-Claude Brunot
(41 ans)

Martine Brunot
(41 ans)

Jean-Paul
(22 ans)

Monique
(20 ans)

Lili
(15 ans)

Philippe
(16 ans)

Anne-Marie
(15 ans)

TABLEAU 43

Jean-Paul et Monique sont leurs **enfants**.

M. Chabrier est le **père** de Jean-Paul.
Mme Chabrier est la **mère** de Jean-Paul.
M. Chabrier est le **mari** de Mme Chabrier.
Mme Chabrier est la **femme** de M. Chabrier.

Voici les grands-parents de Jean-Paul et de Monique.
M. Bernard Chabrier est le **grand-père** de Jean-Paul.
Mme Marie Chabrier est sa **grand-mère**.
M. et Mme Chabrier sont ses **grands-parents**.

Voici les cousins de Jean-Paul et de Monique.

Jean-Paul est le **cousin** d'Anne-Marie.

Monique est la **cousine** d'Anne-Marie.

M. Brunot est l'**oncle** de Jean-Paul.

Mme Brunot est la **tante** de Jean-Paul.

B. *Maintenant, parlons de Lili. Regardez Lili. Elle a quinze ans.*

Qui est sa mère ? Quel âge a-t-elle ?

Qui est son père ? Quel âge a-t-il ?

Qui est sa sœur ? Qui est son frère ? Quel âge ont-ils ?

Qui est son oncle ? Qui est sa tante ? Quel âge ont-ils ?

Qui est son cousin ? Qui est sa cousine ? Quel âge ont-ils ?

C. Au resto-U

MICHEL Alors, qu'est-ce qu'il y a aujourd'hui ?

CHRISTINE Il y a du poisson.

MICHEL Encore du poisson ? Je déteste le poisson.

CHRISTINE Moi, j'adore le poisson. Mais il y a aussi des pizzas.

MICHEL C'est déjà mieux[1]. Moi, j'aime beaucoup les pizzas.

D. Où est mon frère ?

MARIE Tu connais mon frère Marc ?

PIERROT Oui, je connais très bien ton frère.

MARIE Sais-tu où il est ?

PIERROT Oui, il est au stade, avec ses copains.

Compréhension auditive (basée sur la Conversation A)

DIFFÉRENCES

La famille

France tends to be a very family-oriented society. French children grow up in a closely-knit family structure that remains an important part of their social life, even after they become adults and have their own families. In the past especially, most French people married someone within their own geographic, economic, and social milieu, and this to some extent explains why French families have remained so homogeneous even today. The divorce rate is substantially lower than it is in the United States: about 1.59 per population of 1,000, as opposed to the American rate of 4.8 per 1,000.

Most social activities in France revolve around relatives—parents, siblings, grandparents, aunts, uncles, in-laws, cousins and more cousins—as well as childhood friends, rather than neighbors, university friends or business associates. Close friends or relatives, usually of the same age group as the parents, often become a child's godfather (**le parrain**) or godmother (**la marraine**). They share in all the important events in the child's life (baptism, confirmation, school years, engagement, marriage, and so on), and are kept informed by the parents and the child about his or her progress and future plans. Family get-togethers are very common in France, especially on holidays. The traditional **dîner du dimanche**, often resembling a feast that can last as long as three hours, with spirited conversation over food and drink, is an occasion to invite

[1]**mieux** *better*

Une réunion familiale.

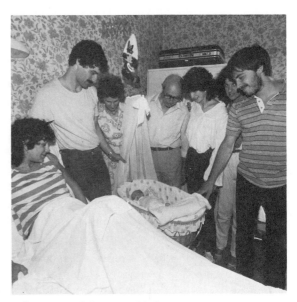

« Je trouve qu'elle ressemble à sa maman. »

members of the clan. French people seldom invite other couples or families to dinner, unless they are very good friends, and business associates are rarely entertained at home. Children celebrate their birthday or their saint's day, but adults rarely do.

The French government has an extensive program of subsidies and benefits for all mothers (as will be discussed in the *Différences* of Lesson 13). In order to counter the declining birthrate, the government encourages large families with generous financial supplements, even though many couples these days prefer to have fewer children. A woman with two or more children is entitled to a certain sum of money (depending on the family income), called **allocations familiales**, every month to defray the expenses of raising her children. Single-income families are often entitled to a single-salary supplement (**allocations de salaire unique**), and single mothers receive an income supplement at the beginning of the school year (**allocations de rentrée scolaire**). Many French women are working mothers and face the same needs for adequate child care that American women do. Children are raised more strictly in France. In the traditional French view, they are to be trained for adulthood, and parents play a definite role in "shaping" their growth. When in the company of adults, they are expected to be as polite and as unobtrusive as possible. Some young men and women continue to live with their parents, rather than move out, until they marry or find a job far from home.

STRUCTURES

8.1 EMPLOIS DE L'ARTICLE DÉFINI

In Lesson 1.3 you learned that the definite article **le**, **la**, **l'**, **les** corresponds to English *the*. However, there are several cases in which the definite article is obligatory in French where *the* is never used in English.[1]

[1]Use of the definite article with days of the week was presented in Lesson 3.2 and will not be repeated here.

1. Names of languages (they are all masculine singular) take **le** or **l'**, except when they are used with the verb **parler** or after the prepositions **de** and **en**. Names of languages in French do not begin with a capital letter (**majuscule** *f*).

Nous apprenons **le français**.	*We are learning French.*
Mon oncle comprend **l'allemand**.	*My uncle understands German.*
Le japonais est très difficile.	*Japanese is very difficult.*
Marie étudie-t-elle **l'espagnol** ?	*Is Marie studying Spanish?*

BUT

Parlez-vous **russe** ?	*Do you speak Russian?*
Voilà mon professeur **de français**.	*There's my French teacher.*
Il pose la question **en français**.	*He asks the question in French.*

2. Abstract nouns, which are usually singular noncount nouns, take the definite article in French.

La vie est belle.	*Life is beautiful.*
La liberté ou **la mort** !	*Freedom or death!*
Mange cela, c'est bon pour **la santé**.	*Eat that, it's good for (your) health.*
La chimie est une science.	*Chemistry is a science.*

3. The idea of *totality* or *generality* is expressed by the definite article. A sentence like **Les chats et les chiens sont des animaux** *Cats and dogs are animals* implies that *all cats* (totality) and *all dogs* (totality) are just *a part* of the animal category (hence ***des animaux***). **Les légumes sont importants pour la santé** *Vegetables are important for health* implies that *vegetables in general* (generality) or *all vegetables* (totality) are important for health (abstract noun).

Les enfants aiment **les** bonbons[1].	*Children like candy.*
Les roses sont **des** fleurs.	*Roses are flowers.*
Je déteste **les** épinards[1].	*I hate spinach.*
Le fer est un métal, et **l'**or aussi.	*Iron is a metal, and so is gold [and gold also].*

« Encore du poisson ? Moi, je déteste le poisson. »

[1]On emploie ces mots au pluriel.

Certain verbs in French express generality: **aimer** *to like*, **adorer** *to love*, **préférer** *to prefer*, and **détester** *to hate*. These verbs take the definite article rather than **des**, **du**, **de la**, or **de l'**.

Jacqueline **aime les chats** ; elle a trois chats.	*Jacqueline likes cats; she has three cats.*
Je ne bois pas de vin ; je n'**aime** pas **le vin**.	*I don't drink wine; I don't like wine.*
Avez-vous des fraises ? J'**adore les fraises** !	*Do you have strawberries? I love strawberries!*
Liliane **préfère le thé au café**.	*Liliane prefers tea to coffee.*
Il ne va pas manger de poisson ; Il **déteste le poisson**.	*He isn't going to eat any fish; he hates fish.*

4. You will need to distinguish between **beaucoup** *a lot* and **beaucoup de** *a lot of*. The first modifies a verb and comes immediately after it, while the second modifies a noun that follows it.

J'**aime beaucoup** les pommes.	*I like apples a lot.*
Il n'**aime** pas **beaucoup** les langues étrangères.	*He doesn't like foreign languages a lot.*
J'achète **beaucoup de pommes**.	*I buy a lot of apples.*
Elle comprend **beaucoup de langues**.	*She understands a lot of languages.*

A   *Répondez aux questions.*

1. Les fraises, les cerises, les bananes et les pommes sont des fruits.
   Quels fruits aimez-vous beaucoup ? Quels fruits mangez-vous souvent ? Quels fruits n'aimez-vous pas ?
2. Les haricots verts, les carottes, les petits pois et les asperges sont des légumes.
   Quels légumes préférez-vous ? Quels légumes n'aimez-vous pas ? Quels légumes voulez-vous pour votre dîner ?
3. Le café, le thé, le chocolat, le lait et le jus de tomate sont des boissons.
   Quelle boisson préférez-vous ? Quelle boisson voulez-vous prendre au petit déjeuner ? Quelle boisson détestez-vous ?
4. La natation, le football, le tennis, le patinage et le basket sont des sports.
   Quel sport aimez-vous beaucoup ? Que faites-vous comme sport ? Quel sport détestez-vous ? Quel sport ne comprenez-vous pas ?
5. Parlons des cours. Quel cours est difficile ?[1] Quel cours est facile ? Quel cours est utile ? Quel cours est intéressant ?
6. Quelles langues parlez-vous ? Quelle langue apprenez-vous ? Quelle langue est difficile ?

B   *Parlons de vos préférences. Faites des phrases d'après ce modèle.*

(ne pas) prendre/thé/parce que (ne pas) aimer/thé
Je prends du thé parce que j'aime le thé.
Je ne prends pas de thé parce que je n'aime pas le thé.

---

[1]Dites, par exemple : **Le cours de chimie** (ou **La chimie**) **est difficile**. (Consultez les *Expressions utiles* de la Leçon 2 (p. 53).)

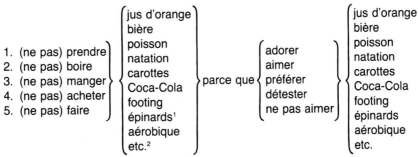

1. (ne pas) prendre
2. (ne pas) boire
3. (ne pas) manger
4. (ne pas) acheter
5. (ne pas) faire

jus d'orange
bière
poisson
natation
carottes
Coca-Cola
footing
épinards[1]
aérobique
etc.[2]

parce que

adorer
aimer
préférer
détester
ne pas aimer

jus d'orange
bière
poisson
natation
carottes
Coca-Cola
footing
épinards
aérobique
etc.

Exercice supplémentaire

8.2 ADJECTIF ATTRIBUT DU SUJET : SINGULIER

Adjectives describe nouns, and in French they agree in gender (*m*/*f*) and number (*s*/*pl*) with the noun. Examine the four forms of the adjective **intelligent** below.

Mon frère est **intelligent**.	*m, s*	*My brother is intelligent.*
Votre sœur est **intelligente**.	*f, s*	*Your sister is intelligent.*
Mes frères sont **intelligents**.	*m, pl*	*My brothers are intelligent.*
Vos sœurs sont **intelligentes**.	*f, pl*	*Your sisters are intelligent.*

In this section, you will learn the masculine and feminine singular forms of adjectives that come after **être** (called **attribut du sujet** because they describe the subject). There are three basic types of adjectives in French: (1) those that do not show any gender distinction; (2) those that make this distinction only in written French; (3) those that make the distinction in both written and spoken French.

1. Some adjectives are *invariable*: They show no distinction between masculine and feminine forms. Nearly all such adjectives end in **-e**.

   Jacques est **optimiste** ; Jacqueline est **optimiste**.
   Ce devoir est **difficile** ; cette question est **difficile**.
   Mon père est **énergique** ; ma mère est **énergique**.
   Ce cours est **utile** ; cette langue est **utile**.
   Mon frère est **jeune** ; ma sœur est **jeune**.

2. Some adjectives show gender distinction in written French, but sound the same in spoken language. The masculine form ends in **-al**, **-el**, **-r**, or a vowel other than **-e**, and the corresponding feminine form ends in **-ale**, **-elle**, **-re**, or **-e**.

   Le projet est **original** ; la réponse est **originale**.
   Ce produit est **naturel** ; cette décision est **naturelle**.
   Son chat est **noir** ; sa voiture est **noire**.
   Le ciel est **bleu** ; la robe est **bleue**.

3. Other adjectives show gender distinction in both written and spoken French. The difference between the masculine and feminine forms occurs mostly in the *final consonant* of the adjective.

   a) If the masculine form ends in **-if** /if/, the feminine form changes the ending to **-ive** /iv/.

---

[1] *spinach (on emploie ce mot au pluriel)*
[2] Vous pouvez utiliser d'autres mots.

Philippe est attentif ; Monique est attentive.

Mon oncle est très actif ; ma tante est très active.

b) If the masculine form ends in a consonant letter (not pronounced), the feminine form usually ends in that consonant plus **-e** (the consonant is now pronounced).

Jean est **discret** ; Jeanne est **discrète**[1].	/diskʀɛ/	/diskʀɛt/
Michel est **heureux** ; sa femme est **heureuse**.	/œʀø/	/œʀøz/
Ce fruit est **mauvais** ; cette viande est **mauvaise**.	/mɔvɛ/	/mɔvɛz/
Ton frère est **grand** ; ta sœur est **grande**.	/gʀɑ̃/	/gʀɑ̃d/
Cet exercice est **long** ; cette leçon est **longue**[2].	/lõ/	/lõg/
Le sucre est **blanc** ; la neige est **blanche**[3].	/blɑ̃/	/blɑ̃ʃ/
Mon père est **gentil** ; ma mère est **gentille**.	/ʒɑ̃ti/	/ʒɑ̃tij/

c) If the masculine form ends in **-n**, the feminine form adds **-e**. The **-n** is doubled if the masculine ending is **-on** or **-ien**. In spoken French, the difference is between a nasal vowel (masculine) and an oral vowel followed by a nasal consonant: /ɛ̃/–/ɛn/, /õ/–/ɔn/.

Il est **américain** ; elle est **américaine**.	/ameʀikɛ̃/	/ameʀikɛn/
Ce vin est **bon** ; cette salade est **bonne**.	/bõ/	/bɔn/
Ce verre est **italien** ; cette voiture est **italienne**.	/italjɛ̃/	/italjɛn/

4. Finally, a few adjectives show more marked differences between the masculine and feminine forms.

Michel est **beau** ; sa sœur est **belle**.		
Ce client est **nouveau** ; cette cliente est **nouvelle**.		
Cet hôtel est **vieux** ; cette maison est **vieille**.	/vjø/	/vjɛj/
Paul est **travailleur** ; Marie est **travailleuse**.	/tʀavajœʀ/	/tʀavajøz/

5. *Cognates*.[4] You have probably noticed that many French adjectives have cognates in English. By learning to recognize them, you can increase your vocabulary considerably.

-iste (*ist*/*-istic*)	**-able** (*-able*)	**-ible** (*-ible*)
idéaliste	acceptable	possible
optimiste	probable	terrible
pessimiste	sociable	visible
-ique (*-ic*/*-ical*)	**-al** (*-al*)	**-el** (*-al*)
énergique	médical	artificiel
logique	national	confidentiel
pratique	régional	intellectuel
-if (*-ive*)	**-ien** (*-ian*)	**-eux** (*-ous*)[5]
actif	canadien	curieux
imaginatif	italien	dangereux
négatif	parisien	sérieux

[1]When the masculine form ends in **e** + consonant, the feminine is **è** + consonant + **e**: **discret/discrète, complet/ complète, léger/légère, premier/première.**

[2]Note that the feminine ends in **-gue.**

[3]Note that the feminine ends in **-che.**

[4]Cognates are words that are spelled more or less alike in two languages and have the same meaning in both languages.

[5]Exceptions in this lesson include **ennuyeux** *boring*, **heureux** *happy*, **malheureux** *unhappy*, and **paresseux** *lazy*.

Cette jeune Canadienne est belle.

Ce jeune homme est sympathique.

A *On va parler d'un couple. C'est un mariage heureux. Le mari ressemble beaucoup à sa femme, et la femme ressemble beaucoup à son mari. Ajoutez des phrases d'après ce modèle.*

Sa femme est belle.
Oui, elle est belle, et lui aussi[1], il est beau.

1. Sa femme est petite.
2. Sa femme est active.
3. Sa femme est jeune.
4. Sa femme est énergique.
5. Sa femme est heureuse.
6. Sa femme est optimiste.
7. Sa femme est travailleuse.
8. Sa femme est parisienne.

B *Répétez les antonymes suivants et donnez les formes masculines d'après ce modèle.*

belle—laide
belle—laide, beau—laid

1. bonne—mauvaise
2. froide—chaude
3. belle—laide
4. grande—petite
5. facile—difficile
6. légère—lourde
7. riche—pauvre
8. longue—courte
9. jeune—vieille
10. discrète—indiscrète
11. contente—mécontente
12. heureuse—malheureuse
13. intelligente—bête
14. intéressante—ennuyeuse
15. travailleuse—paresseuse

C *Maintenant, ajoutez des phrases en employant des antonymes d'après ce modèle.*

Ce cours est-il ennuyeux ?
Ennuyeux ? Au contraire, il est très intéressant !

1. Cet exercice est-il difficile ?
2. Cette leçon est-elle courte ?
3. Cette classe est-elle petite ?
4. Cette chaise est-elle lourde ?
5. (Olivier) est-il paresseux ?
6. (Florence) est-elle bête ?
7. Est-ce que je suis pessimiste ?
8. Est-ce que je suis mécontent(e) ?

[1]**lui aussi** *he too, he also*

D *Maintenant, répondez aux questions d'après ce modèle.*

Êtes-vous paresseux(euse)[1] ?
Paresseux(euse) ? Mais non, je suis très travailleur(euse) !

1. Êtes-vous indiscret(ète) ?
2. Êtes-vous mécontent(e) ?
3. Cette chaise est-elle lourde ?
4. Tom Cruise est-il laid ?
5. La natation est-elle mauvaise pour la santé ?
6. Est-ce que je suis bête ?
7. Lee Iacocca est-il pauvre ?
8. Brooke Shields est-elle vieille ?
9. Beetle Bailey est-il travailleur ?
10. Donald Duck est-il pessimiste ?

 Dictée

 Compréhension auditive

8.3 CONNAÎTRE, SAVOIR

1. The verb **connaître** *to know* is used as an equivalent of *to be familiar with* or *to be acquainted with* (someone or something). It is *always* used with nouns that denote human beings, animals, and places. Note that the sound /s/ occurs only in the stem of the plural forms, and that the *accent circonflexe* (ˆ) occurs only before **t**.

connaître

connais	connaissons
connais	connaissez
connaît	connaissent

Je **connais** Sophie et Jean-Paul.
Tu ne **connais** pas ce journal ?
Il ne **connaît** pas mes parents.

Nous **connaissons** ce restaurant.
Vous **connaissez** bien mon copain.
Ils **connaissent** très bien la ville.

2. The verb **savoir** *to know* is used in the sense of *to find out* (something), or *to know thoroughly* through study, memorization, investigation, and inquiry, that is, more than just being familiar or acquainted with something. **Savoir** is *never* used with direct objects denoting human beings, animals, or places (for which **connaître** must be used). Note that the stem changes to /sav/ throughout the plural forms.

savoir

sais	savons
sais	savez
sait	savent

Je **sais** votre âge.
Tu **sais** la vérité ?
Elle ne **sait** pas la réponse.

Nous **savons** son numéro de téléphone.
Vous **savez** bien votre leçon.
Elles **savent** la date de ma fête.

3. The direct-object slot in statements with **savoir** may be filled by a dependent clause that begins with **que** *that*, **quand** *when*, **si** *if*, **pourquoi** *why*, or other question words. English has similar constructions.

Je sais { **la vérité.** / **que vous parlez espagnol.** / **quand elle va arriver.** }

I know { *the truth.* / *that you speak Spanish.* / *when she is going to arrive.* }

Savez-vous { **mon adresse ?** / **si elle va bien ?** / **pourquoi il est là ?** }

Do you know { *my address?* / *if she is well?* / *why he is there?* }

4. **Savoir** + infinitive corresponds to English *to know how to do (something)*. Note that in English the word *can* may imply either *to be able to* (physically, at a given moment, at a given place) or *to know how to*. But in French, a distinction must be maintained between **pouvoir** *to be able to* and **savoir** *to know how to*.

Je **sais nager**.
Je **peux nager** cet après-midi.

I can swim (I know how).
I can swim (I am able to) this afternoon.

[1]The alternative feminine form of adjectives will be indicated in Lessons 8 through 20.

Savez-vous **jouer** au tennis ?

Êtes-vous libre ? **Pouvez**-vous **jouer** au tennis avec nous ?

Can you play tennis (Do you know how to)?

Are you free? Can you (Are you able to) play tennis with us?

TABLEAU 44 Il ne **sait** pas faire du ski. Il ne **peut** pas faire du ski.

A *Exercice de contrôle*

Je connais bien mon professeur.

1. Nous 2. Tu 3. Les étudiants 4. (Paul)

Je ne connais pas bien Paris.[1]

1. Vous, Tokyo 2. Mon père, Paris 3. Nous, Londres[2] 4. Tu, Mexico[3]

Je ne sais pas toujours la réponse.

1. Les étudiants 2. Le professeur 3. Nous 4. Vous

Savez-vous s'il va neiger ?

1. Tu 2. Nous 3. Vous 4. Le professeur

Vous savez jouer au tennis.

1. Je 2. Nous 3. Tu 4. Mon ami(e)

B *Répondez aux questions.*

1. Connaissez-vous (Jean-Paul) ? Est-ce qu'il connaît vos parents ?
2. Connaissez-vous Paris ? Quelle ville connaissez-vous bien ?
3. Qui est-ce que vous connaissez bien ? Est-ce que je connais cette personne ?
4. Savez-vous ma nationalité ? Est-ce que je sais votre adresse ?
5. Savez-vous que je parle (anglais) ? Est-ce que je sais si vos parents parlent français ?
6. Savez-vous jouer au tennis ? Demandez à (Daniel) s'il sait jouer au basket. Demandez-moi si je sais jouer au golf.
7. Qui sait faire du ski ? Pouvez-vous faire du ski maintenant ? Demain ?

C *Répétez les expressions suivantes en ajoutant **Je sais**, **Je sais que**, ou **Je connais** devant chaque expression.*

1. ... mon voisin de droite.
2. ... il apprend le français.
3. ... son numéro de téléphone.
4. ... quel âge il a.
5. ... ses camarades.
6. ... son adresse.
7. ... mon professeur.
8. ... le journal *New York Times*.
9. ... faire du ski.
10. ... cette leçon.
11. ... compter de 1 à 100.
12. ... le cours n'est pas terminé.

Dictée

[1]Insert the name of each city in each sentence (example: **Vous ne connaissez pas bien Montréal** /mōʀeal/.).

[2]*London*

[3]*Mexico City*

8.4 ADJECTIF ATTRIBUT DU SUJET : PLURIEL ; LE PLURIEL DES NOMS -AUX, -EAUX

1. Most adjectives form their plural by adding **-s** to the singular form.

   Mon cousin est **petit**.   Ma cousine est **petite**.
   → Mes cousins sont **petits**.   → Mes cousines sont **petites**.
   Cet exercice est **long**.   Cette leçon est **longue**.
   → Ces exercices sont **longs**.   → Ces leçons sont **longues**.

2. If the masculine singular form already ends in **-s** or **-x**, no plural marker is added to the plural form. The feminine forms are not affected by this rule.

   Ce fruit est **mauvais**.   Cette orange est **mauvaise**.
   → Ces fruits sont **mauvais**.   → Ces oranges sont **mauvaises**.
   Cet hôtel est **vieux**.   Cette maison est **vieille**.
   → Ces hôtels sont **vieux**.   → Ces maisons sont **vieilles**.
   Cet étudiants est **heureux**.   Cette étudiante est **heureuse**.
   → Ces étudiants sont **heureux**.   → Ces étudiantes sont **heureuses**.

3. If the masculine singular form ends in **-al**, its ending changes to **-aux** in the plural. If it ends in **-eau**, it becomes **-eaux** in the plural. Again, the feminine form is not affected by this rule.

   Ce problème est **régional**.   Cette question est **régionale**.
   → Ces problèmes sont **régionaux**.   → Ces questions sont **régionales**.
   Cet arbre est **beau**.   Cette maison est **belle**.
   → Ces arbres sont **beaux**.   → Ces maisons sont **belles**.

4. If an adjective modifies two or more nouns consisting of masculine as well as feminine genders, the adjective assumes the masculine plural form.

   Paul est **travailleur**.   Il est **intelligent**.
   Marie est **travailleuse**.   Elle est **intelligente**.
   → Paul et Marie sont **travailleurs**.   → Ils sont **intelligents**.

5. *Nouns*. If a noun ends in **-al** or **-eau** in the singular, the plural is formed by changing the ending to **-aux** or **-eaux**. This parallels what you have seen in (3) above. You have already encountered examples such as **journal**/**journaux** and **morceau**/**morceaux**.

C'est un **animal** ; ce sont des **animaux**.	*It's an animal; they're animals.*
Voici un **journal** ; j'achète beaucoup de **journaux**.	*Here is a newspaper; I buy a lot of newspapers.*
Il mange un **morceau** de pain, puis deux **morceaux** de pain.	*He eats a piece of bread, then two pieces of bread.*
Regardez ce **tableau**[1], puis ces deux autres **tableaux**.	*Look at this picture, then at these two other pictures.*

6. *Listing of adjectives*. Look over the **Vocabulaire** of this lesson (p. 184). Note that only the masculine singular form is listed in full. The feminine form of an adjective is given in parentheses. This system—used in many dictionaries—is adopted in our lesson vocabularies as well as in the **Lexique** (*End Vocabulary*, beginning on p. V1). The explanation below is also intended as a summary and a review of the basic differences between the masculine and feminine forms that you have learned.

---

[1]The word **tableau** has several meanings, depending on the context: *blackboard* (also **tableau noir**), *picture*, and *chart*.

a) If there is no indication of the feminine form, then it is identical to the masculine form.

optimiste	*m* **optimiste**, *f* **optimiste**
sympathique	*m* **sympathique**, *f* **sympathique**

b) If the feminine form can be derived by adding **-e** to the masculine form, it is indicated by **(e)**.

petit(e)	*m* **petit**, *f* **petite**
froid(e)	*m* **froid**, *f* **froide**

c) If there is a change in the vowel preceding the last consonant before the addition of the feminine **-e**, the vowel is indicated.

premier(ière)	*m* **premier**, *f* **première**
discret(ète)	*m* **discret**, *f* **discrète**

d) If the masculine form ends in **-eux** or **-eur** and the feminine in **-euse**, the feminine ending is shown by **(euse)**.

heureux(euse)	*m* **heureux**, *f* **heureuse**
travailleur(euse)	*m* **travailleur**, *f* **travailleuse**

e) If the masculine form ends in **-if** and the feminine in **-ive**, the feminine is shown by **(ive)**.

actif(ive)	*m* **actif**, *f* **active**
attentif(ive)	*m* **attentif**, *f* **attentive**

f) If the feminine form doubles the final consonant of the masculine form before adding **-e**, it is shown by **(le)**, **(ne)**.

exceptionnel(le)	*m* **exceptionnel**, *f* **exceptionnelle**
parisien(ne)	*m* **parisien**, *f* **parisienne**

g) When the feminine form differs substantially from the masculine form (the adjective is usually very short), the entire feminine form is given in parentheses.

bon (bonne)	*m* **bon**, *f* **bonne**
long (longue)	*m* **long**, *f* **longue**
blanc (blanche)	*m* **blanc**, *f* **blanche**

A *Mettez le sujet de chaque phrase au pluriel, d'après ce modèle.*

Notre professeur n'est pas bête ; il est intelligent.
(Sophie) **Nos professeurs ne sont pas bêtes.**
(Hervé) **Ils sont intelligents.**

1. Notre professeur n'est pas paresseux ; il est travailleur.
2. Notre cours n'est pas ennuyeux ; il est intéressant.
3. Notre examen n'est pas écrit ; il est oral.
4. Ce problème n'est pas national ; il est régional.
5. Cette question n'est pas régionale ; elle est internationale.

B *Maintenant, ajoutez des phrases en employant les mots indiqués, d'après ce modèle.*

Mes tantes sont généreuses ; mes oncles
Mes oncles sont généreux.

1. Vos étudiantes sont travailleuses ; vos étudiants

2. Ces fêtes sont régionales ; ces journaux
3. Ces photos sont belles ; ces tableaux
4. Les questions sont sociales ; les problèmes
5. Les maisons sont anciennes ; les monuments
6. Ces activités sont orales ; ces exercices

C *Mettez les phrases suivantes au pluriel d'après le modèle.*

C'est un journal français.
Ce sont des journaux français.

1. C'est un animal dangereux.
2. C'est un sénateur libéral.
3. C'est un métal précieux.
4. Ce tableau est amusant.
5. C'est un morceau de pain.
6. Ce tableau est intéressant.
7. C'est un cheval blanc.
8. Cet hôpital est grand.

D *Quelle est votre opinion? Complétez les phrases suivantes avec votre partenaire.*

1. Morgan Fairchild est...
2. Michael Jackson est...
3. Notre campus est...
4. Nos résidences sont...
5. Les repas au resto-U sont...
6. Les chambres à la résidence sont...

📼 *Exercice supplémentaire*

📼 *Compréhension auditive*

📼 *Dictée*

8.5 PARTIR, SORTIR

1. **Partir** *to leave, to depart* and **sortir** *to go out* are conjugated in the same way. The consonant sound /t/ occurs only in the plural forms. These verbs are intransitive: they do not take a direct object and can occur without any other complement. To indicate a place, **partir** may be used with **de** (*from*) or **pour** (*for*), and **sortir**, with **de** (*from*).

partir	
pars	partons
pars	partez
part	partent

sortir	
sors	sortons
sors	sortez
sort	sortent

Je **pars**.
Tu **pars** de la maison.
Il **part** pour Montréal.
Nous **partons** demain soir.
Vous **partez** pour Québec.
Ils **partent** avec leurs parents.

Je **sors**.
Tu **sors** de la maison.
Elle **sort** ce soir.
Nous **sortons** demain soir.
Vous **sortez** de votre hôtel.
Elles **sortent** avec leurs parents.

2. **Quitter** also means *to leave* (a place or a person). It cannot be used without a direct object.

Je **sors** (de ma chambre).	*I go out (of my room).*
Je **pars** (de mon hôtel).	*I leave (my hotel).*
Je **pars** (de la gare) pour mon hôtel.	*I leave (the station) for my hotel.*
Je **quitte la gare** (pour aller à mon hôtel).	*I leave the station (to go to my hotel).*
Elle **quitte son mari.**	*She is leaving her husband.*

Ils partent en voyage.

A *Exercice de contrôle*

Je pars bientôt en vacances[1].
1. Vous
2. Ce touriste
3. Ces touristes
4. Tu

Je ne pars pas pour Montréal.
1. Nous
2. Ces touristes
3. Tu
4. Ce touriste

Je sors de la classe.
1. Nous
2. Tu
3. Les étudiants
4. Le professeur

B *Répondez aux questions.*

1. Sortez-vous ce soir ? Demandez à (Martine) si elle sort ce soir. Demandez-moi si je sors ce soir.
2. À quelle heure avez-vous votre premier cours ? À quelle heure partez-vous de la maison ? À quelle heure sortez-vous de ce cours ?
3. Quand est-ce que les vacances (de Noël)[2] commencent ? Quand partez-vous en vacances ?
4. Voici plusieurs phrases. Répétez chaque phrase. Ensuite, remplacez **partir** ou **sortir** par **quitter** quand c'est possible.

Je pars de Sherbrooke.	Sortez-vous ce soir ?
Elle part pour Montréal.	Nous partons à dix heures.
Sortons de la ville.	Il part en vacances demain.
On va sortir de Paris.	Je pars de Rome avec mes parents.

Compréhension auditive

---

[1]**partir en vacances** *to leave on vacation*
[2]**les vacances (de Noël)** *(Christmas) vacation*; on emploie le mot **vacances** au pluriel comme équivalent de *vacation*.

APPLICATIONS

« Voici ma famille : mon père, ma mère et mes deux sœurs. »

📼 **A** **Situations**

Voilà notre famille.

passer *to spend*

Jean-Paul et Monique invitent Christine à[1] passer° les vacances de Noël chez leurs parents. Ils habitent dans une grande maison près de Tours, une ville importante dans la vallée de la Loire. Les trois étudiants sont dans un café. Jean-Paul et Monique parlent de leur famille.

CHRISTINE   Vous êtes combien dans votre famille?[2]

MONIQUE   Nous sommes cinq. Attends, j'ai une photo dans mon portefeuille. Tiens, regarde.   5

à moustache *with a mustache*

Christine regarde la photo avec beaucoup d'intérêt. Sur la photo, il y a un monsieur à moustache°, une dame blonde, Monique et une autre jeune fille, et Jean-Paul.

[1]**inviter quelqu'un** *to invite someone;* **inviter** *takes* **à** *before an infinitive.*
[2]*How many are in your family?*

	MONIQUE	Voilà notre famille : nos parents, notre sœur et nous deux.
	CHRISTINE	Comment sont vos parents ?
athletic, fond of sports	JEAN-PAUL	Notre père est très gentil et sportif°. Il est architecte.
	CHRISTINE	Votre mère a l'air jeune[1].
	MONIQUE	Elle a quarante-deux ans. Elle est très sportive, comme papa.
	CHRISTINE	Est-ce qu'elle travaille ?
interior decorator	MONIQUE	Oui, elle est décoratrice°. Elle a beaucoup de clients.
What is her name?	CHRISTINE	Votre sœur ressemble beaucoup à Monique. Comment s'appelle-t-elle ?°
l'appelle *calls her*	JEAN-PAUL	Aurélie. Mais tout le monde l'appelle° Lili.
	CHRISTINE	Quel âge a-t-elle ?
	JEAN-PAUL	Elle a quinze ans. Elle est en Seconde au lycée[2].
	CHRISTINE	Elle aussi, elle a l'air sportive.
	MONIQUE	Ah oui, chez nous tout le monde aime le sport.
	JEAN-PAUL	C'est vrai. Lili est aussi très bonne en maths[3] et en physique, comme Monique.
	CHRISTINE	Qu'est-ce qu'elle a sur l'épaule ?
	JEAN-PAUL	C'est sa souris blanche. Elle aime beaucoup les animaux. Elle a aussi des poissons
goldfish		rouges°.
	CHRISTINE	Votre famille a l'air très sympa[4]. J'ai hâte de faire leur connaissance[5].

Répondez aux questions. (lignes 1–7)

1. Où est-ce que Christine va passer ses vacances ?
2. Quelle sorte de maison ont les Chabrier ?
3. Qu'est-ce que Monique a dans son portefeuille ?
4. Comment est-ce que Christine regarde la photo ?

(lignes 8–25)

5. Quelle est la profession de la mère de Monique ?
6. Quel âge a la sœur de Jean-Paul ?
7. Comment s'appelle-t-elle ?
8. À qui est-ce que Lili ressemble beaucoup ?
9. Quel animal a-t-elle sur l'épaule ?
10. Qu'est-ce que Christine a hâte de faire ?

[1]*seems/looks young.* **Avoir l'air** + adjective corresponds to English *to seem/look* + adjective. The adjective may remain invariable (*m, s*), or may agree in gender and number with the subject.

[2]**Lycée** is a public school in France, more or less an equivalent of the American high school. French students begin their education at the age of six. The first grade is **la Onzième**, the second **la Dixième**, the third **la Neuvième**, and so on, counting backwards. The last two grades are **la Première** and **la (Classe) Terminale**, approximately corresponding to the first one or two years of college in the United States in terms of academic work.

[3]**maths** /mat/ = mathématiques

[4]**sympa** = sympathique; **sympa** is invariable, and the same form is used regardless of the noun's gender or number.

[5]**avoir hâte de** + infinitif *to be eager to do*; **faire la connaissance de quelqu'un** *to meet someone* (literally, *to make the acquaintance of someone*)

B   Expressions utiles

La famille

les parents : { le père (papa) } { le mari
              { la mère (maman) } { la femme

les enfants : { le fils } { le frère
             { la fille } { la sœur

les parents[1] : { l'oncle } { le neveu } { le cousin
               { la tante } { la nièce } { la cousine

les grands-parents : { le grand-père
                    { la grand-mère

les petits-enfants : { le petit-fils
                    { la petite-fille

être { marié(e) / divorcé(e)
     { célibataire
     { veuf / veuve

ressembler   }
ne pas ressembler   } (beaucoup) à quelqu'un

avoir l'air { sympathique (sympa)
            { intelligent

Les couleurs (1)[2]

De quelle couleur[3] sont vos yeux ?
→ J'ai les yeux bleus[4] (bruns / noirs / gris).
De quelle couleur sont vos cheveux[5] ?
→ J'ai les cheveux bruns (noirs / blonds / châtains / roux / gris).

C   Pratique

Daniel Jourlait est professeur de français. Il est marié. Il parle de sa famille et de ses parents. Complétez les phrases avec les termes de parenté appropriés.[6]

1. Je suis marié et j'ai deux enfants, Jean-Pierre et Sophie. Jean-Pierre est mon (   ), et Sophie, ma (   ). Je suis leur (   ). Ma femme Anne est leur (   ). Nous sommes leurs (   ).
2. Ma sœur Pascale a une fille. Elle s'appelle Martine. Je suis l'(   ) de Martine, et elle est ma (   ). Pascale est la (   ) de mes enfants. Mes enfants sont les (   ) de Martine.
3. Mes parents habitent près de Paris. Ma mère est la (   ) de mes enfants, et mon père, leur (   ). Sophie est la (   ) de mes parents, et Jean-Pierre est leur (   ). Pascale est ma (   ) et la (   ) de mes parents.

---

[1]**Parents** can mean either *parents* or *relatives*. The context usually clears up any ambiguity.

[2]D'autres adjectifs de couleur sont dans les *Expressions utiles* de la Leçon 11 (p. 250).

[3]*What color*; remarquez l'emploi de **de** dans cette expression.

[4]*I have blue eyes*; remarquez l'emploi de l'article défini.

[5]On emploie le mot **cheveux** *hair* au pluriel.

[6]*Complete the sentences with the appropriate kinship (**parenté**) terms.*

D **Mini-composition** : *Une photo de ma famille. Complétez le passage. Faites attention au genre de chaque nom.*[1]

(1) Vous/ne pas/connaître/mon/famille,/n'est-ce pas ? (2) Je/avoir/un/photo/mon/famille/dans/mon/portefeuille. (3) Mon/père/être/professeur/anglais/et/enseigner[2]/à/université. (4) Mon/mère/avoir/39/ans ;/elle/être/institutrice[3]. (5) Elle/être/très/gentil/et/patient. (6) Ce/jeune fille/entre[4]/mon/père/et/mon/mère/être/mon/sœur. (7) Elle/avoir/16/ans. (8) Elle/être/très/intelligent/et/sportif. (9) Mon/parents/habiter/dans/un/grand/maison/près de/Aix-en-Provence. (10) Ce/voiture/derrière/mon/famille/être/un/Renault[5]. (11) Il y a/un/très/grand/arbre/entre/le/voiture/et/le/maison. (12) Ce/arbre/avoir/90/ans.

E **Questions** : *Ma sœur fait ses études*[6] *en France. Lisez d'abord le passage, puis posez des questions sur les parties soulignées.*

Savez-vous que ma sœur Christine est en France ? Elle habite (1) à Paris. Elle vient d'envoyer (2) cette photo à mes parents. (3) Ma sœur est devant la voiture rouge. Elle a les cheveux (4) bruns. Elle a les yeux (5) bleus. Elle a (6) vingt et un ans. Le jeune homme à gauche de Christine est (7) Jean-Paul. Il étudie (8) la littérature américaine. Monique, sa sœur, est à droite de Christine. Ils sont (9) français. Christine aime beaucoup (10) Jean-Paul et Monique.

F **Portrait** : *Apportez la photo d'une personne. Faites une description de cette personne, y compris*[7] *les renseignements suivants.*

son nom	son passe-temps préféré[8]
son âge	sa personnalité
la couleur de ses yeux	ses défauts
la couleur de ses cheveux	ses qualités

G **Renseignements et opinions**

1. Est-ce que vous sortez ce soir ? Qui ne va pas sortir ce soir ?
2. De quelle couleur sont vos cheveux ? De quelle couleur sont mes cheveux ?
3. De quelle couleur sont vos yeux ? De quelle couleur sont mes yeux ?
4. Est-ce que je connais votre famille ? Combien êtes-vous dans votre famille ? Quels sont les membres de votre famille ? Quel âge ont-ils ?
5. Qui voulez-vous connaître ? Pourquoi ?
6. À qui pensez-vous souvent ? Qui est cette personne ?
7. Qu'est-ce que vous savez de moi ?[9]
8. Qu'est-ce que vous savez du président des États-Unis ?[10]

---

[1] *Pay attention to the gender of each noun*; they are intentionally left masculine throughout this passage; the modifiers of feminine nouns must be changed accordingly (for example: **un photo** must be **une photo**, **mon famille** must be **ma famille**, etc.).

[2] **enseigner** *to teach*

[3] **instituteur** *m*, **institutrice** *f* *schoolteacher*

[4] *between*

[5] All car names are feminine in French.

[6] **faire des études** = étudier

[7] **y compris** *including*

[8] *his/her hobby, favorite pastime* (*pl* **ses passe-temps préférés**)

[9] *What do you know about me?* Par exemple : **Je sais que vous parlez français. Je sais que vous êtes américain(e)**, etc.

[10] Par exemple : **Je sais qu'il habite à la Maison Blanche.**

Compréhension auditive (basée sur l'Application A)

Compréhension auditive (basée sur l'Application B)

Dictée : « Une photo de ma famille » (basée sur les Applications D et E)

H Lecture

The last section of the Applications *in Lessons 8–11 and 13–25 will consist of short reading passages. In order to increase your reading proficiency, you might try the following procedure: it involves at least three readings of the passage: quick–slow–quick.*

1. *Read the text quickly to get a general idea of what it is about. Don't look up any word, but try to guess the meaning from the context.*
2. *Read again, this time carefully, underlining the words and phrases you don't know. Wait until you reach a punctuation mark before looking up the meaning of underlined words. Jot down their meaning in the margin. If there are phrases you simply cannot understand, mark them and ask your instructor about them in class.*
3. *Read again, fairly rapidly, making sure that you understand the text (except for any parts you plan to ask your instructor about). Then do the exercises that are assigned as homework.*

Le climat de la France est très varié.

Où est la France ?

La France, située à l'extrémité occidentale[1] de l'Europe, occupe une situation géographique privilégiée. On la compare souvent à un hexagone. Trois côtés de cet hexagone sont des frontières maritimes avec beaucoup de ports. Deux chaînes de montagnes, les Pyrénées et les Alpes, forment deux autres côtés. Le dernier côté rattache la France à l'Allemagne et à la Belgique. Cette immense plaine commence dans le nord-est de la France et continue à 5
across / up to, until   travers° la Belgique, l'Allemagne et la Pologne jusqu'en° Russie. C'est donc le côté « faible » de la France puisqu'il n'y a pas de « barrière » naturelle qui sépare la France des autres pays.
/Rəljɛf/ *topography*   Le relief° de la France est varié. Les Pyrénées et les Alpes sont des chaînes de très hautes
Other / hence   montagnes. D'autres° montagnes occupent le centre du pays, d'où° leur nom de *Massif Central.*
verdant   Les vallées de ses quatre grands fleuves[2] sont riches et verdoyantes° : La Loire et la Garonne 10
se jeter *to empty*   se jettent° dans l'océan Atlantique, la Seine dans la Manche, et le Rhône dans la mer Méditerranée. Le climat du pays est varié comme son relief : par exemple, il est maritime dans l'Ouest (doux en hiver, frais en été), méditerranéen dans le Sud (très doux en hiver, très sec et chaud en été), continental dans l'Est (très froid et très chaud).
which / cent mille   La France a 34 villes qui° dépassent 100.000° habitants (138 aux États-Unis). Dans la 15

[1]adjectif de **ouest**

[2]A **fleuve** *m* is a river that ends in a sea; a **rivière** *f* is its tributary.

mouth (of a river)

road

hiérarchie des villes, Paris, la capitale politique, économique et culturelle, est au sommet. Viennent ensuite Marseille (un port très important à l'embouchure° du Rhône), Lyon (sur la grande route° entre Paris et Marseille), Toulouse (sur la route entre l'océan Atlantique et la Méditerranée), Nice (sur la Méditerranée), Bordeaux (à l'embouchure de la Garonne), Lille (dans le nord, région industrielle). Le gouvernement favorise leur développement pour réduire 20 la domination de Paris sur la vie du pays entier.

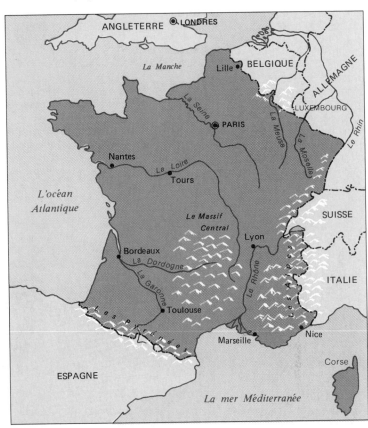

TABLEAU 45

A   *Mettez les mots appropriés dans les parenthèses.*

1. Un (   ) est une forme géométrique qui a six côtés.
2. La chaîne de montagnes qui sépare la France de l'Espagne s'appelle (   ).
3. On trouve (   ) entre la France et l'Italie.
4. Les hivers sont doux dans (   ) et (   ) de la France.
5. Les frontières maritimes de la France sont (   ), (   ) et (   ).
6. La Garonne est (   ), mais la Moselle est (   ).
7. Une frontière sans barrière naturelle sépare la France de (   ) et de (   ).
8. (   ) et (   ) sont à l'embouchure de deux grands fleuves.

B   *Indiquez si chaque commentaire est vrai ou faux. S'il est faux, corrigez le commentaire.*

1. La France a six côtés, et trois de ses côtés sont des frontières maritimes.
2. La Pologne est un des pays voisins de la France.
3. La plaine qui commence dans le nord-ouest de la France continue jusqu'en Russie.
4. Les Pyrénées sont une chaîne de montagnes entre la France et l'Italie.
5. Le Massif Central est une chaîne de montagnes qui occupe le centre de la France.
6. La Seine est une rivière qui se jette dans l'océan Atlantique.
7. Le climat de la France, comme son relief, n'est pas très varié.
8. Marseille, à l'embouchure de la Loire, est un port important.

C *Indiquez le mot qui n'appartient pas à chaque série et dites pourquoi.*

1. la mer, le fleuve, la montagne, l'océan, la rivière
2. la Loire, la Manche, le Rhône, la Seine, la Garonne
3. Marseille, Toulouse, Lyon, Paris, Londres
4. sommet, froid, sec, chaud, frais, doux
5. nord, sud, côté, est, ouest
6. l'Angleterre, la Belgique, la Pologne, la Russie, l'Allemagne

VOCABULAIRE

Noms

une **activité**	activity	la **grand-mère**	grandmother	un **oncle**	uncle
l'**aérobique** f	aerobics	le **grand-père**	grandfather	un papa	dad
un **animal**	animal	les **grands-parents** m	grandparents	le **patinage**	skating
un architecte	architect	la hâte	haste	la **photo**	photo
la **banane**	banana	un intérêt	interest	la physique	physics
le **cheval**	horse	le **journal**	newspaper	le **poisson**	fish
la connaissance	knowledge; acquaintance	la Loire	Loire River	le poisson rouge	goldfish
le(la) **cousin(e)**	cousin	**Londres**	London	le portefeuille	wallet
le décorateur	interior decorator	le lycée	French high school	le **problème**	problem
la décoratrice	interior decorator	les maths f	math	la **santé**	health
une épaule	shoulder	la **matière**	subject	la Seconde	fifth year in lycée
les **épinards** m	spinach	le **métal**	metal		
la **femme**	woman; wife	**Mexico**	Mexico City	le **sénateur**	senator
la **fille**	daughter	le monsieur	gentleman	la souris	mouse
le **fils**	son	**Montréal**	Montreal	la **tante**	aunt
		la moustache	mustache		

Verbes

connaître irrég	to know; to be familiar with	**passer**	to spend	**savoir** irrég	to know (how to)
partir irrég	to leave; to depart	**remplacer**	to replace	**sortir** irrég	to go (come) out
		ressembler (à)	to resemble		

Adjectifs

actif(ive)	active	**grand(e)**	tall; great	**parisien(ne)**	Parisian
amusant(e)	amusing	**heureux(euse)**	happy	**pauvre**	poor
ancien(ne)	old	important(e)	important	**pessimiste**	pessimistic
bête	stupid, dumb	**indiscret(ète)**	indiscreet	**plusieurs**	several
blanc (blanche)	white	**international(e)**	international	**possible**	possible
blond(e)	blond	**laid(e)**	ugly	**précieux(euse)**	precious
composé(e)	mixed; composed	**léger(ère)**	light	**régional(e)**	regional
content(e)	content, glad	**libéral(e)**	liberal	**riche**	rich
court(e)	short	**long (longue)**	long	rouge	red
dangereux(euse)	dangerous	**lourd(e)**	heavy	**social(e)**	social
discret(ète)	discreet	**malheureux(euse)**	unhappy	sportif(ive)	athletic, fond of sports
écrit(e)	written	**mécontent(e)**	dissatisfied	**sympa**	nice, likeable
énergique	energetic	**optimiste**	optimistic	**travailleur(euse)**	hardworking, industrious
ennuyeux(euse)	boring	**oral(e)**	oral	**utile**	useful
généreux(euse)	generous	**paresseux(euse)**	lazy		

Adverbes

bientôt	soon	**mieux**	better

Autres expressions

avoir hâte de + inf	to be eager to + inf	**lui aussi**	he (him) too
avoir l'air + adj	to seem, look + adj	**partir en vacances**	to leave (go) on a vacation
faire la connaissance de qqn	to make somebody's acquaintance		

9 Allons au Canada !

LESSON OBJECTIVES

Theme and Culture

1. City layout, buildings, and monuments
2. French Canada
3. The French in the early history of North America

Communication Skills

1. Reading a simple city map
2. Asking for/Giving street directions
3. Thanking people and responding to thanks
4. Using direct-object pronouns instead of nouns
5. Expressing events and activities in the past (*yesterday, two days ago, last week, last year*)
6. Understanding large numbers and expressing dates

Structures

1. Direct-object pronouns
2. *Passé composé* with **avoir**
3. Agreement of the past participle with the direct object
4. *Passé composé* with **être**
5. Cardinal numbers (beyond 1000) and dates

CONVERSATIONS

A. À Québec

Nous sommes à Québec, capitale du Québec[1]. Quelle ville passionnante ![2] Il y a des remparts, de vieux quartiers[3] avec des maisons pittoresques, aussi bien que[4] des quartiers ultramodernes. Regardez le plan à la page 186. Il montre une partie des vieux quartiers de la ville. La ville est entourée de[5] remparts.

Vous êtes entré(e) dans la ville par la porte Saint-Louis. Vous avez garé votre voiture dans le parking près du bureau de tourisme. Trouvez le bureau de tourisme sur le plan.

Vous voulez d'abord visiter la Citadelle. Vous prenez la rue d'Auteuil jusqu'à[6] la rue Saint-Louis. Là, vous tournez à droite. Puis, juste avant la porte Saint-Louis, vous prenez la première rue à gauche. Elle s'appelle la Côte de la Citadelle. Elle mène à l'entrée de la Citadelle. Maintenant, répondez à ces questions.

[1] **Québec** (sans l'article défini) désigne la ville ; **le Québec** designe la province.
[2] *What an exciting city!*
[3] **vieux quartier**   *Old Town* (les vieux quartiers pittoresques et historiques d'une ville)
[4] **aussi bien que**   *as well as*
[5] *surrounded by, with*
[6] *until, up to*

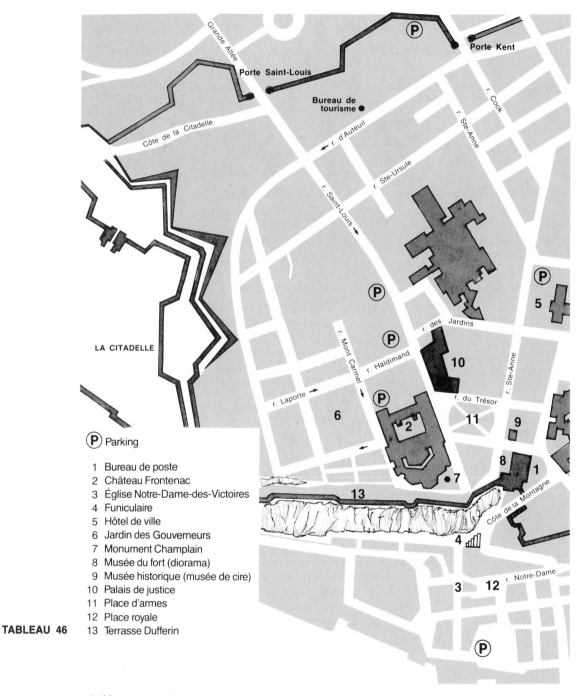

P Parking

1 Bureau de poste
2 Château Frontenac
3 Église Notre-Dame-des-Victoires
4 Funiculaire
5 Hôtel de ville
6 Jardin des Gouverneurs
7 Monument Champlain
8 Musée du fort (diorama)
9 Musée historique (musée de cire)
10 Palais de justice
11 Place d'armes
12 Place royale
13 Terrasse Dufferin

TABLEAU 46

1. Vous venez de visiter la Citadelle. Vous voulez aller au Musée du fort, où il y a un diorama. Trouvez ce musée sur le plan. Comment va-t-on de la Citadelle au Musée du fort ?
2. Vous sortez du Musée du fort. Vous cherchez maintenant un autre musée. Il s'appelle le Musée historique. C'est un musée de figures de cire. Est-il près ou loin du Musée du fort ?

Le Château Frontenac.

3. Vous avez visité le vieux quartier en bas[1] où il y a beaucoup de boutiques de souvenirs. Trouvez le funiculaire. Vous prenez le funiculaire et vous montez. Où êtes-vous maintenant ?[2] Comment s'appelle le grand et beau bâtiment devant vous ?[3]

4. Vous avez soif. Vous allez au café du Château Frontenac et vous prenez quelque chose de rafraîchissant[4]. Maintenant, vous voulez aller à l'Hôtel de ville[5]. Quelles rues prenez-vous ?

B. Je cherche ma montre.

MICHEL   Qu'est-ce que tu cherches ?

ALAIN   Je cherche ma montre.

MICHEL   Attends, je vais t'aider... (*deux minutes plus tard*[6]) Je l'ai trouvée. Elle est dans la cuisine.

ALAIN   Ah oui, c'est vrai. Je l'ai laissée sur la table ce matin.

C. Qu'est-ce que tu as fait dimanche après-midi ?

CLAUDE   Qu'est-ce que tu as fait dimanche après-midi ?

SYLVIE   Mes parents et moi, nous avons joué au golf miniature.

CLAUDE   Ah oui ? Et après ?

SYLVIE   Après, nous sommes allés dans un café.

Compréhension auditive (basée sur la Conversation A)

[1]*down below*

[2]**La terrasse Dufferin** is a wide and long boardwalk in front of the Château Frontenac at the very edge of the cliff overlooking the St. Lawrence River (**le Saint-Laurent**).

[3]*Ce grand hôtel date de la fin du dix-neuvième siècle.*

[4]*something cool and refreshing*

[5]*City Hall*

[6]**plus tard**   *later*

Une des portes de la ville de Québec.

« Voulez-vous visiter le Musée du Fort ? »

DIFFÉRENCES

Je me souviens[1]

France once maintained a vast territory in North America, called **la Nouvelle-France**. (You will read more about the French in early America in the *Lecture* of this lesson.) Britain, through a series of military campaigns and diplomatic moves, eventually took control of **la Nouvelle-France** by the mid-eighteenth century. Through **l'Acte de Québec** (1774), the French retained the rights to their language, civil law, and religion in what was to become the province of Quebec. Today a little over one-quarter of Canada's population consists of French Canadians. Quebec is the largest of the ten provinces in Canada in terms of area, and the second largest after Ontario in population. Montreal is the second largest French-speaking city in the world, after Paris. French is also spoken in parts of New Brunswick, Ontario, and Manitoba.

Much of the industry and natural resources of Quebec have been traditionally in the hands of English-speaking Canadian (about 20% of Quebec's population) and U.S. corporations. Access to high-paying jobs was often denied to French Canadians. The resentment toward the Anglo-Saxon dominance in economy, politics, and culture culminated in the formation of **le Parti Québécois** in 1968. In 1974 the provincial government voted to make French the only official language, and **le Parti Québécois** pledged to seek independence for Quebec. The language legislation was intended to guarantee French as the official language of the province and protect the French-speaking people. But in reality, in terms of commerce and education, it resulted in the departure of some large corporations, as well as part of the English-speaking population, and was subsequently declared unconstitutional by the supreme court of Canada. Recent polls have shown a notable decline in support for the separatist movement. The referendum for the independence of Quebec failed in 1980, and in 1985 **le Parti Québécois** deferred indefinitely the question of sovereignty for Quebec.

[1] *I remember*; official motto (**la devise**) of the province of Quebec (you will find it, for example, on license plates)

STRUCTURES

9.1 PRONOM PERSONNEL COMPLÉMENT D'OBJET DIRECT

The distinction between direct and indirect objects, which you learned in Lesson 6.2, plays a very important role in the use of all pronouns. You applied it to interrogative pronouns in Lessons 6.4 and 7.1. You will learn to apply it to object pronouns in this as well as later lessons. Before proceeding, you might want to review Lesson 6.2, paying special attention to the French verbs that do not have the same patterns as the corresponding verbs in English.

1. *Third person.* The object pronouns for the third person (English *him, her, it, them*) are identical in form with the definite article: **le, la, l', les**. You replace a masculine singular noun with **le**, a feminine singular noun with **la**, and any plural noun with **les**, provided the noun is *not* preceded by an indefinite or a partitive article. The object pronoun is placed immediately before the verb, and **le** or **la** becomes **l'** if the verb begins with a vowel sound.

Je comprends **le professeur**.	*I understand **the professor**.*
→ Je **le** comprends.	*→ I understand **him**.*
Vous savez **la réponse**.	*You know **the answer**.*
→ Vous **la** savez.	*→ You know **it**.*
Daniel aime **la musique**.	*Daniel likes **music**.*
→ Daniel **l'**aime.	*→ Daniel likes **it**.*
Nous connaissons **ces pays**.	*We know **these countries**.*
→ Nous **les** connaissons.	*→ We know **them**.*

Clauses introduced by such words as **que** *that*, **pourquoi** *why*, **quand** *when*, and **où** *where* can be replaced by **le**; it corresponds to English *it*.

Je sais **que Michel est français**.	Savez-vous **quand elle va arriver** ?
→ Je **le** sais.	→ **Le** savez-vous ?
Tu comprends **pourquoi je suis venue**.	Elles savent **où je suis**.
→ Tu **le** comprends.	→ Elles **le** savent.

2. *First and second persons.* The direct-object pronouns for the first- and second-person singular (English *me, you*) are **me** and **te**. Those for the plural (English *us, you*) are **nous** and **vous**. They all come before the verb, and **me** or **te** becomes **m'** or **t'** if the verb begins with a vowel sound.

Robert **me** connaît.	*Robert knows me.*
Mes camarades **m'**attendent.	*My friends are waiting for me.*
Nous **te** comprenons.	*We understand you.*
Jean-Paul **t'**adore.	*Jean-Paul loves you.*
Vos parents **nous** cherchent.	*Your parents are looking for us.*
Parlez. Je **vous** écoute.	*Speak. I'm listening to you.*

3. *Negation and inversion.* In negative sentences, **ne** comes *before* the combination object pronoun + verb, and **pas** after the verb. In inversion, **pas** comes after the inverted subject pronoun.

Tu attends l'autobus.	Vous **me** comprenez.
→ Tu **ne** l'attends **pas**.	→ Vous **ne me** comprenez **pas**.
→ **Ne** l'attends-tu **pas** ?	→ **Ne me** comprenez-vous **pas** ?

4. *With an infinitive.* If an infinitive (preceded by a conjugated verb form) takes a direct-object pronoun, the pronoun is placed immediately before the infinitive.

Je vais **visiter l'Espagne**.	*I'm going to visit Spain.*
→ Je vais **la visiter**.	→ *I'm going to **visit it**.*
Elle peut **apprendre cette leçon**.	*She can learn this lesson.*
→ Elle peut **l'apprendre**.	→ *She can **learn it**.*
Nous ne voulons pas **manger ces pommes**.	*We don't want to eat these apples.*
→ Nous ne voulons pas **les manger**.	→ *We don't want to **eat them**.*

5. When you hear **nous** or **vous** and a verb, do not conclude automatically that it is the *subject* of the sentence. It can also be the *object*. The verb will give you a clue since it must always agree in person (first/second/third) and number (singular/plural) with the subject.

SUBJECT	DIRECT OBJECT
Nous les **attendons**.	Ils **nous** attendent.
Nous ne la **comprenons** pas.	**Nous** comprend-elle ?
Vous me **connaissez**.	Est-ce qu'il **vous** connaît ?
Vous détestez Jean-Pierre.	Jean-Pierre **vous** déteste-t-il ?

6. The expressions **voilà** and **voici** can also take a direct-object pronoun (see Exercise B below).[1]

Où est Marie ? Ah, **la voilà**.	*Where is Marie? Oh, there she is!*
Où sont-ils ? Ah, **les voici**.	*Where are they? Oh, here they are!*
Vous voilà, enfin.	*There you are, finally.*

TABLEAU 47

Le comprend-elle ?
Elle **le** comprend.

A *Remplacez chaque objet direct par le pronom approprié, d'après ce modèle.*

Je comprends le professeur.
Je le comprends.

1. Je comprends mon copain.
2. Je comprends mes parents.
3. Je ne comprends pas la question.
4. Nous aimons Sissy Spacek.

[1]**Voici** *here is/are* is used with persons and objects nearest to the speaker, while **voilà** is generally used for persons and things away from the speaker.

5. Nous aimons beaucoup les vacances.
6. Nous n'aimons pas les examens.
7. Je vais visiter la France.

8. Vas-tu apprendre cette leçon ?
9. Voulez-vous regarder la télé ?
10. Je ne veux pas faire les devoirs.

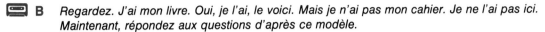

B *Regardez. J'ai mon livre. Oui, je l'ai, le voici. Mais je n'ai pas mon cahier. Je ne l'ai pas ici. Maintenant, répondez aux questions d'après ce modèle.*

Avez-vous votre cahier ?
Mon cahier ? Oui, je l'ai ; le voici. (*ou* Mon cahier ? Non, je ne l'ai pas ici.)

1. Avez-vous votre livre ?
2. Avez-vous votre portefeuille ?
3. Avez-vous votre stéréo ?
4. Avez-vous votre parapluie ?

5. Avez-vous vos cartes de crédit ?
6. Avez-vous votre montre ?
7. Avez-vous vos disques[1] ?
8. Avez-vous votre carte d'identité[2] ?

C *Répondez aux questions.*

1. Est-ce que vous me connaissez ? Est-ce que je vous connais ? Est-ce que je connais vos parents ?
2. Est-ce que je vous comprends ? Me comprenez-vous ? Est-ce que je comprends (le chinois) ?
3. Faites-vous toujours votre lit ? Faites-vous toujours vos devoirs ? Est-ce que le président fait toujours son travail ?
4. À quelle heure allez-vous prendre votre dîner ce soir ? Demandez-moi quand je vais le prendre.
5. Pouvez-vous comprendre mes questions ? Est-ce que je peux comprendre vos questions ?

Exercice supplémentaire

Compréhension auditive

9.2 PASSÉ COMPOSÉ AVEC L'AUXILIAIRE **AVOIR**

The *passé composé* is a verb tense denoting actions completed in the past. In construction, it corresponds to the present perfect in English, that is, *have* + past participle as in *I have spoken*, *She has done*. The *passé composé* consists of two elements: the present tense of the auxiliary ("helping") verb **avoir** or **être**, and the past participle of the verb that expresses the action. Verbs that take **avoir** are discussed below. Those that take **être** will be presented in Lesson 9.4. Review the conjugation of **avoir** first.

avoir

ai	avons
as	avez
a	ont

1. The past participle of regular verbs is formed by replacing the infinitive endings **-er**, **-ir**, **-re** with **-é**, **-i**, **-u**, respectively. Note how **parler**, **finir**, and **répondre** are conjugated in the *passé composé*.

parler → parlé	**finir → fini**	**répondre → répondu**
j'**ai parlé**	j'**ai fini**	j'**ai répondu**
tu **as parlé**	tu **as fini**	tu **as répondu**
il **a parlé**	elle **a fini**	il **a répondu**
nous **avons parlé**	nous **avons fini**	nous **avons répondu**
vous **avez parlé**	vous **avez fini**	vous **avez répondu**
ils **ont parlé**	elles **ont fini**	ils **ont répondu**

[1]*records*
[2]**carte d'identité** *identification (ID) card*

The *passé composé* usually corresponds to three English constructions; the most common equivalent is the first one.

J'ai parlé. ⎰ *I spoke.*
⎱ *I have spoken.*
  I did speak.

Vous avez répondu. ⎰ *You answered.*
⎱ *You have answered.*
  You did answer.

Elle a rencontré son copain. Ils ont bavardé pendant quelques minutes.

2. Below is a list of irregular verbs you have learned so far that are conjugated with **avoir**. This list must be thoroughly memorized.

   a) **-u** ending

avoir	*to have*	J'ai **eu** /y/ un accident.
boire	*to drink*	J'ai **bu** un verre d'eau.
connaître	*to know*[1]	J'ai **connu** plusieurs Français.
pleuvoir	*to rain*	Il a **plu** hier soir.
pouvoir	*to be able*	J'ai **pu** finir mon travail.
savoir	*to know*[2]	J'ai **su** la vérité.
tenir[3]	*to hold, keep*	J'ai **tenu** ma promesse.
vouloir	*to want*	J'ai **voulu** téléphoner à Paul.

---

[1] Le verbe **connaître**, employé au passé composé, signifie *to meet*.

[2] Le verbe **savoir**, employé au passé composé, est un équivalent de *to find out*.

[3] **Venir** *to come* is conjugated with **être** in the *passé composé* (see Lesson 9.4).

b) **-is** ending

apprendre	*to learn*	Vous avez **appris** la leçon.
comprendre	*to understand*	Vous avez **compris** ma question.
prendre	*to take*	Vous avez **pris** mon parapluie.

c) other

être	*to be*	Elle a **été** très contente.
faire	*to do*	Elle a **fait** ses devoirs.

3. *Negation*. The negative construction is subject + **ne** + auxiliary + **pas** + past participle. In other words, you "negate" the auxiliary by putting **ne** and **pas** around it, then you add the past participle.

J'**ai** fini mon travail.

→ Je **n'ai pas** fini mon travail.

Elle **a** voyagé en Espagne.

→ Elle **n'a pas** voyagé en Espagne.

Nous **avons** compris la vérité.

→ Nous **n'avons pas** compris la vérité.

Ils **ont** vendu leur maison.

→ Ils **n'ont pas** vendu leur maison.

4. *Inversion*. Inversion in questions occurs between the subject pronoun and the auxiliary.

AFFIRMATIVE

Tu as voyagé au Canada.

→ **As-tu** voyagé au Canada ?

Vous avez été à Montréal.

→ **Avez-vous** été à Montréal ?

Marie a visité l'Italie.

→ **Marie a-t-elle** visité l'Italie ?

NEGATIVE

Tu n'as pas voyagé au Canada.

→ **N'as-tu pas** voyagé au Canada ?

Vous n'avez pas été à Montréal.

→ **N'avez-vous pas** été à Montréal ?

Marie n'a pas visité l'Italie.

→ **Marie n'a-t-elle** pas visité l'Italie ?

Qu'est-ce que **tu as fait** hier soir ?   Moi ? **J'ai travaillé**.   (Mais non, tu **as regardé** la télévision.)

TABLEAU 48

A   *Exercice de contrôle*

J'ai regardé la télé hier soir.

1. Nous   2. Tu   3. Le professeur   4. Vous

Je n'ai pas fini mon travail.

1. Vous   2. Le professeur   3. Tu   4. Nous

As-tu fait ton travail ?

1. Nous   2. Vous   3. Cet étudiant   4. Ces étudiants

B *Répondez aux questions d'après ce modèle.*

> Allez-vous déjeuner bientôt ?
> **Non, j'ai déjà déjeuné.**[1]

1. Allez-vous travailler bientôt ?
2. Allez-vous manger bientôt ?
3. Allez-vous finir votre travail bientôt ?
4. (Gisèle) va-t-elle prendre son petit déjeuner ?
5. (Robert) va-t-il choisir mon cours ?
6. Allons-nous étudier la Leçon 8 ?

C *Martine Leroux, une étudiante française, veut acheter une voiture d'occasion*[2]. *Elle est avec son copain Laurent. Écoutez ces phrases et mettez chaque verbe au passé composé.*

(1) Nous cherchons le vendeur. (2) Nous attendons le vendeur. (3) Nous parlons au vendeur. (4) Il montre des voitures. (5) Nous regardons plusieurs voitures. (6) Nous posons des questions. (7) Nous choisissons une Toyota. (8) Martine veut essayer la voiture. (9) Le vendeur donne les clés à Martine. (10) Elle prend le volant. (11) J'écoute le moteur. (12) Nous essayons la voiture. (13) Martine achète la voiture. (14) Elle paie la voiture au vendeur.

D *Répondez aux questions d'après ce modèle. Remarquez que votre camarade va être en contradiction avec vous.*

> Avez-vous voyagé en Europe ?
> (Marianne) **Bien sûr, j'ai voyagé en Europe.**
> (Robert) **Mais non, tu n'as pas voyagé en Europe !**

1. Avez-vous visité Tokyo ?
2. Avez-vous appris la Leçon 10 ?
3. Avez-vous voyagé en Afrique ?
4. Avez-vous appris le japonais ?
5. Avez-vous pu aller à Paris ?
6. Avez-vous été à Marseille ?
7. Avez-vous pris votre dîner ?
8. A-t-il plu (hier) ?

E *Maintenant, parlons d'hier soir. Posez des questions à votre partenaire. Ensuite, faites un compte-rendu de votre interview.*

1. À quelle heure as-tu dîné hier soir ? Où as-tu dîné ? Qu'est-ce que tu as mangé ? Qu'est-ce que tu as bu ?
2. Après le dîner, as-tu téléphoné à quelqu'un ? À quelle heure as-tu téléphoné ? Qui est cette personne ?
3. Qu'est-ce que tu as fait hier soir ? As-tu travaillé ? As-tu regardé la télé ? Quelle émission ? As-tu pu faire tes devoirs ?

Compréhension auditive

Compréhension auditive

9.3 ACCORD DU PARTICIPE PASSÉ

1. The past participle of verbs that take a direct object (conjugated with **avoir** in the *passé composé*) agrees in gender (*m/f*) and number (*s/pl*) with the direct object if it *precedes* the verb. There are two cases.

---

[1]Note that **déjà** *already* is placed between the auxiliary verb and the past participle.
[2]**d'occasion** *used, second-hand*

a) The direct object is a pronoun.

J'ai **acheté** cette voiture.

→ Je l'ai **achetée**.

André a **fini** les exercices.

→ André **les** a **finis**.

Nous n'avons pas **vendu** la voiture.

→ Nous ne l'avons pas **vendue**.

Avez-vous **fait** vos devoirs ?

→ Est-ce que vous **les** avez **faits** ?

b) The direct object is a noun preceded by **quel(le)(s)** or **combien de** in questions.

Quelle maison ont-ils **cherchée** ?

Quelles villes a-t-elle **visitées** ?

Combien de pommes avez-vous **mangées** ?

Combien de journaux a-t-il **choisis** ?

There is no agreement if the noun that precedes the verb is *not* a direct object.

À quelle question a-t-il **répondu** ?

À quels enfants as-tu **parlé** ?

De combien d'enfants avez-vous **parlé** ?

À combien de camarades a-t-il **téléphoné** ?

2. With most verbs, the agreement of the past participle is not heard in spoken French. The only exception is with verbs whose past participle ends in a consonant. In such cases, the difference between the masculine and feminine forms can be heard.

MASCULINE

J'ai **compris** le problème.

→ Je l'ai **compris**.

J'ai **fait** mes devoirs.

→ Je **les** ai **faits**.

FEMININE

J'ai **compris** la question.

→ Je l'ai **comprise**.

Elle a **fait** ces robes.

→ Elle **les** a **faites**.

Among the irregular verbs you have learned so far, the following have a past participle ending in a consonant.

faire : fait

prendre, apprendre, comprendre : pris, appris, compris

 A *Remplacez les noms par les pronoms appropriés d'après ce modèle. Dites ensuite si le participe passé est au masculin ou au féminin, au singulier ou au pluriel.*

J'ai posé cette question.

Je l'ai posée : féminin, singulier.

1. J'ai posé les questions.
2. J'ai compris les questions.
3. Avez-vous appris la vérité ?
4. Avez-vous fait votre lit ?
5. Avez-vous fait cette faute ?
6. Nous avons compris la leçon.
7. Nous n'avons pas pris notre dîner.
8. Il a cherché les réponses.
9. Elle n'a pas pris sa montre.
10. Ils n'ont pas appris le français.

B *Maintenant, répondez aux questions en employant les pronoms appropriés.*

1. Avez-vous compris la Leçon 8 ? Avez-vous compris mes questions ? Et la grammaire ? Et les explications ?
2. Avez-vous appris cette leçon ? Et la grammaire ? Et le dialogue de cette leçon ? Et les *Expressions utiles* de cette leçon ?
3. Avez-vous pris votre montre ? Et votre portefeuille ? Et votre parapluie ? Et vos médicaments ?
4. Avez-vous fait votre lit ce matin ? Avons-nous fait les exercices oraux hier ? Regardez cette phrase au tableau. Il y a une faute. Qui a fait cette faute ? Qui a corrigé la faute ?

Compréhension auditive

9.4 PASSÉ COMPOSÉ AVEC L'AUXILIAIRE ÊTRE ; EXPRESSIONS DU TEMPS PASSÉ

1. About a dozen verbs, commonly called "verbs of motion" (**les verbes de mouvement**) are conjugated with **être** in the *passé composé*. You will need to learn the following list thoroughly. Note that some, such as **rester** *to stay, to remain*, do not imply motion as such.[1] These verbs are arranged here more or less in pairs of opposite meanings. Review also the conjugation of **être**.

être

suis	sommes
es	êtes
est	sont

venir	Il est **venu** de Québec.	*He came from Quebec.*
aller	Il est **allé** à Montréal.	*He went to Montreal.*
arriver	Il est **arrivé** ce matin.	*He arrived this morning.*
partir	Il est **parti** hier soir.	*He left last night.*
entrer	Il est **entré** dans la classe.	*He entered the class(room).*
sortir	Il est **sorti** de la classe.	*He went out of the class(room).*
monter	Il est **monté** en haut.	*He went up.*
descendre	Il est **descendu**.	*He came (went) down.*
naître[2]	Il est **né** à Sherbrooke.	*He was born in Sherbrooke.*
mourir[3]	Il est **mort** à Marseille.	*He died in Marseilles.*
tomber	Il est **tombé** dans l'eau.	*He fell into the water.*
rester	Il est **resté** avec Janine.	*He stayed (remained) with Janine.*

Jacques Cartier est arrivé au Canada en 1534.

---

[1]Not all verbs denoting motion are conjugated with **être**: **Il a voyagé à Québec; Il a traversé la rue; Il a marché dans la neige.**

[2]**Naître** is irregular. In the present tense it is conjugated like **connaître** (Lesson 8.3).

[3]**Mourir** is irregular; it will be presented in Lesson 20.5.

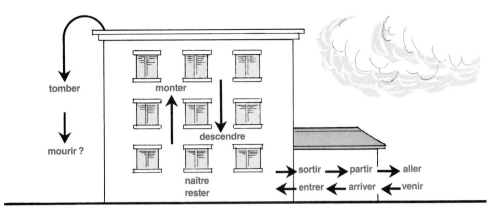

TABLEAU 49

2. Verbs that are derived from those above by the addition of a prefix are also conjugated with **être**.

devenir	Il est **devenu** très riche.	*He became very rich.*
revenir	Il est **revenu** de Paris.	*He came back from Paris.*
repartir	Il est **reparti** ce matin.	*He left again this morning.*
ressortir	Il est **ressorti**.	*He went out again.*
rentrer	Il est **rentré** tard.	*He came (went) home late.*

3. The past participle of verbs conjugated with **être** must agree in gender (*m/f*) and number (*s/pl*) with the *subject* of the sentence, just like an adjective after **être**. Examine the subjects and the past participles in the examples below.

SUBJECT	NUMBER	GENDER	EXAMPLE
Je	*s*	*m*	**Je** suis **allé** au cinéma.
		f	**Je** suis **allée** au cinéma.
Tu	*s*	*m*	**Tu** es **resté** à la maison.
		f	**Tu** es **restée** à la maison.
Il		*m*	**Il** est **parti** cet après-midi.
On	*s*	*m*	**On** est **parti** cet après-midi.
Elle		*f*	**Elle** est **partie** cet après-midi.
Nous	*pl*	*m*	**Nous** sommes **arrivés** ce matin.
		m + f	**Nous** sommes **arrivés** ce matin.
		f exclusively	**Nous** sommes **arrivées** ce matin.
Vous	*s*	*m*	**Vous** êtes **venu** avec Paul.
		f	**Vous** êtes **venue** avec Paul.
	pl	*m*	**Vous** êtes **venus** avec Paul.
		m + f	**Vous** êtes **venus** avec Paul.
		f exclusively	**Vous** êtes **venues** avec Paul.
Ils	*pl*	*m*	**Ils** sont **rentrés** à minuit.
		m + f	**Ils** sont **rentrés** à minuit.
Elles	*pl*	*f* exclusively	**Elles** sont **rentrées** à minuit.

4. The agreement of the past participle is always indicated in written French, but it is not heard in spoken French, except in the case of **mourir**: **mort**, **morts** *m* /mɔR/, but **morte**, **mortes** *f* /mɔRt/.

Es-tu **sortie** hier soir, Sophie ?

— Non, je suis **restée** à la maison.

Mon grand-père est **mort** à Boston.

Ma grand-mère est **morte** à Québec.

Adèle et Marie sont-elles **venues** ?

— Oui, elles sont **venues** hier matin.

Ils sont **morts** l'année dernière.

Elles sont **mortes** l'année dernière.

5. Study these negative and inverted forms of verbs conjugated with **être**. Like verbs that are conjugated with **avoir**, the negation takes place around the auxiliary, and the inversion occurs between the subject pronoun and the auxiliary.

Tu **es** allée chez Gilberte.

→ Tu **n'es pas** allée chez Gilberte.

Est-il allé à Montréal ?

→ **N'est-il pas** allé à Montréal ?

Vous **êtes** resté à la maison.

→ Vous **n'êtes pas** resté à la maison.

Êtes-vous sortis ensemble ?

→ **N'êtes-vous pas** sortis ensemble ?

6. *Expressions of the past.* **Il y a** + time is an equivalent of time + *ago* in English. It can be attached to either the beginning (usually with a comma in written French) or the end of a sentence.

Je suis allée au cinéma **il y a dix jours**.

Il y a six ans, mes parents ont visité le Québec.

I went to the movies ten days ago.

Six years ago, my parents visited (the province of) Quebec.

Here are more expressions. **Dernier** *last* can be used with expressions of time. Note that it becomes **dernière** before a feminine noun.

hier, hier matin, hier soir		*yesterday, yesterday morning, last night*
avant-hier		*the day before yesterday*
dernier(ière) :	**lundi dernier**	*last:* / *last Monday*
	la semaine dernière	*last week*
	le mois dernier	*last month*
	l'été dernier	*last summer*
	l'année dernière	*last year*

Elle **est montée** dans l'autobus.

Ils **sont entrés** dans ma chambre.

Elle **est morte** en 1930.

TABLEAU 50

A *Exercice de contrôle*

Je suis allé(e) au cinéma.
1. Vous   2. Les enfants   3. Nous   4. Tu

Je ne suis pas resté(e) à la maison.
1. Mon camarade   2. Vous   3. Tu   4. Les étudiants

Je ne suis pas rentré(e) tard.
1. Nous   2. Tu   3. Mon frère   4. Mes parents

B *L'été dernier, Barbara, une étudiante américaine, a passé une semaine à Montréal. Voici comment elle a passé sa première journée dans la ville. Mettez chaque verbe au passé composé.*

(1) Je viens à Montréal. (2) J'arrive à une heure. (3) Je vais à mon hôtel. (4) Je monte dans ma chambre. (5) Je reste dans ma chambre. (6) Je descends en ascenseur[1]. (7) Je vais dans les vieux quartiers. (8) J'entre dans une boutique. (9) Je sors de la boutique. (10) Je vais à l'église Notre-Dame. (11) Je reviens à mon hôtel. (12) J'entre dans ma chambre. (13) Je ressors à six heures. (14) Je repars de mon hôtel. (15) Je vais dans un restaurant. (16) Je rentre après le dîner.

C *Regardez le Tableau 33 à la page 126. Mettez chaque phrase au passé composé d'après ce modèle.*

Je traverse la rue.
J'ai traversé la rue.

D *Voici l'histoire d'un voyage. Monique a invité Michel chez ses parents pendant le week-end. Il a fait très mauvais temps et le voyage n'a pas été agréable. Mettez chaque verbe au passé composé.*

(1) Je vais chez mes parents. (2) Je téléphone à ma mère. (3) Nous partons à neuf heures. (4) Il pleut et il neige. (5) Il ne fait pas beau. (6) La chaussée est glissante. (7) Nous ne faisons pas bon voyage[2]. (8) Je ne veux pas continuer. (9) Mais nous arrivons chez mes parents. (10) Nous descendons de la voiture. (11) Mon père sort de la maison. (12) Nous entrons dans la maison. (13) Nous dînons ensemble. (14) Michel parle de sa famille. (15) Nous jouons aux cartes. (16) Je monte dans ma chambre. (17) Je prends un bain chaud. (18) Je sors de ma chambre. (19) Nous mangeons des fruits. (20) Nous regardons la télévision.

E *Répondez aux questions.*

1. À quelle heure êtes-vous parti(e) de la maison ce matin ? À quelle heure êtes-vous arrivé(e) à l'université ?
2. Moi, je suis né(e) (en Floride). Où êtes-vous né(e) ? Où est-ce que vos parents sont nés ?
3. Je suis né(e) il y a (vingt-huit) ans. Demandez à (Jacques) quel âge il a. Demandez à (Jacques) quand il est né.
4. Quand est-ce que vous êtes allé(e) au cinéma ? Demandez à (Jeanne) quand elle est allée au labo.
5. Parlons de samedi dernier. Qui est sorti samedi dernier ? Où êtes-vous allé(e) ? Qu'est-ce que vous avez fait ? Qui est rentré tard ? À quelle heure ? Qui est resté à la maison ?
6. Demandez à votre partenaire ce qu'il (elle)[3] a fait pendant le week-end. Posez au moins[4] cinq questions.

[1]**en ascenseur** *in an elevator*

[2]**faire bon voyage** *to have a good trip*

[3]**ce que** *that which, what* (in questions it becomes **Qu'est-ce que**).

[4]*at least*; You can ask questions similar to No. 5.

⊟ *Exercice supplémentaire*

⊟ *Exercice supplémentaire*

⊟ *Compréhension auditive*

9.5 NOMBRES CARDINAUX (APRÈS 1.000)

1. Study the numbers below. Instead of a comma, a period (**un point**) is used in French with numbers in the thousands and millions.[1] A comma (**une virgule**) is used to indicate the decimal point (2,54 cm). **Mille** does not add an **-s** in the plural. Note that **million** is preceded by **un**, **deux**, etc., and **de** + noun when it is not followed by a smaller number.

1.000	**mille**
2.000	**deux mille**
2.500	**deux mille cinq cents**
3.640	**trois mille six cent quarante**
10.011	**dix mille onze**
258.300	**deux cent cinquante-huit mille trois cents**
1.000.000 francs	**un million de** francs
1.000.500 maisons	**un million cinq cents** maisons
2.000.000 habitants	**deux millions d'**habitants
3.500.000 voitures	**trois millions cinq cent mille** voitures

2. *Dates.* Years between 1100 and 1999 are often read in multiples of **cent(s)**. Unlike its English equivalent, the word **cent(s)** cannot be omitted.[2] See Lesson 4.6 (p. 94) to review when the **s** of **cents** is omitted.

1142	**onze cent quarante-deux**
1789	**dix-sept cent quatre-vingt-neuf**
1870	**dix-huit cent soixante-dix**
1991	**dix-neuf cent quatre-vingt-onze**

A *Répondez aux questions.*

1. Combien d'étudiants est-ce qu'il y a dans notre université ?
2. Quelle est la population de notre ville ?
3. Quelle est la population de notre état ?

B *Lisez le passage suivant à haute voix.*

La France a plus de[3] 55.000.000 d'habitants. Il y a 34 villes qui[4] dépassent 100.000 habitants (138 aux États-Unis). Paris, capitale de la France, a 2.300.000 habitants. Dans son agglomération, il y a 8.550.000 habitants. Dans l'agglomération de Lyon, la deuxième ville de France, il y a 1.171.000 habitants. Après Lyon, c'est Marseille, avec sa population de 1.071.000 habitants. Vient ensuite[5] Lille, avec 936.000 habitants dans l'agglomération.

[1]Sometimes a space replaces the period: **258.300** → **258 300**.

[2]Another way of reading dates is to use **mil**, an alternate spelling for **mille**: **dix-neuf cent quatre-vingt-un** → **mil neuf cent quatre-vingt-un**.

[3]**plus de** *more than*

[4]**qui** *which*

[5]*Then comes*

C *Lisez les phrases suivantes.*

1. Christophe Colomb /kɔlõ/ est venu en Amérique en 1492.
2. Jacques Cartier est venu en Amérique en 1534.
3. Daniel Duluth a commencé son exploration du lac Supérieur[1] en 1678.
4. Jean-Jacques Audubon est né en Louisiane le 4 mai 1780 ; il est mort en 1851.
5. La date de la déclaration de l'indépendance américaine est le 4 juillet 1776.
6. La date de la prise de la Bastille est le 14 juillet 1789.

D *Répondez aux questions.*

1. Quelle est la date de votre anniversaire ? En quelle année êtes-vous né(e) ? Quand est-ce que votre mère est née ?
2. En quelle année êtes-vous entré(e) à l'université ? En quelle année allez-vous terminer vos études ?
3. Quelle est la date de la déclaration de l'indépendance américaine ? Et la date de la prise de la Bastille ?

Dictée

APPLICATIONS

A **Situations**

Pour demander son chemin

L'été dernier, Jean-Paul et Monique sont allés au Canada et aux États-Unis. Ils ont passé quelques jours à Québec. Ils ont trouvé un hôtel pas cher° mais confortable près du jardin des Gouverneurs, à quelques minutes° du Château Frontenac. Quelle ville passionnante ! Il y a des remparts, de vieux quartiers, aussi bien que° des quartiers ultramodernes.

inexpensive
a few minutes (away)
as well as

Jean-Paul descend la rue Notre-Dame et cherche la Place Royale. Il demande son chemin 5
à un passant.

JEAN-PAUL	Pardon, Monsieur. Pour aller Place Royale[2], s'il vous plaît.
LE PASSANT	Mais vous êtes Place Royale[2].
JEAN-PAUL	*(un peu gêné)* Ah bon ! Merci, Monsieur.
LE PASSANT	De rien,° Monsieur.	10

You're welcome.

Monique demande des renseignements à un agent de police.

MONIQUE	Pardon, Monsieur l'agent. Est-ce qu'il y a un arrêt d'autobus° près d'ici ?
L'AGENT	Oui. Allez tout droit jusqu'à la rue du Trésor, puis tournez à droite.
MONIQUE	Merci, Monsieur.
L'AGENT	À votre service,° Mademoiselle.	15

a bus stop
You're welcome

Jean-Paul et Monique cherchent un restaurant pour goûter des spécialités québécoises. Jean-Paul demande le chemin.

| JEAN-PAUL | Excusez-moi, Madame. Où est le restaurant Santenay ? |
| LA PASSANTE | Santenay ? Voyons... continuez tout droit, et puis prenez la troisième rue à gauche. | 20
| JEAN-PAUL | Merci bien, Madame. |
| LA PASSANTE | Je vous en prie,° Monsieur. |

You're welcome

[1]*Lake Superior*

[2]On n'a pas besoin d'employer les prépositions **à**, **sur**, **dans**, etc. et l'article défini avec des verbes comme **aller**, **être** et **habiter** pour indiquer une rue, une avenue, un boulevard, une place, etc.

Jean-Paul et Monique veulent aller à Sainte-Anne-de-Beaupré.

JEAN-PAUL	Excusez-moi, Monsieur. Où est Sainte-Anne-de-Beaupré, s'il vous plaît ?
LE PASSANT	C'est loin d'ici. Vous êtes en voiture ?[1]	25
JEAN-PAUL	Oui.
LE PASSANT	Alors, prenez la première avenue là-bas. Allez jusqu'au boulevard Sainte-Anne et tournez à droite. Puis continuez tout droit sur ce boulevard.
JEAN-PAUL	Je vous remercie, Monsieur.
LE PASSANT	Il n'y a pas de quoi.°	30

You're welcome. (gloss for line 30)

Répondez aux questions. (lignes 1–4)

1. Où est-ce que Jean-Paul et Monique sont allés l'été dernier ?
2. Combien de jours ont-ils passés à Québec ?
3. Qu'est-ce qu'ils ont trouvé près du jardin des Gouverneurs ?
4. Quelle sorte de ville est Québec ?

Qu'est-ce qu'on peut dire dans les situations suivantes ?[2]

1. Vous demandez à un agent de police comment trouver un arrêt d'autobus. Il dit de prendre[3] la première rue à gauche, la deuxième à droite, etc.
2. Vous demandez à un passant comment aller au bureau de poste. C'est un peu compliqué, et la dame veut vous accompagner jusque-là[4].
3. Vous êtes en voiture. Vous venez de visiter une grande ville. Vous voulez prendre une autoroute pour sortir de la ville. Vous interrogez un agent de police.
4. Vous visitez une ville. Vous voulez goûter des spécialités régionales dans un bon restaurant. Vous interrogez quelqu'un.

« Allez tout droit, puis tournez à gauche. »

« Prenez la première rue à droite. »

[1]Avez-vous une voiture ?

[2]Les réponses ne sont pas enregistrées sur la bande magnétique.

[3]*He tells (you) to take* (**dit** : du verbe **dire** *to tell*, Leçon 10.3)

[4]*up to there*

B   **Expressions utiles**

La ville : *Bureaux, bâtiments et monuments*

un bureau de poste / bureau des P.E.T.[1]	un jardin
une cathédrale (une église)	un marché (en plein air)
le centre ville[2]	un monument
un château	un musée
un cinéma	un parc
une fontaine	un parking
une gare	une place
un gratte-ciel[3]	une statue
un hôpital	un syndicat d'initiative[4]
un hôtel	une tour
l'Hôtel de ville	la vieille ville (le vieux quartier)

A pied dans le vieux Québec

Le monument
Le bâtiment ⎬ est ⎨ beau, splendide, extraordinaire, magnifique.
L'édifice *m*   laid, pittoresque, vieux, historique.
                  moderne, ultramoderne.

La ville : *Les chemins*

regarder ⎬ ⎨ un guide
consulter   le plan de la ville

prendre ⎨ une rue / la deuxième rue à gauche
          une avenue / la première avenue à droite
          un boulevard (jusqu'au bout[5])

aller / continuer tout droit

tourner ⎨ à gauche
          à droite

traverser un pont / une place / une rue

Le bureau est ⎨ dans cette rue.
                dans / sur cette avenue.
                sur ce boulevard.

Le musée est ⎨ en face du jardin.
               devant (derrière) le cinéma.
               à côté du cinéma.

VISITEZ LE MUSÉE DE CIRE À QUÉBEC

LA PLACE ROYALE

il fait bon vivre à québec

enjoy your visit in quebec city

50

C   **Pratique**

1. Examinez la liste suivante. Indiquez si ces bureaux et ces monuments existent dans notre ville (utilisez **il y a**, **nous avons** ou **on a**) ; mentionnez aussi près de quel autre bâtiment ou endroit on trouve le bureau, le bâtiment ou le monument.

une cathédrale	un hôpital	un palais
un château	un hôtel	une place
un cinéma	un jardin public	une statue
une fontaine	un marché en plein air	un quartier (une maison)
une gare	un musée	historique

[1]En France, on dit **P.E.T.** ou **P.e.T.** (Postes et Télécommunications) ; le bureau de poste et le bureau des P.E.T. signifient à peu près la même chose.

[2]c'est-à-dire, le centre de la ville (*downtown*)

[3]Le mot ne change pas au pluriel : **des gratte-ciel**.

[4]bureau d'information pour les touristes (On dit aussi **un bureau** ou **un office de tourisme**.)

[5]*until the end*

Il y a des quartiers charmants à Québec.

2. Hier après-midi vous avez envoyé un paquet à vos parents. Comment êtes-vous allé(e) de votre résidence au bureau de poste ?
3. Vous êtes allé(e) au cinéma le week-end dernier. Comment s'appelle le cinéma ? Où est-il ? Quel chemin avez-vous pris pour aller au cinéma ?

D **Mini-composition :** *Monique parle de sa journée à Québec. Complétez le passage en employant le passé composé.*

(1) Nous/sortir/de/hôtel/à/9 h/et/nous/prendre/petit déjeuner/dans petit/café. (2) Après,/ nous/aller/à/vieux quartier/en bas. (3) Nous/descendre/à/Place Royale/et/nous/visiter/ la/église/et/les/maison/historique. (4) Je/acheter/souvenirs/et/Jean-Paul/prendre/photos. (5) À/1 h/nous/prendre/funiculaire/et nous/monter/sur/Terrasse Dufferin. (6) Nous/dé-jeuner/dans/café/de/le/Château Frontenac. (7) Ensuite/nous/aller/à/Citadelle. (8) Après/ visite/de/Citadelle/nous/faire/courses. (9) Je/trouver/cadeaux de Noël/pour/mes/parent. (10) À/6 h,/nous/rentrer/dans/hôtel. (11) Nous/ressortir/à/7 h. (12) Nous/goûter/spé-cialités/québécoise. (13) Après/dîner/nous/aller/cinéma. (14) Journée/être/fatigant,/mais/ très/intéressant.

E **Questions :** *Une visite aux chutes du Niagara. Posez des questions sur les parties soulignées.*

Nous avons quitté Québec (1) <u>il y a quatre jours</u>. Nous avons passé (2) <u>deux jours</u>[1] à Toronto. Hier matin nous avons visité (3) <u>les chutes du Niagara</u>. Nous sommes partis (4) <u>de Toronto</u>[2] à huit heures. Nous sommes montés (5) <u>en haut d'une</u>[3] tour. (6) <u>La tour</u> est très haute. (7) <u>Mon frère</u> a pris beaucoup de photos. Ensuite, nous avons visité le bassin des chutes (8) <u>en bateau</u>. Nous avons acheté (9) <u>des souvenirs et des cartes postales</u>. Nous allons les envoyer (10) <u>à nos amis</u>.

[1]**Combien de temps... ?**
[2]**D'où... ?**
[3]**Où... ?**

F **Composition** : *Choisissez un des sujets suivants et écrivez une composition d'à peu près 120 mots.*[1]

1. Choisissez quelqu'un de célèbre (par exemple, le président des États-Unis, une vedette de cinéma[2] ou le président de votre université). Faites un portrait comique de cette personne : Qui est-ce ? Comment est la personne ? Que fait-elle[3] ? Qu'a-t-elle fait hier ?

2. Vous êtes en France. Vous partagez un appartement avec un(e) Français(e). Vous avez invité des copains à dîner chez vous. Quels copains avez-vous invités ? Qu'est-ce que vous avez préparé comme repas ? Où avez-vous acheté les aliments ? En quelles quantités ? Qu'est-ce que vous avez servi[4] comme boisson ? Qu'est-ce que vous avez fait après le dîner ?

3. Êtes-vous allé(e) au Canada ? Qu'est-ce que vous avez fait ? Qu'est-ce que vous avez vu[5] ? Comment avez-vous trouvé le voyage ?

4. Qu'est-ce que vous avez fait hier, entre dix heures du matin et dix heures du soir ? Employez au moins vingt verbes différents dans votre description.

G **Renseignements et opinions**

1. Donnez une date très importante de votre vie depuis 1982. Pourquoi cette date est-elle importante ?

2. À quelle heure êtes-vous parti(e) de la maison ce matin ? Quel chemin avez-vous pris pour venir en classe ?

3. À quelle heure êtes-vous rentré(e) hier ? Qu'est-ce que vous avez fait après ?

4. Qu'est-ce que vous avez fait hier soir ? Mentionnez deux choses. Qu'est-ce que vous n'avez pas fait ? Mentionnez deux choses.

5. En quelle année êtes-vous entré(e) à l'université ? En quelle année allez-vous terminer vos études?

6. Préparez une question à poser à votre professeur au sujet de[6] la ville ou de la province de Québec.

[1]About one line less than **Application D** in total length.

[2]*movie star*

[3]**Elle** refers to **la personne**, a feminine noun, and not to the sex of the person you are going to describe (who can be a male).

[4]du verbe **servir** *to serve* (Leçon 13.5)

[5]participe passé de **voir** *to see* (Leçon 11.4)

[6]*concerning*

☐ *Compréhension auditive (basée sur l'Application A)*

☐ *Dictée : « Une journée à Québec » (basée sur les Applications B et D)*

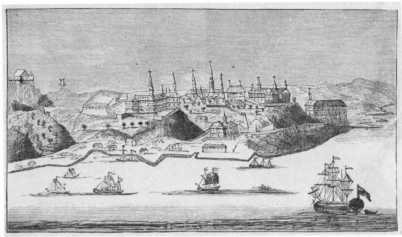

"A VIEW OF THE CITY OF QUEBEC IN NEW FRANCE IN AMERICA."

Drawing (in British Museum) by Margaret Cecil, 1740.

H Lecture

Les Français en Amérique

Vous savez déjà qu'on parle français au Canada, surtout dans la province de Québec. Quand est-ce que les Français sont venus en Amérique du Nord ? L'histoire du Canada français remonte au seizième siècle. À partir de° 1543, Jacques Cartier a fait trois voyages dans le Nouveau-Monde. Pendant son deuxième voyage, il a découvert[1] le Saint-Laurent[2]. Il a planté une grande croix sur une colline et il l'a nommée Mont Réal[3]. Un autre explorateur, Samuel de Champlain, a exploré le golfe du Mexique, la Nouvelle-Angleterre°, et ensuite l'Est du Canada. Il a établi des colonies françaises en Acadie — aujourd'hui les provinces maritimes canadiennes de la Nouvelle-Écosse[4] et du Nouveau-Brunswick — et il a fondé la ville de Québec en 1608. La ville est devenue la capitale de la Nouvelle-France, un vaste territoire français dans le Nouveau-Monde.

    Le dix-septième siècle a été une période d'exploration très active. Le comte de Frontenac, gouverneur de la Nouvelle-France, a demandé à Louis Joliet et au père Marquette d'explorer les régions au sud des Grands Lacs°. Avec des compagnons intrépides, indiens et français, ils sont allés jusque dans le Minnesota, puis ils ont découvert plusieurs grandes rivières : le Wisconsin, l'Illinois, l'Ohio, le Missouri, l'Arkansas. Ils ont fait presque 3.000 milles sur le Mississippi. Le père François-Xavier de Charlevoix, Louis Joliet et Robert de la Salle ont exploré cet immense arrière-pays° à travers les plaines et les prairies. La Salle, après beaucoup de dangers, est arrivé à l'embouchure du Mississippi, sur le golfe du Mexique. Il a pris possession des terres le long du° Mississippi et, en l'honneur de son roi Louis XIV (*quatorze*), il a nommé ce pays la Louisiane.

Beginning (in)

New England

Great Lakes

hinterland

le long de *along*

5

10

15

20

[1]participe passé de **découvrir** *to discover*

[2]*the St. Lawrence River*

[3]In the sixteenth century, **réal** was another spelling for **royal**.

[4]*Nova Scotia* (literally, *New Scotland*)

Lake Superior L'exploration a continué au siècle suivant. Daniel Duluth a exploré le lac Supérieur° et la région qui est aujourd'hui le Minnesota. Antoine de la Mothe Cadillac a fondé Détroit[1]. Auguste Chouteau a établi un village sur le Missouri pour le commerce des fourrures et il a nommé ce village Saint-Louis, en l'honneur de Louis IX, ancêtre de son roi. Le lac Champlain, Duluth, Détroit, Joliet, Charlevoix, Marquette — vous avez remarqué l'origine française de plusieurs noms géographiques. Mais qu'est-ce qui est arrivé à la Nouvelle-France, ce vaste territoire ? Vous allez bientôt apprendre quels événements ont causé la perte des colonies françaises. 25

A *Trouvez dans le texte les équivalents français des noms propres suivants.*

North America	The St. Lawrence River	The Gulf of Mexico
New England	Nova Scotia	Detroit
Louisiana	The New World	Lake Superior

B *Indiquez si chaque commentaire est vrai ou faux. S'il est faux, corrigez le commentaire.*

1. Le Québec est la seule province au Canada où on parle français.
2. L'exploration française du Canada a commencé au seizième siècle.
3. Jacques Cartier a découvert le Saint-Laurent pendant son dernier voyage.
4. Champlain a fondé une ville sur le Saint-Laurent et l'a nommée Montréal.
5. Montréal est devenu ensuite la capitale de la Nouvelle-France.
6. Louis Joliet et le père Marquette ont découvert les grandes rivières du « *Midwest* ».
7. La Salle a nommé « Louisiane » les vastes terres le long du Missouri.
8. Duluth a exploré le lac Supérieur et il a fondé Détroit.

C *Quelle est l'origine des noms propres suivants ?*

Montréal	Marquette (WI)	Charlevoix (MI)
Lake Champlain (NY)	Louisiana	Saint Louis (MO)
Duluth (MN)	Détroit (MI)	Joliet (IL)
Château Frontenac	Cadillac (MI)	

MONTRÉAL
Prenez l'tour du Québec

[1]Literally, *Strait* (connecting Lake Huron and Lake Erie)

VOCABULAIRE

Noms

l'**Afrique** f	Africa	le **disque**	record	la **Louisiane**	Louisiana
une **agglomération**	metropolitan area	une **église**	church	**Marseille**	Marseilles
l'**Amérique** f	America	une **entrée**	entrance	le **médicament**	medicine
un **ascenseur**	elevator	un **état**	state	le **million**	million
une autoroute	highway	une **étude**	study	le **moteur**	motor
la **Bastille**	Bastille	une **explication**	explanation	le **parking**	parking lot
la **capitale**	capital	une **exploration**	exploration	la **partie**	part
la **carte de crédit**	credit card	une **expression**	expression	le **passant**	passer-by
la **carte d'identité**	ID card	une **figure**	figure	la **place**	square
le **château**	castle	la **Floride**	Florida	le **plan**	map
la **chaussée**	pavement, road	le **fort**	fort	la **population**	population
le **chemin**	way	le **funiculaire**	cable car	la **prise**	storming, taking
la **cire**	wax	le gouverneur	governor	le **quartier**	area of city
la **citadelle**	citadel; fort	un **habitant**	inhabitant	**Québec**	Quebec City
la **côte**	hill	un **hôtel**	hotel	le **Québec**	Quebec province
le **crédit**	credit	un **Hôtel de ville**	City Hall	le **rempart**	rampart
le **dialogue**	dialogue	une **identité**	identity	le **renseignement**	information
le **diorama**	diorama	le **lac**	lake	le **souvenir**	souvenir

Noms

la spécialité	specialty	la **vérité**	truth	le **voyage**	trip
le **tourisme**	tourism	le **vieux quartier**	Old Town		
le trésor	treasury; treasure ·	le **volant**	steering wheel		

Verbes

accompagner	to accompany	**laisser**	to leave	**ressortir** irrég	to go out again
aider	to help	**mener à**	to lead to	**revenir** irrég	to come back
dépasser	to exceed	**montrer**	to show	**terminer**	to finish
garer	to park	**naître** irrég	to be born	**tourner**	to turn
goûter	to taste	remercier (de)	to thank (for)		
interroger	to ask	**repartir** irrég	to leave again		

Adjectifs

cher (chère)	expensive	**glissant(e)**	slippery	**pittoresque**	picturesque
compliqué(e)	complicated	**historique**	historical	québécois(e)	of Quebec
confortable	comfortable	**miniature**	miniature	royal(e)	royal
droit(e)	straight	**né(e)**	born	**supérieur(e)**	superior; upper
entouré(e) (de)	surrounded (by)	pas cher (chère)	inexpensive	**ultramoderne**	ultramodern
gêné(e)	embarrassed	**passionnant(e)**	exciting		

Adverbes

hier	yesterday	**juste**	just	tout droit	straight ahead

Prépositions

avant	before	**loin (de)**	far (from)	**pendant**	during, for

Autres expressions

à droite	on/to the right	**hier soir**	last night, yesterday evening
à gauche	on/to the left	Il n'y a pas de quoi.	You're welcome.
à quelques minutes	a few minutes (away)	**il y a** + time	time + ago
aussi bien que	as well as	Je vous en prie.	You're welcome.
À votre service.	You're welcome.	jusque-là	up to there
d'abord	first of all	Merci bien.	Thanks a lot.
en ascenseur	in an elevator	**plus de**	more than
en bas	down below	**Quel(le)... !**	What (a) . . . !
faire bon voyage	to have a good trip		

LA FRANCE ET SES RÉGIONS

Le Grand Canyon du Verdon.

Les moutons des Pyrénées
donnent de la belle laine.

Sur le port
de Marseille.

La Dordogne, avec, au fond,
le village de la Roque-Gageac.

Le Mont Blanc, dans les Alpes.

PARIS, CAPITALE DE LA FRANCE

L'Opéra.

*Une rue animée
dans le Quartier Latin.*

Une jeune Parisienne.

L'Arc de Triomphe.

*La Basilique du Sacré-Cœur,
vue de la rue Lafitte.*

*La Place de la Concorde,
avec, au fond,
l'église de la Madeleine.*

*Un artiste sur les quais,
près de Notre-Dame.*

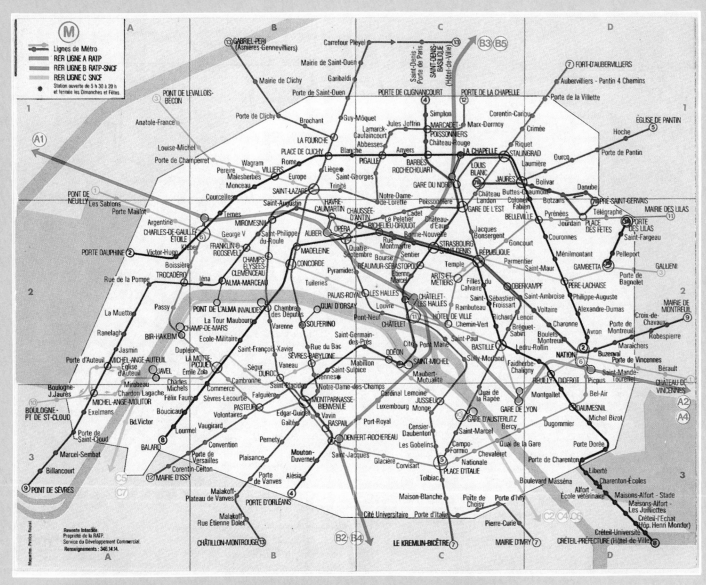

La Défense,
un quartier ultramoderne.

10 Les maisons

LESSON OBJECTIVES

Theme and Culture

1. Houses and rooms (furniture and fixtures in Lesson 14)
2. French heritage in Louisiana

Communication Skills

1. Describing the general plan of a house
2. Expressing habitual or progressing actions in the past (*I used to do*, *I was doing*)
3. Using indirect-object pronouns instead of nouns
4. Contrasting actions and descriptions in the past
5. Expressing negation (*no one, nothing*)

Structures

1. The imperfect tense
2. Indirect-object pronouns
3. **Dire**
4. The *passé composé* and the imperfect
5. Negation: **ne ... personne, ne ... rien**

CONVERSATIONS

A. La maison

Regardez le Tableau 51 à la page 210. Qu'est-ce que c'est ? Oui, c'est une maison française. Entrons dans la maison. L'entrée est à droite. Il y a plusieurs pièces[1] dans cette maison. Au rez-de-chaussée[2] il y a une salle de séjour[3], une salle à manger et une cuisine. Au premier étage[4], il y a des chambres à coucher[5] et une salle de bains[6].

À quel étage est la salle de bains ? Elle est au-dessus de[7] la salle à manger. Regardez la cuisine. Quelle pièce y a-t-il au-dessus de la cuisine ?

À quel étage est la salle à manger ? Elle est au-dessous de[8] la salle de bains. Qu'est-ce qu'il y a au-dessous de la chambre à droite ?

Y a-t-il un sous-sol[9] ? Où est le grenier ? Qu'est-ce qu'il y a au-dessus du grenier ? Dans quelles pièces y a-t-il des lits ?

[1]rooms
[2]*On the first (ground) floor*
[3]*living room* (on dit aussi **un séjour**)
[4]*On the second floor*; **premier** is pronounced like **première** because of liaison with **étage**.
[5]*bedrooms* (on dit aussi **des chambres**)
[6]*bathroom*
[7]/odsyd/ *above*
[8]/odsud/ *below*
[9]*basement*

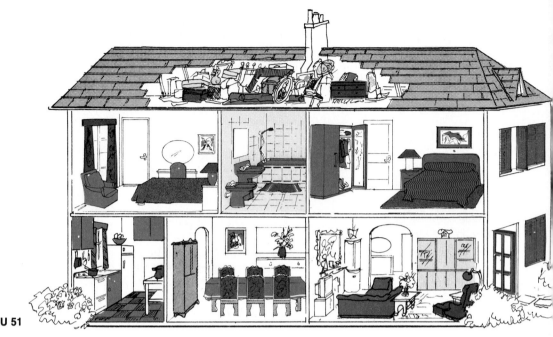

TABLEAU 51

B.   Robert a ma souris[1].

ROBERT   Jeanne, où étais-tu tout l'après-midi[2] ? Je t'ai cherchée partout.

JEANNE   J'étais chez Daniel. Pourquoi me cherchais-tu ?

ROBERT   J'avais besoin de ta souris pour mon programme.

JEANNE   Ma souris ? Je l'ai prêtée à Daniel !

C.   Achille[3] joue avec sa balle.

MME BOSQUET   Jean, réveille-toi[4]. J'entends du bruit dans la cuisine.

M. BOSQUET   Hein ?... Je n'entends rien.

MME BOSQUET   Si. Qu'est-ce qui se passe ?[5] Va voir.[6]

(*Un moment plus tard, le mari revient.*)

M. BOSQUET   Il n'y a personne dans la cuisine. C'est Achille qui joue avec sa balle.

DIFFÉRENCES

Les maisons françaises

Traditional French houses can be recognized easily by their windows with **volets** *m*, external shutters, often louvered, which are closed in the evening for privacy and security. Modern homes have hinged multiple-section metal shutters that are almost invisible when folded against the window jamb or into the header. The windows are hinged vertically to swing inward whereas traditional American houses have windows

[1]*mouse* (for microcomputers)

[2]*all afternoon*

[3]le nom d'un chat

[4]*wake up*

[5]*What's going on?*

[6]*Go (and) see.*

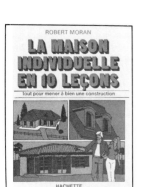

that are raised and lowered or swing outward. Because of the **volets**, curtains are usually thin. Bedrooms normally do not have built-in closets, except in some modern apartments. Instead, the French use **armoires** *f*, very large wardrobes to store shoes and articles of clothing. **La salle de bains** (bathroom), containing a sink and bathtub but no toilet, is where you wash and take a bath. The toilet is in a small, separate room called **les w.-c.** (often pronounced **les vé-cé**), short for "water closet." In polite language, you refer to the **w.-c.** as **les toilettes** (always in the plural in French) or as **le petit coin**. When in need of that facility in public, you ask: **Où sont les toilettes, s'il vous plaît ?**

The French are more energy-conscious than most Americans. The cost of gas and electricity is higher than in the United States, and electricity is the main source of heating energy in winter. The two-tier electricity rate is widespread; it is cheaper between 11 P.M. and 7 A.M. In winter, the thermostats in homes and buildings are kept rather low. People simply wear heavier clothing and use more covers at night. Hot water for the kitchen is produced instantaneously by a tiny gas water heater. Appliances like the washing machine and dishwasher have their own electric heater to heat the water. The large water heater for the **salle de bains** is heavily insulated and designed to heat water during the night and keep it hot throughout the day. In hotels and apartment buildings the stairway and hall light switches are timed to switch off a few minutes after being turned on (the device is called **la minuterie**).

The French seem concerned about how light (**clair**) or dark (**sombre**) a room is. In most apartments, the living room, dining room, and main bedroom are on the street side, while the kitchen, bathroom, and staircase face the courtyard, which is darker. Traditional apartment buildings in large cities have a **concierge**, usually a woman, who is at the same time a doorkeeper, a custodian, and a building manager. She takes care of the mail, messages, and deliveries, keeps the stairs, halls, courtyard, and sidewalk clean, makes certain that no stranger enters the building without her clearance, and, to be sure, keeps up-to-date on all the latest gossip about the residents. Now most

Toutes les fenêtres ont des volets.

Un immeuble ultramoderne à Paris.

modern buildings, especially in the outskirts of a city, have a **gardien(ne)**, a kind of building manager whose main duty is to keep the public areas clean, watch for strangers loitering, and take messages. The access to the foyer of the building is gained either by a key or by punching the code number (**le code**) on a push-button dial located by the door.

STRUCTURES

10.1   IMPARFAIT DE L'INDICATIF

French has two main past tenses. One is the *passé composé*, which you learned in Lesson 9. The other is the *imparfait* (*imperfect* in English), which is presented here. These two tenses have their own different functions and cannot be used interchangeably.

1. To form the imperfect tense, you take the **nous** form of the present indicative, and replace **-ons** with the endings **-ais** /ɛ/, **-ait** /ɛ/, **-ions** /jõ/, **-iez** /je/, and **-aient** /ɛ/. Note that the **je**, **tu**, **il**, **ils** forms are pronounced alike.

nous **parl**ons	nous **finiss**ons	nous **vend**ons
je **parl**ais	je **finiss**ais	je **vend**ais
tu **parl**ais	tu **finiss**ais	tu **vend**ais
il **parl**ait	elle **finiss**ait	il **vend**ait
ils **parl**aient	elles **finiss**aient	ils **vend**aient
nous **parl**ions vous **parl**iez	nous **finiss**ions vous **finiss**iez	nous **vend**ions vous **vend**iez

For verbs like **manger** and **commencer**, the sound /ʒ/ or /s/ is represented by **-ge-** or **-ç-** in all but the **nous** and **vous** forms.[1] A verb such as **étudier** has **-ii-** in the **nous** and **vous** forms.

nous **mange**ons	nous **commenç**ons	nous **étudi**
je **mange**ais	je **commenç**ais	j' **étudi**ais
tu **mange**ais	tu **commenç**ais	tu **étudi**ais
elle **mange**ait	il **commenç**ait	elle **étudi**ait
elles **mange**aient	ils **commenç**aient	elles **étudi**aient
nous **mang**ions vous **mang**iez	nous **commenc**ions vous **commenc**iez	nous **étudi**ions vous **étudi**iez

aller	(nous **all**ons)	j'**all**ais, vous **all**iez
avoir	(nous **av**ons)	j'**av**ais, vous **av**iez
boire	(nous **buv**ons)	je **buv**ais, vous **buv**iez
faire	(nous **fais**ons)	je **fais**ais /f(ə)zɛ/, vous **fais**iez /fəzje/
prendre	(nous **pren**ons)	je **pren**ais, vous **pren**iez
venir	(nous **ven**ons)	je **ven**ais, vous **ven**iez
vouloir	(nous **voul**ons)	je **voul**ais, vous **voul**iez

[1]The general spelling rule is that **g** and **c** are pronounced /ʒ/ and /s/ only before **i** and **e**; before the letters **a**, **o**, and **u**, **g** and **c** must be changed to **ge** and **ç**.

Être is the only verb whose imperfect stem cannot be derived from the **nous** form (**nous sommes**) of the present tense.

j'**étais**	nous **étions**
tu **étais**	vous **étiez**
il **était**	ils **étaient**

The imperfect tense of **pleuvoir** *to rain* is **pleuvait**: **il pleuvait**.

2. One of the functions of the imperfect tense is to denote *habitual* or *repeated* actions in the past. In English, such actions are either implied in the past tense of the verb itself or expressed by the construction *used to/would* + verb.

Il **jouait** souvent avec Jacques quand il **habitait** en Louisiane.	*He played/used to play/would play . . . he lived/used to live*
Elle **parlait** français quand elle **était** petite.	*She spoke/used to speak/would speak . . . she was*
L'année dernière j'**allais** au cinéma deux fois par mois.	*I went/used to go*
Philippe **était** mécontent chaque fois que[1] tu m'**aidais**.	*Philippe was/used to be/would be . . . you helped/used to help . . .*

TABLEAU 52   Nous **jouions** souvent au foot quand nous **étions** petits.

3. Another function of the imperfect tense is to denote a *state of affairs*, that is, *what was going on* in the past. In this sense, the imperfect tense corresponds to the English past progressive construction *was/were* + *doing*.

Qu'est-ce que vous **faisiez** à dix heures ?	*What were you doing at ten o'clock?*
— À dix heures ? Je **prenais** un bain.	*At ten? I was taking a bath.*
Charles **faisait** des courses pendant que je **travaillais**.	*Charles was doing errands while I was working.*

The imperfect tense denotes not only *what was going on* but also *how things were* in the past. In a narration in the past, expressions that are basically *descriptive*, providing the general background (weather, time, date), or verbs that are usually descriptive in function (being, thinking, feeling, knowing, wishing) rather than indicating physical actions, tend to be in the imperfect tense.

Il **faisait** très beau.	*The weather was very nice.*
Il **était** dix heures du matin.	*It was ten o'clock in the morning.*
C'**était** mardi après-midi.	*It was Tuesday afternoon.*
Nous **avions** sommeil.	*We were sleepy.*
Je **voulais** aller en Louisiane.	*I wanted to go to Louisiana.*

[1]**chaque fois que**   *each time (when)*

TABLEAU 53

Tu **regardais** la télévision pendant que je **faisais** mes devoirs.

A *Exercice de contrôle*

Je ne parlais pas français quand j'avais dix ans.
1. Nous   2. Tu   3. Mes camarades   4. Mon camarade

Ils étaient chez eux parce qu'ils étaient malades.
1. Vous   2. Tu   3. Mon copain   4. Nous

J'avais soif et je voulais boire quelque chose.
1. Les touristes   2. Nous   3. Tu   4. Vous

B *Nous allons comparer cette année scolaire et l'année dernière. Ajoutez des phrases d'après ce modèle.*

Je parle français maintenant.
L'année dernière je ne parlais pas français.

1. J'étudie le français maintenant.
2. Je travaille beaucoup maintenant.
3. Nous parlons français maintenant.
4. Vous me connaissez maintenant.
5. Vous comprenez vos étudiants maintenant.
6. Les étudiants vous comprennent maintenant.

C *Parlons de l'époque où[1] vous aviez treize ans. Répondez aux questions.*

1. Dans quelle ville habitiez-vous ? (« J'habitais à... »)
2. Habitiez-vous dans une maison ou dans un appartement ?
3. Combien de pièces y avait-il dans la maison (l'appartement) ?
4. Où était votre chambre ?
5. Qu'est-ce qu'il y avait au-dessus de votre chambre ?
6. Qu'est-ce que vous faisiez comme sport ?
7. Quelle émission regardiez-vous souvent à la télévision ?
8. Maintenant, vous pouvez poser quelques questions sur mon passé.

D *Répondez aux questions.*

1. Combien de cours avez-vous ce semestre (trimestre) ? Combien de cours aviez-vous le semestre (trimestre) dernier ?
2. Quelle est la date aujourd'hui ? Quelle était la date hier ? Quel jour de la semaine est-ce que c'était ?
3. Quelle heure est-il maintenant ? Quelle heure était-il il y a dix minutes ? Qu'est-ce que nous faisions il y a dix minutes ?
4. Quel temps fait-il aujourd'hui ? Quel temps faisait-il hier soir ? Et avant-hier ?
5. Où étiez-vous hier soir à neuf heures ? Qu'est-ce que vous faisiez ? Aviez-vous sommeil ?

[1]**l'époque où** *the time (time period) when*

🖭 *Exercice supplémentaire*

🖭 *Compréhension auditive*

10.2 PRONOM PERSONNEL COMPLÉMENT D'OBJET INDIRECT

1. An indirect object (**à** + noun) designating human beings and animals can be replaced by the pronouns **lui** (s) and **leur** (pl). In negative sentences, **ne** comes before **lui** or **leur**. In the *passé composé*, the past participle does *not* agree with a preceding *indirect* object.

Nous avons parlé **au professeur**.	Je n'ai pas téléphoné **à mes parents**.
→ Nous **lui** avons parlé.	→ Je ne **leur** ai pas téléphoné.
As-tu répondu **à tes cousins** ?	Elle ne ressemblait pas **à sa mère**.
→ **Leur** as-tu répondu ?	→ Elle ne **lui** ressemblait pas.

2. Do not confuse the pronoun **leur** *them* and the possessive adjective **leur/leurs** *their*. The object pronoun precedes a *verb*, and the possessive adjective precedes a *noun*.

Je ne **leur** parle pas souvent.	*I don't speak to them often.*
Je n'ai pas **leurs** adresses.	*I don't have their addresses.*
Vous ne **leur** avez pas répondu.	*You didn't answer them.*
Vous n'avez pas répondu à **leur** lettre.	*You didn't answer their letter.*

3. The pronouns **me/m'**, **te/t'**, **nous**, and **vous**, which you learned as direct-object pronouns in Lesson 9.1, can also be used as indirect-object pronouns. In the examples below, they are indirect objects since each verb takes **à** + noun.[1]

obéir à	Il ne **t'**obéit jamais.	*He never obeys you.*
parler à	Je **te** parle souvent.	*I often speak to you.*
répondre à	Tu ne **me** réponds pas.	*You don't answer me.*
ressembler à	Il ne **vous** ressemble pas.	*He doesn't look like you.*
téléphoner à	Elle **nous** téléphone.	*She phones us.*

You can also use an indirect-object pronoun for verbs that take both direct and indirect-object pronouns.[2]

Avez-vous envoyé la lettre **à Jeanne** ?	*Did you send the letter to Jeanne?*
— Oui, je **lui** ai envoyé la lettre.	*Yes, I sent her the letter.*
Est-ce qu'elle **vous** explique la leçon ?	*Does she explain the lesson to you?*
— Oui, elle **m'**explique la leçon.	*Yes, she explains the lesson to me.*

4. *Inversion.* The object pronoun always comes immediately before the verb when inversion is used.

Vous ressemble-t-il ?	*Does he look like you?*
Leur parlez-vous souvent ?	*Do you speak to them often?*
Ne **lui** répondez-vous pas ?	*Don't you answer him/her?*
Ne **t'**obéit-il pas ?	*Doesn't he obey you?*

In the *passé composé*, the pronoun comes immediately before the auxiliary.

Vous a-t-elle téléphoné ?	*Did she phone you?*
Je ne **lui** ai jamais parlé.	*I have never spoken to him.*
Ne **leur** as-tu pas répondu ?	*Didn't you answer them ?*

[1]Verbs that take **à** + stressed pronoun (**être à**, **penser à**) will be presented in Lesson 12.2.
[2]Use of two object pronouns (direct and indirect) will be presented in Lesson 12.5.

« C'est vrai ? Tu lui as vraiment dit ça ? »

5. If an infinitive takes an indirect-object pronoun, the pronoun comes immediately before the infinitive.

Allez-vous répondre **à Marie** ?	*Are you going to answer Marie?*
— Je vais **lui** répondre demain.	*I'm going to answer her tomorrow.*
Pouvez-vous téléphoner **à mes parents** ?	*Can you phone my parents?*
— Je peux **leur** téléphoner ce soir.	*I can phone them tonight.*

6. Here is a summary of the personal pronouns you have learned so far.

SUJET	OBJET	
	DIRECT	INDIRECT
je **tu**	**me/m'** **te/t'**	
nous **vous**	**nous** **vous**	
il **elle**	**le/l'** **la/l'**	**lui**
ils **elles**	**les**	**leur**

🔲 **A** *Répondez aux questions en employant le pronom objet indirect.*

> *Modèles :* Avez-vous parlé à (Jacques) ?
> **Oui, je lui ai parlé** (*ou* **Non, je ne lui ai pas parlé**).
> M'avez-vous montré vos devoirs ?
> **Oui, je vous ai montré mes devoirs** (*ou* **Non, je ne vous ai pas montré mes devoirs**).

1. Avez-vous téléphoné à (Mireille) ?
2. Ressemblez-vous à vos parents ?
3. (Paul) ressemble-t-il à (Jeanne) ?
4. Obéissez-vous aux agents ?
5. Avez-vous répondu à vos parents ?
6. Qui vous explique la leçon ?
7. Avez-vous donné une pomme à (Jean) ?[1]
8. M'avez-vous donné de l'argent ?[1]

🔲 **B** *Répondez aux questions en employant* **le, la, les, lui** *ou* **leur.**

1. Écoutez-vous votre professeur ?
2. Répondez-vous à votre professeur ?
3. Connaissez-vous mes parents ?
4. Ressemblez-vous à Brooke Shields ?
5. Avez-vous visité la Louisiane ?
6. Avez-vous parlé à Paul Newman ?
7. Allez-vous regarder la télé ce soir ?
8. Pouvez-vous téléphoner à Mickey Mouse ?

C *Répondez aux questions.*

1. Est-ce que je vous parle maintenant ? Avez-vous parlé à vos parents ce matin ? Avez-vous jamais parlé au président de l'université ?
2. Est-ce que je vous ressemble ? Me ressemblez-vous ? Ressemblez-vous à Jacqueline Bisset ?
3. Est-ce que j'ai posé une question à (Jacques) ? Est-ce que (Jacques) m'a répondu ? M'a-t-il donné une réponse ?
4. À qui téléphonez-vous souvent ? Lui (Leur) avez-vous téléphoné hier soir ? Quand allez-vous lui (leur) téléphoner ?
5. Obéissiez-vous toujours à votre père quand vous étiez petit(e) ? Et à votre mère ? Leur obéissez-vous maintenant ?

10.3 **DIRE**

1. Study the conjugation of **dire** *to say, to tell.*

> Je **dis** mon opinion quand je veux.
> Tu ne **dis** pas la vérité à ton ami.
> Il **dit** la vérité à ses parents.
> J'ai **dit** des choses amusantes.[2]
>
> Nous **disons** bonjour au professeur.
> Vous **dites** au revoir aux étudiants.
> Ils me **disent** quelque chose.

dire

dis	disons
dis	*dites*
dit	disent
dit	

Dire is one of three verbs whose **vous** form of the present indicative does not end in **-ez**. Note that the *accent circonflexe* occurs only in **vous êtes**.

être : vous **êtes**   **faire** : vous **faites**   **dire** : vous **dites**

2. **Dire** can be followed by a direct-object noun (as in the sentences above) with or without an indirect object, or by **que, quand, si, pourquoi,** or other words followed by a sentence (such sentences are called *dependent clauses*, while the one containing **dire** is called a *main clause*; you saw this construction with **vouloir dire** in Lesson 5.1). English has similar constructions.

---

[1]Employez **... pas de ...** dans les réponses négatives.

[2]The past participle will be included from now on in the presentation of irregular verbs.

Je vais dire
$\begin{cases} \textbf{mon opinion.} \\ \textbf{que Paul est ici.} \\ \textbf{quand il est parti.} \end{cases}$
I am going to say
$\begin{cases} \textit{my opinion.} \\ \textit{that Paul is here.} \\ \textit{when he left.} \end{cases}$

Dites-moi
$\begin{cases} \textbf{si vous me comprenez.} \\ \textbf{pourquoi elle est là.} \\ \textbf{où vous allez.} \end{cases}$
Tell me
$\begin{cases} \textit{if you understand me.} \\ \textit{why she is there.} \\ \textit{where you are going.} \end{cases}$

3. **Dire** vs. **parler**. **Dire** *to say, tell* usually cannot be used without a direct object (what you tell); an indirect object (to whom you tell) is optional. **Parler** *to speak, talk* does not take a direct object, except for the names of languages, and it can be used with **à** and/or **de** (*to/about*).

J'**ai dit la vérité** (à mon amie).	*I said (told) the truth (to my friend).*
Il **dit** (à ses parents) **qu'il a assez d'argent**.	*He says (tells) (to his parents) that he has enough money.*
Parlez-vous **français** ?	*Do you speak French?*
J'**ai parlé à** Marie ce matin.	*I spoke (talked) to Marie this morning.*
Nous **avons parlé de** notre voyage (à nos parents).	*We spoke (talked) about our trip (to our parents).*

4. **Dire** + **à** + person + **de** + infinitive is an indirect command, corresponding to English *to tell someone to do (something).*

Je vais **dire à** Florence **d'**aller au bureau de poste.	*I am going to tell Florence to go to the post office.*
Dites aux enfants **de** nettoyer leur chambre.	*Tell the children to clean their room.*
Paul, **dis à** Michel **de** fermer la porte.	*Paul, tell Michel to close the door.*

A   *Exercice de contrôle*

Je dis bonjour à mon professeur.
1. Nous   2. Les étudiants   3. L'étudiant   4. Vous

Je dis que j'ai raison.
1. Vous   2. Tu   3. Nous   4. Mes camarades

Je dis à mes camarades de visiter le musée.
1. Cet étudiant   2. Vous   3. Tu   4. Nous

B   *Posez des questions. Puis redites[1] la réponse d'après ce modèle.*

Demandez à (Jean) s'il a faim.
As-tu faim, Jean ?
— Oui, j'ai faim. (Non, je n'ai pas faim.)
Il dit qu'il a faim (qu'il n'a pas faim).

1. Demandez à (Marie) si elle a soif.
2. Demandez à (Mireille) si elle a visité Québec.
3. Demandez à (André) s'il veut aller à Québec.
4. Demandez à (Étienne) s'il vous connaît.
5. Demandez à (Jeanne) si je suis son professeur.
6. Demandez à (Michel) si vous connaissez ses copains.

[1]du verbe **redire** *to say again*

C   *Répondez aux questions.*

1. Qu'est-ce que je dis quand j'arrive dans la classe ? Est-ce j'ai dit bonjour aujourd'hui ?
2. Qu'est-ce que je dis quand je quitte la classe ? Qu'est-ce que j'ai dit quand j'ai quitté la classe hier ?
3. Qu'est-ce qu'on dit quand on rencontre un camarade dans la rue ? Et quand on rencontre un professeur ?
4. Dites-moi quand il va neiger. Dites-moi si vous avez sommeil. Dites à (Christine) où vous allez être ce soir.
5. Qu'est-ce que je dis aux étudiants de faire ? Dites à (Vincent) de regarder sa montre. Dites à (France) de dire bonjour à (Paul).
6. À qui dites-vous « tu » ? À qui dites-vous « vous » ?

à votre copain ?	à votre chien (chat) ?
à votre professeur ?	à un monsieur ?
à l'agent de police ?	à un enfant ?
au douanier ?	à la mère de votre copain ?

   Compréhension auditive

10.4 LE PASSÉ COMPOSÉ ET L'IMPARFAIT

1. The imperfect tense, as you learned in Lesson 10.1, indicates a state of affairs (*what was going on*, *how things were*). Expressions that provide a descriptive function in a narration are usually in the imperfect tense. The wavy lines in the examples below represent what was going on.

Il **faisait** son lit. ～～～～→	*He was making his bed.*
Vous l'**attendiez**. ～～～～→	*You were waiting for him.*
→ Il **faisait** son lit pendant que vous l'**attendiez**.	→ *He was making his bed while you were waiting for him.*
Mes parents **habitaient** une grande maison quand j'**avais** dix ans.	*My parents were living in a large house when I was ten.*
Elle **écoutait** la radio pendant que sa camarade de chambre **travaillait**.	*She was listening to the radio while her roommate was working.*

2. Actions that are not continuous or descriptive, i.e., are not providing a "background" for some other actions, are usually in the *passé composé*. The straight lines below show such actions.

J'**ai donné** la réponse. ⎯⎯↑ ↑	*I gave the answer.*
Elle **a dit** « Bon ». ⎯⎯⏎	*She said "Fine."*
→ Elle **a dit** « Bon » quand j'**ai donné** la réponse.	→ *She said "Fine" when I gave the answer.*
Il **a pris** son blouson et il **est sorti** de sa chambre.	*He took his windbreaker and went out of his room.*
Elle **a prononcé** le mot et nous l'**avons répété**.	*She pronounced the word and we repeated it.*

3. The imperfect and the *passé composé* can occur in the same sentence. The imperfect shows what was going on or how things were, providing "background" information against which certain actions took place.

J'**étais** au lit. ～～～↑～→	*I was in bed.*
Le téléphone **a sonné**. ⎯⎯⏎	*The phone rang.*
→ J'**étais** au lit quand le téléphone **a sonné**.	→ *I was in bed when the phone rang.*

« Ce matin, ma camionette ne marchait pas, alors j'ai attelé mon vieux cheval. »

Il **pleuvait** quand nous **sommes sortis**.	*It was raining when we went out.*
Le professeur **expliquait** la leçon quand je **suis entrée** dans la classe.	*The professor was explaining the lesson when I entered the classroom.*
Il **faisait** froid et il **avait** faim quand il **est parti**.	*It was cold and he was hungry when he left.*
Elle m'**a donné** l'adresse quand je lui **ai dit** que je ne la **savais** pas.	*She gave me the address when I told her that I didn't know it.*

4. The distinction between the *passé composé* and the imperfect can be subtle. It is not something you can learn in a few days. But you will develop a good "feel" for it as you practice using them. Just remember that the *passé composé* denotes an action (answering questions like "What happened?," "What did people do?"), while the imperfect denotes a *condition* or a *situation* (answering questions like "What was going on?," "What was the situation?," "How were things/people?"), and that certain verbs, such as **être**, **avoir**, **savoir**, **vouloir**, **pouvoir**, **penser**, **ressembler**, which usually do not indicate a physical action, often take the imperfect. Before you go over the oral exercises, read the following passage in English, in which a young man describes his afternoon, and decide which verbs would be in the *passé composé* and which would be in the imperfect. Then compare the passage with the French version in the footnote.

(1) It **was** sunny this afternoon. (2) I **returned** to the dorm at three. (3) I **finished** my homework around four. (4) I **was** a little tired, and (5) I **decided** to take a walk. As (6) I **was leaving** my room, (7) the telephone **rang**. (8) It **was** Marie. (9) She **asked** me if (10) I **had** one of her books. (11) I **told** her that (12) I **didn't have** it. (13) Since (*Puisque*) I **wanted** to go out, (14) I **asked** Marie if (15) she **wanted** to take a walk with me. (16) She **accepted** my invitation. (17) I **took** my jacket and (18) I **left** the dorm. (19) Marie **was waiting** for me when (20) I **got to** [= **arrived at**] her apartment. (21) We **went** downtown. (22) We **walked** and **chatted** (*bavarder*) for (*pendant*) an hour and a half. (23) We **were** thirsty. (24) We **found** a café and (25) we **ordered** a Coke. (26) It **was** six when (27) I **returned** home.[1]

---

[1](1) Il **faisait** du soleil cet après-midi. (2) Je **suis rentré** à la résidence à trois heures. (3) J'**ai fini** mes devoirs vers quatre heures. (4) J'**étais** un peu fatigué, et (5) j'**ai décidé** de faire une promenade. Comme (6) je **sortais** de ma chambre, (7) le téléphone **a sonné**. (8) C'**était** Marie. (9) Elle m'**a demandé** si (10) j'**avais** un de ses livres. (11) Je lui **ai dit** que (12) je **ne l'avais pas**. (13) Puisque je **voulais** sortir, (14) j'**ai demandé** à Marie si (15) elle **voulait** faire une promenade avec moi. (16) Elle **a accepté** mon invitation. (17) J'**ai pris** mon blouson et (18) j'**ai quitté**/je **suis sorti** de/je **suis parti** de la résidence. (19) Marie m'**attendait** quand (20) je **suis arrivé** à son appartement. (21) Nous **sommes allés** en ville. (22) Nous **avons marché** et **bavardé** pendant une heure et demie. (23) Nous **avions** soif. (24) Nous **avons trouvé** un café et (25) nous **avons commandé** un Coca-Cola. (26) Il **était** six heures quand (27) je **suis rentré**.

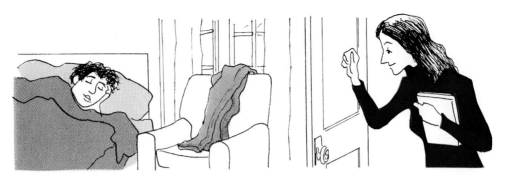

TABLEAU 54   J'**étais** au lit quand elle **a frappé** à la porte.

A *Exercice de contrôle*

J'étais fatigué(e) quand je suis rentré(e).
1. Nous   2. L'étudiant   3. Vous   4. Les étudiants

J'ai fait la sieste¹ parce que j'avais sommeil.
1. Nous   2. Le professeur   3. Les étudiants   4. Vous

J'écoutais la radio quand le téléphone a sonné.
1. Vous   2. Le professeur   3. Tu   4. Nous

J'ai mangé parce que j'avais faim.
1. Tu   2. L'étudiant   3. Nous   4. Vous

B *Avez-vous bonne mémoire ? Nous allons parler de notre premier jour de classe. Répondez à ces questions.*

1. Quelle était la date du premier jour de classe ?
2. Quel temps faisait-il ?
3. Est-ce que vous étiez en classe ?
4. À quelle heure est-ce que le cours a commencé ?
5. Aviez-vous votre livre de français ?
6. Saviez-vous que j'étais votre professeur ?
7. Qu'est-ce que nous avons fait ?
8. Connaissiez-vous (Jacqueline) ?
9. Où êtes-vous allé(e) après le cours ?

C *Répondez aux questions. Faites attention au temps² de chaque verbe.*

1. À quelle heure êtes-vous sorti(e) de la maison ce matin ?
2. Quel temps faisait-il ce matin ?
3. Le cours de français était-il votre premier cours ?
4. À quelle heure êtes-vous venu(e) à notre cours ?
5. Qui était dans la classe quand vous êtes arrivé(e) ?
6. Qu'est-ce que votre voisin(e) faisait quand vous êtes arrivé(e) ?
7. Est-ce que j'étais dans la classe ?
8. Est-ce que (Mireille) était dans la classe ?
9. Qu'est-ce que j'ai dit quand je suis entré(e) ?

¹**faire la sieste**   *to take a nap*
²**temps**   *tense*

D *Écoutez cette histoire. Une étudiante raconte comment elle a passé une soirée. Mettez chaque verbe au passé.*

(1) Mon dernier cours finit à quatre heures. (2) J'ai froid quand je quitte mon cours. (3) Il fait du vent et il fait frais. (4) Je rentre tout de suite[1] à la résidence. (5) Je suis fatiguée et je ne veux pas travailler. (6) Je décide de faire la sieste. (7) Quelqu'un frappe à la porte quand je suis au lit. (8) C'est Marie. Elle demande si je vais bien. (9) Elle veut savoir si je suis libre ce soir. (10) Je suis libre, mais je demande pourquoi. (11) Elle dit qu'il y a un bon film en ville. (12) Nous dînons ensemble à sept heures. (13) Nous quittons la résidence après le dîner. (14) Nous arrivons au cinéma vers huit heures. (15) Il y a une longue queue devant le guichet. (16) Le film est bon, et la salle est bondée. (17) Il pleut quand nous sortons du cinéma. (18) Nous allons dans un café, car nous avons froid. (19) Nous prenons du chocolat. (20) Il est presque minuit quand nous rentrons.

📟 *Exercice supplémentaire*

📟 *Compréhension auditive*

10.5 FORMES NÉGATIVES **NE ... PERSONNE, NE ... RIEN**

1. **Personne** *no one* is the opposite of **quelqu'un** *someone* or **tout le monde** *everyone*; **rien** *nothing* is the opposite of **quelque chose** *something* or **tout** *everything*. The place of these negative words in a sentence depends on their function. Note that **ne** still precedes the verb and **pas** cannot be used with **personne** and **rien**.

a) As the *subject*, they come where a subject should be, i.e., before **ne** and the verb.

Marie ne comprend pas cet enfant.	*Marie doesn't understand this child.*
→ **Personne** ne comprend cet enfant.	→ *No one understands this child.*
Cette ville n'était pas passionnante.	*This city was not exciting.*
→ **Rien** n'était passionnant.	→ *Nothing was exciting.*

b) As the *indirect object* and the *object of a preposition*, they both occupy the same position as the corresponding noun objects.

Nous ne répondons pas **à la cliente**.	Nous ne répondons pas **à sa question**.
→ Nous ne répondons **à personne**.	→ Nous ne répondons **à rien**.
N'as-tu pas parlé **de mon frère** ?	N'as-tu pas parlé **de mon hôtel** ?
→ N'as-tu parlé **de personne** ?	→ N'as-tu parlé **de rien** ?
Je ne comptais pas **sur eux**.	Je ne comptais pas **sur leur aide**.
→ Je ne comptais **sur personne**.	→ Je ne comptais **sur rien**.

c) As the *direct object* of a verb, they are both behind the verb, where a direct object should be, in *simple* tenses (tenses without an auxiliary, i.e., the present or the imperfect).

Je n'achète pas **de souvenirs**.	*I don't buy any souvenirs.*
→ Je n'achète **rien**.	→ *I buy nothing.*
Il ne connaissait pas **ces hommes**.	*He didn't know these men.*
→ Il ne connaissait **personne**.	→ *He knew no one.*

But, in compound tenses (with an auxiliary, i.e., the *passé composé*), **personne** follows the verb; but **rien**, like **pas**, comes between the auxiliary and the past participle.

[1]**tout de suite** *right away*

Je n'ai pas compris **le guide**.	*I didn't understand the guide.*
→ Je n'ai compris **personne**.	→ *I understood no one.*
Je n'ai pas compris **la question**.	*I didn't understand the question.*
→ Je n'ai **rien** compris.	→ *I understood nothing.*

2. If **personne**, **quelqu'un**, **rien**, or **quelque chose** is modified by an adjective, **de** + masculine singular adjective is used.

Tu connais **quelqu'un d'intéressant** ?	*Do you know anyone interesting?*
— Je **ne** connais **personne d'intéressant**.	*I know no one interesting.*
Avez-vous trouvé **quelque chose de bon** ?	*Have you found anything good?*
— Je **n'ai rien** trouvé **de bon**.	*I found nothing good.*

3. Both **personne** and **rien** can be used as single-word negative answers. If the verb in question takes a preposition, that preposition must also precede **personne** and **rien** in the answer.

Qui sait la réponse ?	**Qu'est-ce qui** se passe ?[1]
— **Personne**.	— **Rien**.
De qui parle-t-elle ?	**À quoi** pensait-elle ?
— **De personne**.	— **À rien**.

4. The pronoun **tout** corresponds to *everything* or *all*. Note that in the *passé composé*, it comes immediately before the past participle.

Tout est cher dans ce magasin.	*Everything is expensive in this store.*
Tout est facile dans ce chapitre.	*Everything is easy in this chapter.*
J'achète **tout**.	*I buy everything.*
→ J'ai **tout** acheté.	→ *I bought everything.*
→ Je n'ai pas **tout** acheté.	→ *I did not buy everything.*

Qui regarde la télévision ?
Personne !

[1]*What's going on?*

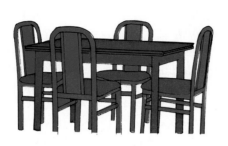

Il **n'**y a **rien** sur la table.
Rien n'est sur la table.

Il **n'**y a **personne** dans la chambre.
Personne n'est dans la chambre.

TABLEAU 55

A *Vous allez être en contradiction avec moi. Ajoutez des phrases négatives d'après ce modèle.*

J'achète tout.
Ce n'est pas vrai, vous n'achetez rien !
Je connais tout le monde.
Ce n'est pas vrai, vous ne connaissez personne !

1. Je sais tout.
2. Je connais tout le monde.
3. J'ai besoin de tout.
4. Je comprends tout le monde.
5. Je pense à tout.

6. Je fais tout.
7. Je parle à tout le monde.
8. J'ai besoin de tout le monde.
9. Je mange tout.
10. Je parle de tout.

Maintenant, ajoutez des phrases d'après ce modèle.

J'ai tout acheté.
Mais non, vous n'avez rien acheté !

J'ai connu tout le monde.
Mais non, vous n'avez connu personne !

B *Répondez négativement d'après ce modèle.*

Apprenez-vous quelque chose d'intéressant ?
Non, je n'apprends rien d'intéressant.

1. Pensez-vous à quelque chose d'important ?
2. Avez-vous besoin de quelque chose ?
3. (Sophie) a-t-elle bu quelque chose ?
4. Avez-vous trouvé quelque chose d'intéressant ?
5. Est-ce que j'ai fait quelque chose de bête ?
6. Y a-t-il quelqu'un de bête dans ce cours ?
7. Est-ce que j'ai parlé de quelque chose d'important ?
8. Est-ce que quelque chose de bizarre est arrivé[1] ?
9. Est-ce que quelqu'un vous a téléphoné à minuit ?
10. Est-ce qu'un accident est arrivé ce matin ?
11. Y a-t-il quelqu'un à la porte ?
12. Est-ce que j'ai quelque chose dans la main ?

Exercice supplémentaire

[1]**arriver** *to happen*

APPLICATIONS

C'est une très vieille maison acadienne. L'escalier est dehors, dans le coin de la véranda. Il mène à la garçonnière.

A Situations
En « Acadiana »[1]

Jean-Paul Chabrier et sa sœur Monique sont allés en Louisiane au cours de[2] leur séjour au
New Orleans *Canada et aux États-Unis. D'abord ils ont visité la Nouvelle-Orléans°. Ils ont fait la connais-*
sance de Bill Broussard, un étudiant qui travaillait dans leur hôtel. Bill leur a montré le Vieux
Carré, quartier pittoresque de la ville où il y a de nombreux[3] cafés, restaurants, boutiques et
nightclubs *boîtes de nuit°. Un jour ils sont allés à Lafayette, « cœur de la Louisiane francophone ». Là,*   5
beginning *ils ont visité une maison du début° du dix-huitième siècle.*

how   MONIQUE   Regarde comme° la salle de séjour est petite.

          JEAN-PAUL On préparait les repas dans cette cheminée autrefois ?

guidebook/separate BILL   Non, d'après le guide°, les femmes faisaient la cuisine[4] dans une cabane à part°,
                          là-bas, à côté de la maison.   10

          MONIQUE   Pendant que les hommes attendaient tranquillement leur repas, je suppose ?

          BILL   Oui, mais après une longue journée de travail. Voilà la chambre des parents et,
                     plus loin[5], la chambre des filles[6].

[1]Les habitants du pays des « Cajuns » préfèrent appeler leur région « Acadiana ». Le mot anglais *Cajun* vient du mot
« Acadien ».

[2]*in the course of* (= pendant)

[3]**de nombreux** = beaucoup de

[4]**faire la cuisine** = préparer un repas

[5]*beyond* (literally, *farther*)

[6]Le mot **fille** signifie *girl* (= **jeune fille**) aussi bien que *daughter* (le contraire de **fils**).

MONIQUE Tu as remarqué, Jean-Paul ? Les filles traversaient la chambre de leurs parents pour aller au lit ! 15

JEAN-PAUL Oui, elles étaient bien surveillées, je suppose.

MONIQUE Et les garçons, où est-ce qu'ils couchaient[1] ?

Above BILL En haut°, dans la garçonnière.

JEAN-PAUL Mais il n'y a pas d'escalier dans la maison.

BILL Il est dehors. Regarde dans le coin de la véranda. 20

MONIQUE Allons voir !

Ils montent l'escalier et regardent la garçonnière.

How dark it is! JEAN-PAUL Comme c'est sombre !° Il n'y a pas de fenêtre.

BILL Oui, c'est un peu déprimant.

MONIQUE Mais les garçons avaient une entrée privée. Ils avaient aussi ce grand grenier 25 comme chambre.

JEAN-PAUL Tu veux dire qu'ils avaient plus de liberté que[2] leurs sœurs.

MONIQUE Exactement.

the poor souls JEAN-PAUL Mais qu'est-ce qu'ils pouvaient faire, les pauvres°, au-dessus des chambres de leurs parents et de leurs sœurs ? Inviter des filles et danser ? Impossible ! 30

Répondez aux questions. (*lignes 1–6*)

1. Dans quelle ville est-ce que Jean-Paul et Monique ont fait la connaissance de Bill ?
2. Où est-ce qu'il y a beaucoup de boîtes de nuit ?
3. Quel quartier est-ce que Bill leur a montré ?
4. Quelle sorte de maison ont-ils visitée ?

(*lignes 7–30*)

5. Comment est la salle de séjour ?
6. Où est-ce que les femmes faisaient la cuisine ?
7. Qu'est-ce que les filles traversaient pour entrer dans leur chambre ?
8. Où est l'escalier ?
9. Qu'est-ce qu'il n'y a pas dans la garçonnière ?
10. Qui avait une entrée privée ?

MIAMI/MIAMI BEACH
et
FLORIDE
USA

WASHINGTON, D.C.
PHILADELPHIE
et le pays de George Washington
USA

MINNEAPOLIS
ST. PAUL
Minnesota, Wisconsin et Iowa
USA

LA NOUVELLE-
ORLEANS
et
LE SUD
USA

SAN FRANCISCO
Nord de la Californie
Nord du Nevada
USA

CHICAGO
DETROIT
et le Pays des Grands Lacs
USA

---

[1]**coucher** = passer la nuit, dormir

[2]**plus de liberté que** *more freedom than*

B Expressions utiles

La maison (1)[1]

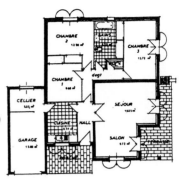

La maison a
{
un toit (rouge, gris-bleu, etc.).
un grenier.
un étage supérieur.
un rez-de-chaussée.
un sous-sol (une cave).
}

Les pièces :
{
une salle de séjour / un séjour (un salon[2])
une cuisine
une salle à manger
une salle de bains[3]
un cabinet de travail / un bureau
une chambre (à coucher)
une chambre d'amis[4]
}

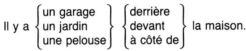

Il y a
{
un garage
un jardin
une pelouse
}
{
derrière
devant
à côté de
}
la maison.

La chambre est
{
au bout[5]
au fond[6]
à gauche
à droite
au-dessus[7]
au-dessous[8]
}
{
du couloir.
de l'escalier.
}

C Pratique

1. Comment s'appelle la pièce où on passe la nuit ? Et la pièce où on prépare les repas ? Et la pièce où on prend le dîner ? Et la pièce où on prend un bain ?

2. Dans quelle pièce fait-on les choses suivantes ?

   prendre une douche
   préparer un repas
   regarder la télé
   faire sa toilette[9]

   aller au lit
   prendre le petit déjeuner
   prendre un bain
   prendre le déjeuner du dimanche

3. Comment s'appelle l'étage qui est au niveau de[10] la rue ? Et l'étage qui est au-dessus ? Et l'étage qui est au-dessous ?

4. Décrivez une maison à deux étages. Puis demandez à vos camarades de dessiner le plan de cette maison.

---

[1]The vocabulary for furniture and fixtures will be presented in Lesson 14.

[2]**un salon**   *a drawing room* (normally found in a very large house)

[3]In most homes, the toilet (**les w.-c., les toilettes, le petit coin**) is in a small, separate room. See *Différences* of this lesson.

[4]*guest room*

[5]**au bout de**   *at the end of*

[6]**au fond de**   *at the end of* (literally, *in the back of*)

[7]**au-dessus de**   *above*

[8]**au-dessous de**   *below*

[9]*to wash and dress*

[10]**au niveau de**   *at the same level as* (literally, *at the level of*)

D **Mini-composition :** *Jean-Paul, Monique et Bill ont passé une journée autour de Lafayette. Complétez le passage en employant les mots indiqués.*

(1) Nous/quitter/la Nouvelle-Orléans/à/8 h. (2) D'abord/nous/visiter/Bâton Rouge,/et/il/être/presque/11 h/demi/quand/nous/arriver/Lafayette. (3) Bill/et/Jean-Paul/avoir faim/et/nous/chercher/restaurant. (4) Bill/inviter/nous/à/goûter/cuisine[1]/créole. (5) Après,/nous/visiter/églises,/vieux/maisons/et/monuments. (6) Nous/poser/beaucoup/question/à/Bill. (7) Je/ne pas/savoir/que/il/connaître/si bien[2]/ce/région. (8) À/Saint-Martinville,/où/il y a/monument/consacré/à/Évangeline,/Bill/raconter/nous/histoire/de/Évangeline. (9)Il/citer/quelques/vers/de/Longfellow. (10) Nous/écouter/les/et/je/trouver/son/récit/émouvant. (11) Nous/visiter/d'autres[3]/village/et/nous/dîner/à/Abbeville/(beaucoup/huître/et/écrevisses !). (12) Il/être/tard/et/nous/être/très/fatigué/quand/nous/rentrer/à/Nouvelle-Orléans.

E **Questions :** *Bill Broussard parle de sa famille. Lisez d'abord le paragraphe, ensuite posez des questions sur les parties soulignées.*

Mes grands-parents habitaient près d'Abbeville (1) il y a soixante ans. Ils cultivaient (2) le riz et le maïs. Ils avaient (3) quatre enfants. Mon père est né en (4) 1932. (5) Tout le monde parlait français dans la famille. Les passe-temps préférés[4] de la famille étaient (6) la chasse et la pêche : on chassait surtout les rats musqués[5] (7) pour vendre leur fourrure. Comme les autres Acadiens, ils adoraient les fêtes. Ils aimaient « laisser le bon temps rouler »[6]. Ils assistaient (8) aux[7] « fais dodo »[8] (bal du samedi soir). Mon père avait (9) vingt ans quand il est parti pour Bâton Rouge. Il est devenu (10) ingénieur-chimiste[9]. (11) Mes grands-parents sont morts il y a cinq ans. Mes parents habitent près de (12) la Nouvelle-Orléans.

F **Renseignements et opinions**

1. Qu'est-ce qu'il y a au-dessus de notre classe ? Qu'est-ce qu'il y a au-dessous de notre classe ?
2. Qui est sorti hier soir ? Où êtes-vous allé(e) ? Quel temps faisait-il ? Quelle heure était-il quand vous êtes rentré(e) ?
3. Préparez une question à poser à votre professeur, ou[10] au sujet de son enfance ou au sujet de sa maison (son appartement).
4. À qui avez-vous téléphoné hier ? Est-ce que vous lui (leur) téléphonez souvent ? Allez-vous lui (leur) téléphoner ce soir ?
5. Où étiez vous hier matin à dix heures et demie ? Qu'est-ce que vous faisiez ? Qu'est-ce que vous avez fait après ?
6. Combien coûtait une place de cinéma il y a cinq ans ? Combien coûte une place aujourd'hui ?

---

[1]ici, *food* ; utilisez l'article partitif.

[2]*so well*

[3]*other* (pluriel de **un autre**)

[4]**passe-temps préféré** *favorite pastime*

[5]*muskrats*

[6]*to have a good time* (expression acadienne)

[7]**assister à** *to attend*

[8]**fais dodo** literally, *go nighty-night* (**faire dodo** means *to go to sleep* in child talk). Parents often brought their small children to these dances and put them to sleep in an adjacent room while they danced.

[9]*chemical engineer*

[10]**ou ... ou ...** *either . . . or . . .*

🔲 *Compréhension auditive (basée sur l'Application A)*

🔲 *Compréhension auditive (basée sur l'Application B)*

🔲 *Dictée : « Un voyage pénible »*

G Lecture

L'Acadie et la Louisiane

Nous avons parlé du vaste pays qui s'appelait[1] la Nouvelle-France. Il était l'objet de conflits économiques et militaires continuels entre la France et l'Angleterre, deux grandes puissances coloniales au dix-huitième siècle. Les Anglais luttaient contre les Français et contre les Indiens, alliés des Français.[2] Les Anglais étaient forts et nombreux. Ils ont pris l'Acadie et la baie d'Hudson, et ils ont occupé Québec et Montréal. Après le traité de Paris en 1763, la France 5
Québécois a cédé toute la rive gauche du Mississippi. Les Anglais ont promis[3] aux Franco-Canadiens° le droit de garder[4] leur langue, leur religion et leur système légal. Aujourd'hui, le Canada reste officiellement bilingue.

Qu'est-ce qui est arrivé aux Acadiens ? Les Anglais n'ont rien promis aux Français qui habitaient en Acadie.[5] Après leur victoire, ils ont déporté et dispersé sur toute la côte Atlantique, 10
West Indies/more than en Louisiane et aux Indes occidentales° plus de° 100.000 Acadiens qui refusaient de leur obéir. Beaucoup d'Acadiens déportés aux Indes occidentales sont morts de maladies tropicales. Vous connaissez peut-être l'*Évangeline* de Longfellow ; ce beau poème raconte l'histoire de deux amants séparés par la déportation et évoque les malheurs des Acadiens. Aujourd'hui, dans le sud de la Louisiane, il y a plus d'un demi-million d'Américains d'origine française et 15
beaucoup de ces Américains parlent encore français. Avez-vous remarqué que le mot *Cajun* vient du mot français « Acadien » ?

Les longues années de guerre au Canada, l'aménagement des vastes territoires cédés par la France, et la réorganisation des colonies en Amérique ont coûté une fortune à l'Angleterre. Les Anglais avaient besoin d'argent. Comment payer leurs dettes ? Ils ont décidé d'im- 20
taxes/colonists poser de nouveaux impôts° aux colons° américains. Pourquoi pas un impôt sur le *thé*, par exemple ? Ainsi, la fin de la Nouvelle-France allait signaler le début de la Révolution américaine.

---

[1]l'imparfait de **s'appeler** *to be called*
[2]Cette série de guerres s'appellent « *French and Indian Wars* » en anglais.
[3]participe passé de **promettre** *to promise*
[4]**le droit de garder**   *the right to keep*
[5]Aujourd'hui les provinces maritimes du Canada (voir la *Lecture* de la Leçon 10)

A *Indiquez si chaque commentaire est vrai ou faux. S'il est faux, corrigez le commentaire.*

1. La Nouvelle-France était victime des conflits continuels entre la France et l'Angleterre.
2. Les Français luttaient contre les Indiens, qui étaient les alliés des Anglais.
3. Les Anglais n'ont rien promis aux Québécois après leur victoire.
4. Les Anglais ont dispersé les Acadiens sur toute la côte Atlantique.
5. Les Anglais ont déporté certains Acadiens aux Indes orientales.
6. Il y a beaucoup de *Cajuns* qui parlent encore français.
7. Si on lit l'*Évangeline*, on apprend l'histoire de deux jeunes gens séparés par la déportation.
8. L'impôt sur le thé a déclenché la guerre de l'indépendance américaine.

B *Que signifient les expressions suivantes ? Expliquez en français.*

un pays bilingue   l'*Évangeline*
la Nouvelle-France   l'Acadie
un conflit militaire   les Franco-Canadiens

VOCABULAIRE

Noms

l' Acadiana *f*	*Louisiana Cajun country*	un escalier	*staircase*	la **queue**	*line*
		un **étage**	*floor, story*	le **rez-de-chaussée**	*ground floor*
un **accident**	*accident*	la garçonnière	*boys' room*	la **salle de bains**	*bathroom*
la **balle**	*ball*	le **grenier**	*attic*	la **salle de séjour**	*living room*
la boîte de nuit	*nightclub*	le **guichet**	*box office; ticket window*	le **séjour**	*stay*
le **bruit**	*noise*			le **semestre**	*semester*
la cabane	*cabin*	le guide	*guidebook; guide*	le siècle	*century*
la **chambre à coucher**	*bedroom*	une journée	*day*	le **sous-sol**	*basement*
la **cheminée**	*chimney; fireplace*	la liberté	*freedom*	le **toit**	*roof*
le cœur	*heart*	la Nouvelle-Orléans	*New Orleans*	le **trimestre**	*quarter*
la cuisine	*cooking*	le **passé**	*past*	la véranda	*porch*
le début	*beginning*	la **pièce**	*room*	le Vieux Carré	*French Quarter*
le **douanier**	*customs official*	la **programme**	*program*		

Verbes

arriver	*to happen*	**expliquer**	*to explain*	**rencontrer**	*to meet*
coucher	*to spend the night*	**se passer**	*to happen*	supposer	*to suppose*
décider	*to decide*	**prêter**	*to lend*		
dire *irrég*	*to say; to tell*	remarquer	*to notice*		

Adjectifs

bizarre	*strange*	impossible	*impossible*	sombre	*dark*
bondé(e)	*crowded*	**malade**	*sick*	surveillé(e)	*watched*
déprimant(e)	*depressing*	nombreux(euse)	*numerous*		
francophone	*French-speaking*	privé(e)	*private*		

Adverbes

autrefois	*long ago, before*	**jamais**	*ever*	plus loin	*farther, beyond*
dehors	*outside*	**partout**	*everywhere*	tranquillement	*peacefully*

Prépositions

au-dessous de	*underneath*	d'après	*according to*
au-dessus de	*above*	**vers**	*around; about*

Autres expressions

à part	*separate(d)*	**ne ... personne**	*nobody*
au cours de	*in the course of*	**ne ... rien**	*nothing*
avant-hier	*the day before yesterday*	pendant que	*while*
dire à qqn de + *inf*	*to tell somebody to* + inf	**quelque chose de** + *adj*	*something* + adj
en haut	*upstairs; above*	**quelqu'un de** + *adj*	*someone* + adj
en ville	*downtown*	**réveille-toi**	*wake up*
faire la cuisine	*to do the cooking*	**tout**	*everything, all*
Hein ?	*What?*	**tout l'après-midi**	*all afternoon*
les pauvres	*poor souls*	**voir** *irrég*	*to see*

Bienvenue en ACADIANA
Atchafalaya Basin

11 Quelle belle robe !

LESSON OBJECTIVES

CONVERSATIONS

A. Les vêtements

Regardez le Tableau 56.[1] Ce sont deux étudiants français. Julien Reynaud est à gauche, et sa fiancée Ignès Lacombe est à droite. Julien porte une chemise (1), un blouson (2) et un blue-jean (5). Il ne porte pas d'imperméable (19). Il n'a pas de parapluie (20).

Regardez Ignès. Elle est à droite de Julien. Elle porte un pull à col roulé (9), une veste (10) et une jupe (11). Elle ne porte pas de manteau (22) ni de[2] gants (23).

Maintenant, répondez aux questions.

Est-ce que Julien porte un pull (18) ? Regardez son blouson. Est-ce que le blouson a des poches (4) ? A-t-il des boutons (3) ?

Est-ce qu'Ignès porte un pantalon (17) ? Porte-t-elle un chemisier (21) ? Porte-t-elle une veste ? La veste a-t-elle des poches ?

Regardez vos camarades. Qui porte un blue-jean ? Qui porte une chemise ? Qui porte un pull ? Quelle sorte de vêtements portez-vous aujourd'hui ?

[1]Le vocabulaire de ce tableau (*Expressions utiles*, p. 250) est sur la bande magnétique.
[2]**ni de** *nor*

TABLEAU 56

Maintenant, regardez mes vêtements. Quelle sorte de vêtements est-ce que je porte ? Est-ce que j'ai des poches ? Combien de poches ? Qu'est-ce qu'il y a dans cette poche ? Devinez.

B. Une vieille photo

MIREILLE	Tiens, qu'est-ce que c'est ?
DANIEL	C'est une photo. Elle est très vieille.
MIREILLE	Ce monsieur à moustache, qui est-ce ?
DANIEL	C'est mon grand-père. Il était pilote.
MIREILLE	Et ce petit garçon ?
DANIEL	C'est mon père. Lui aussi, il est pilote.

« Ce monsieur à moustache, qui est-ce ? »

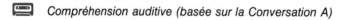 **C. C'est pour mon père.**

JACQUES   Préfères-tu le portefeuille gris ou le portefeuille brun ?
FLORENCE   Je trouve que le gris est plus élégant.
JACQUES   Oui, c'est vrai. Mais il est plus cher.
FLORENCE   Oh, regarde ce portefeuille en croco[1] noir. C'est le plus beau.
JACQUES   Dis donc[2], il coûte 550 F. Je ne suis pas millionnaire !

Compréhension auditive (basée sur la Conversation A)

DIFFÉRENCES

Le système métrique

On utilise le système métrique au Canada.

[1]**croco** = crocodile (*alligator leather*)
[2]*Hey*

The metric system of measurement is used in France, as in the rest of Europe. It was developed by a commission of French scientists shortly after the Revolution of 1789, in an attempt to establish a compatible decimal system for length, weights, and liquid measures. It finally became the obligatory standard of measure in 1840. The meter was originally defined as one ten-millionth of the distance from the earth's pole to the equator. You can still see the original measure, a platinum bar, in the **Bureau International des Poids et Mesures** near Paris. Most other nations have since adopted the metric system, including Britain and Canada. Only a dozen countries in the world have yet to convert to the system: the United States is the only major nation, the rest being mini-states such as Tonga, Oman, and Barbados. In 1975, the U.S. Congress passed the Metric Conversion Act in order to coordinate voluntary conversion. Nowadays most American products are based on metric measurements in order to facilitate their exportation.

Here is a conversion table between the metric and the American systems, which will be used in some of the exercises in this lesson. Note that in French a comma (**une virgule**) indicates a decimal point.

un **pouce** = 2,54 cm	**deux** *centimètres* **cinquante-quatre**
un **pied** = 30,5 cm	**trente** *centimètres* **cinq**
un **mille** = 1,609 km	**un** *kilomètre* **six cent neuf**
un **kilomètre** = 0,621 mille	**zéro** *mille* **six cent vingt et un**
un **mètre** = 39,37 pouces	**trente-neuf** *pouces* **trente-sept**
une **livre** = 454 g	**quatre cent cinquante-quatre** *grammes*
un **kilo** = 2,20 livres	**deux** *livres* **vingt**
un **gallon**[1] = 3,785 l	**trois** *litres* **sept cent quatre-vingt-cinq**

When you travel in Europe, you will often find it necessary to convert the metric system back to the American way. Here are quick formulas to make rough estimates.

kilometers to miles	Multiply kilometers by 0.6
kilograms to pounds	Double the kilos.
meters to feet	Multiply meters by 3.
Celsius to Farenheit	Double Celsius, and add 32.
liters to gallons	Divide by 4.

STRUCTURES

11.1 **METTRE**

1. **Mettre** *to put* (something somewhere) is conjugated somewhat like a third-conjugation verb (**-re**). The sound /t/, represented by **-tt-**, occurs only in the plural forms.[2]

mettre

mets	mettons
mets	mettez
met	mettent
mis	

Je **mets** ce livre sur la table.   Nous **mettons** du lait dans ce thé.
Tu **mets** du sucre dans ton café.   **Mettez** cet argent dans votre poche.
   Il **met** son enfant au lit.   Ils **mettent** les verbes à l'imparfait.
                    J'ai **mis** la lettre dans l'enveloppe.

[1]**un gallon américain** ; il y a 4,545 litres dans un **gallon impérial**.

[2]There are verbs that derive from **mettre** and are conjugated like it, though they do not occur in this lesson: **admettre** *to admit*, **commettre** *to commit*, **compromettre** *to compromise*, **émettre** *to emit, to broadcast*, **permettre** *to permit*, **promettre** *to promise*, **réadmettre** *to readmit*, **remettre** *to postpone*, **soumettre** *to submit*, **transmettre** *to transmit*. Note that many have cognates in English.

« Je vais l'acheter et la mettre ce soir. »

2. **Mettre** also means *to put on* (clothes). **Porter**, as in the **Conversation A** of this lesson (p. 232), means *to wear* (clothes) as well as *to carry, to take (something somewhere)*. **Prendre** means *to take* but not *to take (something) to a place*.

Je **mets** un pull quand j'ai froid.	*I put on a sweater when I am cold.*
On **met** des vêtements légers en été.	*One puts on light clothes in summer.*
Mettez ce pull ; il fait froid ici.	*Put on this sweater; it's cold here.*
Elle **porte** une jolie robe bleue.	*She is wearing a nice blue dress.*
Portez cette valise, s'il vous plaît.	*Please carry this suitcase.*
Portez cela au bureau de poste.	*Take that to the post office.*
Prenez ce parapluie.	*Take this umbrella.*

TABLEAU 57   Il **met** un pull-over.   Elle **porte** une jolie robe.
Elle **met** son sac sur la table.

*« **Portez** ces lettres au bureau de Mme Dupin. »*

A   *Exercice de contrôle*

Nous mettons nos clés sur notre table.
1. Tu   2. Le professeur   3. Les étudiants   4. Vous

Je mets des vêtements légers en été.
1. Tu   2. On   3. Nous   4. Les enfants

Je n'ai pas mis de pull parce qu'il ne faisait pas froid.
1. Vous   2. Les enfants   3. On   4. Nous

B *Répondez aux questions.*

1. Regardez. Voici une lettre et une enveloppe. Je mets la lettre dans l'enveloppe. Qu'est-ce que j'ai fait ? Je mets l'enveloppe sur la table. Où est-ce que j'ai mis l'enveloppe ?
2. Où est-ce que j'ai mis mon cahier ? Où est-ce que j'ai mis mes clés ? Où avez-vous mis votre livre de français ?
3. Quand mettez-vous des gants ? Demandez à (Hélène) quand elle met un maillot de bain[1].
4. Avez-vous des cravates ? Quand mettez-vous une cravate ? Quand avez-vous mis une cravate ?
5. Quand est-ce qu'on met des vêtements chauds ? Quand est-ce qu'on met des vêtements légers ?
6. Demandez à votre partenaire quels vêtements il (elle) porte aujourd'hui. Demandez quels vêtements il (elle) portait hier.
7. (Jean), prenez cette lettre. Avez-vous pris la lettre ? Portez la lettre au bureau de poste, s'il vous plaît. Où allez-vous porter la lettre ?

Exercice supplémentaire

Compréhension auditive

11.2 ADJECTIFS POSTPOSÉS ET PRÉPOSÉS ; EMPLOI DE **IL EST/C'EST**

1. Most adjectives, when they modify a noun directly, come after the noun (**postposé** *"postposed"*). After a singular noun, no liaison can be made between the noun and the adjective (shown by // in the examples below).

   C'est un enfant//**intelligent**.

   Ce médecin//**anglais** est un ami de mon père.

   After a plural noun, liaison is optional between the noun and the adjective (**liaison facultative**, shown by ⌣⌣ in the examples below).

   Vous avez donné des réponses **originales**.

   Il a acheté des journaux **américains**.

2. But about a dozen commonly used adjectives, most of them consisting of only one or two syllables, usually come in front of the nouns they modify (hence **préposé** *"preposed"*). You will need to learn these adjectives thoroughly.

un **gros** livre, une **grosse** voiture	*big (fat)*
un **grand** lit, une **grande** maison	*big, tall*
un **petit** livret, une **petite** table	*small, little*
un **bon** journal, une **bonne** montre	*good*
un **mauvais** fruit, une **mauvaise** pomme	*bad*
un **nouveau** vendeur, une **nouvelle** vendeuse	*new*
un **jeune** homme, une **jeune** femme	*young*
un **vieux** bâtiment, une **vieille** maison	*old*
un **beau** garçon, une **belle** dame	*beautiful*
un **joli** jardin, une **jolie** fleur	*pretty, nice*
un **long** voyage, une **longue** distance	*long*
un **autre** cousin, une **autre** cousine	*other (another)*

[1]*swimsuit*

3. Liaison must always be made between a preposed adjective and a masculine noun beginning with a vowel sound. As a result, in spoken French the masculine form of all the adjectives listed above, except **gros** and **grand**, will sound just like the *feminine* form.

MASCULINE		FEMININE	
Cet hôtel est **petit**.	/pti/	Cette maison est **petite**.	/ptit/
→ C'est un **petit** hôtel.	/ptit/	→ C'est une **petite** maison.	
Cet hôtel est **bon**.	/bõ/	Cette orange est **bonne**.	/bɔn/
→ C'est un **bon** hôtel.	/bɔn/	→ C'est une **bonne** orange.	
Cet exercice est **mauvais**.	/mɔvɛ/	Cette banane est **mauvaise**.	/mɔvɛz/
→ C'est un **mauvais** exercice.	/mɔvɛz/	→ C'est une **mauvaise** banane.	

Beau, **nouveau**, and **vieux** have special *singular* forms that are pronounced like the feminine form.[1]

Cet arbre est **beau**.	/bo/	Cette robe est **belle**.	/bɛl/
→ C'est un **bel** arbre.	/bɛl/	→ C'est une **belle** robe.	
Cet étudiant est **nouveau**.	/nuvo/	Cette étudiante est **nouvelle**.	/nuvɛl/
→ C'est un **nouvel** étudiant.	/nuvɛl/	→ C'est une **nouvelle** étudiante.	
Cet hôtel est **vieux**.	/vjø/	Cette voiture est **vieille**.	/vjɛj/
→ C'est un **vieil** hôtel.	/vjɛj/	→ C'est une **vieille** voiture.	

BUT

Cet homme est **gros**.	/gʀo/	Cette tomate est **grosse**.	/gʀos/
→ C'est un **gros** homme.	/gʀoz/	→ C'est une **grosse** tomate.	
Cet hôtel est **grand**.	/gʀɑ̃/	Cette classe est **grande**.	/gʀɑ̃d/
→ C'est un **grand** hôtel.	/gʀɑ̃t/	→ C'est une **grande** classe.	

4. In the sequence **des** + plural adjective + plural noun, **des** usually becomes **de** or **d'**. Use of **des** is more typical of informal French.[2]

Je connais **un** beau jardin.

→ Je connais { **de** beaux jardins. / **des** beaux jardins.

C'est **un** bon livre.

→ Ce sont { **de** bons livres. / **des** bons livres.

Il y a **une** belle maison.

→ Il y a { **de** belles maisons. / **des** belles maisons.

Voilà **une** bonne réponse.

→ Voilà { **de** bonnes réponses. / **des** bonnes réponses.

5. We saw in Lesson 1.6 that when a noun denoting profession follows **être**, the indefinite article **un**, **une**, or **des** is omitted. However, the indefinite article is used with such a noun if it is modified by an adjective.

Vous êtes **médecin**.

→ Vous êtes *un bon* **médecin**.

Nous sommes **étudiants**.

→ Nous sommes *des* étudiants *sérieux*.

---

[1]Note that **ce** behaves in the same way: **ce monsieur**, **cette dame** /sɛt/, **cet étudiant** /sɛt/.

[2]**Autres** is nearly always used with **d'**: **d'autres livres**. We will be using mostly **de/d'** (rather than **des**) in the rest of the text. There are also a few "compound nouns" in which the combination adjective + noun constitutes a single meaning. In such cases, **des** is always used.

des jeunes filles	*girls*	**des petits-enfants**	*grandchildren*
des grands magasins	*department stores*	**des petits gâteaux**	*cookies*
des grands-parents	*grandparents*	**des petits pois**	*peas*

Tu es **étudiante**.   M. Leroux est **vendeur**.

→ Tu es *une* **étudiante** *travailleuse*.   → M. Leroux est *un* **vendeur** *patient*.

6. **Il est** *vs.* **c'est**. When the subject is in the third person, two patterns occur: **il est** + noun and **c'est** + noun. The **il est** pattern is used with nouns denoting professions, and can be the answer to questions (real or implied) like **Quelle est sa profession ?**. **Il est** is also used with adjectives when referring to a specific person or thing that has already been mentioned.

Quelle est sa profession ?   Comment est ta sœur ?

— **Il est** ingénieur.   — **Elle est** très sportive.

Que fait ta mère ?   Comment avez-vous trouvé le vin ?

— **Elle est** décoratrice.   — **Il était** excellent.

7. The **c'est** pattern is used in all other cases, as shown below.

   a) With a proper name, stressed pronoun (such as **moi**, **toi**)[1], or a noun that is modified by an adjective.

Qui est très travailleur ?   Comment est le cours ?

— **C'est** Mireille.   (proper name)   — **C'est** un cours intéressant.   (noun +

Qui savait la réponse ?   adjective)

— **C'était** moi.   (stressed pronoun)

   b) In response to a question that contains **c'est** or **est-ce**.

Qu'est-ce que **c'est** ?   Qui **est-ce** ?

— **C'est** une souris.   — **C'est** mon frère.

   c) With an adjective when referring to a previously mentioned idea or situation.

Est-ce que Paul va venir avec vous ?   Je trouve qu'il ne travaille pas assez.

— Oui, **c'est** possible.   — **C'est** vrai.

8. *Nationality*. The **il est** pattern is used with adjectives denoting nationality. As adjectives, such words do not begin with a capital letter. The **c'est un** pattern is used with nouns, which, as in English, begin with a capital letter.

ADJECTIVES   NOUNS

Quelle est sa nationalité ?   Qui est cette personne ?

— **Il est** américain.   — **C'est un** Américain.

Est-elle américaine ?   Est-ce une Américaine ?

— Non, **elle est** française.   — Non, **c'est une** Française.

The **c'est un** pattern must be used if the noun denoting profession or nationality is modified by an adjective.

Il est ingénieur. ⎱
Il est imaginatif. ⎰   → **C'est un** ingénieur imaginatif.

Elle est étudiante. ⎱
Elle est exceptionnelle. ⎰   → **C'est une** étudiante exceptionnelle.

Ils sont médecins. ⎱
Ils sont jeunes. ⎰   → **Ce sont de(s)** jeunes médecins.

---

[1]Stressed pronouns will be presented in Lesson 12.2.

Il **est** mécanicien.
C'est un bon mécanicien.

Elle **est** journaliste.
C'est une bonne journaliste.

TABLEAU 58

A *Exercice de contrôle. Faites attention à la place de chaque adjectif.*

Voilà une grande maison.
1. vieille   2. blanche   3. autre   4. jolie

J'ai apporté un joli cadeau.
1. petit   2. imaginatif   3. original   4. beau

C'est un jeune homme.
1. exceptionnel   2. autre   3. gros   4. amusant

Ce sont des réponses imaginatives.
1. originales   2. bonnes   3. intéressantes   4. autres

Nous avons trouvé des journaux anglais.
1. vieux   2. conservateurs   3. ennuyeux   4. bons

B *Ajoutez une phrase en employant* **c'est** *ou* **ce sont** *d'après ces modèles. Faites attention à la place et à la forme de chaque adjectif.*

Ce livre est intéressant.
C'est un livre intéressant.

Ces étudiants sont bons.
Ce sont de bons étudiants.

1. Cette montre est (japonaise).
2. Cette montre n'est pas vieille.
3. Cet étudiant n'est pas nouveau.
4. Cette chaise n'est pas grande.
5. Ces photos sont petites.

6. Cet étudiant n'est pas vieux.
7. Ces exercices sont oraux.
8. Ces étudiants sont jeunes.
9. Ces étudiants sont travailleurs.
10. Cette leçon est longue.

C *Voici une liste de personnes célèbres. Identifiez leur nationalité et leur profession en employant les mots suggérés.[1]*

NATIONALITÉ	PROFESSION
allemand	compositeur
américain	écrivain
anglais	peintre
espagnol	savant[2]
français	
italien	

[1]**en employant les mots suggérés** *by using the words suggested*
[2]*scientist*

Modèle : Debussy

(Frédérique) **Il était français.**

(Jean-Pierre) **Il était compositeur.**

(Jacqueline) **C'était un compositeur français.**

1. Matisse	5. Verdi	9. Goya
2. Bizet	6. Goethe /gøt/	10. Hemingway
3. Dickens	7. Shakespeare	11. Cervantès
4. Pasteur	8. Beethoven	12. Newton

D *Répondez aux questions en employant des adjectifs.*

1. Quelle sorte d'étudiant(e) êtes-vous ? Et (Jacqueline) ? Quelle sorte de professeur est-ce que je suis ?

2. Quelle sorte d'acteur est Clint Eastwood ? Quelle sorte d'actrice est Molly Ringwald ?

3. Quelle sorte d'exercices faisons-nous en classe ? Quelle sorte d'exercices avez-vous faits hier à la maison ?

4. Quelle sorte de vêtements portez-vous en été ? Et en hiver ? En quelle saison mettez-vous un pull ?

5. Y a-t-il un restaurant français dans notre ville ? Connaissez-vous un restaurant chinois (italien) ? Comment s'appelle ce restaurant ?

6. Est-ce que nous avons une bonne équipe de football ? Quelle université a une mauvaise équipe ? Comment le savez-vous ?

E *Décrivez[1] un objet, un animal ou une personne en cinq phrases. Deux de ces phrases commencent par* **il** *ou* **elle,** *et deux autres phrases commencent par* **c'est.**

Modèle : **Voilà la photo de mon chien. Il s'appelle Pepper. C'est un bon chien. C'est un chien très intelligent. Il est très patient avec les enfants.**

Regardez ce blouson. C'est mon blouson préféré. Il est bleu. Il a deux grandes poches. C'est un blouson très confortable.

Voici une photo de mon père. Il est ingénieur. Il a quarante ans. C'est un homme sportif. C'est un ingénieur intelligent.

 Exercice supplémentaire

11.3 COMPARATIF ET SUPERLATIF DE L'ADJECTIF

1. The construction **aussi** + adjective + **que** *as . . . as* expresses equality in comparing two items. Inequality is expressed by **plus** + adjective + **que** *more . . . than* or **moins** + adjective + **que** *less . . . than.* Compare the sentences below with Tableau 59 of the oral exercises.

Jean-Paul est **aussi grand que** sa mère.	*as tall as*
Mme Chabrier est **aussi grande que** son fils.	*as tall as*
Jean-Paul est **plus grand que** Monique.	*taller than*
Monique est **plus grande que** Lili.	*taller than*
Lili est **moins grande que** les autres.	*less tall than (not as tall as)*

2. The comparative form of **bon** is **meilleur** /mɛjœʀ/. Note that **plus** is not used with **meilleur.**

Ce film est **aussi bon que** les autres.	*as good as*
Ce film est **moins bon que** les autres.	*less good than (not as good as)*
Ce film est **meilleur que** les autres.	*better than*

[1]*Describe* (conjugué comme **écrire**) ; apportez une photo si c'est possible.

« Tu es plus grand que ton cousin Michel. »

« Moins cher que des soldes... Est-ce possible ? »

In informal French, the comparative form of **mauvais** is **plus mauvais**. In more formal French, it is often replaced by the irregular form **pire**, which is used without **plus**.

Cet article est **aussi mauvais que** les autres.	*as bad as*
Cet article est **moins mauvais que** les autres.	*less bad than (not as bad as)*
Cet article est **plus mauvais que** les autres.	*worse than*
Cet article est **pire que** les autres.	*worse than*

3. The superlative of adjectives is formed by adding the definite article immediately before the comparative form.

Jean-Paul et sa mère sont **les plus grands**.	*the tallest*
Lili est **la plus petite**.	*the smallest, the shortest*
Jean-Paul et sa mère sont **les moins petits**.	*the least small*
Lili est **la moins grande**.	*the least tall*

The superlative form of **bon** is **meilleur**; the word **plus** occurs in neither the comparative nor the superlative form of **bon**.

Ces croissants sont **bons**.	*good*
Ces croissants sont **meilleurs**.	*better*
Ces croissants sont **les meilleurs**.	*best*

4. The position of the adjective with regard to the noun it modifies usually follows the pattern discussed in Lesson 11.2.

PREPOSED	POSTPOSED
C'est une **belle** maison.	Voilà un étudiant **sérieux**.
→ C'est une **plus belle** maison.	→ Voilà un étudiant **plus sérieux**.
→ C'est **la plus belle** maison.	→ Voilà l'étudiant **le plus sérieux**.
Je connais de **bons** élèves.	J'ai vu un film **intéressant**.
→ Je connais de **meilleurs** élèves.	→ J'ai vu un film **plus intéressant**.
→ Je connais **les meilleurs** élèves.	→ J'ai vu le film **le plus intéressant**.

5. The only preposition used after the superlative of an adjective is **de**. Note below that **sur**, **dans**, and **à** are all replaced by **de**.

Il y a de grands bâtiments **sur** notre campus.

    Mais voilà **le plus grand** bâtiment **de** notre campus.

Il y a des étudiants attentifs **dans** ce cours.

    Mais Michèle est l'étudiante **la plus attentive de** ce cours.

Il y a de très bons professeurs **à** l'université.

    Mais vous êtes **le meilleur** professeur **de** l'université.

TABLEAU 59   Mme Chabrier Jean-Paul Monique   Lili

 A *Regardez le Tableau 59. C'est une photo. M. Chabrier l'a prise il y a quatre ans. Répétez après moi.*

Jean-Paul était aussi grand que sa mère.
Jean-Paul était plus grand que ses sœurs.
Lili et Monique étaient moins grandes que leur frère.
Monique était plus grande que Lili.
Monique et Lili étaient moins grandes que Jean-Paul.
Jean-Paul était le plus grand.
Lili était la plus petite.

> **Chantecler**
> La meilleure table de Nice
> (GUIDE GAULT ET MILLAU)
> 37, Promenade des Anglais
> (NÉGRESCO)   88.39.51 & 88.40.31

Maintenant, répondez à ces questions.

1. Qui était aussi grand que la mère ?
2. Qui était plus grand que Monique ?
3. Qui était le plus petit ?
4. Qui était plus petit que Lili ?[1]

5. Qui était moins petit que Monique ?
6. Qui était plus grand que Lili ?
7. Qui était plus grand que Jean-Paul ?[1]
8. Qui était le plus grand des enfants ?

 B *Regardez le Tableau 43 à la page 164. Répondez aux questions en employant les adjectifs* **âgé**[2] *et* **jeune**.

1. Quel âge a Monique ? Dans sa famille, qui est plus jeune que Monique ? Qui est la plus jeune personne de la famille ?
2. Regardez Mme Brunot. Est-elle plus âgée que son mari ? Qui est le frère de Mme Brunot ? Est-il plus jeune que sa sœur ?
3. Regardez le grand-père. Est-ce la personne la plus âgée ? Quel âge a-t-il ? Combien d'enfants a-t-il ? Combien de petits-enfants a-t-il ? Qui est le petit-enfant le plus âgé ? Et le moins âgé ?

---

[1]Employez **personne ne...** dans vos réponses.

[2]**âgé** *old;* **vieux** is not normally used when comparing the age of people directly.

C *Vous êtes dans plusieurs cours, n'est-ce pas ? Comparez vos cours en employant les adjectifs suivants.*

1. intéressant, plus intéressant, le plus intéressant
2. facile, plus facile, le plus facile
3. utile, moins utile, le moins utile
4. difficile, plus difficile, le plus difficile

D *Répondez aux questions.*

1. Quel âge avez-vous ? Demandez à (Marie) quel âge elle a. Est-elle plus âgée que vous ? Savez-vous mon âge ? Est-ce que je suis moins âgé(e) que vous ?
2. Regardez vos camarades. Qui a les cheveux[1] les plus longs ? Qui a les cheveux les plus courts ?
3. Quand avez-vous dîné dans un restaurant ? N'y a-t-il pas de meilleur restaurant ? Y a-t-il un plus mauvais restaurant ?
4. Qui a regardé la télévision la semaine dernière ? À votre avis[2], quel était la meilleure émission ? Quelle était la plus mauvaise émission ?

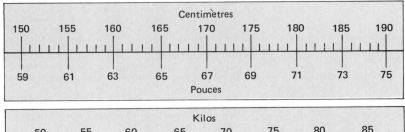

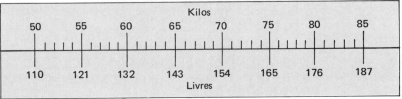

5. Combien mesurez-vous ?[3] Demandez à (Mireille) combien elle mesure. Est-elle plus grande que vous ? Demandez-moi combien je mesure. Est-ce que je suis moins grand(e) que vous ?
6. Combien pesez-vous ?[4] Demandez à (Jacques) combien il pèse. Est-il moins lourd que vous ? Demandez-moi combien je pèse. Est-ce que je suis plus lourd(e) que vous ?

📟 *Exercice supplémentaire*

📟 *Compréhension auditive*

11.4 VOIR, CROIRE

1. **Voir** *to see* can take a direct object or a clause introduced by the conjunction **que** or an interrogative word.[5]

voir	
vois	voyons
vois	voyez
voit	voient
	vu

Je ne **vois** pas souvent Chantal.　　　　Nous **voyons** que vous n'êtes pas libre.
Tu la **vois** une fois par semaine.　　　　Vous **voyez** pourquoi il est venu ?
Elle **voit** Chantal ce soir.　　　　Elles **voient** comment j'ai fait cela.
　　　　J'ai **vu** un très bon film.

[1]*hair* (on emploie ce mot au pluriel)

[2]*In your opinion*

[3]Dites, par exemple : « Je mesure un mètre soixante-douze. »

[4]Dites, par exemple : « Je pèse quatre-vingts kilos. »

[5]Two other verbs derived from **voir**, though not used in the exercises, are conjugated like it: **prévoir** *to foresee*, **revoir** *to see again.*

2. **Croire** means *to think* or *to believe*. It can take a direct object, just like **voir**, or a clause introduced by **que**. **Croire à** means *to believe in (something)*; but *to believe in God* is **croire en Dieu**.

croire	
crois	croyons
crois	croyez
croit	croient
cru	

Je **crois** cet enfant.

Tu me **crois**, j'espère.

Il ne **croit** pas à la magie noire !

Nous **croyons** en Dieu.

Vous **croyez** que Paul a raison ?

Ils **croient** qu'elle est là.

J'ai **cru** que vous étiez malade.

3. **Croire** indicates a "mental process" rather than a physical action. In past events, it tends to be in the imperfect rather than the *passé composé*. The use of the *passé composé* implies something like *I thought/believed for a moment* or *It occurred to me suddenly*.

Je **croyais** que vous étiez malade.	*I thought/believed you were sick.*
Il **croyait** qu'il avait raison ?	*He thought/believed he was right?*
J'**ai cru** que c'était Julien à la porte.	*I thought it was Julien at the door.*

4. In the sentences below, **croire/penser/espérer/dire que oui (non)** corresponds to English *(not) to believe/think/hope/say so*.[1]

Croyez-vous qu'il va neiger ?	*Do you believe (think) it's going to snow?*
— Je **crois que oui**.	*I believe (think) so.*
— Je **crois que non**.	*I don't believe (think) so.*
Pensez-vous qu'il a dit la vérité ?	*Do you think he told the truth?*
— Nous **pensons que oui**.	*We think so.*
— Nous **pensons que non**.	*We don't think so.*
A-t-elle acheté un cadeau ?	*Did she buy a gift?*
— J'**espère que oui**.	*I hope so.*
— J'**espère que non**.	*I hope not.*
Est-ce que Marie a vu son cousin ?	*Did Marie see her cousin?*
— Elle **a dit que oui**.	*She said so.*
— Elle **a dit que non**.	*She said no.*

A *Exercice de contrôle*

Je vois mes copains.

1. Vous   2. Cet enfant   3. Nous   4. Tu

Nous voyons que vous avez raison.[2]

1. Je   2. On   3. Les étudiants   4. Vous

Je crois que j'ai vu ce film.

1. Nous   2. Tu   3. Vous   4. Ces enfants

B *Répondez aux questions.*

1. Regardez autour de[3] vous. Il y a pas mal de[4] choses dans cette classe. Qu'est-ce que vous voyez ?

---

[1]**Penser** means *to think*, as does **croire** (which can also mean *to believe*, as explained above), but it often implies more "thinking" or deliberation than **croire**, almost like *to consider*.

[2]Ne changez pas la deuxième partie de la phrase (**...vous avez raison.**).

[3]*around*

[4]**pas mal de** = beaucoup de

2. Est-ce que je vous ai vu(e) hier ? M'avez-vous vu(e) hier ? Avez-vous vu quelqu'un hier soir ?

3. Qui va voir un film ce week-end ? Quel film allez-vous voir ? Demandez à (Yves) s'il a vu ce film.

4. Est-ce que vous me croyez toujours ? Est-ce que je vous crois toujours ? Qui est-ce que vous ne croyez pas ?

5. Croyez-vous à l'astrologie ? À quoi est-ce que vous ne croyez pas ? Que veut dire[1] « croire quelque chose » en anglais ? Et « croire à quelque chose » ?

6. Croyez-vous au père Noël ?[2] Quand vous étiez petit(e), est-ce que vous croyiez au père Noël ?

7. On dit souvent : « Voir, c'est croire. » Qu'est-ce que cela veut dire ? Donnez des exemples.

C   *Connaissez-vous bien vos camarades dans ce cours ? Je vais poser des questions. Quelle est votre opinion ? Répondez d'après ces modèles.*

(Jacqueline) parle-t-elle français ?
Je crois que oui (*ou* **Je pense que oui**).
(Jacqueline) portait-elle un pull hier ?
Je crois que non (*ou* **Je pense que non**).
(Jacqueline) va-t-elle faire ses devoirs ?
J'espère que oui.
(Jacqueline) vous déteste-t-elle ?
J'espère que non !

1. (Robert) boit-il de la bière ?
2. (Michel) parle-t-il espagnol ?
3. (Jeanne) est-elle née en France ?
4. (Monique) fait-elle du judo ?
5. (Jacques) vous connaît-il bien ?

6. (Claire) est-elle mariée ?
7. (Sophie) vous a-t-elle vu(e) hier ?
8. (Marc) est-il allé au cinéma hier ?
9. (Yves) était-il marié il y a un an ?
10. (Claire) a-t-elle fait ses devoirs ?

11.5   PHRASES EXCLAMATIVES

1. A declarative sentence can be changed into an exclamatory sentence by adding **Comme** or **(Ce) que** at the beginning.[3] They are equivalent to English *How.*

Ils travaillent.	*They work.*
→ **Comme** ils travaillent !	*→ How they work!*
Il fait froid ce matin.	*It's cold this morning.*
→ **Comme** il fait froid ce matin !	*→ How cold it is this morning!*
Elle est belle.	*She is beautiful.*
→ **(Ce) qu**'elle est belle !	*→ How beautiful she is!*

2. **Quel** + noun in an exclamation is equivalent to English *What (a)* + noun. **Quel** must agree in gender and number with the noun. The noun may be modified by an adjective.

Quel homme ! **Quel** enfant !	*What a man! What a child!*
Quelle robe élégante !	*What an elegant dress!*
Quelle belle chambre tu as !	*What a beautiful room you have!*

---

[1] **Que veut dire... ?** = Qu'est-ce que ... veut dire ?

[2] **Il/Elle croit au père Noël** is an expression used sometimes to describe a naïve person.

[3] **Ce que** occurs in more colloquial French.

Quel bâtiment gigantesque,
et comme il est original !
(Paris : Maison de la Radio)

3. The adverb **si** *so, such* intensifies the meaning of the adjective or adverb it precedes. The construction **si** + adjective/adverb may be followed by **que** + clause, corresponding to the English construction *so/such . . . that . . . .*

Votre dessert est **si** délicieux !	*Your dessert is so delicious!*
Elle parle **si** bien français !	*She speaks French so well!*
Il a mangé **si** vite **qu**'il a une indigestion.	*He ate so fast that he has indigestion.*
Il avait un **si** bel appartement **que** tout le monde voulait le voir.	*He had such a beautiful apartment that everyone wanted to see it.*

TABLEAU 60

A *Ajoutez des phrases exclamatives d'après ce modèle.*

Il fait (froid) aujourd'hui.
(Robert) **Qu'il fait (froid) !**
(Janine) **Oui, comme il fait (froid) !**

1. Il fait (beau) aujourd'hui.
2. (Jacques) parle bien français.
3. Nous avons faim.
4. Nous avons sommeil.
5. Vos questions sont difficiles.
6. Mes chaussures sont sales.

B *Vous regardez les vitrines d'un grand magasin[1]. Ajoutez des phrases d'après ce modèle.*

Regardez cette belle robe.
(Michèle) **Ah, quelle belle robe !**
(Daniel) **Ah, comme elle est belle !**

1. Regardez cette robe élégante.
2. Regardez cette jolie broche.
3. Regardez ces petites chaussures.
4. Regardez ce beau tailleur.
5. Regardez ces chapeaux bizarres.
6. Regardez ce grand sac.

C *Maintenant, vous allez parler de moi. Ajoutez des phrases d'après ce modèle.*

Je suis patient(e). Tout le monde m'admire.
Vous êtes si patient(e) que tout le monde vous admire.

1. Je parle vite. Personne ne me comprend.
2. J'ai mangé vite. J'ai une indigestion.
3. Je suis bête. Je ne comprends rien.
4. J'ai sommeil. Je veux rentrer à la maison.
5. Je suis intelligent(e). Tout le monde m'admire.
6. J'étais fatigué(e) ce matin. Je ne voulais pas sortir.

APPLICATIONS

A **Situations[2]**

Vous faites des compliments.

Faites des compliments aux Français. Vous allez voir qu'ils sourient[3] mais ne disent pas « Merci beaucoup » comme le font les Américains. Les Français veulent minimiser l'importance de la chose sur laquelle[4] on les complimente, par[5] politesse ou par modestie. (Mais n'oubliez pas, quand même°, d'exprimer votre appréciation ou de faire des compliments quand cela est nécessaire.) 5

anyway

Monique porte un ensemble élégant.

CHRISTINE   Ton ensemble est très élégant. Il te va très bien.[6]
MONIQUE   Tu trouves ? Je l'ai acheté au Printemps[7]. Il était en solde°.

on sale

Lili a fait sa robe elle-même°.

herself

CHRISTINE   J'aime beaucoup ta robe. Elle est très belle. 10
LILI   Tu trouves ? Je l'ai faite moi-même le mois dernier.

Marc vient de ranger ses affaires[8].

CHRISTINE   Quelle jolie chambre tu as.
MARC   Tu trouves ? Je viens de ranger mes affaires.

[1]*department store*
[2]Les réponses aux questions ne sont pas enregistrées sur la bande magnétique.
[3]du verbe **sourire** *to smile* (Lesson 23.4)
[4]**sur laquelle** *about/concerning which*
[5]*out of* (literally, *through, by*)
[6]**aller bien à quelqu'un** *to become someone, to suit someone*
[7]*un des grands magasins à Paris*
[8]**ranger ses affaires** *to straighten out and put away one's belongings*

Les Georget ont un appartement élégant. 15

CHRISTINE   Quel appartement élégant, et quelles belles aquarelles !

M. GEORGET   Oui, nous aimons beaucoup les belles choses.

Mme Georget aime faire la cuisine.

CHRISTINE   Le déjeuner était sensationnel. Vous êtes un vrai cordon-bleu[1], Madame.

MME GEORGET   Vous êtes trop gentille. J'aime beaucoup faire la cuisine. 20

On a accepté un tableau de Marie.

VOUS   Félicitations ! Je viens d'apprendre qu'on a accepté ton tableau.

MARIE   Oui, je suis très contente. C'est mon tableau préféré.

Qu'est-ce que vous allez dire dans les situations suivantes ?

1. Un de vos camarades vous félicite, parce que vous avez bien réussi à votre examen. Vous avez beaucoup travaillé et, d'ailleurs[2], l'examen n'était pas trop difficile.
2. Après un dîner délicieux, vous faites un compliment à votre hôtesse. Elle vous dit que c'était un repas simple et qu'elle l'a préparé en deux heures.
3. Vous montez dans la voiture de votre hôte. Vous admirez l'élégance et le confort de la voiture. Votre hôte vous dit qu'il l'a depuis quatre ans mais qu'elle roule encore très bien.
4. Chez M. et Mme Vernin vous remarquez qu'il y a beaucoup d'objets d'art dans le séjour. Vous les admirez. M. Vernin mentionne qu'il aime collectionner les belles choses.
5. Vous admirez l'ensemble très élégant de votre amie. Qu'est-ce que vous lui dites ? Qu'est-ce qu'elle vous dit ?
6. Vous admirez la collection de timbres de votre copain. Imaginez la conversation.

« Félicitations ! C'était un très bon match ! »

[1]Un « cordon-bleu » est une personne qui sait faire de la cuisine délicieuse (le Cordon-Bleu est une école de cuisine très célèbre à Paris).

[2]*besides, moreover*

B Expressions utiles

🔲 **Les vêtements** (Tableau 56, page 233)

1. une chemise
2. un blouson
3. un bouton
4. une poche
5. un blue-jean (*pl* des blue-jeans)
6. une ceinture
7. des chaussettes *f*
8. des chaussures *f*
9. un pull à col roulé
10. une veste
11. une jupe (10 + 11 : un tailleur)
12. un collant
13. un sac
14. une cravate

15. un veston
16. un mouchoir
17. un pantalon (15 + 17 : un complet)
18. un pull / un pull-over
19. un imperméable
20. un parapluie
21. un chemisier
22. un manteau
23. des gants *m*
24. des lunettes de soleil *f*
25. un short
26. un maillot (de bain)
27. des bottes *f*
28. un T-shirt /tiʃœʀt/

Les couleurs (2)

beige	gris(e)	rose
blanc (blanche)	jaune	rouge
bleu(e)	noir(e)	vert(e)
brun(e)	orange[1]	violet (violette)

La taille[2]

CHEMISIERS, PULLS		CHEMISES		AUTRES VÊTEMENTS			
				DAMES		HOMMES	
France	U.S.	France	U.S.	France	U.S.	France	U.S.
40	32	36	14	38	10	46	36
42	34	37	14½	40	12	48	38
44	36	38	15	42	14	50	40
46	38	39	15½	44	16	52	42
48	40	40	16	46	18	54	44

C Pratique

1. Vous êtes allé(e) en ville hier soir. Il faisait froid. Il neigeait. Vous avez rencontré Philippe, un de vos camarades. Quels vêtements est-ce qu'il portait ?
2. Vous êtes allé(e) à la piscine. Il faisait chaud. Il faisait du soleil. À la piscine vous avez rencontré Marie-Claire, une de vos camarades. Elle prenait un bain de soleil. Qu'est-ce qu'elle portait ?
3. Vous avez assisté à[3] la réception[4] organisée par le président de l'université. Qu'est-ce que vous avez mis ?

[1]mot invariable : **les jupes orange, les manteaux orange**

[2]Il y a deux mots en français qui indiquent la dimension des vêtements. On dit « la taille » pour les chemises, les chemisiers, les vestons, les vestes, les pulls, etc. L'autre mot, « la pointure », est pour les chaussures, les chaussettes et les gants.

[3]**assister à** *to attend*

[4]*reception, a formal early evening party*

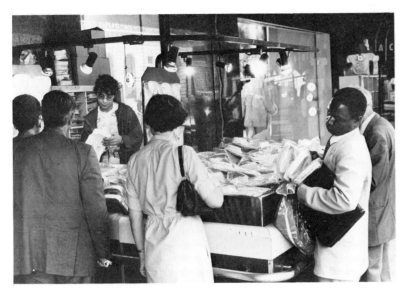

« 38... Oui, c'est bien ma taille. »

4. Regardez les vêtements de vos camarades dans le cours de français. De quelle couleur sont leurs vêtements ?

5. De quelle couleur est le drapeau américain ? Et le drapeau français ? Et le drapeau canadien ?

6. Quelle est votre taille d'après le système français ? Demandez à votre partenaire quelle est sa taille. Est-il(elle) plus grand(e) que vous ? Devinez ma taille.

7. Parlons de la taille des chemises. Est-ce que la taille 14 du système américain est plus grande que la taille 38 du système français ? Trente-huit signifie 38 centimètres de tour de cou[1]. Qu'est-ce que 14 signifie ?

8. Regardez la photo en haut et à droite. Quels vêtements sont en solde[2] ? Combien coûtaient les vêtements ? Quels sont leurs prix maintenant ?

D Mini-composition : *Catherine a acheté un cadeau d'anniversaire. Complétez le passage en employant les mots indiqués.*[3]

(1) Mon/sœur/être/personne/le/moins/âgé/de/notre/famille. (2) Elle/aller/avoir/14 ans/dans/un/semaine. (3) Samedi/dernier/je/être/sortir/de/résidence/pour/chercher/cadeau/pour/elle. (4) Je/vouloir/trouver/quelque chose/petit/et/léger,/car/je/aller/envoyer/le/par avion[4]. (5) D'abord/je/aller/à/les/magasins/autour de/le/campus. (6) Je/aller/dans/plusieurs/magasin/mais/je/ne rien/trouver/intéressant. (7) Ensuite/je/prendre/le/autobus/pour/aller/à/le/centre commercial[5]/près de/la/autoroute. (8) Je/aller/à/le/grand magasin/quand/je/voir/un/nouveau/boutique. (9) Il y a/broches/et/bracelets/dans/le/vitrine. (10) Je/entrer/dans/boutique/et/je/regarder/les/broche. (11) Je/choisir/plus/beau/broche. (12) Ce/être/un/broche/indien,/et/prix/être/raisonnable.

[1]**tour de cou** *around the neck*

[2]*on sale*

[3]Employez l'imparfait et le passé composé sauf dans les deux premières phrases.

[4]*by air (mail)*

[5]*shopping center*

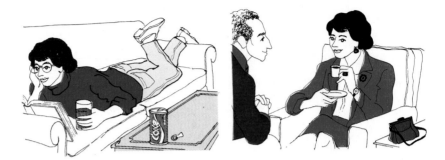

TABLEAU 61

E *Regardez le Tableau 61. Lundi dernier Christine était chez elle. Cet après-midi elle est chez un professeur. Quelles différences trouvez-vous entre ces deux dessins ?*

F **Questions :** *J'ai fait des courses parce que j'avais besoin de vêtements. Lisez le passage suivant et posez des questions sur les parties soulignées.*

(1) L'hiver arrive bientôt. (2) Mes vêtements d'hiver ne sont pas encore arrivés. (3) Je suis allé en ville hier après-midi, (4) car j'avais besoin de vêtements chauds. D'après le journal, il y avait (5) des vêtements en solde dans plusieurs magasins. J'avais besoin (6) de gants. J'avais aussi besoin d'un blouson (7) plus chaud. Je suis allé en ville (8) avec Daniel. (9) Daniel est mon camarade de chambre. (10) Il voulait faire des courses avec moi. Il a acheté (11) des gants et un imperméable. Nous avons pris un taxi pour rentrer (12) parce qu'il commençait à neiger.

G **Renseignements et opinions**

1. Quel temps faisait-il hier soir ? Quelle sorte de vêtements portiez-vous à midi ? Et à sept heures du soir ?
2. Quel est le meilleur magasin de vêtements de notre ville ? Pourquoi ? Et quel est le plus mauvais magasin ? Pourquoi ?
3. À votre avis, quel est le meilleur restaurant de notre ville ? Choisissez plusieurs restaurants et comparez leurs prix, leur ambiance, la qualité du service et de la cuisine.
4. Êtes-vous plus énergique aujourd'hui qu'hier ? Quel jour êtes-vous le (la) plus énergique ? Quel jour êtes-vous le (la) moins énergique ? Pourquoi ?
5. Cinq étudiants veulent faire un cadeau[1] à leur copain pour son anniversaire. Chacun va contribuer cinq dollars. Qu'est-ce qu'ils peuvent acheter comme cadeau ?
6. Comparez les états suivants. Employez *petit* et *grand*.

   le Texas   le Wisconsin   l'Iowa   le Delaware
7. Qui voyez-vous souvent ? Qui est-ce que vous ne voyez pas souvent ? Croyez-vous à l'astrologie ? Qui croit à la magie noire ?

🔲 *Compréhension auditive (basée sur l'Application A)*

🔲 *Compréhension auditive (basée sur l'Application B)*

🔲 *Compréhension auditive*

🔲 *Dictée : « Un cadeau d'anniversaire » (basée sur l'Application D)*

[1]**faire un cadeau** = donner un cadeau

« La semaine dernière, nous avons présenté la nouvelle collection à la presse et aux meilleurs clients. »

H Lecture

high fashion

La haute couture°
Micki est arrivée de Suède il y a deux ans, avec l'intention de devenir mannequin. Elle avait le physique idéal : 1,80m, 57 kilos, les cheveux blonds et les yeux verts. Elle a d'abord fait

advertising

des photos de publicité°, puis elle a posé pour le catalogue des « Trois Suisses[1] ». Enfin, l'année dernière, elle est devenue mannequin pour la maison de couture de Chantal Marion, qui crée des vêtements excentriques et sophistiqués pour les jeunes. Micki parle de son travail : 5

C'est un métier très prestigieux et très bien payé, mais c'est aussi un métier très fatigant. Nous passons des heures debout dans des studios ou des ateliers surchauffés, et même quand nous sommes épuisées, nous devons[2] être belles et souriantes. La semaine dernière, nous avons présenté la nouvelle collection d'hiver à la presse et aux meilleurs clients. Il y 10 avait 300 personnes dans le grand salon décoré d'immenses bouquets roses et blancs. Les clients les plus importants étaient au premier rang. Tout le personnel° était énervé et inquiet°.

staff / nervous and worried
show

Une présentation de mode est un spectacle°, et tout doit[3] être parfait. Le défilé de mode a duré une heure et demie, et nous avons présenté 150 tailleurs, manteaux, robes courtes et

as well as / wedding gown

robes longues, ainsi que° la traditionnelle robe de mariée°. 15

Une présentation de mode demande beaucoup de travail, et les deux dernières semaines ont été les plus dures de l'année. Les mannequins arrivaient à huit heures du matin, et toute la journée nous mettions et remettions les vêtements pendant que Chantal choisissait les accessoires et les bijoux[4] et faisait les changements de dernière minute. J'espère que la collection a été un succès. 20

[1]one of the large mail order houses in France

[2]du verbe **devoir** *must* (Leçon 15.1)

[3]du verbe **devoir** *must*

[4]*jewels* (s **un bijou**)

A   *Indiquez si les commentaires suivants sont vrais ou faux, puis corrigez les commentaires faux.*

1. Micki est une jeune Suédoise qui a quitté son pays il y a deux ans.
2. Elle mesurait un mètre quarante et pesait cinquante-sept kilos.
3. Elle est venue en France pour faire des photos de publicité.
4. Elle trouve que le métier de mannequin est mal payé.
5. Chantal est employée par une dame pour la présentation de ses clients.
6. Il fait très chaud dans les studios et les ateliers où Micki travaille.
7. Micki était debout pendant une heure pendant la présentation de mode.
8. Le grand salon était décoré de bouquets de roses blanches.
9. Micki a travaillé pendant les deux dernières semaines d'hiver.
10. Les mannequins ont choisi leurs bijoux et leurs accessoires.

B   *Trouvez dans le texte l'antonyme des mots suivants. Attention : il y a deux possibilités pour certains de ces mots.*

imparfait	premier	long
noir	prochain	vieux
rien	tranquille	ordinaire
le plus mauvais	calme	minuscule

C   *Trouvez dans le texte les mots qui sont définis ci-dessous.*

1. rigoureux, pas facile
2. assemblage de fleurs
3. très fatigué
4. objet précieux

5. extraordinaire, inhabituel
6. qui a du prestige
7. l'aspect d'une personne
8. qui cause de la fatigue

VOCABULAIRE

Noms

un(e) **acteur (actrice)**	actor (actress)	le confort	comfort	le(la) **millionnaire**	millionaire
les **affaires** f	belongings	le cordon-bleu	gourmet cook	la modestie	modesty
un(e) Américain(e)	American	la **cravate**	tie	un objet d'art	objet d'art, artifact
une appréciation	appreciation	le **croco**	crocodile	le **pantalon**	pants
une aquarelle	watercolor		(alligator leather)	le **peintre**	painter
l'art m	art	un **écrivain**	writer	le **père Noël**	Santa Claus
l'**astrologie** f	astrology	l'élégance f	elegance	les **petits-enfants** m	grandchildren
un **avis**	opinion	un **ensemble**	outfit	le **pilote**	pilot
le **blue-jean**	blue jeans	une **équipe**	team	la politesse	politeness
le **bouton**	button	un **exemple**	example	le Printemps	Printemps department store
la **broche**	brooch, pin	la **fiancée**	fiancée		
le **cadeau**	present	le **gant**	glove	le **pull (à col roulé)**	(turtleneck) sweater
le **chapeau**	hat	un(e) hôte (hôtesse)	host (hostess)	la **robe**	dress
la **chaussure**	shoe	un **imperméable**	raincoat	le **sac**	purse
la **chemise**	shirt	une importance	importance	le **savant**	scientist
le **chemisier**	blouse	une **indigestion**	indigestion	la situation	situation
les **cheveux** m	hair	un **ingénieur**	engineer	la solde	sale
la **chose**	thing	le **judo**	judo	le **tailleur**	suit (for women)
le **col**	collar	la **jupe**	skirt	le timbre	stamp
la collection	collection	le **maillot de bain**	swimsuit	la **veste**	jacket
le compliment	compliment	le **manteau**	coat	les **vêtements** m	clothes, clothing
le **compositeur**	composer	le mètre	meter		

Verbes

accepter	*to accept*	exprimer	*to express*	minimiser	*to minimize*
admirer	*to admire*	féliciter	*to congratulate*	oublier (de + *inf*)	*to forget (to + *inf*)*
collectionner	*to collect*	imaginer	*to imagine*	**peser**	*to weigh*
complimenter	*to compliment*	mentionner	*to mention*	**porter**	*to wear* (clothes);
coûter	*to cost*	**mesurer**	*to measure*		*to carry*
croire (à) *irrég*	*to believe (in);*	**mettre** *irrég*	*to put, place;*	rouler	*to drive; to run* (car)
	to think		*to put on* (clothes)	**voir** *irrég*	*to see*

Adjectifs

âgé(e)	*old*	**espagnol(e)**	*Spanish*	nécessaire	*necessary*
allemand(e)	*German*	**exceptionnel(le)**	*exceptional*	**noir(e)**	*black*
anglais(e)	*English*	**gris(e)**	*gray*	**original(e)**	*original*
bleu(e)	*blue*	**gros (grosse)**	*big, fat*	**patient(e)**	*patient*
brun(e)	*brown*	**imaginatif(ive)**	*imaginative*	**roulé(e)**	*rolled*
chinois(e)	*Chinese*	**italien(ne)**	*Italian*	**sale**	*dirty*
conservateur(trice)	*conservative*	**marié(e)**	*married*	sensationnel(le)	*sensational*
élégant(e)	*elegant*	**meilleur(e)**	*better*		

Autres expressions

aller bien à quelqu'un	*to become someone,*		**Félicitations !**	*Congratulations!*
	to fit someone		**Je crois que oui/non.**	*I think so/I don't think so.*
aussi ... que	*as . . . as*		**le plus**	*the most*
autour de	*around*		**moi-même**	*myself*
à votre avis	*in your opinion*		**moins ... que**	*less . . . than*
(Ce) que... !	*How . . . !*		**ni de**	*nor*
Combien mesurez-vous ?	*How tall are you?*		**pas mal de**	*quite a few*
croire au père Noël	*to believe in Santa Claus,*		**plus ... que**	*more . . . than*
	to be naïve		quand même	*anyway*
d'ailleurs	*besides*		ranger ses affaires	*to put away one's belongings*
depuis	*since, for*		réussir à un examen	*to pass an exam*
Dis donc !	*Say!, Hey!*		**si ... que**	*so/such . . . that*
elle-même	*herself*		(ils) sourient	*(they) smile*
en solde	*on sale*		sur laquelle	*about/concerning which*
faire des compliments	*to pay compliments*			

12 Après les vacances

CONVERSATIONS

A. L'Europe

Connaissez-vous bien la géographie de l'Europe ?[1] Regardez la carte à la page 257 et étudiez les Expressions utiles de cette leçon. Voici un petit test. Après chaque commentaire, dites « C'est vrai » ou « Ce n'est pas vrai ». Ensuite, corrigez les commentaires qui ne sont pas vrais.

1. Paris est la capitale de la France.
2. Les habitants de la France s'appellent[2] les Espagnols.
3. On parle français en Belgique et en Suisse.
4. L'Irlande est moins grande que la France.
5. La capitale de l'Espagne est Rome.
6. On parle italien en Espagne.
7. La capitale du Portugal est Lisbonne.
8. On parle portugais à Lisbonne.
9. Londres est la capitale de l'Angleterre.

---

[1]La première partie des *Expressions utiles* (1–14) est enregistrée sur la bande magnétique.
[2]**s'appellent** *are called* (literally, *call themselves*)

TABLEAU 62

10. On parle anglais en Angleterre.
11. On parle allemand en Allemagne et en Autriche.
12. La capitale de la Suisse est Genève.

Maintenant, préparez un ou deux commentaires « vrais/faux » pour vos camarades.

B. Je ne vais pas inviter Laurence !

MME BOSQUET Est-ce que tu as invité Laurence pour ton anniversaire ?

GÉRALDINE Non, Maman. Je ne veux pas lui parler.

MME BOSQUET Pourquoi ? Vous êtes fâchées ?[1]

GÉRALDINE Oui. Elle ne me téléphone jamais et je ne l'aime plus.

---

[1]*Are you angry (with each other)?*

⌨ **C.** **Loin des yeux, loin du cœur**[1]

JULIEN   Je t'ai vu avec Marianne hier soir. Tu ne sors plus avec Isabelle ?

CLAUDE   Non, elle a déménagé à Marseille.

JULIEN   Ah oui ? Mais tu lui écris, quand même[2] ?

CLAUDE   Non, elle ne m'a jamais donné son adresse.

⌨   *Compréhension auditive (basée sur la Conversation A)*

Tanger, Maroc.   *Tunis, Tunisie.*   *Port-au-Prince, Haïti.*

DIFFÉRENCES

Les pays francophones

French is spoken not only in France but also in many other parts of the world. In Europe it is spoken in parts of Belgium (**la Belgique**) and Switzerland (**la Suisse**), and in Luxemburg (**le Luxembourg**), and Monaco (**Monaco**). As for North America, French is the official language of French Canada, meaning the province of Quebec (**le Québec**). In the past it was spoken in northern New England, especially in Maine, New Hampshire, and Vermont, where more than one-third of the inhabitants are of French origin. A few old-timers in those states still know French. In southern Louisiana (**la Louisiane**) French is the first language of the Cajuns, descendants of French Canadian settlers of over two hundred years ago. The Cajuns have preserved the French language in their homes for all these years, even at a time when it was banned from use in school.

France, like England, pursued a colonial expansion policy in the prosperous nineteenth century, and acquired vast territories in Asia (Indochina), West Africa, and other parts of the world. Nearly all of these colonies are now independent, but most still maintain cultural and/or economic ties with France. The inside of the back cover of your text shows the French-speaking regions of the world. In Africa, French is either

---

[1] proverbe français, équivalent de *Out of sight, out of mind*.

[2] *anyway*

the official language or one of two official languages in **l'Algérie** (Algeria), **Burkina Faso** (formerly **la Haute-Volta**, or Upper Volta), **le Cameroun** (Cameroon), **la Côte-d'Ivoire** (Ivory Coast), **le Congo** (Congo-Brazzaville), **le Gabon** (Gabon), **la Guinée** (Guinea), **Madagascar** (Malagasy Republic), **le Mali** (Mali), **le Maroc** (Morocco), **la Mauritanie** (Mauritania), **le Niger** (Niger), **la République Centrafricaine** (Central African Republic), **le Sénégal** (Senegal), **la Somalie** (Somalia), **le Tchad** (Chad), **le Togo** (Togo), **la Tunisie** (Tunisia), **le Zaïre** (Zaire), and several others. Although they do not carry the same value as French currency, the words **franc** and **centime** are used in most of these countries to designate standard monetary units.

French is also spoken in French Polynesia, where Tahiti is located, and New Caledonia (in Oceania, to the east of Australia), and in four overseas **départements** (administrative units of France): Martinique and Guadeloupe in the West Indies, French Guiana in South America, and the island of Réunion in the western part of the Indian Ocean. Creole French—a mixture of French and Black African languages—is used in Haiti and parts of Louisiana.

STRUCTURES

12.1 NOMS GÉOGRAPHIQUES ET PRÉPOSITIONS

1. First, go over the names of European countries in the *Expressions utiles* of this lesson. Most countries in Europe are feminine, except **le Danemark**, **le Luxembourg**, **les Pays-Bas** (*Holland*), and **le Portugal**. Countries in the plural are rare: **les Pays-Bas**, **les États-Unis**. The prepositions used most often with geographic names are those indicating location.

ENGLISH EQUIVALENTS	CONTINENTS[1]	COUNTRIES			CITIES[2]
		f	m	pl	
in, at, to	en	en	au	aux	à
from	de	de	du	des	de

M. Yewah vient **d'**Afrique et il fait ses études **en** Europe.

Pedro vient **d'**Espagne et il voyage **en** France.

Mlle Yamamoto vient **du** Japon ; elle est **au** Canada.

La mère de Bob vient **des** Pays-Bas ; elle habite **aux** États-Unis.

Mme Brunot vient **de** Paris ; elle est **à** Dijon.

2. *United States.* Some states are feminine in French, and take the same prepositions as feminine countries. Most states do not change their spelling, but the "feminine" states usually do.

la Californie	la Georgie	la Pennsylvanie /pɛsilvani/
la Floride	la Louisiane	la Virginie

---

[1]All the names of continents are feminine in French (**Afrique**, **Amérique**, **Asie**, **Australie**, **Europe**). They may be followed by **du Sud** /syd/ *South*, **de l'Ouest** /wɛst/ *West*, **du Nord** /nɔʀ/ *North*, or **de l'Est** /ɛst/ *East*: **en Amérique du Nord**, **en Afrique du Sud**.

[2]**Dans** *inside* may be used for a location *specifically within a city*.

Un cours de français pour adultes en Algérie.

North and South Carolina and West Virginia are also feminine, but in their case either **en** or **dans la**, and **de** or **de la** can be used.

Mes parents sont **en** Californie, et mes grands-parents sont **en** (**dans la**) Caroline du Nord.

Barbara vient **de** Georgie et elle habite **en** Pennsylvanie.

Bob est né **en** (**dans la**) Virginie de l'Ouest ; il fait ses études à l'université **de** Floride.

The rest of the states are masculine and usually take **dans le/l'** (*in, at, to*) or **du/ de l'** (*of, about, from*).[1]

L'été prochain je vais aller **dans le** Colorado et **dans le** Texas.

Mon frère habite **dans le** Maine, mais ma sœur est **dans l'**Ohio.

L'université **du** Michigan est à Ann Arbor, **dans le** Michigan.

	STATES	
	f	*m*
in, at, to	**en**	**dans le**
of, from, about	**de**	**du**

A *Faites des phrases d'après ce modèle.*

Paris, France, Français
(Jacques) **Paris est la capitale de la France.**
(Marie) **Les habitants de la France s'appellent les Français.**

1. Madrid, Espagne, Espagnols
2. Lisbonne, Portugal, Portugais
3. Londres, Angleterre, Anglais

4. Bruxelles, Belgique, Belges
5. Berne, Suisse, Suisses
6. La Haye, Pays-Bas, Hollandais

---

[1]**Hawaii** is treated like a city: **Je vais à Hawaii ; elle vient de Hawaii.**

B *Ajoutez des phrases d'après ces modèles.*

> Je suis allé(e) à Paris.   Je suis venu(e) de Paris.
> **Ah bon, vous êtes allé(e) en France.**   **Ah bon, vous êtes venu(e) de France.**

1. Je suis allé(e) à Londres.
2. Je suis arrivé(e) d'Ottawa.
3. Je suis rentré(e) de Mexico[1].
4. Je suis venu(e) de Bruxelles.

5. J'ai habité à Tokyo.
6. Je suis rentré(e) de Vienne.
7. Je suis resté(e) à Berne.
8. J'ai voyagé à Rome.

C *Maintenant, parlons de pays européens.*

1. Quelle est la capitale de l'Italie ? Comment s'appellent les habitants de l'Italie ? Quelle langue parle-t-on en Italie ?
2. Quelle est la capitale du Luxembourg ? Comment s'appellent ses habitants ? Quelle langue parle-t-on au Luxembourg ?
3. Quels sont les pays voisins[2] de la France ? Indiquez cinq pays.
4. Dans quels pays d'Europe parle-t-on français ?[3]
5. Dans quels pays est-ce qu'on fabrique les voitures suivantes ?[4]

les Toyota	les Mercedes	les Buick
les Renault	les Citroën /sitʀɔɛn/	les Mazda
les Lincoln	les Volkswagen	les Jaguar

6. Avez-vous visité un pays étranger ? Quel(s) pays ? Quels pays voulez-vous visiter ?

D *Parlons maintenant des États-Unis.*

1. Dans quel état êtes-vous né(e) ? Et vos parents ?
2. Comment s'appelle le président des États-Unis ? De quel état vient-il ? Comment s'appelle le vice-président ? D'où vient-il ?
3. Où est la Louisiane ? Quels sont les états voisins de la Louisiane ?
4. Voici le nom de quelques villes américaines. Dans quel état sont-elles ?

Bâton Rouge	Cœur d'Alène	la Nouvelle-Orléans
Beaumont	Des Moines	Pierre
Détroit	Saint-Louis	Terre Haute
Louisville	Eau Claire	Boisé

12.2 PRONOMS PERSONNELS TONIQUES **MOI**, **TOI**, ETC.

You have seen words such as **moi** and **toi** in the preceding lessons, used in sentences like the following.

Je vais très bien. Et **toi** ?	*I'm fine. And you?*
Moi, je n'ai pas d'idée.	*I have no idea.*
C'est pour **toi**.	*It's for you.*
Lui aussi, il est beau.	*He, too, is handsome.*

Words such as **moi** and **toi** are called stressed personal pronouns since they often occur in a phrase-final (stressed) position.

---

[1]Attention : Mexico est la capitale du Mexique.

[2]*neighboring* (adjectif)

[3]Consultez les *Différences* de cette leçon.

[4]Répondez, par exemple : **On fabrique les Toyota au Japon et aux États-Unis.** Remarquez que toutes les marques de voitures sont au féminin en français et qu'on ne met pas de « s » aux noms propres.

1. The stressed personal pronouns are used after a preposition, except after **à** (the case of **à** will be discussed in the next paragraph).

Je suis chez **moi**.	**Nous** sommes chez **nous**.
Tu es chez **toi**.	**Vous** êtes chez **vous**.
Il est chez **lui**.	**Ils** sont chez **eux**.
Elle est chez **elle**.	**Elles** sont chez **elles**.
On est chez **soi**.	

Je vais voyager avec **eux**.	*I am going to travel with them.*
Nous sommes devant **vous**.	*We are in front of you.*
Vous êtes derrière **nous**.	*You are behind us.*
A-t-elle besoin de **lui** ?	*Does she need him?*

2. As you learned in Lesson 10.2, indirect-object pronouns (**me/m'**, **te/t'**, **lui**, **nous**, **vous**, **leur**) are used with verbs that take **à** + noun. There are, however, a few verbs that require **à** + stressed pronoun. **Penser à** *to think of* and **être à** *to belong to* belong to this category.

MOST VERBS	PENSER À, ÊTRE À
Je **vous** ai répondu.	J'ai **pensé à vous**.
Je vais **leur** parler.	Je vais **penser à eux**/**elles**.
Vous **m'**avez téléphoné ?	Ce livre **est à moi**.
Il **nous** ressemble.	Ces chaises **sont à nous**.

3. In French, subject pronouns (**je**, **tu**, **il**, etc.) cannot be stressed. In order to emphasize a subject pronoun, you must place the corresponding stressed pronoun at either the beginning or end of the sentence, separated by a comma (,) in written language.

Moi, je vais inviter Jean-Paul. ⎫	
Je vais inviter Jean-Paul, **moi**. ⎬	*I am going to invite Jean-Paul.*
Toi, tu veux rester ici ? ⎫	
Tu veux rester ici, **toi** ? ⎬	*Do **you** want to stay here?*

Use of the third-person subject pronoun (**il**, **elle**, **ils**, **elles**) is optional when the stressed pronoun begins the sentence.

Lui(, il) ne le veut pas. ⎫	
Il ne le veut pas, **lui**. ⎬	***He** doesn't want it.*
Elles(, elles) ne fument pas. ⎫	
Elles ne fument pas, **elles**. ⎬	***They** don't smoke.*

4. Stressed pronouns are also used for combined subjects. You give the separate subjects, then summarize with **nous**, **vous**, **ils**, or **elles**. The summary pronouns **nous**, **ils**, and **elles** are optional, while **vous** is usually retained.

Toi et moi(, nous) allons faire cela.	***You and I** are going to do that.*
Paul et moi(, nous) venons à midi.	***Paul and I** are coming at noon.*
Vous et lui, vous parlez anglais.	***You and he** speak English.*
Marie et toi, vous allez à Dijon.	***Marie and you** are going to Dijon.*
Sylvie et lui(, ils) travaillent.	***Sylvie and he** are working.*
Anne et elle(, elles) sont ici.	***Anne and she** are here.*

5. The stressed pronoun can be used as a single-word answer to a question. If the verb in the question takes a preposition, the preposition must precede the stressed pronoun in the answer.

Qui sait la réponse ?	**À qui** pense-t-il ?
— **Moi**, Monsieur.	— **À elle.**
Qui va faire la réservation ?	**Chez qui** allons-nous ?
— **Lui.**	— **Chez eux.**

6. Study the following expressions as short rejoinders to statements.

Je vais réserver une chambre.	*I'm going to reserve a room.*
— **Moi aussi.**	*So am I. (Me, too.)*
— **Pas moi.**	*I'm not. (Not me.)*
Je ne veux pas rester dans cet hôtel.	*I don't want to stay in this hotel.*
— **(Ni) moi non plus.**	*Neither do I. (Me, neither.)*
— **Moi, si.**	*I do.*

TABLEAU 63 Je regarde la télé.   **Pas moi !** Je ne la regarde pas.   **Moi, si.**
                Moi aussi.   **Ni moi non plus.**

A *Exercice de contrôle*

Je vais rentrer chez moi.
1. Ce voyageur   2. Nous   3. Vous   4. Les étudiantes

Je veux rester chez moi.
1. Tu   2. Mes parents   3. Cette dame   4. Vous

Moi, je comprends le français.
1. Eux   2. Nous   3. Lui   4. Toi

Moi, je ne peux pas aller en France cet été.
1. Toi   2. Elle   3. Vous   4. Eux

B *Répondez aux questions en employant des pronoms toniques.*

1. Avez-vous besoin de moi ? Est-ce que j'ai besoin de vous ? Avez-vous besoin de vos professeurs ?
2. Est-ce que vous voulez parler de Molly Ringwald ? Voulez-vous parler de vos camarades ? Voulez-vous parler de moi ?
3. Est-ce que vous et moi, nous parlons français ? (Robert) et (Jeanne) comprennent-ils l'allemand ?
4. Est-ce que (Jacques) et (Paul) habitent dans la même[1] résidence ? (Jeanne), est-ce que vous et (Robert), vous comprenez le chinois ?
5. Pensez-vous souvent à vos parents ? Téléphonez-vous à vos parents ? À qui est ce livre ? À qui est ce cahier ?

[1]**même** *same*

C   *Regardez autour de¹ vous et répondez d'après ce modèle.*

(François), qui porte des lunettes ?
Elle, (Michèle). Lui, (Daniel). Vous. Moi.
Eux, (Michèle et Daniel).

1. (Jean), qui est près de moi ?
2. (Marie), qui est près de la porte ?
3. (David), qui a des cheveux longs ?
4. (Paul), qui a un micro-ordinateur ?

5. (Renée), à qui parlez-vous souvent ?
6. (Lili), de qui avez-vous besoin ?
7. (Michel), qui parle bien français ?
8. (Marie), qui connaissez-vous bien ?

D   *Je vais parler de moi-même². Écoutez bien et ajoutez* **moi aussi**, **pas moi**, **moi non plus** *ou* **moi, si** *après chaque phrase.*

1. Je vais bien aujourd'hui.
2. Je suis professeur de français.
3. Je ne mange pas en classe.
4. Je ne suis pas paresseux(euse).
5. J'ai des amis en France.

6. J'aime beaucoup les escargots.
7. Je fais (de la natation).
8. Je ne comprends pas (le russe).
9. Je bois du vin de temps en temps.
10. Je pose beaucoup de questions.

   *Exercice supplémentaire*

12.3   FORMES NÉGATIVES **NE ... PLUS**, **NE ... JAMAIS**

1. The negation **ne ... pas** can be replaced by **ne ... plus** *no longer*, *not anymore* and **ne ... jamais** *never*. In the present and imperfect tenses, **ne/n'** comes before the verb (before the object pronoun, if there is any), and **pas**, **plus**, or **jamais** after the verb. The indefinite and partitive articles become **de/d'**, as shown below.

Je n'ai **pas** d'argent sur moi.	*I don't have any money on me.*
Il **ne** mangeait **plus** de viande.	*He no longer ate any meat.*
Elle **ne** fait **jamais** de fautes.	*She never makes any mistakes.*

2. In the *passé composé*, **ne/n'** comes before the auxiliary (before the object pronoun, if there is any), and **pas**, **plus**, or **jamais** after the auxiliary. In other words, you put the auxiliary into the negative.

J'ai compris la question.	Ils ont nettoyé la chambre.
→ Je n'ai **pas** compris la question.	→ Ils n'ont **plus** nettoyé la chambre.
Je l'ai comprise.	Ils l'ont nettoyée.
→ Je **ne** l'ai **pas** comprise.	→ Ils **ne** l'ont **jamais** nettoyée.

3. **(Non,) Jamais** *never* and **(Non,) Pas du tout** *not at all* can also be used as short answers to a question. These expressions, unlike **ne ... personne/ne ... rien** (presented in 10.5), do not require a preposition.

Veux-tu parler de Marianne ?	Avez-vous pensé à votre avenir ?
— **(Non,) Jamais !**	— **(Non,) Jamais !**
— **(Non,) Pas du tout !**	— **(Non,) Pas du tout !**
— **(Non,) De personne !**	— **(Non,) À rien !**

¹*around*

²**de moi-même**   *about myself*; **-même(s)** ajouté au pronom personnel tonique correspond à *-self/-selves* en anglais : **moi-même, toi-même, lui-même, elle-même, soi-même, nous-mêmes, vous-même(s), eux-mêmes, elles-mêmes.**

« Avez-vous jamais visité cette région ? »

4. **Jamais** without **ne/n'**, used in *affirmative* questions, is an equivalent of *ever* in English.

Bill a-t-il **jamais** visité Paris ?　　　　*Has Bill **ever** visited Paris?*
— Non, il **n'**a **jamais** été en France.　　*No, he has **never** been to France.*
Êtes-vous **jamais** allé au Canada ?　　　*Have you **ever** gone to Canada?*
— Oui, j'ai visité la ville de Québec.　　　*Yes, I (have) visited Quebec City.*

TABLEAU 64　　　　On **ne** fume **pas**.　　　Il **ne** fume **plus**.　　　Il **ne** fume **jamais**.

A *Je vais parler de quelqu'un. Autrefois, il faisait certaines choses. Maintenant, il ne les fait plus. Ajoutez des phrases d'après ce modèle.*

Autrefois, il mangeait des escargots.
(Mireille)　**Mais il ne mange plus d'escargots.**[1]
(Charles)　**Moi, je n'ai jamais mangé d'escargots.**

1. Autrefois, il mangeait des huîtres.
2. Autrefois, il buvait du jus de carotte.
3. Autrefois, il faisait du footing.
4. Autrefois, il fumait des cigarettes.
5. Autrefois, il allait souvent en Floride.
6. Autrefois, il rentrait très tard.

[1]Attention : **un**, **des**, **du** et **de la** deviennent **de** dans une phrase négative, après **pas**, **plus** et **jamais**.

B *Écoutez, ensuite posez des questions d'après ce modèle.*

> Je n'ai pas visité Madrid.
> **Alors, vous n'êtes jamais allé(e) en Espagne ?**

1. Je n'ai pas visité Rome.
2. Je n'ai pas visité Lisbonne.
3. Je n'ai pas visité Mexico.

4. Je n'ai pas visité Tokyo.
5. Je n'ai pas visité Londres.
6. Je n'ai pas visité Ottawa.

C *Maintenant, répondez aux questions.*

1. Qu'est-ce que vous faisiez souvent quand vous aviez dix ans ? Est-ce que vous faites encore cela ?
2. Quelle émission de télé regardiez-vous souvent quand vous aviez dix ans ? Est-ce que vous la regardez encore ?
3. Avez-vous jamais mangé des escargots ? Qu'est-ce que vous n'avez jamais bu ? Qu'est-ce que vous n'avez jamais acheté ?
4. Avez-vous jamais voyagé en France ? Êtes-vous jamais allé(e) à Dijon ? Qui n'a jamais visité l'Europe ?
5. Qu'est-ce qu'on ne fait jamais dans ce cours ? Indiquez trois choses.

D *Révision. Faites des phrases en utilisant les expressions suivantes.*

1. tous les jours	croire au père Noël
2. toujours	prendre un bain (une douche)
3. souvent	travailler à la bibliothèque
4. de temps en temps	boire du champagne
5. (une) fois par (mois)	aller en France
6. rarement	boire du lait à chaque repas
7. ne jamais	manger des escargots
8. ne plus	aller au cinéma
9. ne pas du tout[1]	étudier la géographie
	manger des croissants
	visiter Montréal

E *Révision. Répondez aux questions en employant* **personne, rien, jamais, pas du tout** *ou* **plus** *d'après ce modèle.*

> Y a-t-il quelqu'un à la porte ?
> (Hervé) **Non, personne.**
> (Marie) **Personne n'est à la porte.**

1. Y a-t-il quelque chose sous cette table ?
2. Avez-vous voyagé en Europe ?
3. Avez-vous téléphoné à quelqu'un ce matin ?
4. Est-ce que quelqu'un est derrière (Monique) ?
5. Avez-vous jamais mangé des escargots ?
6. Voulez-vous sortir à minuit ?
7. Est-ce que tout est facile dans ce livre ?
8. Avez-vous quelque chose dans la main gauche ?
9. Allez-vous encore à l'école secondaire ?

---

[1]**ne ... pas du tout** *not at all*

12.4 **LIRE, ÉCRIRE**

1. The conjugation of **lire** *to read* follows a simple irregular pattern. There is no change in the stem vowel, and the consonant sound /z/, shown by the spelling **-s-**, is heard only in the plural.

lire	
lis	lisons
lis	lisez
lit	lisent
lu	

Je **lis** un journal.　　　　Nous **lisons** des articles.
Tu ne **lis** pas de romans ?　　Vous ne **lisez** pas les instructions ?
Elle **lit** une lettre.　　　　Elles **lisent** beaucoup.
J'ai **lu** votre article.

2. **Écrire** *to write* follows a pattern similar to **lire**, but the past participle is different.

écrire	
écris	écrivons
écris	écrivez
écrit	écrivent
écrit	

Je n'**écris** pas de lettres.　　Nous **écrivons** peu de phrases.
Tu **écris** ta réponse.　　　　Vous **écrivez** un poème ?
Il **écrit** à son ami.　　　　Ils **écrivent** des compositions.
J'ai **écrit** à mes parents.

3. Both **lire** and **écrire** can take direct and/or indirect objects. English has similar constructions.

Elle **lit** la lettre (à sa mère).　　*She is reading the letter (to her mother).*
Vous **écrivez** (la lettre) à Chantal.　*You are writing (the letter) to Chantal.*

Il vient d'écrire une phrase au tableau. (au Zaïre)

Qu'est-ce qu'ils lisent ?

A *Exercice de contrôle*

Je lis beaucoup de livres.
1. Nous　　2. Tu　　3. Vous　　4. Les étudiants

J'écris assez de lettres.
1. Les étudiants　2. Ma mère　　3. Vous　　4. Nous

Je lis et écris beaucoup.
1. Vous　　2. Tu　　3. Nous　　4. Le professeur

B *Répondez aux questions.*

1. Lisez-vous des quotidiens ? Quels quotidiens ? Lisez-vous des hebdomadaires ? Quels hebdomadaires ? À quelles revues êtes-vous abonné(e) ?
2. Lisez-vous des romans ? Qui a lu James Michener ? Quel roman de Michener avez-vous lu ?
3. Avez-vous lu quelque chose hier soir ? Qu'est-ce que vous allez lire ce soir ?
4. Qu'est-ce que vous lisiez souvent quand vous aviez huit ans ? Est-ce que vous lisez toujours cela ?
5. Qu'est-ce que vous écrivez dans votre cahier d'exercices ? Qu'est-ce que vous lisez dans le cahier d'exercices ?
6. Avez-vous jamais écrit au président des États-Unis ? Et au gouverneur de notre état ?

 Compréhension auditive

12.5 PRONOMS PERSONNELS : OBJETS DIRECT ET INDIRECT

1. It is possible to have two pronouns in a sentence. Remember, **le**, **la**, **les** are direct objects, **lui**, **leur** are indirect objects, while **me**, **te**, **nous**, **vous** can be either direct or indirect objects. The sequence of object pronouns is as follows.

a) When the direct object **le/la/les** is used with the indirect object **lui** or **leur**, the indirect object comes after the direct object. In the *passé composé*, the past participle agrees in gender and number with **le/la/les**.

Je donne **le cadeau à Mireille**.
→ Je **le lui** donne.

Il explique **les symptômes au médecin**.
→ Il **les lui** explique.

Il a montré **la lettre à ses parents**.
→ Il **la leur** a montrée.

Il a posé **les questions aux étudiants**.
→ Il **les leur** a posées.

b) When **le/la/les** is used with the indirect object **me**, **te**, **nous**, or **vous**, the indirect object comes before the direct object, and **le/la** becomes **l'** before a vowel sound.

Il **me** donne **son adresse**.
→ Il **me la** donne.

Je t'envoie **cette carte**.
→ Je **te l'**envoie.

Il ne **nous** a pas montré **ses photos**.
→ Il ne **nous les** a pas montrées.

Je **vous** ai dit **la vérité**.
→ Je **vous l'**ai dite.

2. In the *passé composé*, the object pronouns precede the auxiliary verb. The past participle agrees in gender and number with the preceding *direct* object (Lesson 9.3, p. 194). If an infinitive takes object pronouns, they come immediately before the infinitive.

Je dis **la vérité à mon ami**.
→ Je **la lui** ai dite.
→ Je vais **la lui** dire.
Vous **m'**expliquez **la leçon**.
→ Vous **me l'**avez expliquée.
→ Vous n'allez pas **me l'**expliquer.

Je ne vends pas **ma voiture à Jacques**.
→ Je ne **la lui** ai pas vendue.
→ Je ne veux pas **la lui** vendre.
Elle ne **vous** raconte[1] pas **ses ennuis** ?
→ Elle ne **vous les** a pas racontés ?
→ Elle ne peut pas **vous les** raconter ?

[1]**Raconter** means *to tell (about)*, specifically in the sense of telling a story (**raconter une histoire**), an adventure (**une aventure**), problems (**des ennuis**), where **dire** cannot be used.

3. Here is a list of verbs that can take both direct and indirect objects. The indirect object usually denotes human beings or animals.

apporter	to bring	**lire**	to read
demander	to ask for	**montrer**	to show
dire	to say	**payer**	to pay for
donner	to give	**poser (une question)**	to ask (a question)
écrire	to write	**prêter**	to lend
envoyer	to send	**raconter**	to tell
expliquer	to explain	**vendre**	to sell

Le facteur **les lui** apporte.

Je **vous les** paie. Vous **me les** payez.

TABLEAU 65

A *Remplacez les noms par les pronoms appropriés, d'après ces exemples.*

J'apporte le livre à mon ami.
Je le lui apporte.

Il m'a dit la vérité.
Il me l'a dite.

1. Je montre ma photo à mon ami.
2. Je dis la vérité à mes parents.
3. Je vous pose cette question.
4. Il vous explique les symptômes.
5. Il a donné le journal à ses parents.
6. Vous m'avez dit la vérité.
7. Avez-vous vendu la voiture à Marie ?
8. Allez-vous m'expliquer cette leçon ?

B *Répondez aux questions.*

1. Est-ce que je vous explique la grammaire ?
2. Est-ce que je vous prête ma voiture ?
3. Est-ce que je vous raconte mes ennuis ?
4. Est-ce que vous me racontez vos ennuis ?
5. Est-ce que vous m'avez donné votre numéro de téléphone ?
6. Est-ce que (Janine) nous a donné son numéro ?
7. Est-ce que vous voulez me montrer vos devoirs ?
8. Est-ce que (Robert) va vous vendre sa montre ?

C *Répondez aux questions.*

1. Expliquez-vous la leçon à vos camarades ?
2. Montrez-vous vos devoirs à vos camarades ?
3. Avez-vous prêté vos disques à (Marianne) ?
4. Avez-vous vendu votre livre à (Cécile) ?
5. Avez-vous expliqué la grammaire à (Daniel) ?
6. Pouvez-vous expliquer la grammaire à vos camarades ?
7. Allez-vous raconter vos ennuis à vos parents ?
8. Voulez-vous raconter vos ennuis à vos parents ?

🔲 *Exercice supplémentaire*

🔲 *Compréhension auditive*

🔲 *Compréhension auditive*

APPLICATIONS

*Voulez-vous aller
en Grèce ?*

🔲 **A Situations**

Après les vacances

*Les vacances de Noël sont terminées. Après les cours, Ignès, Mayoumi, Jean-Paul et Michel
vont au café près de l'université. Ils parlent de leurs vacances. Pour eux, elles ont duré
presque trois semaines. Ils ont donc eu le temps de faire pas mal de¹ choses.*

MAYOUMI	Qu'est-ce que tu as fait pendant les vacances, Ignès ?
IGNÈS	Julien et moi, nous sommes allés au Maroc.
MAYOUMI	Au Maroc, vraiment ?
IGNÈS	Oui, pendant une semaine. Ahmed nous a invités. Nous avons fait des excursions en voiture autour de Casablanca. Après, nous avons passé trois jours chez sa grand-mère, à Rabat².
JEAN-PAUL	Vous avez de la veine.³
IGNÈS	Et toi, qu'est-ce tu as fait ?
JEAN-PAUL	Eh bien, Monique et moi, nous sommes rentrés chez nous. Nous avons invité Christine à passer les vacances avec nous.
IGNÈS	Vous avez visité les châteaux de la Loire ?
JEAN-PAUL	Oui, et puis nous sommes souvent sortis avec nos copains.
IGNÈS	Et toi, qu'est-ce que tu as fait, Mayoumi ?

5

10

15

¹**pas mal de** = beaucoup de
²Casablanca est la ville la plus importante du Maroc ; Rabat est la capitale du pays.
³**avoir de la veine** *to be lucky*

MAYOUMI	Mes parents sont arrivés en France juste avant Noël. Nous avons passé quelques jours à Paris. Après, nous avons voyagé dans le Midi[1].
JEAN-PAUL	Et ils nous ont rendu visite[2] à Tours.
MAYOUMI	Oui, c'était très gentil de ta part[3] de nous inviter. Nous avons fêté le Nouvel An 20 chez les Chabrier, et puis nous avons visité des châteaux.
JEAN-PAUL	La soirée de la Saint-Sylvestre[4] était vraiment formidable. Nous avons dansé jusqu'à deux heures.
MAYOUMI	Oui, tout était parfait : des amis sympathiques, des quantités de bonnes choses à manger, du champagne... 25
IGNÈS	On me dit que tu es allé en Grèce, Michel. C'est vrai ?
MICHEL	Oui, j'ai trouvé un vol bon marché° à Nouvelles Frontières[5]. J'avais envie de[6] voir Athènes.
IGNÈS	J'aimerais° aller en Grèce un de ces jours.
MICHEL	J'ai pris pas mal de photos. Voulez-vous les voir, demain peut-être ? 30
MAYOUMI	Bien sûr.
MICHEL	Alors, tout le monde a passé de bonnes vacances.
JEAN-PAUL	C'est vrai. Mais maintenant, au travail !

bon marché *cheap* (marginal gloss)

I would like (marginal gloss)

Répondez aux questions. (*lignes 1–3*)

1. Où vont les quatre étudiants après le cours ?
2. De quoi est-ce qu'ils parlent ?
3. Combien de temps est-ce que les vacances ont duré ?

(*lignes 4–33*)

4. Qui a invité Julien et Ignès à aller au Maroc ?
5. Quelles villes ont-ils visitées ?
6. Où est-ce que Christine a passé ses vacances ?
7. Quand est-ce que les parents de Mayoumi sont arrivés ?
8. Chez qui ont-ils passé la nuit de la Saint-Sylvestre ?
9. Où est-ce que Michel est allé pendant les vacances ?
10. Quelle sorte de vol a-t-il trouvé pour aller en Grèce ?

B Expressions utiles

 Pays, capitales, habitants (voir la carte à la page 257)

Pays féminins[7]

1. la France, Paris, Français
2. l'Allemagne de l'Est, Berlin, Allemands
3. l'Allemagne de l'Ouest, Bonn, Allemands
4. l'Angleterre (la Grande-Bretagne), Londres, Anglais
5. l'Autriche, Vienne, Autrichiens
6. la Belgique, Bruxelles /bʀy(k)sɛl/, Belges
7. l'Espagne, Madrid, Espagnols
8. l'Irlande, Dublin /dyblɛ̃/, Irlandais
9. l'Italie, Rome, Italiens
10. la Suisse, Berne, Suisses

[1]Le Midi désigne le sud de la France.
[2]On **visite** quelque chose, mais on **rend visite à** quelqu'un.
[3]*it was very nice of you*
[4]*New Year's Eve* (voir les *Différences* de la Leçon 15)
[5]A French company specializing in worldwide charter flights (**un charter** /ʃaʀtɛʀ/ *charter*)
[6]**avoir envie de** + infinitif *to feel like doing (something)*
[7]Most countries whose names end in **-e** are feminine (exception: **le Mexique**).

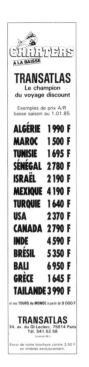

Pays masculins

11. le Danemark, Copenhague, Danois
12. le Luxembourg, Luxembourg, Luxem-
bourgeois

13. les Pays-Bas, La Haye /laɛ/ Hollandais
14. le Portugal, Lisbonne, Portugais

D'autres pays féminins

la Chine, Pékin, Chinois
l'Égypte, le Caire, Égyptiens
la Grèce, Athènes, Grecs (*f* Grecques)
la Norvège, Oslo, Norvégiens
la Pologne, Varsovie, Polonais

la Russie (l'Union Soviétique, l'URSS
/lyʀs/), Moscou, Russes
la Suède, Stockholm, Suédois
la Yougoslavie, Belgrade, Yougoslaves

D'autres pays masculins

le Brésil, Brasilia, Brésiliens
le Canada, Ottawa, Canadiens
les États-Unis, Washington, Américains

l'Israël[1], Jérusalem, Israéliens
le Japon, Tokyo, Japonais
le Mexique, Mexico, Mexicains

Continents[2]

l'Afrique (du Nord / Centrale / du Sud)
l'Amérique (du Nord / Centrale / du Sud)
l'Asie
l'Europe (Occidentale / Centrale / de l'Est)
l'Australie

C **Pratique**

1. La plaque internationale. Si vous voyagez en Europe en voiture, vous achetez une petite plaque ovale qui indique le pays d'immatriculation[3]. Devinez quels pays ces plaques représentent.[4]

TABLEAU 66

[1]**Il va en Israël** ; **Il vient d'Israël.** Lorsque le nom d'un pays commence par une voyelle, on emploie **en** et **d'** comme prépositions.

[2]Tous les continents sont féminins.

[3]**immatriculation** *(title)* registration

[4]Voici les pays (pas dans l'ordre) : Monaco, Belgique, Allemagne, Angleterre, États-Unis, Italie, Autriche, Danemark, France, Espagne, Pays-Bas, Suisse (Confédération Helvétique).

2. Voici les noms de quelques personnes célèbres. Identifiez leur nationalité et leur profession (compositeur, écrivain, poète, peintre, homme d'état[1]).

   Exemple : **Debussy ? C'était un compositeur français.**

Dante Alighieri	F. Chopin	Michel-Ange /mikɛlɑ̃ʒ/
M. Ravel	G. Pompidou	C. Saint-Saëns /sɛ̃sɑ̃s/
P. Cézanne	L. Tolstoï	J. Dos Passos
T. Jefferson	G. Gershwin	L. de Vinci /vɛ̃si/

3. Certaines villes et certains pays sont célèbres pour leurs monuments. Dans quels pays va-t-on pour voir les monuments suivants ?

la Tour Eiffel	la basilique Saint-Pierre
l'Acropole d'Athènes	le palais de Buckingham
les Pyramides	le palais de l'ONU[2]
la Grande Muraille	le palais de Versailles

Les guides Michelin sont très utiles pour les touristes.

D **Mini-composition :** *Cheryl Wilson, une étudiante américaine, a passé le mois de juillet en Europe avec une de ses copines. Complétez le passage en employant les mots indiqués.*

(1) Lisa/et/moi/aller/...[3]/Europe/été/dernier. (2) Nous/trouver/vol/pas cher[4]/et/nous/partir/.../États-Unis/10 juillet. (3) Nous/rester/.../Paris/pendant/1 semaine. (4) Je/acheter/plusieurs/guides Michelin[5]. (5) Ce/guides/être[6]/très/utile :/pour/chaque/région,/ils/donner[6]/plans[7]/de/les/villes,/histoire/et/description/de/les/endroits/intéressant. (6) .../Paris,/nous/voir/pas mal de/monuments/et/musée/et/nous/célébrer/14 juillet. (7) Après,/nous/visiter/régions/autour de/capitale. (8) Puis,/nous/prendre/le train/pour/aller/.../Italie. (9) Nous/visiter/Florence/et/Rome. (10) Nous/voyager/.../Allemagne/pendant/quelques/jour. (11) Au cours de[8]/voyage/nous/rester/dans/plusieurs/Auberges *f* de Jeunesse[9]. (12) Nous/trouver/les/propre/et/assez/confortable. (13) Mais/comme/temps/passer[6]/vite ! (14) Bientôt/ce/être/fin/de/notre/vacances. (15) Nous/revenir/.../États-Unis/16 août ;/nous/être/triste/quand/nous/quitter/France.

[1]*statesman*

[2]**l'ONU** l'Organisation des Nations Unies (ici, le mot **palais** signifie **un beau bâtiment public**)

[3]Remplacez **...** dans le paragraphe par une préposition appropriée.

[4]**pas cher** *inexpensive, cheap*

[5]Ne mettez pas le mot **Michelin** au pluriel.

[6]Employez le présent pour ces verbes.

[7]*maps*

[8]*In the course of, During*

[9]*Youth Hostels* (voir les *Différences* de la Leçon 14)

E Renseignements et opinions

1. Qu'est-ce que vous avez fait hier ? Mentionnez deux choses. Qu'est-ce que vous n'avez pas fait ? Mentionnez une chose.
2. Qu'est-ce que vous avez lu hier ? Avez-vous écrit à quelqu'un ? Est-ce que vous lui (leur) écrivez souvent ?
3. Est-ce que vous et moi, nous sommes étudiants ? Est-ce que vous et moi, nous sommes français(es) ?
4. Avez-vous jamais fumé ? Avez-vous jamais bu de l'alcool ? Qu'est-ce que vous n'avez jamais fait ?
5. Voulez-vous aller en Europe ? Quels pays voulez-vous visiter ? Quelles villes voulez-vous visiter ?
6. Connaissez-vous le Canada ? Quels pays connaissez-vous bien ? Les avez-vous déjà visités ?

Compréhension auditive (basée sur l'Application A)

Compréhension auditive (basée sur l'Application B)

Dictée (les noms des pays francophones)

VOCABULAIRE

Noms

l'**Allemagne** f	Germany	un **hebdomadaire**	weekly magazine	le **portugais**	Portuguese language
l'**allemand** m	German language				
un(e) **Anglais(e)**	Englishman (Englishwoman)	un(e) **Hollandais(e)**	Dutchman (Dutchwoman)	un(e) **Portugais(e)**	Portuguese (person)
l'**Angleterre** f	England	l'**Idaho** m	Idaho	le **Portugal**	Portugal
Athènes	Athens	l'**Indiana** m	Indiana	la quantité	quantity
l'**Autriche** f	Austria	l'**Iowa** m	Iowa	le **quotidien**	daily newspaper
un(e) **Belge**	Belgian (person)	l'**Irlande** f	Ireland	la **revue**	magazine, journal
la **Belgique**	Belgium	l'**Italie** f	Italy	le **roman**	novel
Berne	Bern	l'**italien** m	Italian language	le **russe**	Russian language
Bruxelles	Brussels	un(e) **Italien(ne)**	Italian (person)	la Saint-Sylvestre	New Year's Eve
la **carte**	map	le **Japon**	Japan	la **soirée**	evening; evening party
la **cigarette**	cigarette	le **Kentucky**	Kentucky		
le **commentaire**	comment; commentary	**Lisbonne**	Lisbon	la **Suisse**	Switzerland
		les **lunettes** f	glasses	les **Suisses**	the Swiss (people)
le **croissant**	croissant	le **Luxembourg**	Luxemburg	le **symptôme**	symptom
le **Dakota du Sud**	South Dakota	le **Luxembourgeois(e)**	Luxemburger	le **test**	test
une **école**	school	la **maman**	mom	le **Texas**	Texas
un **ennui**	trouble, problem	le Maroc	Morocco	la **veine**	luck
une **envie**	desire	le **Mexique**	Mexico	le **vice-président**	vice president
un **escargot**	snail	le **Michigan**	Michigan		
l'**Espagne** f	Spain	le **micro-ordinateur**	microcomputer	**Vienne**	Vienna
un(e) **Espagnol(e)**	Spaniard	le Midi	south of France	la **visite**	visit
une excursion	excursion	le **Missouri**	Missouri	le **vol**	flight
Genève	Geneva	**Monaco**	Monaco	le **voyageur**	traveler
la **géographie**	geography	la nuit	night	le **Wisconsin**	Wisconsin
la **Grèce**	Greece	le **pays**	country	les **yeux** m	eyes
La Haye	The Hague	les **Pays-Bas** m	The Netherlands		

Verbes

déménager *to move*
durer *to last*
écrire *to write*

fabriquer *to manufacture*
fumer *to smoke*
indiquer *to indicate*

lire *irrég* *to read*
raconter *to tell*

Adjectifs

bon marché *cheap, inexpensive*
fâché(e) *angry; sorry*

parfait(e) *perfect*
secondaire *secondary*

voisin(e) *neighboring*

Adverbes

peut-être *perhaps*

vraiment *really*

Autres expressions

Au travail ! *Let's get to work!*
avoir de la veine *to be lucky*
avoir envie de + *inf* *to feel like doing (something)*
combien de temps *how long*
de ta part *of you, on your part*
donc *so, therefore*
être abonné(e) (à) *to have a subscription (to)*
être à qqn *to belong to someone*
eux *them*
J'aimerais *I would like*

moi aussi *me too, I also*
Moi non plus. *Neither do I. (Me, neither.)*
Moi, si. *I do.*
ne ... jamais *never*
ne ... pas du tout *not at all*
ne ... plus *no longer, not anymore*
Nouvelles Frontières *f* *a French charter company*
rendre visite à qqn *to visit someone*
un de ces jours *one of these days*

13 Je ne me sens pas bien !

LESSON OBJECTIVES

Theme and Culture

1. Routine activities with regard to parts of the body
2. Personal hygiene and health

Communication Skills

1. Expressing activities that require reflexive constructions (*getting up, getting dressed, going to bed*)
2. Expressing activities associated with parts of the body (*washing hands, brushing teeth*)
3. Expressing activities with regard to their durations (*during, ago, for, since*)
4. Asking/Answering questions about one's health
5. Expressing symptoms of ailments in simple ways

Structures

13.1 Reflexive verbs: present and imperfect
13.2 Use of **depuis**, as contrasted with **il y a** and **pendant**
13.3 Use of the definite article with parts of the body
13.4 Reflexive verbs: *passé composé*
13.5 **Dormir**, **servir**, **sentir**

CONVERSATIONS

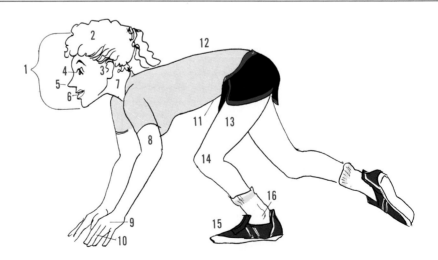

TABLEAU 67

276

A. Le corps humain

Regardez le Tableau 67. Qu'est-ce que c'est ? C'est un corps humain. Répétez les mots après moi...[1] Maintenant, répondez aux questions.

Où est votre tête ? Où sont vos cheveux ? De quelle couleur sont vos cheveux ? (« J'ai les cheveux noirs », etc.)

Où sont vos oreilles ? Où sont vos yeux ? De quelle couleur sont vos yeux ? (« J'ai les yeux bleus », etc.)

Où est votre main gauche ? Levez la main droite. Qu'est-ce que vous faites quand vous avez une question à poser ?[2]

Qu'est-ce que vous faites avec les yeux ? Qu'est-ce que vous faites avec les oreilles ? Et avec la bouche ? Et avec les jambes ?

B. Réveille-toi ![3]

JACQUES Comment ! Tu es encore au lit ? Réveille-toi !

ROBERT Hein ?... D'accord, d'accord, je me lève. Quelle heure est-il ?

JACQUES Il est déjà sept heures. Tu te couches trop tard.

ROBERT Oui, je sais. (*Il bâille.*)

C. J'ai mal au ventre.[4]

MAYOUMI Je vais rentrer à la maison. Je ne me sens pas bien.

MME BOSQUET En effet[5], vous n'avez pas bonne mine[6]. Qu'est-ce qui ne va pas ?[7]

MAYOUMI J'ai mal au ventre.

MME BOSQUET Ce n'est pas grave, j'espère.

Compréhension auditive (*basée sur la Conversation A*)

DIFFÉRENCES

À votre santé[8]

An American complains of an "upset" stomach; a French person suffers from **mal au foie** (an "upset" liver). This term, perhaps derived from the traditional high consumption of wine, is used to cover many symptoms of indigestion (to be distinguished from **une maladie de foie** *a liver ailment*). The French place great faith in the ability of the local **pharmacien** to supply them with a remedy for minor illnesses, and may purchase aspirin or other medicine. In more serious cases, one calls the doctor (some doctors still make house calls in France), goes to **la clinique** (usually private), or, in case of emergency or if hospitalization is required, to the hospital (**l'hôpital** *m*, usually public). The French Social Security reimburses up to 75% of the doctor's fees and the cost of medication, and up to 80% of hospitalization costs, in addition to compensation for lost wages.

The French government is generous in providing health care for mothers to be and new mothers. For example, various kinds of assistance are offered for pregnancy and

[1]Le vocabulaire du Tableau 67 est enregistré sur la bande magnétique.

[2]En France on lève le doigt (l'index) quand on a une question à poser.

[3]*Wake up!*

[4]**Avoir mal à** + definite article + part of body means *to have an ache* or *a pain* in that part of the body.

[5]*Indeed, In fact*

[6]**avoir bonne mine** *to look well*

[7]*What's wrong?*

[8]*To your health* (or **À la bonne vôtre**); said when drinking a toast to someone.

Le pharmacien donne de bons conseils.

childbirth. An expectant mother receives financial aid equivalent to 25% of her husband's salary. Her medical expenses are almost entirely covered, and she even receives a sum of money (about $300, twice) to cover extra expenses for the baby. A working woman receives about sixteen weeks of maternity leave at half pay, while still qualifying for the supplement of 25% of her husband's earnings. The husband himself is given several days of paid leave after the birth of the child in order to assist his wife.

STRUCTURES

13.1 VERBES RÉFLÉCHIS : AUX TEMPS SIMPLES

Reflexive verbs denote an action that is performed by the subject on the subject rather than on another person or thing. In English, *I see myself in the mirror, You will hurt yourself* are reflexive constructions, while *I see you in the mirror, You will hurt him* are not.

1. In French, reflexive verbs are preceded by reflexive pronouns: **me, te, se (m', t', s'** before a vowel sound), **nous** and **vous**. The expressions **il/elle s'appelle** and **ils/elles s'appellent**, which you have been using, are reflexive constructions. Study the examples below. Remember, the verb itself must be conjugated to agree with the subject.

Je **me lave**.	*I wash myself.*	Nous **nous lavons**.	*We wash ourselves.*
Tu **te laves**.	*You wash yourself.*	Vous **vous lavez**.	*You wash yourself/ yourselves.*
Il **se lave**.	*He washes himself.*		
Elle **se lave**.	*She washes herself.*	Ils **se lavent**.	*They wash themselves.*
On **se lave**.	*One washes oneself.*	Elles **se lavent**.	*They wash themselves.*

2. In dictionaries, reflexive verbs are usually listed under the infinitive form preceded by **se**. Below are the reflexive verbs used in the oral and written exercises in Lesson 13. Note that in many cases the English equivalents are nonreflexive.

s'amuser	*to have fun* (literally, *to amuse oneself*)
s'appeler[1]	*to be called, one's name is* (literally, *to call oneself*)
se brosser	*to brush oneself (off)* (in 13.4)
se casser	*to break* (in 13.4)
se coucher	*to go to bed*
se couper	*to cut oneself* (in 13.4)
se dépêcher	*to hurry up*
s'ennuyer[2]	*to be bored* (literally, *to bore oneself*)
se fouler	*to sprain* (in 13.4)
s'habiller	*to get dressed* (literally, *to dress oneself*)
se déshabiller	*to get undressed* (literally, *to undress oneself*)
se faire mal (à)	*to hurt oneself* (in 13.4)
se laver	*to wash (oneself)*
se lever[3]	*to get up* (literally, *to raise oneself*)
se promener[3]	*to take a walk* (literally, *to walk oneself*)
se reposer	*to rest*[4]
se réveiller	*to wake up* (literally, *to wake oneself*)
se sentir	*to feel* (in 13.5)

Je **m'appelle** Michel.

Je **me réveille** à sept heures.

Je **me lève** à sept heures cinq.

TABLEAU 68   Je **m'habille** dans ma chambre.   Je **me repose** sur un banc public.   Je **me couche** à onze heures.

[1]**Appeler** doubles the stem consonant (see Lesson 7.3): **je m'appelle, tu t'appelles, il s'appelle, ils s'appellent,** but **nous nous appelons, vous vous appelez.**

[2]Conjugated like **essuyer** (Lesson 7.3): **je m'ennuie, tu t'ennuies, il s'ennuie, nous nous ennuyons, vous vous ennuyez, ils s'ennuient.**

[3]Conjugated like **acheter** (Lesson 7.3): **je me lève, tu te lèves, elle se lève, nous nous levons, vous vous levez, ils se lèvent.**

[4]Note the meaning of **se reposer**; **rester** means *to stay, to remain.*

Les enfants s'amusent dans la fontaine.

3. Many reflexive verbs are used as nonreflexive verbs if the action is performed by the subject on someone or something else.

Je **m'amuse** au cinéma.	*I have fun at the movies.*
J'**amuse** les enfants	*I amuse the children.*
Je **me lave** dans la salle de bains.	*I wash myself in the bathroom.*
Je **lave** ma voiture	*I wash my car.*
Je **me réveille** à six heures.	*I wake up at six o'clock.*
Je les **réveille** à six heures.	*I wake them up at six o'clock.*

4. *Negation and inversion.* The reflexive pronoun always precedes the verb directly. This means that **ne ... pas** is placed around the combination of reflexive pronoun + verb. In inversion, it will be placed around the combination of reflexive pronoun + verb + subject pronoun.

Vous **vous dépêchez**.	Elle **se lève** à sept heures.
→ **Vous dépêchez**-vous ?	→ **Se lève**-t-elle à sept heures ?
Vous **ne vous dépêchez pas**	Elle **ne se lève pas** à sept heures.
→ **Ne vous dépêchez**-vous **pas** ?	→ **Ne se lève**-t-elle **pas** à sept heures ?

5. *The imperative.* To form a negative command, you simply drop the subject pronoun. For an *affirmative* command, the reflexive pronoun comes *after* the verb, and **te** becomes **toi**. A hyphen is placed between the verb and the inverted reflexive pronoun in written French. (Remember, first-conjugation verbs (**-er**) drop the **-s** of the **tu** form.)

Tu **te** reposes.	Vous **vous** couchez à minuit.
→ Ne **te** repose pas !	→ Ne **vous** couchez pas à minuit !
→ Repose-**toi** !	→ Couchez-**vous** à minuit !
Nous **nous** levons à sept heures.	Vous **vous** réveillez à six heures.
→ Ne **nous** levons pas à sept heures !	→ Ne **vous** réveillez pas à six heures !
→ Levons-**nous** à sept heures !	→ Réveillez-**vous** à six heures !

6. *The infinitive.* If the reflexive verb is in the infinitive form, the reflexive pronoun still agrees with the subject.

Je me **lève** à sept heures.

→ Je vais me **lever** à sept heures.

Tu te **promènes** dans ce parc.

→ Tu peux te **promener** dans ce parc.

Elle se **couche** avant minuit.

Elle peut se **coucher** avant minuit.

Nous nous **habillons**.

→ Nous avons besoin de nous **habiller**.

TABLEAU 69

A *Exercice de contrôle*

Je me couche très tard.
1. Le professeur   2. Nous   3. Tu   4. Vous

Je ne me lève pas très tôt.
1. Nous   2. Les étudiants   3. Vous   4. Tu

Je me lave quand je prends un bain.
1. Tu   2. Vous   3. On   4. Nous

Je vais me reposer chez moi.[1]
1. Les étudiants   2. Nous   3. Tu   4. Vous

B *Écoutez bien et ajoutez des phrases affirmatives ou négatives d'après ces modèles.*

Je ne me lave pas dans la salle de bains.
Mais si, vous vous lavez dans la salle de bains !
Je me repose dans la classe.
Mais non, vous ne vous reposez pas dans la classe !

1. Je ne m'habille pas dans la chambre.
2. Je me lave dans la chambre.
3. Je m'ennuie dans ce cours.
4. Je m'appelle Napoléon Bonaparte.
5. Je ne m'appelle pas (Smith).
6. Je me lève à midi.
7. Je me déshabille dans la classe.
8. Je me couche à midi.

C *Posez des questions d'après ce modèle.*

(Le professeur)   Demandez-moi à quelle heure je me réveille.
(Jacques)   **À quelle heure est-ce que vous vous réveillez ?**
(Le professeur)   **Moi, je me réveille à (sept) heures.**
(Jacques, *aux autres*)   **Vous avez entendu ? Il (Elle) se réveille à (sept) heures.**

1. Demandez-moi à quelle heure je me lève.
2. Demandez-moi à quelle heure je me couche.
3. Demandez-moi comment je m'appelle.
4. Demandez-moi où je m'habille.
5. Demandez-moi où j'aime me promener.

[1]Make **chez moi** agree with the subject as well: **Elle va se coucher chez elle**.

D *Répondez aux questions.*

1. Comment vous appelez-vous ? Demandez-moi comment je m'appelle. Demandez à votre voisin(e) de gauche (droite) comment il (elle) s'appelle.
2. À quelle heure vous levez-vous ? Demandez-moi à quelle heure je me lève. Demandez à (Michèle) à quelle heure elle se lève.
3. À quelle heure vous couchez-vous ? Demandez-moi à quelle heure je me couche. Demandez à (Michel) à quelle heure il se couche.
4. À quelle heure allez-vous vous réveiller demain ? Demandez-moi à quelle heure je vais me réveiller. Demandez à (Suzanne) à quelle heure elle va se réveiller.
5. Tout le monde veut se reposer. Dites-moi de me reposer. Dites à (Jeanne) de se reposer.
6. Je suis fatigué(e). J'ai sommeil. Dites-moi de me coucher. Dites à (Monique) de se coucher.

Exercice supplémentaire

Compréhension auditive

13.2 EMPLOI DE **IL Y A**, **PENDANT**, **DEPUIS**

1. In Lesson 9.4, you learned the expression **il y a** + time (in English, time + *ago*), which indicates the time when an event took place in the past.

Je vous ai vue **il y a deux heures**.	*I saw you two hours ago.*
Elle était ici **il y a dix minutes**.	*She was here ten minutes ago.*

The interrogative expression for **il y a** + time is **quand**.

Quand a-t-elle acheté cette robe ?	*When did she buy this dress?*
— Elle l'a achetée **il y a cinq jours**.	*She bought it five days ago.*

2. **Pendant** + time (English *during/for* + time) indicates the duration of an event in the past, present, or future.[1]

Je suis resté à l'hôpital **pendant trois jours**.	*I stayed in the hospital during/for three days.*
Il travaille au labo **pendant deux jours**.	*He works at the lab during/for two days.*
Je vais être à Paris **pendant deux ou trois mois**.	*I'm going to be in Paris during/for two or three months.*

Pendant can be omitted if number + time unit comes directly after the verb.

Elle a travaillé (**pendant**) **six heures** hier.	*She worked (for) six hours yesterday.*
Je vous ai attendu (**pendant**) **vingt minutes**.	*I waited (for) twenty minutes for you.*

The interrogative expression for **pendant** + time is **(pendant) combien de temps**.

(Pendant) combien de temps allez-vous rester à l'hôpital ?	*(For) how long are you going to stay in the hospital?*
(Pendant) combien de temps a-t-elle travaillé ?	*(For) how long did she work (study)?*

3. **Depuis** + time corresponds to English *since/for* + time. In the examples below, **depuis** corresponds to *since*, indicating the *starting point* of an action. The verb

---

[1] **Pendant** is a preposition and it comes before a noun; **pendant que** is a conjunction and comes before a clause: **Je faisais des courses pendant qu'il était en classe.**

is in the present tense because it expresses an *ongoing* action or event, which began in the past but is still continuing in the present.[1]

J'ai commencé à apprendre le français en septembre.	*I began learning French in September.* (starting point)
J'**apprends** encore le français.	*I am still learning French.* (continuing)
J'**apprends** le français **depuis** septembre.	*I **have been learning** French **since** September.* (continuing)
Il a acheté ce livre en 1987.	*He bought this book in 1987.*
Il **a** encore ce livre.	*He still has this book.*
Il **a** ce livre **depuis** 1987.	*He **has had** this book **since** 1987.*

The interrogative expression for **depuis** + time is **depuis quand** *since when/how long*, and the answer expected is the *starting point* of an action or an event.

Depuis quand travaillez-vous ?	*Since when/How long have you been working?*
— Je travaille ici **depuis mai**.	*I have been working here **since May**.*

4. **Depuis** can also be followed by an expression indicating *the total amount of time elapsed* since the beginning point of an action. **Depuis** + time in the examples below corresponds to *for* + time in English. Note again that the continuing action is expressed by the present tense in French.

Je suis venue en France il y a deux semaines.	*I came to France two weeks ago.* (beginning point)
Je **suis** encore en France.	*I am still in France.* (continuing)
Je **suis** en France **depuis** deux semaines.	*I **have been** in France **for** two weeks.* (continuing)
Il a commencé son travail à dix heures.	*He began his work at ten o'clock.*
Il est midi et il **travaille** encore.	*It's noon and he is still working.*
Il **travaille depuis** deux heures.[2]	*He **has been working for** two hours.*

Ils attendent le train depuis deux heures !

---

[1]Note that English uses *have/has been doing* or *have/has done* rather than the present tense.

[2]Note that the construction **depuis** + number + **heure(s)** is ambiguous: **depuis deux heures** can mean either *for two hours* or *since two o'clock* because **heures** can mean both *hour* and *o'clock*.

The interrogative expression for the amount of time elapsed is **depuis combien de temps** (for) how long.

Depuis combien de temps parlez-vous français ?	*How long have you been speaking French?*
— Je parle français **depuis quatre mois**.	*I have been speaking French for four months.*

TABLEAU 70

Il **faisait** beau à 8 h.

Il **a commencé** à pleuvoir à 10 h.

Il **pleut** maintenant.
Il **pleut depuis** 10 h.

A *Répondez aux questions en employant **il y a** d'après ce modèle. Utilisez les pronoms appropriés dans vos réponses.*

Quand avez-vous pris votre petit déjeuner ?
Je l'ai pris il y a deux heures (trois heures, etc.).

1. Quand avez-vous acheté (ce pull) ?
2. Quand avez-vous fait vos devoirs ?
3. Quand avez-vous parlé à vos parents ?
4. Quand êtes-vous allé(e) chez (Jacques) ?
5. Quand avez-vous regardé la télé ?
6. Quand avez-vous quitté la maison ?

B *Répondez aux questions d'après ce modèle.*

Connaissez-vous (Jacques) ?
Oui, je le connais.
Depuis quand ?
Je le connais depuis janvier (septembre, etc.).
Depuis combien de temps ?
Je le connais depuis deux mois (trois mois, etc.).

1. Connaissez-vous (Marianne) ? Depuis quand ?
2. Me connaissez-vous ? Depuis combien de temps ?
3. Parlez-vous français ? Depuis quand ?
4. Avez-vous votre livre de français ? Depuis quand ?
5. Avez-vous votre montre ? Depuis combien de temps ?
6. Apprenez-vous le français ? Depuis combien de temps ?
7. Connaissez-vous cette université ? Depuis quand ?
8. Quel temps fait-il ? Depuis quand ?

C *Répondez aux questions en employant **il y a**, **pendant** ou **depuis**.*

1. Qui a regardé la télé hier soir ? Pendant combien de temps ? Quelle émission avez-vous vue ?
2. Savez-vous depuis combien de temps je parle français ? Devinez. Savez-vous depuis quand je suis professeur de français ?

3. Qui joue au tennis ? Quand avez-vous appris à jouer au tennis ? Depuis quand jouez-vous au tennis ?

4. Quand êtes-vous entré(e) à l'université ? Depuis combien de temps êtes-vous à l'université ?

5. Qui boit du café ? Quand avez-vous bu du café pour la première fois ? Depuis combien de temps buvez-vous du café ?

6. Qui est allé au cinéma ? Quand ? Quel film avez-vous vu ? Combien de temps est-ce que le film a duré ?

7. À quelle heure vous couchez-vous ? Depuis combien de temps vous couchez-vous à (minuit) ?

Compréhension auditive

13.3 EMPLOI DE L'ARTICLE DÉFINI : PARTIES DU CORPS

In Lesson 8.1 you learned the cases in which French uses the definite article (**le**, **la**, **l'**, **les**) where English does not. In this lesson we will discuss cases concerning parts of the body where French uses the definite article while English uses none or the possessive adjective (*my*, *her*, *your*, etc.).

1. The definite article rather than the possessive adjective is used when the subject is the *possessor* of the part of the body mentioned in a sentence.

Marie a **les** yeux bleus.	*Marie has blue eyes.*
Michel a **les** cheveux blonds.	*Michel has blond hair.*
Fermons **les** yeux.	*Let's close our eyes.*
Levez **la** main, s'il vous plaît.	*Please raise your hand.*
Qu'est-ce qu'il a dans **la** main droite ?	*What does he have in his right hand?*
Avez-vous mal **aux** dents[1] ?	*Do you have a toothache?*

2. If the subject performs an action *to* or *on* a part of someone else's body (i.e., the subject is not the possessor), then the possessor is indicated by an *indirect object*.[2]

Je lave les mains **à Pierrot**.	*I wash Pierrot's hands.*
→ Je **lui** lave les mains.	→ *I wash his hands.*
→ Je les **lui** lave.	→ *I wash them.*
Elle va couper les ongles **à ses enfants**.	*She is going to cut her children's fingernails.*
→ Elle va **leur** couper les ongles.	→ *She is going to cut their fingernails.*
→ Elle va les **leur** couper.	→ *She is going to cut them.*
Peux-tu **me** brosser les cheveux ?	*Can you brush my hair?*
→ Peux-tu **me** les brosser ?	→ *Can you brush it?*

3. If the subject performs an action *to* or *on* a part of his/her own body, the reflexive pronoun (as an *indirect object*) is used; the construction is, then, subject + reflexive pronoun + verb + part of the body. This parallels what was discussed in the preceding paragraph, except that here the possessor is the same as the subject.

Je **me** coupe les ongles.	*I cut my fingernails.*
→ Je **me** les coupe.	→ *I cut them.*
Elle **se** lave la figure.	*She washes her face.*
→ Elle **se** la lave.	→ *She washes it.*

[1]**Avoir mal à** + part of the body means *to have an ache* or *a pain* in that part of the body.

[2]The possessor is expressed by the indirect object, and the part of the body is the direct object of the verb (except in the expression **faire mal à** *to hurt*, where à + part of the body is not a direct object).

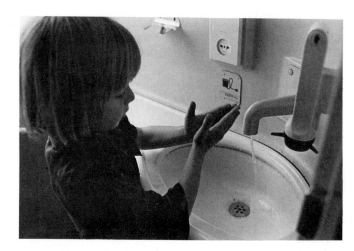

*Minou va se laver
les mains.*

Vous **vous** brossez les dents.	*You brush your teeth.*
→ Vous **vous** les brossez.	*→ You brush them.*
Nous **nous** lavons les mains.	*We wash our hands.*
→ Nous **nous** les lavons.	*→ We wash them.*

4. In imperative sentences, the possessive adjective may be used (as in English) rather than the possessor being indicated by an indirect object.

Lave **ses** mains, s'il te plaît. ⎫ Lave-**lui les** mains, s'il te plaît. ⎬	*Please wash his / her hands.*
Brossons **leurs** cheveux. ⎫ Brossons-**leur les** cheveux. ⎬	*Let's brush their hair.*
Coupez **vos** ongles. ⎫ Coupez-**vous les** ongles. ⎬	*Cut your fingernails.*
Brosse **tes** dents. ⎫ Brosse-**toi les** dents. ⎬	*Brush your teeth.*
Lavons **nos** mains. ⎫ Lavons-**nous les** mains. ⎬	*Let's wash our hands.*

5. There are few verbs that are used in conjunction with parts of the body, but those that are occur in common expressions. Study the list below.

(se) brosser (les dents, les cheveux)	*to brush (one's teeth, hair)*
(se) casser (le bras, la jambe)	*to break (one's arm, leg)*
(se) couper (le doigt, les cheveux)	*to cut (one's finger, hair)*
(se) fouler (le doigt, la cheville)	*to sprain (one's finger, ankle)*
(se) laver (la figure, les mains)	*to wash (one's face, hands)*
(se) faire mal (au genou, à la main)	*to hurt (one's knee, hand)*

In **se faire mal à**, the reflexive pronoun is an indirect object, and **à** + part of the body does *not* become a pronoun.

Il **me fait mal aux mains** !	*He is hurting my hands!*
Elle **se fait mal aux oreilles**.	*She is hurting her ears.*
Tu vas **te faire mal à la jambe**.	*You are going to hurt your leg.*

TABLEAU 71   Il a très mal **aux dents**.   Elle **se** brosse **les dents**.   Elle **se** lave **la figure**.

A *Exercice de contrôle*

J'ai mal au dos.

1. pied   2. dents   3. yeux   4. ventre

Pouvez-vous me laver les cheveux ?

1. couper les cheveux   2. brosser les cheveux   3. couper les ongles

Attention ! Vous allez vous faire mal aux oreilles !

1. dos   2. cou   3. jambes   4. doigt

B *Répondez aux questions.*

1. Avez-vous mal aux dents ? Où avez-vous mal ? Qui a mal à la tête ? Demandez à (Olivier) s'il a mal au dos.
2. Vous êtes chez le coiffeur (la coiffeuse). Qu'est-ce qu'il(elle) vous fait ?
3. Où est-ce que vous vous coupez les ongles ? Demandez-moi quand je me coupe les ongles.
4. Où est-ce que vous vous lavez la figure ? Demandez-moi quand je me lave les mains.
5. Où est-ce que vous vous brossez les cheveux ? Demandez-moi quand je me brosse les dents.
6. Dites-moi de lever la main gauche. Dites-moi de me laver les mains. Dites à (Monique) de fermer les yeux. Dites à (Michel) de se couper les ongles.

13.4   VERBES RÉFLÉCHIS : AUX TEMPS COMPOSÉS

You learned in Lesson 9.4 that, in the *passé composé*, the past participle of verbs conjugated with **être** ("verbs of motion") agrees in gender (*m/f*) and number (*s/pl*) with the subject. In Lesson 9.3, you also learned that the past participle of verbs conjugated with **avoir** agrees with the direct object, if it precedes the past participle.

Pascale et Jacqueline sont **arrivées** ce matin.

Êtes-**vous** jamais **allée** au Canada, **Louise** ?

Regardez **ces robes** ; je **les** ai **achetées** samedi dernier.

Quelle question n'a-t-il pas **comprise** ?

1. All reflexive verbs take **être** as the auxiliary in the *passé composé*. In most cases, the reflexive pronoun is the *direct object* of the verb, and the past participle agrees in gender and number with it.

PRÉSENT	PASSÉ COMPOSÉ
Je **me** lève tôt.	Je **me** suis **levé(e)** tôt.
Tu **t'**amuses au cinéma.	Tu **t'**es **amusé(e)** au cinéma.

Il **se** réveille à sept heures.	Il **s'est réveillé** à sept heures.
Elle **s'**habille rapidement.	Elle **s'est habillée** rapidement.
On **se** couche tard.	On **s'est couché** tard.
Nous **nous** promenons dans le parc.	Nous **nous** sommes **promené(e)s** dans le parc.
Vous **vous** lavez.	Vous **vous** êtes **lavé(e)(s)**.
Ils **se** dépêchent.	Ils **se** sont **dépêchés**.
Elles **se** reposent à la maison.	Elles **se** sont **reposées** à la maison.

2. *Parts of the body.* There are a few verbs for which the reflexive pronoun may not be a direct object. Usually, such verbs have to do with *parts of the body*, as discussed in Lesson 13.3. When the part of the body is not mentioned, the reflexive pronoun is the direct object and the past participle agrees with it (except **se faire mal**, as noted in Lesson 13.3). If the part of the body is mentioned (direct object), the reflexive pronoun is the indirect object and the past participle does not agree with it.[1]

Je **me** suis **lavé(e)**.	*I washed myself.*
Je **me** suis **lavé les mains**.	*I washed my hands.*
Elle **s'est brossée**.	*She brushed herself (off).*
Elle **s'est brossé les cheveux**.	*She brushed her hair.*
Ils **se** sont **coupés**.	*They cut themselves.*
Ils **se** sont **coupé les ongles**.	*They cut their fingernails.*
Elle **s'est fait mal au pied**.	*She hurt her foot.*
Elles **se** sont **fait mal aux mains**.	*They hurt their hands.*

3. *Negation and inversion.* The reflexive pronoun always precedes the auxiliary directly. The inversion takes place between the subject pronoun and the auxiliary.

Je **me suis** dépêché.	Vous **vous êtes** promenés.
→ Je **ne me suis pas** dépêché.	→ **Vous êtes**-vous promenés ?
Il **s'est** lavé la figure.	Elle **ne s'est pas** levée.
→ Il **ne s'est pas** lavé la figure.	→ **Ne s'est**-elle **pas** levée ?

TABLEAU 72   Il **s'est lavé les mains**.   Elle **s'est fait mal au pied**.   Elle ne **s'est** pas encore **levée**.

[1]But if the direct object becomes a pronoun and precedes the verb, then the past participle agrees with it in gender and number.

Il s'est **coupé les ongles**.	Je me suis **brossé les dents**.
→ Il se **les** est **coupés**.	→ Je me **les** suis **brossées**.
On s'est **lavé les mains**.	Tu t'es **foulé la cheville**.
→ On se **les** est **lavées**.	→ Tu te **l'es foulée**.

A *Exercice de contrôle*

Je me suis couché(e) à minuit.
1. Nous   2. Tu   3. Vous   4. Les étudiants

Je ne me suis pas levé(e) très tôt.
1. Les étudiants   2. Vous   3. Tu   4. Nous

Est-ce que vous vous êtes amusé(e) au cinéma ?
1. nous   2. cet enfant   3. tu   4. ces enfants

Ils se sont brossé les dents.
1. Tu   2. Vous   3. Je   4. Nous

Aïe !¹ Je me suis fait mal au pied !
1. genou   2. dos   3. tête   4. cou

B *Mettez les phrases suivantes au passé composé.*

1. Mes parents se lèvent à six heures.
2. Moi, je ne me lève pas à six heures.
3. Je me lave la figure dans la salle de bains.
4. Je ne m'habille pas dans la salle de bains.
5. Ma sœur s'habille dans sa chambre.
6. Je me brosse les dents après le petit déjeuner.
7. Je vais à l'école et mes parents vont au travail.
8. Je ne rentre pas avant quatre heures.
9. Je prends un bain et je me coupe les ongles.
10. Nous nous couchons vers onze heures.

C *C'est une jeune fille qui parle dans ce passage. Mettez chaque phrase au passé.²*

(1) Je me réveille tôt ce matin. (2) Je regarde mon réveil. (3) Il est seulement six heures et demie. (4) Je n'ai plus sommeil. (5) Je décide de me lever. (6) Je me lave la figure. (7) Je m'habille dans ma chambre. (8) Tout le monde est encore au lit. (9) Je regarde par la fenêtre. (10) Il fait beau et le ciel est bleu. (11) Je sors de notre appartement. (12) Je me promène dans la rue pendant un quart d'heure³. (13) Je rencontre Mme Didier, notre voisine. (14) Je lui dis bonjour. (15) Nous bavardons pendant quelques minutes. (16) Il est presque sept heures. (17) Il fait froid et j'ai faim. (18) Quand je rentre dans l'appartement, maman prépare le petit déjeuner. (19) Mon frère Marc est dans la salle de bains. (20) Mon père s'habille dans sa chambre. (21) À sept heures et demie, tout le monde est dans la cuisine. (22) Après le petit déjeuner, je me brosse les dents. (23) Marc part le premier, ensuite mes parents. (24) Marc se dépêche, car ses cours commencent à huit heures. (25) Moi, je reste dans la maison pendant vingt minutes. (26) Mon premier cours au lycée est à huit heures et demie, et je n'ai pas besoin de me dépêcher.

D *Répondez aux questions.*

1. À quelle heure vous êtes-vous couché(e) hier soir ? Demandez-moi à quelle heure je me suis couché(e).
2. À quelle heure vous êtes-vous levé(e) ce matin ? Demandez-moi à quelle heure je me suis levé(e).
3. Vous êtes-vous brossé les dents ? Demandez-moi si je ne me suis pas brossé les dents.
4. À quelle heure êtes-vous allé(e) à votre premier cours ? Vous êtes-vous dépêché(e) ? Demandez-moi si je ne me suis pas dépêché(e).

¹*Ouch!*
²Faites une révision du passé composé et de l'imparfait (Leçon 10.4, p. 219).
³*a quarter of an hour*

5. Est-ce que vous vous êtes jamais cassé le bras ? Vous êtes-vous jamais foulé le doigt ? Vous êtes-vous jamais fait mal au dos ?

6. À quelle heure vous leviez-vous quand vous alliez au lycée ? Demandez à (Sophie) à quelle heure elle se couchait quand elle allait au lycée.

📼 *Exercice supplémentaire*

📼 *Compréhension auditive*

13.5 DORMIR, SERVIR, SENTIR

dormir

dors	dormons
dors	dormez
dort	dorment
dormi	

servir

sers	servons
sers	servez
sert	servent
servi	

sentir

sens	sentons
sens	sentez
sent	sentent
senti	

1. In the present tense, **dormir** *to sleep*, **servir** *to serve*, and **sentir** *to feel, to smell* are conjugated like **partir** and **sortir** (Lesson 8.5): the stem vowel remains the same throughout the conjugation, and the stem-final consonant sound (here /m/ for **dormir**, /v/ for **servir**, and /t/ for **sentir**) occurs only in the infinitive and the plural forms.

Je **dors** beaucoup.	Je **sers** le déjeuner.	Je **sens** une odeur.
Tu **dors** huit heures ?	Tu **sers** le dîner ?	Tu **sens** le parfum.
Il **dort** sept heures.	Elle **sert** de la bière ?	Il **sent** la faim.
Nous **dormons** bien.	Nous **servons** du vin.	Nous **sentons** la chaleur.
Vous **dormez** mal.	Vous **servez** du café.	Vous **sentez** le froid.
Ils **dorment** assez.	Elles **servent** du thé.	Ils **sentent** la soif.
J'ai **dormi** six heures.	J'ai **servi** du rosbif.	J'ai **senti** quelque chose.

2. **Sentir** is also used as an intransitive verb meaning *to smell (good, bad)*. Note that the adjectives **bon** and **mauvais** remain masculine singular.

Ces fleurs **sentent bon**.	*These flowers smell good.*
Cette viande **sent mauvais**.	*This meat smells bad.*

3. **Se sentir** refers to one's mental or physical condition. It is usually followed by **bien** or **mal**, or an adjective that agrees in gender and number with the subject.

Je ne **me sens** pas **bien**.	*I don't feel well.*
Il **se sentait mal**.	*He was feeling sick (bad).*
Nous **nous sentons découragés**.	*We feel discouraged.*
Elles **se sentaient heureuses**.	*They were feeling happy.*

📼 **A** *Exercice de contrôle*

Je ne dors pas assez.

1. Vous   2. Mes parents   3. Mon père   4. Nous

Je n'ai pas très bien dormi.[1]

1. Nous   2. Tu   3. Vous   4. L'étudiant

Je sers du thé à mes amis.

1. Les étudiants   2. Tu   3. Vous   4. L'étudiante

J'ai trop mangé.[1] **Je ne me sens pas bien.**

1. Tu   2. Nous   3. Cet enfant   4. Vous

Elle s'est couchée tôt parce qu'elle ne se sentait pas bien.

1. Vous   2. Tu   3. Les enfants   4. Je

[1]Adverbs such as **bien**, **mal**, **peu**, **assez**, **beaucoup**, **trop** are placed immediately before the past participle: **J'ai bien dormi, J'ai assez dormi, J'ai beaucoup dormi ; J'ai mal dormi ; Je n'ai pas assez mangé, J'ai trop mangé.**

B *Répondez aux questions.*

1. Combien de temps dormez-vous ? Demandez-moi combien de temps je dors.
2. Qui a bien dormi hier soir ? Qui n'a pas assez dormi ? Combien de temps avez-vous dormi ?
3. Qui déjeune au restaurant universitaire ? Qu'est-ce qu'on sert comme boisson ? Et hier, qu'est-ce qu'on a servi comme viande ?
4. Quand vous invitez des amis chez vous, qu'est-ce que vous leur servez comme boisson ? Qu'est-ce que vous ne leur servez pas ?
5. Qu'est-ce que vous faites quand vous sentez la faim ? Et quand vous sentez la soif ? Et quand vous sentez le froid ?
6. Quand est-ce que vous sentez le froid ? Et quand est-ce que vous sentez la chaleur ? Quand est-ce que vous sentez la faim ?
7. Comment est-ce qu'on se sent quand on a bien dormi ? Et quand on a mal dormi ? Et quand on a trop mangé ? Et quand on est malade ?
8. Comment sentent les roses ? Citez deux autres choses qui sentent bon. Citez deux choses qui sentent mauvais.

APPLICATIONS

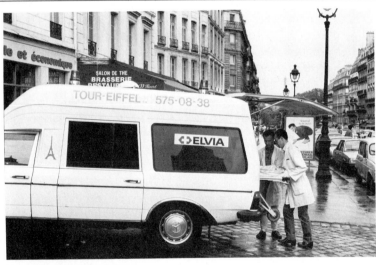

On a appelé une ambulance.

A **Situations**

Je vais appeler le médecin.

Mayoumi ne se sent pas bien depuis hier soir. Hier matin elle allait parfaitement bien. Elle a assisté à ses cours à l'institut et elle a même° joué au tennis pendant deux heures. Mais ce matin elle a très mal au ventre et elle peut à peine° marcher. Christine, qui venait prendre le déjeuner chez Mayoumi, arrive chez elle.

even
hardly

nightgown	CHRISTINE Bonjour, Mayoumi. Tiens, tu viens de te lever ? Tu es encore en chemise de nuit°. 5
	MAYOUMI Bonjour, Christine. Excuse-moi. Je me reposais. Je ne me sens pas bien.
	CHRISTINE Qu'est-ce qui ne va pas ?
	MAYOUMI J'ai très mal au ventre.
	CHRISTINE As-tu appelé un médecin ?

	MAYOUMI	Non, pas encore.	10
general practitioner	CHRISTINE	Je connais un très bon médecin généraliste°. Je vais lui téléphoner.
	MAYOUMI	Merci, Christine.

Christine téléphone à la clinique.

LA VOIX	Allô. Clinique Ravoux.
CHRISTINE	Bonjour, Madame. J'ai une amie qui a très mal au ventre.	15
LA VOIX	Peut-elle se rendre¹ à la clinique ?
CHRISTINE	Je ne crois pas. Elle peut à peine marcher. Est-ce que le docteur² peut venir ici ?
LA VOIX	Quelle est l'adresse ?
CHRISTINE	23, rue des Moines.
LA VOIX	Attendez... Oui, il peut être là vers³ onze heures.	20
CHRISTINE	Très bien. Merci, Madame.
LA VOIX	De rien, Mademoiselle.

Le docteur est dans la chambre de la malade.

LE DOCTEUR	Alors, qu'est-ce qui ne va pas ?
MAYOUMI	J'ai très mal au ventre.	25
LE DOCTEUR	Où, avez-vous mal, exactement ? Ici ?
MAYOUMI	Aïe ! Oui.
LE DOCTEUR	Ouvrez la bouche, s'il vous plaît. Avez-vous d'autres symptômes ?
MAYOUMI	Oui, j'ai de la fièvre et j'ai des nausées⁴.
LE DOCTEUR	Depuis quand avez-vous ces symptômes ?	30
MAYOUMI	Depuis hier soir, Docteur.
LE DOCTEUR	Je vais prendre votre température.
What's the matter with her	CHRISTINE	Qu'est-ce qu'elle a,° Docteur ?
LE DOCTEUR	Je crois que c'est l'appendicite. Je vais appeler une ambulance.
CHRISTINE	Je vais t'accompagner, Mayoumi.	35
MAYOUMI	Je te remercie, Christine. Tu es vraiment gentille.

Répondez aux questions. (lignes 1–4)

1. Depuis quand est-ce que Mayoumi ne se sent pas bien ?
2. Qu'est-ce qu'elle a fait hier ?
3. Où a-t-elle mal ?

(lignes 5–12)

4. Que faisait-elle quand Christine est venue ?
5. Quelle sorte de médecin Christine connaît-elle ?
6. Qu'est-ce qu'elle va faire ?

(lignes 13–22)

7. Pourquoi Mayoumi ne peut-elle pas aller à la clinique ?
8. Quelle est son adresse ?
9. Quand est-ce que le médecin peut venir ?

¹**se rendre** = venir (ou aller)

²Le mot **médecin** désigne la profession et le mot **docteur**, le titre.

³*around* (literally, *toward*)

⁴**avoir des nausées** *to feel nauseous*

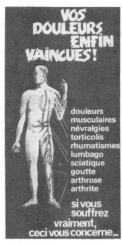

Une étudiante sénégalaise à l'Institut Pasteur.

(lignes 23–36)

10. Quels autres symptômes Mayoumi a-t-elle ?
11. D'après le docteur, qu'est-ce qu'elle a ?
12. Qu'est-ce que Christine va faire ?

B Expressions utiles

 Le corps humain (Tableau 67, page 276)

1. la tête
2. les cheveux *m*
3. l'oreille *f* (gauche / droite)
4. l'œil *m* (*pl* yeux)
5. le nez
6. la bouche
7. le cou
8. le bras (gauche / droit)
9. la main (gauche / droite)
10. le doigt
11. le ventre
12. le dos
13. la jambe (gauche / droite)
14. le genou (*pl* genoux)
15. le pied (gauche / droit)
16. la cheville (gauche / droite)

Autres expressions

les dents *f*
le dos
l'épaule *f*

l'estomac /ɛstɔma/ *m*
le foie
la gorge

la langue
les lèvres *f*
les poumons *m*

La santé

être
tomber } malade : { aller
se sentir } { bien, mieux
mal, plus mal } : aller { voir un médecin
à l'hôpital / à la clinique

le médecin
l'infirmière *f* } : { examiner
soigner
guérir } le / la malade

avoir mal
se faire mal } à la tête, au genou, à la jambe, à la gorge, au ventre, au dos

donner
avoir besoin d' } une ordonnance

prendre des médicaments

se casser } { le bras } : avoir { le bras } dans le plâtre
se fouler } { la jambe }   { la jambe }

C   Pratique

Complétez les phrases suivantes.

1. Nous sentons les odeurs avec ... et goûtons avec...
2. Vous voyez avec ... et marchez avec...
3. Je prends de l'aspirine quand j'ai mal...
4. On a mal ... quand on a une indigestion.
5. Vous ne pouvez pas tourner... ? Vous avez le torticolis !
6. Elle a la jambe dans le plâtre parce qu'elle...
7. On va chez le dentiste quand on a mal...
8. Le médecin donne une ordonnance ; le pharmacien vend...
9. Quand on a une grippe intestinale, on a mal...
10. On a mal ... quand on s'est fait mal...

Jacques dit :[1]

Levez la main droite.
Levez la main gauche.
Montrez vos dents.
Montrez votre langue.
Fermez l'œil droit.
Levez la jambe gauche.

Bouchez-vous les oreilles.
Touchez votre tête avec la main droite.
Touchez votre pied droit avec la main gauche.
Touchez votre oreille gauche avec la main droite.

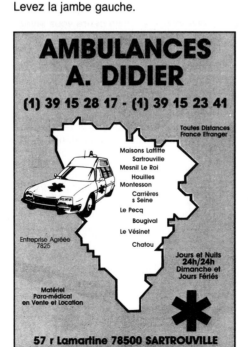

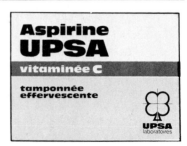

---

[1]On dit aussi « Pierrot dit » ; c'est l'équivalent de « *Simon says* ».

D Mini-composition : *Mireille a la grippe. Complétez le passage en employant les mots indiqués.*

(1) Mireille/rentrer/tôt/hier,/car/elle/ne pas/se sentir/bien. (2) Elle/être/très/fatigué/ et/elle/avoir/mal/à/tête. (3) Elle/ne rien/manger/parce que/elle/ne pas/avoir/de/ appétit. (4) Elle/se coucher/vers/8 h/soir. (5) Pendant/nuit/elle/dormir/très mal/et,/ quand/elle/se réveiller/ce/matin,/elle/avoir/fièvre. (6) Vers/11 h/elle/aller/à/hôpital/ près/son/appartement. (7) Médecin/examiner/la/et/dire/lui/que/elle/avoir/grippe. (8) Il/ donner/lui/ordonnance/et/dire/lui/de/se reposer/pendant/quelques/jour. (9) Elle/aller/ à/pharmacie/et/après,/elle/rentrer. (10) Vers/1 pés h/Pascale,/son/copine,/téléphoner/ lui. (11) Elle/apporter/lui/un/bol/soupe/et/journaux. (12) Mireille/se/sentir/un peu mieux[1] ;/elle/manger/soupe/et/se recoucher.

E Questions : *Pauvre Anne ! Elle a la jambe dans le plâtre depuis deux semaines. Elle s'est cassé la jambe. Lisez d'abord le paragraphe, ensuite posez des questions sur les parties soulignées.*

Anne a la jambe dans le plâtre (1) depuis deux semaines. (2) Cet accident lui est arrivé pendant les vacances de Noël. Elle est allée dans le Colorado (3) avec ses parents. Elle allait faire (4) du ski. Elle espérait aussi rencontrer des (5) jeunes gens sympathiques. Mais elle a eu (6) un accident le troisième jour de ses vacances. Elle est rentrée dans un arbre[2] et elle est tombée (7) la tête la première dans le neige ! Elle ne pouvait plus se relever. Le moniteur[3] (8) l'a emmenée chez le médecin. Elle s'est cassé (9) la jambe. Mais son moniteur était (10) très sympathique. Il est venu (11) la voir chaque soir. Elle est rentrée à la maison (12) il y a trois jours. Le moniteur (13) lui a téléphoné après son retour. Elle lui a écrit (14) deux fois.

F Renseignements et opinions

1. À quelle heure vous couchez-vous ? À quelle heure vous levez-vous ? Combien de temps dormez-vous ?
2. À quelle heure vous êtes-vous couché(e) hier soir ? À quelle heure vous êtes-vous levé(e) ce matin ? Comment vous sentez-vous aujourd'hui ?
3. Depuis quand êtes-vous à l'université ? En quelle année allez-vous terminer vos études ?
4. Comment vous sentez-vous aujourd'hui ? Avez-vous bien dormi ? Vous êtes-vous bien reposé(e) ?
5. Décrivez votre journée d'hier en utilisant les expressions suivantes. Mettez ces expressions dans l'ordre chronologique et indiquez à quelle heure et à quel endroit vous avez fait chaque action.

s'habiller	sortir du dernier cours
dîner	aller à l'université
se coucher	faire les devoirs
déjeuner	prendre le petit déjeuner
se lever	rentrer à la maison
assister au premier cours	se laver la figure

Compréhension auditive (basée sur l'Application A)

Dictée : « Jeanne est malade. »

[1]**mieux** *better* (comparative form of **bien**)
[2]**rentrer dans un arbre** *to hit (bump into) a tree*
[3]*ski instructor*

G Lecture

La cure[1]

Depuis l'antiquité romaine, on reconnaît les vertus thérapeutiques de certaines sources ther-
hot springs *males° pour soigner les maladies de la peau et du système nerveux, les troubles respiratoires*
spas *ou digestifs, les rhumatismes et les allergies. De nombreuses stations thermales° se sont*
développées autour de ces sources : dans le Massif Central, ancienne région volcanique
située au centre de la France, dans les Pyrénées et dans d'autres régions montagneuses. 5
Tous les ans, des milliers[2] de Français viennent se soigner et se reposer à Évian, Vichy,
Vittel, Luchon ou la Bourboule. Certaines villes ont compris que ces malades, assez âgés
pour la plupart, ont envie de[3] s'amuser et de se distraire[4] pendant qu'ils font leur cure. Des
plays *courts de tennis, des terrains de golf, des concerts, des pièces de théâtre° et parfois même*
des casinos sont à la disposition du[5] public. La cure est bonne pour la santé, et on passe 10
de bonnes vacances. M. Lacombe est un curiste à Vichy. Il parle de sa cure.

Ma femme et moi sommes arrivés ici il y a quinze jours[6]. Mon médecin m'a recommandé de
faire une cure car j'ai des rhumatismes. Nous sommes pensionnaires[7] dans un bon hôtel à
dix minutes de l'établissement thermal, et tous les jours j'ai deux heures de soins le matin, et
mud baths deux heures l'après-midi : des massages, des douches et des bains de boue° font partie du[8] 15
traitement quotidien. Ensuite, je rentre à l'hôtel et je me repose pendant une heure avant le
dîner. Tous les pensionnaires de l'hôtel font aussi une cure, et nous avons rencontré des gens
sympathiques de notre âge. Je suis venu à Vichy l'année dernière, et pendant l'hiver, je me
suis senti beaucoup mieux.

A *Indiquez si les commentaires suivants sont vrais ou faux, puis corrigez les commentaires faux.*

1. Les Romains reconnaissaient les vertus thérapeutiques de certaines sources thermales.
2. Il y a beaucoup de stations thermales dans le Midi, qui est une ancienne région volcanique.
3. On trouve des stations thermales surtout dans les régions montagneuses.
4. Rien n'est à la disposition des curistes pour se distraire.
5. C'est son médecin à Vichy qui a recommandé à M. Lacombe de faire une cure.
6. Chaque jour il fait sa cure pendant six heures.
7. M. et Mme Lacombe sont à Vichy depuis deux semaines.
8. Leur hôtel n'est pas très loin de l'établissement où il fait sa cure.
9. Tous les curistes sont pensionnaires à l'hôtel où sont M. et Mme Lacombe.
10. L'année dernière il s'est senti beaucoup mieux après la cure.

B *Cherchez dans le texte l'adjectif qui correspond à chaque nom ci-dessous.*

sympathie	digestion	volcan
montagne	maladie	respiration
Rome	nombre	centre

---

[1] traitement dans une station thermale (*spa*)

[2] *thousands* (du mot **mille** *thousand*)

[3] **avoir envie de** *to feel like (doing something)*

[4] **se distraire** *to entertain oneself*

[5] **être à la disposition de** *to be available to*

[6] deux semaines (**huit jours** = une semaine)

[7] personne qui prend une chambre avec repas dans un hôtel

[8] **faire partie de** *to belong to*

C *Trouvez dans le texte les mots qui sont définis ci-dessous.*

1. personne qui fait une cure thermale
2. eau qui sort de terre
3. de chaque jour
4. endroit où on joue au golf
5. bonne qualité
6. où il y a des montagnes
7. traitement dans une station thermale
8. endroit où on joue au tennis
9. établissement où les jeux d'argent sont autorisés

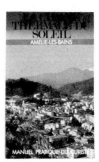

VOCABULAIRE

Noms

une ambulance	*ambulance*	la **dent**	*tooth*	la **mine**	*look*
une appendicite	*appendicitis*	le docteur	*doctor*	la nausée	*nausea*
la **bouche**	*mouth*	le **dos**	*back*	un **œil** (*pl* **yeux**)	*eye*
le **bras**	*arm*	la fièvre	*fever*	un **ongle**	*nail*
la **chaleur**	*heat*	la **figure**	*face*	un **quart d'heure**	*a quarter of an hour*
la chemise de nuit	*nightgown*	le **froid**	*cold*	le **réveil**	*alarm clock*
la clinique	*private hospital*	le **genou**	*knee*	la **rose**	*rose*
le **coiffeur**	*barber, hairdresser*	la **jambe**	*leg*	la température	*temperature; fever*
la **coiffeuse**	*beautician*	le **mal**	*pain*	la **tête**	*head*
le **corps**	*body*	le(la) malade	*patient*	le **ventre**	*stomach, belly*
le **cou**	*neck*	le médecin généraliste	*general practitioner*	la voix	*voice*

Verbes

s'amuser	*to have fun*	**se couper**	*to cut oneself*	**se lever**	*to get up*
s'appeler	*to be called, one's name is*	**se déshabiller**	*to get undressed*	**se promener**	*to take a walk*
		se dépêcher	*to hurry (up)*	se rendre (à)	*to go/come (to)*
assister à	*to attend*	**dormir** *irrég*	*to sleep*	**se reposer**	*to rest*
bavarder	*to chat*	**s'ennuyer**	*to be bored*	**se réveiller**	*to wake up*
se brosser	*to brush oneself (off)*	**se faire mal (à)**	*to hurt oneself*	**sentir** *irrég*	*to feel; to smell*
se casser	*to break*	**se fouler**	*to sprain*	**se sentir** *irrég*	*to feel*
citer	*to cite*	**s'habiller**	*to get dressed*	**servir** *irrég*	*to serve*
se coucher	*to go to bed*	**se laver**	*to wash (oneself)*		

Adjectifs

droit(e) *right*   **humain(e)** *human*

Adverbes

à peine	*hardly*	même	*even*	**tôt**	*early*
mal	*badly*	parfaitement	*perfectly*		

Autres expressions

Aïe !	*Ouch!*	**depuis combien de temps**	*(for) how long*
Attention !	*Careful!*	**depuis quand**	*since when/how long*
avoir bonne mine	*to look well, heatlhy*	**de quelle couleur**	*what color*
avoir de la fièvre	*to have a fever*	**en effet**	*indeed, in fact*
avoir des nausées	*to feel nauseous*	Ouvrez	*Open*
avoir mal à + *part of body*	*to have an ache or a pain in that part of the body*	Qu'est-ce qu'elle a ?	*What's the matter with her?*
Comment !	*What!*	**Qu'est-ce qui ne va pas ?**	*What's wrong?*

14 Comment est la chambre ?

LESSON OBJECTIVES

Theme and Culture

1. Rooms, furniture, and fixtures
2. Hotels and hotel accommodations

Communication Skills

1. Asking/Answering questions about rooms and furniture
2. Making business transactions with regard to hotels (reservations, requests, and complaints)
3. Expressing comparative quantities (*more, less, as many, as much, fewer than, most*) with nouns and pronouns
4. Emphasizing one part of a statement (**Marie** *came, We saw* **you**, *He left* **yesterday**)
5. Drawing generalizations (*all, every, entire*)

Structures

14.1 **Ouvrir**, **offrir**
14.2 Uses of **en**
14.3 Adverbs of quantity
14.4 **C'est ... qui**, **C'est ... que**
14.5 Adjective **tout**; expressions with **monde**

CONVERSATIONS

A. La chambre (à coucher)

Regardez le Tableau 73.[1] C'est une chambre à coucher. Elle est grande et claire. Parlons des meubles de ce tableau.

Regardez la **table de nuit**. Elle est à côté du[2] **lit**. Qu'est-ce que vous voyez sur la table de nuit ?

Voyez-vous la **commode** ? Elle est dans un coin de la chambre. Combien de **tiroirs** a-t-elle ? Qu'est-ce qu'il y a sur la commode ?

Vous venez d'acheter une belle affiche et un flacon de parfum. Où allez-vous les mettre ?

Vous venez d'acheter les choses suivantes. Où est-ce que vous allez les mettre ?

une belle affiche	des sous-vêtements
des mouchoirs	un réveil
une paire de chaussures	un imperméable

[1]Le vocabulaire du Tableau 73 est enregistré sur la bande magnétique.
[2]**à côté de** *next to*

TABLEAU 73

B. La salle de bains

Regardez le Tableau 74. C'est une salle de bains. Les w.-c. sont dans une petite pièce à part[1].

Voyez-vous le **lavabo** ? Où est-ce qu'on se lave la figure ? De quoi a-t-on besoin pour se laver les mains ?

Regardez la **baignoire**. Qu'est-ce qu'on fait dans une baignoire ? Où sont les **serviettes de bain** ?

Quelles sont les différences entre les salles de bains françaises et les salles de bains américaines ?

Décrivez toutes les actions nécessaires pour prendre un bain.

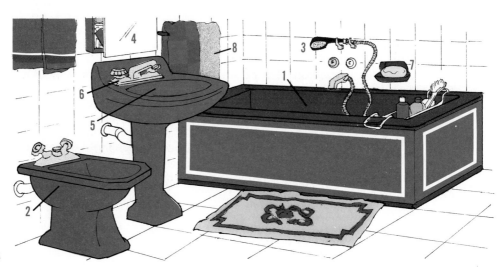

TABLEAU 74

[1]*separate*

« Je crois que maman va gagner. »

 **C. Après une partie¹ de Monopoly**

IGNÈS   J'ai seulement deux mille francs. Combien d'argent as-tu ?

JULIEN   Moi, j'en² ai un peu plus que toi. Deux mille cinq cents francs.

MONIQUE   Moi, j'ai vingt mille francs. Je n'ai pas gagné. Et toi, Michel, combien d'argent as-tu ?

MICHEL   J'en ai autant que toi. Alors, qui est le gagnant³ ?

IGNÈS   Personne ! C'est la banque qui a gagné !

Compréhension auditive (basée sur la Conversation A)

DIFFÉRENCES

Les hôtels

Tourist trade, especially the hotel business, is an important segment of the French economy, and many hotel keepers take pride in offering good service. Most **hôtels de tourisme** are classified by the **secrétariat d'État au Tourisme** into five categories, from a single star to four, and four stars with an **L** (for **luxe**). All rooms must have heating and hot and cold running water. The rating is based on the price of the room as well as the availability of a private shower or bath, toilet, telephone, elevator, and the extent of carpeting on each floor. Many three-star places also offer such amenities as radio, TV, and a mini-refrigerator (**le mini-bar**) with beverages, for which you pay separately.

For a stay of three or more days, there are more than 1,500 rooms in private homes throughout France, called **café-couette** (*bed and breakfast⁴*), with varying comfort and accommodations. Small to medium family-run hotels are often members of **la Fédération Nationale des Logis et Auberges de France**: the **logis** (1–2 stars) offer modern comfort and serve regional as well as the chef's specialties in the dining room, and **auberges** (ungraded), located in small towns, have much simpler accommodations.

---

¹*game*
²**en**   literally, *of it*, referring to **argent**
³*winner*
⁴literally, *coffee and comforter*

Other medium-sized hotels (2–3 stars) may belong to **France-Accueil**, a branch of European-based **Minotel International**, and large ones (3–4 stars) to **Mapotel**, which is associated with the Best Western chain. You can also find historic mansions, old manor houses, and castles (4 stars-4L) that have been renovated as hotels. Usually away from the main roads, they offer high comfort, aristocratic decor, and superior cuisine, and belong to the **Relais de Campagne Châteaux-Hôtels**. Large motels are increasing near major roads and cities, including such chains as **Novotel** (3 stars), **Mercure** (2–3 stars), and **Ibis** (2 stars).

Most students prefer to stay in Youth Hostels (**Auberges ƒ de Jeunesse**), which are considerably cheaper but which have certain restrictions, such as a curfew, no-smoking and no-drinking regulations, separation of the sexes, lack of privacy, and a limited length of stay. During summer, some universities open up their dormitories to traveling students, so it is certainly possible to travel throughout France even if you are on a limited budget.

STRUCTURES

14.1 OUVRIR, OFFRIR

ouvrir

ouvre	ouvrons
ouvres	ouvrez
ouvre	ouvrent
ouvert	

offrir

offre	offrons
offres	offrez
offre	offrent
offert	

1. **Ouvrir** *to open* and **offrir** *to offer* are conjugated like a first-conjugation verb (**-er**) in the present indicative. Note that the past participle ending (**-ert**) cannot be predicted from any of the conjugated forms or the infinitive.[1]

J'**ouvre** la porte.	J'**offre** mon aide à Chantal.
Tu **ouvres** la fenêtre.	Tu **offres** un cadeau à ta mère.
Il **ouvre** son livre.	Elle **offre** la chaise à la dame.
Nous **ouvrons** la valise.	Nous **offrons** des fleurs.
Vous **ouvrez** le cadeau.	Vous **offrez** du vin à vos invités.
Ils **ouvrent** la boutique.	Elles **offrent** la clé à Charles.
J'ai **ouvert** la porte avec la clé.	J'ai **offert** mon aide à Michèle.

2. Both verbs drop the **-s** of the **tu** form in the imperative, just like first-conjugation verbs (Lesson 3.3).

Ouvre la porte, s'il te plaît.	**Offre** un cadeau à Pierre.
N'**ouvre** pas la fenêtre.	N'**offre** pas de vin à Jeanne.

---

[1]Les mots anglais *overt* et *covert* viennent des participes passés **ouvert** et **couvert**.

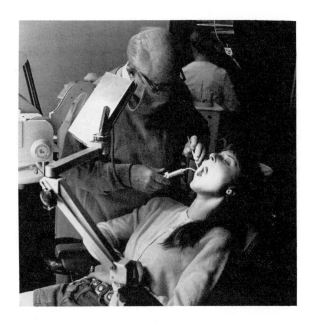

« Ouvrez la bouche un peu plus grand, s'il vous plaît. »

Other verbs conjugated like **ouvrir**:

couvrir (de)   *to cover (with)*
découvrir   *to discover; to uncover*

Another verb conjugated like **offrir**:

souffrir (de)   *to suffer (from)*

 A   *Exercice de contrôle*

J'ouvre la fenêtre quand j'ai chaud.
1. Nous   2. Tu   3. Vous   4. On

L'hôte offre des boissons à ses invités.
1. Tu   2. Nous   3. Je   4. Vous

J'ai ouvert mes valises à la douane.
1. Nous   2. Le voyageur   3. Vous   4. Les voyageurs

B   *Répondez aux questions.*

1. Quand est-ce qu'on ouvre les fenêtres ? Quand est-ce qu'on les ferme ?
2. Regardez la porte. Est-elle ouverte ou fermée ? Est-elle fermée à clé[1] ? Si elle est fermée à clé, avec quoi est-ce que vous allez l'ouvrir ?
3. Qu'est-ce que vous offrez à vos parents à Noël ? L'année dernière, qu'est-ce que vous leur avez offert ?
4. Vous êtes invité(e) à dîner chez des Français. Qu'est-ce que vous leur apportez ? Qu'est-ce que l'hôte vous offre ?
5. Connaissez-vous les mots anglais *overt* et *covert* ? D'où viennent ces mots ?
6. Quand on a mauvaise mine, est-ce qu'on souffre de quelque chose ? Demandez-moi si je souffre d'une maladie grave.
7. En quelle année Christophe Colomb /kɔlō/ a-t-il découvert l'Amérique ? Savez-vous qui a découvert la pénicilline ?

 Dictée

[1]**fermer à clé**   *to lock*

14.2 EMPLOIS DE **EN**

1. The pronoun **en** can replace any noun preceded by the plural indefinite article **des** or the partitive article **du**, **de la**, **de l'** (**de/d'** in negation). In the sentences below, **en** corresponds to English *some* or *any*. Note that the past participle remains masculine singular in the *passé composé*.

Nous apportons **des cadeaux**.	*We are bringing (some) gifts.*
→ Nous **en** apportons.	*→ We are bringing some.*
Elle a servi **du thé**.	*She served (some) tea.*
→ Elle **en** a servi.	*→ She served some.*
J'ai mangé **de la viande**.	*I ate (some) meat.*
→ J'**en** ai mangé.	*→ I ate some.*
Il n'a pas acheté **de pain**.	*He didn't buy (any) bread.*
→ Il n'**en** a pas acheté.	*→ He didn't buy any.*

In the expression **il y a**, **en** comes between **y** and the verb.

Il y a **des hôtels** près d'ici.	*There are (some) hotels near here.*
→ Il y **en** a près d'ici.	*→ There are some near here.*
Il n'y avait plus **de chambres**.	*There were no more rooms.*
→ Il n'y **en** avait plus.	*→ There weren't any more.*

2. In expressions of quantity (such as **beaucoup de**, **trop de**, **assez de**, as you learned in Lesson 7.4), **de** + noun can be replaced by **en**. In the following sentences, **en** corresponds to *of them* or *of it* (usually omitted in English).

Nous avons **trop de lits**.	*We have too many beds.*
→ Nous **en** avons **trop**.	*→ We have too many [of them].*
Vous n'avez pas **assez d'argent**.	*You don't have enough money.*
→ Vous n'**en** avez pas **assez**.	*→ You don't have enough [of it].*
Il y avait **peu de chambres**.	*There were few rooms.*
→ Il y **en** avait **peu**.	*→ There were few [of them].*

3. **En** can also replace any count noun that is preceded by a *number*, including the indefinite article **un** and **une**. The number itself must be retained. In the sentences below, **en** corresponds to English *of them*.

J'ai **une stéréo** chez moi.	*I have a stereo at home.*
→ J'**en** ai **une** chez moi.	*→ I have one [of them] at home.*
Il a vu **deux films** hier soir.	*He saw two movies last night.*
→ Il **en** a vu **deux** hier soir.	*→ He saw two [of them] last night.*
Il y a **vingt étudiants** ici.	*There are twenty students here.*
→ Il y **en** a **vingt** ici.	*→ There are twenty [of them] here.*
Nous avons **cinq fauteuils**.	*We have five armchairs.*
→ Nous **en** avons **cinq**.	*→ We have five [of them].*

Note, however, that **un**, **une**, or the number is usually dropped in *negative* sentences, especially as answers to questions.

Avez-vous **des frères** ?	*Do you have brothers?*
— Oui, j'**en** ai **un**.	*Yes, I have one.*
— Non, je n'**en** ai **pas**.	*No, I don't have any.*

Y avait-t-il encore **des chambres** ?	*Were there still some rooms?*
— Oui, il y **en** avait encore **deux**.	*Yes, there still were two.*
— Non, il **n'y en** avait **plus**.	*No, there no longer were any.*

4. The preposition **de** means *of*, *about*, or *from*. **De** + noun denoting a thing or a place can be replaced by **en**.

Je parle **de ma chambre**.	*I'm speaking about my room.*
→ J'**en** parle.	*→ I'm speaking about it.*
Avez-vous besoin **de cette chaise** ?	*Do you need this chair?*
→ **En** avez-vous besoin ?	*→ Do you need it?*
Charles a peur **des**[1] **examens**.	*Charles is afraid of tests.*
→ Charles **en** a peur.	*→ Charles is afraid of them.*
Il est venu **du magasin**.	*He came from the store.*
→ Il **en** est venu.	*→ He came from it.*

But **de** + person is replaced by **de** + stressed pronoun.

Je parle **de mes camarades**.	*I'm speaking of my friends.*
→ Je parle **d'eux**.	*→ I'm speaking of them.*
Avez-vous besoin **de Daniel** ?	*Do you need Daniel?*
→ Avez-vous besoin **de lui** ?	*→ Do you need him?*
Charles a peur **de cette femme**.	*Charles is afraid of this woman.*
→ Charles a peur **d'elle**.	*→ Charles is afraid of her.*

5. *Pronoun order.* When **en** is used with an indirect-object pronoun (s **me**, **te**, **lui**; pl **nous**, **vous**, **leur**), **en** comes between the indirect-object pronoun and the verb. As you have seen in 14.2.1, the past participle remains masculine singular in the *passé composé*.

NO AGREEMENT	AGREEMENT
Il **m'**a apporté **de la bière**.	Il **m'**a apporté **cette bière**.
→ Il **m'en** a apport**é**.	→ Il **me l'**a apport**ée**.
Tu **nous** as donné **deux bouteilles**.	Tu **nous** as donné **ces bouteilles**.
→ Tu **nous en** as donn**é deux**.	→ Tu **nous les** as donn**ées**.

As with all other object pronouns, **en** can also occur before an infinitive.

Je peux acheter **des journaux**.	Je veux parler **de mes vacances**.
→ Je peux **en** acheter.	→ Je veux **en** parler.
Je vais écrire **beaucoup de lettres**.	Je vais avoir besoin **de ce livre**.
→ Je vais **en** écrire **beaucoup**.	→ Je vais **en** avoir besoin.

m'/t'/lui/nous/vous/leur	+	en

A *Répondez aux questions en employant le pronom* **en**.

1. Buvez-vous du lait au petit déjeuner ?
2. Avez-vous mangé des œufs au petit déjeuner ?
3. Quand est-ce que vous buvez de l'eau ?
4. Est-ce que je vous pose des questions ?
5. Voulez-vous manger des escargots ?
6. Y a-t-il des chaises dans la classe ?
7. Y a-t-il des chiens dans la classe ?
8. Est-ce que les végétariens mangent de la viande ?

---

[1]**avoir peur de**   *to be afraid of*

Il a une **voiture**.   Il parle **de sa voiture**.   Elle a une **sœur**.   Elle parle **de sa sœur**.
Il **en** a une.   Il **en** parle.   Elle **en** a une.   Elle parle **d'elle**.

TABLEAU 75

B *Cette fois, répondez en employant* **trop, beaucoup, assez, (un) peu,** *etc. et le pronom* **en,** *d'après ce modèle.*

Avez-vous de l'imagination ?
De l'imagination ? J'en ai beaucoup (*ou* J'en ai assez, etc.).

1. Avez-vous de la patience ?
2. Avez-vous du travail aujourd'hui ?
3. Est-ce que Lee Iacocca a de l'argent ?
4. Avez-vous de l'argent sur vous ?
5. Est-ce que je vous donne des examens ?
6. (Daniel), est-ce que je vous ai posé des questions ?
7. Mangiez-vous des bonbons[1] quand vous étiez petit(e) ?
8. Lisiez-vous des romans quand vous aviez quinze ans ?

C *Faites une interview de votre voisin ou voisine, d'après ce modèle.*

Combien/frère/avoir ?
(Michel)   **Combien de frères as-tu ?**
(Jeanne)   **J'en ai un (*ou* Je n'en ai pas).**
(Michel, *aux autres*)   **Elle en a un (*ou* Elle n'en a pas).**

1. Combien/frère/avoir ?
2. Combien/sœur/avoir ?
3. Combien/micro-ordinateur/avoir ?
4. Combien/montre/avoir ?
5. Combien/repas/prendre/par jour ?
6. Combien/cours/avoir/aujourd'hui ?
7. Combien/lit/il y a/dans ta chambre ?
8. Combien/camarade de chambre/avoir ?

D *Répondez aux questions.*

1. Avez-vous peur des examens ? Demandez à (Olivier) s'il a peur des examens. Avez-vous peur de vos professeurs ?
2. Est-ce que je vous parle de mes parents ? Me parlez-vous de vos parents ? Me parlez-vous de votre ami(e) ?
3. J'ai besoin de mon livre de français. Avez-vous besoin de votre livre ? Avez-vous besoin de vos parents ?
4. Je connais quelqu'un qui aime beaucoup le Coca-Cola. Il en boit à chaque repas. Et vous, qu'est-ce que vous aimez comme boisson ? En buvez-vous à chaque repas ?
5. Moi, j'adore Paris. J'en parle souvent. Est-ce que je vous en ai parlé hier ? M'en avez-vous parlé hier ?
6. Moi, j'adore les (pommes). J'en mange souvent. M'en avez-vous apporté aujourd'hui ? Demandez à (Simone) si elle m'en a apporté.
7. Je réponds toujours à vos questions, n'est-ce pas ? M'en avez-vous posé hier ? Demandez à (Jean) s'il m'en a posé hier.

[1]*candy*; on emploie ce mot au pluriel.

▭ *Exercice supplémentaire*

14.3 ADVERBES DE QUANTITÉ

1. The adverbs in boldface type in the sentences below indicate quantity or degree (extent).

Monique écrit **trop**.	*too much*
Monique écrit **beaucoup**.	*a lot, very much*
Jean-Paul écrit **assez**.	*enough*
Marc écrit (**très**) **peu**.	*(very) little*

In the *passé composé*, these adverbs come between the auxiliary and the past participle (in negation, after **pas**).

Nous ne parlons pas **trop**.	Vous ne mangez pas **assez**.
→ Nous n'avons pas **trop** parlé.	→ Vous n'avez pas **assez** mangé.
Je travaille **beaucoup**.	Philippe dort **très peu**.
→ J'ai **beaucoup** travaillé.	→ Philippe a **très peu** dormi.

2. Study the comparative and superlative forms. The definite article **le** in **le plus** and **le moins** does not change since these expressions modify a verb, not a noun.

Jean-Paul écrit **autant que** Lili.	*as much as*
Monique écrit **plus que** Lili.	*more than*
Marc écrit **moins que** Jean-Paul.	*less than*
Monique écrit **le plus**. /ply(s)/[1]	*the most*
Marc écrit **le moins**.	*the least*

3. Adverbs of quantity can be followed by **de** + noun to indicate the quantity of a noun. You learned most of the following expressions in Lesson 7.4.

Jean-Paul a **beaucoup de** livres.	*a lot of, many*
Jean-Paul a **trop de** livres.	*too many*
Monique a **assez de** livres.	*enough*
Marc a (**très**) **peu de** livres.	*(very) few*
Jean-Paul a **tant de** livres !	*so many*

The construction **de** + noun can also be used to form the comparative and superlative; **de** + noun can also be replaced by **en**.

Monique a **plus de** livres **que** Marc. ⎫ Elle **en** a **plus que** lui. ⎭	*more . . . than*
Monique a **autant de** livres **que** Lili. ⎫ Elle **en** a **autant qu'**elle. ⎭	*as many . . . as*
Marc a **moins de** livres **que** Lili. ⎫ Il **en** a **moins qu'**elle. ⎭	*fewer . . . than*
Jean-Paul a **le plus de** livres. ⎫ Il **en** a **le plus**. ⎭	*the most*
Marc a **le moins de** livres. ⎫ Marc **en** a **le moins**. ⎭	*the fewest*

[1]**Plus** can be pronounced /plys/ at the end of a phrase or sentence, but not in **plus de** or **plus que**.

« Des notes ? J'en ai pris autant que toi. Regarde. »

4. **Plus de** and **moins de** can be used with numbers, as an equivalent of expressions such as *more/fewer than* + number. Note that **de** + number corresponds to *than* + number in English.

Nous achetons **plus de** livres. We buy **more** books.
Nous achetons **plus de dix** livres. We buy **more than ten** books.
La maison a **moins de** pièces. The house has **fewer** rooms.
La maison a **moins de six** pièces. The house has **fewer than six** rooms.

TABLEAU 76   Jean-Paul   Monique   Lili   Marc

A *Regardez le Tableau 76 et répondez aux questions.*

1. Regardez les quatre lettres. Qui a écrit le plus ? Et qui a écrit le moins ?
2. Qui a écrit autant que Lili ? Qui a écrit moins qu'elle ? Qui a écrit plus que Marc ?
3. Qui a écrit plus de deux pages ? Qui a écrit moins de deux pages ?
4. Regardez les livres. Qui a autant de livres que Monique ? Qui en a moins qu'elle ?
5. Qui a le plus de livres ? Qui en a le moins ?
6. Qui a plus de trois livres ? Qui a moins de trois livres ?

B *Répondez aux questions.*

1. J'ai (dix) dollars sur moi. Demandez à (Gilberte) combien d'argent elle a sur elle. Qui en a plus que moi ? Qui en a moins que moi ?
2. Chaque jour je prends (une tasse de café). Qui ne prend pas de (café) ? Qui en prend autant que moi ? Qui en prend plus que moi ?
3. J'ai dormi (huit) heures. Qui a dormi moins que moi ? Qui a dormi autant que moi ? Qui a dormi plus que moi ?
4. (Lundi) dernier j'ai travaillé (six) heures. Qui a travaillé autant que moi ? Qui a travaillé plus que moi ? Qui n'a pas travaillé ?
5. (Philippe), demandez à (Marie) si elle a plus de vingt ans. (Jeanne), demandez à vos camarades qui a moins de vingt ans.
6. Qui va au cinéma plus d'une fois pas mois ? Qui va à la bibliothèque moins de deux fois par semaine ?

   Exercice supplémentaire

   Compréhension auditive

14.4 EMPLOI DE **C'EST ... QUI**, **C'EST ... QUE**

In English it is possible to emphasize any part of a sentence by placing a heavy stress on it.

I answered them yesterday.	(maybe no one else answered them)
*I answered **them** yesterday.*	(*they*, if no one else, got my answer)
*I answered them **yesterday**.*	(not today or the day before yesterday)

In French, similar meanings are conveyed by the construction **c'est ... qui** and **c'est ... que**.

1. **C'est ... qui** is used when the *subject* of a sentence is to be emphasized. The verb following **qui** agrees with the word preceding **qui**, which can be a noun or a stressed pronoun. **C'est** becomes **ce sont** before a third-person plural noun or pronoun.

   Je vais nettoyer la chambre.

   → **C'est moi qui** vais nettoyer la chambre.

   La réceptionniste nous a donné la clé.

   → **C'est la réceptionniste qui** nous a donné la clé.

   Vous avez garé cette voiture.

   → **C'est vous qui** avez garé cette voiture.

   Ils ont trouvé cet hôtel.

   → **Ce sont eux qui** ont trouvé cet hôtel.

   If the subject to be stressed is a pronoun, a corresponding stressed pronoun can be added at the beginning of the sentence. This construction (discussed in Lesson 12.2) is not as emphatic as **c'est ... qui**.

   Quelle sorte de chambre veux-tu ?

   —**Moi**, je veux une chambre avec salle de bains.

2. **C'est ... que** is used when an element other than the subject of a sentence needs emphasis: the direct or indirect object, the object of a preposition, an adverb or adverbial phrase of place and time. The object pronoun placed in **c'est ... que** must be in the stressed form.

« Vous dites que c'est moi qui suis responsable ? Ah non ! C'est vous qui avez brûlé le feu rouge ! »

Je **les** ai vus à la gare ce matin.

→ **C'est eux que** j'ai vus à la gare ce matin.

Vous avez donné la clé **à Jeanne**.

→ **C'est à Jeanne que** vous avez donné la clé.

Elle va voyager en Italie **avec eux**.

→ **C'est avec eux qu'**elle va voyager en Italie.

Nous avons garé la voiture **devant l'hôtel**.

→ **C'est devant l'hôtel que** nous avons garé la voiture.

Les clients vont partir **ce matin**.

→ **C'est ce matin que** les clients vont partir.

Est-ce **toi** qui as cassé le vase ?
— Ce n'est pas **moi** qui l'ai cassé, c'est **lui** !

TABLEAU 77

🔊 **A** *Exercice de contrôle*

C'est moi qui ai nettoyé la chambre.

1. vous   2. mon camarade   3. eux   4. nous

C'est derrière l'hôtel qu'on va garer la voiture.

1. nous   2. je   3. vous   4. tu

C'est samedi dernier que nous sommes allés au cinéma.

1. tu   2. vous   3. mon camarade   4. je

C'est à Paris que je veux aller.

1. vous   2. mon camarade   3. nous   4. tu

B   *Répondez aux questions en employant* **c'est ... qui** *d'après ce modèle.*

Quel cahier est sur la table ?
C'est votre cahier qui est sur la table.

1. Quelle montre est sur la table ?
2. Qui vient de répondre à la question ?
3. Qui a écrit ces mots au tableau ?
4. Quelle langue vous intéresse le plus ?
5. Quel pays vous intéresse le plus ?

C   *Répondez aux questions en employant* **c'est ... que** *d'après ce modèle.*

Apprenez-vous le chinois ?
(Jean-Jacques)   **Non, ce n'est pas le chinois que nous apprenons.**
(Marie-Claire)   **C'est le français que nous apprenons.**

1. Apprenez-vous le japonais ?
2. Faisons-nous un exercice écrit ?
3. Notre cours finit-il à (dix) heures ?
4. Sommes-nous dans un cours de chimie ?
5. Faites-vous les exercices écrits au labo ?
6. Êtes-vous né(e) en 1950 ?
7. Les vacances d'été commencent-elles en avril ?
8. Répondez-vous aux questions de (Charles) ?

D   *Complétez les phrases suivantes avec votre partenaire.*

1. C'est avant-hier que...
2. C'est en 1986 que...
3. C'est demain matin que...
4. C'est en 1992 que...
5. C'est le président des États-Unis qui...
6. C'est à la bibliothèque que...
7. Ce sont mes parents qui...

Exercice supplémentaire

14.5   L'ADJECTIF **TOUT** ; EXPRESSIONS AVEC **MONDE**

1. The singular forms **tout** and **toute** correspond to English *entire*, *whole*, or *all*. These forms are followed by a determiner and a singular noun.

Tout l'hôtel était moderne.	*The entire hotel*
Elle a **tout son argent** à la banque.	*all her money*
Vous avez compris **toute la leçon**.	*the entire lesson*
Toute la famille voyage en Suisse.	*The whole family*

2. The plural forms **tous** and **toutes** correspond to English *all* or *every*.

Où allez-vous **tous les jours** ?	*every day*
Tous mes livres sont sur l'étagère.	*All my books*
Je connais **toutes ces étudiantes**.	*all these students*
Toutes les chambres sont claires.	*All the bedrooms / Every bedroom*

3. The word **monde** usually means *world*. Used as a noncount noun, it refers to people in general.

Tout le monde est ici.	*Everyone*
Il y avait **du monde** là-bas !	*some people / a lot of people*

Je connais **beaucoup de monde**.   *a lot of people*
Tu as invité **trop de monde**.   *too many people*

📟 **A** *Répondez aux questions en employant* **tout** *ou* **toute** *d'après ce modèle.*

Avez-vous compris la leçon ?
Oui, j'ai compris (*ou* **Non, je n'ai pas compris**) **toute la leçon.**

1. Avez-vous appris la leçon ?
2. Pouvez-vous voir le tableau ?
3. Ce livre est-il facile ?
4. Avez-vous votre argent ici ?
5. Où est votre famille ?
6. Où êtes-vous l'après-midi ?

📟 **B** *Répondez aux questions d'après ce modèle.*

Avez-vous étudié les exemples ?
Oui, j'ai étudié (*ou* **Non, je n'ai pas étudié**) **tous les exemples.**

1. Avez-vous compris les exemples ?
2. Comprenez-vous mes questions ?
3. Avez-vous regardé ces photos ?
4. Faites-vous les exercices écrits ?
5. Avez-vous besoin de vos livres ?
6. Faisons-nous les exercices oraux ?

C *Voici encore des questions.*

1. Combien d'étudiants y a-t-il dans cette classe ? Y a-t-il beaucoup de monde, assez de monde, ou peu de monde ? Est-ce que tout le monde comprend le français ?
2. Connaissez-vous tout le monde dans ce cours ? Est-ce que je connais tous les étudiants ?
3. Pouvez-vous répondre à toutes mes questions ? Est-ce que je réponds à toutes vos questions ?
4. Que faites-vous tous les matins ? Mentionnez deux choses.
5. Que faites-vous tous les soirs ? Mentionnez deux choses.

APPLICATIONS

📟 **A** **Situations**

Dans un hôtel

full *Vous êtes en vacances et vous voyagez en France. Vous avez trouvé une chambre dans un hôtel pas trop cher[1]. L'hôtel est presque complet°. Vous remarquez qu'il y a pas mal de touristes étrangers dans l'hôtel.*

front desk À la réception°

/vese/ toilettes	L'ÉTRANGER	J'ai réservé une chambre avec salle de bains et w.-c°. 5
	LE RÉCEPTIONNISTE	À quel nom[2], s'il vous plaît ?
	L'ÉTRANGER	Yazdi. Y-A-Z-D-I.
	LE RÉCEPTIONNISTE	Un moment, s'il vous plaît... Il n'y a pas de réservation à ce nom, Monsieur.
How's that (possible)?	L'ÉTRANGER	Comment cela ?° Je vous ai téléphoné moi-même il y a trois jours.
very sorry	LE RÉCEPTIONNISTE	Attendez... Non, Monsieur. Je suis désolé°. Êtes-vous sûr que vous avez 10 téléphoné à l'Hôtel des Iris ?
	L'ÉTRANGER	Des Iris ? Non, c'est à l'Hôtel Ibis que j'ai téléphoné.

[1]**pas trop cher** = qui ne coûte pas trop
[2]*What is the name? (literally, In whose name?)*

Où avez-vous réservé une chambre ?

À la réception d'un grand hôtel.

Dans le couloir (voici une traduction en français)

L'ÉTRANGÈRE	Est-ce qu'on ne nous a pas dit que la chambre était au deuxième ?
SON MARI	Je crois que si.
L'ÉTRANGÈRE	Je ne trouve pas le numéro 212.
SON MARI	On doit[1] monter encore un étage, ma chérie. Nous sommes au premier[2].

15

Dans la chambre (une traduction)

a sleepless night

L'ÉTRANGÈRE	Ah ! quel bruit dans la rue ! Je vais passer une nuit blanche° !
SON MARI	On m'a dit qu'il n'y avait plus de chambre qui donne sur[3] le jardin.
L'ÉTRANGÈRE	Mais pourquoi n'as-tu pas inspecté la chambre avant de[4] la prendre ?
SON MARI	Je ne savais pas que c'était possible.
L'ÉTRANGÈRE	Je suis fatiguée. Je veux faire la sieste.

20

Go ahead.

SON MARI	Vas-y.° C'est une bonne idée.
L'ÉTRANGÈRE	Ces rideaux sont trop transparents et la lumière me gêne.
SON MARI	Je vais fermer les volets. Ça va maintenant ?
L'ÉTRANGÈRE	Oui. Merci, mon chéri.

25

À la réception

Visa card

hotel bill

L'ÉTRANGER	Quelles cartes de crédit acceptez-vous ?
LA RÉCEPTIONNISTE	Nous acceptons la Carte Bleue° et American Express.
L'ÉTRANGER	Bon. Voici ma Carte Bleue.
LA RÉCEPTIONNISTE	Et voilà la note°.
L'ÉTRANGER	(*Il examine la note.*) Je crois qu'il y a une erreur sur la note.
LA RÉCEPTIONNISTE	Ah oui ?
L'ÉTRANGER	Je n'ai pas pris de petit déjeuner ce matin.

30

35

[1]*must* (du verbe **devoir**, Leçon 15.1)

[2]En France, le premier étage est au-dessus du rez-de-chaussée (*the ground floor*).

[3]**donner sur**   *to open out on*

[4]**avant de** + infinitif   *before doing (something)*

LA RÉCEPTIONNISTE   Le petit déjeuner est compris¹ dans le prix de la chambre, Monsieur.

L'ÉTRANGER   Ah bon. Et qu'est-ce que c'est ? Seize francs pour le garage ?

LA RÉCEPTIONNISTE   Oui, Monsieur. C'est un garage payant².

Répondez aux questions. (*lignes 1–3*)

1. Dans quelle sorte d'hôtel avez-vous trouvé une chambre ?
2. Comment est l'hôtel ?
3. Quelle sorte de touristes voyez-vous ?

(*lignes 4–12*)

4. Comment s'appelle l'étranger ?
5. Qu'est-ce que le réceptionniste ne peut pas trouver ?
6. Quand l'étranger a-t-il fait une réservation ?
7. À quel hôtel a-t-il téléphoné ?

(*lignes 13–27*)

8. Quel est l'équivalent américain du « deuxième étage » ?
9. Comment s'appelle l'étage qui est au niveau de la rue ?
10. Qu'est-ce que le mari a négligé de faire³ ?
11. Dans un hôtel américain, peut-on voir la chambre avant de la prendre ?
12. Dans un hôtel américain, qu'est-ce qu'il y a à la place des⁴ volets ?

(*lignes 28–38*)

13. Qu'est-ce que le client examine ?
14. Aux États-Unis, est-ce que le petit déjeuner est compris dans le prix de la chambre ?
15. Qu'est-ce que le client a oublié de vérifier ?
16. Dans un hôtel américain, est-ce que le garage est toujours gratuit ?

B   Expressions utiles

La maison (2)⁵

 la chambre (à coucher) (Tableau 73)

1. une affiche / un poster   /pɔstɛʀ/
2. une armoire⁶
3. des bibelots *m*
4. une chaise
5. une coiffeuse (avec une glace)
6. une commode (avec des tiroirs *m*)
7. une étagère
8. un fauteuil
9. une (porte-)fenêtre
10. une lampe
11. un lit
    une couverture
    un drap
    un oreiller
12. un réveille-matin / un réveil
13. un rideau
14. une table de nuit
15. une stéréo
16. des disques *m*
17. un poste de télévision

---

¹**compris**   *included*; le prix de la chambre et le prix du petit déjeuner, s'il n'est pas compris, sont toujours affichés à la porte de la chambre.

²**payant**   contraire de **gratuit**

³**négliger de** + infinitif   *to neglect to do (something)*

⁴**à la place de**   *instead of*; aux États-Unis des rideaux épais ou des stores vénitiens (*venetian blinds*) remplacent les volets.

⁵Voir aussi les *Expressions utiles* de la Leçon 10 (p. 227) et la salle à manger dans la Leçon 6.5 (p. 133).

⁶Dans beaucoup d'appartements modernes les chambres sont petites, et on a souvent **un placard** ou **une penderie** (*closet*) au lieu d'une armoire.

la salle de bains (Tableau 74)

1. une baignoire
2. un bidet
3. une douche
4. une glace

5. un lavabo
6. un robinet (d'eau chaude / froide)
7. du savon
8. une serviette de bain

la cuisine

une cuisinière[1] { électrique
{ à gaz

un évier
un four

un frigo (un réfrigérateur)
un lave-vaisselle[2]
une machine à laver[3]

Dans un hôtel

réserver { une chambre
{ une chambre à deux lits } pour { une personne
{ deux personnes

une chambre { avec } { salle de bains
{ sans } { douche
{ balcon
{ cabinet de toilette[5] } qui donne sur[4] { la cour
{ la rue
{ la rivière

Le prix comprend[6] { le petit déjeuner.
{ le parking.
{ le service.

Le chauffage
Le climatiseur
La radio / la télévision
Le robinet d'eau chaude / froide
Les volets } ne marche(nt) pas.

[1]*stove, range*

[2]*dishwasher*

[3]*washing machine* (on met souvent la machine à laver dans la cuisine)

[4]**donner sur** *to open out on*

[5]En général on a les w.-c. s'il y a une salle de bains. La salle de bains sans les w.-c. s'appelle **un cabinet de toilette**.

[6]**comprendre** *to include*

C Pratique

1. En général, dans quelle pièce trouve-t-on :

   un canapé ?   une armoire ?   un buffet ?
   un tableau ?   un réveil ?   une stéréo ?
   un frigo ?   un lit ?   une baignoire ?
   une table de nuit ?   une étagère ?   une table ?
   une commode ?   un lavabo ?   un évier ?

2. Quelle est la différence entre un lavabo et un évier ?
3. Quelle est la différence entre une armoire et un placard (une penderie) ?
4. Faites des phrases avec les mots suivants. Mettez les phrases dans l'ordre logique.

   a) prendre une douche   *h)* entrer dans l'hôtel
   b) aller à la réception   *i)* entrer dans la chambre
   c) ouvrir la porte de la chambre   *j)* garer la voiture
   d) prendre la clé de la chambre   *k)* prendre l'ascenseur
   e) remplir la fiche de voyageur   *l)* ouvrir les valises
   f) réserver une chambre   *m)* arriver à l'hôtel
   g) fermer la porte de la chambre   *n)* chercher la chambre

5. Imaginez une conversation entre vous et la réceptionniste d'un hôtel.

   Vous voulez savoir s'il y a une chambre (vous allez lui dire, bien sûr, quelle sorte de chambre vous voulez).

   Vous lui demandez où se trouve la chambre (par exemple : à quel étage, à gauche ou à droite de l'escalier (de l'ascenseur), etc.).

   Vous lui téléphonez parce que certaines choses ne marchent pas dans votre chambre.

6. Regardez la photo à la page 314. Qu'est-ce que vous voyez sur cette photo ?

D Mini-composition : *Christine a passé ses vacances chez les Chabrier. Elle décrit son premier après-midi à Tours.*

(1) Nous/arriver/à/Tours/à/1 h/demi. (2) Je/avoir/2/valises/et/Monique/et/Jean-Paul/ avoir/en/1/chacun[1]. (3) Il/faire/froid/quand/train/arriver/gare. (4) Mme Chabrier/attendre/ nous/quand/nous/descendre/train. (5) Nous/monter/dans/son/voiture/et/nous/partir/tout de suite/pour/son/maison. (6) Mme Chabrier/dire/me/que/je/aller/partager/chambre/Monique. (7) Je/mettre/mon/vêtements/dans/son/grand/armoire. (8) Je/remarquer/que/son/ chambre/être/grand/et/clair. (9) Il y a/autant/posters/et/tableaux/sur/murs/et/plus/bibelots/que/dans/mon/chambre/à/les/États-Unis. (10) Tout/le/membres/de/famille/être/à/ maison/vers/5 h. (11) M. Chabrier/rapporter/un/bouteille/champagne/pour/célébrer/début/vacances/de/les/enfants.

E Fiche de voyageur : *Si vous voyagez en France et allez dans un hôtel, vous remplissez une « fiche de voyageur ». Posez une question qui correspond à chaque numéro.[2]*

1. Nom (écrire en majuscules) :
2. Prénom :
3. a. Né le _____ (date)   b. à _____ (lieu)
4. Pays :
5. Profession :
6. Domicile habituel :
7. Nationalité :
8. a. Passeport : Numéro _____   b. delivré[3] le _____ (date)   c. à _____ (lieu)

[1]*each (of them)*

[2]Par exemple : 1. **Quel est votre nom ?** ou **Comment vous appelez-vous ?** 6. **Quel est votre domicile habituel** *(permanent address)* **?** ou **Où habitez-vous ?**

[3]*issued*

F **Composition :** *Choisissez un des sujets suivants et écrivez une composition d'à peu près 150 mots.*

1. Faites la description de votre chambre, puis décrivez ce que[1] vous avez fait dans la chambre dimanche dernier.
2. Faites la description d'un petit appartement, y compris le plan de l'appartement et la description des meubles. Décrivez ce qu'on a fait dans cet appartement il y a plusieurs jours.
3. Avez-vous été malade récemment ? Qu'est-ce qui n'allait pas ? Qu'est-ce que vous avez fait ?
4. Écrivez le monologue d'une personne qui croit qu'elle a un rhume. C'est un vendredi et elle a pas mal de choses à faire pendant le week-end. Va-t-elle se reposer et annuler tous ses projets ?
5. Avez-vous jamais visité un pays étranger ? Quand et pour quelles raisons ? Faites une description de votre voyage (ou d'une journée dans votre voyage).
6. Racontez un incident amusant qui vous est arrivé récemment.
7. Avez-vous acheté des vêtements récemment ? Pourquoi ? Où êtes-vous allé(e) ? Qu'est-ce que vous avez acheté ?

TABLEAU 78   Hôtel Terminus   Hôtel Clair Soleil

G *Vous voyagez en France depuis plusieurs jours. Hier vous avez passé la nuit à l'Hôtel Terminus. Ce soir vous êtes à l'Hôtel Clair Soleil. Comparez ces deux chambres.*

H **Renseignements et opinions**

1. Regardez la porte de la classe. Quand est-ce qu'on l'ouvre ? Quand est-ce qu'on la ferme ? Est-elle ouverte ou fermée maintenant ? Peut-on la fermer à clé ? Combien de clés portez-vous ? Quelles portes ouvrent-elles ?
2. Qui habite à la résidence ? Comment est votre chambre ? (claire ? petite ? confortable ? propre ?) Qu'est-ce que vous avez dans votre chambre ? Nommez trois objets.
3. Combien d'argent aviez-vous hier ? Avez-vous autant d'argent aujourd'hui qu'hier ? Devinez si j'ai plus d'argent que vous aujourd'hui.
4. Est-ce que tous les étudiants sont ici aujourd'hui ? Est-ce que tout le monde est ici ?
5. Un de vos camarades va passer une semaine à Paris. Il n'a jamais étudié le français. Choisissez dix expressions importantes pour lui.

[1]*what (that which)*

Compréhension auditive (basée sur l'Application A)

Compréhension auditive (basée sur l'Application B et la lecture)

Compréhension auditive (basée sur l'Application B et la lecture)

I Lecture

Chez les Pineau[1]

Christine Johnson habite chez les Pineau. Elle décrit leur appartement dans une lettre à son professeur de français, qui est aux États-Unis. Voici un extrait de sa lettre.

(...) Les Pineau habitent dans un grand appartement au troisième étage d'un immeuble rue Saint-Dominique, près des Invalides[2]. M. Pineau travaille comme expert financier dans une banque. Mme Pineau fait des traductions à la maison et s'occupe en même temps de[3] ses deux enfants, Denis, dix-huit mois, et Mathilde, quatre ans. Tout l'appartement est moderne. À droite du couloir central se trouvent le bureau°, puis les w.-c., une cuisine bien équipée, la salle de bains et la chambre des parents. À gauche la grande salle de séjour communique avec[4] la salle à manger, puis deux chambres. Au bout du couloir se trouve un grand placard°. Ma chambre est spacieuse et claire. La porte-fenêtre° s'ouvre sur un balcon. J'ai une grande armoire, une commode ancienne°, un petit bureau et un fauteuil. Sur un des murs il y a une étagère avec la collection de livres d'art de Mme Pineau. J'ai autant de confort que dans ma chambre aux États-Unis. Je me sens bien chez moi[5] dans cette pièce agréable°.

Les Français font beaucoup plus attention que nous à[6] ne pas gaspiller l'électricité. J'ai remarqué, par exemple, que les ampoules électriques° sont moins fortes que chez nous°. On a une minuterie dans l'entrée et dans l'escalier de l'immeuble : on appuie sur le bouton pour allumer la lumière, et une minute plus tard, elle s'éteint[7] automatiquement. D'après Mme Pineau, l'électricité coûte moins cher après onze heures du soir, et le grand chauffe-eau de la salle de bains s'allume seulement la nuit°. C'est parfois après onze heures que Mme Pineau utilise la machine à laver et le lave-vaisselle.[8] L'eau chaude pour la cuisine est fournie[9] par un petit chauffe-eau ; il s'allume chaque fois qu'on a besoin d'eau chaude. L'appartement est moins chauffé qu'un appartement américain. Tout le monde porte des vêtements plus chauds...

Margin glosses:
- ici, *study*
- *walk-in closet*
- *French door (large glass door)*/*antique*
- *pleasant*
- *light bulbs*/dans notre pays
- pendant la nuit

Line numbers: 5, 10, 15, 20

---

[1]Pour le deuxième paragraphe, consultez d'abord les *Différences* de la Leçon 10 (p. 211).

[2]un des grands monuments de Paris

[3]**s'occuper de** *to take care of*; **en même temps** *at the same time*

[4]**communiquer avec** *to be connected with*

[5]**se sentir chez soi** *to feel at home*

[6]**faire attention à ne pas faire** *to be careful not to do*

[7]*goes out* (du verbe **s'éteindre**, Leçon 24.1)

[8]**machine à laver** *washing machine*; **lave-vaisselle** *dishwasher*; ces machines ont un chauffe-eau électrique pour chauffer l'eau froide.

[9]*supplied* (du verbe **fournir** *to furnish, supply*); ce chauffe-eau utilise le gaz pour chauffer l'eau.

Mme Pineau fait des traductions à la maison.

A *Indiquez si chaque commentaire est vrai ou faux. S'il est faux, corrigez le commentaire.*

1. Mme Pineau sait au moins une langue étrangère.
2. Il y a quatre chambres dans l'appartement des Pineau.
3. Denis Pineau a deux ans et sa sœur Mathilde, quatre ans.
4. La chambre de Christine se trouve à droite du couloir central.
5. La chambre de Christine est moins confortable que sa chambre aux États-Unis.
6. Les Français gaspillent moins d'électricité que les Américains.
7. Mme Pineau utilise la machine à laver et le lave-vaisselle après onze heures pour ne pas gaspiller d'électricité.
8. En général, les maisons sont plus chauffées aux États-Unis qu'en France.

B *On utilise parfois la construction* verbe + nom (objet direct) *pour créer des mots nouveaux.[1] Trouvez l'équivalent anglais des mots suivants.*

gratte-ciel	*nutcracker*
chasse-mouches	*water heater*
tourne-disque	*dishwasher*
chauffe-eau	*flyswatter*
lave-vaisselle	*key ring*
porte-clés	*record player*
casse-noisette	*skyscraper*

C *Projets*

1. Faites un plan approximatif de l'appartement des Pineau. Indiquez quels meubles on peut trouver dans chaque pièce.
2. Si on ne fait pas attention, on peut gaspiller beaucoup d'essence, de gaz et d'électricité. Dites comment on peut gaspiller ces ressources d'énergie et comment on peut éviter le gaspillage.

---

[1]Ces mots ne changent pas au pluriel : un **gratte-ciel**, des **gratte-ciel** ; ce **chauffe-eau**, ces **chauffe-eau**.

VOCABULAIRE

Noms

une **action**	action	la **lampe**	lamp	le(la) réceptionniste	clerk (hotel)
une **affiche**	poster	le **lavabo**	bathroom sink	la réservation	reservation
la **baignoire**	bathtub	la **lumière**	light	le **réveille-matin**	alarm clock
la **banque**	bank	la **maladie**	illness	le rideau	curtain
le **bidet**	bidet	le **meuble**	piece of furniture	le **robinet**	faucet
les **bonbons** m	candy	le **Monopoly**	Monopoly	le **savon**	soap
la **Carte Bleue**	Visa card	le **mouchoir**	handkerchief	la **serviette de bain**	bath towel
le(la) chéri(e)	darling	le niveau	level	les **sous-vêtements** m	underwear
la **commode**	dresser	la note	bill	le store vénitien	Venetian blind
la **différence**	difference	la **paire**	pair	la **table de nuit**	nightstand
le **dollar**	dollar	le **parfum**	perfume	le **tiroir**	drawer
la **douane**	customs	la **partie**	game	la traduction	translation
un **équivalent**	equivalent	la **patience**	patience	la **valise**	suitcase
une **erreur**	mistake	la **pénicilline**	penicillin	le volet	shutter
un(e) **étranger(ère)**	foreigner; stranger	la **peur**	fear	les **w.-c.** m	toilet
le **flacon**	bottle	le prix	price		
le(la) **gagnant(e)**	winner	la **réception**	front desk		

Verbes

découvrir irrég	to discover	gêner	to bother	réserver	to reserve
décrire irrég	to describe	inspecter	to inspect	**souffrir (de)** irrég	to suffer (from)
donner sur	to open out on	négliger (de)	to neglect	vérifier	to check
examiner	to examine	**offrir** irrég	to offer		
gagner	to win	**ouvrir** irrég	to open		

Adjectifs

clair(e)	bright	**fermé(e) à clé**	locked	**tout (toute, tous, toutes)**	all, whole,
complet(ète)	full	payant(e)	pay; not for free		entire, every
désolé(e)	sorry	sûr(e)	sure	transparent(e)	transparent, sheer
épais(se)	thick				

Adverbes

autant que	as much as, as many as	**moins de**	less	**peu**	little
le moins	the least	**moins que**	less than	**plus que**	more than

Autres expressions

à la place de	instead of	**c'est ... que**	it's . . . that/who
À quel nom ?	What is the name?	**c'est ... qui**	it's . . . that/who
au niveau de	on the level of	on doit	we must
avant de + inf	before + pres part	passer une nuit blanche	to spend a sleepless night
avoir mauvaise mine	to look sick	Vas-y.	Go ahead.
avoir peur (de)	to be afraid (of)		

15 Les soirées

LESSON OBJECTIVES

Theme and Culture

1. Social get-togethers
2. Christmas and New Year's festivities

Communication Skills

1. Expressing obligations and conjectures (*must, had to, must have*)
2. Introducing people
3. Leave-taking at get-togethers
4. Accepting/Declining offers for food and drinks
5. Expressing future events and activities
6. Replacing locative and other expressions with an adverbial (*there, to it, it*)

Structures

15.1 **Recevoir**, **devoir**
15.2 Future tense (1)
15.3 Use of **y**
15.4 Future tense (2): irregular verbs
15.5 Interrogative form: inversion with subject nouns

CONVERSATIONS

TABLEAU 79

320

A. Elle ne peut pas venir.

MME BOSQUET   J'ai reçu une lettre de Martine ce matin.

M. BOSQUET   Ah oui ? Qu'est-ce qu'elle dit ?

MME BOSQUET   Elle ne peut pas assister à la réception[1].

M. BOSQUET   C'est dommage.[2] Dit-elle pourquoi ?

MME BOSQUET   Oui, elle doit aller à Marseille.

B. Viens à la surprise-party[3].

CHANTAL   Veux-tu venir chez moi samedi ? Je donne une surprise-party.

MONIQUE   Je veux bien.[4] Est-ce que je connais les gens que[5] tu vas inviter ?[6]

CHANTAL   Bien sûr. Tu connais presque tout le monde.

MONIQUE   C'est à quelle heure, ta surprise-party ?

CHANTAL   Vers 17 heures. Alors, tu viens ?

MONIQUE   Oui, d'accord. Et merci de ton invitation.

C'est une soirée sympathique.

C. Je t'aiderai demain après-midi.

ROLAND   Alors, tu m'aideras à faire[7] cette traduction ?

MARTINE   Oui, j'apporterai mon dictionnaire d'informatique[8].

ROLAND   N'oublie pas. J'y compte beaucoup, tu sais.

MARTINE   Non, non. Je n'oublierai pas.

---

[1]**assister à**   *to attend*; **réception**   a fairly formal late afternoon or early evening party

[2]*It's a pity, That's too bad.*

[3]réunion amicale de jeunes gens

[4]**vouloir bien**   *to be willing*

[5]**que**   *that, whom*

[6]Ce n'est pas un signe d'indiscrétion de poser cette question ; Monique ne veut pas être avec des gens qu'elle ne connaît pas.

[7]**aider quelqu'un à faire**   *to help someone do*

[8]**informatique** *f*   *computer science*

« Regarde ce que le Père Noël m'a apporté. »

DIFFÉRENCES

Joyeux Noël et Bonne Année !

Christmas is a festive holiday in France. In large cities, store windows display seasonal decorations, while streets in shopping districts are illuminated by thousands of small light bulbs. On Christmas Eve, Catholic families attend **la messe de minuit** (*midnight mass*) and afterward celebrate with the traditional dinner known as **le réveillon**. Dessert calls for **la bûche de Noël**, a chocolate cake shaped like a Yule log. In the morning, families gather around **l'arbre de Noël** (*Christmas tree*) and open presents. Children are delighted by the gifts **Père Noël** (*Santa Claus*) has left in their shoes.

La nuit de la Saint-Sylvestre (*New Year's Eve*) is an occasion for parties, dinners, and dancing with friends and relatives. People are likely to don masks or funny hats and carry on their revelry until 4 or 5 in the morning. **Restaurants**, **brasseries** (**café-restaurants**), and **discothèques** feature entertainment and a special menu for the evening and early morning hours. Traditional culinary delicacies include oysters, foie gras (pâté made from the livers of specially fattened geese), and champagne.

In some families, celebrating the New Year culminates with **la Fête de l'Épiphanie** (*Epiphany*) on January 6 or on the first Sunday in January, when family members exchange small gifts to commemorate the coming of the Magi. Some families also set up a miniature **crèche** *f* (*manger*) with **santons** *m*, small, hand-painted clay figurines, on Christmas Eve. On January 7, they move the **santons** of the three wise men inside the **crèche**. It is also the time for small parties with the traditional **galette des rois**, a special flat round cake with a bean in it. The person who finds the bean (**la fève**) in his or her piece of cake becomes king or queen of the party. The bean can also be a small plastic object representing a crown, a scepter, a baby, or a four-leaf clover. Here are some commonly used greetings of the Christmas and New Year season.

Joyeux Noël (et Bonne Année) !

Bonnes fêtes et bonne année !

Bonne et heureuse année !

Bonne année et bonne santé !

Je vous souhaite un joyeux Noël (une bonne année).

(Mes) meilleurs vœux pour Noël (et la nouvelle année).

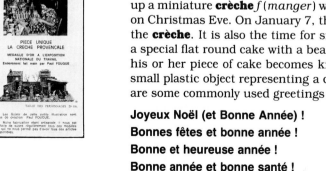

STRUCTURES

15.1 **RECEVOIR, DEVOIR**

1. **Recevoir** *to receive* and **devoir** are conjugated alike in the present indicative, and somewhat like **pouvoir**: the stem-final consonant /v/ occurs only in the infinitive and the plural forms, and the **nous** and **vous** forms have a stem based on the infinitive and different from all the other forms. The basic meaning of **devoir** + noun is *to owe (something)*. **Recevoir** can also mean *to entertain (someone) at home.*

recevoir	
reçois	recevons
reçois	recevez
reçoit	reçoivent
reçu	

devoir	
dois	devons
dois	devez
doit	doivent
dû	

Je **reçois** des lettres.
Tu **reçois** un cadeau.
Il **reçoit** de bonnes notes[1].
Nous **recevons** des amis.
Vous **recevez** vos étudiants.
Ils **reçoivent** leurs parents.
J'ai **reçu** une lettre anonyme !

Je **dois** cent francs à Anne.
Tu ne me **dois** rien.
Elle ne **doit** rien à personne.
Nous **devons** une fortune !
Vous me **devez** un déjeuner.
Elles **doivent** de l'argent à Jacques.
Je lui ai **dû**[2] cet argent.

Ils ont reçu leur courrier.

2. A much more important use of **devoir** is with an infinitive. **Devoir** + infinitive has two distinct meanings.

a) Obligation, corresponding to English *must, have (got) to*

Je **dois partir** ce matin.
Vous **devez vous reposer**.
Nous avons **dû partir** avant midi.

I must/have to leave this morning.
You must/have to rest.
We had to leave before noon.

---

[1]*good grades*

[2]Remarquez l'emploi de l'accent circonflexe pour distinguer le participe passé de **devoir** de l'article partitif **du** ou de la contraction de + **le** → **du**. Le mot anglais *due* vient de la forme féminine de **dû**.

b) Conjecture (guessing): the speaker is making a guess, and it corresponds to *must* (in the past tense, *must have*).

Elle parle bien français ; elle **doit être** française.	*She speaks French well; she must be French.*
Vous n'étiez pas là ; vous avez **dû rentrer** à la maison.	*You weren't there; you must have gone home.*
C'est le passeport du client ; il a **dû** l'**oublier**.	*It's the customer's passport; he must have forgotten it.*

3. In the imperfect tense, **devoir** often corresponds to English *was/were (supposed) to*, implying obligation whether or not the action took place. In the *passé composé*, it means *had to* (obligation) or *must have* (conjecture).

Je **devais** nettoyer ma chambre.	*I was supposed to clean my room.*
J'**ai dû** nettoyer ma chambre.	*I had to clean my room.*
Vous **deviez** partir vers midi.	*You were supposed to leave around noon.*
Vous **avez dû** partir vers midi.	*You had to leave/must have left around noon.*

Elle **a dû travailler** toute la nuit.
Elle **doit être** très fatiguée !

TABLEAU 80

A *Exercice de contrôle*

Je reçois des cadeaux à Noël.

1. Nous   2. Tu   3. Vous   4. Les enfants

Je dois aller à la bibliothèque.

1. Vous   2. Le professeur   3. Nous   4. Les étudiants

Je devais sortir hier soir.

1. Nous   2. Tu   3. Vous   4. Le professeur

J'ai dû travailler à la maison.

1. Vous   2. Tu   3. Nous   4. Les étudiants

B *Répondez aux questions.*

1. Qu'est-ce que vous recevez à Noël ? Combien de cartes de Noël avez-vous reçues l'année dernière ?

2. Quelles notes recevez-vous dans vos cours ? De très bonnes notes, de bonnes notes ou d'assez bonnes notes ?

3. Recevez-vous des amis chez vous ? Demandez à (Jeanne) si elle reçoit des amis chez elle.

4. Avez-vous jamais reçu une lettre anonyme ? Qui a jamais reçu un coup de téléphone[1] anonyme ?

[1]**un coup de téléphone**   *a phone call*

5. À quelle heure devez-vous venir à ce cours ? À quelle heure est-ce que le cours doit commencer ?
6. Ce matin, j'ai dû (aller à la bibliothèque). Qu'est-ce que vous avez dû faire ce matin ?
7. Ce matin, je devais (jouer au tennis), mais j'étais trop occupé(e). Qu'est-ce que vous deviez faire ce matin ? L'avez-vous fait ?

C *Écoutez ces phrases et faites des conjectures, d'après les modèles.*

Je veux boire de l'eau.
Vous devez avoir soif.

Elle a beaucoup travaillé.
Elle doit être fatiguée.

1. Je veux manger quelque chose.
2. La dame parle très bien français.
3. Je ne veux pas de boisson.

4. Il n'a pas bonne mine.
5. Ils habitent dans un château.
6. Voici le blouson de Jacques.[1]

Exercice supplémentaire

Dictée

15.2 FUTUR DE L'INDICATIF (1)

The construction **aller** + infinitive (**le futur proche**), which you learned in Lesson 4.3, is normally used to express actions or events in the near future. The future tense is used either for a more distant future or for any narration in the future, in which a repeated use of **aller** + infinitive would be awkward. In English, you put the auxiliary *will* or *shall* before the verb: *I will speak, I shall be in town.* In French, you use special verb endings: **-ai**, **-as**, **-a** for the singular, and **-ons**, **-ez**, **-ont** for the plural. (Note that the endings **-ai**, **-as**, **-a**, **-ont** are identical to the forms of the present tense of **avoir**.)[2]

1. For second- and third-conjugation verbs, you attach the future endings to the *infinitive*. The third-conjugation verbs drop the final **-e** of the infinitive. Note that written French has six different endings, while spoken French has only three: /ʀa/ for **-ras** and **-ra**, /ʀe/ for **-rai** and **-rez**, and /ʀõ/ for **-rons** and **-ront**.

finir		vendre	
je **finirai**	/finiʀe/	je **vendrai**	/vãdʀe/
tu **finiras**	/finiʀa/	tu **vendras**	/vãdʀa/
il **finira**	/finiʀa/	elle **vendra**	/vãdʀa/
nous **finirons**	/finiʀõ/	nous **vendrons**	/vãdʀõ/
vous **finirez**	/finiʀe/	vous **vendrez**	/vãdʀe/
ils **finiront**	/finiʀõ/	elles **vendront**	/vãdʀõ/

2. In principle, the future tense of first-conjugation verbs is also formed by adding the future endings to the infinitive. In terms of spoken French, however, it is more practical to say that you add **-rai**, **-ras**, **-ra**, **-rons**, **-rez**, **-ront** to the **je** form of the present indicative.[3]

donner	/dɔne/	payer	/pɛje/
je **donne**	/dɔn/	je **paie**	/pɛ/
je **donnerai**	/dɔn/ + /ʀe/	je **paierai**	/pɛ/ + /ʀe/
nous **donnerons**	/dɔn/ + /ʀõ/	vous **paierez**	/pɛ/ + /ʀe/

---

[1]Employez **oublier** dans la réponse.

[2]The future-perfect tense will be discussed in Lesson 24.3.

[3]In other words, if there is any pronunciation and/or spelling change in the present indicative of the **je** form, it will show up in *all* the forms of the future tense (see Lesson 7.3). The **répéter** type is the only exception in terms of *spelling*.

acheter	/aʃte/		**appeler**	/aple/
j'**achète**	/aʃɛt/		j'**appelle**	/apɛl/
j'**achèter**ai	/aʃɛt/ + /ʀe/		j'**appeller**ai	/apɛl/ + /ʀe/
nous **achèter**ons	/aʃɛt/ + /ʀõ/		vous **appeller**ez	/apɛl/ + /ʀe/

The only exception is the verbs whose infinitive ends in **é** + consonant + **er**. In spoken French, the forms of their future tense are quite regular (derived from the **je** form of the present); in spelling, however, the stem vowel /ɛ/ is spelled -**é**- in all the forms.

répéter	/ʀepete/		**préférer**	/pʀefeʀe/
je **répète**	/ʀepɛt/		je **préfère**	/pʀefɛʀ/
je **répéter**ai	/ʀepɛt/ + /ʀe/		je **préférer**ai	/pʀefɛʀ/ + /ʀe/
elles **répéter**ont	/ʀepɛt/ + /ʀõ/		ils **préférer**ont	/pʀefɛʀ/ + /ʀõ/

3. The future stem of the following irregular verbs is based on the infinitive. If the infinitive ends in **-e**, the **-e** is dropped before the future endings are added.[1]

INFINITIVE	FUTURE STEM	JE FORM		INFINITIVE	FUTURE STEM	JE FORM
boire	**boir-**	je **boirai**		**offrir**	**offrir-**	j'**offrirai**
connaître	**connaîtr-**	je **connaîtrai**		**ouvrir**	**ouvrir-**	j'**ouvrirai**
dire	**dir-**	je **dirai**		**partir**	**partir-**	je **partirai**
dormir	**dormir-**	je **dormirai**		**prendre**	**prendr-**	je **prendrai**
écrire	**écrir-**	j'**écrirai**		**sentir**	**sentir-**	je **sentirai**
lire	**lir-**	je **lirai**		**servir**	**servir-**	je **servirai**
mettre	**mettr-**	je **mettrai**		**sortir**	**sortir-**	je **sortirai**

4. *Inversion.* The rules you learned in Lesson 5.4 regarding inversion also apply to the future tense: there is no inversion for the **je** form (**Est-ce que** must be used), and **-t-** must be inserted for the third-person singular pronouns **il**, **elle**, and **on**.

J'inviterai Isabelle.
→ **Est-ce que j'inviterai** Isabelle ?
Tu serviras du café.
→ **Serviras-tu** du café ?
Elle aura du champagne.
→ **Aura-t-elle** du champagne ?
On organisera une soirée.
→ **Organisera-t-on** une soirée ?

Nous boirons du champagne.
→ **Boirons-nous** du champagne ?
Vous parlerez aux invités.
→ **Parlerez-vous** aux invités ?
Ils apporteront des disques.
→ **Apporteront-ils** des disques ?
Elles arriveront plus tard.
→ **Arriveront-elles** plus tard ?

JE FERAI MES DEVOIRS, ENSUITE JE MANGERAI LE SANDWICH.

TABLEAU 81   D'abord il **fera** ses devoirs, ensuite il **mangera** le sandwich.

[1]Verbs with future stems that are unpredictable from the infinitive or the **je** form of the present indicative are presented in Lesson 15.4.

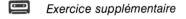

A *Exercice de contrôle*

J'inviterai mes copains chez moi.
1. Nous   2. Tu   3. Vous   4. L'étudiant

Je rentrerai tard et je me coucherai tard.
1. Vous   2. Les étudiants   3. Tu   4. Nous

D'abord je finirai mon travail, ensuite je sortirai.
1. les étudiants   2. nous   3. l'étudiant   4. tu

B *Faites des phrases d'après ce modèle.*

regarder la télé ; je
(Jacques)   **Hier j'ai regardé la télé.**
(Marianne)   **Aujourd'hui je regarde la télé.**
(Claudine)   **Demain je regarderai la télé.**

1. écouter la radio ; je
2. parler français ; nous
3. ne pas aller au labo ; (Marie)
4. ne pas dormir ; vous

5. ne pas travailler ; je
6. venir au cours ; vous
7. rentrer tard ; tu
8. travailler à la bibliothèque ; (Paul)

C *Deux étudiants vont inviter quelques copains chez eux. Mettez toutes les phrases au futur d'après ce modèle.*

Nous <u>allons dîner</u> ensemble.
Nous dînerons ensemble.

(1) Nous <u>allons inviter</u> des copains. (2) Je <u>vais nettoyer</u> le séjour. (3) Robert, tu <u>vas nettoyer</u> la salle de bains. (4) Nous <u>allons préparer</u> un bon repas. (5) Je <u>vais acheter</u> des steaks. (6) Michel <u>va apporter</u> le dessert. (7) Il <u>va arriver</u> vers six heures. (8) Nous <u>allons dîner</u> vers sept heures. (9) Tu <u>vas servir</u> du café. (10) Après le dîner, nous <u>allons jouer</u> aux cartes. (11) Nous <u>allons aussi regarder</u> la télé. (12) Nos invités <u>vont partir</u> vers minuit.

D *Parlons de demain. Posez des questions à votre partenaire, d'après ce modèle.*

À quelle heure/se lever/demain ?
À quelle heure te lèveras-tu demain ?

1. À quelle heure/se lever/demain ?
2. Quelle sorte de vêtements/mettre ?
3. À quelle heure/commencer/premier cours ?
4. À quelle heure/finir/dernier cours ?
5. Quand/rentrer/à la maison ?
6. Que/faire/après le dîner ?

Exercice supplémentaire

15.3 EMPLOIS DE **Y**

1. The basic meaning of **y** is *there*. It can replace any expression of location such as **à**, **dans**, **devant**, **derrière**, **en** + noun denoting a thing or place.

Je vais **à Marseille** demain.
→ J'**y** vais demain.

Elle n'habite pas **en France**.
→ Elle n'**y** habite pas.

Il entre **dans sa chambre**.
→ Il **y** entre.

Nous sommes **devant l'hôtel**.
→ Nous **y** sommes.

2. **Y** can also replace the *indirect object* (**à** + noun) when it denotes a thing or an idea. In this construction, **y** no longer means *there*, as shown in the English equivalents below.

Vous obéirez **aux règles**.	*You will obey the rules.*
→ Vous **y** obéirez.	*→ You will obey them.*
A-t-elle répondu **à la question** ?	*Did she answer the question?*
→ **Y** a-t-elle répondu ?	*→ Did she answer it?*
Je téléphonerai **à mon hôtel**.	*I will call my hotel.*
→ J'**y** téléphonerai.	*→ I will call it.*
Il n'a pas pensé **à ta suggestion**.	*He did not think of your suggestion.*
→ Il n'**y** a pas pensé.	*→ He did not think of it.*

3. But **à** + noun denoting human beings and animals is replaced by **lui** or **leur** or, in the case of **penser à** and **être à**, by **à** + stressed pronoun (both points were discussed in Lesson 12.2).

Vous obéirez **à l'agent**.	*You will obey the policeman.*
→ Vous **lui** obéirez.	*→ You will obey him.*
A-t-il répondu **à la réceptionniste** ?	*Did he answer the front desk clerk?*
→ **Lui** a-t-il répondu ?	*→ Did he answer her?*
Je téléphonerai **à mes parents**.	*I will call my parents.*
→ Je **leur** téléphonerai.	*→ I will call them.*
Ne dis rien **à cet enfant**.	*Don't say anything to this child.*
→ Ne **lui** dis rien.	*→ Don't say anything to him.*

BUT

Nous pensons **à nos invités**.	*We are thinking of our guests.*
→ Nous pensons **à eux**.	*→ We are thinking of them.*
Cette voiture est **à Danielle**.	*This car belongs to Danielle.*
→ Cette voiture est **à elle**.	*→ This car belongs to her.*

4. When used with a direct-object pronoun, **y** comes after it and immediately before the verb (which may be an infinitive).

Je mets **la lettre dans ce tiroir**.	Je ne **vous** ai pas vu **à la réception**.
→ Je l'**y** mets.	→ Je ne **vous y** ai pas vu.
Je vais envoyer **la lettre à Paris**.	Il ne peut pas **nous** attendre **à l'hôtel**.
→ Je vais l'**y** envoyer.	→ Il ne peut pas **nous y** attendre.
Je m'habitue[1] **à ma nouvelle vie**.	Elle s'habituera **à tout cela** bientôt.
→ Je m'**y** habitue.	→ Elle s'**y** habituera bientôt.

m'/t'/l'/s'/nous/vous/les	+	**y**

---

[1]**s'habituer à**   *to get used to*

TABLEAU 82

Elle répond **à la lettre**.
Elle **y** répond.

Elle répond **à la dame**.
Elle **lui** répond.

Elle pense **à son ami**.
Elle pense **à lui**.

Elle pense **à sa lettre**.
Elle **y** pense.

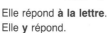 **A** *Répondez aux questions en employant* **y**.

1. Allez-vous au cinéma ? Combien de fois par mois y allez-vous ?
2. Êtes-vous jamais allé(e) en France ? Voulez-vous y aller ?
3. Êtes-vous dans votre chambre maintenant ? Quand y êtes-vous ?
4. Êtes-vous dans le cours de français ? Quels jours y êtes-vous ?
5. Avez-vous jamais habité en France ? Et à New York ?
6. Vos camarades ont-ils voyagé au Canada ? Et en Europe ?

B *Modifiez les phrases suivantes en employant le pronom* **y**.

1. Je pense aux vacances.
2. Je n'ai pas obéi aux ordres.
3. Nous avons téléphoné à Chicago.
4. Nous répondons à vos questions.
5. Vous penserez à ce problème.
6. Je m'habitue à la vie universitaire.

C *Remplacez chaque nom par le pronom approprié d'après ces modèles.*

Je réponds à la question.
J'y réponds.
Je parle à mon professeur.
Je lui parle.

Je pense à mon oncle.
Je pense à lui.

1. Je pense à mon avenir.
2. Je parle à mon professeur.
3. Je ne réponds pas à mon copain.
4. Je n'ai pas répondu à sa lettre.
5. Je vais téléphoner à ma sœur.
6. Je pense à mes parents.
7. Je me suis habitué(e) à tout cela.
8. Je n'ai pas obéi aux règles.
9. Je ne veux pas obéir aux règles.
10. Je ne peux pas parler à ma sœur.

D *Répondez aux questions en employant des pronoms appropriés.*

1. (Daniel), regardez cette photo. (Suzanne), est-ce que je montre la photo à (Daniel) ? Est-ce que je vous la montre ?
2. À qui est ce crayon ? À qui est ce livre ? À qui est cette montre ? À qui sont ces clés ? À qui est ce stylo ?
3. Voici mes clés. Est-ce que j'ai mis les clés sur la table ? Est-ce que je les ai mises dans ma poche ?
4. Avez-vous fait vos devoirs ? Est-ce que vous les avez faits à la maison ? Est-ce que vous les avez montrés au professeur ?
5. Qui avez-vous vu dans le couloir ? M'avez-vous vu(e) dans le couloir ? Avez-vous vu (René) dans le couloir ?
6. Est-ce que la vie à l'université est difficile ? Vous vous y êtes habitué(e) ? Est-ce que tout le monde s'y est habitué ?

 Exercice supplémentaire

15.4 FUTUR DE L'INDICATIF (2)

1. Here is a list of verbs that have irregular future stems.

avoir	aur-	j'aurai	/ɔʁe/
être	ser-	je serai	/s(ə)ʁe/
aller	ir-	tu iras	/iʁa/
devoir	devr-	tu devras	/dəvʁa/
envoyer[1]	enverr-	il enverra	/ɑ̃vɛʁa/
faire	fer-	elle fera	/f(ə)ʁa/
pouvoir	pourr-	on pourra	/puʁa/
recevoir	recevr-	nous recevrons	/ʁəsvʁõ/
savoir	saur-	nous saurons	/sɔʁõ/
venir	viendr-	vous viendrez	/vjɛ̃dʁe/
voir	verr-	vous verrez	/vɛʁe/
vouloir	voudr-	ils voudront	/vudʁõ/
pleuvoir	pleuvr-	il pleuvra	/plœvʁa/

Il y aura beaucoup de bonnes choses à manger à la soirée.

2. **Si** *clause.* In a statement referring to a future event, the verb in the **si** *clause* (introduced by **si** *if*) remains in the present, while the verb in the *main clause* is in the future. Note that, as in English, the **si** clause can be either at the beginning or at the end of the main clause.

S'il **pleut**, je **prendrai** un parapluie.	*If it rains, I will take an umbrella.*
Si vous **restez** ici, je vous **aiderai**.	*If you stay here, I will help you.*
Elle ne **viendra** pas **s'**il **pleut**.	*She will not come if it rains.*
Ils **viendront s'**ils **sont** libres.	*They will come if they are free.*

3. **Quand** *clause.* If the *main clause* is in the future tense, then a clause introduced by **quand** *when* or **dès que** and **aussitôt que** *as soon as* must also be in the future. Note that in English such clauses are in the present rather than in the future.

[1]This verb is irregular only in the future stem. In the present and imperfect tenses, it is conjugated like **employer** and **nettoyer**.

Je les **verrai quand** ils **viendront**.	*I will see them when they come.*
Je vous **téléphonerai dès que** nous **arriverons** à Paris.	*I will call you as soon as we arrive in Paris.*
Elle **cherchera** une chambre **aussitôt qu**'elle **sera** à Rome.	*She will look for a room as soon as she is in Rome.*

	SI vs. **QUAND**	MAIN CLAUSE
SI **QUAND**	present ‾ future	future

A *Mettez chaque phrase au futur.*

1. je mange	7. vous venez	13. il pleut
2. nous faisons	8. tu dors	14. je sors
3. elle veut	9. nous voyons	15. je lis
4. j'ai	10. elle sait	16. j'envoie
5. vous faites	11. ils ont	17. tu vas
6. nous buvons	12. je peux	18. vous savez

B *Nous parlons d'une étudiante américaine. Elle ira en Europe cet été. Elle voudra faire beaucoup de choses. Mettez chaque phrase au futur.*

(1) Je voyage en France cet été. (2) Je passe six semaines en Europe. (3) Je pars avec mes parents. (4) Nous prenons un avion. (5) Nous allons à Paris. (6) Mes parents vont en Italie. (7) Je veux rester à Paris. (8) Je suis donc à Paris. (9) Je sais bien parler français. (10) Je vois mes parents plus tard. (11) Il fait chaud à Paris. (12) Il ne pleut pas souvent. (13) Je connais bien Paris. (14) Je prends beaucoup de photos. (15) J'envoie des cartes postales. (16) J'écris des lettres. (17) Je reçois des lettres. (18) Je vais à Rome en juillet. (19) Je peux voir mes parents. (20) Nous devons rentrer en juillet.

C *Répondez aux questions en employant le futur.*

1. Quel temps va-t-il faire demain ?
2. Allez-vous être en classe demain ?
3. Vos parents vont-ils vous envoyer de l'argent ?
4. Allez-vous voir un film ce week-end ?
5. Allez-vous avoir assez d'argent cet été ?
6. Qu'est-ce que vous allez faire l'été prochain ?

D *Faites des phrases d'après ces modèles.*

Je/aller/cinéma/si/je/être/libre.
J'irai au cinéma si je suis libre.
Je/aller/cinéma/quand/je/être/libre.
J'irai au cinéma quand je serai libre.

1. Je/voir/ce film/si/je/avoir/le temps.
2. Je/voir/ce film/dès que/je/avoir/le temps.
3. Nous/aller/à la plage/si/il/faire beau.
4. Nous/aller/à la plage/quand/il/faire beau.
5. On/pouvoir/sortir/si/on/être/libre.
6. On/pouvoir/sortir/aussitôt que/on/être/libre.
7. Vous/s'amuser/quand/vous/aller/Paris.
8. Tu/prendre/taxi/si/tu/être/pressé(e).

POUR VOTRE FÊTE

JE VOUS COUVRIRAI DE BIJOUX

JE SERAI VOTRE ESCLAVE

VOUS SEREZ CHOYÉE COMME UNE REINE

VOUS AUREZ VOTRE VOITURE PERSONNELLE

E *Peut-on prédire l'avenir ? Voici une boule de cristal. Complétez les phrases suivantes avec votre partenaire en employant le futur.*

1. L'année prochaine, vous...
2. L'année prochaine, (Michèle)...
3. Quand vous aurez soixante ans, vous...
4. Quand (André) aura quarante ans, il...
5. En l'an 2000,...

🔲 *Exercice supplémentaire*

🔲 *Compréhension auditive*

15.5 FORME INTERROGATIVE : INVERSION AVEC LE NOM SUJET

1. This lesson concerns the use of question words (**où**, **quand**, **que**, **comment**, etc.) with a subject noun. In Lesson 5.4 you learned the inversion of subject pronouns with verbs when the subject is a noun.

Marie va à la soirée.	Gisèle a parlé à tout le monde.
→ Où **Marie va-t-elle** ?	→ À qui **Gisèle a-t-elle parlé** ?
Daniel obéit à cet ordre.	Les invités arrivent vers midi.
→ À quoi **Daniel obéit-il** ?	→ Quand **les invités arrivent-ils** ?

The construction above is a little complicated because of the inversion using a pronoun that must correspond to the noun in question. This is why many speakers of French prefer to use the **est-ce que** form.

Où Marie va-t-elle ?	À qui Gisèle a-t-elle parlé ?
→ Où **est-ce que Marie va** ?	→ À qui **est-ce que Gisèle a parlé**?
À quoi Daniel obéit-il ?	Quand les invités arrivent-ils ?
→ À quoi **est-ce que Daniel obéit** ?	→ Quand **est-ce que les invités arrivent** ?

2. But there are cases when the use of **est-ce que... ?** is awkward, and a direct inversion of the verb with the *subject noun* is not only possible but is definitely *preferable*, especially for rhythmic reasons. In French, the "stress" (more like lengthening of the vowel) falls on the last syllable of a sentence,[1] and the sentence should not end with a verb of one or two syllables if the subject is longer. A *short element* must usually precede a *long element*. Sentences like those on the left below are very awkward in French, and those on the right are preferred.

USE OF **EST-CE QUE**	INVERSION WITH THE SUBJECT NOUN
Comment **est-ce que votre père va** ?	→ Comment **va votre père** ?
Où **est-ce que Jean-Pierre va** ?	→ Où **va Jean-Pierre** ?
Qu'**est-ce que ces étudiants font** ?	→ Que **font ces étudiants** ?
Combien de frères **est-ce que Jean a** ?	→ Combien de frères **a Jean** ?
Quel âge **est-ce que leur mère a** ?	→ Quel âge **a leur mère** ?
À quelle heure **est-ce que le cours de français commence** ?	→ À quelle heure **commence le cours de français** ?
De quel hôtel **est-ce que ces deux clients parlent** ?	→ De quel hôtel **parlent ces deux clients** ?

[1]See **Prononciation** Lesson 2 of your **Cahier d'exercices**.

3. This kind of inversion is usually limited to verbs that are short, especially in the present tense. There are three cases in which the inversion is not possible. First, **pourquoi** cannot take the construction verb + subject noun.

Pourquoi **est-ce que Marie est** là ?
$\begin{cases} \rightarrow \text{Pourquoi } \textbf{Marie est-elle } \text{là ?} \\ \rightarrow \text{~~Pourquoi }\textbf{est Marie }\text{là ?~~} \end{cases}$

In contrast to **pourquoi**, **que** cannot be followed by the subject noun.

Qu'est-ce que **ces enfants font** ?
$\begin{cases} \rightarrow \text{~~Que }\textbf{ces enfants font-ils}\text{ ?~~} \\ \rightarrow \text{Que }\textbf{font ces enfants}\text{ ?} \end{cases}$

Second, the inversion cannot be made if it results in two nouns coming next to each other (the subject noun and the direct-object noun).

Où est-ce que **Michel** gare **la voiture** ?
$\begin{cases} \rightarrow \text{Où }\textbf{Michel }\text{gare-t-il }\textbf{la voiture}\text{ ?} \\ \rightarrow \text{~~Où gare }\textbf{Michel la voiture}\text{ ?~~} \end{cases}$

À qui est-ce que **Sylvie** donne **la clé** ?
$\begin{cases} \rightarrow \text{À qui }\textbf{Sylvie }\text{donne-t-elle }\textbf{la clé}\text{ ?} \\ \rightarrow \text{~~À qui donne }\textbf{Sylvie la clé}\text{ ?~~} \end{cases}$

Third, the inversion cannot be made if it results in ambiguous sentences.

Qui est-ce que **Cécile connaît** ?
$\begin{cases} \rightarrow \text{Qui }\textbf{Cécile connaît-elle}\text{ ?} \\ \rightarrow \text{~~Qui }\textbf{connaît Cécile}\text{ ?~~}^1 \end{cases}$

Quel enfant est-ce que **Jeanne attend** ?
$\begin{cases} \rightarrow \text{Quel enfant }\textbf{Jeanne attend-elle}\text{ ?} \\ \rightarrow \text{~~Quel enfant }\textbf{attend Jeanne}\text{ ?~~}^1 \end{cases}$

Où **est-ce que** cet enfant va ?
Où cet enfant **va-t-il** ?
Où **va** cet enfant ?

TABLEAU 83

 A *Voici un touriste qui arrive à Paris. Écoutez bien, et posez trois questions d'après ce modèle.*[2]

Le touriste habite à New York ; où
(Mireille) **Où est-ce que le touriste habite ?**
(Daniel) **Où le touriste habite-t-il ?**
(Pierre) **Où habite le touriste ?**

1. Le touriste voyage en avion ; comment
2. Son avion arrive ce matin ; quand
3. Le touriste cherche un taxi ; que
4. Le touriste parle au chauffeur ; à qui
5. Le touriste entre dans un hôtel ; où
6. La réceptionniste parle au touriste ; à qui
7. La chambre coûte 400 francs ; combien
8. La réceptionniste donne la clé au touriste ; que

[1]The only acceptable interpretation of these sentences is that **Qui** and **Quel enfant** are the subjects: *Who knows Cécile?, What child is waiting for Jeanne ?*

[2]On the tape, only the inversion with noun is practiced; when it is impossible, the student is to use **est-ce que**.

B *Nous parlons d'une réception. Modifiez chaque phrase d'après ce modèle.*

À quelle heure est-ce que la réception commence ?
À quelle heure commence la réception ?

1. À quelle heure est-ce que les invités arrivent ?
2. Où est-ce que la maison de l'hôte se trouve ?
3. Quel âge est-ce que l'hôte et l'hôtesse ont ?
4. Quelles boissons est-ce que l'hôtesse sert ?
5. Qu'est-ce que les invités disent quand ils arrivent ?
6. À qui est-ce que l'hôte et l'hôtesse parlent ?
7. Comment est-ce que la soirée est ?
8. Qu'est-ce que les invités disent quand ils partent ?

 Exercice supplémentaire

APPLICATIONS

« Le punch est délicieux. »

A Situations[1]

Un cocktail[2] chez les Chabrier
Les parents de Jean-Paul ont décidé de donner une petite soirée. Ils ont invité une quinzaine
some *d'amis[3]. Jean-Paul et Monique, eux aussi, ont invité quelques-uns° de leurs copains. Il est cinq heures et demie et les invités commencent à arriver.*

Introductions *Présentations° : Jean-Paul présente Christine au docteur[4] Bloch, un neurologue.*

[1]Les réponses aux questions ne sont pas enregistrées sur la bande magnétique.

[2]*A cocktail party* (but not necessarily serving cocktails)

[3]*about fifteen;* **Une** + nombre + **-aine** + **de** indique un nombre approximatif.

[4]In French, most professional titles before a proper name are preceded by the definite article: **le docteur Bloch** /blɔk/, **le professeur Raymond, le général Joubet.** It is dropped only in direct address: **Je parlerai au docteur Bloch,** but **Bonsoir, Docteur Bloch.**

JEAN-PAUL   Docteur Bloch, permettez-moi de vous présenter Christine Johnson.   5
LE DOCTEUR   Très heureux de faire votre connaissance, Mademoiselle.
CHRISTINE   Enchantée,[1] Monsieur.

Monique présente Christine à une copine.

MONIQUE   Mireille, je te présente Christine.
MIREILLE   Bonjour, Christine. Monique m'a souvent parlé de toi.   10
CHRISTINE   Bonjour.

Accepterez-vous ou refuserez-vous ? : M. Chabrier offre du Dubonnet[2] à Christine.

M. CHABRIER   Un peu de Dubonnet, Christine ?
or else   CHRISTINE   Oui, volontiers. Je n'en ai jamais goûté. (*ou bien*° : Non merci, Monsieur. Je ne
/alkɔl/ *alcohol*   bois pas d'alcool°.   15
M. CHABRIER   À votre bon séjour en France.
CHRISTINE   Merci, et à votre santé.

Monique offre des cacahouètes à Bernard, un des copains de son frère.

MONIQUE   Tu en veux ?
BERNARD   Oui, s'il te plaît. Elles sont très bonnes.   20

Mme Chabrier offre un morceau de quiche[3] à Christine.

MME CHABRIER   Vous en voulez, Christine ?
just a little bit   CHRISTINE   Je veux bien[4]. Seulement un tout petit peu°, s'il vous plaît. (*ou bien* : Merci
                 beaucoup, mais j'ai assez mangé. Tout était délicieux.)

Jean-Paul offre encore de l'[5]apéritif aux invités.   25

JEAN-PAUL   Veux-tu encore du Dubonnet ?
CHRISTINE   Non merci.
JEAN-PAUL   Tu es sûre ?
Tout à fait *Quite*   CHRISTINE   Tout à fait° sûre.

Les invités commencent à partir : Le docteur Bloch doit partir. Il parle à Mme Chabrier.   30

LE DOCTEUR   Au revoir, chère amie. Je vous remercie de[6] cette excellente soirée[7].
What a pity!   MME CHABRIER   Vous devez déjà partir ? Quel dommage !°
LE DOCTEUR   Oui, hélas ! Mais j'espère vous revoir bientôt.
MME CHABRIER   Oui, à bientôt, Docteur.

Bernard dit au revoir à Jean-Paul.   35

BERNARD   C'était vraiment réussi, ta soirée.
JEAN-PAUL   Tu pars déjà ? Tu ne veux pas rester encore un petit moment ?
I would like to   BERNARD   J'aimerais bien°, mais j'ai encore des devoirs à faire.
JEAN-PAUL   Dommage ! Alors, à bientôt.
BERNARD   Oui, à bientôt. Et merci encore. C'était très sympa.   40

[1]C'est-à-dire, **Je suis enchantée de faire votre connaissance**. On dit rarement toute la phrase.
[2]vin très doux et sucré
[3]pie shell baked with a mixture of eggs and cream, and often bacon, onions or cheese
[4]Volontiers (littéralement, *I'm willing*)
[5]**encore de** + article défini *some more*
[6]**remercier quelqu'un de** *to thank someone for*
[7]Attention : **soirée** a deux significations en anglais : *evening* et *party*. Ici, le contexte suggère qu'il est question de
evening.

Répondez aux questions. (*lignes 1–11*)

1. Vous êtes chez votre professeur de français. Vous avez amené un de vos copains. Présentez votre copain au professeur.
2. Présentez votre camarade de chambre à un de vos copains.
3. Présentez vos parents à votre professeur.
4. Présentez quelqu'un à votre professeur.

(*lignes 12–29*)

5. Votre professeur vous offre un apéritif. Qu'est-ce que vous lui direz ?
6. Votre professeur vous offre encore un morceau de gâteau, mais vous n'en voulez plus. Qu'est-ce que vous direz ?
7. Votre amie vous offre du café. Est-ce que vous en voulez ? Qu'est-ce que vous direz à votre amie ?

(*lignes 30–40*)

8. Vous avez passé une excellente soirée chez votre professeur. Vous devez partir maintenant. Qu'est-ce que vous lui direz ? Quelle sera sa réponse ?
9. Un(e) de vos camarades a donné une surprise-party. Vous y êtes, mais vous devez partir maintenant. Pour quelle raison ? Imaginez une petite conversation entre votre camarade et vous.

B   Expressions utiles

La soirée

L'hôte et l'hôtesse

donner }
organiser } { une réception
            un cocktail
            une soirée
            une surprise-party

Les invités

Il y a { assez
        beaucoup } de monde.
        trop

On { sonne à la porte.
     présente ses amis aux autres invités.
     boit, mange, chante, danse, bavarde.
     enlève son veston et sa cravate.

Les conversations

faire la connaissance de }
reconnaître / voir }   { quelqu'un
rencontrer }   la plupart } des invités
                            quelques-uns }

trouver quelqu'un { charmant, sympathique, très cultivé
                    bavard, arrogant, timide, ennuyeux

chercher (désespérément) }
trouver (heureusement) }   un sujet de conversation

parler }   { de n'importe quoi / n'importe qui[1]
discuter } { d'un problème économique / social / régional

---

[1]**n'importe quoi** *anything,* **n'importe qui** *anyone*

Le buffet et les rafraîchissements[1]

des canapés	du punch /põʃ/
des petits gâteaux	un bol de punch
des amuse-gueule (*pl* invar)[2]	des verres
des cacahouètes	

C Pratique

1. Quelle différence y a-t-il entre un cocktail et une surprise-party ?
2. Décrivez le comportement des personnes suivantes.

une personne timide	une personne arrogante
une personne très cultivée	une personne bavarde

3. Quelle est la meilleure façon de trouver des sujets de conversation quand on vient de faire la connaissance de quelqu'un ? Quelle sorte de sujets est-ce qu'on évite ?
4. Nous allons donner une surprise-party. Quelle sorte de rafraîchissements achèterons-nous ? Qui va préparer le buffet ? Qu'est-ce que nous allons servir ?

« À ta santé ! »

D Mini-composition : *Plusieurs étudiants organisent une surprise-party. Complétez le passage en employant le futur.*

(1) Nous/donner/un/surprise-party/samedi/prochain. (2) Nous/inviter/y/une vingtaine de[3]/copain. (3) Elle/commencer/à/9 h,/mais/la plupart de[4]/les/invité/venir/un peu/plus/tard. (4) Samedi/matin,/nous/aller/à/supermarché. (5) Nous/acheter/y/boissons/rafraîchissant,/salami,/fruits,/verres/en plastique,/etc. (6) Avant/surprise-party,/nous/devoir/emprunter/chaises/

---

[1]Pour les boissons, consultez les *Expressions utiles* des Leçons 5 et 6.

[2]de petits sandwichs, des biscuits salés, des chips, etc.

[3]Voir la note 3 à la page 334.

[4]*most of*

[5]**emprunter quelque chose à** *to borrow something from*

à[5] notre/voisins. (7) Robert/faire/un/bol/punch/avec/jus[1]/fruits. (8) Moi,/je/avoir besoin/faire/petit/sandwichs. (9) Michel/pouvoir/s'occuper de[2]/autre/choses. (10) On/boire,/danser/et/bavarder. (11) On/discuter/de/les/problème/social,/national/et/international. (12) Vous/voir/que/tout le monde/s'amuser/bien. (13) Nous/être/fatigué/quand/nous/se coucher. (14) Nous/ne pas/nettoyer/appartement/avant/dimanche/après-midi.

E   Renseignements et opinions

1. Recevez-vous beaucoup de lettres ? Qui a reçu une lettre hier ? Qui n'a pas reçu de lettres ? Qui a reçu plus de trois lettres ? Qu'est-ce que vous recevrez à Noël ?
2. Qu'est-ce que vous avez dû faire hier soir ? Qu'est-ce que vous deviez faire hier soir ? Qu'est-ce que vous avez fait ?
3. Que ferez-vous ce week-end ? Mentionnez trois ou quatre choses dans l'ordre chronologique.
4. Si vous voulez faire quelque chose d'original l'été prochain, que ferez-vous ? Pourquoi est-ce que ce sera original ?
5. De qui voulez-vous faire la connaissance ? Pourquoi ? Quand est-ce que vous avez fait ma connaissance ?
6. Où serez-vous l'année prochaine ? Et l'année d'après ? Quand irez-vous en Europe ?

 Compréhension auditive (*basée sur l'Application A*)

 Compréhension auditive (*basée sur le premier paragraphe de la Lecture*)

À la surprise-party de Carole, les filles seront en jean et en T-shirt.

F   Lecture

Les soirées

first of all / In spite of

Aimez-vous les soirées ? Moi aussi. Voulez-vous savoir comment les jeunes Français organisent leurs soirées ? Je vais vous parler tout d'abord° des surprises-parties. En dépit de° ce mot « surprise », ce ne sont pas des réunions imprévues ou à l'improviste[3]. Ce sont surtout des réunions amicales entre amis et copains.[4]

[1]Ce mot est au pluriel.

[2]*to take care of*

[3]**imprévues ou à l'improviste**   *unexpected (unforeseen) or impromptu*

[4]Quelquefois on les appelle aussi « surboums » ou « surpattes ».

Carole Taillefer, une de mes camarades de Terminale[1], donnera une surprise-party demain [5]
soir. J'irai chez elle demain après-midi pour l'aider. Nous déplacerons quelques meubles et
nous roulerons le tapis de la salle de séjour pour pouvoir danser. Nous y installerons aussi
spotlights des spots° de différentes couleurs pour créer une atmosphère de discothèque. Il y aura une
trentaine d'[2]invités. Ils arriveront vers neuf heures. Les garçons porteront des blue-jeans et
des chemises, mais pas de cravates, et les filles seront en jean et en T-shirt.[3] Robert apportera [10]
des disques de danse, car il en a une collection impressionnante. Il y aura un buffet : des
cheese crackers sandwichs, des chips, des cacahouètes et des petits gâteaux au fromage°. Il y aura aussi du
Coca-Cola, des jus de fruits, de la bière et des pichets de sangria[4]. On écoutera de la musique,
on bavardera et on dansera jusqu'à une heure du matin. Et les parents de Carole ? Ils iront
probablement au cinéma et rentreront vers minuit. Ensuite ils iront se coucher, mais je ne sais [15]
pas s'ils pourront dormir avec tout le bruit qu'on va faire.

Les gens plus âgés donnent un « cocktail » ou un « pot[5] ». Mon frère Jean et sa femme
Monique en ont donné un pour une vingtaine de personnes la semaine dernière. Jean est
both (of them) ingénieur et Monique, institutrice. Ils ont 26 ans tous les deux°. Les invités sont arrivés vers
sept heures. Jean a servi du porto, du Dubonnet, du Martini,[6] du scotch et des jus de fruits. [20]
Sur la table dans le coin de la salle à manger il y avait des petits fours, des petits gâteaux[7],
eggs in aspic / very thin de petits sandwichs, des œufs en gelée° et de fines tranches° de salami. J'ai fait la connais-
slices sance de deux couples qui connaissaient bien les États-Unis et qui échangeaient leurs impressions. Cela m'a beaucoup intéressée puisque j'espère aller un jour aux États-Unis. Les invités
ont passé une excellente soirée[8] et ils sont partis vers neuf heures. Jean, Monique, un [25]
autre couple et moi, nous sommes allés dîner dans un petit restaurant. Il était onze heures
et demie quand je suis rentrée chez mes parents.

A *Indiquez si chaque commentaire est vrai ou faux. S'il est faux, corrigez le commentaire.*

1. Les surprises-parties sont des réunions à l'improviste entre amis et copains.
2. La soirée chez Carole durera à peu près[9] quatre heures.
3. Les invités danseront dans la salle à manger où on installera les spots.
4. La seule boisson alcoolisée de la soirée sera la sangria.
5. Les parents de Carole sortiront parce qu'ils ne voudront pas déranger les jeunes invités.
6. Parmi les invités de Jean et Monique il y avait deux couples qui venaient de faire un voyage
   aux États-Unis.
7. Monique enseigne dans une école primaire.
8. La personne qui vous décrit ces deux soirées est une jeune fille.

B *Indiquez l'expression qui n'appartient pas à chaque série.*

1. du salami—des petits fours—des cacahouètes—de la sangria
2. des blue-jeans—des œufs en gelée—des T-shirts—des cravates
3. du porto—de la sangria—du Dubonnet—du Coca-Cola
4. un invité—un ingénieur—un meuble—une institutrice
5. une surprise-party—une soirée—une réception—un tapis

[1]**La Terminale** est la dernière année au lycée. On prépare le Baccalauréat (examen national qui donne accès à
l'université).

[2]Voir la note 3 à la page 334.

[3]Parmi les jeunes Français, il est très à la mode de porter des blue-jeans.

[4]boisson faite de vin rouge et de tranches d'oranges

[5]Un **pot** dans ce contexte est comme une « *cocktail party* » aux États-Unis, mais plus intime.

[6]**porto** *port wine*; **Dubonnet** *a sweet wine somewhat like cocktail sherry*; **Martini** *sweet vermouth*

[7]**petits fours** *miniature cakes*; **petits gâteaux** *cookies* (L'emploi de **des** devant ces expressions est obligatoire ; voir
la Leçon 11.2.4, page 238, note 2).

[8]**Soirée** signifie ici *evening* (voir la note 7 à la page 335).

[9]*approximately, about*

C *Révision des verbes*

1. Décrivez la soirée chez Carole au passé.
2. Décrivez la soirée chez Jean et Monique au futur.

VOCABULAIRE

Noms

l'**avenir** *m*	*future*	le Dubonnet	*Dubonnet*	la **présentation**	*introduction; presentation*
un **avion**	*airplane*	le gâteau	*cake*	la quiche	*quiche*
la cacahouète	*peanut*	l'**informatique** *f*	*computer science*	la quinzaine	*about fifteen*
la **carte postale**	*postcard*	une **invitation**	*invitation*	la raison	*reason*
le **chauffeur**	*chauffeur; driver*	le neurologue	*neurologist*	la **réception**	*formal party*
le cocktail	*cocktail party*	la **note**	*grade*	la **règle**	*rule*
le **coup de téléphone**	*phone call*	l'**ordre** *m*	*order*	la **surprise-party**	*party*
le **dictionnaire**	*dictionary*	la **plage**	*beach*	la **vie**	*life; living*

Verbes

aider à + *inf*	*to help* + inf	permettre de + *inf*	*to allow to* + inf	refuser de + *inf*	*to refuse to* + inf
devoir *irrég*	*to owe; to have to, must*	**recevoir** *irrég*	*to receive; to entertain* (at home)	revoir *irrég*	*to see again*
s'habituer à	*to get used to*			**se trouver**	*to be located*

Adjectifs

anonyme	*anonymous*	excellent(e)	*excellent*	**pressé(e)**	*in a hurry*
enchanté(e)	*delighted, thrilled*	**occupé(e)**	*busy*	réussi(e)	*successful*

Adverbe

y *there*

Autres expressions

aussitôt que	*as soon as*		Quel dommage !	*What a pity!*
à votre santé	*to your health*		quelques-uns	*a few*
C'est dommage.	*It's a pity; That's too bad.*		tout à fait	*quite*
dès que	*as soon as*		un tout petit peu	*just a little bit*
Dommage !	*It's a pity!*		volontiers	*gladly*
Hélas !	*Alas!*		**vouloir bien**	*to be willing*
ou bien	*or else*			

16 Allons à Paris !

LESSON OBJECTIVES

Theme and Culture

1. Visits to monuments
2. Well-known sites in Paris

Communication Skills

1. Asking/Answering questions about monuments
2. Asking/Answering questions using all personal pronouns
3. Expressing ideas in complex sentence patterns by use of relative pronouns
4. Asking/Answering questions using the passive voice

Structures

16.1 **Conduire**, **construire**
16.2 Object pronouns: summary
16.3 Relative pronoun **qui**
16.4 Relative pronoun **que**
16.5 The passive voice

CONVERSATIONS

A. C'est un plan utile.

SOPHIE Regarde ce plan. Tous les monuments de la ville y sont indiqués.
MICHEL Oui, en effet[1]. C'est un plan utile.
SOPHIE C'est pour toi. Je te le donne.
MICHEL Tu me le donnes ? Tu n'en as pas besoin ?
SOPHIE Non, j'en ai acheté deux.
MICHEL Merci. Tu es gentille.

TABLEAU 84

B. Au voleur !

MLLE ROCHE Monsieur l'agent ! Monsieur l'agent ! Quelqu'un m'a volé[2] mon sac.
L'AGENT Avez-vous vu la personne qui vous l'a volé ?
MLLE ROCHE Oui, il était plus grand que vous, Monsieur l'agent... mais pas aussi beau.
L'AGENT Je vais vous aider tout de suite, Mademoiselle !

C. Quel beau bâtiment !

LE TOURISTE Ah, quel beau bâtiment ! Qu'est-ce que c'est ?
LE GUIDE C'est l'Hôtel de Cluny. Il a été construit au quinzième siècle.
LE TOURISTE Vraiment ? Qu'est-ce qu'il y a à l'intérieur ?
LE GUIDE Il y a un musée du Moyen Âge[3].

DIFFÉRENCES

Le pourboire

One of the problems you face when you travel in France is whom to tip and how much, as the custom of tipping is far more widespread than in North America. Not only do you tip waiters, porters, and taxicab drivers, but also ushers in movie theaters, guides

---

[1]*indeed*

[2]**voler quelque chose à quelqu'un** *to steal something from someone*

[3]*Middle Ages*

in museums and monuments, and attendants in public restrooms. Tips are supposed to be a gratuity that these workers receive in addition to their wages. In reality, however, most of them depend on tips because their wages are so low. So how much does one tip? Here is what is expected of a customer in France.

Restaurants and cafés. All restaurants and cafés are required by law to post the menu and prices and to indicate whether or not the 12–15% service charge is included (**service compris** or **service non compris**). If it is not included, the amount will be added automatically to the bill. In addition, some customers leave the small change left after paying the bill (2–5 francs per person for a meal if the service has been excellent, or around 30 centimes per drink in a café).

Hotels. A service charge of 12–15% is usually included in the price of the room, except for the baggage porter. Some hotels charge extra for the garage, and may include a continental breakfast whether you want it or not. If you spend several nights in the same small or medium-sized hotel with good service, you might leave a tip of around 10–20 francs for the **femme de chambre** (*cleaning woman*) if the service was satisfactory.

Baggage porters. They should be tipped at least 10–15 francs for each piece of baggage in hotels, railroad stations, and airports. In some airports and railroad stations, the fee is posted. Coin-operated rental carts (**chariots** *m*) are becoming popular as there is usually a scarcity of porters.

Theaters, concerts, and movies. You do not walk in and find your own seat. A woman usher (**l'ouvreuse**) will take you to your seat or find you a seat, and will expect a tip of 2–3 francs per person for a group of three or more, or about 10% of the ticket price for one or two.

Taxis. The usual tip is 10–20% of the fare, depending on the distance and the quality of service.

Museums and monuments. After a guided tour (**visite guidée/accompagnée**), most visitors tip the guide from 2–5 francs, depending on the quality of the tour. There are usually signs posted to remind you to do this (for example, **N'oubliez pas le guide**).

Public restrooms. Public restrooms, including those in large restaurants and hotels, are kept clean by elderly attendants. The tip expected is about 1 franc.

Gas stations. Some people give 4–5 francs for the attendant who fills up the gas tank. If the attendant checks your tires, washes the windshield, etc., 5–10 francs are expected. Many self-service stations (where no tipping is necessary) have windshield cleaning equipment for your use.

STRUCTURES

16.1 CONDUIRE, CONSTRUIRE

1. Study the conjugation of **conduire** *to drive, to lead* and **construire** *to construct, to build*. The **-ui-** of the stem is pronounced /ɥi/, as a single syllable, as in **lui** /lɥi/, **nuit** /nɥi/, and **suis** /sɥi/. In the present indicative, the consonant sound /z/ occurs only in the plural forms. Beginning with this lesson, the future stem of irregular verbs will be indicated in the **je** form.

conduire

conduis	conduisons
conduis	conduisez
conduit	conduisent
conduit	
conduirai	

construire

construis	construisons
construis	construisez
construit	construisent
construit	
construirai	

Je **conduis** cette voiture.
Tu **conduis** pour moi.
Elle **conduit** un camion.
Nous **conduisons** prudemment[1].
Vous **conduisez** trop vite.
Elles **conduisent** à 110 km/h[2].
J'ai **conduit** la voiture à Paris.
Je **conduirai** plus prudemment.

Je **construis** un château de sable[3].
Tu **construis** une maison de poupée[4].
Il **construit** un garage.
Nous **construisons** une maison.
Vous **construisez** de longues phrases.
Ils **construisent** une maquette[5].
J'ai **construit** cela moi-même.
Je **construirai** un bâtiment.

Savez-vous conduire un autobus ?

2. Unlike the English verb *to drive*, you cannot use **conduire** + destination meaning *to drive to somewhere*; for an equivalent expression, **aller** + destination + **en voiture** is used. **Conduire** + person + destination corresponds to *to drive/take someone somewhere*.

Je **suis allé** à Paris **en voiture**.   *I went to Paris by car/I drove to Paris.*
J'**ai conduit** ma sœur **à Paris**.[6]   *I drove my sister to Paris.*

Other verbs conjugated like **conduire** and **construire**:

produire *to produce*   **détruire** *to destroy*
traduire *to translate*

A *Exercice de contrôle*

On conduit prudemment quand il neige.
1. Nous   2. Je   3. Vous   4. Tu

Vous traduisez une phrase en anglais.
1. Tu   2. Nous   3. Les étudiants   4. On

Cet enfant construit un château de sable.
1. Les enfants   2. Je   3. Nous   4. Vous

[1]/pʀydamɑ̃/ *prudently, carefully*
[2]kilomètres (à l')heure
[3]*sand castle*
[4]*dollhouse*
[5]*scale model*
[6]**J'ai conduit ma voiture à Paris** is possible, but it means *I drove my car in Paris* (and not *to Paris*).

B *Répondez aux questions.*

1. Savez-vous conduire ? Depuis combien de temps ? Comment conduisez-vous quand il neige ?
2. Avez-vous jamais conduit un camion ? Voulez-vous conduire une ambulance ? Pourquoi (pas) ?
3. Est-ce que nous traduisons beaucoup de phrases dans ce cours ? Comment traduit-on « *I drove to Paris* » ?
4. Est-ce que le Japon produit plus d'autos que les États-Unis ? Est-ce que les États-Unis produisent plus de pétrole que la France ?
5. Avez-vous jamais construit une maison de poupée ? Aimez-vous construire des châteaux de sable ?

16.2 PRONOMS PERSONNELS COMPLÉMENTS : RÉVISION

1. The chart below summarizes all the forms of the personal pronouns you have learned.

	SUJET	OBJET DIRECT	OBJET INDIRECT	RÉFLÉCHI	TONIQUE
	je tu		me/m' te/t'		moi toi
	nous vous		nous vous		
	il elle	le/l' la/l'	lui		lui elle
	on	—	—	se/s'	soi
	ils elles	les	leur		eux elles
Leçon	1.6	9.1	10.2	13.1	12.2

a) The *subject* pronouns are **je**, **tu**, **il**, **elle**, **on** (singular), and **nous**, **vous**, **ils**, **elles** (plural). The indefinite pronoun **on** was presented in Lesson 7.2.

b) The pronouns **me**, **te** (**m'**, **t'** before a vowel sound), **nous**, **vous** can be either *direct* or *indirect* object pronouns. They can also be *reflexive* pronouns. In the third person, however, you must distinguish between *direct* (**le**, **la**, **l'**, **les**) and *indirect* (**lui**, **leur**) object pronouns. The *reflexive* pronoun **se** (**s'** before a vowel sound) is used for both singular and plural subjects.

c) The stressed pronouns are **moi**, **toi**, **lui**, **elle**, **soi** (singular), and **nous**, **vous**, **eux**, **elles** (plural). Note that gender distinction is maintained only in the third person.

2. The pronoun **y** replaces the indirect object **à** + noun (*denoting a thing*) as well as any locative preposition + noun. The pronoun **en** replaces the indefinite article **des** as well as the partitive article **du**, **de la**, **de l'** and a noun. It also replaces the preposition **de** + noun (*denoting a thing*) as well as a noun that follows a number.

3. No more than two object pronouns can be used before a verb, and they occur in the following order.

me te se nous vous	+	le la les	+	lui leur y	+	en

A *Regardez le Tableau 16 à la page 64 et répondez d'après ce modèle.*

Est-ce que je suis arrivé(e) à la boutique ?
Oui, vous y êtes arrivé(e).

B *Regardez le Tableau 33 à la page 126 et répondez d'après ce modèle.*

Est-ce que vous avez traversé la rue ?
Non, je ne l'ai pas traversée.

C *Vous allez en ville. Vous entrerez dans un magasin et vous achèterez une montre. Répondez affirmativement en employant le futur et les pronoms appropriés, d'après ce modèle.*

Achetez-vous cette montre ?
Oui, je l'achèterai.

1. Sortez-vous de la maison ?
2. Avez-vous besoin d'argent ?
3. Prenez-vous le métro ?
4. Montez-vous dans la voiture ?
5. Descendez-vous de la voiture ?
6. Entrez-vous dans le magasin ?
7. Parlez-vous au vendeur ?
8. Répondez-vous à ses questions ?
9. Regardez-vous des montres ?
10. Choisissez-vous une montre ?
11. Finissez-vous vos courses ?
12. Rentrez-vous à la maison ?

D *Voici l'histoire d'une soirée sympathique. M. Dubois, le professeur de français, a invité ses étudiants chez lui. Votre camarade de chambre y est allé, et maintenant il vous en parle. Ajoutez une question après chaque phrase en employant les pronoms appropriés.*

Modèle : J'ai vu Barbara chez le professeur.
Ah oui ? Tu l'as vue chez lui ?

1. Je suis allé chez le professeur.
2. J'y ai emmené Robert et Marie.
3. J'ai présenté mes camarades au professeur.
4. Il y avait vingt étudiants chez le professeur.
5. Je n'ai pas vu Jacques.
6. M. Dubois nous a montré des diapos.[1]
7. Nous avons vu les diapos dans le séjour.
8. Mme Dubois a fait des crêpes[2] délicieuses.
9. Nous avons beaucoup aimé ses crêpes.
10. Je n'ai pas bu de vin.
11. J'ai dit à Mme Dubois que la soirée était très agréable.[3]
12. J'ai quitté leur maison avec Robert et Marie.

Exercice supplémentaire

Compréhension auditive

[1]**diapositives** *f* slides

[2]**crêpes** *f* very thin pancakes made of milk, sugar, flour, and eggs, sometimes rolled up, and served with jam or liqueur.

[3]Toute la proposition après **que** devient **le** (Leçon 9.1).

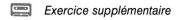

16.3 PRONOM RELATIF **QUI**

Relative pronouns are used to "embed" one sentence into another when both sentences share the same noun. The sentence that is embedded is known as the *relative clause* (**la proposition relative**), and the sentence that contains the relative clause is known as the *main clause* (**la proposition principale**). The relative clause is always embedded immediately after the same noun in the main clause, known as its *antecedent* (**l'antécédent** *m*), which the relative clause serves to describe. The corresponding noun in the relative clause becomes a relative pronoun, which is always placed at the beginning of the clause. Examine the English examples below. The sentences to be embedded and the relative clauses are in italics.

There's **the guide**. ***The guide*** *speaks English.*

→There's **the guide *who*** *speaks English.*

       (antecedent) (relative pronoun)

The museum is on the right bank. ***The museum*** *is well known.*

→ The museum, ***which*** *is well known*, is on the right bank.

1. In French, the relative pronoun **qui** replaces the subject of the relative clause. It is used for both persons and things and corresponds to English *who, which,* or *that.*

    Voilà **le guide**. ***Le guide*** *parle anglais.*

    → Voilà **le guide *qui*** *parle anglais.*

    Je cherche **le monument**. ***Le monument*** *est sur la rive droite*[1].

    → Je cherche **le monument *qui*** *est sur la rive droite.*

2. The relative clause does not necessarily come at the end of the main clause. In the examples below, the antecedent is the subject of the main clause, separated from the rest of the sentence by the relative clause.

    Le guide parle anglais. ***Le guide*** *est absent.*

    → **Le guide *qui*** *parle anglais* est absent.

    Le musée est sur la rive droite. ***Le musée*** *est très connu.*

    → **Le musée *qui*** *est très connu* est sur la rive droite.

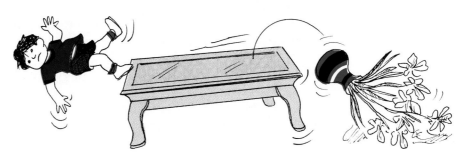

Voilà le garçon **qui** tombe de la table !   Voilà le vase **qui** tombe de la table !

TABLEAU 85

[1]*right bank*

🔲 **A** *Voulez-vous aller à Paris ? Bon, vous êtes un(e) touriste et vous êtes à Paris. Reliez[1] les deux phrases d'après ce modèle.*

> J'ai trouvé un hôtel. L'hôtel était près de la gare.
> **J'ai trouvé un hôtel qui était près de la gare.**

1. J'ai trouvé un hôtel. L'hôtel n'était pas loin de la gare.
2. Je suis dans un quartier. Le quartier a beaucoup de monuments.
3. Voilà un agent. L'agent pourra me donner des renseignements.
4. J'ai vu la cathédrale Notre-Dame. Elle date du Moyen Âge.
5. J'ai visité un monument. Le monument m'intéressait.
6. J'ai cherché un café. Le café était célèbre.

B *Reliez les deux phrases d'après ce modèle.[2]*

> Les touristes étaient japonais. Les touristes étaient dans l'autocar[3].
> **Les touristes qui étaient dans l'autocar étaient japonais.**

1. Les touristes étaient allemands. Les touristes étaient dans l'autocar.
2. Le quartier était près d'ici. Le quartier avait beaucoup de monuments.
3. Les autocars étaient là-bas. Les autocars étaient pour les touristes.
4. La visite était en français. La visite a commencé à onze heures.
5. Le guide n'était pas là. Le guide parlait bien anglais.
6. Le musée était fermé. Le musée m'intéressait.

C *Répondez aux questions en employant le pronom relatif **qui**.*

1. Regardez votre livre de français. Quelle est la photo en couleur qui vous intéresse ?[4]
2. Regardez les photos des monuments à la page 357. Quel est le monument qui vous intéresse le plus ? Quel est le bâtiment qui vous intéresse le moins ?
3. Regardez autour de vous. Quels sont les étudiants qui ont des cheveux courts ? Quel (Quelle) est l'étudiant(e) qui travaille beaucoup ?
4. Quelle est la personne qui n'a pas de montre ? Et quelle est la personne qui n'habite pas à la cité ?

16.4 PRONOM RELATIF **QUE**

Study the English examples below. They illustrate how a direct-object noun in the relative clause becomes a relative pronoun (which is often deleted).

There's **the lady**. *You know **the lady** well.*

→ There's **the lady (whom)** *you know well.*

The monument is on the left bank. *I saw **the monument** yesterday.*

→ **The monument (which/that)** *I saw yesterday* is on the left bank.

1. In French, the relative pronoun **que** (**qu'** before a vowel sound) replaces the direct object of the verb in the relative clause and is placed at the beginning of the relative clause. It is used for both persons and things, and corresponds to English *whom*, *which*, or *that*. While these relative pronouns are often omitted in English, **que** cannot be omitted in French.

---

[1]**relier** = mettre ensemble

[2]Dans toutes ces phrases, la proposition relative vient immédiatement après le sujet de la proposition principale.

[3]**L'autocar** est un autobus de grand confort, utilisé comme transport interurbain ou pour les excursions.

[4]Commencez vos réponses par **Voilà**.

Voilà **la dame**. *Vous connaissez bien **la dame**.*

→ Voilà **la dame q̆ue** *vous connaissez bien.*

Le monument est sur la rive gauche. *J'ai visité **le monument** hier.*

→ **Le monument q̆ue** *j'ai visité hier* est sur la rive gauche.

2. The past participle of the transitive verb in the relative clause must agree in gender (*m/f*) and number (*s/pl*) with the preceding direct object. In relative clauses, the direct object is the pronoun **que**, which has replaced a noun.

Je cherche les touristes **que** *vous avez vus ce matin.*

La jeune fille **que** *nous avons vue* parle allemand.

Les étudiantes **que** *j'ai présentées à Paul* sont américaines.

J'ai acheté les journaux **que** *vous avez mentionnés*.

TABLEAU 86   Voilà le garçon **qu'**elle cherche.   Voilà le vase **qu'**elle cherche.

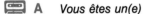

A *Vous êtes un(e) touriste qui visite Paris. Reliez les deux phrases d'après ce modèle.[1]*

J'ai acheté le guide[2]. Mon copain m'a recommandé le guide.
J'ai acheté le guide que mon copain m'a recommandé.

1. J'ai acheté le plan de Paris. Mon copain m'a recommandé le plan.
2. J'ai trouvé l'hôtel. Mon copain m'a mentionné l'hôtel.
3. J'ai cherché le monument. Je voulais voir le monument.
4. Je suis allé(e) à l'église. On venait de restaurer l'église.
5. Voici les photos du quartier. J'ai visité le quartier.
6. Voici les photos. J'ai pris ces photos.

B *Reliez les deux phrases d'après ce modèle.[3]*

Le guide était très utile. J'ai acheté le guide.
Le guide que j'ai acheté était très utile.

1. Le plan de la ville était très utile. J'ai acheté le plan.
2. La chambre était confortable. J'ai pris la chambre.
3. Le quartier était loin. J'allais visiter le quartier.
4. Le monument était fermé. Je voulais voir le monument.
5. La cathédrale était magnifique. J'ai visité la cathédrale.
6. Les photos étaient en couleur. J'ai pris les photos.

---

[1]Faites attention à l'accord du participe passé avec l'objet direct qui le précède.

[2]Le mot **guide** signifie deux choses : le *livre* qui donne des renseignements touristiques et la *personne* qui accompagne les touristes. Ici, il s'agit d'un livre.

[3]Dans toutes ces phrases, la proposition relative vient immédiatement après le sujet de la proposition principale. Faites attention à l'accord du participe passé.

C *Maintenant, reliez les deux phrases avec **qui** ou **que** selon le cas, d'après ces modèles.*

Le quartier était loin. Le quartier m'intéressait.
Le quartier qui m'intéressait était loin.
Le quartier était ancien. J'ai visité le quartier.
Le quartier que j'ai visité était ancien.

1. Le quartier était loin. J'allais visiter le quartier.
2. L'autobus était bondé. J'ai pris l'autobus.
3. L'agent ne parlait pas anglais. L'agent m'a donné des renseignements.
4. L'église était ouverte. Je voulais visiter l'église.
5. Les maisons étaient anciennes. Les maisons étaient sur la place.
6. Les maisons étaient belles. J'ai vu les maisons.
7. J'ai trouvé le musée. Le musée était près de la cathédrale.
8. Le musée était dans un bâtiment. Le bâtiment date du Moyen Âge.

D *Complétez les phrases suivantes avec votre partenaire.*

1. (Marie) est l'étudiante qui...
2. (Jean-Paul) est l'étudiant que...
3. Nous sommes dans un cours qui...
4. Notre professeur est une personne que...
5. Nous faisons un exercice oral qui...
6. Paris est une ville que...

 Compréhension auditive

16.5 VOIX PASSIVE

All sentences can be classified into two basic types: those in the *active voice* (**la voix active**) and those in the *passive voice* (**la voix passive**). In the active voice, the subject performs the action expressed by the verb. In the passive voice, however, the action is *performed on the subject* by someone or something else, often referred to as the "agent" of the sentence. In English, sentences like *Paul writes a letter* and *Bill liked Nancy* are in the active voice, whereas *A letter is written by Paul* and *Nancy was liked by Bill* are in the passive voice.

1. The passive construction in French is very similar to that of English: it consists of **être** + past participle. The subject of the active voice becomes the *agent* of the passive voice, usually introduced by **par** *by*. The direct object of the active voice becomes the subject in the passive voice.

SUBJECT	VERB	DIRECT OBJECT	
Jean-Paul	écrit	**ce mot.**	*Jean-Paul* writes **this word.**
Ce mot	est écrit	**par Jean-Paul.**	*This word is written **by Jean-Paul.***
SUBJECT	VERB	AGENT	

L'étudiant copie le mot.   The student copies the word.
→ **Le mot** est copié **par l'étudiant**.   → *The word is copied by the student.*
Michel ne fait pas **le lit**.   *Michel doesn't make the bed.*
→ **Le lit** n'est pas fait **par Michel**.   → *The bed is not made by Michel.*

2. You have learned two types of verbs that are conjugated with **être**. The first was "verbs of motion" (Lesson 9.4).

Je **suis allé** au cinéma.   *I went to the movies.*
Elle **est rentrée** à minuit.   *She returned home at midnight.*

The second type was reflexive verbs (Lesson 13.4).

Je **me suis levé** à sept heures.	*I got up at seven (o'clock).*
Elle **s'est lavé** les mains.	*She washed her hands.*

Do not confuse the passive construction with the *passé composé* of these verbs. The "verbs of motion" are all *intransitive verbs*; they cannot take a direct object. All reflexive verbs must have a reflexive pronoun before **être**. In the passive voice, *all* past participles are *transitive verbs*, i.e., in the corresponding active voice the verb requires a direct object (which becomes the subject in the passive voice). Moreover, in the passive voice, the past participle must agree in gender and number with the subject, as if it were an adjective.

Le douanier inspecte toutes les valises.

→ **Toutes les valises** sont **inspectées** par le douanier.

Les étudiants posent quelques questions.

→ **Quelques questions** sont **posées** par les étudiants.

The indefinite subject pronoun **on** (Lesson 7.2) cannot be used after any preposition, including **par**; hence it is omitted in the passive voice as the agent.

On nettoie tout l'appartement.	**On a restauré** le bâtiment.
→ Tout l'appartement **est nettoyé**.	→ Le bâtiment **a été restauré**.

3. *Tense.* The tense of the passive voice is indicated by **être**; in other words, the tense of **être** in the passive voice is *identical* to that of the verb in the active voice.

PRESENT

Le garçon **sert** le repas.	*serves/is serving*
→ Le repas **est servi** par le garçon.	→ *is served, is being served*

IMPERFECT

L'agent **inspectait** la voiture.	*was inspecting*
→ La voiture **était inspectée** par l'agent.	→ *was being inspected*

PASSÉ COMPOSÉ

Paul **a réparé** ma montre.	*repaired/has repaired*
→ Ma montre **a été réparée** par Paul.	→ *was repaired/has been repaired*

FUTURE

Elle **paiera** la voiture.	*will pay*
→ La voiture **sera payée** par elle.	→ *will be paid*

Il y a eu un accident. Deux personnes ont été blessées.

4. Keep in mind that in French, only the *direct object* of the active voice can become the subject of the passive voice. This means that, unlike English, an indirect object or the object of a preposition cannot be used as the subject in the passive voice. In such cases, **on** is used in the active voice.

répondre à

On a répondu **à la question**.   *The question was/has been answered.*

offrir quelque chose **à**
On lui a offert de l'argent.   *He/She was offered some money.*

parler de
On a parlé **de cela**.   *That was/has been talked about.*

5. The meaning of the passive voice can be conveyed in two other ways. When the implied agent is a human being, the active voice with the indefinite subject pronoun **on** can be used. With a few verbs (such as **dire**, **faire**, **vendre**, **manger**), a reflexive construction may be used, provided the subject of the passive voice is an *inanimate* object and the implied agent is a human being.

On ne **dit** pas cela en français. ⎫
Cela ne **se dit** pas en français. ⎭   *That is not said in French.*

On ne **fait** pas cela au Québec. ⎫
Cela ne **se fait** pas au Québec. ⎭   *That is not done in (the province of) Quebec.*

On vend du pain à la boulangerie. ⎫
Le pain[1] **se vend** à la boulangerie. ⎭   *Bread is sold at the bakery.*

On mange ça ? ⎫
Ça **se mange** ? ⎭   *Can that be eaten (Is it edible)?*

TABLEAU 87   La poupée **est cassée par** le garçon.   Le garçon **est puni par** la mère.

🔊 **A**   *Mettez les phrases suivantes à la voix passive, d'après ce modèle.*

Le professeur explique la leçon.
La leçon est expliquée par le professeur.

1. Le professeur écrit la phrase.
2. Le professeur a écrit la phrase.
3. Le professeur écrivait la phrase.
4. Le professeur écrira la phrase.

5. Les étudiants copient le mot.
6. Les étudiants ont copié le mot.
7. Les étudiants copiaient le mot.
8. Les étudiants copieront le mot.

[1]*Bread* (in general). For the use of the definite article to express totality or generality, see Lesson 8.1.

La Tour Eiffel a été construite vers la fin du dix-neuvième siècle.

B *Vous connaissez la Tour Eiffel, n'est-ce pas ? Elle est considérée comme le symbole de Paris par beaucoup de touristes. Elle a été construite il y a un siècle. Mettez les phrases suivantes à la voix passive d'après ces modèles.*

On a construit la Tour vers la fin du dix-neuvième siècle.
La tour a été construite vers la fin du dix-neuvième siècle.
Beaucoup de touristes utilisent les ascenseurs.
Les ascenseurs sont utilisés par beaucoup de touristes.

1. Gustave Eiffel a proposé le projet pour la Tour.
2. On a achevé la construction en 1889.
3. On a utilisé plus de 7.000 tonnes d'acier.
4. On a installé trois ascenseurs.
5. On a installé un escalier de 1.710 marches.
6. Naturellement, peu de touristes utilisent l'escalier.
7. Plus tard, on a ajouté des antennes de radio et de télévision.
8. Les touristes considèrent la Tour comme le symbole de Paris.
9. On repeint[1] la Tour tous les sept ans[2].

C *Modifiez les phrases suivantes d'après ce modèle.*

On achète du bœuf à la boucherie.
Le bœuf s'achète à la boucherie.

1. On achète du veau à la boucherie.
2. On achète du porc à la charcuterie.
3. On vend de l'aspirine à la pharmacie.
4. On vend des timbres au bureau de tabac.
5. On mange des croissants au petit déjeuner.
6. On mange du fromage avec un morceau de pain.
7. On comprend cela facilement.

[1]*repaints, paints again* (du verbe **peindre**, Leçon 24.1)
[2]*every seven years*

D *Répondez aux questions en employant la voix passive.*

1. Qui corrige vos compositions ? Vos compositions ont-elles été corrigées par (Jacqueline) ?
2. Regardez la porte de la classe. Est-elle ouverte ou fermée ? Par qui a-t-elle été fermée (ouverte) ?
3. Regardez le tableau. Qui a effacé le tableau ? Par qui est-ce que le tableau a été effacé ?
4. Vous sortez de la douane. Qu'est-ce que le douanier vous a dit ?[1] Par qui vos valises ont-elles été inspectées ?
5. Connaissez-vous bien votre université ? En quelle année a-t-elle été fondée ?

🔲 *Exercice supplémentaire*

🔲 *Compréhension auditive*

APPLICATIONS

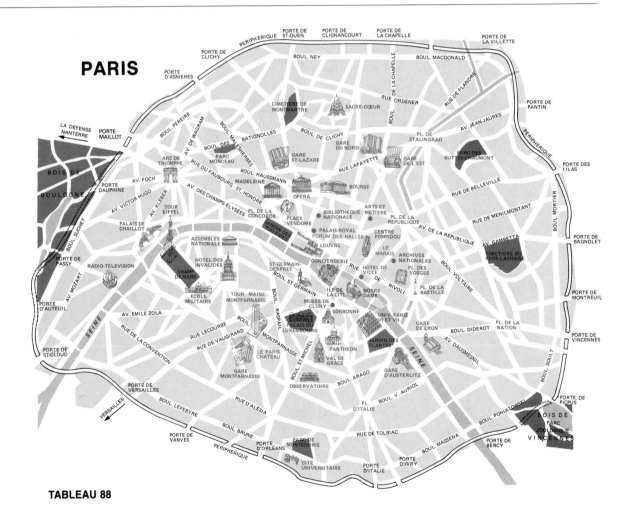

PARIS

TABLEAU 88

---

[1]Dites : « N'avez-vous rien à déclarer ? ».

Paris, vu du haut de Notre-Dame.

A Situations

Les grands monuments de Paris

Il est impossible de vous donner une liste de tous les grands monuments de Paris, qui sont Instead of *très nombreux. À la place d'°une conversation, nous vous offrons une liste d'une quinzaine* in the manner of *de monuments et de sites célèbres, à la manière d'°un guide touristique. Quelques autres sites seront présentés dans les leçons suivantes.*

L'Arc de Triomphe. Commencé par Napoléon en 1806 et terminé longtemps après sa mort. 5
Plus haut qu'un bâtiment de quinze étages, le monument est couvert de sculptures qui commémorent ses victoires. Sous l'Arc se trouve le tombeau du Soldat Inconnu.

Romanesque-Byzantine **La Basilique du Sacré-Cœur.** Grande église de style romano-byzantin°, située sur la butte
Montmartre et construite vers la fin du XIXᵉ siècle. Sa haute silhouette domine toute la capitale.

La Cathédrale Notre-Dame. Une des premières cathédrales gothiques construites en Europe 10
(1163–1345) ; elle se trouve dans l'Île de la Cité, une des deux îles de la Seine qui constituent
le cœur de la ville.

Le Centre Pompidou[1]**.** Extraordinaire bâtiment où se trouvent à l'extérieur tous les éléments
air conditioning qu'on cache d'habitude : les grosses poutres, les gros tuyaux de ventilation et de climatisation°,
les escaliers, les escalators... Il abrite un musée d'art moderne, une cinémathèque[2], un théâtre, 15
une bibliothèque.

La Conciergerie. Ancien[3] palais royal qui date du Moyen Âge et qui se trouve dans l'Île de
courthouse la Cité. On a démoli la plus grande partie du palais pour construire le Palais de Justice°. La
partie qui existe était une prison pendant la Révolution de 1789. La Sainte-Chapelle, construite
par le roi Saint-Louis, date également du Moyen Âge. 20

L'Église Saint-Germain-des-Prés. Située tout près du Quartier Latin[4]. Le clocher de cette
Romanesque église romane° est un des plus anciens de France.

[1]Officiellement, il s'appelle le Centre National d'Art et de Culture Georges Pompidou ; G. Pompidou (1911–1974) était
un homme d'état et président de la République (1969–1974).

[2]une sorte de « bibliothèque » pour le cinéma, où on conserve et projette des films

[3]L'adjectif **ancien**, placé devant le nom, signifie *former* (placé après le nom, il signifie *old*) : **l'ancien palais** *the former
palace*, **le palais ancien** *the old palace.*

[4]Ainsi appelé parce que la Sorbonne (l'ancienne Université de Paris) est dans ce quartier. Les professeurs et les étudiants
y parlaient latin au Moyen Âge.

L'Arc de Triomphe.

La Place de la Concorde.

Le Forum des Halles. Vaste centre commercial souterrain et ultramoderne, à plusieurs étages, qui occupe le grand espace laissé vide par les anciennes Halles[1]. En surface° se trouve une immense place pour piétons.

On the street level

25

L'Hôtel des Invalides. Ainsi appelé parce que Louis XIV l'a construit pour y loger les soldats blessés. Ce groupe de bâtiments abrite le musée de l'Armée et le tombeau de Napoléon ainsi que° les tombeaux de ses généraux.

ainsi que *as well as*

Le Louvre. Ancien palais royal qui abrite une vaste collection d'art de tous les pays et de toutes les époques depuis l'Antiquité.[2]

30

Le Palais de Chaillot. Construit pour l'Exposition de 1937. On y trouve plusieurs musées et une grande salle de théâtre. De la terrasse entre ses deux ailes, on a une belle vue sur les jardins qui descendent jusqu'à la Tour Eiffel.

La Place Charles de Gaulle. On l'appelle aussi L'Étoile (son ancien nom), parce que douze magnifiques avenues partent de cette grande place circulaire ; au centre se trouve l'Arc de Triomphe.

35

La Place de la Concorde. Une vaste place où circulent plus de 160.000 voitures par jour. Pendant la Révolution de 1789, Louis XVI, Marie-Antoinette, et plus tard Danton et Robespierre y ont été guillotinés. L'obélisque de Louksor, offert par le vice-roi d'Égypte en 1829, se trouve au centre de la place. Cet obélisque a plus de trente siècles.

40

La Tour Eiffel. Construite par l'ingénieur Gustave Eiffel pour l'exposition de Paris en 1889. (Voir la Leçon 16.5, exercice B.)

panorama, view **La Voie Triomphale.** Vaste perspective° qui va du Louvre jusqu'à l'Arc de Triomphe (à peu près 4 km) ; sur cette voie se trouvent le Jardin des Tuileries, la Place de la Concorde et l'avenue des Champs-Élysées.

45

[1]**halles** *f* grand marché couvert ; le marché des Halles Centrales (qu'on appelait « le ventre de Paris ») se trouve maintenant au sud de Paris, près de l'aéroport d'Orly.

[2]On parlera des musées célèbres de Paris dans la Leçon 18.

L'Hôtel des Invalides.

Le Sacré-Cœur.

La Conciergerie.

Le Forum des Halles.

La Cathédrale Notre-Dame.

Répondez aux questions.[1]

1. Qu'est-ce qui se trouve au centre de la Place de la Concorde ?
2. Qu'est-ce qui se trouve au centre de la Place Charles de Gaulle ?
3. Où se trouve le tombeau du Soldat Inconnu ?
4. Où se trouve le tombeau de Napoléon ?
5. Quels bâtiments datent du Moyen Âge ?
6. Quels monuments sont des bâtiments religieux ?
7. Est-ce que tous ces bâtiments datent du Moyen Âge ?
8. Est-ce que le Palais de Chaillot était un palais royal ?
9. Quels bâtiments abritent des musées ?
10. Quels bâtiments datent du dix-neuvième siècle ?

B Expressions utiles

Les monuments

visiter $\begin{cases} \text{un quartier} \begin{cases} \text{historique / touristique / pittoresque} \\ \text{résidentiel / commercial / industriel} \end{cases} \\ \text{le vieux quartier (la vieille ville)} \end{cases}$

Le monument a été $\begin{cases} \text{construit} \\ \text{détruit} \\ \text{sauvegardé} \\ \text{restauré} \end{cases} \begin{cases} \text{au début} \\ \text{vers le milieu} \\ \text{à la fin} \end{cases}$ du XIXe siècle.

La visite (est) $\begin{cases} \text{guidée (accompagnée).} \\ \text{sur demande.} \\ \text{suspendue / interdite (on ne visite pas).} \end{cases}$

$\left.\begin{matrix} \text{s'adresser} \\ \text{se renseigner} \end{matrix}\right\}$ au $\begin{cases} \text{bureau d'information} \\ \text{syndicat d'initiative} \end{cases}$

C Pratique

1. A-t-on besoin de donner un pourboire au guide après une visite accompagnée ?
2. Définissez ces mots :

   un quartier résidentiel   un quartier industriel
   un centre commercial   le centre ville

3. Vous visitez un château. Au bout d'un couloir vous trouvez une porte avec cette pancarte : ACCÈS INTERDIT. Qu'est-ce que cela veut dire ?
4. Vous voulez visiter une vieille tour. Sur la porte d'entrée on a affiché ceci : VISITE SUR DEMANDE. S'ADRESSER AU SYNDICAT D'INITIATIVE. Qu'est-ce que vous allez faire si vous voulez la visiter ?
5. Y a-t-il des monuments ou des quartiers historiques dans votre ville qui ont été sauvegardés ou restaurés ?

[1]Les réponses aux questions ne sont pas enregistrées sur la bande magnétique.

D *Inventions ou découvertes célèbres : Par qui ces choses ont-elles été inventées ou découvertes ?*

le paratonnerre (1752)
le phonographe (1877)
la pénicilline (1928)
le télégraphe (1843)
la dynamite (1866)
le vaccin anti-polio (1953)
l'écriture pour les aveugles (1786)
l'imprimerie (1436)
le stylo (1884)
le téléphone (1876)

a) Alexander Fleming
b) Johannes Gutenberg
c) Lewis Waterman
d) Louis Braille
e) Thomas Edison
f) Benjamin Franklin
g) Jonas Salk
h) Samuel Morse
i) Alfred Nobel
j) Alexander Graham Bell

E *Regardez le Tableau 89. Que faisait le jeune couple ? Qu'est-ce qui leur est arrivé ? Que disent-ils à l'agent ?*

TABLEAU 89

F *Il y a beaucoup de rues à Paris qui portent le nom de personnes célèbres. Pouvez-vous identifier la profession de chacune des personnes suivantes ? (par exemple : artiste, compositeur, écrivain et savant)*

rue Berlioz	rue Louis-Braille	rue Degas
rue Gounod	avenue Victor-Hugo	rue Lavoisier
avenue Molière	rue Édouard-Manet	boulevard Pasteur
avenue Rodin	avenue Émile-Zola	rue Saint-Saëns /sɛ̃sɑ̃s/

G *Paris est divisé en 20 arrondissements. Savez-vous dans quel quartier se trouvent les monuments et les sites suivants ? Pour vous orienter, consultez d'abord le plan de Paris à la page 354 (Tableau 88). Les quatre lettres vous offrent des points de repère[1].*

A: la gare Saint-Lazare
B: la gare de l'Est

C: la gare de Lyon
D: la gare Montparnasse

a) l'Arc de Triomphe
b) l'avenue des Champs-Élysées
c) le Centre Pompidou
d) la Cathédrale Notre-Dame
e) l'Église Saint-Germain-des-Prés
f) le Forum des Halles

g) l'Hôtel des Invalides
h) le Louvre
i) le Palais de Chaillot
j) la Place de la Concorde
k) la Tour Eiffel
l) la Sorbonne

[1]*reference points*

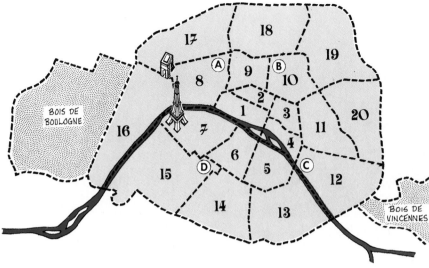

TABLEAU 90　　　　　　　　　　Les arrondissements de Paris.

H　Renseignements et opinions

1. Y a-t-il un monument historique dans notre ville ? Pourquoi est-il historique ?
2. Vous rencontrez au resto-U un étudiant qui vient de la Côte-d'Ivoire[1]. Décrivez le climat de notre région ainsi que les monuments et les endroits intéressants de notre ville.
3. Avez-vous jamais été en France ? Si vous voyagez en France, combien d'argent allez-vous laisser aux personnes suivantes comme pourboire ?[2]

   À la femme de chambre d'un hôtel où vous venez de passer cinq jours et où le service était excellent.
   Au guide, après la visite d'un château.
   À l'ouvreuse du cinéma où votre place a coûté trente francs.
   Au garçon de café ; vous avez commandé une boisson qui a coûté 12 F, service compris.
4. Voici les réponses à quelques questions. Quelles étaient les questions ?

Mais je l'ai déjà visitée !	Je vais vous les montrer.
Il m'en parlera demain.	Je l'y ai mise ce matin.
Non, je n'y pense pas souvent.	Elle le lui apportera ce soir.

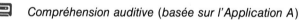 *Compréhension auditive (basée sur l'Application A)*

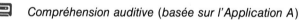 *Compréhension auditive*

---

[1] *Ivory Coast* (un des pays francophones d'Afrique)
[2] Consultez les *Différences* de cette leçon.

Le quartier de la Défense.   *La Place des Vosges.*   *Rue de la chaussée d'Antin.*

❙ Lecture

Paris

Paris est une ville vraiment extraordinaire. C'est non seulement le centre politique mais aussi le centre culturel et économique d'un pays très centralisé. Au Moyen Âge, Paris était déjà une *thanks to/traffic* grande ville grâce à° la circulation° des bateaux sur la Seine, à la réputation des grands maîtres de la Sorbonne, et aux rois qui aimaient séjourner à Paris. Voulez-vous visiter la ville ? Mais quel Paris voulez-vous visiter ? 5

Le plus beau, le plus célèbre est le Paris des touristes et de l'histoire, avec les grands monuments du passé : Notre-Dame, le Louvre, les Invalides, l'Arc de Triomphe, la Tour Eiffel... Mais il y a aussi le Paris des affaires[1] — ces quartiers grouillants[2] du centre, autour de la *Stock Market* Bourse° et des Grands Boulevards... Vous trouverez le Paris des étudiants dans le Quartier Latin, sur la rive gauche de la Seine, et le Paris du grand luxe sur la rive droite, dans le 10 Faubourg Saint-Honoré, célèbre pour ses maisons de haute couture[3] et ses boutiques de bijoux somptueux... Si vous cherchez le Paris des artistes, allez à Montmartre, pittoresque colline qui domine la ville, ou sur les quais[4] de la Seine... Si vous voulez voir le Paris des bourgeois[5] avec ses grands immeubles élégants, allez dans le 16e arrondissement[6]. Il y a *slums* aussi le Paris des taudis°, le Paris des ouvriers, le Paris des usines. Et cette énumération 15 peut continuer !

beyond Mais au delà de° cette immense variété, on distingue nettement un vieux Paris et un Paris moderne. Comme exemple du vieux Paris on peut citer le quartier du Marais. Tout près de la Seine, sur la rive droite, le Marais est resté tel qu'il[7] était il y a plus de 300 ans. On y trouve *groupes de bâtiments* de très beaux ensembles° d'architecture classique : la Place des Vosges, qui était, au 17e 20 siècle, le centre de la vie aristocratique, et de nombreux hôtels particuliers[8] qui ont été restaurés récemment. La plupart des rues sont très étroites. On n'y voit pas un seul immeuble moderne.

Il y a aussi le Paris du 20e siècle, visible, par exemple, dans le quartier Montparnasse dominé par la silhouette de la Tour Maine-Montparnasse (le plus haut immeuble d'Europe).

[1]*business*; on emploie ce mot au pluriel dans ce sens.

[2]*teeming* (du verbe **grouiller** *to swarm*)

[3]*high fashion* (par exemple, les créations de Cardin, Courrèges, Chanel, Dior, Lanvin, Saint-Laurent)

[4]**quais** *streets that run along any body of water*

[5]**les bourgeois** *upper middle class people*

[6]Paris est divisé en 20 arrondissements.

[7]**tel que** *such as, just as*

[8]domiciles privés (*private*) très somptueux

Le plus impressionnant est le quartier de la Défense : prenez à la Place Charles de Gaulle 25
cette immense avenue qui traverse la Seine. Soudain, vous vous trouverez dans une vaste
jungle de gratte-ciel[1]. Il y a des immeubles d'affaires et d'habitation gigantesques, un énorme
palais d'exposition, une grande station de métro, des gares pour les trains et pour les autocars.

On the other hand
twisting

Mais, pour les Parisiens comme pour beaucoup de touristes, le charme de Paris n'est pas
dans ses quartiers neufs, car on retrouve ce style d'architecture à New York, à Paris, ou à 30
Tokyo. Par contre°, un quartier comme Saint-Germain-des-Prés reste uniquement parisien.
Une vieille église, une place, un grand boulevard, de petites rues tortueuses°, avec beaucoup
de terrasses de café, de restaurants, de bistrots, de librairies, d'antiquaires, et une animation
constante... Voilà ce qui fait le charme et la vie d'un quartier parisien.

A *Indiquez si chaque commentaire est vrai ou faux. S'il est faux, corrigez le commentaire.*

1. La Seine a beaucoup contribué au développement de Paris comme centre économique
   de la France au Moyen Âge.
2. Parmi les grands monuments du passé que les touristes visitent sont Notre-Dame, le Louvre,
   la Bourse et la Défense.
3. Le Quartier Latin se trouve sur une pittoresque colline qui domine la ville.
4. Le quartier du Marais est resté tel qu'il était au Moyen Âge.
5. La Place des Vosges est un bel ensemble d'architecture classique.
6. Beaucoup d'hôtels particuliers du Marais ont été restaurés.
7. La Place Charles de Gaulle se trouve au centre du quartier le plus moderne de Paris.
8. L'immeuble le plus haut d'Europe se trouve dans le quartier de Montmartre.

B *Quels aspects de Paris sont représentés par les quartiers suivants ?*

ASPECT	QUARTIER
le Paris des affaires	a) le Quartier Latin
le Paris des artistes	b) le Faubourg Saint-Honoré
le Paris des étudiants	c) le quartier de la Bourse
le Paris de la haute couture	d) le 16e arrondissement
le Paris du 17e siècle	e) Montmartre
le Paris ultramoderne	f) le quartier du Marais
le Paris des bourgeois	g) le quartier de la Défense
le Paris des Parisiens	h) le quartier de Saint-Germain-des-Prés

C *Trouvez dans le texte les antonymes des mots suivants.*

nouveau   gauche
public   large
loin (de)   bas

[1]*skyscrapers* (le mot est invariable au pluriel : un **gratte-ciel**, des **gratte-ciel**)
[2]Il y a plusieurs mots dans le texte qui signifient « très grand ».
[3]*straight*

VOCABULAIRE

Noms

l'**acier** *m*	steel	une **auto(mobile)**	automobile, car	la cinéma-thèque	film library
une aile	wing	la basilique	basilica	la climatisation	air conditioning
une **antenne**	antenna	la butte	hill	le clocher	steeple
l'Antiquité *f*	Antiquity	le **camion**	truck	la **composition**	composition
un arc	arch	la **cathédrale**	cathedral	la **construction**	building, construction
une armée	army	le centre (commercial)	(shopping) center		
un **autocar**	bus (interurban or sightseeing)	la chapelle	chapel	la **crêpe**	crepe

le **croissant**	croissant	la manière	manner; way	le Sacré-Cœur	basilica in Paris
la **diapo(sitive)**	slide	la **marche**	step	la sculpture	sculpture
l'Égypte f	Egypt	le **métro**	subway	la Seine	Seine River
un élément	element	la mort	death	la silhouette	silhouette, outline
une époque	era	le **Moyen Âge**	Middle Ages	le site	site
un escalator	escalator	un obélisque	obelisk	le soldat	soldier
un espace	space	le palais	palace; large public	le style	style
une étoile	star		building	la surface	surface
une exposition	exhibition	le Palais de	courthouse	le **symbole**	symbol
l'extérieur m	outside, exterior	Justice		le théâtre	theater
la fin	end	la perspective	perspective; pano-	le tombeau	tomb, grave
le forum	forum		rama, view	la **tonne**	ton
la **gare**	station	le **pétrole**	petroleum	la **tour**	tower
le général	general	le piéton	pedestrian	le triomphe	triumph
Les Halles f	wholesale food	la **poupée**	doll	le tuyau	pipe
	market	la poutre	beam	la ventilation	ventilation
une île	island	la prison	jail, prison	le vice-roi	viceroy
l'**intérieur** m	inside, interior	le **projet**	project	la victoire	victory
Les Invalides m	former residence	le Quartier Latin	Latin Quarter	la voie	way
	for war veterans	la **radio**	radio	le **voleur**	thief
la liste	list	la révolution	revolution	la vue	view, sight
Louksor	Luxor	le roi	king		
le Louvre	Louvre museum	le **sable**	sand		

Verbes

abriter	to shelter; to house	**construire** irrég	to build; to construct	**intéresser**	to interest
achever	to finish	**dater (de)**	to date (back to)	loger	to house
ajouter	to add	**déclarer**	to declare	occuper	to occupy
cacher	to hide	démolir	to demolish	**produire** irrég	to produce; to give
circuler	to go around; to drive	dominer	to dominate	**proposer**	to propose
	around	**emmener**	to take	**recommander**	to recommend
commémorer	to commemorate	exister	to exist	**restaurer**	to restore
conduire irrég	to drive; to lead	**fonder**	to found	**traduire** irrég	to translate
considérer	to consider	guillotiner	to guillotine	**voler**	to steal
constituer	to make up; to represent	**installer**	to install, set up		

Adjectifs

agréable	pleasant	gothique	Gothic	sacré(e)	sacred
ancien(ne)	former	**haut(e)**	high	situé(e)	located
blessé(e)	wounded	immense	immense, huge	souterrain(e)	underground
célèbre	famous	inconnu(e)	unknown	touristique	(of) tourist
circulaire	circular	**indiqué(e)**	indicated	triomphal(e)	triumphant
commercial(e)	commercial	religieux(euse)	religious	vaste	vast
couvert(e) (de)	covered (with)	roman(e)	Romanesque	vide	empty
extraordinaire	extraordinary	romano-byzantin(e)	Romanesque-Byzantine		

Adverbes

ainsi	so, thus	**facilement**	easily	**prudemment**	prudently, carefully
à peu près	approximately	longtemps	(for) a long time		
également	likewise, also	**naturellement**	naturally		

Autres expressions

ainsi que	as well as	d'habitude	usually
à la manière de	in the manner of	en surface	on the street level
à l'extérieur	outside	**on repeint**	they repaint
à l'intérieur	inside	**qui**	who; what
aller + destination + **en voiture**	to drive to somewhere	**tous les sept ans**	every seven years
au centre de	in the center of	tout près (de)	very close (to)
Au voleur !	Thief!		

17 Prenons le métro !

LESSON OBJECTIVES

Theme and Culture

1. Urban transportation
2. Public transportation in Paris

Communication Skills

1. Reading a subway map
2. Comparing ways of performing a task (*better, best*, etc.)
3. Modifying statements with adverbs describing manners (*slowly, carefully, legibly*)
4. Making polite requests (*Would you/Could you . . . ?*)
5. Making hypothetical statements (*If I were . . .*)
6. Making generalizations (*It is good to do . . .*)
7. Asking/Answering questions about definitions
8. Apologizing and accepting apologies

Structures

17.1 Formation of adverbs
17.2 Comparative and superlative of adverbs
17.3 The present conditional
17.4 Impersonal expressions
17.5 **Qu'est-ce que c'est que... ?**

CONVERSATIONS

A. Le métro[1]

Regardez le Tableau 91 à la page 366. C'est une très petite partie du plan du métro de Paris. Les stations de correspondance[2] sont marquées par la lettre C. Vous avez une chambre dans un hôtel près de la station Wagram. Aujourd'hui vous allez visiter quelques grands monuments de Paris.

D'abord vous voulez voir l'Arc de Triomphe, qui se trouve au centre de la Place Charles de Gaulle. Vous prenez donc la direction Gallieni[3] et vous changez de ligne à Villiers. Là, vous prenez la direction Porte Dauphine et vous descendez à Charles de Gaulle-Étoile.

[1]officiellement, le Chemin de fer métropolitan

[2]Les stations où on peut changer de ligne.

[3]Toutes les lignes de métro sont numérotées. Mais, en général, on mentionne le nom des terminus de chaque ligne au lieu des numéros : **prendre la ligne Étoile-Nation, prendre la direction Porte Dauphine**, etc.

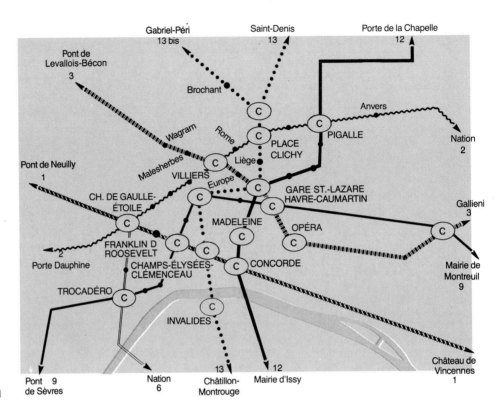

Station de correspondance

TABLEAU 91

Vous venez de visiter l'Arc de Triomphe. Vous voulez aller voir la Tour Eiffel, qui est près de la station Trocadéro. Comment[1] allez-vous de la Place Charles de Gaulle à la station Trocadéro ?

Après la visite de la Tour Eiffel, vous voulez aller aux Invalides. Vous voulez voir le tombeau de Napoléon. Comment est-ce que vous y allez ?

Après la visite des Invalides, vous voulez aller à Montmartre. Vous voulez visiter ce quartier pittoresque. Une des stations les plus proches de Montmartre, c'est Anvers. Comment allez-vous des Invalides à Anvers ?

C'est la fin de l'après-midi. Vous êtes fatigué(e) et vous voulez rentrer à votre hôtel. Quelles lignes prendrez-vous pour rentrer ?

B. Après un match de tennis

MICHEL   Dis donc[2], Monique. Tu joues très bien.

MONIQUE   Mais toi, tu joues beaucoup mieux que moi.

MICHEL   Un peu mieux que toi, peut-être. C'est Christine qui joue le mieux.

MONIQUE   Tu as raison. C'est elle la meilleure joueuse.

---

[1]Il y a une liaison interdite après **comment** : **Comment//aller**, **Comment//est-ce que**. (**Comment allez-vous ?** est une exception.)

[2]*Say*

Le métro est un moyen de transport très rapide.

C. Elle voudrait aller aux Galeries Lafayette[1].

LA TOURISTE   Excusez-moi, Monsieur l'agent. Pourriez-vous m'indiquer comment aller aux Galeries Lafayette ?

L'AGENT   Aller où, Madame ?

LA TOURISTE   Je voudrais aller aux Galeries Lafayette.

L'AGENT   Alors, vous voyez ce grand bâtiment là-bas ? C'est l'Opéra. Allez jusque-là, puis tournez à droite.

Compréhension auditive (basée sur la Conversation A)

DIFFÉRENCES

Le métro

Both buses and the **métro** (*subway*) in Paris are run by RATP (**Régie Autonome des Transports Parisiens**), a transit authority. The dense network of bus lines boasts more than 4,000 stops, but the **métro**, inaugurated in 1900 (the present-day **Ligne 1**), offers the fastest means of getting around the city and today serves more than one billion passengers annually. Some lines have been extended far into the suburbs to facilitate commuting. For commuters, there are reduced fares (**la carte orange**), while tourists can buy **un billet de tourisme**, which is good for one to several days of unlimited travel. Anyone can buy **un carnet de tickets** (*a book of tickets*), which

[1]un des grands magasins de Paris

Une station de métro classique (Abbesses).

Une station du R.E.R. (Charles de Gaulle-Étoile).

consists of ten tickets at a reduced price. A popular expression depicting the daily life of those working in Paris goes like this: « **métro, boulot, dodo** »[1].

In order to allow even more rapid movement in and out of Paris, three new subway lines have been constructed, two running roughly east-west and one going north-south. Called R.E.R. (**le Réseau Express Régional**), they are 20–25 meters underground with fewer stations, and large, fast trains. These lines interconnect with some of the old **métro** lines within the city, and with suburban train lines at each end.

While the **métro** map appears complicated at first glance (see the map facing p. 369), all lines run basically either east-west (parallel with the Seine) or north-south. On some lines the trains roll smoothly and quietly on pneumatic tires, an innovation that has been exported to other countries such as Canada and Mexico. It is said that no point in Paris is farther than 500 meters from a **métro** station. Some stations are beautifully decorated (Charles de Gaulle-Étoile, Louvre, Varenne, Franklin D. Roosevelt) and large ones have underground shopping centers (Gare Saint-Lazare, Chaussée d'Antin). All main stations have electric maps which light up to help you find the shortest route to your destination. Some now have a computer terminal called SITU: you type in the address or the name of a monument to which you want to go, and it prints out directions when you choose one of the four options: (1) **Pour y aller le plus vite possible**, (2) **Pour marcher le moins possible**, (3) **Pour prendre Métro et RER seulement**, (4) **Pour prendre le bus seulement**.

STRUCTURES

17.1 FORMATION DES ADVERBES

Most adverbs modify verbs, describing in what way the action denoted by the verb is performed. In English, many adverbs are formed by adding *-ly* to adjectives: *quick → quickly, natural → naturally, frank → frankly*. Similarly, many adverbs in French are formed by adding **-ment** /mã/ to adjectives.

1. Most adverbs are formed by adding **-ment** to the *feminine* form of the adjective.

> **seul, seule**
> Nous avons **seulement** dix francs sur nous. *only*
>
> **lent, lente**
> Nous nous promenons **lentement** dans la rue. *slowly*
>
> **sérieux, sérieuse**
> Ils doivent travailler **sérieusement**. *seriously*
>
> **naturel, naturelle**
> **Naturellement**, je n'ai pas pris l'autobus. *naturally*
>
> **excessif, excessive**
> Sa question était **excessivement** difficile. *excessively*
>
> **oral, orale**
> Répondez **oralement** à ces questions. *orally*
>
> **franc, franche**
> **Franchement**, je ne sais pas où il est allé. *frankly*

[1] literally, *métro, job, bed*

LA FRANCE ET SON PASSÉ

*Le château de Versailles
date du 17ᵉ siècle.*

*Le vieux quartier de Colmar,
une ville en Alsace.*

*Carcassonne, ville fortifiée
bâtie au Moyen Âge.*

*Semur-en-Auxois, une ville
pittoresque en Bourgogne.*

Rocamadour, un des centres de pèlerinage
au Moyen Âge (dans le Périgord).

Le Mont-Saint-Michel.

Rue du Gros Horloge,
centre du vieux quartier
de Rouen (en Normandie).

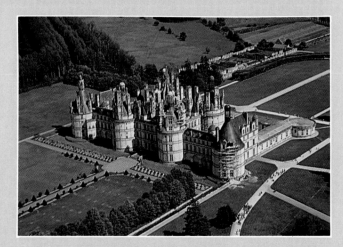

Le château de Chambord
a été construit au 16e siècle.

ON PARLE FRANÇAIS...

...au Zaïre (Kisangani)...

...au Maroc (Casablanca)...

...en Belgique (Bruxelles)...

...à Haïti...

...à Québec...

...en Tunisie (Kairouan)...

...au Niger (Niamey)...

...au Sénégal (Dakar)...

...en Côte-d'Ivoire
(Bogouina).

Elle est montée rapidement dans l'autobus.

2. If the masculine form of the adjective has two or more syllables and ends in **-ant** or **-ent** (both pronounced /ɑ̃/), the corresponding adverb is formed by changing these endings to **-amment** or **-emment** (both pronounced /amɑ̃/).

constant, constante
    Ce monsieur parle **constamment**.   /kõstamɑ̃/   *constantly*
élégant, élégante
    Cette dame s'habille **élégamment**.   /elegamɑ̃/   *elegantly*
intelligent, intelligente
    Vous lui avez répondu **intelligemment**.   /ɛ̃tɛliʒamɑ̃/   *intelligently*
récent, récente
    Vous les avez vus **récemment**.   /ʀesamɑ̃/   *recently*

3. If the masculine form of the adjective ends in the vowel sound /e/, /ɛ/, /i/, or /y/, the corresponding adverb is formed by adding **-ment** to the *masculine* form.

séparé, séparée   /e/
    Je vais lui écrire **séparément**.   *separately*
vrai, vraie   /ɛ/
    Le métro est **vraiment** rapide.   *really*
poli, polie   /i/
    Elle nous a répondu **poliment**.   *politely*
absolu, absolue   /y/
    Le métro était **absolument** bondé.   *absolutely*

4. Some adverbs are not formed in any of the three ways mentioned above.

précis, précise
    Dites **précisément** où vous voulez aller.   *precisely*
gentil, gentille   /ʒɑ̃ti/, /ʒɑ̃tij/
    Elle nous a répondu **gentiment**.   *nicely*
bref, brève
    Parlez **brièvement** de vos projets d'été.   *briefly*

A *Donnez l'adverbe qui correspond à chaque adjectif.*

1. vrai
2. franc
3. négatif
4. constant
5. lisible
6. gracieux
7. frugal
8. fréquent
9. élégant
10. patient
11. bref
12. absolu

B *Répondez aux questions d'après ce modèle.*

> (Monique) est gracieuse. Comment danse-t-elle ?
> **Elle danse gracieusement.**

1. (Françoise) est intelligente. Comment travaille-t-elle ?
2. (Philippe) est sérieux. Comment étudie-t-il ?
3. (Yves) est discret. Comment parle-t-il ?
4. (Marion) est élégante. Comment s'habille-t-elle ?
5. (René) est franc. Comment parle-t-il ?
6. Vous êtes patient(e). Comment travaillez-vous ?
7. Votre écriture est lisible. Comment écrivez-vous ?
8. Mon repas est frugal. Comment est-ce que je mange ?
9. Votre réponse sera affirmative. Comment répondrez-vous ?
10. Vous serez énergique demain. Comment travaillerez-vous ?

C *Maintenant, répondez à ces questions.*

1. Comment est-ce que vous vous habillez quand vous assistez à un mariage ?
2. Comment est-ce que vous mangez quand vous êtes en retard ?
3. Comment est-ce que vous marchez quand vous faites une promenade ?
4. Comment est-ce qu'on travaille avant un examen ?
5. Qu'est-ce que je dois faire fréquemment ?
6. Qu'est-ce que nous devons faire constamment ?

D *Complétez les phrases suivantes avec votre partenaire. Utilisez l'adverbe qui correspond à chaque adjectif.*

1. Nous parlons (discret) quand...
2. Nous parlons (poli) quand...
3. Nous travaillons (énergique) quand...
4. Nous devons (absolu) nous reposer quand...
5. Nous nous habillons (élégant) quand...

Compréhension auditive

17.2 COMPARATIF ET SUPERLATIF DE L'ADVERBE

1. The comparative and superlative of the adverb are similar to the comparative and superlative of the adjective (Lesson 11.3), except that adverbs are always invariable and have no gender/number agreement with any noun. **Aussi ... que** corresponds to English *as . . . as*, and **plus ... que/moins ... que** to *more . . . than/less . . . than*.

Jeanne écrit **lisiblement**.	*legibly*
Elle écrit **aussi lisiblement que** sa sœur.	*as legibly as*
Elle écrit **plus lisiblement que** son frère.	*more legibly than*
Mais elle écrit **moins lisiblement que** sa mère.	*less legibly than*

The superlative is formed by adding **le** before **plus** or **moins**. This **le** is invariable.

La mère de Jeanne écrit **le plus lisiblement**.	*the most legibly*
Le frère de Jeanne écrit **le moins lisiblement**.	*the least legibly*

2. The adverb **bien** has an irregular comparative form: **mieux**.[1]

Danielle chante **aussi bien que** sa sœur.	*as well as*
Elle chante **mieux que** moi.	*better than*
Mais Françoise chante **le mieux**.	*the best*

Be careful to distinguish between the adverb **mieux** (from **bien**) and the adjective **meilleur(e)(s)** (from **bon**). Both correspond to *better* or *best* in English, but **meilleur**, an adjective, must agree in gender (*m/f*) and number (*s/pl*) with the noun it modifies.

Vous avez répondu **mieux** que moi.	*You answered better than I (did).*
Vos réponses étaient **meilleures** que mes réponses.	*Your answers were better than my answers.*
Votre voiture marche **bien** ; elle marche **mieux** que ma voiture. Mais c'est la voiture de Paul qui marche **le mieux**.	*Your car runs well; it runs better than my car. But it's Paul's car that runs the best.*
Votre idée est **bonne** ; elle est **meilleure** que mon idée. Mais c'est l'idée de Paul qui est **la meilleure**.	*Your idea is good; it is better than my idea. But it's Paul's idea that is the best.*

Ariane patine **mal**.

Henri patine **mieux**. Caroline patine **le mieux**.

TABLEAU 92

Pierre patine **aussi bien que** Caroline.

 A *Répondez aux questions d'après ce modèle.*

(Jeanne), vous êtes l'étudiante la plus patiente. Comment travaillez-vous ?
Je travaille le plus patiemment.

1. Vous êtes l'étudiant le plus sérieux. Comment travaillez-vous ?
2. Vous êtes l'étudiante la plus diligente. Comment travaillez-vous ?
3. Vous êtes l'étudiant le plus discret. Comment parlez-vous ?
4. Vous êtes l'étudiante la plus élégante. Comment vous habillez-vous ?
5. Vous êtes les étudiants les plus énergiques. Comment travaillez-vous ?
6. Vous êtes les meilleurs étudiants. Comment travaillez-vous ?

[1]The adverb **mal** also has an irregular form: **pis** /pi/. It is rarely used in colloquial French, and is usually replaced by **plus mal** and **le plus mal**, except in idiomatic expressions such as **Tant pis !** *So much the worse!, Too bad!.*

B   *Répondez aux questions.*

1. (Daniel), allez au tableau et écrivez le mot « lisiblement ». (Anne), faites la même chose. Est-ce que j'écris assez lisiblement ? Qui écrit plus lisiblement que moi ? Qui écrit moins lisiblement que moi ? Alors, qui écrit le plus lisiblement ?[1]

2. Est-ce que je parle trop vite ? Qui parle plus vite que moi ? Et qui parle moins vite que moi ? Alors, qui parle le plus vite ?

3. Qui sait patiner ? Est-ce que vous patinez aussi bien que Scott Hamilton ? Qui patine mieux que lui ? Qui patine le mieux ?

4. Qui fait du tennis ? Est-ce que vous jouez aussi bien que Chris Evert ? Qui joue mieux qu'elle ? Qui joue le mieux ?

5. Moi, je me lève à (sept) heures. Qui se lève plus tôt que moi ? À quelle heure vous couchez-vous ? Qui se couche plus tard que (Jeanne) ?

6. Dans une grande ville, quel est le moyen de transport[2] pour se déplacer le plus rapidement : le taxi, l'autobus ou le métro ? Comparez ces trois moyens de transport en employant le verbe « se déplacer ».[3]

📼   *Exercice supplémentaire*

📼   *Compréhension auditive*

17.3   LE MODE CONDITIONNEL : PRÉSENT

1. The conditional mood has two tenses, the present and the past.[4] The conjugation of the present tense is a "combination" of the future and the imperfect tenses: you take the *future stem* of a verb (Lesson 15.2 and 15.4) and attach to it the *imperfect endings* (Lesson 10.1). Compare the various endings of the verbs **parler**, **finir**, and **vendre** in the following examples.[5]

FUTURE INDICATIVE	IMPERFECT INDICATIVE	PRESENT CONDITIONAL
je **parlerai**	je **parlais**	je **parlerais**
tu **parleras**	tu **parlais**	tu **parlerais**
elle **parlera**	elle **parlait**	elle **parlerait**
nous **parlerons**	nous **parlions**	nous **parlerions**
vous **parlerez**	vous **parliez**	vous **parleriez**
elles **parleront**	elles **parlaient**	elles **parleraient**
je **finirai**	je **finissais**	je **finirais**
tu **finiras**	tu **finissais**	tu **finirais**
il **finira**	il **finissait**	il **finirait**
nous **finirons**	nous **finissions**	nous **finirions**
vous **finirez**	vous **finissiez**	vous **finiriez**
ils **finiront**	ils **finissaient**	ils **finiraient**
je **vendrai**	je **vendais**	je **vendrais**
tu **vendras**	tu **vendais**	tu **vendrais**
elle **vendra**	elle **vendait**	elle **vendrait**
nous **vendrons**	nous **vendions**	nous **vendrions**
vous **vendrez**	vous **vendiez**	vous **vendriez**
elles **vendront**	elles **vendaient**	elles **vendraient**

2. *The stem.* As has just been mentioned, the stem of the present conditional is *identical* with that of the future tense. Any verb whose future stem is irregular will also have the same irregular stem in the conditional. (Because only the **conduire** and **construire** type of irregular verb has been presented since the future tense

---

[1]Utilisez la construction **C'est ... qui**.

[2]*means of transportation*

[3]Par exemple : **On se déplace moins rapidement en autobus qu'en métro.**

[4]The past conditional will be presented in Lesson 24.2.

[5]The future ending **-ai** is pronounced /e/, while the imperfect/conditional ending **-ais** is pronounced /ɛ/.

was introduced, you should review Lesson 15.2 and 15.4 for other irregular stems.) Here are a few examples.

INFINITIVE	CONDITIONAL	INFINITIVE	CONDITIONAL
essayer	on **essaierait**	**acheter**	on **achèterait**
nettoyer	on **nettoierait**	**appeler**	on **appellerait**

IRREGULAR VERBS WITH A "REGULAR" FUTURE/CONDITIONAL STEM

boire	je **boirais**	**ouvrir**	j'**ouvrirais**
dire	je **dirais**	**conduire**	je **conduirais**

VERBS WITH AN IRREGULAR FUTURE/CONDITIONAL STEM

avoir	vous **auriez**	**recevoir**	vous **recevriez**
être	vous **seriez**	**savoir**	vous **sauriez**
aller	vous **iriez**	**venir**	vous **viendriez**
devoir	vous **devriez**	**voir**	vous **verriez**
envoyer	nous **enverrions**	**vouloir**	nous **voudrions**
faire	nous **ferions**	**pleuvoir**	il **pleuvrait**
pouvoir	nous **pourrions**		

3. The present conditional often corresponds to English *would* + verb, and has three main uses: (*a*) the "polite" use; (*b*) the so-called "future in the past" statements; and (*c*) in "contrary-to-fact" statements. In all of these, the conditional corresponds fairly closely to the English construction just mentioned.

a) *The "polite" use.* It is often used instead of the present indicative to "soften" the meaning of a verb. It is very prevalent with verbs such as **aimer**, **vouloir**, **pouvoir**, and **devoir**, followed by an infinitive.

Je **veux** prendre l'autobus.	*I want to take the bus.*
Je **voudrais** prendre l'autobus.	*I would like to take the bus.*
J'**aimerais** prendre l'autobus.	*I would like to take the bus.*
Pouvez-vous nous aider ?	*Can you help us?*
Pourriez-vous nous aider ?	*Could you help us?*

Note the various degrees of politeness in making requests (English has parallel structures).

Indiquez-moi le chemin !	*Show me the way!*
Indiquez-moi le chemin, **s'il vous plaît**.	*Please show me the way.*
Pouvez-vous m'indiquer le chemin ?	*Can you show me the way?*
Pourriez-vous m'indiquer le chemin ?	*Could you show me the way?*
Pourriez-vous m'indiquer le chemin, **s'il vous plaît** ?	*Could you please show me the way?*

Note below that the English equivalent of **devoir** in the conditional is *should* or *ought to* ("softer" in nuance than *must, have to*).

Je **dois** partir maintenant.	*I must (have to) leave now.*
Je **devrais** partir maintenant.	*I should (ought to) leave now.*
Ne **devriez**-vous pas partir maintenant ?	*Shouldn't you leave now?*

b) *"Future in the past."* The future indicative tense in the dependent clause, often introduced by the conjunction **que** *that*, is replaced by the present conditional when the verb in the main clause is in the past (i.e., in the imperfect or *passé composé*).

Je **sais** qu'il **pleuvra**.	*I know it will rain.*
→ Je **savais** qu'il **pleuvrait**.	→ *I knew it would rain.*

Elle **dit** qu'elle **viendra**.	*She says she will come.*
→ Elle **a dit** qu'elle **viendrait**.	→ *She said she would come.*
Espères-tu qu'il **partira** ?	*Are you hoping that he will leave?*
→ **Espérais**-tu qu'il **partirait** ?	→ *Were you hoping that he would leave?*

c) "Contrary-to-fact" statements. In English, a clause introduced by *if* implies either a "real" (potential) supposition or an "unreal" (contrary-to-fact) supposition.[1]

If I am busy, I won't come.   (real, potential—it may happen)
If I were a bird, I would fly.   (unreal, contrary to fact—it wouldn't happen since no one can be a bird)

A similar distinction exists in French. The tenses used for real suppositions are the *present* in the **si** clause and the *future* in the "result" (main) clause. (This construction was presented in Lesson 15.4, p. 330.) Note that the **si** clause may come before or after the "result" clause, as in English.

S'il **pleut**, je ne **sortirai** pas.	*If it rains, I won't go out.*
S'il **est** occupé, il ne **viendra** pas.	*If he is busy, he won't come.*
Que **ferez**-vous **si** elle **est** fâchée ?	*What will you do if she is angry?*
Je **serai** triste **si** tu **pars**.	*I will be sad if you leave.*

The tenses used for unreal or contrary-to-fact suppositions are the *imperfect* in the **si** clause and the *present conditional* in the "result" (main) clause. Compare the verb tenses in the sentences below with those in the examples given above.

S'il **pleuvait**, je ne **sortirais** pas.	*If it were raining, I would not go out.*
S'il **était** occupé, il ne **viendrait** pas.	*If he were busy, he wouldn't come.*
Que **feriez**-vous **si** elle **était** fâchée ?	*What would you do if she were angry?*
Je **serais** triste **si** tu **partais**.	*I would be sad if you left.*

SITUATION	*SI* CLAUSE	"RESULT" (MAIN) CLAUSE
real, possible	present indicative	future
contrary to fact	imperfect	present conditional

TABLEAU 93   Qu'est-ce qu'ils **feraient** s'ils **avaient** assez d'argent ?

---

[1]Some English speakers use *will* and *would* even in the if clause: *If you will do this,* . . . or *If he would go there,* . . . . For such people the neat parallel between the English and French tenses discussed here will not work.

A *Exercice de contrôle*

Pourrais-tu aider cet enfant ?
1. nous   2. on   3. vous   4. elle

Je ne savais pas que je serais en retard.
1. Vous   2. On   3. Nous   4. Tu

Je prendrais le métro si j'étais pressé(e).
1. Nous   2. On   3. Vous   4. Les étudiants

B *Modifiez les phrases suivantes en employant le conditionnel d'après ce modèle.*

Voulez-vous faire une promenade ?
Voudriez-vous faire une promenade ?

1. Pouvez-vous m'aider ?
2. Je veux boire quelque chose.
3. Je peux répéter la question.
4. J'aime aller en France.
5. Nous voulons vous aider.
6. Ne devez-vous pas travailler ?
7. Nous devons visiter le Louvre.
8. Vous devez vous reposer.

C *Modifiez les phrases suivantes d'après ces modèles.*

« On parlera français », c'est ce que[1] vous avez dit.
Vous avez dit qu'on parlerait français.
« Nous verrons des diapos de Paris », c'est ce que j'espérais.
J'espérais que nous verrions des diapos de Paris.

1. « Il n'y aura pas d'examens », c'est ce que vous avez dit.
2. « Le cours sera facile », c'est ce que je pensais.
3. « Nous apprendrons beaucoup de choses », c'est ce que vous avez promis.[2]
4. « Les examens seront faciles », c'est ce que vous avez annoncé.
5. « J'aurai de bonnes notes », c'est ce que j'espérais.
6. « On fera beaucoup de progrès[3] », c'est ce que j'ai dit.
7. « Il y aura de bons étudiants », c'est ce que vous pensiez.
8. « Le cours ne sera pas difficile », c'est ce qu'on espérait.

D *Ajoutez des phrases d'après ce modèle.*

S'il fait beau, on fera une promenade.
S'il faisait beau, on ferait une promenade.

1. S'il ne fait pas mauvais, on fera une promenade.
2. Si vous êtes malade, vous ne serez pas en classe.
3. Si je n'apprends pas le français, je ne serai pas ici.
4. Si nous avons faim, nous mangerons quelque chose.
5. Je mets un pull s'il fait froid.
6. Vous achèterez un château si vous êtes millionnaire.
7. On fera une promenade s'il ne pleut pas.
8. On ira au cinéma si on est libre.

E *Complétez les phrases suivantes avec votre partenaire.*

1. Si nous étions malades,...
2. Nous irions au cinéma si...
3. Le professeur nous a dit que...
4. Nous voudrions...
5. Si nous avons le temps demain,...

[1]**ce que** *that which, what* (Leçon 18.5)
[2]participe passé du verbe **promettre** *to promise*
[3]**faire des progrès** *to make progress*

Exercice supplémentaire

Compréhension auditive

17.4 EXPRESSIONS IMPERSONNELLES

1. To make generalizations, you can begin with an infinitive clause as the subject of your sentence. In this construction, the pronoun **ce** is used to sum up the infinitive clause before the verb **être**.

Se promener ici, **c**'est agréable.	*To take a walk here is pleasant.*
Prendre le métro, **c**'était facile.	*To take the subway was easy.*
Arriver à l'heure, **ce** sera important.	*To arrive on time will be important.*
Dire la vérité, **ce** serait pénible.	*To tell the truth would be painful.*

2. A more common way to make generalizations is to begin a sentence with **il est** + adjective,[1] followed by **de** + infinitive. It corresponds to English *it is* + adjective + *to do (something)*. This construction is called *impersonal* because **il** does not denote a person.

Il est agréable de se promener ici.	*It is pleasant to take a walk here.*
Il était facile de prendre le métro.	*It was easy to take the subway.*
Il sera important d'arriver à l'heure.	*It will be important to arrive on time.*
Il serait pénible de dire la vérité.	*It would be painful to tell the truth.*

3. A short statement with **ce** + adjective can sum up a previous statement, including **de** + infinitive of an impersonal construction.

Ils ont passé toute la journée[2] au musée.
— Mais **ce** n'est pas possible !
Est-il nécessaire **de prendre l'autobus** ?
— Non, **ce** n'est pas nécessaire.
Il est agréable **de boire quelque chose de rafraîchissant**.
— Oui, **c**'est toujours agréable.

TABLEAU 94

[1]In colloquial French, **il est** and **c'est** are used interchangeably in this construction: **Il est/C'est important de finir ce travail.**

[2]*all day*

A *Modifiez les phrases suivantes d'après ce modèle.*

Apprendre le français, c'est utile.
Il est utile d'apprendre le français.

1. Parler français, c'est assez facile.
2. Comprendre le français, ce n'est pas facile.
3. Préparer un examen[1], c'est pénible.
4. Passer un examen[2], c'est désagréable.
5. Parler anglais en classe, c'est défendu[3].
6. Dormir en classe, c'est interdit[3].
7. Répondre aux questions, c'est simple.
8. Quitter la classe, ce sera triste.

TABLEAU 95

B *Voici quelques panneaux. On les voit souvent quand on se promène dans la rue. Qu'est-ce qu'ils signifient ? Utilisez* **il est interdit de** *ou* **il est défendu de** *dans votre explication.*[4]

C *Maintenant, faites des phrases avec votre partenaire.*

1. Il était pénible de...
2. Il est important de...
3. Il n'est pas bon de...
4. Il sera agréable de...
5. Il serait très désagréable de...
6. Il serait dangereux de...

Compréhension auditive

17.5 QU'EST-CE QUE C'EST QUE... ?

1. **Qu'est-ce que c'est que... ?** *What is/are . . . ?* is used when asking for a definition or a description. It is used with both singular and plural nouns. The answer usually begins with **C'est** or **Ce sont** and often contains a relative pronoun.

Qu'est-ce que c'est qu'une horloge ?[5]
— **C'est** un instrument qui indique l'heure.

Qu'est-ce que c'est que des hors-d'œuvre ?
— **Ce sont** des plats qu'on sert au début d'un repas.

[1]**préparer un examen**   *to prepare for a test*

[2]**passer un examen**   *to take a test*

[3]**défendu, interdit**   *forbidden*

[4]Panneau 8 : **Défense de tourner à droite** ; panneau 9 : **Stationnement interdit**

[5]Une **horloge** est un instrument qui indique l'heure (terme général) ; une **pendule** est une petite horloge.

2. In a dependent clause, **Qu'est-ce que c'est que... ?** becomes **ce que c'est que...** *what . . . is/are* or **ce que c'est** *what it is/they are.*

Qu'est-ce que c'est qu'un plan ?	*What is a map?*
Savez-vous ce que c'est qu'un plan ?	*Do you know what a map is?*
Dites-moi ce que c'est.	*Tell me what it is/they are.*
Je ne sais pas ce que c'est.	*I don't know what it is/they are.*

 A *Je vais vous donner quelques définitions. Écoutez bien et posez-moi une question d'après ce modèle.*

C'est un employé du bureau de poste qui distribue les lettres.
Qu'est-ce que c'est qu'un facteur ?

1. C'est un petit instrument qui indique l'heure.
2. C'est une personne qui sert des boissons dans un café.
3. Ce sont des personnes qui vendent des légumes et des fruits.
4. C'est un magasin où on peut acheter du veau et du bœuf.
5. C'est un magasin où on vend toutes sortes de choses[1].
6. Ce sont des plats qu'on sert au début d'un repas.
7. C'est quelqu'un qui ne peut pas voir.   (aveugle)
8. C'est quelqu'un qui ne peut pas entendre.   (sourd)
9. C'est l'endroit où on prépare les repas.
10. C'est l'endroit où on prend un bain.

B *Maintenant, donnez la définition de ces mots.*

1. Qu'est-ce que c'est qu'une serveuse ?
2. Qu'est-ce que c'est qu'un restaurant ?
3. Qu'est-ce que c'est qu'une pendule ?
4. Qu'est-ce que c'est qu'un professeur de français ?
5. Qu'est-ce que c'est qu'un bon étudiant ?
6. Dites-moi ce que c'est qu'une librairie.
7. Dites-moi ce que c'est qu'une boulangerie.
8. Dites à (Thierry) ce que c'est qu'un hôtel.

Compréhension auditive

APPLICATIONS

A **Situations**[2]

Les mésaventures de Julien

rush hour

Julien va chez M. et Mme Moreau. Il donne des leçons particulières° d'anglais à leur fille Sophie, qui a dix ans. Aujourd'hui, la leçon commence à six heures. Malheureusement, c'est le début des heures de pointe°, et le métro est absolument bondé. Il veut descendre à la prochaine station pour changer de ligne.

Let me through

JULIEN Pardon, s'il vous plaît. Pardon, Madame. Laissez-moi passer°, s'il vous   5
plaît.

Ouch! UNE VIEILLE DAME Aïe !° Vous m'avez marché sur le pied !

on purpose JULIEN Je suis désolé, Madame. Je ne l'ai pas fait exprès°.

[1]*all kinds of things*
[2]*Les réponses aux questions ne sont pas enregistrées sur la bande magnétique.*

C'est le début des heures de pointe.

LA VIEILLE DAME   Ce n'est pas grave.

Il essaie d'atteindre la portière.   10

UN MONSIEUR   Ne me bousculez pas, jeune homme.

à la prochaine station   JULIEN   Excusez-moi. Vous descendez à la prochaine° ?

LE MONSIEUR   Non.

JULIEN   Alors, laissez-moi passer, s'il vous plaît.

LE MONSIEUR   D'accord, d'accord ! Voilà.   15

laisser tomber   *to drop*   *Julien se heurte à une jeune fille qui porte un tas de¹ livres. Elle laisse tomber° tous ses livres.*

livres (en langage familier)   LA JEUNE FILLE   Attention ! Mes bouquins° !

JULIEN   Ah, je suis vraiment navré.

LA JEUNE FILLE   Ça ne fait rien. Ce n'est pas grave. Pouvez-vous m'aider ?

JULIEN   Bien sûr... (*Il aide la jeune fille à ramasser ses livres.*) Voilà.   20

Pauvre Julien ! Il a manqué sa station et il arrive finalement chez les Moreau, en retard de vingt minutes.

JULIEN   Bonsoir, Madame. Je suis désolé d'arriver en retard.

MME MOREAU   Ne vous inquiétez pas. Entrez.

JULIEN   Merci. Le métro était absolument bondé et j'ai manqué ma station.   25

MME MOREAU   Oh ! quel dommage ! Passez au salon. Sophie vous attend.

Julien va tout de suite dans le salon, où Sophie l'attend.

JULIEN   Bonsoir, Sophie. Je m'excuse d'arriver en retard.

SOPHIE   Ça ne fait rien.

where are we   JULIEN   (*Il ouvre son livre.*) Alors, où en sommes-nous° ?   30

SOPHIE   À la page 130. Mais je voudrais faire une révision du conditionnel d'abord.

JULIEN   Bon, d'accord.

De combien de façons² peut-on dire les phrases suivantes en français ?

1. I am (very) sorry/Excuse me.
2. It's OK/Don't worry.

---

¹beaucoup de (**un tas**   littéralement, *a pile*)
²*In how many ways*

Qu'est-ce que vous diriez dans les situations suivantes ?

1. Il est 19 h et vous êtes dans le métro. Vous êtes coincé(e) à l'arrière de[1] la voiture et vous devez descendre à la prochaine station. Qu'est-ce que vous dites ?
2. Même situation que ci-dessus.[2] Vous avez laissé tomber un gros paquet sur le pied d'un vieux monsieur. Il est en colère[3].
3. Vous arrivez en retard chez les parents de votre fiancé(e). Vous n'avez pas pu trouver de taxi.
4. Vous rencontrez un copain. Il a l'air ennuyé. Il vous dit qu'il a perdu[4] la clé de sa voiture.
5. Vous prenez le thé chez M. et Mme Moreau. Vous avez renversé votre tasse de thé sur le tapis du salon.
6. Votre copain a l'air bouleversé. Il vient de recevoir un coup de téléphone[5]. Son oncle préféré est mort subitement d'une crise cardiaque. Il avait seulement quarante-deux ans.
7. Vous êtes pressé(e). Vous marchez rapidement et vous bousculez un enfant, qui laisse tomber ses jouets par terre[6].

B Expressions utiles

Une station de métro

Avant de monter dans le train

consulter } { un plan }
regarder } { une carte } du métro ; utiliser SITU[7]

acheter { un ticket[8] } de { première (classe) } au guichet
{ un carnet (de tickets) } { deuxième (classe) }

passer le péage / le composteur automatique[9]

Dans le train

aller } en { première }
voyager } { deuxième } (classe)

prendre { la direction } Nation
{ la ligne }

arriver { sur le quai
{ au terminus
{ à la station (de correspondance)

prendre une correspondance }
changer (de train / de ligne) } à la Madeleine
sortir de la bouche[10] de métro }

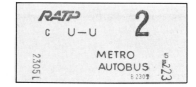

[1]**à l'arrière de** *in the back of*

[2]*Same situation as above.*

[3]**être en colère** *to be angry*

[4]participe passé du verbe **perdre** *to lose*

[5]**un coup de téléphone** *a phone call*

[6]**par terre** *on the ground*

[7]**SITU** calcule la meilleure façon de se déplacer et propose quatre choix : trajet en autobus, en métro et R.E.R., trajet le plus rapide par combinaison des modes, et trajet qui minimise la marche à pied (voir les photos à la page 382).

[8]En général, on dit **un ticket de métro**, **d'autobus**, **de cinéma**, **de musée**, **de vestiaire** (*cloakroom*), mais **un billet** /bijɛ/ **d'avion**, **de train**.

[9]**péage** literally, *toll*; **le composteur automatique** in the **métro** is an electromagnetic device that validates the ticket and opens the gate for the passenger.

[10]**bouche** *entrance in the street*

Un arrêt d'autobus

chercher ⎫
prendre ⎭ la ligne 14[1]

composter le ticket[2] (mettre le ticket dans le composteur)

utiliser   ⎫ ⎧ un ticket pour chaque section[3]
composter ⎭ ⎩ deux tickets pour le trajet

L'autobus est ⎧ (à moitié) vide.
              ⎨ (absolument) bondé.
              ⎩ complet[4].

Le réseau d'autobus est très dense.

C   **Pratique**

1. Où peut-on acheter des tickets de métro ? Est-ce qu'on les achète avant d'aller sur le quai ?
2. Qu'est-ce que c'est qu'un composteur ?
3. Comment s'appelle la plate-forme d'où on monte dans le train ?
4. Qu'est-ce qu'on fait à une station de correspondance ?
5. Que veut dire le mot « terminus » ?
6. Pourquoi l'autobus peut-il coûter plus cher que le métro ?[5]
7. Mettez les phrases suivantes dans l'ordre logique.

   a) composter le ticket
   b) acheter un ticket
   c) arriver sur le quai
   d) chercher une bouche de métro
   e) sortir de la station
   f) descendre du train pour faire la correspondance[6]

   g) chercher la sortie
   h) attendre le train
   i) descendre du train
   j) monter dans un autre train
   k) descendre à la station
   l) chercher une place libre[7]

[1]Toutes les lignes d'autobus à Paris sont numérotées.

[2]**composter** *to punch (a ticket)* ; les voyageurs doivent mettre leurs tickets dans le composteur pour les valider quand ils montent dans l'autobus.

[3]La plupart des lignes sont divisées en deux ou trois sections, selon la distance ou la longueur du trajet.

[4]*full* (il n'y a plus de places)

[5]Voir le deuxième paragraphe de la *Lecture* de cette leçon.

[6]**faire la correspondance** = changer de ligne

[7]*an unoccupied (free) seat*

```
SITU
---------------------------------
RATP / 2EME VOITURE


       LUNDI 27 JUIN 1988 12H13

    VOUS ETES 29 RUE DE RIVOLI
    VOUS ALLEZ 21 RUE DES MOINES
    ATTENTION, VOUS AVEZ ECRIT :
               21-DES-MOINES
    VOTRE CHOIX POUR ALLER LE PLUS
                 VITE POSSIBLE

     PRENEZ LE METRO LIGNE 1
     DIRECTION PT DE NEUILLY
              A HOTEL DE VILLE
       JUSQU'A CHAMPS ELYSEES
               CLEMENCEAU
    PUIS
      PRENEZ LE METRO LIGNE 13
      DIRECTION ASNIERES GENNEVILLIERS
        JUSQU'A BROCHANT

    VOUS METTREZ ENVIRON UNE DEMI-
    HEURE.
```

```
SITU
---------------------------------
RATP / 2EME VOITURE


      MERCREDI 29 JUIN 1988 11H59

    VOUS ETES 3 BOULEVARD SAINT
              MICHEL
    VOUS ALLEZ 100 BOULEVARD DE
               ROCHECHOUART
    VOTRE CHOIX POUR MARCHER LE MOINS
                 POSSIBLE

     PRENEZ LE METRO LIGNE 4
     DIRECTION PTE DE CLIGNANCOURT
              A ST MICHEL
       JUSQU'A BARBES ROCHECHOUART
    PUIS
      PRENEZ LE BUS LIGNE 30
      DIRECTION TROCADERO
        A BARBES-ROCHECHOUART
          (6 BD DE ROCHECHOUART)
        JUSQU'A ROCHECHOUART-MARTYRS

    VOUS METTREZ 20-25 MINUTES.
```

8. Vous allez de l'Opéra à la Place Charles de Gaulle-Étoile avec Soledad, qui vient d'arriver du Panama. Vous lui expliquez ce qu'on fait à chaque étape de votre trajet. (Consultez le Tableau 91, à la page 366.)

D **Mini-composition :** *C'est une étudiante américaine qui parle d'une soirée qu'elle a passée avec sa cousine. Complétez le passage.*

(1) Je/rentrer/hier/vers/4 h/et/je/trouver/un/message/téléphonique. (2) Ce/être/de/un/de/mon/cousines ; /elle / aller/passer/nuit / à/Paris / et / elle/vouloir/voir/me. (3) Je/téléphoner/lui/et/elle/dire/me/que/son/hôtel/ne pas/être/loin/de/le/gare Saint-Lazare. (4) Ce/être/heures de pointe,/et/je/se dire[1] : (5) « Si/je/ne pas/prendre/métro,/je/ne jamais/pouvoir/se déplacer[2]/rapidement ». (6) Alors,/je/consulter/plan/métro/et/je/sortir. (7) En route[3],/je/devoir/changer/de/ligne/2 fois. (8) Je/descendre/à/gare Saint-Lazare. (9) Puisque/je/ne pas/connaître/ce/quartier,/je/demander/chemin/à/un/passante. (10) Elle/parler/avec/un/accent/étranger/et/je/ne pas/comprendre/la/très/bien. (11) Puis/un/autre/dame/dire/me/que/elle/aller/de ce côté[4]/et/demander/me/si/je/vouloir/suivre[5]/la. (12) Mon/cousine/attendre/me/quand/je/arriver/à/hôtel. (13) Elle/inviter/me/à/dîner/dans/restaurant. (14) Il/être/agréable/revoir/la/et/sortir[6]/avec/elle.

E **Questions :** *Deux touristes parlent de leur après-midi à Paris. D'abord lisez le paragraphe, ensuite posez des questions sur les parties soulignées.*

Après le déjeuner, (1) <u>ma mère et moi</u>, nous sommes allées à l'Arc de Triomphe. (2) <u>Douze</u> grandes avenues partent de la Place Charles de Gaulle, avec l'Arc de Triomphe au milieu. (3)

[1] *to say to oneself*
[2] *move (around)*
[3] *On the way*
[4] *in that direction*
[5] *to follow*
[6] *Répétez la préposition* **de**.

« Si j'arrive en retard, maman sera en colère. »

Puisqu'il y avait une longue queue devant l'ascenseur, nous avons décidé de prendre l'escalier. Quelle montée ! Nous étions complètement (4) hors d'haleine[1] quand nous sommes enfin arrivées sur la plate-forme. (5) De la plate-forme[2], la vue était vraiment magnifique, surtout sur les Champs-Élysées. Nous avons pris (6) le métro pour aller de l'Arc de Triomphe au Trocadéro — on se déplace (7) moins vite en autobus qu'en métro. (8) La queue devant l'ascenseur n'était pas très longue. Nous sommes montées (9) jusqu'en haut de la Tour[3]. Le panorama sur Paris, vu du haut de la Tour, était splendide. (10) Grâce au[4] plan de « Paris-Monuments »[5], nous avons pu identifier pas mal de monuments.

F *Cause et effet. Lisez les phrases suivantes et corrigez les phrases qui ne vous semblent pas logiques.*

1. Si j'avais froid, je mettrais un pull.
2. Si je mangeais quelque chose, j'aurais faim.
3. Je ferais une promenade s'il faisait beau.
4. J'aurais soif si je buvais un verre d'eau fraîche.
5. Je viendrais au cours si j'étais malade.
6. Si je prenais le métro, je me déplacerais plus rapidement.
7. Je ne saurais pas conduire si je n'achetais pas cette voiture.
8. Je ne serais pas dans ce cours si j'apprenais le français.

G Renseignements et opinions

1. Avez-vous jamais pris le métro dans une grande ville ? Dans quelle ville ? Dans quelle ville des États-Unis y a-t-il un métro ? Pourquoi a-t-on besoin d'un métro ?
2. Quelle ville connaissez-vous mieux que moi ? Quel(s) pays est-ce que je connais mieux que vous ?

[1]*out of breath*
[2]Employez **D'où** dans votre question.
[3]Employez **Jusqu'où**.
[4]*Thanks to* ; employez **Comment**, **Pourquoi**, ou **Grâce à quoi**.
[5]a map of Paris showing a bird's-eye view of monuments

3. Qu'est-ce que vous faites fréquemment ? Et qu'est-ce que vous faites rarement ? Pourquoi ?
4. Que feriez-vous si vous gagniez deux mille dollars à la loterie ? Et si vous gagniez cinquante mille dollars ?
5. Qu'est-ce qu'il est important de faire chaque matin ? Qu'est-ce qu'il n'est pas nécessaire de faire tous les jours ?
6. Préparez une question à poser à votre professeur au sujet du métro de Paris.

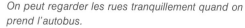 *Compréhension auditive* (*basée sur l'Application A*)

Compréhension auditive (*basée sur les Applications B et C*)

Dictée (*noms de quelques stations de métro*)

On peut regarder les rues tranquillement quand on prend l'autobus.

Paris est la ville des embouteillages.

H   Lecture

se déplacer

Comment circuler° dans Paris[1] ?

Le métro est le moyen le plus économique et le plus rapide de se déplacer dans Paris. Il est à tarif unique°, c'est-à-dire qu'avec un seul billet vous pouvez aller n'importe où[2] dans Paris et prendre n'importe quelle correspondance[3]. Le métro a pourtant deux gros inconvénients° : aux heures de pointe[4] il est absolument bondé, et les voyageurs sont serrés comme des sardines ; de plus°, l'accès aux trains par les couloirs souterrains est parfois long et fatigant, même si beaucoup de stations sont équipées d'escaliers roulants°, de tapis roulants° et d'ascenseurs.

single fare (**tarif** *fare, rate*)
le contraire de « avantages »
moreover
escalators / moving ramps

[1]**Dans** est utilisé spécifiquement quand on parle de l'intérieur d'une ville (voir la note 2 à la page 259).
[2]*anywhere* (littéralement, *no matter where*)
[3]*any connection* (littéralement, *no matter what connection*)
[4]*rush hour* (entre 7 et 8 heures du matin et 5 et 8 heures du soir)

traveled Le réseau d'autobus est très dense. Mais, bien sûr, ce moyen de transport est beaucoup moins rapide, car Paris est la ville des embouteillages. De plus, l'autobus est plus cher, car le prix des tickets varie selon la distance parcourue°. Si vous êtes pressé(e), ou si vous 10 connaissez mal la ville, vous pouvez prendre un taxi. Les taxis sont à tarif assez raisonnable et ils se déplacent un peu plus rapidement que les autobus. Les chauffeurs sont généralement bavards et font souvent des commentaires sur la politique ou les événements du jour si vous engagez la conversation.

masterpiece Le plan de Paris rend la circulation difficile. Un chef-d'œuvre° d'architecture comme la Place 15 Charles de Gaulle devient, aux heures de pointe, un véritable cauchemar pour les automobilistes. Douze grandes avenues y débouchent, et les voitures y entrent constamment. Si vous

tourner en rond *to go around and around* êtes trop timide, vous tournerez en rond° pendant dix ou quinze minutes sans pouvoir en sortir ! De plus, il n'y a pas assez de ponts pour faciliter la circulation Nord-Sud. Malgré les

wide larges° boulevards et la voie express le long de la Seine[1], tous les soirs vers six heures, plus 20

*traffic lights (s **feu**)* de 100.000 voitures sont immobilisées dans le centre de Paris par plus de 800 feux°. Même

expressway le Périphérique, grande autoroute° moderne qui encercle la ville, n'est plus suffisant. Il est complètement saturé aux heures de pointe et vous verrez des embouteillages monstrueux, surtout à chaque entrée et à chaque sortie. Paris n'a pas été construit pour l'automobile, et

what, that which c'est justement ce qui° fait son charme. Mais aujourd'hui l'automobile envahit tout. Le charme 25 de Paris pourra-t-il résister longtemps ?

A *Indiquez si chaque commentaire est vrai ou faux. S'il est faux, corrigez le commentaire.*

1. Le prix des tickets de métro varie selon la distance parcourue.
2. Le métro est absolument bondé aux heures de pointe.
3. Dans certaines stations, les couloirs qui donnent accès aux trains sont très longs.
4. On peut se déplacer plus rapidement en taxi qu'en autobus.
5. L'autobus est à tarif unique et coûte moins cher que le métro.
6. La Place de la Concorde devient un cauchemar pour les automobilistes timides.
7. Il n'y a pas assez de ponts sur la Seine pour traverser Paris d'est en ouest.
8. La circulation est presque immobilisée à la plupart des entrées et des sorties du Périphérique.

B *Trouvez dans le texte les mots qui sont définis ci-dessous.*

1. aller d'un endroit à l'autre
2. qui est sous terre
3. changer de ligne (de métro)
4. remarquable œuvre d'art
5. personne qui conduit une voiture
6. très mauvais rêve
7. situation où la circulation est presque immobilisée
8. contraire de « avantage »
9. heures où beaucoup de gens se déplacent
10. endroit par où on peut sortir

---

[1]Sur cette petite autoroute (*expressway*) de la rive droite on peut traverser le centre de Paris sans rencontrer de feux (*traffic lights*).

VOCABULAIRE

Noms

l'arrière *m*	back, rear	un **instrument**	instrument	le **plat**	dish
un **aveugle**	blind man	le jouet	toy	la portière	door
le bouquin *fam*	book	la **joueuse**	player	le **progrès**	progress
la colère	anger	la **librairie**	bookstore	la **promenade**	walk
le conditionnel	conditional	la ligne	line	la révision	review
la **correspondance**	change; transfer	le marchand (de	(vegetable)	le salon	sitting room
la crise cardiaque	heart attack	primeurs)	merchant	le **sourd**	deaf man
la **direction**	direction	le mariage	marriage	la station	subway station
l'**écriture** *f*	writing	le match	game	le tapis	rug, carpet
un **endroit**	place	la mésaventure	misadventure	le tas	pile
le **facteur**	mailman	le moyen	means	la terre	earth; ground
le fiancé	fiancé	le **moyen de transport**	means of trans-	le **transport**	transportation
l'**herbe** *f*	grass		portation		
les heures de pointe *f*	rush hour	l'**Opéra** *m*	Opera		

Verbes

afficher	to post, display	**distribuer**	to distribute	**marquer**	to mark
annoncer	to announce	s'excuser	to apologize	**patiner**	to skate
bousculer	to bump	se heurter à	to bump into	perdre	to lose
changer (de)	to change	s'inquiéter	to worry; to be concerned	**promettre** *irrég*	to promise
comparer	to compare	laisser tomber	to drop	ramasser	to pick up
se **cracher**	to spit	manquer	to miss	renverser	to spill
déplacer	to move; to travel	marcher sur	to step on	**stationner**	to park

Adjectifs

absolu(e)	absolute	**diligent(e)**	diligent	navré(e)	very sorry
affirmatif(ive)	affirmative	ennuyé(e)	bothered, upset; annoyed	**négatif(ive)**	negative
bouleversé(e)	very upset	**franc (franche)**	frank	particulier(ière)	private
bref (brève)	brief	**fréquent(e)**	frequent	**pénible**	painful; difficult
coincé(e)	stuck	**frugal(e)**	frugal	**poli(e)**	polite
constant(e)	constant	**gracieux(euse)**	gracious	**proche**	near
défendu(e)	forbidden	**interdit(e)**	forbidden	**sérieux(euse)**	serious
désagréable	unpleasant	**lisible**	legible	**triste**	sad

Adverbes

absolument	absolutely	**franchement**	frankly	**mieux que**	better than
affirmativement	affirmatively	**fréquemment**	frequently	**négativement**	negatively
brièvement	briefly	**frugalement**	frugally	**patiemment**	patiently
constamment	constantly	**gracieusement**	gracefully	**poliment**	politely
diligemment	diligently	**intelligemment**	intelligently	**rapidement**	quickly
discrètement	discreetly	**lentement**	slowly	**sérieusement**	seriously
élégamment	elegantly	**lisiblement**	legibly	subitement	suddenly
énergiquement	energetically	malheureusement	unfortunately		
finalement	finally	**le mieux**	the best		

Autres expressions

à l'arrière de	in the back of	**faire une promenade**	to take a walk
atteindre *irrég*	to reach	les **Galeries Lafayette**	large department store in Paris
Ça ne fait rien.	It doesn't matter.	laissez-moi passer	let me through
ci-dessus	above	Où en sommes-nous ?	Where are we?
courir *irrég*	to run	par terre	on the ground
De combien de façons	In how many ways	**passer un examen**	to take an exam
en employant	while using	**préparer un examen**	to prepare for an exam
être en colère	to be angry	**qu'est-ce que c'est que... ?**	what is...?
faire des progrès	to make progress	un tas de	a bunch of
faire exprès	to do on purpose		

18 Allons au Louvre !

LESSON OBJECTIVES

Theme and Culture

1. Various kinds of museums and works of art
2. Well-known museums in Paris

Communication Skills

1. Giving commands or making requests using pronouns (*give it to me, please do it*)
2. Expressing ideas in complex sentences (with relative pronouns)
3. Modifying statements about the past by use of adverbials
4. Offering/Accepting services
5. Various ways of thanking for gifts and services

Structures

18.1 Relative pronoun **dont**
18.2 Relative pronouns **à qui**, **auquel**, etc.
18.3 Pronoun sequences in the imperative
18.4 Place of adverbs in compound tenses
18.5 Relative pronouns after **ce**

Il y a toujours beaucoup de monde au Louvre.

CONVERSATIONS

A. Devant une galerie d'art

MME LEROUX   Regarde, mon chéri. Voilà le tableau auquel je pensais.

M. LEROUX   Ah oui, c'est le tableau dont tu m'as parlé hier ?

MME LEROUX   N'est-ce pas qu'il est magnifique ?

M. LEROUX   Oui, mais inutile[1] d'y penser, ma chérie. Regarde le prix !

B. On vient de déménager.

L'OUVRIER   Je mets ces chaises dans le séjour ?

MME BOSQUET   Ah non, ne les y mettez pas !

L'OUVRIER   Alors, dans la salle à manger ?

MME BOSQUET   Oui, mettez-les-y, s'il vous plaît.

C. Roland a besoin de disquettes.

JACQUES   Denise t'a dit qu'elle apporterait des disquettes ?

MIREILLE   Oui, c'est ce qu'elle m'a dit.

JACQUES   Trois disquettes, c'est tout ce dont[2] tu as besoin ?

MIREILLE   Oui, je n'ai plus de disquettes, et le magasin est fermé.

DIFFÉRENCES

Les musées de Paris

The first public museum in France dates from the Revolution of 1789. Opened in the former royal palace of **le Louvre**, it displayed collections of royal and aristocratic families as well as treasures taken away from the Church. Ever since, **le musée du Louvre** has grown and become one of the best known museums in the world, now housing more than 250,000 works of art from the Orient, Middle East, Europe, and Greco-Roman antiquities. Statistics show that in France, during the period 1870–1914, museums multiplied at the rate of one every two years, and between 1918 and 1939, one *every year*. There are more than eighty museums within the city of Paris, and you will find brief descriptions of the most famous ones in the *Lecture* of this lesson. Museums charge a small entrance fee, but students and those under 18 or over 65 can usually get in for half price. Nearly all national museums are free on Sundays and consequently are very crowded that day. Most museums are closed on Tuesdays (sometimes on Monday), so make your plans accordingly.

It has been said that for every special interest there is a museum in Paris. Among the more curious ones are: **le musée de la Serrurerie** (keys and locks), **le musée du Pain**, **le musée des lunettes et des lorgnettes** (glasses and spectacles), **le musée de la Police**, **le musée de la Contrefaçon** (counterfeits, fraudulent imitations), **le musée de la Monnaie** (coins), **le musée Postal**, **le musée instrumental** (musical instruments, including those played by clockworks), and **le musée du Vin** (where you can learn how to taste good wine). Some of these museums began long ago as private collections and are housed in resplendent former mansions.

---

[1] **inutile** = il est inutile

[2] *all* (littéralement, *all that which*)

« Tiens, voici la statue dont Claude m'a parlé. » (Musée Picasso)

STRUCTURES

18.1 PRONOM RELATIF **DONT**

1. If the verb in the relative clause takes the preposition **de**, then **de** + noun becomes **dont** *of whom, of which*. **Dont**, like other relative pronouns, is placed at the beginning of the relative clause and is used for both persons and things.

   Voilà **la dame**. *Nous avons parlé de la dame*.

   → Voilà la dame **dont** nous avons parlé.
   There is the lady (whom) we spoke of.

   Le livre est sur la table. *Vous avez besoin du livre*.

   → Le livre **dont** vous avez besoin est sur la table.
   The book (which) you need (have need of) is on the table.

2. Here are some of the expressions that take **de** + noun.

avoir besoin de	*to need*
avoir peur de	*to be afraid of*
être content de	*to be satisfied with*
être mécontent de	*to be dissatisfied with*
discuter de	*to discuss*
parler de	*to speak about*

Je connais l'homme **dont tu as peur**.	*I know the man you are afraid of.*
Le musée **dont il parle** est loin.	*The museum he is talking about is far away.*
Voilà le problème **dont on a discuté**.	*There's the problem we discussed.*
C'est la voiture **dont elle n'était pas contente**.	*It's the car she was not satisfied with.*

3. **Dont** is also an equivalent of English *whose* in a relative clause, still replacing **de** + noun. Unlike English, which deletes *the* after *whose*, the definite article must be retained after **dont**.

Comment s'appelle **le pays** ? *La capitale **du pays** est Ottawa.*

→ Comment s'appelle **le pays** *dont la capitale est Ottawa* ?
   What is the name of the country whose capital is Ottawa?

L'enfant ne sera pas en classe. *La mère **de l'enfant** est malade.*

→ **L'enfant** *dont la mère est malade* ne sera pas en classe.
   The child whose mother is sick will not be in class.

TABLEAU 96   Voilà la lettre **dont** elle a besoin !   Voilà le garçon **dont** elle parle !

A *Reliez les deux phrases avec **dont** d'après ce modèle.*

Voilà le cahier. J'ai besoin de ce cahier.
Voilà le cahier dont j'ai besoin.

1. Voilà les livres. J'ai besoin de ces livres.
2. Où est le musée ? Vous avez parlé de ce musée.
3. Je vois la statue. Vos enfants ont peur de cette statue.
4. Le problème est sérieux. On a discuté de ce problème.
5. Où est le vin ? Le client était satisfait de ce vin.
6. Je parle de la visite au musée. Vous étiez content de cette visite.

B *Reliez les deux phrases avec **dont** d'après ce modèle.*

La région est magnifique. J'ai la carte[1] de cette région.
La région dont j'ai la carte est magnifique.

1. La ville est intéressante. J'ai le plan[1] de cette ville.
2. Voilà le musée. J'ai le plan[1] de ce musée.
3. J'ai visité la cathédrale. Le trésor de la cathédrale est bien connu.
4. Le pays s'appelle la Suisse. La capitale de ce pays est Berne.
5. Où sont les enfants ? Le père de ces enfants est médecin.
6. La valise est là. La clé de cette valise a été perdue.

C *Nous sommes à l'aéroport. Reliez les deux phrases en utilisant **qui**, **que** ou **dont**.[2]*

1. L'avion est arrivé. Vous attendez l'avion.
2. L'avion est français. Vous voyez l'avion.

[1]**carte** *(geographic) map*; **plan** *map*, meaning *layout* (of a building or city)
[2]La première phrase devient la proposition principale et la deuxième devient la proposition relative.

3. L'avion est en retard. Vous parlez de l'avion.
4. L'hôtesse[1] est là. Tout le monde est content de l'hôtesse.
5. L'hôtesse est occupée. Nous avons besoin de l'hôtesse.
6. L'hôtesse parle allemand. Nous cherchons l'hôtesse.
7. Le taxi n'est pas libre. On voit le taxi.
8. Le taxi est là. Je connais le chauffeur du taxi.
9. Le taxi ira à Versailles. Le taxi est là.

18.2 PRONOMS RELATIFS À QUI, AUQUEL, ETC.

1. When the noun to be replaced with a relative pronoun is preceded by a preposition other than **de**, it is necessary to distinguish between persons and things. A noun denoting human beings is replaced by preposition + **qui**

    Voilà **la dame**. *J'ai parlé à la dame hier.*

    → Voilà **la dame à qui** *j'ai parlé hier.*

    There's the lady (whom) I spoke to yesterday.

    Le jeune homme est mon cousin. *Elle a dansé avec le jeune homme.*

    → **Le jeune homme avec qui** *elle a dansé* est mon cousin.

    The young man (whom) she danced with is my cousin.

2. A noun that does not denote human beings is replaced by **lequel**, **laquelle** for singular, or **lesquels**, **lesquelles** for plural.[2]

    Où est **la lettre** ? *J'ai répondu à la lettre.*

    → Où est **la lettre à laquelle** *j'ai répondu* ?

    Where is the letter (that) I answered?

    Je te donnerai **le livre**. *Tu trouveras la réponse dans le livre.*

    → Je te donnerai **le livre dans lequel** *tu trouveras la réponse.*

    I will give you the book in which you will find the answer.

3. If the preposition is **à**, then **lequel**, **lesquels**, and **lesquelles** combine with it to form **auquel**, **auxquels**, and **auxquelles** (just as **à** + **le** or **les** becomes **au** or **aux**).

    Le musée est loin d'ici. *Vous pensez au musée.*

    → **Le musée auquel** *vous pensez* est loin d'ici.

    The museum (that) you are thinking about is far from here.

    Où sont **les lettres** ? *Je dois répondre aux lettres.*

    → Où sont **les lettres auxquelles** *je dois répondre* ?

    Where are the letters (that) I must answer?

4. Expressions of place and time are normally replaced by **où**, which corresponds to *where* as well as *when* in English.

    La ville est Paris. *On trouve beaucoup de musées dans la ville.*

    → **La ville où** *on trouve beaucoup de musées* est Paris.

    The city where one finds a lot of museums is Paris.

---

[1] ici, *flight attendant*

[2] Preposition + **lequel/laquelle/lesquels/lesquelles** can also be used for nouns denoting human beings: **Voilà le jeune homme avec lequel/avec qui elle est sortie.**

Je parle de **l'époque**. *Tout le monde était heureux à l'époque*.

→ Je parle de **l'époque où** *tout le monde était heureux*.

I'm talking about the time when everyone was happy.

5. Here is a summary of the relative pronouns you have learned.

	Sujet	Objet Direct	Après **de**	Après d'autres prépositions
Personne	qui	que	dont	préposition + **qui**
Chose				préposition + **lequel**, etc.

TABLEAU 97   Où est la lettre **à laquelle** elle pense ?   Où est le garçon **à qui** elle pense ?

A *Reliez les deux phrases en employant le pronom relatif approprié d'après ces modèles.*

Je connais l'agent. Vous avez parlé à l'agent.
Je connais l'agent à qui vous avez parlé.
Je cherche la lettre. Je dois répondre à la lettre.
Je cherche la lettre à laquelle je dois répondre.

1. J'ai le livre. Vous pensez au livre.
2. Je connais la dame. Vous avez parlé à la dame.
3. Voici la lettre. Vous pensiez à la lettre.
4. Voilà la jeune fille. Vous avez dansé avec la jeune fille.
5. La question était difficile. J'ai répondu à la question.
6. L'agent parle anglais. Vous avez répondu à l'agent.
7. Je cherche le garçon. Je comptais sur le garçon.
8. J'ai la réponse. Vous comptez sur la réponse.

B *Lisez le passage suivant et mettez le pronom relatif approprié dans chaque parenthèse.*

Regardez cette photo. C'est une photo de l'appartement (1) j'habitais[1] quand j'étais étudiant à Aix-en-Provence. Il était au quatrième étage d'un grand immeuble (2) datait du dix-huitième siècle. Le garçon (3) vous voyez près du frigo est Daniel. L'autre garçon (4) est à ma droite est Robert. Oui, ce sont les étudiants français (5) je partageais cet appartement et (6) je vous ai souvent parlé. La jeune fille (7) je parle est Martine, une cousine de Daniel. L'autre, (8) vous voyez la tête derrière moi, est Nicole, une amie de Robert. C'est une photo (9) on a prise juste avant la surprise-party (10) on a donnée et (11) a duré quatre heures. C'était une année (12) était pleine de surprises et de joies. C'était l'époque (13) j'étais très heureux et (14) je pense fréquemment.

[1]On peut dire **habiter un appartement** ou **habiter dans un appartement**.

🔲 *Exercice supplémentaire*

🔲 *Compréhension auditive*

18.3 IMPÉRATIF ET PRONOMS COMPLÉMENTS

1. Imperative sentences can be either affirmative or negative. In *negative* commands, you drop the subject pronoun (**tu**, **nous**, or **vous**) but retain the same sequence of object pronouns as in declarative sentences (summarized in Lesson 16.2). The **-s** of the **tu** form of first-conjugation verbs, as well as that of **aller**, **ouvrir**, and **offrir**, is deleted.[1]

Ne +	**me** **te** **nous** **vous**	+	**le** **la** **les**	+	**lui** **leur** **y**	+	**en**	+	verb	+	**pas**

Tu **me** montres **cette photo**.
→ Tu ne **me la** montres pas.
→ Ne **me la** montre pas !

Tu offres **des bonbons aux enfants**.
→ Tu ne **leur en** offres pas.
→ Ne **leur en** offre pas !

Nous allons **au Louvre** demain.
→ Nous n'**y** allons pas demain.
→ N'**y** allons pas demain !

Vous **vous** couchez à minuit.
→ Vous ne **vous** couchez pas à minuit.
→ Ne **vous** couchez pas à minuit !

2. Affirmative commands also drop the subject pronoun, but they differ from the negative commands in several ways: (*a*) the object pronouns come *after* the verb and are connected to it with a hyphen; (*b*) the order of the first group of pronouns (**me**, **te**, **nous**, **vous**) and the second group (**le**, **la**, **les**) is reversed; (*c*) if **me** or **te** is the last pronoun, it becomes **moi** or **toi**; (*d*) the **-s** of the **tu** form of first-conjugation verbs and that of **aller**, **ouvrir**, and **offrir** is retained if **y** or **en** comes immediately after it.[2]

Verb +	**le** **la** **les**	+	**me (moi)** **te (toi)** **nous** **vous**	+	**lui** **leur** **y**	+	**en**

Tu **me** montres **cette photo**.
→ Tu **me la** montres.
→ Montre-**la-moi** !

Vous **me** donnez **du papier**.
→ Vous **m'en** donnez.
→ Donnez-**m'en** !

Nous allons **à Marseille**.
→ Nous **y** allons.
→ Allons-**y** !

Vous **nous** posez **la question**.
→ Vous **nous la** posez.
→ Posez-**la-nous** !

Tu **nous** envoies **des cartes**.
→ Tu **nous en** envoies.
→ Envoie-**nous-en** !

Tu ouvres **des enveloppes**.
→ Tu **en** ouvres.
→ Ouvres-**en** !

[1]Reminder: the exclamation mark (**!**) is often used to distinguish imperative sentences from statements (**.**) and questions (**?**). It does not mean that the speaker is shouting.

[2]When **y** or **en** immediately follows the verb in an affirmative command, an obligatory liaison occurs, and **y** and **en** are pronounced /zi/ and /zã/: **Vas-y, Allons-y, Allez-y; Parles-en, Parlons-en, Parlez-en.**

3. **Être**, **avoir**, and **savoir** have special imperative forms.

être	**Sois** gentil !	*Be kind.*
	Soyons patients !	*Let's be patient.*
	Soyez à l'heure !	*Be on time.*
avoir	N'**aie** /ɛ/ pas peur de moi !	*Don't be afraid of me.*
	N'**ayons** /ɛjõ/ pas peur d'eux !	*Let's not be afraid of them.*
	Ayez /ɛje/ confiance en[1] moi !	*Trust me.*
savoir	**Sache** que je suis ton ami !	*Know that I am your friend.*
	Sachons la vérité !	*Let's know (find out) the truth.*
	Sachez la réponse !	*Know the answer.*

NE LA LUI DONNE PAS! DONNE-LA-MOI!

VOICI UNE POUPÉE; JE TE LA DONNE.

TU ME LA DONNES? MERCI BEAUCOUP.

TABLEAU 98

A   *Regardez le Tableau 33 à la page 126. Ajoutez des phrases d'après ce modèle.*

On va traverser la rue ?
(Janine)   **Non, ne la traversons pas !**
(Michel)   **Si, traversons-la !**

B   *Répondez aux questions d'après ce modèle.*

Je vous montre cette photo ?
(Solange)   **Non, ne me la montrez pas !**
(Daniel)   **Alors, montrez-la moi !**

1. Je vous montre cette lettre ?
2. Je vous parle des mes vacances ?
3. Je vous donne ces bonbons ?
4. Je vous offre des fleurs ?
5. Je vous présente mes amis ?
6. Je vous envoie de l'argent ?

C   *Écoutez les phrases et donnez des conseils à l'impératif, d'après ces modèles.*

Vous parlez à un enfant. Il est timide.
Ne sois pas timide.
Vous êtes avec vos camarades. Ils ne savent pas la vérité.
Sachez la vérité.

1. Vous parlez à un enfant. Il a peur de ce chien.
2. Vous êtes avec votre copain. Il ne sait pas la vérité.
3. Vous êtes avec vos copains. Ils sont impatients.
4. Nous avons un examen. Nous en avons peur.

---

[1]**avoir confiance en**   *to have confidence in; to trust*

5. Vous parlez à un professeur. Il n'a pas confiance en (Jean-Jacques).
6. Nous cherchons la vérité. Nous ne la savons pas.
7. Vous voyez un enfant. Il n'est pas gentil avec son chat.
8. Votre copain a perdu sa clé. Il s'inquiète[1].

D *Faites des phrases impératives en employant les pronoms appropriés.*

1. Voici une carte postale. (Marianne), voulez-vous la voir ? Alors, dites-moi que vous voulez la voir. Dites-moi de vous la montrer.
2. (Paul), voulez-vous voir la carte, vous aussi ? Dites à (Marianne) de vous la passer.
3. (Jacques), dites à (Paul) de vous montrer la carte. (Mireille), dites à (Jacques) de la rendre[2] au professeur.
4. (Rose), demandez à (Bernard) s'il a peur de moi. Dites-lui de ne pas[3] avoir peur de moi. Dites-lui d'avoir confiance en moi.
5. (Michel), dites à (Sylvie) d'avoir de la patience. (Jean), dites à (Sylvie) d'être gentille. Dites-lui de savoir la vérité.
6. (Daniel), dites à (Sophie) de rentrer tôt et de se coucher tôt. (Sophie), dites à Daniel de ne pas rentrer tard et de ne pas se coucher tard.

🔲 *Exercice supplémentaire*

🔲 *Exercice supplémentaire*

🔲 *Compréhension auditive*

18.4 PLACE DE L'ADVERBE DANS UNE PHRASE

1. As in English, adverbial expressions of time or place normally come at the end of a sentence.

J'ai pris le métro **hier**.	*I took the subway yesterday.*
Je prends l'autobus **aujourd'hui**.	*I'm taking the bus today.*
On parle français **ici**.	*French is spoken here.*
J'ai vu des touristes **là-bas**.	*I saw some tourists over there.*

Also as in English, when an adverb of time or place needs some emphasis or highlighting, it is often placed at the beginning of a sentence.

Hier, j'ai pris l'autobus.	*Yesterday, I took the bus.*
Aujourd'hui, je prendrai le métro.	*Today, I'll take the subway.*
Ici, on parle français.	*Here, French is spoken.*
Là-bas, j'ai vu des touristes.	*Over there, I saw some tourists.*

2. In simple tenses, most adverbs are usually placed immediately after the verb; unlike English, they *never* come directly before the verb.

Elle parle **souvent** de vous.	*She often speaks of you.*
Nous prenons **toujours** le métro.	*We always take the subway.*
Tu parles **très bien** français.	*You speak French very well.*
Il parle **probablement** deux langues.	*He probably speaks two languages.*

---

[1]**s'inquiéter** *to be concerned; to worry*

[2]**rendre** *to return, give back*

[3]When an infinitive is negated, both **ne** and **pas** come in front of it.

3. In compound tenses, most adverbs that neither end in **-ment** nor denote time or place occur immediately before the past participle.

Nous dormons **trop**.   Il me parle **souvent** de vous.
→ Nous avons **trop** dormi.   → Il m'a **souvent** parlé de vous.
Vous mangez **déjà** ?   Il ne dit pas **toujours** la vérité.
→ Vous avez **déjà** mangé ?   → Il n'a pas **toujours** dit la vérité.
Elle prend **enfin** un taxi.   Paul ne comprend pas **encore** la situation.
→ Elle a **enfin** pris un taxi.   → Paul n'a pas **encore** compris la situation.

4. Adverbs ending in **-ment** usually come after the past participle.[1]

Elle a parlé **longuement** de ses ennuis.   *She spoke at length about her problems.*
J'ai marché **rapidement** vers la maison.   *I walked rapidly toward the house.*
Il a parlé **brièvement** de ce projet.   *He spoke briefly about this project.*
Il nous a téléphoné **récemment**.   *He called us recently.*

Of the adverbs ending in **-ment**, a few such as **vraiment**, **certainement**, and **probablement** are usually placed before the past participle, like **bien** and **trop**.

A-t-il **vraiment** dit cela ?   *Did he really say that?*
Tu as **certainement** vu cette photo. *You certainly saw this photo.*
Elle a **probablement** pris un taxi.   *She probably took a cab.*

 **A** *Exercice de contrôle*

J'ai déjà parlé de mes ennuis.
1. trop   2. sérieusement   3. assez   4. franchement

Nous sommes souvent allés dans ce café.
1. enfin   2. vraiment   3. fréquemment   4. probablement

J'ai répondu prudemment à la lettre.
1. aujourd'hui   2. bien   3. là-bas   4. récemment

B *Un touriste prend le métro. Mettez le verbe de chaque phrase au passé composé d'après ce modèle. Faites attention à la place de chaque adverbe.*

Il prend souvent le métro.
Il a souvent pris le métro.

1. Il prend le métro aujourd'hui.   5. Il change de ligne là-bas.
2. Il consulte brièvement le plan du métro. 6. Il se déplace rapidement.
3. Il descend déjà sur le quai.   7. Il aime vraiment le métro.
4. Il va directement à l'Opéra.   8. Il préfère toujours le métro.

C *Répondez aux questions.*

1. Qu'est-ce que nous avons déjà fait aujourd'hui ? Qu'est-ce que vous n'avez pas encore fait ?
2. Avez-vous vraiment travaillé hier soir ? (Michel) a-t-il probablement travaillé ? Qui a travaillé brièvement ?
3. De quoi est-ce que j'ai trop parlé aujourd'hui ? De quoi est-ce que je n'ai pas assez parlé ?
4. Avez-vous bien compris cette leçon ? Qui d'autre[2] l'a bien comprise ? Qui ne l'a pas bien comprise ?

---

[1]Such adverbs may come before the past participle if they need *highlighting*: **Elle a longuement parlé de ses ennuis**; **J'ai rapidement marché vers la maison**.

[2]*Who else*

5. Comment dit-on en français « *I didn't understand you* » ? Et « *I didn't understand you very well* » ?

18.5 PRONOM RELATIF : **CE** COMME ANTÉCÉDENT

1. The invariable pronoun **ce** can be used as the antecedent of a relative clause when referring to things and ideas. **Ce** is grammatically masculine singular. **Ce** + relative pronoun corresponds to English *that which*, or more commonly, *what*. **Ce qui** is the subject of a relative clause.

Je vois **le tableau qui** vous intéresse.	*I see the painting that interests you.*
→ Je vois **ce qui** vous intéresse.	*→ I see what interests you.*
Voici **l'incident qui** est arrivé.	*Here is the incident that happened.*
→ Voici **ce qui** est arrivé.	*→ Here is what happened.*

2. **Ce que** is the direct object of a verb in a relative clause. Since **ce** is masculine singular, the past participle remains masculine singular.

Voilà **les tableaux** que j'ai **achetés**.	*There are the paintings I bought.*
→ Voilà **ce que** j'ai **acheté**.	*→ There is what I bought.*
La statue que vous avez **vue** m'inté-resse.	*The statue you saw interests me.*
→ **Ce que** vous avez **vu** m'intéresse.	*→ What you saw interests me.*

3. If the verb in the relative clause takes **de**, the relative pronoun is **ce dont**.

Il verra **les tableaux dont** j'ai parlé.	*He will see the paintings I spoke of.*
→ Il verra **ce dont** j'ai parlé.	*→ He will see what I spoke of.*
Le cahier dont elle a besoin est là.	*The notebook she needs is there.*
→ **Ce dont** elle a besoin est là.	*→ What she needs is there.*

4. When **ce** + relative pronoun begins a sentence and the verb in the main clause is **être**, the entire relative clause is often summed up with the pronoun **ce** before **être**.

Ce qui m'intéresse, **c'est** le musée du Louvre.	*What interests me is the Louvre museum.*
Ce que nous avons visité hier, **c'est** la Tour Eiffel.	*What we visited yesterday was [is] the Eiffel Tower.*

C'est ce que tout le monde regarde. (au musée du Louvre)

5. For emphasis, **tout** can be added before **ce qui**, **ce que**, or **ce dont**. This construction corresponds to English *all* or *everything*.

Aller au Louvre, c'est **tout ce qui** m'intéresse.	*Going to the Louvre is all I'm interested in (all that interests me).*
Racontez-moi **tout ce que** vous avez fait ce matin.	*Tell me everything (all) that you did this morning.*
Tout ce dont j'ai besoin, c'est mon dictionnaire.	*All I need is my dictionary.*
Deux disquettes, c'est **tout ce dont** nous avons besoin.	*Two diskettes are all we need.*

Voilà **ce dont** j'ai besoin.
C'est **ce que** je vais acheter.

Voilà **ce qui** m'intéresse.
C'est **ce que** je veux.

TABLEAU 99

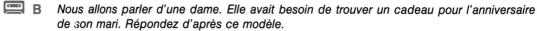

A *Modifiez les phrases suivantes d'après ces modèles.*

J'ai apporté le livre qui vous intéresse.
J'ai apporté ce qui vous intéresse.
Je vois sur la table la montre qui est à moi.
Je vois sur la table ce qui est à moi.

1. J'ai apporté le tableau qui vous intéresse.
2. Je comprends la chose que vous avez dite.
3. Je n'ai pas le livre dont vous avez besoin.
4. Ne comptez pas sur quelque chose qui est impossible.
5. Ne dites à personne la chose que je vous ai racontée.
6. La chose dont j'ai besoin, c'est un ordinateur.

B *Nous allons parler d'une dame. Elle avait besoin de trouver un cadeau pour l'anniversaire de son mari. Répondez d'après ce modèle.*

A-t-elle acheté un cadeau ?
Oui, c'est ce qu'elle a acheté.

1. Voulait-elle trouver un cadeau ?
2. Avait-elle besoin d'argent ?
3. A-t-elle pris le métro ?
4. A-t-elle cherché une galerie d'art ?
5. A-t-elle regardé des tableaux ?
6. Lui a-t-on montré des statuettes ?
7. Les gravures l'ont-elles intéressée ?
8. A-t-elle choisi une gravure ?

C   *Répondez aux questions d'après ce modèle.*

> Avez-vous acheté autre chose[1] ?
> **Non, c'est tout ce que j'ai acheté.**

1. Avez-vous besoin d'autre chose ?
2. Avez-vous d'autres choses à déclarer ?[2]
3. Y a-t-il autre chose qui vous intéresse ?
4. Voudriez-vous parler d'autres problèmes ?
5. A-t-il dit autre chose ?
6. Voulez-vous autre chose ?[3]

D   *Complétez les phrases suivantes avec votre partenaire, d'après ce modèle.*

> Aller au cinéma, c'est ce que...
> **Aller au cinéma, c'est ce que nous voulons faire (ce que nous ne pouvons pas faire ce soir, ce que nous avons fait, etc.).**

1. Faire les devoirs, c'est ce que...
2. Voir la statue de la Liberté, c'est ce que...
3. Visiter le musée du Louvre, c'est ce qui...
4. Un micro-ordinateur, c'est ce dont...
5. Manger des escargots, c'est ce que...

 Compréhension auditive

APPLICATIONS

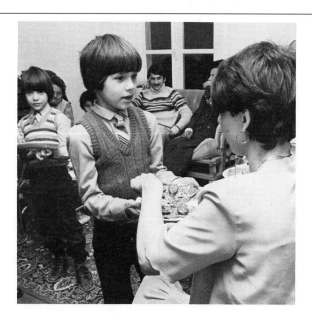

 A   **Situations[4]**

Vous remerciez quelqu'un.
Il y a mille façons (nous exagérons, bien sûr) de remercier quelqu'un qui vous a fait un cadeau ou qui vous a rendu service. Voici quelques exemples.[5]

---

[1]Remarquez la distinction entre **une autre chose** *another thing* et **autre chose** *something else / anything else.*

[2]*Do you have other things to declare?* (**D'autres choses** est le pluriel de **une autre chose**. Imaginez ici que vous passez la douane *the customs.*)

[3]*Would you like anything else?* (On entend souvent cette question quand on achète quelque chose dans un magasin.)

[4]Les réponses aux questions ne sont pas enregistrées sur la bande magnétique.

[5]Voir les *Situations* de la Leçon 9 (*Pour demander son chemin*) pour d'autres expressions de remerciement.

C'est le jour de votre anniversaire.

JULIEN Bon anniversaire ! Voici un petit cadeau. Je l'ai rapporté du Maroc.
VOUS Ah, comme c'est gentil ! Merci beaucoup.   5

Vous venez de déménager.

MME PINEAU C'est un petit quelque chose pour votre appartement. J'ai pensé que ça vous ferait plaisir[1].
VOUS Vous êtes trop aimable... Quelle belle gravure ! Je suis confuse[2]...

Après les vacances   10

d'excellentes vacances

MICHEL Tu as passé de bonnes vacances ?
VOUS Oui, d'excellentes°. Et toi ?
MICHEL Le voyage en Grèce était formidable. Voici quelque chose que je t'ai rapporté.
VOUS Ah, merci. C'est trop gentil...

Vous avez laissé vos clés au bureau de poste.   15

LA DAME Mademoiselle, Mademoiselle, vous avez oublié vos clés.
VOUS Oh, merci, Madame. Merci beaucoup.
LA DAME Il n'y a pas de quoi, Mademoiselle.

Vous avez un tas de paquets et vous avez du mal à[3] ouvrir la porte de votre appartement.

LE VOISIN Je vous donne un coup de main ?[4]   20
VOUS Oui, s'il vous plaît.
LE VOISIN Donnez-moi votre clé... Voilà.
VOUS Merci, Monsieur.
LE VOISIN Je vous en prie.

Vous êtes à la gare. Vous voulez envoyer une valise à Rome.   25

VOUS Excusez-moi, Monsieur. Je ne sais pas comment remplir cette fiche. Pourriez-vous m'aider ?
L'EMPLOYÉ Avec plaisir, Mademoiselle.
VOUS Merci, Monsieur.

Vous voyez une vieille dame qui porte deux grosses valises.   30

VOUS Excusez-moi, Madame. Est-ce que vous allez à la gare routière[5] ?
LA DAME Oui. C'est là-bas.
VOUS J'y vais, moi aussi. Si vous voulez, je peux porter une de vos valises.
LA DAME C'est très gentil de votre part.[6] Je vous remercie, Mademoiselle.

Que diriez-vous dans les situations suivantes ?

1. Un de vos copains vient de vous aider à terminer un travail. Il a travaillé trois heures avec vous.
2. Vous venez de déménager. Vous achetez quelques meubles pour votre nouvel appartement. Un de vos copains vous donne une aquarelle. Un autre vous apporte un vase.

[1]**faire plaisir à qqn** *to please someone*
[2]*I don't know what to say* (**confus(e)** littéralement, *embarrassed*)
[3]**avoir du mal à** + infinitif *to have trouble doing (something)*
[4]**donner un coup de main** = aider
[5]**gare routière** = gare pour autocars
[6]*It is very nice (kind) of you.*

3. Vous êtes malade. Mme Bosquet, chez qui vous habitez, vous apporte un bol de soupe et des fleurs.

4. Vous êtes à l'Hôtel de ville. Vous allez remplir un formulaire[1], mais vous avez oublié votre stylo.

5. Un de vos voisins a du mal à ouvrir la porte de sa chambre. Vous lui demandez si vous pouvez lui donner un coup de main.

6. Vous êtes à la terrasse d'un café. Vous avez laissé tomber une pièce de dix francs. Elle est sous la table voisine, qui est occupée. Vous demandez à votre voisin(e) de se déplacer un peu.

7. Vous êtes dans une station de métro. Vous avez perdu votre portefeuille. Vous voulez emprunter assez d'argent à quelqu'un[2] pour acheter un ticket.

B Expressions utiles

Les musées

Il y a toutes sortes de musées : musées consacrés...

à l'architecture	à la musique
aux armes et armures	à la peinture
à un(e) artiste	à la photographie
à l'aviation	à une région
au chemin de fer[3]	aux sciences
aux costumes	aux sciences naturelles
à l'histoire	à la sculpture /skyltyʀ/
aux jouets	à la tapisserie
à la marine[4]	aux transports
au mobilier et objets d'art	

aller à
assister à } { une exposition[5]
voir   { un vernissage

l'entrée (est) : { dix francs
                  { gratuite   } le dimanche et les jours fériés
                  { à mi-tarif[6]

Dans la vitrine sont exposé(e)s { des maquettes[7] *f.*
                                 { des reproductions *f.*
                                 { des objets d'art *m.*
                                 { des documents *m.*

faire
exposer } { un tableau
          { une peinture
          { une aquarelle   } : { un nu
          { une gravure   { un portrait
          { une fresque   { une nature morte[8]
          { une statue / statuette { un paysage
          { un buste   { une marine[9]

[1]*form*

[2]**emprunter qqch à qqn**   *to borrow something from someone*

[3]*railroad*

[4]**la marine**   things concerning maritime navigation, transportation, etc.

[5]*exhibit, exhibition* (**exposer**   *to exhibit*)

[6]*half price* (**tarif**   *rate*)

[7]*scale models*

[8]*still life*

[9]*seascape*

Le Musée Rodin, dans un coin tranquille de Paris.

C Pratique

1. Dans quelle sorte de musée va-t-on pour voir les choses suivantes ?

   des poupées
   des locomotives, réelles et en modèles réduits
   des avions, réels et en modèles réduits
   des maquettes de bateaux
   des vêtements du Moyen Âge
   des armoires et des chaises du dix-septième siècle

2. Qu'est-ce qu'on peut voir au musée des sciences naturelles ?
3. Qu'est-ce qu'on peut voir au musée Rodin ? Et au musée Victor Hugo ?
4. Quel jour est-ce que la plupart des musées publics sont fermés aux États-Unis ? Et en France ?[1]
5. Expliquez à un enfant de six ans ce que sont les choses suivantes.

un buste	une statuette	un auto-portrait[2]
un nu	une marine	une nature morte

6. Y a-t-il des musées dans notre ville ? Comment s'appellent-ils ? Qu'est-ce qu'on peut y voir ?

D *Voici les noms de quelques chefs-d'œuvre[3]. Pouvez-vous identifier les artistes qui les ont créés ?*

Le déjeuner sur l'herbe (un tableau)	*a)* Van Gogh /vãgɔg/
La Vénus de Milo (une statue)	*b)* Botticelli
Le Penseur (une statue)	*c)* Bartholdi
La Joconde (un tableau)	*d)* Manet
La Création d'Adam (une fresque)	*e)* Rodin
La Liberté éclairant[4] le monde (une statue)	*f)* Michel-Ange /mikɛlãʒ/
La Naissance de Vénus (un tableau)	*g)* Léonard de Vinci /vɛ̃si/
Auto-portrait à l'oreille coupée (un tableau)	*h)* artiste inconnu (découverte dans une île en Grèce)

[1]le mardi et parfois les jours fériés (*legal holidays*)

[2]*self-portrait*

[3]un **chef-d'œuvre**, des **chefs-d'œuvre** ; le **f** ne se prononce pas dans ce mot.

[4]*lighting*

E   *Jouez des rôles. Voici des annonces d'événements publics. Choisissez-en un. Vous allez inviter un copain (une copine) à y aller.*

1. MUSÉE DU LOUVRE (M[o1] Palais-Royal et Louvre). Tlj sf mar[2] de 9 h 45 à 17 h. Entrée 16 F, dim : gratuit. *Expositions : Nouvelles acquisitions du département des objets d'art.*

2. ARCHIVES NATIONALES, 60, rue des Francs-Bourgeois (M[o] Rambuteau). *Exposition : La Belle Époque : documents, photos, lithographies.* Tlj sf mar de 14 h à 17 h. Entrée : 9 F. Dim 4,50 F.

3. CLUNY, 6, place Paul-Painlevé (M[o] Saint-Michel). Tlj sf mar de 9 h 45 à 12 h 30 et de 14 h à 17 h 15. Entrée : 9 F, dim : 4,50 F. *Exposition : Archéologie urbaine (jusqu'au 2 mars).*

4. PALAIS DE LA DÉCOUVERTE, avenue F.-D. Roosevelt (M[o] Franklin-Roosevelt et Champs-Élysées-Clémenceau). Tlj sf lun de 10 h à 18 h. Entrée : 11 F. Étud, −18 ans[3] : 7 F. *Planétarium,* suppl.[4] 10 F : Tlj à 14 h, 15 h 15, 16 h 30 ; en supplément les sam et dim à 11 h 30 et à 17 h 45. *Une nouvelle salle : le système solaire.*

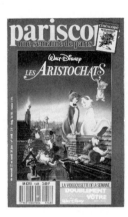

F   **Composition :** *Choisissez un des sujets suivants et écrivez une composition d'à peu près 200 mots.*

1. Y a-t-il des musées dans votre ville ? Choisissez-en un et faites une description de ce qu'on peut y voir. Décrivez aussi une de vos récentes visites.

2. Que feriez-vous si vous gagniez dix milles dollars à la loterie et si vous aviez quinze jours de vacances ?

3. Avez-vous donné une surprise-party récemment ?[5] Qui avez-vous invité ? Qu'est-ce que vous avez servi ? Où avez-vous acheté ces choses ? Comment vous êtes-vous assuré(e) que tout le monde passerait une très bonne soirée ?

4. Quels sont vos projets pour les vacances de Noël (d'été, de printemps) ? Que ferez-vous ? Où serez-vous ? Où irez-vous ? Qui verrez-vous ?[6]

[1]Métro (ici, la ou les stations de métro)
[2]Tous les jours sauf mardi
[3]moins de 18 ans (les personnes qui ont moins de 18 ans)
[4]supplément (ici, *additional charge*)
[5]Vous pouvez parler d'une surprise-party que vous allez donner en employant le futur ou d'une fête imaginaire en employant le conditionnel.
[6]Vous pouvez parler de projets imaginaires en employant le conditionnel.

5. Imaginez un incident qui s'est passé dans le métro et dont vous avez été témoin. Décrivez cet incident (par exemple : un vol, une dispute, une rencontre, l'arrestation d'un criminel).
6. Vous êtes allé(e) à Rome et, en route, vous avez passé 24 heures à Paris. Décrivez ce que vous y avez fait. (Soyez réaliste ; on ne peut pas faire trop de choses en si peu de temps !)[1]

G Renseignements et opinions

1. Qu'est-ce que vous avez toujours voulu faire, mais que[2] vous n'avez jamais fait ? Mentionnez deux choses.
2. La personne à qui je pense souvent est (mon mari). Qui est la personne à qui vous pensez souvent ?
3. Qu'est-ce que vous avez déjà fait aujourd'hui ? Et qu'est-ce que vous n'avez pas encore fait ?
4. Aller en France, c'est ce qui m'intéresse. Qu'est-ce qui vous intéresse ? Qu'est-ce qui ne vous intéresse pas ?
5. Me coucher tôt, c'est ce que je veux faire ce soir. Qu'est-ce que vous voulez faire ce soir ? Qu'est-ce que vous ne voulez pas faire ?

Compréhension auditive (basée sur l'Application A)

Compréhension auditive (basée sur les Applications B, C et D)

Compréhension auditive (basée sur les Applications B et C)

Dictée

H Lecture

Les musées de Paris

La mère
Vous voulez visiter des musées pendant votre séjour à Paris ? Alors, vous pourriez commencer par le plus grand et le plus connu : le Louvre. C'est un des plus beaux musées du monde. Vous y verrez des sculptures, des peintures, des œuvres d'art de toutes sortes qui datent de l'Antiquité jusqu'au XIXe siècle. Tout le monde veut voir la Joconde[3], la Vénus de Milo[4] et la   5
Victoire de Samothrace[5]. Et puis, si vous aimez les impressionnistes, allez au musée d'Orsay. C'est là qu'on voit les toiles de Degas, Renoir, Van Gogh, Cézanne, Monet... et d'autres artistes de la Belle Époque[6].

Le père
Il y a aussi le musée Rodin, avec un très beau jardin. Il est dans un coin caché et tranquille   10
complètement de Paris, pas très loin des Invalides. Et, dans un genre tout à fait° différent, il y a le Centre Pompidou. À mon avis, c'est un scandale, une horreur, mais tout le monde veut aller voir ça.

L'enfant
Mais non, Papa, ce n'est pas une horreur, c'est formidable. Il y a toujours quelque chose d'intéressant qui se passe sur la place — des musiciens, des magiciens, des clowns, des   15
beaucoup de acrobates — et à l'intérieur il y a des tas de° choses pour les enfants. Et puis on peut monter et descendre sur les escaliers roulants. C'est très amusant !

[1]Vous pouvez parler d'un voyage imaginaire à Paris en employant le conditionnel.
[2]*which*
[3]célèbre portrait de Mona Lisa del Giocondo (**la Joconde** en français), une dame de Florence, par Léonard de Vinci
[4]statue découverte dans l'île de Milo (Grèce) au XIXe siècle
[5]statue découverte dans l'île de Samothrace (Grèce) au XIXe siècle
[6]vers la fin du XIXe siècle et le début du XXe siècle

Le père

indeed   C'est bien° ce que je disais. Ce n'est pas un musée, c'est un cirque !

La mère   20

Eh bien   Mais enfin°, allez-y quand même. Au quatrième étage se trouve le musée d'art moderne, avec les œuvres des artistes du XXe siècle : Braque, Matisse, Picasso, Chagall, Dali... Il y a aussi de bonnes expositions de photos et d'affiches.

L'enfant

Et puis n'oublie pas le Palais de la Découverte. C'est le musée que je préfère. Tu verras un   25
grand planétarium, des salles d'expériences[1], des maquettes. Ah, il y a aussi le musée des
Techniques. Tu pourras y voir toutes sortes de machines anciennes. Il y en a beaucoup qui
se mettent en marche[2] quand tu appuies sur un bouton. Ah oui, n'oublie pas d'aller au musée
Grévin. Il est plein de figures de cire : Marie-Antoinette en prison, Marat assassiné dans sa
baignoire, la reine d'Angleterre, Brigitte Bardot, le général de Gaulle...   30

Le père

Oui, oui, mais ça, ce n'est pas de la culture. Si c'est la civilisation médiévale qui vous intéresse,
je vous recommande le musée de Cluny, dans une grande maison du XVe siècle très bien
restaurée. Vous y trouverez des bijoux, des armes, des meubles et de très belles tapisseries,

Lady with a unicorn   en particulier les tapisseries de la Dame à la licorne°. Ensuite allez au musée des Monuments   35
Français. À mon avis, c'est le musée le plus extraordinaire de Paris. Vous y découvrirez des
portails d'églises et de cathédrales, des fontaines, des façades de maisons, des quantités de

replicas   fresques. Ce sont des reconstitutions°, bien sûr, mais ce sera une bonne introduction à l'architecture avant de voir les originaux quand vous visiterez la France. Ensuite vous pourriez
aller au musée Carnavalet, dans le quartier du Marais, qui est le musée historique de la ville   40
de Paris.

La mère

Il y a plus de quatre-vingts musées à Paris, pas tous célèbres, mais tous excellents. Vous
reviendrez à Paris, et, à chaque séjour, vous aurez l'occasion d'en visiter d'autres.

Vous   45

assez de choses pour   Me voici bien conseillée et renseignée. Je vous remercie. J'aurai de quoi° m'occuper pendant
au moins deux semaines à Paris.

Le musée du Louvre.   *Le Centre Pompidou.*   *Le musée d'Orsay.*

[1]*large rooms with machines that one can operate (**expériences** experiments)*
[2]**se mettre en marche** *to start working/moving*

A *Indiquez si chaque commentaire est vrai ou faux. S'il est faux, corrigez le commentaire.*

1. Dix musées sont mentionnés ou décrits dans cette lecture.
2. C'est au musée d'Orsay qu'on trouve les œuvres d'artistes contemporains.
3. Il y a des reconstitutions de portails d'églises médiévales au musée de Cluny.
4. On va au musée Grévin si on veut voir le tableau de Marat assassiné dans sa baignoire.
5. La *Vénus de Milo* est une statue qu'on a découverte en Grèce.
6. Il y a toutes sortes de machines anciennes au Palais de la Découverte.
7. Il y a toujours quelque chose d'intéressant qui se passe sur la place du Centre Pompidou.
8. Une belle maison du XVᵉ siècle abrite un musée consacré à l'art du Moyen Âge.
9. La licorne est un animal fabuleux qui a trois cornes et qui ressemble à un cheval.
10. La personne qui écoute les conseils de la famille est une étrangère.

B *Où peut-on aller pour voir les choses suivantes ?*

1. Peintures du seizième siècle, y compris la Joconde
2. Reproduction des peintures murales d'églises romanes
3. Appareil qui reproduit le mouvement des planètes et des étoiles
4. Œuvres d'artistes contemporains
5. Figures de cire qui représentent des personnages célèbres
6. Toiles d'artistes de la Belle Époque
7. Belles tapisseries du Moyen Âge
8. Documents sur Paris à l'époque de la Révolution
9. Sculptures de Rodin et documents sur sa vie
10. Tableaux impressionnistes

VOCABULAIRE

Noms

la **confiance**	trust, confidence	la **gravure**	engraving, etching	le **quai**	platform (railroad); pier
le **coup de main**	help; helping hand	une **hôtesse**	flight attendant	la **statue**	statue
le **formulaire**	form	un **immeuble**	building	la **statuette**	statuette
le **frigo**	refrigerator	la **joie**	joy	la **surprise**	surprise
la **galerie (d'art)**	(art) gallery	un(e) **ouvrier(ière)**	worker	le **vase**	vase
la **gare routière**	bus station	la **pièce**	coin		

Verbes

consulter	to consult	emprunter (à)	to borrow (from)	rapporter	to bring back
déclarer	to declare	exagérer	to exaggerate	**rendre**	to give back
discuter (de)	to discuss	**partager**	to share		

Adjectifs

aimable	kind	**inutile**	useless	**satisfait(e) (de)**	satisfied (with)
confus(e)	embarrassed	**plein(e) (de)**	full (of)	**timide**	timid, shy
impatient(e)	impatient	routier(ière)	of road		

Adverbes

directement	directly	**pas encore**	not yet
enfin	finally	**récemment**	recently

Autres expressions

autre chose	something else	**dont**	of whom, which; whose
avoir confiance (en)	to have confidence (in); to trust	faire plaisir (à)	to please
avoir du mal à + *inf*	to have trouble + pres part	pourriez-vous	could you
Bon anniversaire !	Happy Birthday!	**qui d'autre**	who else
c'est très gentil de votre part	it's very nice of you	rendre service (à)	to do a favor (for)
donner un coup de main	to give a hand; to assist		

19 À la gare

LESSON OBJECTIVES

Theme and Culture

1. Means of travel, especially by rail
2. Basic means of transportation in France

Communication Skills

1. Expressing opinions for desirability (*one must*, *it is better not to* . . .)
2. Expressing requirements (*it takes*, *one needs* . . .)
3. Expressing opinions (*it is important/time/good that you do* . . .)
4. Expressing volition about other people (*I want him to do* . . .)
5. Reading train schedules and choosing different kinds of accommodations

Structures

19.1 **Falloir, valoir**

19.2 The subjunctive: after impersonal expressions

19.3 Irregular subjunctive forms

19.4 Subjunctive after main verbs of wish and command

19.5 **S'asseoir**

CONVERSATIONS

TABLEAU 100

A. À la gare

Regardez le Tableau 100 à la page 407. Il y a une dame à gauche, un jeune homme au milieu et une jeune fille à droite.

La dame à gauche est au guichet. Que fait-elle ?
Le jeune homme est à la consigne. Que fait-il ?
Où va la jeune fille ? Que fait-elle ?

B. Dans une grande gare

Vous voyez beaucoup de panneaux et de pancartes. Regardez le Tableau 101 et dites ce que signifie chaque panneau ou pancarte.

1 ENTRÉE
2 SORTIE
3 CONSIGNE
4 ASCENSEUR
5 DAMES
6 RÉSERVATIONS
7 OCCUPÉ

8 LIBRE
9 POUSSEZ
10 FUMEUR
11 FERMÉ
12 TIREZ
13 ACCÈS INTERDIT

14 RENSEIGNEMENTS
15 COMPOSTEUR
16 SORTIE DE SECOURS
17 ACCÈS AUX QUAIS
18 BUREAU DES OBJETS TROUVÉS

TABLEAU 101

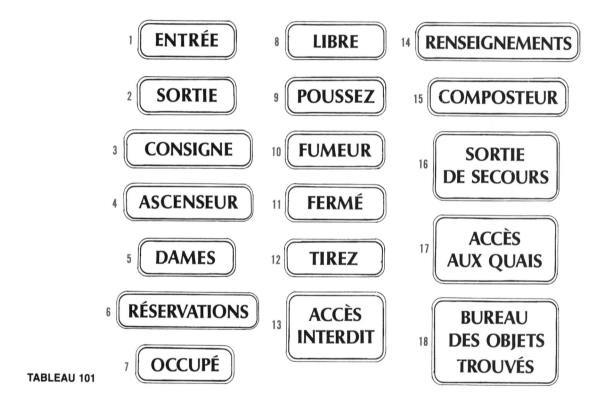

TABLEAU 102

C. **Dans le train**

Regardez le Tableau 102. À gauche, c'est une voiture ordinaire. Au milieu, c'est une voiture-restaurant. À droite, c'est une voiture-couchettes.

Combien de personnes voyez-vous dans la voiture à gauche ? Que font les passagers ?

Que fait le garçon ? Savez-vous dans quelle sorte de trains il y a une voiture-restaurant ?

Regardez le compartiment à droite. Combien de passagers voyez-vous ? Que font-ils ? Y a-t-il quelqu'un sur la couchette supérieure ? Et sur la couchette du milieu ? Et sur la couchette inférieure ?

 Compréhension auditive (*basée sur la Conversation B*)

DIFFÉRENCES

Les voyages en France

With its great variety of geological formations, ever-changing landscapes, and well-preserved historical sites, France encompasses some of the most beautiful visual delights in the world. All of that combined with its renowned gastronomic tradition of the finest cuisine and wine explains why this small country has attracted tourists for centuries. France caters to travelers, both foreign and domestic, and has provided an excellent railroad network and good roads that make it possible to travel around the country fast and efficiently. It also offers convenient air travel between major cities.

The train is still the most popular way to travel in France, especially for students. French trains are for the most part modern, comfortable, fast, and reliable. You may have heard of the TGV (**trains à grande vitesse**)—the ultrarapid trains reaching speeds of up to 160 miles per hour. If you plan to travel extensively in Europe, you should consider purchasing a Eurailpass, or Eurail Youthpass, which allows three weeks to three months of unlimited rail travel in thirteen European countries. **Eurotrain**, a student organization in Europe, will also get you reduced fares (15–30%) for point-to-point travel. For unlimited travel within France, consider **France-Vacances**, issued by the French National Railroads (**la SNCF**[1]). In addition, complementing the railroad, there is good bus service with varying degrees of comfort and luxury.

If you travel by car, you can fully enjoy the scenic routes and picturesque villages in the more remote areas without being bound by train and bus schedules. The drawback is that renting a car can be quite expensive. On top of the rental charge, there is a value-added tax (**TVA**[2]) of almost 35%. Insurance (**la carte verte**) is mandatory and costly. For three or more weeks, you will find leasing much more economical, that is, "buying" a brand-new car with a guaranteed repurchase by the dealer. But whether you rent or lease, you still have to buy gasoline, which is sold by the liter as in the rest of Europe and costs about two and a half times as much as in North America. Traffic rules are generally similar to those in North America except at crossroads of equal status, where the car on your right *always* has the right of way (**la priorité à droite**). International signs are standard.

For air travel, there are the government-owned **Air France** and two other main companies: **Air-Inter** and **UTA**[3]. Although regular airline fares are extremely costly in Europe, these companies offer a wide range of fare reductions for travel within France. For a more leisurely pace, you can rent or buy a 10-speed bicycle or a moped. There is also a network of canals linking seas and rivers. They are no longer of any commercial use today, but you can rent houseboats—many are converted from barges and are luxurious—and float through the country.

[1]**Société Nationale des Chemins de Fer**

[2]**Taxe à la Valeur Ajoutée**; in Belgium and Luxembourg, it is about 20%.

[3]**Union des Transports Aériens**

La signalisation routière

STRUCTURES

19.1 FALLOIR, VALOIR

1. The basic meaning of **falloir** is *to necessitate* or *to require*. It is used only with the impersonal subject pronoun **il**. **Il faut** + infinitive denotes a compulsory action, corresponding to English *it is necessary* or *one must (do something)*.

Il faut parler français ici.	*One must speak French here.*
Il faut arriver à l'heure.	*One must arrive on time.*

The negative form **il ne faut pas** also implies a compulsory action or strong necessity, corresponding to *it is necessary not to* or *one must not*.[1]

Il ne faut pas manger en classe.	*One must not eat in class.*
Il ne faut pas cracher par terre.	*One must not spit on the ground.*

2. **Il faut** + noun followed by **pour** + infinitive indicates that something is necessary in order to complete an action. It is equivalent to English *It takes* + noun or *one needs* + noun followed by *to do (something)*. Note in the last two examples below that **il faut** can also take an indirect object.

Il faut sept heures pour aller de New York à Paris en avion.	*It takes (One needs) seven hours to go from New York to Paris by plane.*
Il faut beaucoup d'argent pour voyager autour du monde.	*It takes (One needs) a lot of money to travel around the world.*
Il faut une heure à Anne **pour aller** à la gare.	*It takes Anne (Anne needs) one hour to go to the railroad station.*
Il leur faut douze mille francs pour aller aux États-Unis.	*It takes them (They need) twelve thousand francs to go to the United States.*

---

[1]*It is not necessary to do* or *One does not have to do* is **Il n'est pas nécessaire de** + infinitive or **On n'a pas besoin de** + infinitive.

« *Il me faut une plaque "chien méchant".* »

3. **Valoir** means *to be worth*. **Il vaut mieux** + infinitive corresponds to *It is better to do (something)*. Note in the second example below that **ne** and **pas** are placed together in front of an infinitive (i.e., **ne pas** + infinitive) when the infinitive is negated (this construction will be used in Exercise C). **Ça/Cela**[1] **vaut la peine** corresponds to *It is worth the trouble.*

Il vaut mieux prendre un parapluie.	*It is better to take an umbrella.*
C'est trop loin ; **il vaut mieux** ne pas y **aller** à pied.	*It is too far; it is better not to go there on foot.*
Ce voyage **vaut** bien le prix.	*This trip is certainly worth the price.*
Ce tableau ne **vaut** rien.	*This painting is worth nothing.*
Ça (ne) **vaut** (pas) **la peine**.	*That / It is (not) worth the trouble.*

4. Here are the future, conditional, and imperfect forms and the past participles of **falloir** and **valoir**.

Il **faudra** changer de train.	*One will have to change trains.*
Il **faudrait** attendre dix minutes.	*One would have to wait ten minutes.*
Il **fallait** sortir de la gare.	*One had to go out of the station.*
Il m'**a fallu** une heure pour le faire.	*It took me one hour to do it.*
Ça **vaudra** bien le prix.	*That will be well worth the price.*
Il **vaudrait** mieux ne pas le faire.	*It would be better not to do it.*
Il **valait** mieux se dépêcher un peu.	*It was better to hurry a little.*
Ça **a** bien **valu** la peine.	*It was well worth the trouble.*

TABLEAU 103   Il **ne faut pas** fumer !   Il **vaut mieux** prendre un parapluie.

[1]**Cela** and **ça** literally mean *that*; **ça** is more informal than **cela**.

A   *Il y a des choses qu'il faut ou qu'il ne faut pas faire en classe. Répondez aux questions d'après ces modèles.*

On peut parler français en classe ?	On peut dormir en classe ?
Oui, il faut parler français.	**Non, il ne faut pas dormir.**

1. On peut écouter le professeur ?
2. On peut poser des questions ?
3. On peut manger en classe ?

4. On peut parler anglais ?
5. On peut répondre aux questions ?
6. On peut cracher en classe ?

B   *Qu'est-ce qu'il faut ou ne faut pas faire dans un musée ? Ajoutez il faut ou il ne faut pas devant chaque phrase.*

1. parler à haute voix
2. écouter le guide
3. regarder attentivement
4. toucher les objets exposés

5. faire du bruit
6. consulter le plan
7. fumer
8. courir[1]

C   *Je vais parler de quelqu'un qui est paresseux. Donnez votre opinion sur lui en employant* **il vaudrait mieux faire** *ou* **il vaudrait mieux ne pas faire** *d'après ces modèles.*

Il est en retard tout le temps.
Il vaudrait mieux ne pas être en retard tout le temps.
Il nettoie sa chambre une fois par mois.
Il vaudrait mieux nettoyer sa chambre[2] plus souvent.

1. Il regarde la télévision tout le temps.
2. Il ne se brosse pas les dents tous les matins.
3. Il nettoie sa chambre une fois par mois.[3]
4. Il laisse ses clés dans sa voiture.
5. Il prend une douche une fois par semaine.[3]
6. Il change de vêtements une fois par semaine.
7. Il se lave les cheveux une fois par mois.[3]
8. Il écoute la radio tout le temps.

D   *Maintenant, répondez aux questions.*

1. Vous voyagez en avion de temps en temps, n'est-ce pas ? Combien de temps faut-il pour aller de New York à San Francisco ? Combien de temps faut-il pour aller de New York à Paris ?
2. Ce matin, j'ai quitté ma maison à (huit heures) et je suis arrivé(e) à l'université à (huit heures vingt). Combien de temps est-ce qu'il m'a fallu pour venir à l'université ?
3. Aimez-vous les sports ? Combien de joueurs faut-il pour former une équipe de base-ball ? Pour former une équipe de football ? Pour former une équipe de basket ?
4. Est-ce qu'il vaux mieux faire ses[4] devoirs tous les jours, ou est-ce que cela ne vaut pas la peine ?
5. Citez deux choses qu'il vaut mieux faire. Citez deux choses qu'il vaut mieux ne pas faire.

19.2   SUBJONCTIF : APRÈS DES EXPRESSIONS IMPERSONNELLES

Like the indicative and the conditional, the subjunctive is a *mood* (**le mode**). It is used instead of the indicative in dependent clauses after certain types of expressions. The main uses of the subjunctive will be discussed in the next two lessons. (For an overview,

---

[1]verbe irrégulier (Leçon 20.5)
[2]The meaning implied here is *one's room* rather than *his room*.
[3]Utilisez **plus souvent** dans vos réponses.
[4]*one's*

you might first glance over Lesson 21.1.) The subjunctive has four tenses: *present*, *past*, *imperfect*, and *pluperfect*. The last two tenses are used only in written, formal language and will be presented in Lesson 25.5. A word of caution: you should not try to equate the subjunctive with any comparable construction in English.[1] Any attempt to do so will only make your learning task more complicated.

1. Let's first look at the forms: the present-subjunctive endings for the singular are **-e**, **-es**, **-e**, and for the plural, **-ions**, **-iez**, **-ent**. The stem for the **je**, **tu**, **il**, **ils** forms is derived from the third-person plural form (**ils**, **elles**) of the *present indicative*; the **nous** and **vous** forms are identical with those of the *imperfect indicative* (Lesson 10.1).

parler : ils **parlent**[2]	finir : ils **finissent**	vendre : ils **vendent**
je **parle**	je **finisse**	je **vende**
tu **parles**	tu **finisses**	tu **vendes**
elle **parle**	il **finisse**	elle **vende**
elles **parlent**	ils **finissent**	elles **vendent**
nous **parlions**	nous **finissions**	nous **vendions**
vous **parliez**	vous **finissiez**	vous **vendiez**

prendre : ils **prennent**	boire : ils **boivent**	venir : ils **viennent**
je **prenne**	je **boive**	je **vienne**
tu **prennes**	tu **boives**	tu **viennes**
il **prenne**	elle **boive**	il **vienne**
ils **prennent**	elles **boivent**	ils **viennent**
nous **prenions**	nous **buvions**	nous **venions**
vous **preniez**	vous **buviez**	vous **veniez**

2. The subjunctive occurs in dependent clauses introduced by the conjunction **que** after *impersonal expressions*.[3]

Il est bon que nous **partions** maintenant.

Il est dommage[4] qu'elle ne me **comprenne** pas.

Il est douteux que je **prenne** le métro.

Il est étonnant que tu **viennes** avec nous.

Il est important qu'il **finisse** le travail.

Il est juste qu'elle **réponde** à la question.

Il est naturel qu'on ne **comprenne** pas cela.

Il est nécessaire que nous **buvions** du lait.

Il est temps[5] que vous **partiez** pour la gare.

Il faut qu'ils **voient** l'horaire.

Il vaut mieux qu'elles **viennent** ensemble.

---

[1]Some people consider the verbs in the dependent clause of sentences like the following to be in the "subjunctive": *It is important that this **be done** at once; I suggest that he **stay** here tonight; I will help you so that you **may succeed**; Think of an alternative lest the plan **should fail**.* Note, however, that it is more common to use the "indicative" mood and say *this is done, he stays, you will succeed, lest (in case) the plan fails*.

[2]The singular forms as well as that of the third-person plural of first-conjugation verbs are identical with those of the present indicative.

[3]In colloquial French, **Il est** is sometimes replaced with **C'est**.

[4]also **C'est dommage** *It's too bad, It's a pity*

[5]*It is time*

The impersonal expressions you learned in 17.4, using the infinitive, express *general* opinions (you might consider the subject of the infinitive to be a pronoun like **on**), while the ones shown above, with a subject pronoun and a verb in the subjunctive, refer *specifically* to that subject.

Il est important de prendre ce train.	*It is important to take this train*. (everyone concerned must take it)
Il est important que vous preniez ce train.	*It is important that you take this train* (you in particular).

3. Note, however, that the subjunctive does not occur if the impersonal expression denotes *certainty*.

Il est certain qu'elle **apprend** l'anglais.

Il est clair que tout le monde **prend** le train.

Il est évident que Julien **viendra** avec elle.

Il est sûr que nous **irons** au supermarché.

Il est vrai que vous **connaissez** bien cette ville.

The expression **il est probable** takes the indicative, but **il est possible** takes the subjunctive (a greater degree of uncertainty).

Il est probable que Marie **comprend** la vérité.

Il est possible que Marie **comprenne** la vérité.

But if the expressions of certainty are in the negative, the subjunctive is normally used.

Il n'est pas certain qu'elle **apprenne** l'anglais.

Il n'est pas évident que Julien **vienne** avec elle.

Il n'est pas vrai que vous **connaissiez** bien cette ville.

Il n'est pas probable que Marie **comprenne** la vérité.

4. The present subjunctive can refer to both *present* and *future* events (it does not have a future tense).

Il est douteux qu'elle **vienne**.	*It is doubtful that* $\begin{cases} \textit{she comes.} \\ \textit{she is coming.} \\ \textit{she will come.} \end{cases}$
Est-ce que Jean prend le métro ?	*Does Jean take the subway?*
— Il est douteux qu'il le **prenne**.	*It's doubtful he takes it.*
Est-ce que Jean prendra l'autobus ?	*Will Jean take the bus?*
— Il est possible qu'il le **prenne**.	*It's possible he will take it.*

TABLEAU 104   **Il est douteux** qu'il **prenne** son parapluie.   **Il est certain** qu'il **n'a** pas son parapluie.

$$\text{Il} + \left\{ \begin{array}{l} \text{certainty} \\ \text{other expressions} \end{array} \right\} + \textbf{que} + \text{subject} \left\{ \begin{array}{l} \text{indicative} \\ \text{subjunctive} \end{array} \right.$$

A *Exercice de contrôle*

Il est bon que vous disiez la vérité.
1. Il est juste   2. Il est temps   3. Il est clair   4. Il est étonnant

Il est important qu'il parte aujourd'hui.
1. Il faut   2. Il est certain   3. Il vaut mieux   4. Il est évident

Il est naturel qu'on finisse le travail.
1. Il est sûr   2. Il est douteux   3. Il n'est pas sûr   4. Il n'est pas certain

B *Répondez aux questions d'après ce modèle.*

Vous comprenez le français ; est-ce bon ?
Il est bon que je comprenne le français.

1. Vous répondez à mes questions ; est-ce nécessaire ?
2. (Marie) comprend le chinois ; est-ce sûr ?
3. (Robert) dort en classe ; est-ce douteux ?
4. Je vous connais : est-ce certain ?
5. Nous finissons cette leçon ; est-ce important ?
6. Je vous comprends ; est-ce remarquable ?

C *Une jeune fille va rendre visite à ses grands-parents. Elle va prendre le train. Écoutez ces phrases et modifiez-les d'après le modèle.*

Elle regardera l'horaire ; c'est important.
Il est important qu'elle regarde l'horaire.

1. Elle rendra visite à ses grands-parents ; c'est vrai.
2. Elle partira cet après-midi ; c'est probable.
3. Elle prendra assez d'argent ; c'est important.
4. Elle mettra son manteau ; c'est douteux.
5. Elle consultera l'horaire ; c'est nécessaire.
6. Elle choisira le train de midi ; c'est probable.
7. Elle achètera un journal ; c'est possible.
8. Elle lira le journal dans le train ; c'est sûr.
9. Son amie ne viendra pas avec elle ; c'est étonnant.
10. Elle attendra le train ; c'est clair.

Exercice supplémentaire

Compréhension auditive

19.3   SUBJONCTIF : VERBES IRRÉGULIERS

1. The verbs below have special subjunctive stems. Note that the special stems for **avoir**, **être**, and **savoir** are identical with those of the imperative (Lesson 18.3). The **nous** and **vous** forms of **aller** and **vouloir** are identical with those of the imperfect indicative. In the following list, **...que** is shown to remind you that the subjunctive usually occurs in a dependent clause introduced by **que**.

avoir

...que j'**aie** /ɛ/
...que tu **aies**
...qu'elle **ait**
...qu'elles **aient**
...que nous **ayons** /ɛjõ/
...que vous **ayez** /ɛje/

être

...que je **sois**
...que tu **sois**
...qu'il **soit**
...qu'ils **soient**
...que nous **soyons**
...que vous **soyez**

savoir[1]

...que je **sache**
...que tu **saches**
...qu'elle **sache**
...qu'elles **sachent**
...que nous **sachions**
...que vous **sachiez**

aller

...que j'**aille** /aj/
...que tu **ailles**
...qu'il **aille**
...qu'ils **aillent**
...que nous **allions**
...que vous **alliez**

vouloir

...que je **veuille** /vœj/
...que tu **veuilles**
...qu'elle **veuille**
...qu'elles **veuillent**
...que nous **voulions**
...que vous **vouliez**

faire

...que je **fasse**
...que tu **fasses**
...qu'il **fasse**
...qu'ils **fassent**
...que nous **fassions**
...que vous **fassiez**

pouvoir

...que je **puisse**
...que tu **puisses**
...qu'elle **puisse**
...qu'elles **puissent**
...que nous **puissions**
...que vous **puissiez**

pleuvoir

...qu'il **pleuve**

falloir

...qu'il **faille**

valoir

...qu'il **vaille**

2. The past subjunctive (**le passé composé du subjonctif**) consists of the auxiliary verb **avoir** or **être** in the present subjunctive and the past participle of the verb denoting the action.

...que j'**aie** voyagé
...que tu **aies** voyagé
...qu'il **ait** voyagé
...que nous **ayons** voyagé
...que vous **ayez** voyagé
...qu'ils **aient** voyagé

...que je **sois** parti(e)
...que tu **sois** parti(e)
...qu'elle **soit** partie
...que nous **soyons** parti(e)s
...que vous **soyez** parti(e)(s)
...qu'elles **soient** parties

The present subjunctive can refer to both *present* and *future* events. But the past subjunctive usually refers to *past* events.

Il est douteux qu'il **pleuve**.

It's doubtful that { *it rains.*
{ *it is raining.*
{ *it will rain.*

Il est douteux qu'il **ait plu**.

It's doubtful that { *it has rained.*
{ *it rained.*

A *Ajoutez* **il faut que** *devant chaque phrase et mettez les verbes au subjonctif.*

1. Vous avez de la patience.
2. Vous êtes à l'heure[2].
3. Vous pouvez nous comprendre.
4. Vous savez où j'habite.
5. Vous faites votre travail.
6. Je sais ma leçon.
7. Je vais à la bibliothèque.
8. Je fais mes devoirs.
9. Je veux réussir.
10. Je finis cet exercice.

[1]The **nous** and **vous** forms of the imperative do not have the **-i-**: **sachons, sachez**.
[2]*on time*

B *Quelqu'un va voyager en train. Modifiez les phrases suivantes d'après ce modèle.*

> Il ira à Versailles aujourd'hui ; c'est possible.
> **Il est possible qu'il aille à Versailles aujourd'hui.**

1. Il est libre aujourd'hui ; c'est bon.
2. Il veut aller à Versailles ; c'est naturel.
3. Il pourra y rester toute la journée ; c'est possible.
4. Il prendra le train ; c'est certain.
5. Il a déjà regardé l'horaire ; c'est juste.
6. Il saura à quelle heure le train partira ; c'est utile.
7. Il ne pleuvra pas et il fera beau[1] ; c'est important.
8. Il ira à la gare vers neuf heures ; c'est nécessaire.

C *Répondez aux questions suivantes d'après ce modèle.*

> J'arrive toujours à l'heure. Est-ce important ?
> **Il est important (*ou* Il n'est pas important) que vous arriviez toujours à l'heure.**

1. Je fais toujours mon lit. Est-ce nécessaire ?
2. J'ai téléphoné à Paris ce matin. Est-ce possible ?
3. J'ai dû travailler hier soir. Est-ce dommage ?
4. Je suis toujours à l'heure. Est-ce bon ?
5. Je peux vous aider. Est-ce important ?
6. J'ai bien préparé la leçon. Est-ce évident ?

🎞 *Exercice supplémentaire*

🎞 *Exercice supplémentaire*

🎞 *Compréhension auditive*

19.4 SUBJONCTIF : APRÈS LES EXPRESSIONS DE VOLONTÉ

1. When the verb in the main clause expresses volition of some sort (*will*, *desire*, *wish*, *command*, *permission*) concerning someone or something else, the verb in the dependent clause is in the subjunctive.[2]

Je **veux** que vous **soyez** ici demain.	*I want*
Je **voudrais** (J'**aimerais**) que vous **partiez**.	*I would like*
Tu **exiges** que tout le monde **vienne** demain.	*You demand*[3]
Il **désire** qu'on **fasse** le travail maintenant.	*He wishes*
Nous **demandons** que vous **arriviez** à l'heure.	*We ask*
Vous **défendez** qu'on **soit** en retard.	*You forbid*
Elles **permettent** que tu **ailles** au cinéma.	*They permit/allow*

Many of the French patterns you see above conflict with those of English, which often uses an infinitive (*to* + verb).

Je **veux** que vous le **fassiez**.	*I want you to do it.* (literally, *I want that you do it.*)
Il **défend** que je **sorte**.	*He forbids me to go out.* (literally, *He forbids that I go out.*)

[1]Répétez **que** devant chaque proposition : **qu'il ne pleuve pas et qu'il...**
[2]Use of an infinitive instead of a dependent clause with the subjunctive will be discussed in Lesson 22.3.
[3]Note that *to demand* is **exiger**, while **demander** means *to ask (for)*.

Il **aimerait** que nous le **voyions**.

He would like for us to see him. (literally, He would like that we see him.)

2. Note the use of an infinitive with **désirer** and **vouloir** when the subject of the infinitive is the same as the one for **désirer** and **vouloir**.

SAME SUBJECT

Je désire... J'irai à Rome. — *I wish . . . I will go to Rome.*
→ **Je désire aller** à Rome. — → *I wish to go to Rome.*
Je veux... Je prendrai le train. — *I want . . . I will take the train.*
→ **Je veux prendre** le train. — → *I want to take the train.*

DIFFERENT SUBJECTS

Je désire... Vous irez à Rome. — *I wish . . . You will go to Rome.*
→ **Je désire** que **vous alliez** à Rome. — → *I want you to go to Rome.*
Il veut... Je prends le train. — *He wants . . . I take the train.*
→ **Il veut** que **je prenne** le train. — → *He wants me to take the train.*

Subject	+	Wish Command Permission	{ que	+	Different subject	+	Subjunctive
			(de)	+	(Same subject → 0)	+	Infinitive

TABLEAU 105

🔲 **A** *Exercice de contrôle*

Voulez-vous que je fasse mon travail ?
1. Demandez-vous   2. Savez-vous   3. Voyez-vous   4. Permettez-vous

Exige-t-elle que vous sachiez la vérité ?
1. Désire-t-elle   2. Permet-elle   3. Sait-elle   4. Défend-elle

J'espère qu'il fera beau demain.
1. Je dis   2. Je veux   3. Je crois   4. Je voudrais

🔲 **B** *Voici une mère qui parle à son enfant. Modifiez chaque phrase d'après ce modèle.*

Fais ton lit maintenant.
Je veux que tu fasses ton lit maintenant.

1. Fais tes devoirs maintenant.
2. Bois ton lait maintenant.
3. Sois plus gentil avec le chat.
4. Ne sois pas si impatient.
5. Viens tout de suite.
6. Ne fais pas tant de bruit.
7. Prends un bain maintenant.
8. Obéis à ta maîtresse[1].
9. Apprends ta leçon.
10. Va dans ta chambre.

[1]*schoolteacher*

C *Maintenant, répondez aux questions.*

1. Quand êtes-vous entré(e) à l'université ? Qui voulait que vous alliez à l'université ? Qui voulait que vous appreniez le français ?
2. Qu'est-ce que je veux que vous fassiez dans ce cours ? Mentionnez plusieurs choses.
3. Qu'est-ce que je demande que vous ne fassiez pas ? Mentionnez plusieurs choses.
4. Maintenant, regardez la liste. Qu'est-ce que j'exige que vous fassiez ? Qu'est-ce que je défends que vous fassiez ?

D *Complétez les phrases suivantes avec votre partenaire.*

1. Nous aimerions que dans ce cours...
2. Nous voudrions que le professeur...
3. Pourquoi est-il important que nous...
4. Le professeur ne permettra pas que nous...
5. Nos parents demandent que nous...

Exercice supplémentaire

19.5 S'ASSEOIR

asseoir	
assieds	asseyons
assieds	asseyez
assied	asseyent
assis	
assiérai	

1. Study the conjugation of **s'asseoir** /saswaʀ/ *to sit down.* The singular and plural forms have different stem vowels in the present indicative.

Je m'**assieds** sur la chaise. /asje/	Nous nous **asseyons** là-bas.	/asɛjõ/
Tu t'**assieds** près de moi.	Vous vous **asseyez** ici.	/asɛje/
Il s'**assied** dans un fauteuil.	Ils s'**asseyent** dans le coin.	/asɛj/

Je me suis **assis(e)** près de vous.
Je m'**assiérai** là-bas.

2. The verbs **s'asseoir** *to sit down* and **se lever** *to get up* denote actions. **Être assis(e/es)** *to be seated* and **être debout** *to be standing* denote state of being.[1] **Debout** is an adverb and remains invariable.

LE PROFESSEUR Levez-vous, s'il vous plaît.
L'ÉTUDIANTE Oui, Monsieur.

Elle se lève. Elle est debout maintenant.

LE PROFESSEUR Merci, Mademoiselle. Asseyez-vous.
L'ÉTUDIANTE Bien, Monsieur.

Elle s'assied. Elle est assise maintenant.

A *Exercice de contrôle*

Je m'assieds près de la porte.

1. Nous   2. Tu   3. On   4. Vous

Je ne m'assieds pas au fond de[2] la classe.

1. Vous   2. On   3. Personne[3]   4. Nous

Je suis assis(e) ; je ne suis plus debout.

1. Vous   2. On   3. (Jacqueline)   4. Les étudiants

---

[1]As a result, in the past **être assis(e/es)** and **être debout** are usually in the imperfect tense: **Il s'est levé; Il était debout; Il s'est assis; Il était assis**.

[2]*in the back of*

[3]Il n'est pas nécessaire d'employer **pas**, puisque **personne** exprime une négation.

B *Répondez aux questions.*

1. Est-ce que je suis debout ou assis(e) ? Dites-moi de m'asseoir. Dites-moi de me lever.
2. Quelle sorte d'étudiants s'asseyent au fond de la classe ? Quelle sorte d'étudiants s'asseyent près du professeur ?
3. Dites à (Charles) de se lever. Est-il assis ou debout ? Dites-lui de s'asseoir. Est-il assis ou debout ?
4. Voulez-vous que je m'asseye ici ? Là-bas ? Où voulez-vous que je m'asseye ?
5. Où étiez-vous assis(e) hier ? Qui était assis près de vous ?

APPLICATIONS

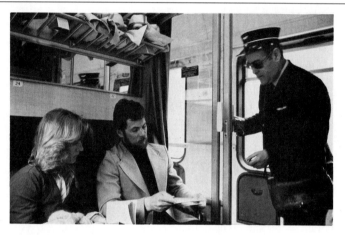

« Vos billets, s'il vous plaît. »

A Situations

Asseyez-vous !
Vous avez passé deux jours à Lyon. Cet après-midi vous allez à Avignon, vieille ville encore entourée de remparts. Vous voulez réserver votre place dans le train, car vous avez marché toute la matinée° dans la ville et vous êtes fatiguée.

all morning

VOUS	Un billet pour Avignon, s'il vous plaît.	
L'EMPLOYÉ	Quelle classe ?°	5
VOUS	Deuxième.	
L'EMPLOYÉ	Aller-retour[1] ?	
VOUS	Non, un aller[2] seulement.	
L'EMPLOYÉ	Voilà. Ça fait cent quatre-vingts francs.	
VOUS	Merci. Est-ce que je peux réserver ma place ?	10
L'EMPLOYÉ	Au guichet numéro cinq, à droite.	

= En quelle classe ?

Le train vient de quitter la gare. Il est bondé, mais heureusement il n'y a personne dans votre compartiment ! Vous mettez vos bagages dans le filet° et vous vous asseyez près de la fenêtre. Vous voilà maintenant toute seule et confortablement installée. Soudain, la porte s'ouvre et une dame entre, accompagnée de quatre enfants. Ils portent des valises, des 15 *paniers, des ballons, des filets à crevettes[3], des sacs à dos°...*

filet (à bagages)
luggage rack

backpacks

[1]*round trip;* on dit aussi **aller et retour**.
[2]*one-way ticket;* on dit aussi **un aller simple**.
[3]*fishing* (literally, *shrimp*) *net* (to catch crayfish, small fish, etc.)

diminutif de Pierre — PIERROT° Je vais m'asseoir près de la fenêtre.

diminutif de Patrick — PATOU° Moi aussi, je veux m'asseoir près de la fenêtre.

LA MÈRE Excusez-moi, Mademoiselle. Pourriez-vous m'aider à mettre cette grosse valise dans le filet ? Merci.

MARTINE Maman, Maman, j'ai oublié ma poupée. Est-ce qu'on peut retourner à la maison ?

JANINE Non, ta poupée est dans la grosse valise.

MARTINE Maman, donne-moi ma poupée.

boisson gazeuse à l'orange ou au citron — PIERROT Maman, j'ai soif. Achète-moi un Pschitt°.

PATOU Moi aussi, Maman. J'ai soif.

LA MÈRE Je ne veux pas que vous fassiez tant de bruit. Asseyez-vous ! Patou, tu t'assiéras près de la fenêtre plus tard.

MARTINE Je veux ma poupée.

aller aux toilettes — PATOU Je veux faire pipi°, Maman.

LA MÈRE Oh ! là ! là ! Vous êtes fatigants ! Mademoiselle, pourriez-vous surveiller les enfants pendant que je vais aux toilettes avec Patou ?

VOUS ...

Répondez aux questions. (*lignes 1–11*)

1. Où voulez-vous aller cet après-midi ?
2. Pourquoi êtes-vous fatiguée ?
3. Quelle sorte de billet achetez-vous ?

(*lignes 12–16*)

4. Y a-t-il quelqu'un dans votre compartiment ?
5. Où est-ce que vous mettez vos bagages ?
6. Qu'est-ce qui s'ouvre soudain ?
7. Qui entre dans le compartiment ?

(*lignes 17–32*)

8. Qui va s'asseoir près de la fenêtre ?
9. Qu'est-ce que la mère voudrait que vous fassiez ?
10. Où est la poupée de Martine ?
11. Qu'est-ce que la mère ne veut pas que les enfants fassent ?
12. Qui veut aller aux toilettes ?
13. Qu'est-ce que la mère voudrait que vous fassiez pendant qu'elle va aux toilettes avec Patou ?

B Expressions utiles

Moyens de transport

aller / arriver / partir / venir / voyager
- à pied
- à bicyclette
- par le / en train
- en voiture
- en avion
- en bateau
- en autobus
- en autocar

faire de l'auto-stop[1]

[1] *to hitchhike*

Il faut composter son billet avant de passer sur le quai.

À la gare

consulter ⎫
regarder ⎬ l'horaire *m* et choisir un train

aller au guichet et acheter un billet
mettre des pièces (de monnaie)[1] dans la machine
faire l'appoint *m*[2]

un billet ⎰ de première (classe), ⎱ ⎰ aller-retour[3]
          ⎱ de deuxième / seconde (classe), ⎰ ⎱ aller / simple

laisser ⎫ ses ⎰ bagages ⎱ à la consigne (automatique)
récupérer ⎭   ⎱ valises ⎰

composter[4] le billet avant d'arriver sur le quai[5]
Les billets sont contrôlés dans le train par le contrôleur.

Les voies et les trains ⎫
Les wagons / voitures et les compartiments ⎬ sont numérotés.

Dans le train

Il y a ⎰ une locomotive.
       ⎱ un wagon / une voiture. ⎰ bar.[6]
       ⎱ un wagon- / une voiture- ⎰ restaurant.
                                    ⎱ lits / couchettes.[7]

N'OUBLIEZ PAS DE COMPOSTER

DO NOT FORGET TO STAMP YOUR TICKET ③
VERGESSEN SIE NICHT, IHREN FAHRSCHEIN ZU ENTWERTEN ③
RICORDATEVI DI OBLITERARE IL VOSTRO BIGLIETTO ④
NO OLVIDE FORMALIZAR SU BILLETE ④
NÃO SE ESQUEÇA DE VALIDAR O SEU BILHETE ⑤
VERGEET NIET UW BILJET AF TE STEMPELEN ⑤

SNCF

[1] **pièces de monnaie**   *coins* (**monnaie**   *change*)

[2] *to give exact change* (The ticket-vending machine will flash this message when it is out of change: **FAITES L'APPOINT**.)

[3] *round-trip*

[4] *to punch* (*with an automatic punching machine*)

[5] *platform*

[6] On y sert des sandwichs, des plats froids, des boissons froides et chaudes.

[7] On peut voyager plus économiquement dans une couchette (mais les wagons-lits offrent plus de confort et de « *privacy* »).

Dans le compartiment il y a $\left\{\begin{array}{l}\text{une fenêtre.}\\ \text{des banquettes.}\\ \text{des filets (à bagages).}\\ \text{des couchettes (des lits).}\\ \text{une porte (entre le compartiment et le couloir).}\end{array}\right.$

le TEE[1] : train international très rapide, avec des voitures de première classe seulement
le TGV[2] : train ultramoderne et exceptionnellement rapide
le TAC[3] : train qui transporte les voitures des passagers qui voyagent en couchettes
le train rapide : train à longue distance ; s'arrête seulement dans les grandes villes
le train express[4] : s'arrête dans les petites villes (moins rapide que le train rapide)
le train omnibus : s'arrête à toutes les gares
le train de marchandises : transporte des marchandises

Le TGV : le train le plus rapide du monde.

C   Pratique

1. Qu'est-ce que c'est qu'un composteur ? Pourquoi y en a-t-il dans toutes les gares en France ?
2. Qu'est-ce qu'on peut faire dans une voiture-bar ? Quelle est la différence entre une voiture-couchettes et une voiture-lits ?

[1]Trans-Europ-Express
[2]Train à Grande Vitesse (vitesse maximum de 260 km/heure)
[3]Train-Autos-Couchettes
[4]On dit « le train direct » en Belgique et en Suisse.

3. Quelle est la différence entre un train rapide et un train express ? Et entre le TEE et le TGV ? Y a-t-il un équivalent du TGV aux États-Unis ?[1]

4. Dans quelle sorte de trains trouve-t-on des wagons-lits ou des wagons-couchettes ? Et des wagons-restaurants ? Les trains omnibus sont rarement des trains à longue distance. Pourquoi ?

5. Qu'est-ce que c'est qu'une consigne (automatique) ? Qu'est-ce que c'est qu'un guichet ?

6. Mettez les phrases suivantes dans l'ordre logique.

   a) Il est naturel que vous vous asseyiez à votre place.
   b) Il faut que vous compostiez votre billet.
   c) Il est nécessaire que vous passiez sur le quai.
   d) Il est important que vous cherchiez votre place dans le train.
   e) Il est bon que vous sachiez sur quelle voie s'arrête le train.
   f) Il vaut mieux que vous achetiez votre billet à l'avance[2].
   g) Il est normal que vous mettiez vos bagages dans le filet.
   h) Il est naturel que vous arriviez à la gare à temps[3].
   i) Il est temps que vous montiez dans le train.

7. Regardez les photos à cette page. Que font ces gens ?

D Horaire : *Regardez cet horaire entre 17 h et 23 h. Vous êtes à Paris (gare d'Austerlitz) et vous voulez aller à Toulouse.*

1. Comparez les trains numéros 9655 et 4417. Quelles différences y a-t-il entre ces deux trains ?

2. Si vous voulez voyager en couchette, quel train prendrez-vous ? Mentionnez l'heure de départ et d'arrivée de ce train.

3. Si vous voulez voyager en voiture-lit, quel train prendrez-vous ? Mentionnez l'heure de départ et d'arrivée de ce train.

4. Combien de trains y a-t-il sans places assises[4] entre 17 h 05 et 22 h 18 ?

5. Si vous voulez arriver à Toulouse avant minuit, quel train prendrez-vous ?

6. Vous avez réservé deux places, en deuxième, dans le train N° 1113. Mais vous avez manqué ce train ! Pourquoi avez-vous manqué le train ? Où vous renseignerez-vous sur le prochain train ? Que ferez-vous pour « tuer le temps » jusqu'au départ de ce train ?

[1]Savez-vous ce que c'est que le *Metroliner* ?

[2]*ahead of time*

[3]*in time* (cf. **à l'heure** *on time*)

[4]Pas de/sans places assises signifie qu'il y a seulement des voitures-couchettes et des voitures-lits ; en général, ce sont des trains de luxe.

Symboles

A Arrivée
D Départ

- Couchettes
- Voiture-lits
- Voiture-restaurant
- Grill-express
- Restauration à la place
- Bar
- Vente ambulante

- Facilités handicapés
- Jeune Voyageur Service
- Train Famille
- Loisirail

Cabine 8

Remarque
Certains trains circulant rarement ne sont pas repris dans cette fiche

Services offerts dans les gares

	information	Réservation	[handicap]	Parcotrain	Location de voitures	Location de vélos	Buffet	Change
Brive-la-Gaillarde	55.23.50.50	55.74.23.97	●	●	●		●	
Cahors	65.22.50.50	65.35.20.41	●	●	●		●	
Caussade (T.-et-G.)	63.63.50.50		●					
Chateauroux	54.27.50.50	54.34.18.51	●	●	●		●	
Gourdon	65.41.02.19	65.41.02.19	●	●	●		●	
Les Aubrais-Orléans	38.53.50.50		●	●	●		●	
Limoges-Bénédictins	55.01.50.50	55.77.72.34	●	●	●		●	
Montauban-Ville-Bourbon	63.63.50.50	63.63.05.14	●	●			●	
Paris-Austerlitz	(1) 45.82.50.50	45.65.60.60	●	●	●		●	●
Souillac	55.23.50.50	65.32.78.21	●	●			●	
Toulouse-Matabiau	61.62.50.50	61.62.85.44	●	●	●		●	●
Vierzon	48.65.50.50	48.75.06.14	●	●	●		●	

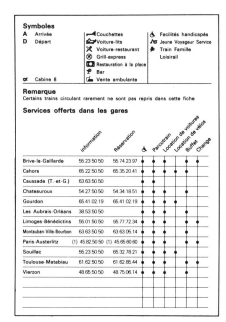

Numéro du train	6201	1386/7	97441	97441	6455/4	4431	97447	4461	4411	4479	77	6471	4427	9655	4415	1113	4417	175	4425
Notes à consulter	1	2	3	4	5		6	18	19	20	21	22	23	24	25	26	27	28	29
Paris-Austerlitz D								17.05	17.17	17.47	18.00	20.03	20.09	21.00	21.06	21.31	22.18	22.53	22.56
Les Aubrais-Orléans D											21.13		22.10	22.40	23.27	23.58			00.01
Vierzon D								18.36					21.56	22.56		00.17			00.55
Chateauroux D								19.09		19.46			22.34	23.35		00.52			01.36
Limoges-Bénédictins D	04.29					06.22		20.20	20.8	20.53	20.53		00.00		01.00	01.17	02.12		03.03
Brive-la-Gaillarde D	05.34	06.04	06.10	06.10		07.30	10.42	21.32	21.34	21.54	21.54	01.10	03.01	02.08		04.26	04.15		04.26
Souillac A	06.02	06.30	06.36	06.36		07.54	11.10									04.52			04.52
Gourdon A			06.57	06.57		08.11	11.29									05.11			05.11
Cahors A	06.44	07.15	07.33	07.33		08.38	11.59	22.33	22.36	22.54	22.54		02.15			05.41	05.29		05.41
Caussade (T.-et-G.) A				08.04		09.04	12.34									06.11			06.11
Montauban-Ville-Bourbon A	07.24	07.55		08.23	08.32	09.20	12.53	23.10	23.15	23.31	23.31		02.56		03.56	06.31	06.20		06.31
Toulouse-Matabiau A	07.54	08.30			08.58	09.50	13.35	23.40	23.45	23.59	23.59	03.20	03.30	06.06	04.28	04.45	07.03	07.00	07.03

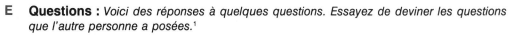

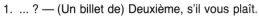

Les trains circulant tous les jours ont leurs horaires indiqués en gras
Tous les trains offrent des places assises en 1re et 2e classe, sauf indication contraire dans les notes.

Notes :

1. Circule:du 30 juin au 1er sept 88 : les jeu. 2°CL.
2. Circule:les mar et sam. 2°CL.
3. Circule:les sam.
4. Circule:tous les jours sauf les sam, dim et fêtes.
5. CORAIL.
6. Circule:les dim.
7. Circule:tous les jours sauf les dim et sauf le 15 août 88. A supplément. 1°CL certains jours.
8. Circule:du 24 juin au 4 sept 88 : tous les jours. Ne prend pas de voyageurs pour Les Aubrais-Orléans. CORAIL.
9. Circule:jusqu'au 23 juin 88 et à partir du 5 sept 88 : tous les jours. Ne prend pas de voyageurs pour Les Aubrais-Orléans. CORAIL certains jours.
19. Circule:les ven sauf le 15 juil 88;Circule le 13 juil 88. Ne prend de voyageurs à Paris-Austerlitz que pour Brive-la-Gaillarde et au-delà. CORAIL. certains jours.
20. Circule:les sam. CORAIL.
21. Circule:tous les jours sauf les sam. Conditions d'admission 'Renseignez-vous'.A supplément de Paris-Austerlitz à Brive-la-Gaillarde. 1°CL certains jours.
22. Circule:les 30 juin, 1, 2, 3 et 13 juil 88;du 29 juil au 2 août 88 : tous les jours;le 12 août 88. 2°CL.
23. Circule:les ven sauf le 15 juil 88;Circule le 13 juil 88.
24. Conditions d'admission 'Renseignez-vous'.Places couchées uniquement. 2°.
26. Ne prend pas de voyageurs en 2eme classe.Ne prend pas de voyageurs en couchettes à Paris-Austerlitz pour Perpignan.Ne prend pas de voyageurs pour Les Aubrais-Orléans.
27. Circule:jusqu'au 23 juin 88 et à partir du 5 sept 88 : tous les jours sauf les ven et dim.

Nota : A Paris-Austerlitz, l'office de tourisme de Paris assure un service d'information touristique et de réservation hotelière.

E Questions : *Voici des réponses à quelques questions. Essayez de deviner les questions que l'autre personne a posées.*[1]

1. ... ? — (Un billet de) Deuxième, s'il vous plaît.
2. ... ? — Deux voitures en avant[2].
3. ... ? — Oui, Mademoiselle. Il faut changer de train à Saumur.
4. ... ? — Non, Monsieur. Le train ne s'arrête pas à Épernay.
5. ... ? — Sur la voie numéro six.
6. ... ? — Oui, Madame. Trois voitures en arrière[3].
7. ... ? — Je suis désolé, mais il vient de partir.
8. ... ? — Non, le train est en retard de dix minutes.
9. ... ? — Cette place est occupée. Je crois que le passager est allé dans la voiture-bar.
10. ... ? — À quinze heures dix.

F Renseignements et opinions

1. Pour un voyage assez court, est-il nécessaire de réserver sa place dans le train ? Et pour un voyage assez long ? Pourquoi (pas) ?
2. Quand vous étiez petit(e), qu'est-ce que votre mère voulait que vous fassiez ? Le faites-vous encore ?
3. Quelle est la différence entre la première classe et la classe touriste dans un avion ?
4. Avez-vous jamais fait de l'auto-stop ? Quels sont les avantages et les inconvénients (et même les dangers !) de l'auto-stop ?
5. Y a-t-il des trains de voyageurs aux États-Unis ? Comment sont-ils ? En avez-vous pris ? Pourquoi (pas) ?

[1]Il y aura quelquefois plusieurs questions possibles : par exemple, pour le numéro 2 : **Où est mon compartiment (ma place**, **la voiture-restaurant**, **la voiture-bar**, etc.).

[2]*forward, in front*

[3]*down, back*

6. Quels sont les avantages et les inconvénients d'un voyage en groupe accompagné d'un(e) guide ?
7. À votre avis, est-il nécessaire qu'une femme mariée perde son nom de jeune fille ? Quels avantages et inconvénients y voyez-vous ?

Compréhension auditive (basée sur l'Application A)

Compréhension auditive (basée sur l'Application B)

Compréhension auditive

Compréhension auditive

Le cyclomoteur est un moyen de transport très pratique.   *Le Concorde est le seul avion commercial supersonique du monde.*

G   Lecture

Les transports

Pour commencer par le commencement, un des moyens de locomotion qui a presque disparu[1] aux États-Unis mais qui est encore utilisé en France, c'est la marche à pied. Une grande partie de la population habite dans des villages et des petites villes. D'autre part°, les villes importantes sont divisées en quartiers. Chaque quartier est comme un village — les habitants peuvent facilement se rendre° à pied dans les magasins, à l'école ou à l'église. De plus°, les   5
rues sont souvent agréables : on flâne, on regarde les vitrines, on fait des courses, on voit des visages familiers, on s'arrête pour bavarder un moment.

Pour aller un peu plus loin, c'est le vélo° ou le cyclomoteur° qui est le plus pratique. Les cyclomoteurs ont un grand succès en France : ils ne coûtent pas cher, ils consomment très peu d'essence, on n'a pas besoin de permis de conduire° pour les utiliser. Pour circuler dans   10
une grande ville ou dans sa banlieue on peut prendre l'autobus. Les villages sont reliés entre eux par un réseau d'autocars. Pour les voyages plus longs, on a le choix — et beaucoup de gens prennent leur voiture. Les routes nationales sont en général très belles, souvent bordées de grands arbres, mais insuffisantes à la circulation du dimanche soir ou des vacances. Les autoroutes sont à péage° ; elles ressemblent aux autoroutes d'Allemagne ou des États-Unis   15
— très monotones mais parfaites pour les gens pressés !

On the other hand

aller / Moreover

bicyclette / une bicyclette équipée d'un très petit moteur   driver's license

toll (sauf autour d'une grande ville)

[1]participe passé de **disparaître** *to disappear*, conjugué comme **connaître** et **paraître**

Corporation, Company

voies ferrées = chemins de fer

dans le Sud, vers la mer Méditerranée/tempting familles de trois enfants et plus/passes

avoir recours à   *to have recourse to*

Indiscutablement, le point fort de la France, ce sont ses trains. La Société° Nationale des Chemins de Fer (la SNCF), sous contrôle de l'État, gère[1] remarquablement le réseau de voies ferrées° et le modernise constamment. Presque toutes les grandes lignes partent de Paris et relient la capitale à toutes les villes importantes de France et d'Europe. Les trains sont ponc-   20
tuels, rapides et confortables. Les wagons-restaurants, les wagons-lits et les couchettes rendent les longs voyages plus agréables et moins fatigants. La SNCF encourage le public à voyager en train — des affiches colorées l'invitent au pays du soleil°, à la mer et à la montagne. Les avantages économiques sont encore plus tentants° : tarifs réduits pour les étudiants, les enfants, les militaires, les familles nombreuses°, billets de groupe, billets touristiques, cartes   25
d'abonnement° pour les gens qui voyagent régulièrement en train, prix spéciaux pour les vacances en famille, pour les sports d'hiver, etc.

Les grandes villes sont reliées entre elles par un réseau aérien. La plus grande ligne aérienne s'appelle Air France et elle aussi est sous contrôle de l'État. Les Français commencent à s'habituer aux voyages en avion, et sont souvent obligés d'y avoir recours°. Mais dans   30
l'ensemble, contrairement aux Américains, ils préfèrent, sauf peut-être pour les affaires[2], voyager sur la terre ferme. Il est à remarquer, d'ailleurs, que les distances à parcourir à l'intérieur du pays sont assez courtes et que les trains *rapides* sont vraiment rapides. Le TGV, qui roule à la vitesse maximum de 260 km/heure, va de Paris à Lyon (385 km) en deux heures !

A   *Indiquez si chaque commentaire est vrai ou faux. S'il est faux, corrigez le commentaire.*

1. Les Français aiment se promener dans les rues plus que les Américains.
2. Il faut un permis de conduire pour conduire un cyclomoteur.
3. Les vélos consomment plus d'essence que les cyclomoteurs.
4. Les trains en France sont renommés pour leur ponctualité, leur rapidité et leur confort.
5. Quand les Français doivent se déplacer, ils aiment mieux voyager en avion qu'en voiture.
6. Les distances à parcourir à l'intérieur du pays sont moins longues aux États-Unis qu'en France.
7. Tous les chemins de fer et toutes les lignes aériennes en France sont sous contrôle de l'État.
8. Les routes nationales ne sont pas suffisantes à la circulation des vacances ou du dimanche soir.

B   *Trouvez dans le texte l'antonyme des mots suivants.*

faible	court	inconvénient
extérieur	inconnu	suffisant
petit	désagréable	échec
régional	couper	lent

C   *Trouvez dans le texte les mots qui sont définis ci-dessous.*

1. grande route sans feux sur laquelle on peut rouler vite
2. la région sud de la France, près de la mer Méditerranée
3. wagon où on peut prendre un repas
4. une bicyclette équipée d'un très petit moteur
5. se déplacer, voyager
6. autorisation écrite nécessaire pour conduire une voiture
7. famille qui a trois enfants ou plus
8. qui concerne l'air ou l'aviation

[1]du verbe **gérer** *to manage*
[2]*business* (toujours employé au pluriel dans ce sens)

VOCABULAIRE

Noms

un **accès**	access	la crevette	shrimp	le panier	basket
un aller	one-way ticket	le filet (à bagages)	(luggage) rack	le **panneau**	panel, board
un aller-retour	round-trip ticket	le filet à crevettes	fishing (literally, shrimp) net	le **passager**	passenger
les bagages *m*	baggage			la **peine**	trouble
le ballon	ball; balloon	le **fond**	back; bottom	le pipi	pee
le **billet**	ticket	le **fumeur**	smoker	le Pschitt	fruit-flavored soda
le **compartiment**	compartment	un **horaire**	timetable, schedule		
le **composteur**	ticket-punching machine	le **joueur**	player	la **sortie (de secours)**	(emergency) exit
		la **maîtresse**	schoolteacher	les toilettes *f*	rest room
la consigne	checkroom, locker	la matinée	morning	la **voiture-couchettes**	economy sleeping car
la **couchette**	economy-class berth	le **milieu**	middle		
		la **pancarte**	sign; billboard	la **voiture-restaurant**	dining car

Verbes

s'asseoir *irrég*	to sit down	**falloir** *irrég*	to be necessary; to require	**signifier**	to mean; to signify
composter	to punch (ticket)			surveiller	to watch
défendre (de)	to forbid	**former**	to form	**tirer**	to pull
désirer	to wish	s'ouvrir *irrég*	to open up	**valoir** *irrég*	to be worth
exiger	to demand	**pousser**	to push		

Adjectifs

assis(e)	seated, sitting	**exposé(e)**	exhibited	**ordinaire**	ordinary
certain(e)	certain	fatigant(e)	tiring	**probable**	probable
clair(e)	clear	**inférieur(e)**	lower	**remarquable**	remarkable
douteux(euse)	doubtful	installé(e)	settled	seul(e)	alone
étonnant(e)	astonishing	**juste**	just, right		
évident(e)	obvious	**naturel(le)**	natural		

Adverbes

attentivement	attentively	**debout**	standing	soudain	suddenly
confortablement	comfortably	heureusement	fortunately	**tant de**	so much; so many

Autres expressions

accès interdit	no entry		faire pipi	to pee
à haute voix	out loud		**il est temps**	it is time
au fond de	at the back of		**il faut**	it is necessary; one must
au milieu de	in the middle of		**il ne faut pas**	one must not
cela ne vaut pas la peine	it's not worth the trouble		**il vaudrait mieux**	it would be better
être à l'heure	to be on time		**il vaut mieux**	it is better
être debout	to be standing		**valoir la peine**	to be worth the trouble
faire du bruit	to make noise			

[1]Angers est dans la région ouest de la France, à 310 km de Paris.

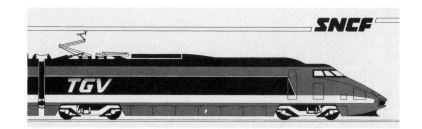

20 Au restaurant

LESSON OBJECTIVES

Theme and Culture

1. Menu items
2. Restaurants and home cooking

Communication Skills

1. Expressing one's opinions and reactions about other people and events (*I'm glad, I'm sorry, I don't think*)
2. Expressing ideas in complex sentence patterns (using conjunctions rather than prepositions)
3. Inviting people to do something together
4. Accepting/Declining invitations
5. Understanding typical restaurant menus

Structures

20.1 Adjective + **de** + infinitive
20.2 Subjunctive: after expressions of emotion
20.3 Subjunctive: after negation and expressions of doubt
20.4 Subjunctive: after certain conjunctions
20.5 **Courir, mourir**

CONVERSATIONS

A. Dans un restaurant français[1]

Avez-vous jamais voyagé en France ? Avez-vous jamais dîné dans un restaurant français ? Essayez de répondre aux questions suivantes. Si vous ne savez pas la réponse, dites ce qu'on fait aux États-Unis, puis demandez au professeur comment on fait en France.

1. Qu'est-ce que c'est que les hors-d'œuvre ? Quand est-ce qu'on les sert ?
2. Quelle sorte de boisson peut-on commander avant le dîner ? Est-il nécessaire qu'on commande une boisson ?
3. En général, avec quelle sorte de plat est-ce qu'on commande du vin blanc ? Et du vin rouge ?
4. Dans quelle main est-ce qu'on tient sa fourchette ? Et son couteau ?
5. Vous avez pris un morceau de pain. Où allez-vous le poser ? Y a-t-il du beurre sur la table ?

---

[1]La carte des *Expressions utiles* est enregistrée sur la bande magnétique.

Ils déjeunent en haut de la Tour Eiffel.

6. Vous voulez prendre du café. Quand est-ce que le garçon vous en apporte ?
7. Quand est-ce qu'on mange de la salade verte ? Est-ce qu'il y a une variété de sauces pour la salade comme aux États-Unis ?
8. Est-ce qu'on sert le fromage avant ou après le dessert ? Avec quoi mange-t-on le fromage ?
9. Est-il possible de savoir combien coûte un repas avant d'entrer dans un restaurant ?
10. Qu'est-ce que cela veut dire quand le menu indique que le service est compris ? Et quand le menu dit : « 15 % service non compris »[1] ou « 15 % service en sus /ɑ̃sys/ » ?
11. Si on n'a pas très faim, peut-on commander tout simplement un sandwich et une boisson rafraîchissante ?
12. Si on est pressé ou si on n'a pas très faim, peut-on commander un ou deux plats avec une boisson ?

B. Je meurs de faim !

ÉTIENNE   Je meurs de faim. Veux-tu que nous nous arrêtions pour déjeuner ?
MIREILLE   Je veux bien, mais je ne crois pas qu'il y ait de restaurant dans cette rue.
ÉTIENNE   Il y a un petit bistrot pas très loin d'ici. Allons-y.
MIREILLE   D'accord. Je suis contente que tu connaisses bien la ville.

Compréhension auditive (basée sur la Conversation A)

DIFFÉRENCES[2]

Le menu ou la carte ?
The fame of French cuisine has spread to all corners of the world. Included in its great variety is everything from cheeses to meats cooked in the finest sauces and the most

---

[1]Quand le service n'est pas compris, il est ajouté automatiquement à l'addition (le client doit le payer).
[2]This is the last lesson in which *Différences* appears.

delicate pastries. When you travel in France, you will find that dining in a restaurant can be a gastronomic delight. But first it helps to distinguish between **le menu (à prix fixe)** and **la carte**. **Le menu** consists of complete dinners at several different prices: **le menu à 80 francs** and **le menu à 120 francs**, for example. Each menu has its own choice of hors d'oeuvres, entrées, and desserts, and both the food and the choices become better as the price goes up. A **menu gastronomique** may have as many as six courses: (1) hors d'oeuvres; (2) entrée (a small quantity of shellfish, grilled fish, a quiche, or an omelette); (3) **le plat de résistance** (the main dish of meat, fowl, or fish with vegetables); (4) green salad; (5) **plateau de fromages** or **fromages assortis** (*assorted cheeses*); and (6) dessert. It is said that gourmets order a different kind of wine with each course! This, as you can imagine, is too much food, and most full menus consist of four courses: (1), (2) or (3), (4) or (5), and (6).

If you don't like the choices offered in the **menus**, you can order from **la carte** (cf. the English expression *to order à la carte*). This will cost you much more, if you order all the courses offered—although just a few dishes will normally suffice—but there is a much wider choice of hors d'oeuvres, meat dishes, vegetables, and desserts. By law, all restaurants in France must post, both inside and outside, the prices of the menus of the day and indicate whether the service charge is included or not. (It usually is.) Not all French families have the same eating habits or the same opinions about food and cooking. In the *Lecture* of this lesson you will find three people expressing rather different attitudes.

STRUCTURES

20.1 ADJECTIF + **DE** + INFINITIF

1. Many adjectives can be followed by **de** + infinitive when the subject of the main clause is the same as that of the infinitive.

Je suis certain... J'irai à Rome.	*I'm certain . . . I will go to Rome.*
→ Je suis **certain d'aller** à Rome.	*I'm certain to go to Rome.*
Nous sommes fatigués... Nous mangeons des carottes.	*We are tired . . . We eat carrots.*
→ Nous sommes **fatigués de manger** des carottes.	*We are tired of eating carrots.*

capable	capable	**fier (fière)**	proud
certain(e)	certain	**heureux(euse)**	happy
content(e)	satisfied; glad	**malheureux(euse)**	unhappy
mécontent(e)	dissatisfied	**obligé(e)**	obliged
curieux(euse)	curious	**satisfait(e)**	satisfied
enchanté(e)	delighted	**sûr(e)**	sure
étonné(e)	astonished	**surpris(e)**	surprised
fatigué(e)	tired		

Je suis **enchantée de** vous **voir**.	*I am delighted to see you.*
Elle est **sûre de venir** à temps.	*She is sure to come in time.*
Nous sommes **étonnés de** le **savoir**.	*We are astonished to know it.*
Êtes-vous **content d'être** à Paris ?	*Are you satisfied to be in Paris?*

2. All the adjectives above, except **obligé(e)**, can also take **de** + noun.

Je suis **enchantée de cette nouvelle**.	*I am delighted with this news.*
Elle est **sûre de sa réponse**.	*She is sure of her answer.*
Nous sommes **étonnés de son absence**.	*We are astonished by his/her absence.*
Êtes-vous **content de votre hôtel** ?	*Are you satisfied with your hotel?*

Both **de** + infinitive and **de** + noun can be replaced by the pronoun **en**.

Je suis très heureux **de vous voir ici.**
Je suis très heureux **de votre présence.** } J'**en** suis très heureux.

Marie est certaine **de vous répondre.**
Marie est certaine **de sa réponse.** } Marie **en** est certaine.

3. *Compound infinitive.* The infinitive can be "compounded" with the auxiliary **avoir** or **être** if the event it expresses precedes the time (tense) of the main verb (here **être** + adjective). Note that in negation **ne** and **pas** come in front of both simple and compound infinitives.[1]

Je suis enchanté de vous **voir**.	*I am delighted to see you.*
Je suis enchanté de vous **avoir vu**.	*I am delighted to have seen you.*
Elles sont heureuses de **venir**.	*They are happy to come.*
Elles sont heureuses d'**être venues**.	*They are happy to have come.*
Il est malheureux de **ne pas** le **faire**.	*He is unhappy about not doing it.*
Il est malheureux de **ne pas** l'**avoir fait**.	*He is unhappy about not having done it.*

JE SUIS ENCHANTÉE DE VOUS VOIR.

JE SUIS CONTENTE DE L'AVOIR VU.

TABLEAU 106

 A *J'ai très faim et je vais déjeuner dans un restaurant. Écoutez bien et modifiez les phrases d'après ce modèle.*[2]

Je verrai tant de bonnes choses ; j'en serai étonné(e).
Vous serez étonné(e) de voir tant de bonne choses.

1. Je mange des sandwichs ; j'en suis fatigué(e).
2. Je déjeunerai dans un restaurant ; j'en suis sûr(e).
3. Je demanderai la carte ; j'en suis certain(e).
4. Je verrai tant de bonnes choses ; j'en serai étonné(e).
5. Je commencerai par des escargots ; j'en serai content(e).
6. Je boirai un litre de vin ; j'en serai capable !
7. Je ne commanderai pas de poulet ; j'en suis sûr(e).
8. Je n'aurai pas faim après ce repas ; j'en suis certain(e).

---

[1]Other negative constructions with infinitives will be discussed in Lesson 21.3.

[2]This is the last lesson in which the reminder to use the feminine forms of nouns and adjectives, such as **étudiant(e)** and **certain(e)**, when appropriate, will be indicated in exercises.

« *Nous sommes contents de dîner dans ce restaurant. La cuisine est excellente.* »

B *D'abord remplacez les noms par les pronoms appopriés, ensuite mettez chaque infinitif au passé, d'après ce modèle.*

> Je suis content(e) de faire ce travail.
> (Monique) **Je suis contente de le faire.**
> (Jacques) **Je suis content de l'avoir fait.**

1. Je suis content(e) de voir ce film.
2. Êtes-vous heureux(euse) d'aller au musée ?
3. Nous sommes surpris(es) de rencontrer ces enfants.
4. Le professeur est certain de ne pas manger d'escargots.
5. Je suis enchanté(e) de voir vos amis à la soirée.
6. Elle sera satisfaite d'acheter ce cadeau dans ce magasin.

C *Répondez aux questions.*

1. Parlons du déjeuner. Qu'est-ce que vous êtes certain(e) de boire ? Qu'est-ce que vous êtes fatigué(e) de manger ?
2. Parlons du dîner. Où est-ce que vous êtes obligé(e) de dîner ? Où est-ce que vous seriez heureux(euse) de dîner ?
3. Parlons d'hier. Qu'est-ce que vous étiez certain(e) de faire ? L'avez-vous fait ? Êtes-vous content(e) de l'avoir fait ? Qu'est-ce que vous êtes mécontent(e) de ne pas avoir fait ?
4. Qui avez-vous vu ce matin ? Êtes-vous heureux(euse) d'avoir vu cette personne ? Êtes-vous surpris(e) de l'avoir vu(e) ?

20.2 SUBJONCTIF : APRÈS LES EXPRESSIONS D'ÉMOTION

1. The subjunctive occurs in the dependent clause when the verb in the main clause expresses emotion (such as feelings of *joy, regret, sorrow, anger, surprise,* and *fear.*

Je **suis heureux** que vous **puissiez** venir.	*I am happy (glad)*
Je **suis content** qu'on **ait choisi** ce restaurant.	*I am satisfied*
Je **regrette** que la soupe ne **soit** pas chaude.	*I am sorry*
Je **suis désolé** que le service **soit** mauvais.	*I am very sorry*
Je **suis malheureux** que le garçon ne me **comprenne** pas.	*I am unhappy*
Je **suis furieux** que le steak **soit** si dur.	*I am furious*
Je **suis mécontent** qu'il n'y **ait** pas de fruits.	*I am dissatisfied*

« Je ne suis pas contente qu'on l'ait servie la première. J'étais devant elle. »

Je **suis fâché**[1] que le vin ne **soit** pas bon.	*I am angry (sorry)*
Je **suis surpris** que le repas **soit** médiocre.	*I am surprised*
Je **suis étonné** qu'on **ait recommandé** ce restaurant.	*I am astonished*
J'**ai peur** que ce **soit** une soirée perdue.[2]	*I am afraid*

2. The expressions above take **de** + infinitive instead of a dependent clause when the subject of the main clause is the same as that of the infinitive (Lesson 20.1).

SAME SUBJECT

Je suis heureux : **je** suis ici.

→ **Je** suis heureux **d'être** ici.

Il est désolé : **il** ne viendra pas.

→ **Il** est désolé **de ne pas venir**.

Je suis surpris : **je** vous vois.

→ **Je** suis surpris **de** vous **voir**.

DIFFERENT SUBJECTS

Je suis heureux : **vous** êtes ici.

→ **Je** suis heureux **que vous soyez** ici.

Il est désolé : **elle** ne viendra pas.

→ **Il** est désolé **qu'elle** ne **vienne** pas.

Elle est surprise : **on** l'a vue.

→ **Elle** est surprise **qu'on** l'**ait vue**.

3. Both **que** + dependent clause and **de** + infinitive can be replaced by the pronoun **en**, except in the case of **regretter**, which takes **le**.

Êtes-vous contente **que nous puissions dîner avec vous** ?

→ Oui, j'**en** suis très contente.

Êtes-vous contente **de dîner dans ce restaurant** ?

→ Oui, j'**en** suis très contente.

Est-il surpris **que nous l'ayons vu** ?

→ Non, il n'**en** est pas surpris.

Est-il surpris **de nous voir** ?

→ Non, il n'**en** est pas surpris.

---

[1]Depending on the context, **fâché** can mean *angry* or *sorry*.

[2]In very formal French, **ne** is added before the subjunctive after **avoir peur que** even if the subjunctive is in the affirmative:
J'ai peur que ce ne soit une soirée perdue *I am afraid it is a lost evening* (discussed in Lesson 25.3).

BUT

Regrettez-vous **que nous n'ayons pas choisi ce restaurant** ?

→ Oui, je **le** regrette beaucoup.

Regrettez-vous **de ne pas dîner dans ce restaurant** ?

→ Non, je ne **le** regrette pas.

Subject +	Emotions	+	**que** + Different subject	+	Subjunctive
			de + (Same subject → 0)	+	Infinitive

TABLEAU 107 « Mais entrez donc, je **suis heureuse** que vous **ayez pu** venir. »

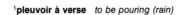 **A** *Julien a invité Ignès à faire une promenade. Ils sortent ensemble mais, malheureusement, il commence bientôt à pleuvoir. Reliez les deux phrases d'après ce modèle.*

Je suis désolé : il pleut à verse[1].
Je suis désolé qu'il pleuve à verse.

1. Je suis content : tu peux venir.
2. Je suis heureux : tu es venue.
3. Je regrette : il ne fait pas beau.
4. Je suis fâché : il pleut.
5. Je suis désolé : nous avons oublié nos parapluies.
6. Je suis étonné : il pleut à verse.
7. Je suis malheureux : nous sommes mouillés.
8. Je suis surpris : tu ne veux pas rentrer ?

B *Vous êtes dans un restaurant que quelqu'un vous a recommandé. Mais le repas est médiocre et le service est mauvais. Vous êtes très mécontent(e). Reliez les deux phrases d'après ce modèle.*

Le repas est si médiocre. Je suis fâché(e).
Je suis fâché(e) que le repas soit si médiocre.

1. Vous pouvez sortir avec moi. Je suis heureux(euse).
2. Le restaurant n'est pas bondé. Je suis surpris(e).
3. Le garçon ne me comprend pas. Je suis furieux(euse).
4. La soupe n'est pas chaude. Je ne suis pas content(e).
5. La viande est dure comme du caoutchouc[2]. Je suis fâché(e).
6. La salade n'est pas fraîche. Je le regrette.
7. Il n'y a pas de glace au chocolat[3]. Je suis mécontent(e).
8. Le repas a coûté cher[4]. Je suis étonné(e).

[1]**pleuvoir à verse** *to be pouring (rain)*

[2]/kautʃu/ *rubber*

[3]*chocolate ice cream*

[4]**coûter cher** = coûter beaucoup d'argent

C *Répondez aux questions d'après ces modèles. Vous n'avez pas besoin de répondre affirmativement.*

> Vous êtes dans ce cours ; en êtes-vous content(e) ?
> **Je (ne) suis (pas) content(e) d'être dans ce cours.**
> Je parle français avec vous : en êtes-vous content(e) ?
> **Je (ne) suis (pas) content(e) que vous parliez français avec moi.**

1. Vous apprenez le français ; en êtes-vous heureux(euse) ?
2. Je parle français avec vous ; en êtes-vous mécontent(e) ?
3. Vous êtes dans ce cours ; le regrettez-vous ?
4. Je vous comprends très bien ; en êtes-vous surpris(e) ?
5. Vous avez fait des progrès ; est-ce que j'en suis content(e) ?
6. J'adore manger des escargots ; en êtes-vous étonné(e) ?
7. Je suis votre professeur ; est-ce que j'en suis malheureux(euse) ?
8. Nous parlons de la cuisine française ; en êtes-vous heureux(euse) ?

D *Complétez les phrases suivantes avec votre partenaire.*

1. Nous sommes content(e)s que vous...
2. Nous ne sommes pas étonné(e)s que le cours...
3. Nous sommes heureux(euses) de...
4. Nous regrettons que vous...
5. Nous sommes surpris(es) que...

📼 *Exercice supplémentaire*

📼 *Compréhension auditive*

20.3 SUBJONCTIF : APRÈS LA NÉGATION ET LES EXPRESSIONS DE DOUTE ET D'INCERTITUDE

1. When the verb in the main clause expresses any kind of negative thinking or feeling (*denial, doubt, uncertainty*), the subjunctive occurs in the dependent clause.

Je **nie** que le repas **ait été** mauvais.	*I deny*
Je **ne dis pas** que tu **sois** paresseuse.	*I am not saying*
Je **ne crois pas** qu'il **pleuve** ce soir.	*I don't believe (think)*
Je **ne pense pas** qu'elle **puisse** venir.	*I don't think*
Je **n'espère pas** qu'il **fasse** froid ce soir.	*I am not hoping*
Je **doute** que vous m'**ayez vu.**	*I doubt*
Je **ne suis pas sûr** qu'elle **soit rentrée.**	*I am not sure*
Il **n'est pas certain** que tu m'**aies compris.**[1]	*It is not certain*
Il **n'est pas clair** que ce **soit** vrai.[1]	*It is not clear*

2. Note, however, that all of the expressions above take the indicative if the element of denial, doubt, or uncertainty is removed from the main clause.

Je **ne nie pas** que le repas **a été** mauvais.	*I don't deny (= I affirm)*
Je **dis** que tu **es** paresseuse.	*I'm saying*
Je **crois**[2] qu'il **pleuvra** ce soir.	*I believe (think)*
Je **pense**[2] qu'elle **pourra** venir.	*I think*
J'**espère**[2] qu'il **fera** froid ce soir.	*I hope*

[1]The impersonal expressions denoting uncertainty were presented in Lesson 19.2.

[2]**Croire, penser,** and **espérer** never take the subjunctive in *affirmative* statements, even if a degree of uncertainty may be implied.

Je **ne doute pas** que vous m'**avez vu**.   *I don't doubt (= I'm certain)*

Je **suis sûr** qu'elle **est rentrée**.   *I am sure*

Il **est certain** que tu m'**as compris**.   *It is certain*

Il **est clair** que c'**est** vrai.   *It is clear*

3. You may hear the subjunctive in *questions*, after some of the expressions above. The mood of the verb in the dependent clause often depends on the speaker's feeling. The subjunctive is used if the speaker feels *doubt* or *uncertainty* about the event. The indicative occurs if the speaker feels either *neutral* or *certain* about it.

Croyez-vous qu'il **pleuve** ce soir ?   (I *doubt* it will rain)

Croyez-vous qu'il **pleuvra** ce soir ?   (I think it will/I have no idea)

Pensez-vous qu'elle **soit** heureuse ?   (I *don't think* she is)

Pensez-vous qu'elle **est** heureuse ?   (I think so/I really don't know)

Est-il clair qu'elle t'**ait compris** ?   (I *don't think* it's clear)

Est-il clair qu'elle t'**a compris** ?   (I think it's clear/I don't know)

Subject + Uncertainty / Negation / Doubt + **que** + Different subject + Subjunctive

TABLEAU 108   **Je ne crois pas** qu'il **ait fini** ses devoirs. Le croyez-vous ?

 A   *Je parle d'un touriste. Il a beaucoup marché ce matin et il est fatigué. Mais il est encore trop tôt pour déjeuner. Qu'est-ce qu'il va faire ? Reliez les deux phrases d'après ces modèles.*

Est-il fatigué ? Je pense que oui.[1]

Je pense qu'il est fatigué.

Veut-il déjeuner ? J'en doute.[2]

Je doute qu'il veuille déjeuner.

1. Est-il fatigué ? Je crois que oui.
2. Veut-il déjeuner ? J'en doute.
3. A-t-il faim ? Je pense que non.
4. A-t-il soif ? Je pense que oui.
5. Va-t-il dans un café ? Je crois que oui.
6. Connaît-il ce café ? Je ne le dis pas.
7. Boira-t-il du café ? Je n'en suis pas sûr(e).
8. Prendra-t-il une boisson rafraîchissante ? J'espère que oui.

---

[1]Voir la Leçon 11.4 pour cette construction.

[2]Le verbe **douter** prend **de** + nom ou **que** + proposition ; tous les deux peuvent être remplacés par le pronom **en** : **Je doute de sa sincérité → J'en doute** ; **Je doute qu'il soit venu → J'en doute**.

B   *Répondez aux questions.*

1. Croyez-vous qu'il fera beau demain ? Demandez à (Yves) s'il croit qu'il pleuvra ce soir.
2. Pensez-vous que le français est facile ? Demandez à (Marianne) si elle pense que le français est difficile.
3. Dites-vous que je suis intelligent(e) ? Demandez à (Jacques) s'il dit que je suis bête.
4. Doutez-vous que je sache votre adresse ? Demandez à (Robert) s'il doute que je connaisse ses parents.
5. Espérez-vous que je serai malade ? Demandez à (Mireille) si elle espère que je serai malade.

C   *Est-ce que vous me connaissez bien ? Donnez votre opinion en employant les expressions suivantes, d'après ce modèle.*

>   Je suis né(e) en France.
>   **Je crois que vous êtes né(e) en France.**
>   **Je ne crois pas que vous soyez né(e) en France.**

Je crois / Je ne crois pas	Je suis certain(e) / Je ne suis pas certain(e)
Je pense / Je ne pense pas	Je suis sûr(e) / Je ne suis pas sûr(e)
Je doute / Je ne doute pas	Je nie / Je ne nie pas

1. Je suis né(e) aux États-Unis.	5. J'ai des enfants.
2. J'ai quarante ans.	6. Je parle trois langues.
3. J'adore la cuisine chinoise.	7. J'ai une voiture japonaise.
4. Je suis professeur depuis six ans.	8. J'habite dans une maison.

D   *Faites des phrases en employant les expressions suivantes.*

1. Je suis content(e)		vous/être allé(e)/Europe.
2. Je ne suis pas heureux(euse)		il/faire/très beau/ce week-end.
3. Je sais depuis longtemps		vous/être/un(e) millionnaire.
4. Je ne crois pas		vous/aimer/manger/escargots.
5. Je ne suis pas étonné(e)		il/pleuvoir/demain.
6. J'espère bien	que	la cuisine/resto-U/être/mauvaise.
7. Je ne pense pas		(Michèle)/avoir voyagé/...[1]
8. Je crois certainement		(Daniel)/être/très...[2]
9. Je ne veux pas		tant de monde/avoir voté/pour...[3]
10. Je souhaite		vous/s'appeler/Napoléon Bonaparte.
11. Je doute vraiment		ma chambre/être/plus...[2]
12. Je suis certain(e)		...[4]

 Exercice supplémentaire

 Compréhension auditive

---

[1]Ajoutez le nom d'un pays.

[2]Ajoutez un adjectif.

[3]Ajoutez le nom d'un homme d'état.

[4]Ajoutez votre propre phrase. (**propre** *own*)

20.4   SUBJONCTIF : APRÈS CERTAINES CONJONCTIONS

1. Conjunctions are used to connect two or more sentences together. Some conjunctions require the subjunctive. Here are some common ones.

à moins que[1]	*unless*	**jusqu'à ce que**	*until*
avant que[1]	*before*	**pour que**	*so that*
bien que	*although*	**pourvu que**	*provided*

Je vais faire une promenade **à moins qu'**il **pleuve**.

Finissez ce travail **avant qu'**elle **vienne**.

Elle n'est pas là **bien que** tout le monde l'**attende**.

Il restera ici **jusqu'à ce que** vous **arriviez**.

Nous l'aidons **pour qu'**il **puisse** réussir.

Il pourra réussir **pourvu que** nous l'**aidions**.

2. **Avant que** and **pour que** are not used when the subject of the dependent clause is the same as that of the main clause. In such a case, **avant de/pour** + infinitive is used.

Je sortirai **avant de déjeuner**.	*before eating lunch*
Je suis chez elle **pour l'aider**.	*in order to help her*

3. Other conjunctions, most of which you have learned before this lesson, take the indicative.

Je travaillais **pendant que** tu **dormais**	*while*
Il se lève tard **puisque** c'**est** samedi.	*since*
Elle se repose **parce qu'**elle **est** fatiguée.	*because*
Elle parlait français **quand** elle **était** petite.	*when*
J'irai au cinéma **si** je ne **suis** pas occupé.	*if*

Subject	Any expression	Some conjunctions / Other conjunctions	Different subject	Subjunctive / Indicative

TABLEAU 109   Il veut sortir **bien qu'il pleuve**.   Moi, je veux attendre **jusqu'à ce qu'il fasse** beau.

[1]In very formal French, these expressions require **ne** before the subjunctive in the affirmative: **Je vais faire une promenade à moins qu'il ne pleuve** *I am going to take a walk unless it rains*; **Finissez ce travail avant qu'elle ne vienne** *Finish this work before she comes* (discussed in Lesson 25.3).

A *C'est un jeune homme qui parle. Il va aller dans une discothèque avec son amie. Reliez les deux phrases en employant la conjonction indiquée, d'après ce modèle.*

Je sortirai ce soir. Martine est occupée.   (à moins que)
Je sortirai ce soir à moins que Martine soit occupée.

1. Je sortirai ce soir. Martine est libre.   (si)
2. Je lui téléphonerai. Elle me répondra.   (jusqu'à ce que)
3. Nous irons dans une disco. Elle veut aller ailleurs.   (à moins que)
4. Martine choisira la disco. Elle aime danser.   (parce que)
5. Nous prendrons l'autobus. Nous n'avons pas de voiture.   (puisque)
6. Nous quitterons la disco. Martine pourra rentrer avant minuit.   (pour que)
7. Nous appellerons un taxi. Il commence à pleuvoir.   (parce que)
8. Je rentrerai chez moi. Il pleuvra à verse.   (avant que)

B *Répondez aux questions en employant les conjonctions indiquées, d'après ce modèle.*

Voulez-vous dîner dans un restaurant ?   (Oui, pourvu que)
Oui, pourvu que j'aie assez d'argent (*ou* que je sois libre, que je ne sois pas occupé(e), etc.).

1. Voulez-vous aller au cinéma ?   (Oui, pourvu que)
2. Voulez-vous faire une promenade ?   (Oui, avant que)
3. Voulez-vous aider votre partenaire ?   (Oui, bien que)
4. Voulez-vous sortir ce soir ?   (Non, parce que)
5. Voulez-vous quitter la classe ?   (Non, à moins que)
6. Voulez-vous faire vos devoirs ce soir ?   (Oui, avant de)
7. Voulez-vous rester dans la classe ?   (Oui, jusqu'à ce que)
8. Voulez-vous savoir l'adresse de (Morgan Fairchild) ?   (Oui, pour que)

C *Maintenant, complétez les phrases suivantes avec votre partenaire.*

1. Nous sortirons samedi soir à moins que...
2. Nous irons au labo avant de...
3. Nous ferons notre travail pourvu que...
4. Nous serons à l'université jusqu'à ce que...

 Compréhension auditive

20.5 COURIR, MOURIR

1. **Courir** *to run* is conjugated with **avoir** in compound tenses. The double **r** in the future and conditional is pronounced twice as long as the single **r** in the other tenses.

courir

cours	courons
cours	courez
court	courent
couru	
courrai	

Je **cours** à la maison.
Tu **cours** trop vite.
 Il **court** cent mètres.

Nous **courons** ensemble.
Vous **courez** plus vite que moi.
 Ils **courent** un kilomètre.

J'ai **couru** vers la gare.
Je **courrai** /kurre/ avec toi.

2. *To run* in the sense of *to function* or *to work* is **marcher**.

Votre voiture **marche** bien.	*Your car runs well.*
Cette pendule ne **marche** plus.	*This clock no longer works.*
L'ascenseur ne **marche** pas ; il est en panne.[1]	*The elevator isn't running/working; it's out of order.*

3. Study the conjugation of **mourir (de)** *to die (of, from)*. Only the **nous** and **vous** forms of the present indicative are similar to those of **courir**. **Mourir** is conjugated with **être** in compound tenses. Like **courir**, the double **r** in the future and conditional is pronounced twice as long as the single **r** in the other tenses.

mourir

meurs	mourons
meurs	mourez
meurt	meurent
mort	
mourrai	

Je **meurs** de faim.
Tu **meurs** de soif.
Elle **meurt** d'ennui.

Nous **mourons** de fatigue.
Vous **mourez** de curiosité.
Elles **meurent** de peur.

Il est **mort** il y a dix ans.
Je **mourrai** /murre/ d'ennui si je reste ici.

A *Exercice de contrôle*

Je cours quand je suis en retard.

1. Nous   2. On   3. Vous   4. Tu

J'ai chaud et je meurs de soif !

1. Vous   2. Tu   3. Nous   4. On

Vous n'avez pas couru dans le marathon de Boston.

1. Ce jeune homme   2. Tu   3. Ces femmes   4. Je

B *Répondez aux questions.*

1. Courez-vous à la porte quand le cours est terminé ? Quand est-ce qu'on court ? Avez-vous couru hier ?
2. Est-ce que « courir » est synonyme de « se dépêcher » ? Est-ce que « faire du footing » est synonyme de « courir » ?
3. Combien de temps est-ce qu'il vous faut pour courir cent mètres ? Qui a jamais participé à un marathon ?
4. Qui a une voiture ? Comment marche votre voiture ? Voici un ascenseur. Que veut dire cette pancarte ?
5. Que faites-vous quand vous mourez de faim ? Et quand vous mourez de soif ? Et quand vous mourez de fatigue ?
6. Est-ce que vous mourez d'ennui[2] dans ce cours ? Est-ce que vous mourez de peur dans ce cours ?
7. Savez-vous où Jeanne d'Arc est morte ? Savez-vous comment Marie-Antoinette est morte ?
8. Regardez la photo à la page 440. Imaginez qu'on l'a prise hier. Qu'est-ce qui s'est passé ?

Compréhension auditive

---

[1]The sign **EN PANNE** is an equivalent of *OUT OF ORDER.*

[2]*boredom*

APPLICATIONS

« As-tu envie de prendre un pot avec nous ? »

A   Situations[1]

Invitation : Accepterez-vous ou refuserez-vous ?
Quand des amis vous invitent à déjeuner, à aller voir un spectacle ou à faire quelque chose avec eux, il faut accepter ou refuser cette invitation. Si vous ne pouvez pas accepter, il est normal que vous donniez la raison de votre refus.

Jean-Paul vous invite à prendre un pot.

JEAN-PAUL   As-tu envie d'aller[2] prendre un pot ?   5
    VOUS   Oui, avec plaisir. Où veux-tu aller ? (*ou bien* : Non, pas maintenant. J'ai rendez-vous avec Christine dans un quart d'heure.)

M. Chabrier vous invite à déjeuner.

M. CHABRIER   Je connais un bon restaurant pas très loin d'ici. Voulez-vous déjeuner avec nous ?   10
    VOUS   Volontiers. Merci de votre invitation. (*ou bien* : Je suis désolée, mais j'ai promis à ma camarade de chambre de rentrer avant midi et demi. Je vous remercie de votre invitation.)

Mme Chabrier vous invite à dîner.

MME CHABRIER   Pourriez-vous venir dîner chez nous samedi prochain ?   15
    VOUS   Ça me ferait grand plaisir. Merci beaucoup. (*ou bien* : C'est très gentil de votre part°, mais je vais passer le week-end chez des amis.)

It's very nice of you

[1]Les réponses aux questions ne sont pas enregistrées sur la bande magnétique.
[2]**avoir envir de** + infinitif   *to feel like (doing something)*

M. Pineau vous invite au concert.

How nice (kind) of you.

M. PINEAU Est-ce que vous êtes libre jeudi ? Nous avons trois billets pour *Carmen*.

VOUS Vous êtes trop aimable.° Justement, j'avais très envie d'aller voir cet opéra. (*ou* 20 *bien* : Je regrette beaucoup, mais je ne suis pas libre jeudi.)

Mme Pineau vous invite au théâtre.

MME PINEAU Est-ce que cela vous intéresserait d'aller au théâtre ? Nous avons trois billets pour samedi soir.

VOUS Merci beaucoup. J'aimerais beaucoup aller avec vous. (*ou bien* : C'est vraiment 25 dommage, mais mon amie Cécile m'a invitée à dîner.)

Monique vous invite à faire une promenade.

un petit tour = une petite promenade

MONIQUE Voilà le jardin du Luxembourg[1]. Veux-tu faire un petit tour° ?

VOUS Je veux bien. Allons-y. (*ou bien* : Désolée, mais il faut que je rentre tout de suite. Les Pineau m'attendent.) 30

Que diriez-vous dans les situations suivantes ?

1. Vous êtes devant un monument et vous prenez des photos. Un jeune couple vous offre de prendre une photo de vous avec votre appareil[2]. Que disent-ils ? Que dites-vous ?
2. M. Paillard, un ami de vos parents, vous invite à déjeuner avec lui et sa femme dans un restaurant.
3. Il fait très beau. Un de vos camarades vous téléphone et vous invite à aller faire une promenade dans le jardin public.
4. Il y a un très bon film en ville. Un de vos copains vous invite à aller le voir. Vous lui donnez rendez-vous[3] (ou vous ne pouvez pas y aller).
5. Un de vos copains va donner une surprise-party et il vous invite. Il vous dit d'y amener un copain (une copine) si vous voulez.
6. Il y a une exposition intéressante au musée. Un ami de vos parents vous invite à y aller.
7. Il fait chaud. Un de vos copains vous invite à aller à la piscine. Il vous dit d'amener un copain (une copine).
8. Un de vos copains vous invite à jouer au tennis[4].

B Expressions utiles[5]

Le menu

MENU PROMOTIONNEL[6] (TOURISTIQUE)	MENU GASTRONOMIQUE
ḥors-d'œuvre	ḥors-d'œuvre
viande ou poisson	entrée
légumes	viande ou poisson
fromage ou dessert	salade
	fromage
	dessert

---

[1]Très grand et beau jardin près du Quartier Latin
[2]**appareil** = appareil photo *camera*
[3]**donner rendez-vous à quelqu'un** *to make an arrangement to meet someone*
[4]Voir les *Situations* de la Leçon 4 (p. 95).
[5]Voir aussi les *Expressions utiles* des Leçons 5 et 6 (pp. 115 et 138).
[6]*special-priced menu*

La carte[1]

Service 15 % compris[2]

HORS-D'ŒUVRE

Carottes râpées[3]	12,10	Œuf dur en gelée[7]	14,00
Salade de concombres	12,20	Escargots de Bourgogne (6)[8]	28,40
Salade niçoise[4]	28,50	Huîtres (6)	32,00
Salade de tomates	14,00	Saumon fumé	70,10
Assiette de crudités[5]	15,70	Foie gras de canard[9]	66,00
Pâté de campagne[6]	17,50	Jambon cru de campagne[10]	33,50

POTAGES

Consommé chaud au vermicelle	12,50
Soupe à l'oignon gratinée	20,00
Soupe du jour	14,30

ŒUFS

Œufs brouillés[11] au foie de volaille	21,00
Œufs brouillés aux champignons	21,00
Omelette nature[12]	21,00
Omelette (jambon, fromage ou champignons)	24,50

POISSONS/COQUILLAGES

Sole meunière[13]	42,00	Truite meunière	24,00
Fruits de mer	52,00	Saumon poché beurre fondu	56,00
Sardines grillées	21,00	Cuisses de grenouille[14]	32,00

VIANDES

Jambon garni[15]	31,00	Côte de porc garnie	33,90
Poulet rôti	31,00	Escalope[18] de veau	32,00
Steak frites[16]	52,00	Steak Tartare	49,00
Steak haché[17] frites	32,00	Confit d'oie[19]	73,00

[1]Rappel : les équivalents anglais des *Expressions utiles* sont dans votre **Cahier d'exercices**.

[2]On dit aussi **prix nets**.

[3]*grated* (with vinaigrette dressing)

[4]Vegetable salad (lettuce, sliced tomatoes and onions, sometimes cooked green beans) with black olives, tuna, and sometimes hard-boiled eggs

[5]Raw vegetables, with vinaigrette dressing

[6]Country-style [liver] pâté

[7]*Hard-boiled egg in aspic*

[8]Snails baked in shell with butter, garlic, minced parsley, and shallot

[9]liver of specially fattened duck

[10]Very thin-sliced country-style raw ham

[11]*scrambled*

[12]*Plain omelette*

[13]meunière : lightly breaded with flour, sauteed and seasoned with lemon and parsley

[14]*Frog legs*

[15]**Garni** normally means that the meat dish comes with a vegetable and sometimes with potatoes.

[16]**frites** = pommes de terre frites ; On peut commander le steak **saignant** (*rare*), **à point** (*medium*) ou **bien cuit** (*well-done*).

[17]*ground*

[18]*Cutlet*

[19]Goose cooked in its own fat and preserved

PLATS DU JOUR

Cassoulet[1] au confit de canard	49,30
Côte d'agneau grillée à la provençale	53,60
Brochettes mixtes (bœuf-agneau)	60,00
Faux-filet[2] grillé maître d'hôtel[3]	56,00

LÉGUMES

Pommes[4] frites	14,00	Champignons provençale[6]	20,50
Pommes vapeur[5]	12,50	Haricots verts au beurre	16,00
Salade de saison	14,50	Asperges à la crème	23,00
Artichaut à la vinaigrette	21,50	Poêlée de cèpes[7]	41,00

DESSERTS

Plateau de fromages	19,50	Pâtisserie du jour	19,50
Coupe de glace[8]	14,80	Tarte aux pommes	14,00
Sorbet aux fruits[9]	17,50	Mousse au chocolat	14,00
Crème au caramel[10]	14,80	Corbeille de fruits	21,50

VOIR AU VERSO LA LISTE DE NOS VINS

La maison n'est pas responsable des vêtements perdus, échangés du tachés.

C   Pratique

1. Quelle est la différence entre le « menu promotionnel » ou « touristique » et le « menu gastronomique » ? Préparez ces deux sortes de menus à partir de[11] la carte que vous avez ici.
2. Regardez la carte et indiquez ce que vous voulez commander. Dites pourquoi vous choisissez chaque plat et combien le repas coûtera. (N'oubliez pas la ou les boissons.[12])
3. Qu'est-ce que vous commanderiez si vous étiez pressé(e) et si vous vouliez prendre seulement deux plats ?
4. Qu'est-ce que vous commanderiez si vous aviez seulement 100 F et si vous aviez très faim ?

[1]Beans baked with meats such as pork, sausages, **confit d'oie** (preserved goose); typical of southwestern France

[2]*Sirloin*

[3]**maître d'hôtel** = with butter flavored with parsley and lemon

[4]Pommes de terre

[5]**vapeur** *steamed*

[6]**provençale** = à la provençale ; Provençal-style cooking is usually done with olive oil, garlic, tomatoes, and a lot of herbs and spices.

[7]*Pan-fried cèpes* (wild mushrooms)

[8]par exemple : **glace à la vanille, glace au chocolat, glace au café**

[9]par exemple : **sorbet au cassis, sorbet à la poire, sorbet au citron**

[10]Custard with caramel sauce

[11]**à partir de** *based on*

[12]Un pichet d'eau ne coûte rien. Le prix d'une demie (bouteille) d'eau minérale (40 cl) est 10–12 F ; une boisson gazeuse, 6–9 F ; un café, thé ou une infusion, 7–10 F ; un pichet de vin de table (vin ordinaire) rouge, blanc, ou rosé (33 cl), 12–14 F.

5. Décrivez chaque plat avec un ou deux des adjectifs suivants.

cru	salé	chaud	épais	gras
cuit	sucré	froid	mince	maigre

pommes vapeur	glace au chocolat	salade de concombres
saucisson	soupe à l'oignon	escargots de Bourgogne
crudités	mousse au chocolat	jambon cru de campagne
sorbet aux fraises	tarte aux pommes	fromage de Roquefort
pâtisseries	steak frites	saumon fumé

D **Mini-composition :** *Cindy est une jeune Américaine qui fait des études à Toulouse. Mme Wilson, son ancien professeur de français, va lui rendre visite avec son mari. Voici une partie de ce que Cindy a écrit à Mme Wilson.*

(1) Je/être/très/content/que/vous/pouvoir/passer/quelques/jour/à/Toulouse. (2) Je/réserver/chambre/dans/un/petit/hôtel/confortable/près/notre/appartement. (3) Malheureusement,/je/être[1]/à/université/à/heure/de/votre/arrivée,/mais/ne pas/s'inquiéter. (4) Mireille Arnoud,/avec/qui/je/partager/appartement,/être[1]/à/gare/pour/accueillir/vous. (5) Il/être/dommage/que/vous/avoir/seulement/3 jours/à/Toulouse,/car/Mireille/et/moi/vouloir[2]/montrer/vous/pas mal de/sites/intéressant. (6) Nous/vouloir[2]/aussi/que/vous/goûter/des/spécialité/de/région. (7) On/faire[1]/en/chez/nous,/bien sûr,/mais/nous/vouloir[2]/emmener/vous/à/*Le Cathare*[3]/pour que/vous/essayer/le/cassoulet[4]. (8) Je/ne pas/croire/que/il y a/meilleur/restaurant. (9) Les/parent/de/Mireille,/qui/habiter/à/Albi,/vouloir[2]/que/vous/passer/un/après-midi/chez/eux. (10) Je/souhaiter/vous/bon/voyage[5] ;/je/attendre/avec/impatience/votre/arrivée.

E **Questions :** *Deux touristes ont dîné dans un restaurant. Lisez d'abord le paragraphe, ensuite posez des questions sur les parties soulignées.*

Nous avons dîné dans un restaurant (1) près de la gare. Nous y sommes allés (2) vers six heures et demie et il n'était pas encore ouvert.[6] Nous avons demandé (3) à quelle heure il serait ouvert. (4) Le maître d'hôtel nous a dit : « à 19 heures ». Nous nous sommes promenés dans le quartier (5) pendant plus d'une demi-heure. Il y avait déjà (6) cinq ou six clients dans le restaurant quand nous y sommes revenus. Nous avons commandé (7) des escargots comme hors-d'œuvre. Ensuite nous avons commandé le cassoulet, qui est (8) la spécialité du restaurant. Le cassoulet était (9) vraiment délicieux. (10) Les légumes, à la provençale, étaient excellents aussi. Nous avons passé (11) presque deux heures au restaurant. (12) Après ce repas, qui n'a pas coûté trop cher, nous sommes allés à la gare. Nous y sommes allés (13) parce que nous voulions vérifier l'heure de départ de notre train.

F **Renseignements et opinions**

1. Qu'est-ce que vous êtes content(e) de manger tous les jours ? Qu'est-ce que vous êtes fatigué(e) de manger ?

[1]Employez le futur.
[2]Employez le présent du conditionnel.
[3]nom d'un restaurant
[4]Voir la note 1 à la page 445.
[5]N'employez pas d'article.
[6]La plupart des restaurants en France servent le dîner à partir de 19 heures ou de 19 h 30.

2. Y a-t-il un restaurant japonais dans notre ville ? Êtes-vous surpris(e) qu'il y en ait (qu'il n'y en ait pas) ?

3. À votre avis, quels plats sont typiquement américains ? Quels plats sont typiquement italiens ? Quels plats sont typiquement allemands ?

4. Quel est le meilleur restaurant de notre ville ? Qui doute que ce soit le meilleur ? Qui pense que la cuisine à la résidence est bonne ?

5. Quels sont les avantages et les inconvénients de manger dans un restaurant libre-service[1] ?

6. Qui pense que je meurs de faim en ce moment ? Qui est certain que je peux courir cent mètres en dix secondes ?

7. Utilisez-vous des conserves[2] ? Quelles sortes de conserves ? Qui utilise des produits surgelés[3] ? Quelles sortes de surgelés ?

🔲 *Compréhension auditive* (*basée en partie sur l'Application A*)

🔲 *Compréhension auditive* (*basée sur l'Application B*)

🔲 *Compréhension auditive*

🔲 *Dictée :* « *Pierre a dîné dans un grand restaurant.* »

G Lecture

Les Français et la cuisine

Une dame

J'ai toujours aimé faire la cuisine et, en plus, mon mari est un vrai gourmet. Il est enchanté qu'il je sois un « cordon-bleu »[4]. Je prépare mes repas avec beaucoup de soin et j'achète seulement des produits de meilleure qualité dans des magasins spécialisés. Ce matin je suis allée chez Fauchon[5] pour acheter du foie gras[6], des truffes, du saumon fumé° et du jambon   5
de Bayonne°. Une fois par mois nos enfants viennent déjeuner avec nous et je fais un grand repas. Mon mari choisit quelques bonnes bouteilles et nous restons à table de midi et demi jusqu'à trois heures. Dimanche dernier j'ai préparé des escargots de Bourgogne[7], du canard à l'orange°, des asperges à la crème et de la mousse au chocolat. Bien sûr, tout cela a pris beaucoup de temps, mais comme je disais, j'adore faire la cuisine. Tous les ans, pour fêter   10
notre anniversaire de mariage, nous allons dans un restaurant trois étoiles[8]. Cette année, nous avons dîné à la Tour d'Argent[9].

smoked salmon
thin-sliced raw ham from Bayonne

roast duckling in orange sauce

Un monsieur sportif

La grande cuisine traditionnelle, c'est bien° pour certaines personnes, mais dans notre famille nous faisons très attention à notre santé et à notre ligne°. Nous sommes contents que la   15
nouvelle « cuisine minceur »° soit à la mode°, car nous comptons les calories. Le cholestérol est notre ennemi numéro un ! Nous mangeons des choses très simples et, autant que possible,

fine, OK
shape
low-calorie cooking / popular

[1]**restaurant libre-service** (ou **self-service**) *cafeteria*

[2]*canned food*

[3]*frozen food*; On dit aussi **des surgelés**.

[4]Le Cordon-Bleu est une école de cuisine célèbre à Paris. Un « cordon-bleu » est une personne qui sait faire de la cuisine délicieuse.

[5]magasin à Paris qui vend des produits alimentaires de luxe

[6]*liver* (of specially fattened geese)

[7]baked with butter, garlic, minced parsley, and shallot

[8]Dans le *guide Michelin rouge* (guide touristique et gastronomique très connu), les meilleurs restaurants sont signalés par trois étoiles. Il y a seulement une vingtaine de restaurants trois étoiles dans toute la France.

[9]un des restaurants parisiens de renom international

whole wheat bread
skimmed milk/chemical
fertilizers

des produits naturels achetés au marché ou dans des magasins de régime[1] : pain complet°, lait écrémé°, légumes cultivés sans engrais chimiques°, poulets élevés en liberté. Nous ne buvons pas d'alcool. Vous ne pensez pas qu'il soit possible de préparer des plats délicieux 20 avec de tels[2] ingrédients ? Si, bien sûr ! La santé avant tout !

Une jeune fille
Croyez-vous que j'aie envie de faire de la grande cuisine quand je rentre chez moi à sept heures et demie, après une journée au bureau et une heure de train ? Certainement pas ! En général, je fais mes achats une fois par semaine au supermarché, sauf pour le pain et les 25 fruits. D'ailleurs, la charcuterie du coin a pas mal de bons plats cuisinés[3]. Au supermarché j'achète beaucoup de conserves[4] et d'aliments surgelés qui sont prêts en quelques minutes. Certains sont délicieux, d'ailleurs. En avez-vous goûté ? Pour moi, se nourrir est une nécessité et ne mérite pas une telle dépense de temps et d'argent. L'année dernière, je me suis acheté[5] un petit four à micro-ondes[6]. Avec ça, mes repas sont très vite préparés. Je mange tran- 30

news

quillement et regarde en même temps les informations° à la télévision. De temps en temps je reste à Paris après mon travail, et je vais chez McDonald pour manger un hamburger et des frites avec quelques amis. Eux aussi trouvent que c'est une perte de temps de passer deux heures à table tous les jours ou de dépenser tant d'argent au restaurant. Nous préférons aller au cinéma ou danser dans une disco. 35

Fauchon est un des magasins préférés des gourmets.

« Pour notre anniversaire de mariage, nous avons dîné à la Tour d'Argent. Le canard était délicieux. »

Quand on est pressé, on peut aller chez McDonald.

[1]*health-food stores* (**régime** *diet*)
[2]**un(e) tel(le)** (*pl* **de tel(le)s**) *such (a)*
[3]ici, plats préparés par le charcutier : rôti de porc, poulets rôtis, pâtés, salades, etc.
[4]aliments conservés, surtout en boîte (*canned*)
[5]**s'acheter** *to buy oneself (something)*
[6]**four (à) micro-ondes** *microwave oven*

A *Indiquez si chaque commentaire est vrai ou faux. Sil est faux, corrigez le commentaire.*

1. Ce que dit la dame qui parle en premier suggère qu'elle est assez riche.
2. Les meilleurs restaurants sont signalés par cinq étoiles dans le *guide Michelin.*
3. La dame choisit ses aliments avec soin, car elle fait très attention aux calories.
4. Le monsieur sportif ne mange pas de poulets élevés en liberté, car il évite les engrais chimiques.
5. D'après lui, il est possible de préparer des plats délicieux avec des aliments naturels.
6. La jeune fille n'achète rien dans les magasins spécialisés de son quartier, car elle préfère aller au supermarché.
7. Elle ne veut pas passer beaucoup de temps à préparer son dîner.
8. Pour elle, dîner dans un bon restaurant est une perte de temps et d'argent.

B *Répondez aux questions.*

1. La dame qui parle en premier est assez riche. Comment le sait-on ? Comment sait-on qu'elle ne fait pas attention aux calories ?
2. Le monsieur sportif fait très attention à ce qu'il mange. Quelle sorte d'aliments ne mangerait-il jamais ?
3. Suggérez un menu facile et rapide à la jeune fille qui n'aime pas faire la cuisine.

VOCABULAIRE

Noms

l'appareil *m*	camera	la **glace**	ice cream	la **sauce**	sauce, dressing
le **bistrot**	café, bar	le jardin du Luxembourg	Luxemburg garden	le spectacle	show
le **caoutchouc**	rubber			le **synonyme**	synonym
la **disco**	discotheque	le **marathon**	marathon	le tour	walk
l'**ennui** *m*	boredom	le pot *fam*	drink	la **variété**	variety
la **fatigue**	fatigue	le refus	refusal		

Verbes

s'arrêter	to stop	**marcher**	to work, function, run	**participer (à)**	to participate (in)
courir *irrég*	to run	**mourir (de)** *irrég*	to die (from)	**regretter**	to be sorry, regret
douter (de)	to doubt	**nier**	to deny	**souhaiter**	to wish

Adjectifs

capable	able	**médiocre**	mediocre	public (**publique**)	public
étonné(e)	surprised	**mouillé(e)**	wet	**surpris(e)**	surprised
frais (fraîche)	fresh	normal(e)	normal	**vert(e)**	green
furieux(euse)	furious	**obligé(e)**	obliged		

Adverbes

ailleurs	elsewhere, somewhere else	**simplement**	simply

Conjonctions

à moins que	unless	**jusqu'à ce que**	until	**puisque**	since
avant que	before	**pour que**	so that		
bien que	although	**pourvu que**	provided that		

Autres expressions

coûter cher	to cost a lot	faire un petit tour	to take a short walk
de votre part	of you, on your part	**Jeanne d'Arc**	Joan of Arc
donner rendez-vous à qqn	to make an arrangement to meet someone	**mourir de faim**	to starve
		mourir de soif	to die of thirst
en sus	extra	**pleuvoir à verse**	to be pouring (rain)
être content(e) de + inf	to be satisfied/glad + inf	prendre un pot	to have a drink

21 Au bureau de poste

LESSON OBJECTIVES

Theme and Culture

1. Postal service
2. Telephone

Communication Skills

1. Making statements in complex sentence patterns, with a dependent infinitive (*ready to do, prefer to do, decide to do, continue to do*)
2. Modifying an object with an infinitive (*a book to read, difficult to learn*)
3. Transacting business at the post office
4. Making/Receiving telephone calls

Structures

21.1 The subjunctive: review
21.2 Adjective + **à** + infinitive
21.3 Verb + infinitive
21.4 Verb + **de** + infinitive
21.5 Verb + **à** + infinitive

On utilise les télécartes dans des cabines spécialement équipées.

CONVERSATIONS

A. Vous avez le mauvais numéro.

ROBERT Allô !¹ C'est l'Hôtel Central ?

UNE VOIX Pardon ? J'entends à peine². Parlez plus fort, s'il vous plaît.

ROBERT Est-ce que c'est l'Hôtel Central, en face de³ la gare ?

LA VOIX Ah non. Vous avez le mauvais numéro.

ROBERT Ah, excusez-moi.

LA VOIX Je vous en prie.

B. Daniel téléphone à son professeur.

DANIEL Allô ! Je suis bien chez le Professeur⁴ Martinet ?

MME MARTINET Oui. Qui est à l'appareil, s'il vous plaît ?

DANIEL Ici⁵ Daniel Moreau, un de ses étudiants. Est-ce que le professeur est là ?

MME MARTINET Ne quittez pas. (*Un moment plus tard*) Je suis désolée, mais il n'est pas là. Voulez-vous laisser un message ?

C. Une lettre difficile à écrire

MIREILLE Alors, tu as accepté d'écrire cette lettre ?

JACQUES Non, j'ai décidé de ne pas l'écrire.

MIREILLE Mais pourquoi ne veux-tu pas le faire ?

JACQUES Moi, je ne suis pas habitué à écrire ce genre de lettre !

STRUCTURES

21.1 SUBJONCTIF : RÉVISION

Generally speaking, the subjunctive is used to reflect the speaker's mental attitude—wish, uncertainty, denial, and emotions. It usually occurs in dependent clauses, which are introduced by a conjunction. Here are the most important "signals" that call for the use of the subjunctive.

A) *Impersonal expressions*, except a few that express certainty (Lesson 19.2).
B) Verbs in the main clause expressing *wish* or *command* (Lesson 19.4), *emotions* (Lesson 20.2), *doubt*, *uncertainty*, or *denial* (Lesson 20.3).
C) Certain conjunctions (Lesson 20.4).

MAIN CLAUSE   DEPENDENT CLAUSE

Subject	+	Verb	+	**que**	+	Subject	+	Verb (subjunctive)
(A)		(B)		(C)				

¹On emploie cette expression seulement quand on parle au téléphone.

²*hardly*

³*opposite, across from*

⁴On emploie l'article défini avec les titres sauf dans le discours direct : **Je cherche le Professeur Durand**, mais **Bonjour, Professeur Durand**.

⁵*This is . . . speaking*

A *Exercice de contrôle*

Il est important que vous sachiez mon adresse.

1. Il est bon
2. Il est vrai
3. Il est douteux
4. Il est temps
5. Il est évident
6. Il faut

Je voudrais que tu ailles à la poste[1] maintenant.

1. Je sais
2. Je suis content
3. Je demande
4. Je suis surpris
5. Je vois
6. Je permets

Je doute que vous m'ayez compris.

1. Je suis certain
2. Je ne suis pas sûr
3. Je ne crois pas
4. J'espère
5. Je suis sûr
6. Je ne pense pas

Je vais travailler à moins qu'il fasse beau.

1. pendant que
2. parce que
3. pourvu que
4. bien que
5. puisque
6. à moins que

B *Répondez aux questions en employant dans chaque réponse une proposition subordonnée.[2]*

Modèles : Qu'est-ce que vous demandez ?
Je demande que vous parliez moins vite.
Qu'est-ce qu'il est important de faire ?
Il est important que nous finissions cet exercice.
De quoi êtes-vous étonné ?
Je suis étonné que mon partenaire soit absent.

1. Qu'est-ce que vous voulez ?
2. Qu'est-ce qu'il faut faire ?
3. De quoi êtes-vous sûr ?
4. Qu'est-ce que vous ne croyez pas ?
5. De quoi êtes-vous surpris ?
6. Qu'est-ce que vous espérez ?
7. Qu'est-ce que vous demandez ?
8. Qu'est-ce qu'il est impossible de faire ?

C *Complétez les phrases suivantes avec votre partenaire.*

1. (Robert) et moi, nous pensons que vous...
2. (Robert) et moi, nous doutons que vous...
3. (Robert) et moi, nous sommes contents que vous...
4. Il est bon que (Robert) et moi, nous...
5. (Robert) et moi, nous... à moins que...

21.2 ADJECTIF + À + INFINITIF

1. Most adjectives are followed by **de** + infinitive when the subject of the infinitive is the same as that of **être** + adjective (Lesson 20.1). However, there are a few that require **à** instead. In the second group of examples below, use of the definite article makes the adjective act as a noun.

Je suis **habitué à me lever** tôt.	*I am used to, accustomed to . . .*
Elle est **prête à sortir.**	*She is ready . . .*
Vous êtes **lent à me répondre.**	*You are slow . . .*
Tu es **la première à me téléphoner.**	*You are the first (one) . . .*
André était **le dernier à partir.**	*André was the last (one) . . .*
Nous sommes **les seuls à rester.**	*We are the only ones . . .*

---

[1]**à la poste** = au bureau de poste
[2]In other words, your answer must include **que** + clause.

2. In one other case, adjectives other than those listed above may take **à** + infinitive. This construction is similar to noun + **à** + infinitive, where the infinitive carries a passive meaning (*something to do, something to be done*). In both constructions, the infinitive must be a *transitive* verb, and the noun or pronoun before **à** + infinitive is its direct object.

(Nous **enverrons ce colis**.)	We will send this package.
Nous avons **un colis à envoyer**.	We have a package to send (to be sent).
Le colis sera **difficile à envoyer**.	The package will be difficult to send.
(J'**ai écrit deux lettres**.)	I wrote two letters.
J'avais **deux lettres à écrire**.	I had two letters to write (to be written).
Elles étaient **pénibles à écrire**.	They were painful to write.

NOUN + **à** + INFINITIVE	NOUN + **être** + ADJECTIVE + **à** + INFINITIVE
J'ai **des devoirs à faire**.	**Les devoirs** sont **pénibles à faire**.
J'ai **un article à écrire**.	**L'article** sera **facile à écrire**.
Il y a **un film à voir**.	**Le film** sera **agréable à voir**.
Il y a **un livre à lire**.	**Le livre** est **difficile à lire**.

« Mon Dieu, ce bouquin est difficile à comprendre ! »

A *Exercice de contrôle*

Je serai surpris de recevoir une lettre du président.

1. le seul	3. prêt	5. certain
2. heureux	4. le premier	6. content

Elle n'était pas sûre d'écrire au président.

1. la dernière	3. contente	5. obligée
2. lente	4. la seule	6. prête

B *Répondez aux questions.*

1. Qui est prêt à répondre à ma question ? Qui ne sera pas lent à répondre à ma question ?

2. Qui était le premier à arriver au cours aujourd'hui ? Qui était le dernier à arriver ?
3. Est-ce que je suis le seul à parler français en classe ? Est-ce que je suis toujours le premier à parler français ?
4. Qui est habitué à faire les devoirs ? Êtes-vous content de les faire ? Êtes-vous le seul à les faire ?

C   *Êtes-vous d'accord ? Dites votre opinion d'après ce modèle.*

Il est facile d'apprendre le français.
Oui, le français est facile à apprendre (*ou* **Non, le français n'est pas facile à apprendre**).

1. Il est difficile de comprendre le français.
2. Il est ennuyeux de faire les devoirs.
3. Il est pénible de passer les examens.
4. Il est désagréable de boire du jus de carotte.[1]
5. Il est bon de manger des escargots.[1]
6. Il est amusant de voir des films comiques.[1]

   Compréhension auditive

21.3   VERBE + INFINITIF

You have noticed that some verbs in French are followed directly by an infinitive, while others take **de** or **à** before an infinitive.[2] In all these cases the subject of the conjugated verb is also the subject of the infinitive (that is, the same subject performs the action expressed by the infinitive).

Je **dois acheter** des timbres.	*I have to buy some stamps.*
Je **commençais à m'inquiéter.**	*I was beginning to worry.*
J'ai **décidé d'aller** à la poste.	*I decided to go to the post office.*

1. The verbs below take the construction verb + infinitive, without any preposition. You have already encountered these verbs.

aimer	*to like*	**pouvoir**	*can*
aller	*to be going to*	**préférer**	*to prefer*
désirer	*to wish*	**savoir**	*to know how*
détester	*to hate*	**vouloir**	*to want*
devoir	*must*	**il faut**	*one must*
espérer	*to hope*	**il vaut mieux**	*it is better*

Moi, je **vais envoyer** cette lettre et Paul **désire envoyer** ce colis.
Pierre **voudrait sortir** ce soir, mais moi, je **préfère rester** à la maison.
Monique **aime écouter** la radio, mais son frère **déteste** l'**écouter**.
Je **devrais rappeler** Marie, mais je ne **peux** pas la **rappeler** maintenant.
Nous **espérons aller** au cinéma, mais d'abord nous **devons travailler**.

2. *Object pronouns.* If the infinitive takes object pronouns, they are placed immediately before the infinitive.[3]

Je dois envoyer **cette lettre.**	Allez-vous **m'envoyer des cartes** ?
→ Je dois l'**envoyer.**	→ Allez-vous **m'en** envoyer ?

[1]Employez l'article défini dans votre réponse ; les commentaires que vous faites sont des généralisations (voir la Leçon 8.1).

[2]English also has verbs that take different constructions: *He insists on staying* (not *He insists to . . .*), *I ended up by doing* (not *I ended up to . . .*), *You may leave* (not *You may to . . .*), *He decided to come* (not *He decided coming*), etc.

[3]The sequence of object pronouns was summarized in Lesson 16.2.

Je peux téléphoner **à mes amis**.

→ Je peux **leur** téléphoner.

Elle déteste aller **au bureau de poste**.

→ Elle déteste **y** aller.

Je voudrais **vous** montrer **ces photos**.

→ Je voudrais **vous les** montrer.

Elle mettra **le timbre sur l'enveloppe**.

→ Elle **l'y** mettra.

3. *Negation.* If the infinitive is negated, **ne pas**, **ne plus**, and **ne jamais** come immediately before the infinitive or object pronoun(s) + infinitive.

Je préfère **ne pas** envoyer **la lettre**.

→ Je préfère **ne pas** l'envoyer.

Il vaut mieux **ne pas** faire **de fautes**.

→ Il vaut mieux **ne pas en** faire.

Elle désire **ne plus** écrire **à Jean**.

→ Elle désire **ne plus lui** écrire.

Il espère **ne jamais** revoir **cette femme**.

→ Il espère **ne jamais la** revoir.

Personne always follows the infinitive and is placed where a corresponding object noun would be.

J'espère **ne** voir **personne** ce matin.   (*direct object*)

Je préfère **ne** parler **à personne**.   (*indirect object*)

Je voudrais **ne** travailler **pour personne**.   (*object of a preposition*)

Rien as a direct object precedes the infinitive as **ne rien**, just like **ne pas**, **ne plus**, and **ne jamais**. If the infinitive takes a preposition, preposition + **rien** follows the infinitive (just like **personne**).

Je préfère **ne rien** faire ce soir.   (*direct object*)

J'espère **ne** répondre **à rien**.   (*indirect object*)

Je voudrais **ne** compter **sur rien**.   (*object of a preposition*)

A *Répondez aux questions.*[1]

1. N'aimez-vous pas voyager ? Où voulez-vous aller ?
2. Ne voudriez-vous pas aller en Suisse ? Quand désirez-vous y aller ?
3. N'allez-vous pas dîner ce soir ? Où voulez-vous dîner ?
4. Ne devez-vous pas travailler ce soir ? Que préférez-vous faire ?
5. Ne savez-vous pas nager ? Pouvez-vous nager aujourd'hui ?
6. N'aimez-vous pas écrire des lettres ? À qui aimeriez-vous écrire ?

[1]Employez **si** (au lieu de **oui**) si vous répondez affirmativement aux questions négatives.

B *Répétez les phrases suivantes en remplaçant les noms par les pronoms.*

> *Modèle :* Je peux aller au cinéma ce soir.
> **Je peux y aller ce soir.**

1. Je dois aller au bureau de poste.
2. Je vais acheter des timbres à deux francs[1].
3. Je ne peux pas écrire de cartes postales.
4. Je préfère ne pas téléphoner à mon camarade.
5. J'espère ne jamais téléphoner à (Éric) en PCV[2].
6. Je désire ne plus vous parler de mes ennuis.
7. J'aimerais ne recevoir personne à la maison.
8. Je voudrais ne rien montrer à mes camarades.

C *Répondez aux questions.*

1. Qu'est-ce que vous aimiez faire quand vous aviez dix ans ?
2. Qu'est-ce que vous détestiez faire quand vous aviez dix ans ?
3. Qu'est-ce que vous vouliez faire hier soir ? L'avez-vous fait ?
4. Qu'est-ce que vous deviez faire hier soir ? L'avez-vous fait ?
5. Qu'est-ce que vous n'avez pas pu faire hier ? Qu'est-ce que vous avez fait ?
6. Quand est-ce que vous voulez ne rien faire ? Quand est-ce que vous préférez ne voir personne ?
7. Regardez la photo à la page 455. Où doit-on mettre lès lettres ? Qu'est-ce que la machine de gauche distribue ? Et la machine du milieu ? Où met-on les pièces de monnaie ?

21.4 VERBE + **DE** + INFINITIF

1. The verbs below take the construction **de** + infinitive.

accepter	*to accept*	**négliger**	*to neglect*
cesser[3]	*to stop*	**oublier**	*to forget*
décider	*to decide*	**refuser**	*to refuse*
essayer	*to try*	**regretter**	*to regret, to be sorry*
finir[4]	*to finish*	**venir**[5]	*to have just (done)*

Jacques **a**-t-il **décidé d'écrire** la lettre ?

— Oui, et il **a accepté de** l'**envoyer** en recommandé[6].

Est-ce que Janine **a refusé de** leur **téléphoner** ?

— Non, je crois qu'elle **a** tout simplement **oublié de** le **faire**.

Tu **regrettes** toujours **d'avoir écrit** cette lettre ?

— Oui, j'**essaie de** l'**oublier**.

---

[1]*two-franc stamps*

[2]**PCV** = percevoir ; **en PCV** *collect (call)*

[3]**Cesser** *to stop* suggests that the action is over or has been discontinued, while **s'arrêter** implies a momentary stop: **Il s'est arrêté de parler** *He stopped speaking (for a moment)*; **Il a cessé de me parler** *He stopped speaking to me (for good)*.

[4]**Finir de** means *to finish (doing)*, while **finir par** means *to end up by doing*: **Il a fini de travailler** *He finished working*; **Elle a fini par accepter** *She ended up by accepting*.

[5]**Venir de** expresses action occurring in the immediate past (see Lesson 6.6).

[6]*by registered mail*

2. The following expressions with **avoir** also require **de** before an infinitive.

avoir besoin	*to need*	**avoir peur**	*to be afraid*
avoir envie	*to feel like*	**avoir raison**	*to be right*
avoir l'intention	*to intend*	**avoir tort**	*to be wrong*

Avez-vous **l'intention d'aller** au cinéma ?

— Non, j'**ai besoin de travailler**.

J'**avais peur de poser** cette question.

— Tu **avais tort de** ne pas la **poser**.

3. When the infinitive is preceded by **de** and the direct-object pronoun **le** or **les**, **de** and the pronoun do *not* contract to **du** or **des**.

J'ai décidé **de le** faire. (*not* **du**)	*I decided to do it.*
Elle refusera **de les** voir. (*not* **des**)	*She will refuse to see them.*
Tu as besoin **de le** lire. (*not* **du**)	*You need to read it.*

4. If the action expressed by the infinitive took place before the action expressed by the main verb, the infinitive becomes **avoir/être** + past participle. This construction was presented in Lesson 20.1.

Il regrette de ne pas t'**avoir écrit**.	*He regrets not having written to you. (He's sorry he didn't write to you.)*
Vous avez tort de ne pas **avoir parlé**.	*You are wrong not to have spoken.*
Je suis contente d'**être venue**.	*I am happy to have come (that I came).*

 **A** *Exercice de contrôle*

J'ai oublié d'aller chez le dentiste.

1. Je ne veux pas	3. Je déteste	5. J'accepte finalement
2. J'ai peur	4. Mais je dois	6. Quand même, je regrette

J'ai l'intention de téléphoner en PCV.

1. J'espère	3. Je vais essayer	5. Je préfère
2. J'ai raison	4. Je regrette	6. Je refuse

B *Répondez aux questions.*

1. Avez-vous oublié de vous laver la figure ce matin ? Qu'est-ce que vous oubliez de faire de temps en temps ?
2. Qu'est-ce que vous avez envie de faire ce week-end ? Avez-vous l'intention de le faire ? Avez-vous peur de le faire ?
3. Avez-vous jamais refusé de faire quelque chose ? Avez-vous jamais accepté de faire quelque chose ?
4. Avez-vous cessé d'aller au labo ? Qui a décidé de ne pas y aller ? Qui a besoin d'y aller ?
5. Qui vient de répondre à la dernière question ? Qui avait l'intention de répondre à la question ?

C *Complétez les phrases suivantes avec votre partenaire.*

1. Nous/aller/essayer/téléphoner/à .../avec préavis[1]/parce que...
2. Nous/avoir l'intention/envoyer/ce colis/en recommandé/parce que...
3. Nous/avoir raison/ne pas/répondre/au téléphone/quand...
4. Nous/avoir décidé/téléphoner/à .../en PCV/parce que...
5. Nous/regretter/ne pas/avoir répondu/à .../parce que...

[1]*person to person*

21.5 VERBE + À + INFINITIF

1. The verbs below require the construction **à** + infinitive.

apprendre	*to learn*	**hésiter**	*to hesitate*
commencer	*to begin*	**passer (le temps)**	*to spend (time)*
consentir[1]	*to consent, agree*	**réussir**	*to succeed*
continuer	*to continue*	**servir**	*to be used for*
être habitué	*to be used (to)*		

Laurent **a**-t-il **commencé à apprendre** l'allemand ?

— Oui, mais il **hésite à** vous **parler** en allemand.

Est-ce que vous **continuez à utiliser** l'appareil[2] de Solange ?

— Oui, j'**ai réussi à prendre** de belles photos.

Jacques **a**-t-il **consenti à** vous **aider** ?

— Oui, il va **passer** deux heures **à** m'**aider**.

Servir à *to be used for* (literally, *to serve for*) usually occurs in the third person.

À quoi est-ce que cela **sert** ?	*What is that used for?*
— Cela **sert à** faire du café.	*That is used for making coffee.*
— Cela ne **sert à** rien.	*That is used for nothing (It is useless).*
À quoi **servent** ces machines ?	*What are these machines used for?*
— Ces machines **servent à** envoyer des messages.	*These machines are used for sending messages.*

2. When the infinitive is preceded by **à** and the direct-object pronoun **le** or **les**, **à** and the pronoun do *not* contract to **au** or **aux**.

Il n'a pas hésité **à le** voir. (*not* **au**)	*He did not hesitate to see him/it.*
J'ai enfin réussi **à le** faire. (*not* **au**)	*I finally succeeded in doing it.*
Elle continuera **à les** écouter. (*not* **aux**)	*She will continue to listen to them.*

Savez-vous à quoi sert un écouteur ?

[1]conjugué comme **sentir**

[2]**appareil (photographique)** *camera*

TABLEAU 110   Je **dois** écrire cette lettre.   J'**hésite à** l'écrire.   Je **commence à** l'écrire.

A *Exercice de contrôle*

Je ne voulais pas faire ce travail.

1. D'abord j'ai refusé   3. Mais je devais   5. J'ai commencé
2. Puis, j'ai hésité   4. Alors, j'ai décidé   6. J'ai continué

Nous avons appris à utiliser ce micro-ordinateur.

1. D'abord nous avons refusé   4. Nous avons réussi
2. Puis nous avons hésité   5. Nous avons continué
3. Nous avons consenti   6. Maintenant, nous sommes habitués

B *Répondez aux questions d'après ce modèle.*

À quoi sert une fourchette ?
Une fourchette sert à manger.

1. À quoi servent les stylos ?   5. À quoi sert un couteau ?
2. À quoi sert une brosse à dents ?   6. À quoi sert une machine à laver ?
3. À quoi servent les ciseaux ?   7. À quoi sert une calculatrice ?[1]
4. À quoi servent les montres ?   8. À quoi sert cela ?

C *Répondez aux questions.*

1. À quel âge avez-vous appris à conduire ? Est-ce que vous hésitez à conduire aux heures de pointe ?
2. Quand avez-vous commencé à apprendre le français ? Est-ce que vous continuez toujours à l'apprendre ?
3. Hésitez-vous à dîner au resto-U ? Allez-vous y dîner ce soir ? Allez-vous continuer à y dîner ?
4. Avez-vous réussi à faire tous vos devoirs ? Combien de temps avez-vous passé à les faire ?

D *Voici un exercice de révision.*

1. Donnez six verbes qui sont suivis d'un[2] infinitif sans préposition. Parlez des étudiants dans ce cours en employant ces verbes.[3]
2. Donnez huit verbes qui sont suivis de la préposition **de** devant un infinitif. Parlez de moi en employant ces verbes.
3. Donnez six verbes qui sont suivis de la préposition **à** devant un infinitif. Parlez de quelqu'un de célèbre en employant ces verbes.

Compréhension auditive

Compréhension auditive

[1]Employez l'expression **calculer des chiffres** *to calculate numbers/figures.*

[2]**suivi de** *followed by* (du verbe **suivre**, Leçon 24.4)

[3]Dites, par exemple : « (Barbara) aime faire ses devoirs », « (Robert) déteste manger du poisson ».

APPLICATIONS

CABINES TÉLÉPHONIQUES

POSTE RESTANTE RENSEIGNEMENTS

TIMBRES AU DÉTAIL TIMBRES DE COLLECTIONS

COLIS POSTAUX INTERNATIONAUX

TABLEAU 111

A Situations

Au bureau de poste

Christine vient d'écrire plusieurs lettres. Comme elles sont assez longues, elle décide d'aller au bureau de poste pour les faire peser°. En route, elle rencontre Mayoumi et Ahmed. Mayoumi porte un colis.

faire peser *to have weighed*

au bureau de poste | CHRISTINE | Bonjour ! Vous allez à la poste°, vous aussi ?
| MAYOUMI | Oui, je vais envoyer un cadeau d'anniversaire de mariage à mes parents. 5

out of order | AHMED | Moi, je vais téléphoner à ma grand-mère. Mon téléphone est en panne° depuis hier.
| CHRISTINE | Alors, si nous y allions¹ ensemble ?

une boisson | AHMED | Pourquoi pas ? Et si on prenait un pot° après ?
| MAYOUMI | Oui, bonne idée. 10

Le bureau de poste est bondé.

| AHMED | Pour ton colis, Mayoumi, c'est le guichet numéro 5.
| CHRISTINE | Moi, je vais au guichet numéro 3.
| MAYOUMI | Bon, à tout à l'heure.

Au guichet N° 5 15

| MAYOUMI | Bonjour, Madame. J'aimerais envoyer ce colis au Japon.
| L'EMPLOYÉE | Par avion ou par bateau ?
| MAYOUMI | Par avion.
| L'EMPLOYÉE | Remplissez la fiche de douane. Et ceci pour la poste.

Au guichet N° 3 20

| CHRISTINE | J'aimerais envoyer ces lettres aux États-Unis et au Mexique.
| L'EMPLOYÉ | (*Il pèse les lettres et cherche les tarifs postaux.*) Alors... 9,30 F² et 13,60 F pour les États-Unis, et 16,80 F pour le Mexique. Ça fait 39,70 F.

labels | CHRISTINE | D'accord. Et donnez-moi aussi dix timbres à 2,60 F et des étiquettes° « par avion », s'il vous plaît. 25

¹*Suppose we go there* (**Si** + imparfait est un équivalent de *Suppose one does* ou *How about doing*.)
²Lisez : neuf francs trente.

« Donnez-moi aussi six timbres à 2,60 F, s'il vous plaît. »

Au guichet Nº 6

AHMED   J'aimerais téléphoner au Maroc, s'il vous plaît.

booth/dial tone   L'EMPLOYÉE   D'accord. Prenez la cabine° 5, faites le 19[1], attendez la tonalité°, puis composez
party (on phone)   le 212 et le numéro de votre correspondant°.

AHMED   Merci, Mademoiselle.   30

L'EMPLOYÉE   De rien, Monsieur.

Répondez aux questions. (lignes 1–10)

1. Qu'est-ce que Christine vient de faire ?
2. Pourquoi décide-t-elle d'aller au bureau de poste ?
3. Qu'est-ce que Mayoumi va envoyer à ses parents ?
4. Pourquoi Ahmed ne peut-il pas se servir de[2] son téléphone ?

(lignes 11–31)

5. Comment Mayoumi va-t-elle envoyer le colis ?
6. Où Christine doit-elle envoyer les lettres ?
7. Quelle sorte de timbres achète-t-elle ?
8. Combien vont coûter les lettres et les timbres en tout[3] ?
9. Quelle cabine Ahmed va-t-il prendre ?
10. Comment va-t-il téléphoner à sa grand-mère ?

B   Expressions utiles

Au bureau de poste

écrire $\left\{\begin{array}{l}\text{le nom de l'expéditeur / l'expéditrice}\\ \text{le nom du / de la destinataire}\\ \text{l'adresse } f \text{ et le code postal}\\ \text{« poste restante}^4 \text{ »}\\ \text{« prière de faire suivre}^5 \text{ »}\end{array}\right\}$ sur l'enveloppe *f*

---

[1]**faire le** = composer le *to dial* ; le premier groupe de chiffres (19) indique la communication internationale, et le deuxième (212), le code du pays (ici, le Maroc).

[2]**se servir de** = utiliser

[3]*altogether*

[4]*general delivery* (mail sent c/o the post office); usually kept for two weeks before being discarded

[5]*Please forward*

$$\text{mettre la lettre} \begin{cases} \text{dans une boîte (aux lettres)}^1 \\ \text{à la poste} \end{cases}$$

$$\text{chercher le guichet pour} \begin{cases} \text{les timbres(-poste) } m \\ \text{les colis postaux (internationaux)} \\ \text{(le retrait des) les lettres recommandées}^2 \\ \text{la poste restante} \\ \text{les télégrammes} \\ \text{les cabines téléphoniques} \end{cases}$$

$$\text{acheter} \begin{cases} \text{un timbre à 2,60 F} \\ \text{une carte postale} \\ \text{un timbre de collections} \\ \text{un aérogramme}^3 \end{cases} \qquad \text{envoyer une lettre} \begin{cases} \text{par avion} \\ \text{par bateau} \\ \text{en recommandé} \end{cases}$$

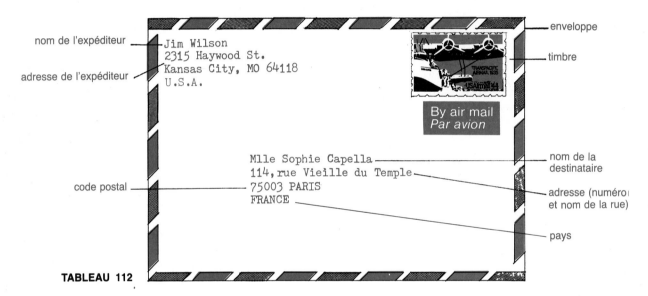

- nom de l'expéditeur — Jim Wilson
- adresse de l'expéditeur — 2315 Haywood St. / Kansas City, MO 64118 / U.S.A.
- enveloppe
- timbre
- By air mail / Par avion
- nom de la destinataire — Mlle Sophie Capella
- code postal — 114, rue Vieille du Temple / 75003 PARIS / FRANCE
- adresse (numéro et nom de la rue)
- pays

TABLEAU 112

Pour téléphoner
How to phone

Le téléphone

$$\left.\begin{array}{l} \text{téléphoner à} \\ \text{appeler} \\ \text{rappeler} \end{array}\right\} \text{quelqu'un} \begin{cases} \text{en PCV}^4 \\ \text{avec préavis}^5 \end{cases}$$

$$\text{chercher} \begin{cases} \text{un téléphone} \\ \text{une cabine téléphonique} \end{cases}$$

$$\left.\begin{array}{l} \text{consulter} \\ \text{chercher le numéro dans} \end{array}\right\} \text{l'annuaire}^6 \ m$$

attendre la tonalité

$$\left.\begin{array}{l} \text{décrocher} \\ \text{raccrocher} \end{array}\right\} \text{le récepteur}$$

PUBLIPOSTE. Pour construire votre campagne marketing direct. De A jusqu'à Z.

---

¹**boîte (aux lettres)** *mailbox*
²*registered letters*
³*air letter*
⁴*collect* (du verbe **percevoir**)
⁵*person to person*
⁶*phone directory*

mettre de la monnaie[1] dans la fente

composer le / faire le ⎫
                         ⎬ numéro[2]
avoir le bon / le mauvais ⎭

Pour acheter
Pour vendre
PAGES JAUNES Pour vous informer

voyez les PAGES JAUNES

C   Pratique

1. Vous êtes au bureau de poste. Voici ce que vous entendez. À quel guichet sont ces gens ?

   a) « Avez-vous du courrier au nom de Wilson ? »
   b) « J'aimerais envoyer cette lettre en recommandé. »
   c) « Combien coûte cette carte par avion pour les États-Unis ? »
   d) « J'aimerais envoyer ce paquet au Canada. »
   e) « Donnez-moi six timbres à 3,20 F, s'il vous plaît. »
   f) « J'aimerais téléphoner à San Francisco. »

2. Vous entendez les monologues suivants. Qu'est-ce que ces gens veulent ou vont faire ?

   a) « Zut ! La ligne est encore occupée. »
   b) « Où est l'annuaire ? »
   c) « Non, je ne veux pas laisser de message ! C'est la dernière fois que j'appelle ! »
   d) « Allô ! Allô ! Je n'entends pas. La communication est mauvaise. Je vous rappelle dans cinq minutes. »
   e) « Allô ! C'est la réception ? Passez-moi la ligne extérieure, s'il vous plaît. »
   f) « Zut ! Personne ne répond. Est-ce que j'ai le mauvais numéro ? »

3. Vous allez écrire une lettre. Mettez les actions suivantes dans l'ordre logique.

   a) recevoir une lettre
   b) coller le timbre
   c) écrire votre nom et votre adresse sur l'enveloppe
   d) écrire votre réponse
   e) écrire la date
   f) chercher du papier à lettre[3]
   g) mettre la lettre dans une enveloppe
   h) écrire l'adresse du destinataire sur l'enveloppe
   i) mettre la lettre dans une boîte aux lettres

4. Vous allez téléphoner pour réserver une chambre d'hôtel. Mettez les actions suivantes dans l'ordre logique.

   a) raccrocher le récepteur
   b) composer le numéro
   c) consulter l'annuaire
   d) attendre la réponse
   e) entendre la tonalité
   f) chercher une cabine téléphonique
   g) décrocher le récepteur
   h) dire « Au revoir »
   i) mettre de la monnaie dans la fente
   j) dire « Allô ! »

5. Regardez la photo de droite à la page 464. Que fait la jeune femme ? Que dit-elle ?

D   *Pour téléphoner à l'étranger[4], voici ce qu'il faut faire.*

De la France aux États-Unis, automatique
Décrocher ...... [tonalité] + 19 [communication internationale] ...... [tonalité] + 11 [indicatif[5] des États-Unis] + 212 [indicatif de la zone, ici la ville de New York] + 767.23.27 [numéro du correspondant]

---

[1]*coin(s)*
[2]Tous les numéros de téléphone en France ont huit chiffres.
[3]*stationery*
[4]*abroad*
[5]*code*

Le bureau de poste est toujours bondé.

Des États-Unis en France (à Paris), automatique

Décrocher ...... [tonalité] + 011 [communication internationale] ...... [tonalité] + 33 [indicatif de la France] + 1 [indicatif de Paris] + 42.38.71.21 [numéro du correspondant]

Indicatifs d'autres pays

Canada	1	Italie	39	Suisse	41
Espagne	34	Japon	81	URSS	7

1. Vous êtes français et vous habitez à Paris. Comment allez-vous téléphoner de votre appartement à votre oncle qui est à Chicago ? Qu'est-ce que vous allez lui dire ?
2. Vous habitez à Philadelphie. Vous voulez téléphoner à Paris pour réserver deux chambres d'hôtel. Comment allez-vous le faire ?
3. Vous êtes à Bordeaux. Vous voulez téléphoner à votre ami qui habite à Madrid (tél. 429.64.85). Qu'est-ce que vous allez faire ?
4. Vous avez besoin de prendre contact avec une Française qui est à Tokyo (tél. 03.765.8596). Qu'est-ce que vous allez faire ?

E   Est-ce logique ? : *Lisez chaque phrase et corrigez les phrases qui ne vous semblent pas logiques.*[1]

1. Je vais commander du vin puisque j'ai cessé de boire de l'alcool.
2. J'hésitais à leur téléphoner, car je ne les connaissais pas très bien.
3. Elle a dû téléphoner en PCV parce qu'elle avait assez d'argent sur elle.
4. Paul était le dernier à me téléphoner, parce que Sophie m'a téléphoné tout de suite après.
5. Elle a oublié de lui téléphoner avec préavis parce qu'elle voulait être absolument sûre de lui parler.
6. Je regrette d'avoir acheté cet appareil, car c'était ce que je voulais.
7. J'ai essayé de leur téléphoner, mais la ligne n'était pas occupée.
8. Elle n'était pas la seule à venir me voir, car personne d'autre n'est venu.
9. Je commençais à m'inquiéter, car mon fiancé devait arriver avant six heures.
10. Je n'ai pas refusé de faire ce travail, parce que j'étais habitué à le faire.

---

[1]Remarquez qu'il y a trois conjonctions employées dans ces phrases : **parce que** *because*, **puisque** *since* et **car** *for*.

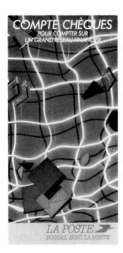

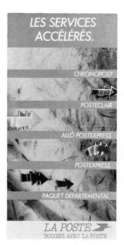

F *Résolutions du Nouvel An. C'est la veille du Nouvel An et vous voulez prendre quelques bonnes résolutions. Faites des phrases en employant les expressions à gauche et les expressions à droite.*

À partir du premier janvier :

je cesserai...	emprunter de l'argent à mes camarades.
j'essaierai...	prendre une douche tous les jours.
je refuserai...	faire mes devoirs.
je n'hésiterai plus...	boire trop de bière.
je n'oublierai jamais...	nettoyer ma chambre régulièrement.
j'accepterai toujours...	ne pas avoir peur des examens.
je ne vais plus...	essayer de comprendre mes parents.
je commencerai...	me lever à sept heures du matin.
j'apprendrai...	dire « Je t'aime » à mon ami(e).
je ne détesterai plus...	regarder la télé jusqu'à minuit.
etc.	manger quatre ou cinq fois par jour.
	dormir jusqu'à neuf heures du matin.
	écrire plus souvent à mes parents.
	manger des chips et des bonbons.
	etc.

G **Renseignements et opinions**

1. Qui est toujours le premier à arriver au cours ? Qui n'est jamais le dernier à arriver ? Qui est toujours prêt à quitter la classe ?
2. Qu'est-ce que vous aviez peur de faire quand vous étiez petit ? En avez-vous encore peur ? Pourquoi (pas) ?

3. Qu'est-ce que vous aimez faire quand il fait beau ? Qu'est-ce que vous préférez faire quand il fait mauvais ?
4. Qu'est-ce que vous refusez de faire dans notre cours ? Et qu'est-ce que vous continuez à faire ? Êtes-vous prêt à faire cela maintenant ?
5. Avez-vous jamais collectionné des timbres ? Quand avez-vous commencé à en collectionner ? Le faites-vous toujours ?
6. Avez-vous jamais reçu une lettre ou un coup de téléphone anonyme ? Décrivez les circonstances.
7. Combien de fois par jour utilisez-vous le téléphone ? Quand est-ce qu'on téléphone en PCV ? Et avec préavis ? Quelle sorte de gens ont besoin d'un répondeur[1] ?

🔲 *Compréhension auditive* (*basée sur l'Application A*)

🔲 *Compréhension auditive* (*basée sur les Applications B et C*)

🔲 *Dictée* (*adresses et numéros de téléphone*)

Avec son uniforme bleu et sa casquette, le facteur fait sa tournée à pied.

H Lecture

Postes et Télécommunications (PET)

Pour beaucoup de Français, les PET, c'est avant tout le facteur. Avec son uniforme bleu et son indispensable casquette, le facteur est souvent sympathique et fait sa tournée dans une petite camionnette jaune, quelquefois à vélomoteur (jaune aussi), ou même à pied. Près de 500.000 employés travaillent « dans les postes », et le budget des PET détient la deuxième place dans le budget national, tout de suite après celui° de la Défense.   5

Il est vrai que les PET remplissent de multiples fonctions. La distribution du courrier et des colis est, bien sûr, la plus importante, mais on va au bureau de poste pour beaucoup d'autres raisons : pour envoyer un télégramme, par exemple, ou pour expédier un mandat télégraphique. Si vous n'arrivez pas à° trouver une boîte solide pour faire un colis, allez à la poste et on vous en vendra une, en carton jaune, très astucieuse[2], qui reste fermée sans ficelle ni   10 ruban adhésif. Pour beaucoup de gens, la poste fait aussi fonction de° banque. Il est possible d'ouvrir un compte d'épargne[3] pour vos économies°, et, si vous voulez, les PET paieront

that (le budget)

Si vous ne pouvez pas

faire fonction de *to work as (a)/savings*

---

[1]*answering machine*

[2]*clever, cleverly done*; on plie un carton selon les indications imprimées pour en faire une boîte.

[3]*savings account* (Caisse Nationale d'Épargne)

bills
Treasury Bonds
stand in line
abroad

directement vos factures° de gaz et d'électricité avec l'argent placé sur ce compte. Vous pouvez aussi acheter des Bons du Trésor°. La poste est donc un endroit plein d'activité, et il n'est pas étonnant qu'on doive faire la queue° au guichet pour obtenir ce qu'on veut.   15

Si vous voyagez, et si vous avez besoin de téléphoner à l'étranger°, il ne faut surtout pas téléphoner de votre hôtel, qui peut vous demander une somme exorbitante pour un coup de téléphone international. Le plus simple est d'aller à la poste la plus proche ou dans une cabine téléphonique. Les cabines sont faciles à trouver, dans les stations de métro, près des arrêts d'autobus ou de taxis, dans les bureaux de tabac ou les cafés. Depuis 1985, tous les numéros 20 de téléphone sont composés de huit chiffres groupés par deux, par exemple, 35.82.44.63.

entitles you to
small, lighted panel
pièces de monnaie coins

La « télécarte » vient de faire son apparition récemment. On peut l'acheter à la poste pour 40 ou 100 francs. Partout en France, dans des cabines spécialement équipées, on peut téléphoner avec cette carte qui vous donne droit à° un certain nombre d'appels. Un petit voyant lumineux° vous indique votre « crédit ». Vous pouvez ainsi téléphoner partout, 25 même à l'étranger, sans utiliser de pièces de monnaie°.

perfectionné
appuyer sur to press,
push / keys / prices at the
Stock Exchange

Une autre innovation qui est en train de révolutionner la vie des Français, c'est le Minitel. Ce petit ordinateur, mis au point° par les PET, rend des services nombreux et variés : en appuyant sur° quelques touches°, vous pouvez obtenir un numéro de téléphone, vérifier votre compte en banque ou le cours de la Bourse°, faire des réservations ou commander des 30 chaussures que vous avez vues dans un catalogue. Les enfants l'utilisent pour des jeux électroniques, et il sert aussi à envoyer ou à recevoir des messages.

Les PET se modernisent !

A Indiquez si chaque commentaire est vrai ou faux. S'il est faux, corrigez le commentaire.

1. Pour beaucoup de Français, c'est la poste qui représente les facteurs.
2. Les véhicules utilisés par les PET sont jaunes.
3. Le budget des PET détient la première place dans le budget national de la France.
4. Pour envoyer un colis, il est obligatoire d'utiliser les boîtes jaunes vendues à la poste.
5. On peut aller au bureau de poste pour envoyer de l'argent.
6. On doit aller à la banque pour envoyer de l'argent.
7. Le bureau de poste est souvent bondé et il faut faire la queue au guichet.
8. Quand on voyage, la façon la plus économique de téléphoner à l'étranger est d'utiliser le téléphone dans sa chambre d'hôtel.
9. En France, certains numéros de téléphone se composent de neuf chiffres.
10. On peut utiliser la télécarte pour expédier un mandat télégraphique.
11. On peut acheter les télécartes dans un bureau de tabac.
12. Le Minitel est un poste de télévision[1] en miniature qui sert à envoyer des colis.

[1]television set

Avec le Minitel, on peut
obtenir toutes sortes de
renseignements.

B *Trouvez dans le texte les mots qui sont définis ou dont on trouve les synonymes ci-dessous.*

1. immédiatement
2. excessif
3. vêtement obligatoire pour un groupe d'employés
4. endroit où s'arrête l'autobus
5. essentiel et obligatoire
6. lettres envoyées ou à envoyer
7. carte utilisée pour faire un appel télé-phonique
8. objet mis dans une boîte, à être envoyé et livré
9. transmission d'information à distance
10. argent qu'on épargne (qu'on ne dépense pas et qu'on met de côté)
11. employé de la poste qui distribue les lettres et les colis

VOCABULAIRE

Noms

un anniversaire de mariage	*wedding anniversary*	le **colis**	*package*	la **pièce de monnaie**	*coin*
le bateau	*ship*	le correspondant	*party (on phone)*	la **poste**	*post office*
la **boîte aux lettres**	*mailbox*	une étiquette	*label*	la **préposition**	*preposition*
la **brosse à dents**	*toothbrush*	le **genre**	*kind*	la route	*road, way*
la cabine	*booth*	un **infinitif**	*infinitive*	le tarif	*rate*
la **calculatrice**	*calculator*	une **intention**	*intention*	la tonalité	*dial tone*
le **chiffre**	*number, figure*	la **machine (à laver)**	*(washing) machine*		
		le **message**	*message*		

Verbes

calculer	*to calculate*	**consentir (à)**	*to consent, agree (to)*	**servir à**	*to be used for, useful for*
cesser (de)	*to stop*	**hésiter (à)**	*to hesitate*		
composer	*to dial*	**nager**	*to swim*	se servir de	*to use*

Adjectifs

absent(e)	*absent*	**habitué(e) à**	*used to*	postal(e)	*postal*
comique	*comical*	**lent(e)**	*slow*	**suivi(e) de**	*followed by*

Adverbe
fort *loudly*

Préposition
en face de *opposite, across from*

Autres expressions

avec préavis	*person to person*	en tout	*in all, altogether*
avoir le mauvais numéro	*to have the wrong number*	**être habitué(e) à**	*to be used to*
avoir l'intention de + *inf*	*to intend to* + inf	**Ne quittez pas.**	*Hold the line.*
en PCV	*collect (call)*	par avion	*by air mail*
en recommandé	*by registered mail*	par bateau	*by surface mail*
en route	*on the way*	**Qui est à l'appareil ?**	*Who is speaking?*

22 Faisons des achats !

LESSON OBJECTIVES

Theme and Culture

1. Markets and department stores
2. Banking transactions

Communication Skills

1. Asking/Answering questions about two or more people or objects (*which one(s)?*, *this one*, *that one*)
2. Expressing possession (*mine, yours, his, hers, ours, theirs, Marie's*)
3. Making indirect requests (*to ask/tell/suggest someone to do*)
4. Making statements involving other people (*to excuse/ thank someone for doing*; *to help/invite/encourage someone to do*)
5. Expressing simultaneous actions or means (*while walking, by reading*)
6. Shopping and bargaining
7. Cashing checks

Structures

22.1 Interrogative pronoun **lequel**; use of **ce ...-ci**, **ce ...-là**

22.2 Demonstrative pronoun **celui**

22.3 Verb + person + **de/à** + infinitive

22.4 Possessive pronouns **le mien**, etc.

22.5 Present participle and **être en train de**

469

CONVERSATIONS

A. Quelle carte de crédit ?

LA VENDEUSE	Voulez-vous autre chose ?
LE CLIENT	Non merci, ce sera tout. Combien est-ce que je vous dois ?
LA VENDEUSE	Ça fait 880 francs.
LE CLIENT	Mon Dieu, je n'ai pas assez d'argent. Acceptez-vous les cartes de crédit ?
LA VENDEUSE	Laquelle, Monsieur ?
LE CLIENT	Celle-ci.
LA VENDEUSE	Ah oui, bien sûr.

B. Le rayon des chaussures

THIERRY	Le rayon des chaussures est au quatrième[1].
DANIEL	Bon. Prenons cet escalator-là.
THIERRY	Mais on y arrivera plus vite en prenant l'ascenseur.
DANIEL	C'est vrai. Montons en ascenseur.

« Donnez-moi deux billets de cinquante francs, s'il vous plaît. »

C. À la banque

LA TOURISTE	Bonjour, Monsieur. Où est-ce que je peux changer des chèques de voyage ?
L'EMPLOYÉ	Au guichet N° 5, là-bas. Vous verrez la pancarte « CHANGE ».
LA TOURISTE	Quel est le cours du dollar[2] ?
L'EMPLOYÉ	Il est posté là-bas. Le dollar est à 6,27 francs aujourd'hui.
LA TOURISTE	Merci, Monsieur.
L'EMPLOYÉ	De rien, Madame.

Elle va au guichet et fait la queue[3]. Bientôt c'est son tour.

LA TOURISTE	Je voudrais changer des chèques de voyage.
L'EMPLOYÉE	Combien voulez-vous changer ?

[1]au quatrième étage
[2]*exchange rate of the dollar*
[3]**faire la queue** *to stand in line*

LA TOURISTE   Cinq cents dollars.

L'EMPLOYÉE   Je suis désolée, Madame. Pour les chèques de voyage, la limite est de 350 dollars.

LA TOURISTE   D'accord. Voici mon passeport. J'aimerais aussi changer ces francs belges.

L'employée fait les calculs, remplit une fiche.

L'EMPLOYÉE   Voilà, Madame. Passez à la caisse, s'il vous plaît. Elle est là-bas, à votre gauche.

STRUCTURES

22.1   PRONOM INTERROGATIF **LEQUEL** ; EMPLOI DE **CE ...-CI, CE ...-LÀ**

1. In questions, the combination **quel** + noun (Lesson 3.5) can be replaced by the pronoun **lequel**. Like **quel**, the pronoun **lequel** has four forms that agree in gender and number with the noun they replace: **lequel, laquelle, lesquels, lesquelles**. They correspond to English *which, which one(s)*.

Quel magasin préférez-vous ?	*Which store do you prefer?*
→ **Lequel** préférez-vous ?	→ *Which (one) do you prefer?*
Quelle vendeuse connaissez-vous ?	*Which saleslady do you know?*
→ **Laquelle** connaissez-vous ?	→ *Which (one) do you know?*
Quels livres viennent de paraître ?	*Which books have just come out?*
→ **Lesquels** viennent de paraître ?	→ *Which (ones) have just come out?*
Quelles robes a-t-elle achetées ?	*Which dresses did she buy?*
→ **Lesquelles** a-t-elle achetées ?	→ *Which (ones) did she buy?*

   The interrogative pronoun may be followed by **de** + determiner + noun, similar to English. The gender of the pronoun agrees with the noun mentioned.

Lesquelles des montres est-ce que tu préfères ? (**des** = **de** + **les**)	*Which of the watches . . .*
Laquelle de ces photos est à vous ?	*Which of these photos . . .*
Lesquels de vos cousins sont ici ?	*Which of your cousins . . .*
Lesquelles de mes photos veut-elle ?	*Which of my photos . . .*

2. **Le** and **les** combine with the prepositions **de** and **à** to form **du, des** and **au, aux**. Similarly, **lequel, lesquels, lesquelles** combine with **de** to form **duquel, desquels, desquelles**, and they combine with **à** to form **auquel, auxquels, auxquelles**.

(**de** + **lequel**)	Voilà deux reçus. **Duquel** avez-vous besoin ?
(**de** + **lesquels**)	On a vu beaucoup de films. **Desquels** parle-t-elle ?
(**de** + **lesquelles**)	**Desquelles** de ces banques ont-elles parlé ?

(**à** + **lequel**)	Voilà deux magasins. **Auquel** voulez-vous aller ?
(**à** + **lesquels**)	Voilà les enfants. **Auxquels** avez-vous parlé ?
(**à** + **lesquelles**)	**Auxquelles** de ces questions allez-vous répondre ?

3. In Lesson 5.2 you learned that the demonstrative adjective in French can correspond to English *this, that, these,* or *those*. When it becomes necessary to distinguish between two or more similar things or groups of similar things, **ce** alone no longer suffices, and **ce** + noun-**ci** and **ce** + noun-**là** are used for more clarity. The first construction, derived from **ici** *here*, corresponds to *this/these*, and the second, derived from **là** *there*, to *that/those*.

Cette banque-**ci** est plus proche.	*This bank is closer.*
Montrez-moi **cet** appareil-**là**.	*Show me that camera.*
Ces stylos-**ci** sont à moi, et **ces** stylos-**là** sont à Jeanne.	*These pens are mine, and those pens are Jeanne's.*
Regardez. Lequel de ces livres est à moi ?	*Look. Which of these books is mine?*
— **Ce** livre-**là** ; **ce** livre-**ci** est à lui.	*That book; this book is his.*

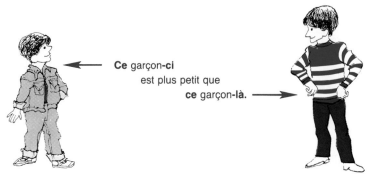

Ce garçon-**ci** est plus petit que **ce** garçon-**là**.

TABLEAU 113

A *Posez des questions d'après ce modèle. Faites attention aux prépositions.*

Je cherche un vendeur.
(Marianne)   **Quel vendeur cherchez-vous ?**
(Robert)   **Oui, lequel cherchez-vous ?**

1. Je cherche un magasin.
2. Je lis une réclame[1].
3. Je connais des magasins.
4. Je pense à un ordinateur.
5. Je paie avec une carte de crédit.
6. J'ai besoin de deux stylos.
7. Je suis allé à une boutique.
8. J'ai répondu à deux questions.
9. J'ai téléphoné à trois bureaux.
10. J'ai parlé à trois vendeuses.

B *Répondez aux questions d'après ce modèle.*

Il y a beaucoup de chaises ici. Laquelle est pour vous ?
Cette chaise-ci est pour moi.
Laquelle est pour moi ?
Cette chaise-là est pour vous.

1. Il y a beaucoup de chaises ici. Laquelle est pour vous ? Laquelle est pour moi ?
2. (Jacques), donnez-moi votre livre, s'il vous plaît. Regardez ces deux livres. Lequel est à moi ? Lequel est à (Jacques) ?
3. Regardez ces stylos. Lequel est à (Mireille) ? Lequel est à (Daniel) ? Lequel est à moi ?
4. Voici des lettres. Lesquelles est-ce que j'ai écrites ? Lesquelles est-ce que j'ai reçues ?
5. Voici deux étudiants. Vous les connaissez bien, n'est-ce pas ? Comment s'appellent ces étudiants ?

Compréhension auditive

[1]*advertisement*

22.2 PRONOMS DÉMONSTRATIFS **CELUI**, **CELLE**, **CEUX**, **CELLES**

The demonstrative pronoun is used to avoid repetition of the same noun. It has four forms—**celui**, **celle**, **ceux**, **celles**—to agree in gender and number with the noun it replaces. You will see that the English equivalents of the demonstrative pronoun vary considerably, depending on how it is used.

1. The demonstrative pronoun can occur with **-ci** or **-là** (Lesson 22.1) and replaces **ce/cet/cette/ces** + noun-**ci**/noun-**là**. It corresponds to English *this (one)*, *that (one)*, *these*, and *those*.

Ce disque-ci est à Jean, et **ce disque-là** est à Monique.	*This record . . . that record . . .*
→ **Celui-ci** est à Jean, et **celui-là** est à Monique.	*This (one) . . . that (one) . . .*
Lesquelles de ces fleurs voulez-vous ?	
— Je voudrais **ces fleurs-là**.	*. . . those flowers*
→ Je voudrais **celles-là**.	*. . . those*
Auxquels de ces étudiants pensiez-vous ?	
— Je pensais à **ces étudiants-ci**.	*. . . these students*
→ Je pensais à **ceux-ci**.	*. . . these*

« Celui-ci ?
— Non, celui-là. »

2. In the following examples, the demonstrative pronoun replaces definite article + noun, and is followed by **de** + noun indicating the possessor. The basic English equivalent is *that/those of* + possessor, but more commonly, possessor + *'s*.

Mon frère et **celui** (= le frère) **de Marie** sont arrivés.	*that of Marie → Marie's*
Ta voiture est rouge, mais **celle** (= la voiture) **de Paul** est blanche.	*that of Paul → Paul's*
Mes parents habitent à Paris ; **ceux** (= les parents) **de Jeanne** sont à Tours.	*those of Jeanne → Jeanne's*
Les valises de Marc sont plus légères que **celles** (= les valises) **de Lili**.	*those of Lili → Lili's*

3. When the demonstrative pronoun, replacing definite article + noun, is followed by a relative clause, it corresponds to English *the one(s)*, or *those*.

Je ne connais pas ce magasin ; **celui** (= le magasin) **que** je connais est près de la gare.

the one (= the store)

La jeune fille qui est assise est ma sœur ; **celle** (= la jeune fille) **qui** est debout est notre cousine.

the one (= the girl)

Vos livres sont sur la table ; mais **ceux** (= les livres) **dont** j'ai besoin ne sont pas là.

the ones, those (= the books)

Je ne connais pas ces étudiantes ; **celles** (= les étudiantes) **que** je connais ne sont pas venues.

the ones, those (= students)

TABLEAU 114

Voilà deux valises ; **celle** de Robert est légère, mais **celle** de Jeanne est très lourde !

 A *Répondez aux questions en employant les pronoms démonstratifs.*

1. Regardez ces murs. Lequel est le plus proche de (Jeanne) ? Lequel est le plus proche de moi ?
2. Voici deux livres. Duquel avez-vous besoin ? Duquel est-ce que j'ai besoin ?
3. Regardez ces photos en couleur dans notre livre. Laquelle vous intéresse le plus ? Pourquoi ? Laquelle vous intéresse le moins ? Pourquoi ?
4. Pensez à un monument de Paris. Regardez la page 357. Auquel avez-vous pensé ? Demandez à (Charles) auquel il a pensé.
5. Vous connaissez tous les étudiants dans ce cours, n'est-ce pas ? Choisissez deux étudiants et dites comment ils s'appellent.

 B *Répondez aux questions d'après ce modèle.*

Savez-vous mon âge ?
Non, mais je sais celui de (Janine).

1. Savez-vous mon âge ?
2. Savez-vous mon adresse ?
3. Voyez-vous mon stylo ?
4. Voyez-vous mon dos ?
5. Connaissez-vous mes amis ?
6. Pouvez-vous regarder ma montre ?
7. Pouvez-vous voir mes pieds ?
8. Avez-vous regardé mon livre ?

C *J'ai dîné dans un restaurant médiocre. Vous, au contraire, vous avez dîné dans un très bon restaurant. Nous allons parler de nos impressions. Dites le contraire de ce que je vous raconte.*

> *Modèle :* Le restaurant que j'ai trouvé était loin de chez moi.
> **Celui que j'ai trouvé n'était pas loin de chez moi.**

1. Le repas que j'ai commandé était mauvais.
2. La soupe qu'on m'a servie n'était pas chaude.
3. Le steak qu'on m'a apporté était trop cuit[1].
4. Le garçon à qui j'ai commandé le repas ne m'a pas bien compris.
5. Les légumes que j'ai choisis n'étaient pas frais.
6. Les fromages que j'ai mangés étaient mauvais.
7. Les verres qu'on nous a apportés n'étaient pas propres[2].
8. L'addition que j'ai demandée avait des erreurs.

D *Faisons des comparaisons.*

1. Comparez les cheveux de (Marie) et ceux de (Sophie).
2. Comparez la montre de (Jacques) et celle de (Chantal).
3. Comparez le cours de français et un autre cours.
4. Comparez la maison du président de l'université et celle du président des États-Unis.
5. Comparez le portefeuille que j'ai acheté et celui que (Paul) a acheté.
6. Comparez l'émission que vous avez regardée et celle que (Sylvie) a regardée.

 Exercice supplémentaire

22.3 VERBE + PERSONNE + DE/À + INFINITIF

1. The verbs below take the construction **à** + person + **de** + infinitive. With the exception of **promettre**, the person named in **à** + person is the one who performs the action expressed by the infinitive. **À** + person can be an indirect-object pronoun (**me, te, lui, nous, vous,** or **leur**).

conseiller	*to advise*	**permettre**	*to permit/allow*
défendre	*to forbid*	**promettre**	*to promise*
demander	*to ask*	**suggérer**[3]	*to suggest*
dire	*to say/tell*		

Le professeur **a suggéré à Louise d'aller** en Europe.

— Ah oui ? Quels pays **lui a-t-il conseillé de visiter** ?

Et ses parents **lui ont permis d'aller** en France.

— Ah bon ! **Leur a-t-elle promis d'écrire** souvent ?

Note that the construction above, with most of the verbs, can also have dependent clauses with the subjunctive (see Lesson 19.4).

Il **me défend de servir** de la bière.	Elle **nous permet de rester** ici.
→ Il **défend que je serve** de la bière.	→ Elle **permet que nous restions** ici.
Je **vous demande de m'aider.**	Je **leur suggère d'aller** au marché.
→ Je **demande que vous m'aidiez.**	→ Je **suggère qu'ils aillent** au marché.

---

[1]*too well-done*

[2]**propre** clean (contraire de **sale**)

[3]The two **g**'s are pronounced /gʒ/: **je suggère** /sygʒɛʀ/, **vous suggérez** /sygʒeʀe/.

2. The verbs below take the construction person + **de** + infinitive. The person can be a direct-object pronoun (**me**, **te**, **le/la**, **nous**, **vous**, **les**).

empêcher	*to prevent, to stop*	**prier**[1]	*to ask*
excuser	*to excuse*	**remercier**	*to thank*

J'espère qu'il **m'excusera d'arriver** en retard.
— Bien sûr, il **vous remerciera d'être** venu.
Je vous **prie de** ne pas **faire** tant de bruit.
— Ah, excusez-moi. Je ne savais pas que vous étiez là.

3. The following verbs take the construction person + **à** + infinitive. Again, the person can be a direct-object pronoun.

aider	*to help*	**inviter**	*to invite*
encourager	*to encourage*		

Nos parents **ont invité Christine à passer** les vacances de Noël chez eux, et nous **l'avons encouragée à accepter** leur invitation. Nous espérons **l'aider à connaître** la région.

A *Exercice de contrôle*

Est-ce que vous encouragez vos étudiants à aller en Europe ?

1. vous conseillez		3. vous empêchez		5. vous dites	
2. vous demandez		4. vous invitez		6. vous suggérez	

Est-ce que vous dites à vos étudiants de parler français ?

1. vous défendez		3. vous aidez		5. vous encouragez	
2. vous priez		4. vous permettez		6. vous invitez	

Excusez-vous vos étudiants de parler anglais ?

1. Permettez-vous		3. Remerciez-vous		5. Encouragez-vous	
2. Défendez-vous		4. Dites-vous		6. Conseillez-vous	

B *Nous allons parler d'un étudiant. Écoutez chaque phrase, puis ajoutez une autre phrase.*

Modèle: Il n'écrit pas à ses parents.   (dire)
Disons-lui d'écrire à ses parents.

1. Il ne fait pas ses devoirs.   (dire)
2. Il hésite à aller en Europe.   (encourager)
3. Il ne va pas au labo.   (conseiller)
4. Il a aidé son copain à faire ses devoirs.   (remercier)
5. Il boit du vin dans sa chambre.   (défendre)
6. Il n'a pas fait pas son lit.   (excuser)
7. Il ne lit jamais de journaux.   (suggérer)
8. Il ne déjeune pas au resto-U.   (inviter)

C *Répondez aux questions.*

1. Qu'est-ce que je vous défends de faire en classe ? Mentionnez trois choses. Qu'est-ce que je vous encourage à faire ? Mentionnez trois choses.
2. Qui vous a conseillé d'apprendre le français ? Qui vous a suggéré de choisir ce cours ? Qui vous a demandé d'être dans mon cours ?
3. Est-ce que quelqu'un vous aide à faire votre devoir de français ? Aidez-vous quelqu'un à faire son devoir de français ?
4. Avez-vous jamais encouragé quelqu'un à faire quelque chose ? Avez-vous jamais défendu à quelqu'un de faire quelque chose ?

---

[1]**Prier** (literally, *to pray/beg*) is more polite in meaning than **demander** when making a request. **Prière de** + infinitive is a very common expression (see Exercise C).

5. Regardez le Tableau 115. Que veulent dire ces panneaux ?

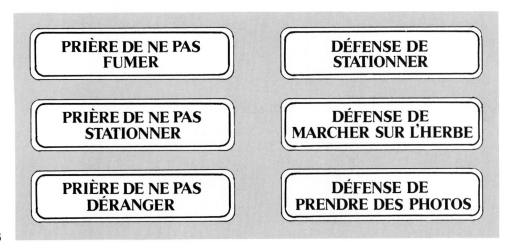

PRIÈRE DE NE PAS FUMER	DÉFENSE DE STATIONNER
PRIÈRE DE NE PAS STATIONNER	DÉFENSE DE MARCHER SUR L'HERBE
PRIÈRE DE NE PAS DÉRANGER	DÉFENSE DE PRENDRE DES PHOTOS

TABLEAU 115

22.4   PRONOMS POSSESSIFS **LE MIEN, LE TIEN,** ETC.

1. The combination of a possessive adjective and a noun can be replaced by a possessive pronoun (in English *my book → mine, your cousins → yours, our house → ours, her answer → hers,* etc.). In French, the possessive pronouns are always preceded by **le, la,** or **les,** and agree in gender and number with the noun they replace. Note below that the first- and second-person singular (*mine, yours*) have four forms.

mon sac, **mes** sacs	*my purse, my purses*
→ **le mien, les miens**	*→ mine*
ma valise, **mes** valises	*my suitcase, my suitcases*
→ **la mienne, les miennes**	*→ mine*
ton couteau, **tes** couteaux	*your knife, your knives*
→ **le tien, les tiens**	*→ yours*
ta clé, **tes** clés	*your key, your keys*
→ **la tienne, les tiennes**	*→ yours*

The third-person singular also has four forms. Each of these forms corresponds to *his* or *hers,* depending on the context, just as the possessive adjectives (**son, sa, ses**) can correspond to either *his* or *her.*

le frère **de Jean** le frère **d'Anne**	→ **son** frère	→ **le sien**	*his/her brother*	*→ his/hers*
les frères **de Jean** les frères **d'Anne**	→ **ses** frères	→ **les siens**	*his/her brothers*	*→ his/hers*
la sœur **de Jean** la sœur **d'Anne**	→ **sa** sœur	→ **la sienne**	*his/her sister*	*→ his/hers*
les sœurs **de Jean** les sœurs **d'Anne**	→ **ses** sœurs	→ **les siennes**	*his/her sisters*	*→ his/hers*

As-tu **ton portefeuille** ?
— Oui, voilà **le mien**. As-tu **le tien** ?
Où sont **tes valises** ? Et **les valises de Robert** ?
— **Les miennes** sont ici ; **les siennes** sont là-bas.

« Mon billet a coûté 55 francs. Et le tien ? »

2. The possessive pronouns for the first-, second-, and third-person plural (*ours*, *yours*, *theirs*) consist of two forms each. Gender distinction is shown only in the singular forms, by **le** and **la**; the plural forms are the same.

notre cours, **nos** cours
→ **le nôtre, les nôtres**[1]
votre sac, **vos** sacs
→ **le vôtre, les vôtres**[1]
leur magasin, **leurs** magasins
→ **le leur, les leurs**

notre résidence, **nos** résidences
→ **la nôtre, les nôtres**[1]
votre pendule, **vos** pendules
→ **la vôtre, les vôtres**[1]
leur table, **leurs** tables
→ **la leur, les leurs**

3. The definite article **le, les** will combine with the preposition **de** or **à** to form **du, des** or **au, aux**.

Regarde mon portefeuille. Il ressemble beaucoup **au tien**, mais pas à celui d'Anne-Marie.

Je viens de recevoir mon passeport. Avez-vous reçu **le vôtre** ?

Voici nos passeports. Je n'ai pas besoin **du mien**. As-tu besoin **du tien** ?

Elle était contente de mes réponses. Était-elle contente **des vôtres** ?

4. French does not use possessive pronouns in expressions corresponding to English *a friend of mine, a book of yours, an uncle of his*, and so forth.

Un de mes camarades étudie le russe.   *A friend of mine (One of my friends)* . . .
J'ai reçu **deux de vos lettres**.   *. . . two letters of yours (two of your letters)*
Un de vos amis m'a téléphoné.   *A friend of yours (One of your friends)* . . .

---

[1]These pronouns are pronounced with /o/: /notR/, /votR/; the possessive adjectives are pronounced with /ɔ/: /nɔtR/, /vɔtR/.

TABLEAU 116

A *Répondez aux questions d'après ces modèles.*

> Voilà mon livre. Où est votre livre ?   Où est le livre de (Marie) ?
> **Voilà le mien.**   **Voilà le sien.**

1. Voilà mon cahier d'exercices. Où est votre cahier ? Où est le cahier de (Jean-Jacques) ?
2. Voilà mes stylos, sur la table. Où sont vos stylos ? Où sont les stylos de (Marie-Claire) ?
3. Voilà ma chaise. Où est votre chaise ? Où est la chaise de (Vincent) ?
4. Voici mon permis de conduire[1]. Avez-vous votre permis de conduire ? Demandez à (Charles) s'il a son permis de conduire.
5. Voici mon mouchoir. Où est votre mouchoir ? Demandez à (Nicole) où est son mouchoir.
6. Voici ma montre. Où est votre montre ? Où est la montre de (Bernard) ?
7. Voici mes cartes de crédit. Où sont vos cartes de crédit ? Demandez à (Alain) s'il a ses cartes de crédit.
8. Voici mes clés. Où sont vos clés ? Demandez à (Brigitte) où elle a mis ses clés.

B *Nous allons comparer ma chambre et la vôtre. Ajoutez des phrases d'après ce modèle.*

> Ma chambre est trop sombre.
> **La vôtre est sombre ? La mienne aussi (*ou* La mienne est claire, La mienne n'est pas sombre, etc.)**

1. Ma chambre est trop petite.
2. Ma chambre est assez claire.
3. Mon lit est trop mou.
4. Ma commode a huit tiroirs.
5. Mes fenêtres sont trop petites.
6. Mes rideaux sont trop sales.
7. Mon placard n'est pas assez grand.
8. Ma chambre est toujours propre.

C *Répondez aux questions en employant les pronoms possessifs appropriés.*

1. Est-ce que j'ai mon livre de français ? Avez-vous votre livre ? (Marie et Jacques) ont-ils leurs livres ?
2. Regardez ces trois stylos. Lequel est mon stylo ? Lequel est votre stylo ? Lequel est celui de (Robert) ?
3. Regardez autour de vous. Est-ce que notre classe est grande ? Est-ce que notre classe est claire ? Ma table est-elle grande ? Vos chaises sont-elles confortables ?
4. De quelle couleur est (ma chemise) ? De quelle couleur est (votre chemise) ? De quelle couleur est (la chemise de Marianne) ?
5. Mon poste de télévision[2] est petit. Est-ce que votre poste est grand ? Est-ce que votre poste est en couleur ?

[1]*driver's license*
[2]*television set*

📼 *Exercice supplémentaire*

📼 *Compréhension auditive*

22.5 PARTICIPE PRÉSENT ; **ÊTRE EN TRAIN DE**

1. The present participle ends in **-ant**. The stem derives from the **nous** form of the present indicative (just like the imperfect indicative tense): you take the **nous** form, remove the ending **-ons**, and add the present participle ending **-ant**.

nous **parlons**	→ **parl**ant		nous **prenons**	→ **pren**ant
nous **finissons**	→ **finiss**ant		nous **buvons**	→ **buv**ant
nous **vendons**	→ **vend**ant		nous **lisons**	→ **lis**ant
nous **allons**	→ **all**ant		nous **servons**	→ **serv**ant

The only exceptions are **être**, **avoir**, and **savoir**.

(nous **sommes**)	étant	(nous **savons**)	sachant
(nous **avons**)	ayant /ɛjɑ̃/		

2. You have seen the construction **en** + present participle in some of the directions for exercises in this book.

Répondez aux questions **en employant** le pronom démonstratif.
Écrivez un paragraphe **en employant** les mots indiqués.

Basically, **en** + present participle has two distinct equivalents in English.

a) The construction **en** (or **tout en** for emphasis) + present participle implies simultaneous or near-simultaneous action. The action expressed by the present participle takes place at the same time as the action of the main verb, and both actions are performed by the same subject. This construction corresponds to English *while doing (something)*.

Il chante ; il prend sa douche en même temps.	*He sings; he takes his shower at the same time.*
→ Il chante **en prenant** sa douche.	*→ He sings while taking his shower.*
→ Il prend sa douche **en chantant**.	*→ He takes his shower (while) singing.*
Je regarde la télé ; je prends mon repas en même temps.	*I watch TV; I eat my meal at the same time.*
→ Je regarde la télé **en prenant** mon repas.	*→ I watch TV while eating my meal.*
→ Je prends mon repas **en regardant** la télé.	*→ I eat my meal while watching TV.*
J'écoute la radio ; je travaille en même temps.	*I listen to the radio; I work at the same time.*
→ J'écoute la radio **en travaillant**.	*→ I listen to the radio while working.*
→ Je travaille **en écoutant** la radio.	*→ I work while listening to the radio.*

b) **En** + present participle can also indicate the *method* or *means* through which the action of the main verb results. In English, a comparable meaning is expressed by the construction *by doing (something)* or *upon doing (something)*.

Vous apprendrez la vérité **en lisant** cette lettre.	*You will learn the truth by reading this letter.*

Nous y arriverons plus vite **en prenant** le métro.	*We will arrive there more quickly by taking the subway.*
On connaîtra mieux la France **en apprenant** le français.	*One will get to know France better by learning French.*

3. **Être en train de.** In contrast to English, French never uses the present participle **-ant** to express an action in progress. Normally the context can indicate whether or not a given verb, in the present or imperfect tense, denotes an ongoing action. But when it becomes necessary to emphasize the fact that an action is in progress, the construction **être en train de** + infinitive can be used. It corresponds to English *to be in the act/process of doing (something).*

Je **vais** chez Sophie ce soir.	*I'm going to Sophie's tonight.*
Écoutez-la ! Elle **parle** !	*Listen to her. She's speaking!*
Il **pleuvait** quand je suis rentré.	*It was raining when I came home.*

BUT

Chut ! / ʃyt, ʃt/ Il **est en train de travailler** !	*Sh! He's (in the process of) working!*
Il **était en train de téléphoner** à Jean quand je suis arrivée.	*He was (in the process of) calling Jean when I arrived.*

Elle regarde la télé **en prenant** son café.

Rappelle-moi dans dix minutes.
Je **suis en train de** manger.

TABLEAU 117

 A *Modifiez les phrases suivantes d'après ce modèle.*

Je travaille ; je mange en même temps.
Je travaille en mangeant.

1. Je mange ; je lis un journal en même temps.
2. Vous dites bonjour ; vous entrez dans le magasin en même temps.
3. Il a chanté ; il a pris une douche en même temps.
4. J'ai corrigé mes fautes ; j'ai regardé le tableau en même temps.
5. Elle a dit au revoir ; elle a quitté le magasin en même temps.
6. Nous avons vérifié nos réponses ; nous avons regardé les clés[1].

B *Modifiez les phrases suivantes d'après ce modèle.*

Vous apprendrez la vérité si vous lisez cette lettre.
Vous apprendrez la vérité en la lisant.

1. Nous monterons plus vite si nous prenons l'ascenseur.
2. Vous aurez chaud si vous mettez ce pull.

[1] *answer keys*

3. Elle saura la vérité si elle parle à son ami.
4. Vous composterez votre billet si vous allez sur le quai.
5. Il se sentira mieux s'il prend des médicaments.
6. Vous grossirez si vous mangez des frites tout le temps.

C *Répondez aux questions d'après ce modèle.*

Est-ce que je regarde le tableau ?
Oui, vous êtes en train de le regarder.

1. Est-ce que je vous parle ?
2. Est-ce que vous m'écoutez ?
3. Est-ce que je pose des questions ?
4. Est-ce que vous me répondez ?

5. Est-ce que je regarde mon livre ?
6. Regardez-vous cette photo ?
7. Regardez bien. Qu'est-ce que je fais ?

D *Répondez aux questions.*

1. Vous êtes à la gare. Le train que vous attendez est en retard de vingt minutes. Qu'est-ce que vous pouvez faire en attendant le train ?
2. Aimez-vous voyager ? Quels états traverse-t-on en allant de Chicago à New York ? Et en allant de Denver à San Francisco ?
3. Il est possible de faire deux choses en même temps. Par exemple, on peut manger en écoutant la radio. Qu'est-ce qu'on peut faire en lisant un journal ? Que faites-vous en regardant la télé ?
4. Qu'est-ce que vous êtes en train de faire ? Et moi, qu'est-ce que je suis en train de faire ? Et (Jean-Paul) ?

Compréhension auditive

Compréhension auditive

APPLICATIONS

A Situations

Faisons des achats !
Christine est dans une maroquinerie[1] près de la Place Vendôme. Elle vient de s'acheter un sac en cuir et elle décide de choisir un portefeuille comme cadeau d'anniversaire pour sa sœur.

LA VENDEUSE	Voulez-vous autre chose, Mademoiselle ?	
CHRISTINE	Oui, j'ai besoin d'un portefeuille.	5
LA VENDEUSE	Voilà, Mademoiselle. Ceux-ci coûtent 250 F.	
CHRISTINE	Oh ! là ! là ! C'est un peu cher. Qu'est-ce que vous avez pour cent cinquante francs environ ?	
LA VENDEUSE	Ceux-là sont en solde en ce moment. Cent quarante francs.	
CHRISTINE	Montrez-moi celui-là. Non, non, celui qui est en bas, le bleu.	10
LA VENDEUSE	Celui-ci ?	
that's right CHRISTINE	Oui, et le rouge, celui-là... non, celui qui est à gauche... oui, c'est ça°. Merci.	

Christine a terminé ses achats.

Visa card CHRISTINE	Vous acceptez la Carte Bleue°, n'est-ce pas ?	
LA VENDEUSE	La Carte Bleue ? Ah oui, bien sûr.	15

[1]*fancy leather products store* (leather = **cuir** *m*); La Place Vendôme est tout près du Faubourg Saint-Germain, quartier connu pour ses boutiques chic.

« *Vous acceptez la Carte Bleue, n'est-ce pas ? »*

« *Deux cents francs, c'est tout ce que je peux vous en donner.* »

Julien et Ignès sont au Marché aux Puces[1]. C'est un des endroits les plus curieux de Paris et ils aiment flâner dans les ruelles en regardant les gens et les stands°, où on vend toutes sortes d'objets d'occasion°. Ils s'arrêtent un moment et écoutent une cliente qui cherche un couteau de poche° pour son fils.

/stād/ *booths*	
d'occasion *second-hand*	
camping knife (on dit	
aussi un **couteau suisse**)	

LE MARCHAND   Regardez celui-là, Madame. Il est très solide, et celui-là est magnifique, et en 20
parfait état.

LA CLIENTE   Et celui-ci coûte combien ?

LE MARCHAND   Cent francs, Madame.

machin *gizmo ("what-*   LA CLIENTE   Comment ça, cent francs pour ce petit machin° ? C'est trop cher !
chamacallit")   LE MARCHAND   Bon, ben[2]... Si vous préférez quelque chose de moins cher, prenez celui-ci. Il 25
a trois lames, vous voyez, et aussi un tire-bouchon. Pour vous, c'est 60 francs.

LA CLIENTE   Vous vous fichez de moi[3]. C'est trop cher.

It's a real bargain.   LE MARCHAND   Mais c'est donné,° Madame. Soyez raisonnable.
truc = machin   LA CLIENTE   Non, c'est vraiment trop cher pour un petit truc° comme ça.

LE MARCHAND   Il est comme neuf, Madame. Vous paieriez le double au BHV[4]. 30

LA CLIENTE   Quarante francs. C'est tout ce que je peux vous en donner.

LE MARCHAND   Cinquante francs, et on n'en parle plus.[5] Tenez, je vous donne cette petite
boussole en plus, d'accord ? Ça va ? Vous le prenez ?

LA CLIENTE   Bon, alors, d'accord. Je le prends.

---

[1]*Flea market* (Au nord de Paris, juste au delà de la Porte de Clignancourt, il y a un grand marché aux puces, avec plus de 2.000 stands de brocanteurs, où on vend toutes sortes d'objets.)

[2]**ben** /bɛ̃/ = bien ; **bon, ben** *oh, well*

[3]**se ficher de** = se moquer de *to make fun of*

[4]**Bazar de l'Hôtel de Ville** *a popular discount store near Paris City Hall*

[5]**(Je voudrais qu')on n'en parle plus.** *Let's not talk any more about it; That's my last offer.*

Répondez aux questions. (*lignes 1–15*)

1. Qu'est-ce que Christine vient d'acheter ?
2. Pourquoi regarde-t-elle les portefeuilles ?
3. Combien coûtent ceux qui sont en solde ?
4. Comment paie-t-elle ses achats ?

(*lignes 16–34*)

5. Qu'est-ce qu'on vend au Marché aux Puces ?
6. Qu'est-ce que la cliente regarde ?
7. Combien finit-elle[1] par payer ?
8. Qu'est-ce que le marchand lui donne en plus ?

Projets

1. Vous êtes dans un grand magasin, au rayon des (bijoux). Vous voulez acheter un cadeau pour votre mère. Imaginez votre conversation avec la vendeuse.
2. Vous êtes au Marché aux Puces. Vous cherchez une pendule (une table de nuit, etc.). Imaginez votre conversation avec le marchand.
3. Vous êtes au guichet des réclamations[2] dans un grand magasin. Vous avez rapporté une chemise (un chemisier) qui a un défaut. Vous avez le reçu. Imaginez votre conversation avec l'employé(e).

B Expressions utiles

Dans un grand magasin

aller au / chercher le } rayon {
- des chemises / des chaussures / des jouets / des parfums
- des vêtements pour { hommes / dames
- des articles de { camping / sport / jardin / ménage
- spécial des produits hors taxe[3]

acheter {
à crédit (utiliser une carte de crédit)
au comptant (payer en espèces[4])

La robe va { bien / mal } à la cliente.

La marchandise est {
bon marché[5] / meilleur marché.
en solde.
de bonne / meilleure / mauvaise qualité.

Le prix est {
trop élevé (la marchandise coûte trop cher).
raisonnable.
avantageux / intéressant.
imbattable.

[1]**finir par** + infinitif   *to end up (by) doing/to finally do*

[2]*complaint department*

[3]hors taxe (*tax-exempt*) pour les voyageurs étrangers (voir la *Lecture* de cette leçon)

[4]*in/with cash*

[5]*cheap, inexpensive* (expression invariable)

$$
\text{payer}
\begin{cases}
\text{la caissière} \\
\text{à la caisse}
\end{cases}
$$

$$
\left.
\begin{array}{l}
\text{garder} \\
\text{demander} \\
\text{montrer}
\end{array}
\right\}
\begin{cases}
\text{le reçu} \\
\text{la facture}
\end{cases}
$$

$$
\left.
\begin{array}{l}
\text{rapporter} \\
\text{échanger}
\end{array}
\right\}
\text{une marchandise (qui a un défaut)}
$$

C Pratique

1. À quel rayon faut-il aller pour trouver les articles suivants ?

des bottes	un complet	un chemisier
une poupée	des verres	un sac de couchage[2]
des sandales	une jupe	un ballon
une tondeuse	une raquette de tennis	des patins à roulettes[3]
le jeu de Monopoly	un réchaud de camping[1]	un pantalon

2. Avez-vous une carte de crédit ? Laquelle ? Quand est-ce que vous l'utilisez ? Quand est-ce que vous ne voulez pas l'utiliser ? Quels sont les avantages et les inconvénients d'une carte de crédit ?

3. Qu'est-ce que c'est que le « cours » quand on parle d'argent ? Quel est le cours du dollar cette semaine ?

4. Avez-vous jamais acheté des marchandises en solde ? Étaient-elles bon marché ? Étaient-elles de bonne qualité ?

D Mini-composition : *Cindy, une amie de Christine, est allée aux Galeries Lafayette. Écrivez un paragraphe en employant les mots indiqués.*

(1) Hier/après-midi,/Christine et moi,/nous/aller/dans/un/grand magasin. (2) À/lequel/nous/aller ? (3) À/les/Galeries/Lafayette,/près/l'Opéra. (4) Je/avoir/besoin/plusieurs/chose/et/c'est/Christine/qui/suggérer/me/aller/y. (5) Elle/conseiller/me/prendre/mon/passeport,/car/je/avoir l'intention/changer/chèques/voyage/et/acheter/produits hors taxe/comme/cadeaux/pour/mon/famille. (6) D'abord/je/toucher/mon/chèques[4],/ensuite/nous/aller/à/magasin. (7) Je/acheter/un/paire/sandales. (8) En/passant/près/rayon/vêtements,/je/remarquer/il y a/chemisiers/en solde. (9) Christine/aider/me/choisir/en/deux,/et/ceux/que/je/acheter/être/de/bon/qualité. (10) Nous/aller/à/plusieurs/autre/rayon. (11) Je/décider/ne pas/chercher/cadeaux,/car/je/avoir/encore/un/semaine/passer/Paris/avant de/rentrer/à/États-Unis. (12) D'ailleurs,/il/être/presque/5/heure/quand/nous/sortir/de/magasin. (13) Je/remercier/Christine/avoir/accompagner/me/et/avoir/aider/me/faire/courses. (14) Je/inviter/la/prendre/pot,/et/je/rentrer/à/mon/hôtel/vers/6/heure.

[1] *camping stove*
[2] *sleeping bag*
[3] *roller skates*
[4] **toucher un chèque** *to cash a check*

E *Vous faites des courses. Lisez chaque phrase et dites où vous êtes.*

a) Chez l'horloger. *d*) À la librairie. *g*) Au bureau de tabac.
b) À la pharmacie. *e*) À la charcuterie. *h*) Au bureau de poste.
c) À la papeterie. *f*) À la boucherie. *i*) À la banque.

1. Donnez-moi un kilo de côtelettes de veau[1], s'il vous plaît.
2. Est-il possible de l'acheter sans ordonnance ?
3. Donnez-moi 400 grammes de ce jambon, s'il vous plaît.
4. Je voudrais dix timbres à 2,85 F.
5. Avez-vous un dictionnaire anglais-français ?
6. Je voudrais changer des dollars. Quel est le cours[2] ?
7. Qu'est-ce que vous avez comme désinfectant ?
8. J'ai laissé tomber cette montre, et elle ne marche plus. Pouvez-vous la réparer ?
9. Je voudrais téléphoner aux États-Unis en PCV.
10. Je désire du scotch[3] et des enveloppes.
11. Avez-vous le *guide Michelin vert* pour l'Allemagne ?
12. Est-ce que vous avez des agendas[4] pour l'année prochaine ?
13. Est-ce que je peux toucher un chèque de voyage ?
14. J'aimerais envoyer ce télégramme au Canada.
15. Je cherche un réveil, aussi petit que possible.
16. Donnez-moi 500 grammes de cette salade de tomates.
17. Qu'est-ce que vous recommandez comme livres de linguistique pour débutants[5] ?
18. Donnez-moi un paquet de Marlboro, s'il vous plaît.
19. Avez-vous des brosses à dents ?
20. Est-ce que vous avez des piles pour cette montre ?

F **Composition :** *Choisissez un des sujets suivants et écrivez une composition d'à peu près 200 mots.*

1. Imaginez les aventures (et les mésaventures) de quelqu'un qui a fait de l'auto-stop pour aller d'une ville à l'autre et décrivez-les d'une façon aussi humoristique que possible.
2. Avez-vous fait un voyage en avion ou en train récemment ? Décrivez votre voyage depuis le moment où vous êtes arrivé à l'aéroport ou à la gare jusqu'au moment où vous êtes arrivé à votre destination.
3. Quel est le meilleur restaurant de votre ville ? (Ou lequel est le plus mauvais ?) Pourquoi ? Décrivez le repas que vous y avez pris récemment, la qualité du service et l'ambiance.
4. Racontez la vie d'un serveur ou d'une serveuse de restaurant. Décrivez aussi ce qui s'est passé récemment sur son lieu de travail.
5. Quel est votre magasin préféré en ville ? Pourquoi le préférez-vous ? Qu'est-ce que vous y avez acheté récemment ? Pourquoi le recommanderiez-vous ?
6. Racontez la vie d'un(e) employé(e) dans un grand magasin. À quel rayon travaille-t-il(elle) ? Que pense-t-il(elle) de son travail ? Qu'est-ce qui s'est passé récemment dans son travail ?

[1]*veal cutlets*
[2]**le cours (du change)** *exchange rate*
[3]*Scotch tape*
[4]*appointment book* (**l'ordre du jour** *agenda*)
[5]*beginners*

G Renseignements et opinions

1. Avez-vous un travail que vous êtes en train d'achever ? Lequel ? Avez-vous une date limite[1] pour ce travail ?
2. Est-ce que je vous encourage à parler français en classe ? Quand est-ce que je vous permets de parler anglais ?
3. Qu'est-ce que vous étiez en train de faire il y a dix minutes ? Et qu'est-ce que j'étais en train de faire ?
4. Un(e) de vos camarades va passer une semaine en France cet été. Qu'est-ce que vous lui suggéreriez de faire ? Et qu'est-ce que vous lui conseilleriez de ne pas faire ?
5. Y a-t-il des grands magasins dans notre ville ? Comment s'appellent-ils ? Lequel est votre magasin préféré ? Pourquoi ?
6. Quand est-ce qu'on peut ou ne peut pas marchander ? Quelles sont quelques-unes[2] des expressions nécessaires pour marchander ?

Compréhension auditive (basée sur l'Application A)

Compréhension auditive

Dictée : « Un appareil photo »

[1]*deadline*
[2]*some*

Les Galeries Lafayette.

Le Printemps.

H Lecture

On fait des achats.

Mayoumi va bientôt rentrer au Japon et elle voudrait acheter de jolis cadeaux pour ses parents et ses amis. Elle a entendu dire[1] que les étrangers peuvent économiser pas mal d'argent en faisant leurs achats dans des boutiques spécialisées. Elle demande à sa camarade Anne de lui suggérer dans quels magasins elle devrait aller.

Anne   5
Si tu achètes tes cadeaux dans un magasin ordinaire, tu vas payer 17 % de TVA[2], qui est une taxe imposée par le gouvernement sur tous les produits qui ne sont pas considérés comme absolument indispensables, par exemple les parfums, les foulards de soie, les articles en cuir. Pour éviter de payer cette taxe, il y a une solution, qui est un peu compliquée : nous irons au

tax-exempt, duty-free rayon hors-taxe° d'un grand magasin où tu choisiras ce que tu veux. Il faut que tu dépenses   10
un minimum de 1.200 F pour bénéficier de la réduction. À la caisse, en sortant, tu demanderas un formulaire de remboursement. En quittant la France, tu montreras tes achats, les formulaires et les reçus à la douane. Tu enverras les formulaires au magasin, et plus tard, tu recevras un mandat qui te remboursera 17 % de tes achats. Tu comprends ?

Mayoumi   15
Ça a l'air un peu compliqué. Est-ce que tu peux venir avec moi ? Tu m'aideras à choisir mes cadeaux et à expliquer la situation à la caissière. Dans quel magasin veux-tu aller ?

Anne
Celui que je préfère, c'est le Printemps. Alors, allons-y cet après-midi.

Anne est en train de faire des courses dans son quartier et elle rencontre Mme Leroux, sa   20
voisine. C'est une jeune femme sympathique qui a demandé plusieurs fois à Anne de garder

garder les enfants *to* *ses deux enfants°. Elle est en train de rentrer chez elle après sa journée de travail dans un*
babysit *grand magasin.*

[1]**entendre dire que**   *to hear (someone say) that*
[2]**Taxe à la Valeur Ajoutée** ; elle varie de 17 % à 33 % selon les produits ou les services.

Mme Leroux
Ah ! Bonsoir, Anne.   25

Anne
Bonsoir, Madame. Votre journée s'est bien passée ?

Mme Leroux
Oui, très bien, merci, mais je suis fatiguée parce que nous avons eu pas mal de clients
aujourd'hui. Comme les vacances approchent, beaucoup de jeunes sont venus acheter des   30
I must have sold sleeping bags ballons, des raquettes de tennis ou des articles de camping. Et j'ai dû vendre° au moins douze
sacs de couchage° !

Anne
backpacks Est-ce que vous avez des sacs à dos° ? Le mien est en mauvais état. Je viendrai vous voir
un de ces jours et vous me montrerez ceux que vous avez. Aussi, j'ai reçu un chèque de ma   35
microwave oven grand-mère pour mon anniversaire, et j'ai envie d'acheter un petit four à micro-ondes° pour
faire la cuisine dans ma chambre. Qu'est-ce que vous en pensez ?

Mme Leroux
Je vous conseille d'en acheter un. Celui que ma belle-mère m'a offert à Noël est formidable.
home appliance Allez au rayon électro-ménager° et demandez à Mme Boucheron de vous aider à choisir. Elle   40
convenir à *to suit* trouvera certainement celui qui vous convient° le mieux. Et puis venez me dire un petit bonjour
au rayon « jouets » et « camping ».

A *Indiquez si les commentaires suivants sont vrais ou faux, puis corrigez ceux qui sont
faux.*

1. Les étrangers économisent peu d'argent en faisant leurs achats dans des boutiques spécialisées.
2. Les touristes étrangers ne sont pas obligés de payer la TVA au rayon hors-taxe d'un grand magasin.
3. On trouve les boutiques hors-taxe seulement dans les aéroports internationaux.
4. En quittant le pays, il suffit de¹ montrer les reçus à la douane pour être remboursé de 17 % sur le prix de ses achats.
5. Le grand magasin qu'Anne préfère, c'est le BHV².
6. Mme Leroux a eu une journée exceptionnellement fatigante.
7. Anne voudrait acheter un nouveau sac à dos parce que le sien n'est plus en bon état.
8. Anne a besoin d'un sac de couchage parce qu'elle va faire du camping.
9. Anne voudrait acheter un four à micro-ondes pour sa cuisine.
10. Mme Leroux ne pense pas que ce soit une bonne idée d'acheter un four à micro-ondes.
11. Pour un four à micro-ondes, Mme Leroux conseille à Anne d'aller voir Mme Boucheron, qui travaille au rayon électro-ménager de son magasin.
12. Mme Leroux travaille au rayon des vêtements pour dames.

B *Indiquez le mot ou l'expression qui n'appartient pas à chaque série.*

1. foulards de soie—caissière—articles en cuir—parfums
2. sac de couchage—sac à dos—formulaire—ballon
3. douane—magasin—boutique—grand magasin
4. taxe—remboursement—reçu—four
5. achats—magasins—meilleurs—reçus
6. économiser—faire des achats—dépenser—approcher
7. aider—payer—rembourser—dépenser
8. chèque—remboursement—mandat—cuir

¹*it suffices, it is enough*
²le Bazar de l'Hôtel de Ville (un des grands magasins de Paris)

VOCABULAIRE

Noms

un achat	purchase	le couteau de poche	camping knife	le **placard**	closet
le BHV	Le Bazar de l'Hôtel de Ville (department store in Paris)	le cuir	leather	le **poste (de télévision)**	(television) set
		le double	twice the amount		
		la lame	blade	la puce	flea
la boussole	compass	le machin	gizmo, whatchamacallit	le **rayon**	department
la **caisse**	cash register			la **réclame**	advertisement, ad
le **calcul**	figuring, computation	le marchand	merchant	la ruelle	narrow street
		le Marché aux Puces	Flea market	le stand	booth
le **chèque (de voyage)**	(traveler's) check	la maroquinerie	fancy leather shop	le tire-bouchon	corkscrew
				le **tour**	turn
la **clé**	answer key	le **passeport**	passport	le truc	gizmo
le **cours**	exchange rate	le **permis de conduire**	driver's license		

Verbes

s'acheter	to buy for oneself	**encourager (à)**	to encourage	**grossir**	to put on weight
chanter	to sing	**excuser (de)**	to excuse	**prier (de)**	to ask, beg
conseiller (de)	to advise	se ficher de	to make fun of	**suggérer (de)**	to suggest
déranger	to disturb	finir par + inf	to end up + pres part		
empêcher (de)	to prevent (from)	flâner	to wander leisurely		

Adjectifs

belge	Belgian	neuf (neuve)	brand-new	solide	strong
cuit(e)	cooked	**posté(e)**	posted	**trop cuit(e)**	too well-done
curieux(euse)	curious	**propre**	clean		
mou (molle)	soft	raisonnable	reasonable		

Adverbe

environ   about; around

Autres expressions

Bon, ben...	Oh, well . . .	**en même temps**	at the same time
ce ...-ci	this	en plus	besides, in addition
ce ...-là	that	**être en train de** + inf	to be in the process of + pres part
celui, celle, ceux, celles	this (one), that (one), these, those	faire des achats	to go shopping
		faire la queue	to stand in line
c'est ça	that's right, that's it	**faire les calculs**	to do the figuring
c'est donné	it's a bargain	**lequel, laquelle, lesquels, lesquelles**	which, which one(s)
Défense de + inf	Do not + verb		
d'occasion	second-hand, used	**Prière de ne pas** + inf	Please do not + verb
en + pres part	while/by doing (something)		

23 Que pensez-vous de ce film?

LESSON OBJECTIVES

Theme and Culture

1. Television programs
2. Movies and other forms of entertainment

Communication Skills

1. Expressing likes and dislikes (*to like, not to like*) and attitudes (*to laugh (at), to smile (to)*)
2. Negating statements with regard to two people or objects (*neither . . . nor . . .*)
3. Expressing duration of time (*the entire morning, the whole day*)
4. Making statements with restrictive *only* (*I only know him, I only paid ten francs*)
5. Making statements regarding events prior to other past events (*He had already left when I got there*)
6. Eliciting/Giving opinions and agreeing/disagreeing

Structures

23.1 **Plaire, rire**
23.2 Negation **ne ... ni ... ni ...**
23.3 Use of **matin, matinée, jour, journée**
23.4 Use of **ne ... que**
23.5 The pluperfect indicative

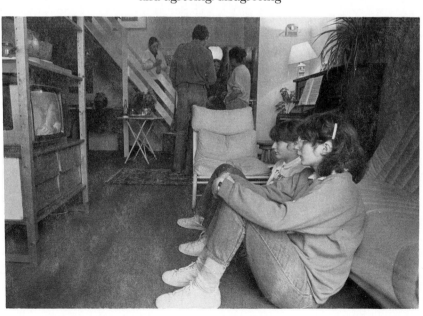

CONVERSATIONS

A. La télévision

Avons-nous parlé de la télévision récemment ? Il y a des gens qui la regardent tous les jours, et il y en a d'autres qui la regardent de temps en temps. Répondez aux questions.

Qui a un poste de télévision ? Est-ce que c'est un poste en couleur ou en noir et blanc ? Depuis combien de temps l'avez-vous ?

Qui n'a pas de poste de télévision ? Où est-ce que vous regardez la télévision ? À qui appartient le poste ?

En quelle saison regardez-vous la télévision le plus souvent ? En quelle saison est-ce que vous la regardez le moins souvent ? Pourquoi ?

Quelle est votre émission[1] préférée ? À quelle heure commence cette émission ? Depuis combien de temps regardez-vous cette émission ?

Quel jour y a-t-il beaucoup de dessins animés[2] ? Est-ce que vous les regardez ? À quel âge avez-vous cessé de les regarder ?

Qui aime les sports ? Pendant quels mois peut-on regarder les matchs de football ? Et les matchs de basket ? Et les matchs de base-ball ?

B. Le film m'a plu énormément.

FRANCE   Où étais-tu hier après-midi ? Je t'ai téléphoné plusieurs fois.
DANIEL   Je suis allé à la cinémathèque[3] avec Michel.
FRANCE   Ah oui ? Quel film avez-vous vu ?
DANIEL   *Kagemousha* ; c'est un film japonais.
FRANCE   On dit que c'est un bon film.
DANIEL   Oui, il m'a plu énormément.

C. Jean-Jacques est fatigué.

ANNE-MARIE   Alors, qu'est-ce que tu as fait aujourd'hui ?
JEAN-JACQUES   J'ai passé toute la journée à la bibliothèque.
ANNE-MARIE   Sans blague[4] ? Et qu'est-ce que tu vas faire ce soir, travailler encore ?
JEAN-JACQUES   Non, je vais me reposer toute la soirée !

23.1 PLAIRE, RIRE

1. The expressions **s'il vous plaît** and **s'il te plaît**, which you learned earlier, come from the verb **plaire** *to please, to appeal.* **Plaire** takes an indirect object, and the

---

[1]**Émission** refers to individual TV programs (**un film, un concert, un match de basket, les actualités**, etc.), while **programme** refers to an entire program for a day, an evening, etc.: **le programme de la soirée**.

[2]*cartoons*

[3]La cinémathèque est une sorte de bibliothèque pour le cinéma où on conserve et projette des films ; à Paris, il y a deux grandes cinémathèques, au Palais de Chaillot et au Centre Pompidou.

[4]*No kidding*

plaire

plais	plaisons
plais	plaisez
plaît	plaisent
plu	
plairai	

accent circonflexe occurs only in the third-person singular form of the present indicative. Note that the past participle is identical with that of **pleuvoir** *to rain*.

Je **plais** à mes amis.   Nous **plaisons** à nos professeurs.
Tu **plais** à mes parents.   Vous **plaisez** à cette dame.
Cela **plaît** à tout le monde.   Les films **plaisent** aux spectateurs.
Le film m'a **plu** énormément.
Cela ne leur **plaira** pas du tout.

Other verbs conjugated like **plaire**:

déplaire (à)   *to displease*   **se taire**[1]   *to be (become) silent*

2. **Plaire** is often used in the sense of *to like* (because of some inherent quality of an object or a person). Compare the two sentences below. The direct object of **aimer** becomes the subject of **plaire**, and the subject of **aimer** becomes the indirect object of **plaire**.

Martine a beaucoup aimé **ce film**.   *Martine liked this movie a lot.*
Ce film a beaucoup plu **à Martine**.   *Martine liked this movie a lot (this movie appealed a lot to Martine).*

Comment avez-**vous** trouvé **la pièce**[2] ?
— **Elle m'**a plu énormément.
Est-ce que **Marion** aime **les films d'épouvante**[3] ?
— Non, **ce genre de film** ne **lui** plaît pas du tout.

rire

ris	rions
ris	riez
rit	rient
ri	
rirai	

3. **Rire (de)** *to laugh (at)* and **sourire (à)** *to smile (at)* are conjugated alike.

Je ne **ris** pas.   Nous **rions** souvent.
Ne **ris** pas de lui !   Vous **riez** trop.
Elle **rit** rarement.   Elles **rient** de tout.
J'ai **ri** quand il a dit cela.
Je ne **rirai** plus.

Note that the **nous** and **vous** forms of **rire** and **sourire** have **-ii-** in the imperfect indicative and present subjunctive.

Nous **riions** chaque fois que nous entendions cette histoire.
Je suis surpris que vous ne lui **souriiez** plus.

[1]Il n'y a pas d'accent circonflexe à la troisième personne du singulier : **il se tait**.
[2]**pièce (de théâtre)** *play*
[3]**film d'épouvante** = film d'horreur

TABLEAU 118   Ils **rient** beaucoup. Cette émission leur **plaît**.

A *Exercice de contrôle*

Je plais à mon patron¹.
1. Vous   2. Cet employé   3. Ces employés   4. Tu

Je me tais quand je n'ai rien à dire.
1. Nous   2. On   3. Vous   4. Tu

Je ris quand j'entends quelque chose de drôle.
1. Vous   2. On   3. Nous   4. Tu

Je souris à ceux qui me plaisent.²
1. Nous   2. Les gens   3. Vous   4. Tu

Je ne ris pas de lui, je lui souris.
1. Vous   2. Tu   3. Nous   4. On

B *Plusieurs étudiants sont allés au cinéma. Ils parlent de leurs impressions. Modifiez chaque phrase en employant le verbe* **plaire***.*

> *Modèle :*   Nous avons beaucoup aimé ce film.
> **Ce film nous a beaucoup plu.**

1. J'ai beaucoup aimé le film.
2. As-tu aimé la fin du film ?
3. Les critiques n'aiment pas le film.
4. J'aime tous les films de ce réalisateur³.
5. Nous aimons les films de science-fiction.
6. N'avez-vous pas aimé la musique ?
7. Il paraît que personne n'aime ce film.
8. Je n'aime pas ce genre de film.

C *Répondez aux questions.*

1. Qui a regardé la télévision hier soir ? Quelle émission avez-vous vue ? Est-ce que cela vous a plu ?
2. Quelle émission vous plaît le plus ? À quelle heure est cette émission ? Quelle émission vous déplaît ?

¹*boss*: Make the possessive adjective agree with the subject.
²Make the indirect object agree with the subject.
³*(film) producer*

3. Est-il possible de parler et de se taire en même temps ? Qu'est-ce que vous faites quand vous n'avez rien à dire ?

4. Que dites-vous à votre camarade quand il dit des bêtises ? Que dites-vous à vos camarades quand ils disent des bêtises ?

5. Quand est-ce qu'on rit ? Quand est-ce qu'on ne doit pas rire ?

6. Est-ce que nous rions souvent dans ce cours ? Quand est-ce que nous avons ri ? De quoi avons-nous ri ?

7. Quand est-ce qu'on sourit ? Quand est-ce qu'il est nécessaire de sourire à quelqu'un ?

8. Regardez-moi. Est-ce que je vous souris ? Regardez (Jacqueline). Est-ce qu'elle vous sourit ? Dites à (Jean) de sourire.

9. Regardez la photo à la page 494. Que font ces gens ?

23.2 FORME NÉGATIVE **NE ... NI ... NI ...**

1. The construction **ne ... ni ... ni ...** corresponds to English *neither . . . nor . . .* (or *not . . . either . . . or . . .*). **Ne** comes before the verb, as in all other negative constructions, and **ni** immediately precedes the phrase that is to be negated.

   Elle a vu cette pièce et ce film.

   → Elle **n'**a vu **ni** cette pièce **ni** ce film.

   Il a corrigé mon travail et le tien.

   → Il **n'**a corrigé **ni** mon travail **ni** le tien.

   Vous avez parlé à mon oncle et à ma tante.

   → Vous **n'**avez parlé **ni** à mon oncle **ni** à ma tante.

   Note below that both the indefinite and partitive articles are omitted after **ni ... ni ....**[1]

   J'ai un frère et une sœur.

   → Je **n'**ai **ni** frère **ni** sœur.

   Daniel met du sucre et du lait dans son café.

   → Daniel **ne** met **ni** sucre **ni** lait dans son café.

2. If **ni ... ni ...** modifies an object pronoun (which comes before the verb), the object pronoun is expressed by its stressed form after **ni ... ni ....**

   Je **le** connais. Je connais **Marie** aussi.

   → Je ne connais **ni lui ni Marie.**

   Elle **m'**a parlé brièvement, et à **vous** aussi.

   → Elle n'a parlé **ni à moi ni à vous.**

3. **Ni ... ni ...** can begin a sentence when used with two subject nouns. If used with two singular nouns, the verb is also in the singular. Note that **ne/n'** still comes before the verb.

   Robert et Danielle ont vu ce film.

   → **Ni** Robert **ni** Danielle **n'**a vu ce film.

   Ce film et cette pièce leur ont plu.

   → **Ni** ce film **ni** cette pièce **ne** leur a plu.

   Mes parents et les tiens ne veulent pas sortir.

   → **Ni** mes parents **ni** les tiens **ne** veulent sortir.

---

[1]Another construction with the same meaning, **pas de ... ni de ...** , does require the negative partitive article: **Je n'ai pas de frère ni de sœur ; Il ne met pas de sucre ni de lait dans son café**.

TABLEAU 119

Il **ne** fume **ni** cigarettes **ni** cigares.

A *Ajoutez des phrases d'après ce modèle.*

> Je n'ai pas de sœur. Je n'ai pas de frère.
> **C'est vrai ? Vous n'avez ni sœur ni frère ?**

1. Je suis fatigué aujourd'hui. Je n'ai pas de patience. Je n'ai pas d'énergie.
2. J'ai très bien mangé aujourd'hui. Je n'ai pas faim. Je n'ai pas soif.
3. Je n'ai pas beaucoup voyagé aux États-Unis. Je ne connais pas (Chicago). Je ne connais pas (San Francisco).
4. Quand je suis entré dans la classe, (Robert) ne m'a pas dit bonjour. Et (Marie) non plus !
5. Mes parents ne m'ont pas téléphoné. Mes amis ne m'ont pas téléphoné non plus.
6. Je connais un végétarien. Il ne mange pas de viande. Il ne mange pas de poisson.
7. Le week-end dernier, j'ai vu une pièce et un film à la télévision. La pièce ne m'a pas plu, et le film non plus.
8. Je ne connais pas toute l'Europe. Je ne suis pas allé en Angleterre. Je ne suis pas allé en Espagne non plus.

B *Vous allez entendre des questions qui sont plutôt[1] bêtes. Répondez-y d'après ce modèle.*

> Y a-t-il des chiens ou des chats dans cette classe ?
> **Mais non, il n'y a ni chiens ni chats dans la classe !**

1. Y a-t-il des lapins ou des poulets dans cette classe ?
2. Avez-vous des grenouilles ou des escargots dans votre poche ?
3. Êtes-vous paresseux et bête ?
4. Apprenez-vous le chinois ou le japonais dans ce cours ?
5. Est-ce votre père ou votre mère qui fait vos devoirs pour vous ?
6. Avez-vous jamais parlé au président des États-Unis ou au président de la France ?
7. Avez-vous jamais dîné avec Michael Jackson ou avec Kathleen Turner ?
8. Êtes-vous jamais sorti avec Meryl Streep ou avec Michael Douglas ?

Exercice supplémentaire

23.3 EMPLOI DE MATIN, MATINÉE, JOUR, JOURNÉE

1. **Matin**, **soir**, **jour** are used to express normal *division* of time into such units. To emphasize the entire *duration* of time, **matinée**, **soirée**[2], **journée** are used. **Après-midi** can be used for both division and duration of time. The idea of duration is often reinforced by the use of **toute** + article before these nouns.

> Je suis allé dans un grand magasin ce **ma-tin**.　　*I went to a department store this morning.*

---

[1]**plutôt** *rather* (cf. **plus tôt** *sooner*)
[2]**Soirée** also means *evening party*.

Elle va écrire à ses parents ce **soir**.	She is going to write to her parents this evening (tonight).
Je passerai deux **jours** au Louvre.	I will spend two days at the Louvre.
Je vais regarder un match de football cet **après-midi**.	I'm going to watch a soccer game this afternoon.
J'ai passé **toute la matinée** dans ce grand magasin.	I spent all morning in this department store.
J'ai passé une excellente **soirée** chez Michel.	I had (spent) an excellent evening at Michel's.
Elle était fatiguée, et la **journée** semblait interminable.	She was tired, and the day seemed endless.
Il a passé **tout l'après-midi** à écouter la radio.	He spent the entire afternoon listening to the radio.

2. French does not usually use prepositions for the expressions corresponding to English *in* with division of time.

Le matin je vais au bureau de poste.	In the morning I go to the post office.
L'après-midi je ferai des courses.	In the afternoon I will do errands.
Je serai à la maison **le soir**.	I will be at home in the evening.
Je sais où j'étais **le jour** de ton anniversaire.	I know where I was on your birthday.

3. As you learned in Lesson 3.2, French does not use any preposition corresponding to English *on* before nouns denoting days of the week. The definite article **le(s)** placed before the noun implies *every*.

Nous reviendrons **mercredi**.	We will come back on Wednesday.
Je n'ai pas de cours **le jeudi**.	I don't have any classes on Thursday.
Les musées sont fermés **le(s) mardi(s)**.	Museums are closed on Tuesdays.

As you learned in Lesson 3.2, all dates are preceded by **le**.

| Demain, ce sera **le quatre mars**. | Tomorrow will be March fourth. |
| Je serai à Paris **du 14 juin au 10 juillet**. | I will be in Paris from June 14 to July 10. |

4. The word **an** *year* is usually preceded by a numeral. **Année** is used with adjectives denoting indefinite numbers (**des** *some*, **quelques** *a few*, **plusieurs** *several*, **combien de** *how many*), ordinal numbers (**premier**, **deuxième**, **dixième**), and the possessive, demonstrative, or interrogative adjectives (**mon**, **notre**; **ce**; **quel**).

Julien a passé **un an** en Angleterre et **deux ans** aux États-Unis.

Il a **vingt-quatre ans**, et sa fiancée **vingt-trois ans**.

Leur cousin va passer **quelques années** aux États-Unis.

C'est sa **quatrième année** à l'université.

Il a beaucoup voyagé **cette année** et l'**année dernière**.

A *Ajoutez des phrases d'après ce modèle.*

J'ai travaillé de huit heures du matin jusqu'à midi.
Mon Dieu, vous avez travaillé toute la matinée !

1. Je suis fatigué. J'ai travaillé de neuf heures du matin jusqu'à six heures.
2. J'ai passé sept heures au Louvre. J'y suis allé à dix heures et j'en suis sorti à cinq heures.
3. J'ai regardé la télévision de sept heures du soir jusqu'à minuit.
4. Samedi dernier, j'ai dormi jusqu'à onze heures et demie.

5. J'ai passé douze mois en France.
6. Je suis allé chez un ami à six heures du soir. Je suis rentré à onze heures.
7. Je serai dans mon bureau d'une heure jusqu'à cinq heures et demie.

B *Répondez aux questions.*

1. Où étiez-vous hier matin ? Où avez-vous passé la matinée ?
2. Où étiez-vous hier soir ? Où avez-vous passé la soirée ?
3. Qu'est-ce que vous faites le dimanche matin ? Et le samedi soir ?
4. Est-ce que c'est votre première année à l'université ? Dans combien d'années allez-vous terminer vos études ?
5. Quel jour est le plus fatigant pour vous ? Quel est le moment le plus fatigant de votre journée ?
6. Connaissez-vous l'expression « faire la grasse matinée » ? Cela veut dire « se lever très tard ». Avez-vous jamais fait la grasse matinée ? Quand faites-vous la grasse matinée ?
7. Si vous aviez toute une journée à passer à Paris, que feriez-vous ?

 Compréhension auditive

23.4 EMPLOI DE **NE ... QUE**

1. The construction **ne ... que** *only* expresses the idea of restriction or limitation, rather than true negation.

Je **ne** fais **pas** ce travail.	*I don't do this work.*
Je **ne** fais **que** ce travail.	*I only do this work.*
Elle **ne** parle **pas** de son fiancé.	*She doesn't talk about her fiancé.*
Elle **ne** parle **que** de son fiancé.	*She only talks about her fiancé.*

While true negative expressions such as **ne ... pas/plus/jamais** change the indefinite article (**un**, **une**, **des**) and partitive article (**du**, **de la**, **de l'**) to **de**, the construction **ne ... que** does not.

TRUE NEGATION	NE ... QUE
Je **n'**ai **pas de** sœur(s).	Je **n'**ai **qu'une** sœur.
Je **ne** vois **pas d'**étudiant(s).	Je **ne** vois **que des** étudiants.
Je **ne** bois **plus de** café.	Je **ne** bois **que du** café.
Je **n'**ai **jamais** bu **de** bière.	Je **n'**ai bu **que de la** bière.

2. **Ne**, like other negative constructions, is placed immediately before the verb. The position of **que** varies: it is placed immediately before the word or phrase to which the restriction applies.

Il **ne** parle **que de son voyage**.	*. . . only about his trip* (about nothing else)
Il **ne** parle **que rarement** de son voyage.	*. . . only rarely . . .* (not very often)
Il **ne** parle de son voyage **qu'à ses parents**.	*only to his parents* (to nobody else)
Il **ne** parle de son voyage à ses parents **que quand il est heureux**.	*. . . only when he is happy* (at no other time)

3. Personal object pronouns usually come before the verb. But if the restriction applies to a personal object pronoun, then the pronoun must be moved *behind* the verb and **que**, and is changed to the corresponding stressed pronoun. Pronouns referring to things or ideas are replaced by **cela** or **ça**.

*« Il faut que je me dépêche.
Je n'ai que cinq minutes
pour changer de train. »*

Je **vous** connais.

→ Je **ne** connais **que vous**.

Je **te** dis la vérité.

→ Je **ne** dis la vérité **qu'à toi**.

Je **lui** parle en français.

→ Je **ne** parle **qu'à lui** en français.

Je **le** crois.

→ Je **ne** crois **que lui**.

Je **le** fais tous les matins.

→ Je **ne** fais **que cela** tous les matins.

J'**en** parle à Marianne.

→ Je **ne** parle **que de ça** à Marianne.

A *Répondez aux questions en employant la locution* **ne ... que**.

1. Moi, je n'ai qu'une montre. Combien de montres avez-vous ?
2. Je n'ai visité que la France. Quels pays avez-vous visités ?
3. Y a-t-il beaucoup de lits dans votre chambre ?
4. Avez-vous mille dollars sur vous ?
5. Avez-vous deux nez ? Avez-vous trois yeux ?
6. J'ai (deux) magnétophones. Combien est-ce que vous en avez ?

B *Répondez aux questions d'après ce modèle.*

Pensez-vous à votre ami(e) ?
Je ne pense qu'à lui (à elle).

1. Déjeunez-vous avec vos camarades ?
2. Prenez-vous (du jus d'orange) au petit déjeuner ?
3. Téléphonez-vous à vos parents quand vous avez besoin d'argent ?
4. Pensez-vous aux examens à la fin du semestre ?
5. Est-ce que je vous regarde en ce moment ?
6. Est-ce que je vous parle en ce moment ?

C *Expliquez la différence entre les deux phrases. Voici un exemple.*[1]

Je ne vois que mon ami pendant le week-end.
Je vois seulement mon ami, et personne d'autre, pendant le week-end.
Je ne vois mon ami que pendant le week-end.
**Je vois mon ami seulement pendant le week-end, et pas pendant les autres jours de
la semaine.**

1. Je ne sors qu'avec mon ami pendant le week-end.
   Je ne sors avec mon ami que pendant le week-end.

---

[1]Il y a d'autres réponses possibles. Par exemple, pour la première phrase, on peut dire : **Pendant le week-end, la seule
personne que je vois est mon ami** ; **Je vois mon ami et je ne vois personne d'autre pendant le week-end**.

2. Il ne boit du lait qu'avec son petit déjeuner.
   Il ne boit que du lait avec son petit déjeuner.
3. Cet étudiant ne va au labo qu'avant un examen.
   Cet étudiant ne va qu'au labo avant un examen.
4. Nous ne jouons aux cartes que pour nous détendre.
   Nous ne jouons qu'aux cartes pour nous détendre.
5. Je ne parle que français quand je suis dans ce cours.
   Je ne parle français que quand je suis dans ce cours.

23.5   PLUS-QUE-PARFAIT DE L'INDICATIF

1. The pluperfect tense (**le plus-que-parfait**), also known as the "past perfect," consists of the auxiliary **avoir** or **être** in the *imperfect* tense and the past participle of the verb expressing the action. Study the conjugation of **parler** and **rentrer** below.

j'**avais** parlé	j'**étais** rentré(e)
tu **avais** parlé	tu **étais** rentré(e)
elle **avait** parlé	il **était** rentré
nous **avions** parlé	nous **étions** rentré(e)s
vous **aviez** parlé	vous **étiez** rentré(e)(s)
elles **avaient** parlé	ils **étaient** rentrés

2. In English, the pluperfect is expressed by *had* + past participle (*I had given, you had gone, she had gone*). In both French and English, the pluperfect is used with other past tenses and denotes an action that had already taken place *before* another past action.[1] Compare the tenses of the verbs in the following examples.

Il **a dit** ce matin que son frère **était parti** lundi dernier.	*He said this morning that his brother had left last Monday.* (**partir** took place before **dire**)
Hier elle **portait** le pull que sa mère lui **avait envoyé** en août.	*Yesterday she was wearing the sweater that her mother had sent her in August.* (**envoyer** took place before **porter**)

3. *Sequence of tenses.* The verb tense in the dependent clause is often determined by its time relationship to the action expressed in the main clause. In reference to the main verb, the action of the verb in the dependent clause (*a*) may have taken place already (*anterior*), (*b*) may be taking place at the same time (*simultaneous*), or (*c*) may take place afterward (*posterior*). You will note that English also has a similar sequence of tenses.

MAIN VERB IN THE PRESENT

Je **sais** que...	*I know that . . .*
Daniel **était** là. (*anterior*)	*Daniel was there.*
Marie **est arrivée**. (*anterior*)	*Marie (has) arrived.*
vous m'**attendez**. (*simultaneous*)	*you are waiting for me.*
tu **partiras** bientôt. (*posterior*)	*you will leave soon.*
Laurent **dit** que...	*Laurent says that . . .*
tu me **cherchais**. (*anterior*)	*you were looking for me.*
Renée m'**a téléphoné**. (*anterior*)	*Renée (has) phoned me.*
son frère **est** malade. (*simultaneous*)	*his brother is sick.*
sa mère **sera** en retard. (*posterior*)	*his mother will be late.*

---

[1] Colloquial English tends to replace the past perfect with the simple past: *She was wearing the sweater I (had) sent her; The road was slippery because it (had) rained.*

Compare the examples above with those given below. The changes in the verb tenses of the dependent clause are caused by the change of tense in the main verb.[1]

MAIN VERB IN THE PAST

Je **savais** que...   *I knew that . . .*

     Daniel **avait été** ici. (*anterior*)   *Daniel had been here.*

     Marie **était arrivée**. (*anterior*)   *Marie had arrived.*

     vous m'**attendiez**. (*simultaneous*)   *you were waiting for me.*

     tu **partirais** bientôt. (*posterior*)   *you would leave soon.*

Laurent **a dit** que...   *Laurent said that . . .*

     tu m'**avais cherché**. (*anterior*)   *you had looked for me.*

     Renée m'**avait téléphoné**. (*anterior*)   *Renée had phoned me.*

     son frère **était** malade. (*simultaneous*)   *his brother was sick.*

     sa mère **serait** en retard. (*posterior*)   *his mother would be late.*

4. The tense relationships between the verb of the main clause and the verb in the dependent clause are summarized below.

MAIN CLAUSE	DEPENDENT CLAUSE	
present	(*anterior*)	imperfect/*passé composé*
	(*simultaneous*)	present
	(*posterior*)	future
past (imperfect/ *passé composé*)	(*anterior*)	pluperfect
	(*simultaneous*)	imperfect/*passé composé*
	(*posterior*)	conditional

TABLEAU 120   La chaussée **était** glissante, car il **avait plu.**   Il s'**etait** déjà **couché** quand je **suis rentre.**

A   *Exercice de contrôle*[2]

     J'ai oublié que je n'avais pas mangé.

1. Nous   2. Tu   3. Mon copain   4. Vous

     Je ne savais pas que j'avais fait une faute.

1. Vous   2. Cet étudiant   3. Nous   4. Tu

     J'ai dit que j'étais arrivé à l'heure.

1. Cet enfant   2. Nous   3. Tu   4. Vous

     Je croyais que j'avais déjà répondu à la question.

1. Nous   2. Tu   3. Vous   4. Le professeur

[1]The use of the conditional to indicate "the future in the past" was discussed in Lesson 17.3.

[2]Utilisez le même sujet dans les propositons principales et subordonnées.

B *Mettez le verbe de chaque phrase d'abord au passé composé, ensuite à l'imparfait, et finalement au plus-que-parfait.*

> *Modèle :* J'arrive en retard.
> (Jeanne) **Je suis arrivée en retard.**
> (Paul) **J'arrivais en retard.**
> (Sophie) **J'étais arrivée en retard.**

1. Je sors ce soir.
2. Nous allons au cinéma.
3. On voit un film.
4. J'achète les billets.

5. Le film commence.
6. Le film est amusant.
7. Nous rentrons tard.
8. Je me couche tard.

 C *Un de vos camarades veut voir un film. Mettez les verbes de la principale au passé d'après ce modèle.*[1]

> Il déclare que le film sera intéressant.
> **Il a déclaré que le film serait intéressant.**

1. Il dit qu'il veut sortir ce soir.
2. Il dit qu'il y a un film suédois en ville.
3. Il croit que le film sera bon à voir.
4. J'affirme que j'ai déjà vu le film.
5. Je sais qu'il ne l'a pas encore vu.
6. Je sais qu'il voudra le voir.
7. Il déclare qu'il ira au cinéma.
8. J'espère qu'il a fini son travail.

D *Modifiez les phrases suivantes d'après ce modèle.*

> Je suis à l'heure parce que je me suis dépêché.
> **J'étais à l'heure parce que je m'étais dépêché.**

1. Je suis en retard parce que je suis rentré tard.
2. J'ai faim parce que je n'ai pas déjeuné.
3. Il fait froid, car il a neigé.
4. Je mets le pull que ma mère m'a envoyé.
5. Je téléphone à Marie ; elle m'a donné son numéro.
6. Je sais son adresse ; elle me l'a donnée.
7. J'arrive chez Marie, mais elle est déjà partie.
8. Je trouve le message qu'elle m'a laissé.

  Exercice supplémentaire

  Compréhension auditive

APPLICATIONS

A **Situations**[2]

 Comment exprimer votre opinion
Comme vous l'avez peut-être remarqué, les Français sont très individualistes. C'est le général de Gaulle qui a dit : « Comment gouverner un pays qui fabrique quatre cents sortes de

---

[1]Mettez **dire**, **déclarer** et **affirmer** au passé composé et les autres verbes à l'imparfait.

[2]Les réponses aux questions ne sont pas enregistrées sur la bande magnétique.

fromages ? » Les Français ont une opinion personnelle sur tout, et ils aiment discuter de ce qu'ils pensent sur n'importe quel[1] sujet. La France est un pays où on aime les discussions animées. Voici quelques façons de demander ou d'exprimer des opinions personnelles. 5

À la sortie du cinéma

JACQUES Ouf ! Quel film ennuyeux ! Je suis content de sortir. Qu'est-ce que tu en penses ?[2]

film de mauvaise qualité — MARYSE Ce que j'en pense ? Je trouve que c'est un vrai navet° !

JEAN-PAUL N'exagérons pas, quand même. Ce n'est pas un film d'art, bien sûr, mais il y avait des moments amusants. 10

JACQUES Moi, je suis d'accord avec Maryse. Franchement, si vous voulez mon opinion, c'était une soirée perdue.

That's for sure!/film director/car chase scenes — MARYSE Ah oui alors !° C'était nul ! Comme le metteur en scène° n'avait rien à dire, il a remplacé les dialogues par des scènes de poursuite en voiture°.

JEAN-PAUL En voiture, en moto, en hélicoptère... Si je ne me trompe pas, il y en avait au 15 moins une dizaine !

Après un documentaire à la télévision

IGNÈS Alors, qu'est-ce que vous pensez de cette émission ?

en ce qui concerne *concerning*/le Syndrome d'immunité déficiente acquise (*AIDS*)/intended for/general public — AHMED À mon avis, trop superficielle, surtout en ce qui concerne° le problème du SIDA° dans certains pays d'Afrique. 20

MAYOUMI Peut-être, mais n'oublie pas que l'émission était destinée au° grand public°, qui n'est pas très bien informé sur cette question.

IGNÈS Je crois que tu as raison, Mayoumi. D'ailleurs, ce n'est que le début d'une série d'émissions sur le SIDA.

AHMED Il faudrait regarder le reste de la série avant de juger. 25

IGNÈS Alors, si on se réunissait[3] ici vendredi pour regarder la prochaine émission ?

MAYOUMI Oui, bonne idée.

En sortant d'un nouveau restaurant

JEAN-PAUL Moi, j'ai trouvé que l'ambiance était bonne, le service très convenable, mais la cuisine ne m'a pas beaucoup plu. Quelle est ton opinion, Monique ? 30

MONIQUE Je n'ai aimé ni la soupe ni le poisson ; et j'ai trouvé que c'était plutôt cher !

AHMED Moi, j'ai bien aimé le décor et la musique, mais on était trop serré.

MONIQUE Et comment as-tu trouvé la cuisine ? Elle était bonne, à ton avis ?

« Moi, je ne suis pas d'accord avec toi. »

[1]**n'importe quel** *any* (littéralement, *no matter what*)

[2]**Que pensez-vous de...** est un équivalent de **Quelle est votre opinion sur...** (très différent de **À quoi pensez-vous ?**).

[3]**se réunir** *to meet (by arrangement)* cf. **rencontrer** *to meet (by chance)*

AHMED   Je ne dirais ni oui ni non... passable, je suppose.

JEAN-PAUL   Eh bien, à votre avis, est-ce qu'on devrait revenir une autre fois ?   35

MONIQUE   Franchement, je ne crois pas.

AHMED   Ni moi non plus. La prochaine fois, essayons un restaurant vietnamien.

Questions

1. Que dites-vous quand vous voulez demander son avis à quelqu'un ?
2. Que dites-vous quand votre opinion est différente de celle d'une autre personne ? Et quand vous partagez la même opinion ?
3. Si vous voulez donner votre opinion, par quelle sorte de phrases pouvez-vous commencer ?
4. Quand donneriez-vous les réponses suivantes ?

   Je n'en sais absolument rien.
   Je n'ai aucune[1] idée.
   Je n'ai aucune opinion là-dessus[2].
   Franchement, je ne sais pas de quoi il s'agit[3].

Projets

1. Choisissez une émission à la télévision. Demandez à vos camarades leur opinion sur cette émission. Dites la vôtre aussi.
2. Choisissez un film (qui est peut-être passé récemment à la télévision). Demandez à vos camarades ce qu'ils en pensent. Dites votre opinion.
3. Parlez de quelques restaurants de votre ville. Demandez à vos camarades ce qu'ils pensent de la cuisine, de la qualité du service et de l'ambiance de ces établissements.
4. Choisissez une personne qui est très connue (une vedette de film, un homme politique, une chanteuse, etc.). Demandez à vos camarades ce qu'ils pensent de cette personne.
5. Choisissez un sport qui est souvent (ou régulièrement) télévisé en direct[4]. Que pensez-vous de ce sport ? Et que pensez-vous des joueurs ?

B   Expressions utiles

Au cinéma

prendre / acheter :
  un billet
  deux fauteuils d'orchestre
  trois fauteuils de / au balcon

les spectateurs :
  être emballés / être déçus[5]
  applaudir / siffler

le film : être
  un grand succès / un vrai triomphe
  un échec (total)
  triste, amusant, profond, ennuyeux

Dans le film, il s'agit d'
  un événement historique / fictif.
  un problème social / politique / psychologique.
  un meurtre / un vol.

C'est un film
  en couleur / en noir et blanc.
  en version originale.
  avec des sous-titres / doublé en français.
  tourné à Rome.

---

[1]**Ne ... aucun(e)** est un équivalent de **pas un(e) seul(e)**, plus emphatique que **pas de**.

[2]**là-dessus**   *concerning/about it*

[3]**de quoi il s'agit**   *what it's about* (**il s'agit de**   *it is a question/matter of*)

[4]*live*

[5]du verbe **décevoir**   *to disappoint* (conjugué comme **recevoir**)

les genres

C'est
$\begin{cases} \text{une comédie / une tragédie.} \\ \text{une comédie musicale.} \\ \text{un drame (psychologique / sentimental).} \\ \text{un dessin animé.} \\ \text{un western.} \end{cases}$

un film
$\begin{cases} \text{comique} \\ \text{policier} \\ \text{de critique sociale} \\ \text{à grand spectacle} \\ \text{à suspens} \quad \text{/syspɑ̃/} \\ \text{interdit aux « moins de 13 / 18 ans »} \end{cases}$

un film
$\begin{cases} \text{de catastrophe} \\ \text{d'espionnage} \\ \text{de guerre} \\ \text{d'épouvante / d'horreur} \\ \text{de science-fiction} \end{cases}$

À la télévision[1]

le téléspectateur
la téléspectatrice
$\Big\}$.
$\begin{cases} \text{allumer} \\ \text{fermer (éteindre[2])} \end{cases}$
$\begin{cases} \text{le poste (de télévision)} \\ \text{la télévision / la télé} \end{cases}$

choisir
voir / regarder
$\Big\}$
$\begin{cases} \text{une émission} \\ \text{une rediffusion[3]} \\ \text{une réémission[3]} \end{cases}$
$\begin{cases} \text{à la télévision} \\ \text{sur la deuxième chaîne} \end{cases}$

le programme (voir aussi *les genres* de film)

un documentaire / reportage sur...
le bulletin météorologique / la météo
un sport (un match de football)
une publicité
un dessin animé
un débat sur...
un feuilleton[4]
une série[5]
une pièce (de théâtre)

un film
un spectacle de variétés / des variétés
un concert
un magazine[6]
un jeu[7]

les
$\begin{cases} \text{actualités} \\ \text{informations} \end{cases}$
$\Big\}$
$\begin{cases} \text{régionales} \\ \text{nationales} \\ \text{internationales} \end{cases}$

une émission en direct[8]

C Pratique

1. Donnez le titre d'un film qui représente chacun des genres suivants.

un western
un dessin animé
un film de guerre
un film à suspens

une comédie musicale
un film de catastrophe
un film de science-fiction
un film d'épouvante

[1]Autrefois, il n'y avait que trois chaînes de télévision (TF1, Antenne 2, France 3), sous contrôle de l'Office de Radiodiffusion-Télévision Française (L'O.R.T.F.). Aujourd'hui il y en a six : Canal +, La 5 et M 6 en plus des trois chaînes mentionnées. En France les gens qui possèdent un poste de télévision paient un impôt annuel.

[2]verbe irrégulier (Leçon 24.1, p. 512)

[3]*rerun*

[4]drame qui paraît par fragments à la télévision (comme *Dallas* ou *Dynasty* aux États-Unis)

[5]aventure qui paraît en série (comme *Cagney & Lacey* et *Highway to Heaven*)

[6]interviews on special timely topics

[7]*game* (par exemple, *La roue de la fortune*)

[8]**en direct** *live*

« Est-ce que ce film est doublé, ou en version originale ? »

« Il y a beaucoup de concerts cette semaine. »

2. Donnez un exemple d'émission de télévision dans chaque catégorie suivante.

un sport	un spectacle de variétés
un feuilleton	un documentaire
un jeu	un dessin animé
une comédie	les actualités

3. Allez-vous au cinéma ? Aimez-vous les films américains ? Regardez cette liste. Certains de ces films sont des classiques. Donnez le titre original de chaque film et indiquez à quel(s) genre(s) il appartient.

a) *Psychose*

b) *Le jour le plus long*

c) *Un Américain à Paris*

d) *Les 101 Dalmatiens*

e) *Rencontre du troisième type*

f) *2000, l'odyssée de l'espace*

g) *Les trois jours du Condor*

h) *La conquête de l'Ouest*

i) *Le Parrain*

j) *Cendrillon*

k) *Aéroport 80 Concorde*

l) *Chantons sous la pluie*

m) *La guerre des étoiles*

n) *Le syndrome chinois*

o) *Les aventuriers de l'arche perdue*

p) *La Belle au bois dormant*

q) *La nuit des morts-vivants*

r) *Le crime de l'Orient-Express*

s) *Certains l'aiment chaud*

t) *Le retour de Jedi*

u) *Autant en emporte le vent*[1]

v) *Les dix commandements*

4. Que préférez-vous, un film français doublé en anglais ou un film français avec des sous-titres ? Quels sont les avantages et les inconvénients de ces deux sortes de films ?

[1]*Gone with the wind*

D *Regardez le programme de télévision sur TF 1 à cette page.*

1. Laquelle de ces émissions vous intéresse ? À quelle heure commence-t-elle ? À quelle heure finit-elle ?
2. À quelle heure commence la première émission ? À quelle heure se termine la dernière émission ?
3. Y a-t-il des séries américaines ? Lesquelles ? Connaissez-vous ces séries ?
4. Quelles émissions sont destinées aux enfants ?
5. À quelle heure peut-on regarder le « journal télévisé » ?
6. Combien de jeux y a-t-il, et à quelle heure ?
7. Si on veut savoir quel temps il va faire, à quelle heure regarde-t-on la télé ?

6.27 UNE PREMIÈRE
Présentation : Robert Namias.
MÉTÉO AGRICOLE A 6.27
JOURNAL A 6.30, 6.45, 7.00, 7.25
MÉTÉO A 6.42, 6.57, 7.14, 7.28
LES RUBRIQUES
Voir lundi.

7.30 CLUB DOROTHÉE
[JEUNES] *Présentation : Dorothée et son équipe.*
DESSIN ANIMÉ
Candy : « Une longue marche ».
SÉRIE
Holmes et Yoyo : « Le témoin ».
LES RUBRIQUES
Voir lundi.

8.27 FLASH

8.30 LE MAGAZINE DE L'OBJET
Présentation : Pierre Bellemare.

9.00 HAINE ET PASSIONS
Feuilleton américain.
Nola .... Lisa Brown
Vanessa .... Maeve Kinkead
197. Quinton et Nola débarquent dans une charmante auberge irlandaise pour y passer leur lune de miel.

9.40 SURTOUT LE MATIN
Présentation : Eric Galliano.
Invitée : **Sabine Paturel**
VARIÉTÉS
Patsy, le groupe **Assouad, Philippe Lavil.**
LES RUBRIQUES
Gym – Beauté – Gadgets – Cuisine cocktail. Et les rubriques habituelles, voir lundi.

10.30 C'EST DÉJA DEMAIN
Feuilleton américain
Martin .... John Aniston
197. Brian n'est pas satisfait de la façon dont Ted, Martin et Granite s'occupent de lui.

10.50 SURTOUT LE MATIN
Suite.

11.15 PARCOURS D'ENFER
Jeu. Présentation : Pierre Bellemare.

11.40 ON NE VIT QU'UNE FOIS
Feuilleton américain.
Viki .... **Erika Slezak**
Clint .... **Clint Ritchie**
201. Viki devient la complice de Stick, son ravisseur, pour faire payer à Clint une rançon de deux millions de dollars.

12.00 TOURNEZ... MANÈGE
Présentation : Evelyne Leclercq, Jean Amadou, José Sacré, Fabienne Egal et Simone Garnier.
FLASH A 12.30

13.00 JOURNAL

13.30 MÉTÉO

13.35 LA BOURSE

13.45 COTE OUEST
Feuilleton américain.
Val .... Joan Van Ark
Gary .... Ted Shackelford
59. Pour effectuer la promotion de son livre, Val doit se rendre à Dallas au moment où Gary s'y trouve pour connaître les dispositions du testament de Jock le concernant.

14.30 LA CHANCE AUX CHANSONS
Présentation : Pascal Sevran.
LES 30 ÉTÉS DE NOS NOSTALGIES
Voir lundi. Invités : **François Deguelt, Rachel, Zanini, Evelyne Leclercq, Anny Gould.**

15.10 LA CROISIÈRE S'AMUSE
Série américaine.
A VOS ORDRES
Julie .... **Lauren Tewes**
Cap. Stabing .... **Gavin MacLeod**
Julie et Gopher envisagent sérieusement de se marier, mais la visite d'un ancien ami du collège de Gopher risque de contrarier leurs projets. Trois anciens combattants jettent dans les bras de leur ex-sergent une jolie hôtesse afin de ne pas être importunés par l'autoritarisme de leur camarade.

16.00 L'APRÈS MIDI AUSSI
Présentation : Eric Galliano.
VARIÉTÉS
Eric Bahmy
LES RUBRIQUES
Mode des jeunes créateurs – C'est si bon – Dorlottez-vous – Tarots.

16.45 CLUB DOROTHÉE
[JEUNES] **DESSINS ANIMÉS**
Rémi : « Nous n'oublions jamais ». – **Goldorak** : L'espion qui venait de Vega ». – **Dragon ball.**
LE JEU DE L'A.B.C.

18.05 CHIPS
Série américaine.
LES VOLONTAIRES
Jon .... **Larry Wilcox**
Ponch .... **Erik Estrada**
Les habitants d'une petite ville interdisent le passage à un camion transportant un dangereux chargement de produits chimiques toxiques, Jon et Ponch sont alors chargés d'escorter le convoi sur une route éloignée de montagne, déserte et accidentée.

19.30 LA ROUE DE LA FORTUNE
Jeu. Présentation : Christian Morin.

20.00 JOURNAL

20.30 MÉTÉO

20.35 TAPIS VERT
Jeu. Proposé par la Loterie nationale.

23.45 JOURNAL

23.57 LA BOURSE

0.00 LES ENVAHISSEURS
Série américaine.
LA RECHERCHE DE LA PAIX
David Vincent .... Roy Thinnes
Edgard Scoville .... Kent Smith
Un officier supérieur de l'armée américaine est convaincu, par David Vincent, de la présence sur terre des étrangers venus de l'espace.

0.50 MINUIT SPORT
(SPORTS) *Sujets annoncés sous réserve :*
Échecs : Coupe du monde à Belfort. – **Tennis** : le tournoi de Wimbledon.

1.50 LE CHEMIN DES INDIENS MORTS
Emission proposée et réalisée par Jean Artaud et Michel Perrin.
LE MONDE D'ISHO
Par une approche intimiste, le film révèle le monde des indiens Guahiro au spectateur occidental de la même manière qu'Isho, le vieux Guahiro, sut le faire découvrir à Michel Perrin durant les sept années de leur dialogue.

2.50 HISTOIRES NATURELLES
Emission proposée par Igor Barrère, Jean-Pierre Fleury et Etienne Lalou.
THON ROUGE – THON BLANC EN MÉDITERRANÉE
La mer Méditerranée est l'un des hauts lieux de la pêche du thon : des thons rouges qui pèsent plusieurs centaines de kilos aussi bien que des thons blancs qui pèsent dix kilos en moyenne.

3.20 SAVOIR CHASSER AVEC SON CHIEN
A la ferme des Amourettes, toute proche de la baie de Somme, on sait qu'il n'y a rien de plus faux que l'adage « Un chasseur doit savoir chasser sans son chien ».

3.50 FIN

E **Mini-composition :** *Christine est allée voir Faust à l'Opéra vendredi dernier. Écrivez un paragraphe en employant les mots indiqués.*

(1) Le/semaine/dernier/les Pineau/inviter/me/aller/voir/le/représentation/de/*Faust*/à/l'Opéra. (2) Avant/mon/départ/de/les-États-Unis,/je/ne que/voir/quelques/comédie musicale. (3) Je/ne jamais/voir/opéra. (4) Je/dire/Mme Pineau/que/je/ne ni ni/écouter/voir/

Faust,/mais heureusement/elle/avoir/le/libretto. (5) Elle/prêter/me/le/pour que/je/pouvoir/comprendre/ce qui/se passer/dans/chaque/scène. (6) Je/passer/tout un/soirée/à/lire/le. (7) Jeudi/dernier/elle/jouer/piano/et/chanter/quelques-uns/de/les/arias *f*/en/faisant/une/parodie/très/amusant/de/le/opéra. (8) Nous/rire/beaucoup,/M. Pineau,/les/enfant/et/moi,/parce que/elle/être/si/drôle ! (9) Vendredi/soir,/quand/nous/arriver/à/l'Opéra,/la plupart de/les/spectateur/être/déjà/là. (10) Le/intérieur/de/bâtiment/être/vraiment/splendide,/et/rappeler/me/Palais/de/Versailles. (11) Représentation/plaire/beaucoup/spectateur. (12) À/chaque/scène,/on/applaudir/et/crier/« Bravo ! »/pendant/longtemps. (13) Après,/nous/aller/dans/restaurant/(il/être/déjà/presque/11/heure !). (14) Nous/dîner/légèrement/en/échangeant/notre/impressions/sur/représentation.

F Renseignements et opinions

1. À peu près combien de cinémas y a-t-il dans notre ville ? Comment s'appellent-ils ? Quels films est-ce qu'on y projette cette semaine ? Lequel voulez-vous voir ? Pourquoi ?
2. Il y a beaucoup d'annonces publicitaires à la télévision. Lesquelles vous plaisent ? Pourquoi ? Lesquelles vous déplaisent ? Pourquoi ?
3. J'ai beaucoup de projets. En ce moment, je suis en train (d'écrire un article). Quel projet êtes-vous en train d'achever ?
4. Qui aime les films comiques ? Lesquels avez-vous vus ? Quel film vous a fait beaucoup rire[1] ?
5. Qui a un poste de radio ? Le mien est à la maison. Où est le vôtre ? Demandez à votre voisin de gauche où est le sien.
6. Hier soir je n'ai vu ni les actualités ni la météo à la télévision. Qui n'a vu ni les actualités ni la météo ?
7. Qui n'a qu'un lit dans sa chambre ? Qui en a deux ? Pourquoi ? Qui en a trois ?
8. Quelle est la différence entre « taisez-vous ! » et « tais-toi ! » ? Quand est-ce qu'on emploie ces expressions ?

📼 *Compréhension auditive* (*basée sur l'Application A*)

📼 *Compréhension auditive* (*basée sur l'Application B*)

📼 *Compréhension auditive*

📼 *Dictée : « Je suis allé à l'Odéon. »*

G Lecture

entertainment **Les Français et leurs distractions°**

Marc

Moi, j'ai onze ans, et j'adore aller au cinéma. J'aime qu'il y ait beaucoup d'action, des bagarres,
car chases des poursuites en voiture°, des gadgets formidables, comme dans les films de James Bond. Le dernier[2] était super ! J'aime aussi les films de science-fiction, comme *Star Trek*, et aussi les films d'horreur — mais certains sont trop violents et il faut avoir treize ans pour les voir.   5 Je regarde souvent les vieux westerns à la télé. Bientôt, on va avoir le câble ; alors je pourrai
videocassette recorder regarder plus de films.[3] Et puis les parents de Patou vont acheter un magnétoscope°, et on
(VCR) pourra louer tous les films qu'on aime. Ça sera chouette !

Éric

je m'intéresse beaucoup à Comme beaucoup de jeunes, je me passionne pour° le cinéma et je vois environ deux films   10 par semaine. Mais pas n'importe quoi ! Ce sont en général des films d'art qu'on passe dans des cinémathèques et que seuls les initiés apprécient vraiment. Ce qui m'intéresse, c'est
directing surtout la qualité des dialogues, de la photographie, de la mise en scène°. Si c'est un film

---

[1]**faire rire** *to make (one) laugh*

[2]c'est-à-dire, le dernier film de James Bond

[3]Canal + /plys/, sur le câble, montre plus de films que toutes les autres chaînes.

subtitles étranger, je ne veux le voir qu'en version originale avec des sous-titres°, car je déteste les films doublés. Vous imaginez Humphrey Bogart parlant japonais ? Ridicule, n'est-ce pas ? Je 15 sais que j'agace souvent mes copains avec mes idées puristes. Eux vont au cinéma pour se détendre, pour oublier leurs ennuis — c'est normal — ou bien ils regardent des films à la télé. Il est vrai qu'avec le câble, on a pas mal de choix et que beaucoup de gens préfèrent rester chez eux plutôt que d'aller au cinéma. Pour moi, le cinéma est un art, et je ne veux accepter aucun compromis. 20

Mme Leloup
Depuis que nous sommes à la retraite, mon mari et moi regardons la télé tous les jours. Nous avons six chaînes maintenant, il est donc assez facile de trouver quelque chose qui nous plaît. Si nos petits-enfants viennent passer la journée avec nous, ils veulent voir les dessins animés à cinq heures. Autrement, nous n'allumons le poste que dans la soirée, sauf s'il y a 25 un tournoi de tennis ou un grand match de football que mon mari veut regarder. En général, nous regardons les actualités nationales à 20 heures, puis la météo régionale, et ensuite un film, une pièce de théâtre ou une émission culturelle. Celle que nous préférons est *Apostrophes*[1] sur la chaîne 2, parce que nous adorons lire et que les invités de Bernard Pivot sont toujours des gens brillants et pleins d'humour. Nous ne regardons ni les feuilletons américains, ni les 30 jeux comme *La roue de la fortune* que je trouve franchement idiots. Malheureusement, il y a

more and more/com- de plus en plus de° publicité° à la télévision, surtout sur les chaînes privées, et je trouve ça
mercials très agaçant. J'avais dit à mon mari qu'on ne verrait jamais ça en France, mais je m'étais trompée. Que voulez-vous, il faut toujours qu'on imite les Américains !

A *Indiquez si les commentaires suivants sont vrais ou faux. Corrigez le sens de ceux qui sont faux.*

1. Il y a certains films d'horreur qui sont interdits aux moins de treize ans.
2. Si on a un magnétophone, on peut louer tous les films qu'on aime.
3. Éric voit à peu près deux films par semaine.
4. Ce qui intéresse Éric, c'est surtout l'action et les bagarres.
5. Éric préfère les films doublés aux films avec des sous-titres.
6. Beaucoup de Français préfèrent aller au cinéma plutôt que de voir des films à la télévision.
7. Les petits-enfants de Mme Leloup rendent visite à leurs grands-parents de temps en temps.
8. Les actualités nationales commencent à 20 heures.
9. Les Leloup se couchent tout de suite après la météo régionale.
10. Les Leloup s'intéressent beaucoup aux feuilletons américains.
11. Autrefois, en France, il y avait peu de publicité à la télévision.
12. Mme Leloup trouve que la publicité qu'on voit souvent à la télévision est amusante.

B *Répondez aux questions.*[2]

E.T.	*L'Exorciste*
Les 101 Dalmatiens	*Dallas*
Apostrophes	*La conquête de l'Ouest*
Galactica	*La roue de la fortune*
Soudain, l'été dernier	*Ben-Hur*
Les aventures de Mickey	*Dracula*
La cage aux folles	*Le crime de l'Orient-Express*

1. Lesquels de ces films plaisent à Marc ?
2. Lesquels de ces films plaisent à Éric ?
3. Lesquels de ces films plaisent aux copains d'Éric ?
4. Laquelle ou lesquelles de ces émissions plaisent aux Leloup ?
5. Lesquels de ces films plaisent aux petits-enfants des Leloup ?

[1]A literary show in which the host, Bernard Pivot, invites several writers and asks them questions about their latest book.
[2]Il est possible qu'un film ou une émission plaise à plus d'un seul groupe des personnes mentionnées.

VOCABULAIRE

Noms

une ambiance	atmosphere	le grand public	the general public	la **pièce**	play
la **bêtise**	foolishness; stupidity	la **grenouille**	frog	le **poulet**	chicken
la **blague**	joke	un hélicoptère	helicopter	la poursuite	chase
le **critique**	critic	le **lapin**	rabbit	le public	the public
le décor	decor	le metteur en scène	film director	le **réalisateur**	(film) producer
le **dessin**	drawing	la moto	motorcycle	le reste	the rest
le **dessin animé**	cartoon	le navet	bad movie	la **science-fiction**	science fiction
la discussion	discussion	le **nez**	nose	la série	series
la dizaine	about ten	une opinion	opinion	le SIDA	AIDS
le documentaire	documentary	le **patron**	boss	le sujet	subject

Verbes

affirmer	to affirm, assert	juger	to judge	**rire (de)** irrég	to laugh (at)
appartenir (à) irrég	to belong (to)	**paraître** irrég	to seem, appear	**sourire (à)** irrég	to smile (at)
concerner	to concern	penser de	to have an opinion about	**se taire** irrég	to be silent, become silent
déplaire (à) irrég	to displease	**plaire (à)** irrég	to please; to appeal	se tromper	to be mistaken
se détendre	to relax	se réunir	to get together		
gouverner	to govern				

Adjectifs

animé(e)	animated	informé(e)	informed	**suédois(e)**	Swedish
convenable	acceptable	nul(le)	zero	superficiel(le)	superficial
destiné(e) (à)	intended (for)	passable	acceptable	vietnamien(ne)	Vietnamese
gras(se)	fat	personnel(le)	personal		
individualiste	individualistic	serré(e)	crowded		

Adverbes

énormément	very much	plutôt	rather
là-dessus	concerning it	surtout	above all, especially

Autres expressions

Ah oui alors !	That's for sure!
de quoi il s'agit	what it's about
dire des bêtises	to say stupid things
en ce qui concerne	concerning
être d'accord avec	to agree with
faire la grasse matinée	to sleep late
il paraît que...	it seems that . . .
ne ... aucun(e)	not any, not a single
ne ... ni ... ni	neither . . . nor . . .
ne ... que	only
Ni moi non plus.	Neither do I.
n'importe quel(le)	any
Ouf !	Whew!
personne d'autre	nobody else
sans	without
Sans blague ?	No kidding?

« Mon mari et moi, nous regardons la télévision de temps en temps. »

24 Cherchez-vous un emploi ?

LESSON OBJECTIVES

Theme and Culture

1. Different kinds of work
2. Job interviews

Communication Skills

1. Expressing reciprocal actions
   (*to see each other, to help one another*)
2. Expressing a future event that will have been completed before another future event (*I will have left, he will have finished*)
3. Making "contrary-to-fact" statements for past events (*I would have come if you had phoned me*)
4. Talking about different kinds of work
5. Asking/Answering questions in job interviews

Structures

24.1 **Craindre**, **éteindre**
24.2 Expressions of reciprocity
24.3 The future perfect
24.4 **Suivre**, **vivre**
24.5 The past conditional

CONVERSATIONS

A.   Ils se voient presque tous les jours.

MME DIDIER   Est-ce que vous voyez mon neveu à l'université ?

DANIEL   Ah oui, nous nous voyons presque tous les jours. Nous déjeunons souvent ensemble au resto-U.

MME DIDIER   Vous aimez déjeuner au resto-U ?

DANIEL   Ah non, pas du tout ! Tout le monde se plaint de la cuisine !

B.   J'ai de quoi me plaindre.

FRANCE   Veux-tu aller chez Alain ce soir ?

JACQUES   Désolé, mais je ne peux pas. J'ai encore deux bouquins à lire.

FRANCE   Pour le cours de Crussot ? Il paraît qu'il est très exigeant.

JACQUES   Trop exigeant. Je ne sais pas pourquoi j'ai décidé de suivre son cours.

C.   Je n'aurais pas su...

MICHEL   Alors, ça s'est bien passé, ton interview ?

CHANTAL   J'espère que oui. En tout cas il faut que je te remercie.

MICHEL   Me remercier ? Pourquoi ?

CHANTAL   Je n'aurais pas su qu'il y avait un poste si tu ne me l'avais pas dit.

STRUCTURES

24.1   CRAINDRE, ÉTEINDRE

1. Here is the conjugation of **craindre** *to fear*. Note that **-gn-** /ɲ/ occurs only in the plural forms in the present, and that before /ɲ/ the preceding vowel is not nasal. **Craindre** may take a direct object, **que** + subjunctive, or **de** + infinitive.

craindre	
crains	craignons
crains	craignez
craint	craignent
craint	
craindrai	

Je ne **crains** pas le tonnerre.   /kʀɛ̃/
Tu ne **crains** pas les examens ?
Elle **craint** que vous ayez tort.
Nous **craignons** qu'il soit malade.   /kʀɛɲõ/
Vous **craignez** de passer la nuit ici.   /kʀɛɲe/
Elles **craignent** de rester dans cet hôtel. /kʀɛɲ/
Je n'ai **craint** personne.
Je **craindrai** de sortir à minuit.

Other verbs conjugated like **craindre**:

plaindre   *to pity*   **se plaindre (de)**   *to complain (about)*

2. **Éteindre** *to extinguish, to turn off* (opposite of **allumer** *to light, to turn on*) is also conjugated like **craindre**.

éteindre	
éteins	éteignons
éteins	éteignez
éteint	éteignent
éteint	
éteindrai	

J'**éteins** le feu.   Nous **éteignons** la radio.
Tu **éteins** la lumière.   Vous **éteignez** la télévision.
Il **éteint** sa cigarette.   Ils **éteignent** le magnétophone.
J'ai **éteint** le micro-ordinateur.
J'**éteindrai** la lampe.

« Je crains que ce genre de travail ne soit pas bien payé. »

Another verb conjugated like **éteindre**:

peindre   *to paint*

A   *Exercice de contrôle*

Nous ne craignons personne.

1. Cet enfant   2. Je   3. Vous   4. Ces enfants

Est-ce que ces employés se plaignent de quelque chose ?

1. vous   2. tu   3. cet employé   4. ces clients

J'éteins la lumière quand je me couche.

1. Nous   2. Tu   3. Vous   4. On

Je peins les murs de ma chambre.

1. Vous   2. Tu   3. Nous   4. Ces garçons

B   *Répondez aux questions.*

1. Craignez-vous quelqu'un ? Craignez-vous quelque chose ? Qu'est-ce qu'on craint vers la fin de chaque semestre (trimestre[1]) ?
2. Quand j'étais petit, je craignais le tonnerre. Qu'est-ce que vous craigniez quand vous étiez petit ?
3. On se plaint de la chaleur en été. On se plaint du froid en hiver. Est-ce que vous vous plaignez de quelque chose en automne ? Et au printemps ?

[1]*quarter*

4. Si je suis à la maison, quand est-ce que j'éteins la lumière ? Qu'est-ce que vous allumez et éteignez dans votre chambre, outre[1] la lumière ?

5. Est-ce que vous plaignez quelqu'un ? Quelle sorte de personne plaignez-vous ? Aimez-vous être plaint ?

6. Qui a peint le portrait de Mona Lisa ? Pourquoi est-ce qu'on appelle ce portrait « la Joconde » en français ?

Compréhension auditive

24.2 EXPRESSIONS DE RÉCIPROCITÉ

1. Verbs taking a direct or indirect object can express reciprocal actions (*each other, one another*) by means of the reflexive pronouns **nous**, **vous**, and **se** when the subject is in the plural.[2] In compound tenses, the auxiliary verb **être** is used, and the past participle agrees in gender and number with the reflexive pronoun if it is the *direct object* of the verb.

DIRECT OBJECT

Nous **nous comprenons** bien.	*We understand each other well.*
Vous êtes-vous **vus** hier soir ?	*Did you see each other last night?*
Ils **se** sont **rencontrés** ce matin.	*They met one another this morning.*

INDIRECT OBJECT

Nous **nous parlons** souvent.	*We often speak to each other.*
Vous êtes-vous **écrit** ?	*Did you write to each other?*
Elles **se** sont **répondu**.	*They answered each other.*

2. The reciprocal construction can lead to ambiguity. **Nous nous aimons** can mean *we love each other* (reciprocal) or *we love ourselves* (reflexive). If the *reciprocal* action needs to be stressed, the phrase **l'un(e) l'autre** for two people can be added to transitive verbs. The forms **l'une l'autre** and **les unes les autres** are used when the subjects are exclusively feminine.

Daniel et Anne **s'aiment** (**l'un l'autre**).
Est-ce que Michel et toi, vous **vous** aidez (**l'un l'autre**) ?
Michèle et sa mère **se** comprennent (**l'une l'autre**).

If either one or both of the subjects are in the plural, **les un(e)s les autres** is used.

Ces chiens et ces chats **se** détestent (**les uns les autres**).
Nous **nous** comprenons (**les un(e)s les autres**).
Cette vendeuse et ces clientes **se** connaissent (**les unes les autres**).

For verbs taking **à** + noun, **l'un(e) à l'autre** or **les un(e)s aux autres** may be added.

Ces enfants **s'écrivent** souvent (**l'un à l'autre**).
Marie et Yannick **se** plaisent (**l'une à l'autre**).
Vous **vous** posez des questions (**les uns aux autres**).
Elle et ses voisines **se** parlent (**les unes aux autres**).

3. Verbs that take a preposition other than **à** (such as **compter sur** and **avoir besoin de**) cannot take the reflexive pronouns **nous**, **vous**, and **se**. Instead, **l'un(e)** +

---

[1]*other than*

[2]The subject may also be **on**, referring to **nous**: **On s'est vu ce matin** *We saw each other this morning.*

preposition + **l'autre** or **les un(e)s** + preposition + **les autres** must be added after the verb. The preposition **de** combines with **les** and becomes **des** before **autres**.

J'ai besoin **de** toi, et tu as besoin **de** moi.

→ (Toi et moi,) nous avons besoin **l'un de l'autre**.

Le professeur compte **sur** ses étudiants, et ses étudiants comptent **sur** lui.

→ Le professeur et les étudiants comptent **les uns sur les autres**.

Ils parlent **d'**elles, et elles parlent **d'**eux.

→ (Eux et elles,) ils parlent **les uns des autres**.

TABLEAU 121   Il **se** gratte.   Ils **se** grattent (**l'un l'autre**).

A *Répondez aux questions d'après ce modèle.*

Connaissez-vous (Marie) ?
Oui, (Marie) et moi, nous nous connaissons (bien).

1. Connaissez-vous (Bernard) ?
2. Est-ce que vous parlez à (Nicole) en français ?
3. Est-ce que vous avez rencontré (Philippe) dans le couloir ?
4. Dites-vous bonjour à (Jean-Paul) ?
5. Avez-vous dit bonjour à (Mireille) ?
6. Avez-vous rencontré (Jacques) dans le couloir ?

B *Jacques et Josette sont étudiants en psychologie. Ils se connaissent depuis deux ans. Ils sont de très bons amis et ils travaillent ensemble. Modifiez les phrases suivantes d'après ce modèle.*

Jacques connaît Josette depuis deux ans ; Josette connaît Jacques depuis deux ans.
Jacques et Josette se connaissent depuis deux ans.

1. Jacques a rencontré Josette il y a deux ans ; Josette a rencontré Jacques il y a deux ans.
2. Jacques voit souvent Josette ; Josette voit souvent Jacques.
3. Jacques comprend bien Josette ; Josette comprend bien Jacques.
4. Jacques plaît beaucoup à Josette ; Josette plaît beaucoup à Jacques.
5. Jacques a vu Josette plusieurs fois cette semaine ; Josette a vu Jacques plusieurs fois cette semaine.
6. Jacques avait besoin de Josette ; Josette avait besoin de Jacques.
7. Jacques comptait sur Josette ; Josette comptait sur Jacques.
8. Jacques a aidé Josette à préparer ses examens ; Josette a aidé Jacques à préparer ses examens.

C *Modifiez les phrases suivantes d'après ce modèle.*

> J'ai parlé à (Marc), et (Marc) m'a parlé.
> **Vous et (Marc), vous vous êtes parlé.**

1. J'ai compris (Cécile), et elle m'a compris.
2. J'ai souri à (Alain), et il m'a souri.
3. J'ai dit bonjour à (Brigitte), et elle m'a dit bonjour.
4. J'ai posé des questions aux étudiants, et ils m'ont posé des questions.
5. J'ai besoin de mes étudiants, et ils ont besoin de moi.
6. Je compte sur mes étudiants, et ils comptent sur moi.
7. Je suis content de mes étudiants, et ils sont contents de moi.
8. J'ai parlé de mes étudiants, et ils ont parlé de moi.

 *Exercice supplémentaire*

24.3 FUTUR ANTÉRIEUR

1. The future-perfect tense (**le futur antérieur**) indicates a future action that will have been completed *before* another future action. It consists of the future tense of the auxiliary **avoir** or **être** and the past participle of the verb expressing the action. It is equivalent to English *(will) have* + past participle. (See Lesson 15.2, p. 325, and 15.4, p. 330, for the future tense.)

j'**aurai** terminé	je **serai** arrivé(e)
tu **auras** téléphoné	tu **seras** rentré(e)
il **aura** déjeuné	elle **sera** sortie
nous **aurons** fini	nous **serons** revenu(e)s
vous **aurez** répondu	vous **serez** descendu(e)(s)
ils **auront** vu	elles **seront** reparties

J'**aurai fini** ce travail avant six heures.	*I will have finished this work before six o'clock.*
Ils **seront partis** bien avant l'arrivée de leur patron.	*They will have left well before their boss's arrival.*
Nous **aurons déjeuné** avant qu'elle nous téléphone.	*We will have eaten lunch before she phones us.*

2. The future perfect occurs often after conjunctions such as **quand**, **aussitôt que**, **dès que**, and **après que**. Note that English does not use the future tense after equivalents of these conjunctions.

Je vous **écrirai quand** je **serai arrivé** à Rome.	*I will write to you when I have arrived in Rome.*
Nous **partirons aussitôt que** tu **seras rentrée**.	*We will leave as soon as you have come home.*
Elle vous **téléphonera dès qu**'elle **aura trouvé** un emploi.	*She will call you as soon as she has found a job.*
Viens nous voir **après que** tu **auras fini** tes devoirs.	*Come see us after you have finished your homework.*

3. **Après** and **avant**. **Après** + compound infinitive can be used instead of **après que** when the subject of the verb after **après** is the same as that of the main clause.

Je te téléphonerai **après que j'aurai copié** les réponses.	*I will call you after I have copied the answers.*

Je te téléphonerai **après avoir copié** les réponses.	*I will call you after copying the answers.*
Il est sorti tout de suite **après qu'il s'était levé**.	*He went out immediately after he had gotten up.*
Il est sorti tout de suite **après s'être levé**.	*He went out immediately after getting up.*

Avant que requires the subjunctive (Lesson 20.4) when there are two different subjects in the sentence. When the two subjects are the same, **avant de** + infinitive is used.

Nous **aurons terminé** notre travail **avant qu'**elle **vienne**.	*We will have finished our work before she comes.*
Je **serai arrivé avant qu'**il **pleuve**.	*I will have arrived before it rains.*
Nous **aurons déjeuné avant de partir**.	*We will have eaten lunch before leaving.*

JE MANGERAI LE SANDWICH QUAND J'AURAI FINI MES DEVOIRS.

TABLEAU 122

A *Exercice de contrôle*

Je téléphonerai à mes parents quand j'aurai trouvé un emploi.

1. Nous 2. Tu 3. Vous 4. Mes copains

Je viendrai après qu'elles auront fini le travail.[1]

1. vous 2. on 3. nous 4. tu

Je vous paierai dès que j'aurai reçu mon argent.

1. Nous 2. Cet employé 3. Ces employés 4. On

Nous serons partis avant que le directeur soit ici.

1. Je 2. Vous 3. Tu 4. On

B *Répondez aux questions.*

1. Aurez-vous terminé vos études avant 1995 ?
2. Demandez à (Jacques) ce qu'il fera quand il aura terminé ses études.
3. Demandez-moi si j'aurai terminé tout mon travail avant de me coucher.
4. Qu'est-ce que vous aurez fait aujourd'hui avant de rentrer à la maison ?
5. Que ferez-vous aussitôt que vous serez rentré à la maison ?
6. Qu'est-ce que vous aurez fait avant minuit ?

[1]Change the second subject (**elles**) with the cue words.

C   *Complétez les phrases suivantes avec votre partenaire.*[1]

1. Nous chercherons un emploi quand...
2. Nous irons à la bibliothèque dès que...
3. Nous serons rentrés à la cité avant que...
4. Nous regarderons la télé après que...
5. Nous dînerons aussitôt que...
6. Nous prendrons le petit déjeuner après...
7. Avant l'âge de quarante ans, nous...
8. Avant l'an 2000, nous...

24.4   SUIVRE, VIVRE

1. **Suivre** means *to follow*. You have seen its present participle used as an adjective in phrases like **les mots suivants** and **les questions suivantes**. **Suivre un cours** means *to take a course* (at school). Note that the first-person singular **je suis** is identical with that of **être**; the context usually clears up any ambiguity. The plural forms have a stem-final consonant /v/, which is not heard in the singular forms.

suivre	
suis	suivons
suis	suivez
suit	suivent
suivi	
suivrai	

Je **suis** un cours de français.   Nous **suivons** un camion.
Tu ne **suis** pas mes conseils[2]?   Vous **suivez** quatre cours.
Elle **suit** le mouvement politique.   Elles **suivent** vos conseils.
J'ai **suivi** cinq cours le trimestre dernier.
J'en **suivrai** deux l'été prochain.

2. Here is the conjugation of the verb **vivre** *to live*. Note that like **suivre**, the stem-final consonant /v/ occurs only in the plural forms in the present indicative. The past participle (**vécu**) is very different from that of **suivre**.

vivre	
vis	vivons
vis	vivez
vit	vivent
vécu	
vivrai	

Je **vis** aux États-Unis.   Nous **vivons** en paix.
Tu **vis** à la campagne.   Vous **vivez** dans une ville.
Il **vit** chez ses parents.   Ils **vivent** en Europe.
J'ai **vécu** six ans au Canada.
Je **vivrai** très longtemps.

3. The common expression **Vive/Vivent** + noun uses the present subjunctive form. It is understood to be preceded by **Nous souhaitons que** or **Nous voulons que**.

Vive la République !   *Long live the Republic!*
Vivent les vacances !   *Long live (Hurray for) vacations!*

The opposite expression uses **À bas**.

À bas le despotisme !   *Down with despotism!*
À bas les examens !   *Down with exams!*

A   *Exercice de contrôle*

Je suis un cours de français.
1. Nous   2. Tu   3. Ces étudiants   4. Vous

Je suis les conseils de mon patron.
1. Vous   2. Cet employé   3. Nous   4. Tu

Je vis aux États-Unis.
1. Nous   2. Les Américains   3. Tu   4. Vous

---

[1]Make sure one event will have happened before another future event, except in 7 and 8.

[2]On peut employer ce mot au singulier et au pluriel : **Il suit mon conseil** ; **Tu suivras mes conseils**.

Mon grand-père a vécu quatre-vingt-neuf ans.

1. Ma grand-mère   2. Mes grands-parents   3. Cet homme   4. Ces femmes

B *Répondez aux questions.*

1. Combien de cours suivez-vous ce semestre (trimestre) ? Combien de cours avez-vous suivis le semestre dernier ?
2. Quels cours suivrez-vous le semestre prochain ? Quels cours ne voulez-vous pas suivre ?
3. Quelles rues suivez-vous pour aller de notre bâtiment à l'Hôtel de ville ? Et pour aller au bureau de poste ?
4. Qui aime les sports ? Quels événements sportifs suivez-vous ?
5. Dans quel pays vivons-nous ? Si vous aviez un an à passer à l'étranger, dans quel pays voudriez-vous vivre ?
6. Quelle est la différence entre « manger pour vivre » et « vivre pour manger » ? Est-ce que vous mangez pour vivre, ou vivez-vous pour manger ?
7. Savez-vous qui est Mathusalem ? D'après la Bible, combien de temps a-t-il vécu ?
8. Que veut dire ceci : « L'Homme ne vit pas seulement de pain » ?
9. Qu'est-ce qu'on doit faire pour vivre en paix avec ses voisins ?
10. Complétez ces phrases :

    Vive... !   Vivent... !   À bas... !

Compréhension auditive

Compréhension auditive

24.5 LE PASSÉ DU CONDITIONNEL

1. Before going over this lesson, you might review the formation of the present conditional (**le présent du conditionnel**) in Lesson 17.3. The past conditional consists of the auxiliary verb in the present conditional and the past participle of a verb. It often corresponds to English *would have* + past participle.

   j'**aurais** compris   je **serais** arrivé(e)
   tu n'**aurais** pas cru   tu ne **serais** pas rentré(e)
   elle **aurait** protesté   il **serait** reparti
   nous **aurions** parlé   nous **serions** venu(e)s
   N'**auriez**-vous pas dîné ?   Ne **seriez**-vous pas revenu(e)(s) ?
   elles **auraient** fini   ils **seraient** descendus

J'**aurais aimé** vous voir là-bas.	*I would have liked to see you over there.*
Qu'est-ce que vous **auriez fait** ?	*What would you have done?*
Elles **seraient parties** ce matin.	*They would have left this morning.*

2. The main use of the past conditional is in "contrary-to-fact" statements referring to past events. In such sentences, the *pluperfect indicative* occurs in the **si** clause, and the *past conditional* in the "result" (main) clause. In the examples below, (*a*) refers to a real or possible situation in the present or future, (*b*) to an unreal or "contrary-to-fact" situation, also in the present or future, and (*c*) to an unreal or "contrary-to-fact" situation in the past.

a) Que **ferez**-vous s'il **neige** ?	*What will you do if it snows?*
b) Que **feriez**-vous s'il **neigeait** ?	*What would you do if it snowed?*
c) Qu'**auriez**-vous **fait** s'il **avait neigé** ?	*What would you have done if it had snowed?*

a) Il ne **viendra** pas s'il **est** occupé.
He won't come if he is busy.

b) Il ne **viendrait** pas s'il **était** occupé.
He wouldn't come if he were busy.

c) Il ne **serait** pas **venu** s'il **avait été** occupé.
He wouldn't have come if he had been busy.

a) Si je **sais** la vérité, je vous la **dirai**.
If I know the truth, I will tell it to you.

b) Si je **savais** la vérité, je vous la **dirais**.
If I knew the truth, I would tell it to you.

c) Si j'**avais su** la vérité, je vous l'**aurais dite**.
If I had known the truth, I would have told it to you.

The following chart summarizes the tense and mood relationship of **si** clauses and main clauses.

TYPE OF SUPPOSITION	TIME REFERENCE	SI CLAUSE	"RESULT" CLAUSE
REAL, POTENTIAL	*present* *future*	present indicative	future indicative
UNREAL, CONTRARY-TO-FACT	*present* *future* *past*	imperfect indicative pluperfect indicative	present conditional past conditional

3. **Devoir** and **pouvoir** in the present conditional correspond to English *should/ought to* and *could*, respectively (Lesson 17.3). In the past conditional, they correspond to *should have/ought to have* and *could have*.

Je **dois** trouver un emploi.
I must find a job.

→ Je **devrais** trouver un emploi.
→ *I should find a job.*

→ J'**aurais dû** trouver un emploi.
→ *I should have found a job.*

Vous **pouvez** m'aider.
You can help me.

→ Vous **pourriez** m'aider.
→ *You could help me.*

→ Vous **auriez pu** m'aider.
→ *You could have helped me.*

« Quelle journée fatigante ! J'aurais dû prendre un taxi. »

TABLEAU 123   Il **aurait pu** éviter cet accident.   Zut ! J'**aurais dû** prendre mon parapluie.

A   *Exercice de contrôle*

Si j'avais été malade hier, je ne serais pas allé au travail.
1. nous   2. on   3. vous   4. tu

Qu'est-ce qu'ils auraient fait s'ils avaient trouvé mille dollars ?
1. tu   2. nous   3. je   4. vous

J'aurais dû me dépêcher ; j'aurais pu attraper le train.
1. Nous   2. Tu   3. Vous   4. On

Nous n'aurions pas dû nous coucher si tard.
1. Je   2. Vous   3. Tu   4. On

B   *Faites des phrases d'après ce modèle.*[1]

avoir besoin d'argent ... chercher un emploi
(Michel) **Si j'avais besoin d'argent, je chercherais un emploi.**
(Sophie) **Si j'avais eu besoin d'argent, j'aurais cherché un emploi.**

1. avoir besoin d'argent ... aller à l'agence de travail
2. aller à l'agence ... trouver un emploi
3. trouver un bon emploi ... gagner beaucoup d'argent
4. gagner beaucoup d'argent ... aller en Europe
5. aller en Europe ... visiter Paris
6. visiter Paris ... prendre des photos
7. prendre des photos ... vous en montrer
8. vous en montrer ... être content

C   *Modifiez les phrases suivantes d'après ce modèle.*

Vous vouliez apprendre le français ; vous vous êtes inscrit à[2] ce cours.
Si je n'avais pas voulu apprendre le français, je ne me serais pas inscrit à ce cours.

1. Vous n'êtes pas paresseux ; vous vous êtes inscrit à ce cours.
2. Vous vouliez obtenir un diplôme ; vous êtes entré à l'université.
3. Vous n'aviez pas de travail ; vous êtes allé au cinéma.
4. Vous n'avez pas fait vos devoirs ; j'étais mécontent.
5. Je ne vous ai pas posé de questions ; vous étiez heureux.
6. Je vous ai parlé en chinois ; vous ne m'avez pas compris.

[1]On the tape, the first student's response (Michel) is to be changed to the second student's (Sophie).
[2]**s'inscrire à**   *to register for* (a course)

D *Répondez aux questions.*

1. Que feriez-vous aujourd'hui si vous n'aviez pas de cours ?
2. Qu'est-ce que vous auriez fait hier si vous n'aviez pas eu de cours ?
3. Que mettriez-vous s'il faisait (chaud) aujourd'hui ? Qu'est-ce que vous auriez fait s'il avait fait (chaud) hier ?
4. Qu'est-ce que vous avez fait hier ? Qu'est-ce que vous auriez dû faire hier ? Que devriez-vous faire aujourd'hui ?
5. Qu'est-ce que vous pourriez faire ce soir ? Qu'est-ce que vous auriez pu faire hier soir ?
6. Qu'est-ce que vous auriez dû faire l'été dernier ? Auriez-vous pu le faire ?

Exercice supplémentaire

Compréhension auditive

APPLICATIONS

Elle a presque fini de remplir les formulaires.

A **Situations**

Un emploi d'été
Laurence Savin, une étudiante en linguistique, cherche un emploi d'été. Elle espère trouver un poste dans lequel elle pourrait utiliser sa connaissance des langues étrangères. C'est lundi matin, et elle rencontre Julien Bosquet dans un café...

want ads	JULIEN	Pourquoi lis-tu les petites annonces° ? Tu veux acheter quelque chose ?
	LAURENCE	Non, je cherche un emploi d'été.
	JULIEN	Ah bon ! Tu connais l'agence de voyage où je travaille ? Il y a un poste ; tu
faire une demande *to* *apply*		pourrais faire une demande°.
	LAURENCE	Ah oui ? Tu es gentil de me le dire. Je vais téléphoner tout de suite.

5

prendre rendez-vous *to make an appointment*
Laurence téléphone à l'agence et prend rendez-vous° pour le lendemain. C'est mercredi. La voilà maintenant à l'agence de voyage.

10

LAURENCE	Bonjour, Madame. J'ai rendez-vous avec le directeur du personnel à dix heures et demie.
L'EMPLOYÉE	Ah oui, vous êtes Mlle Savin ? Asseyez-vous. Remplissez ces formulaires, s'il vous plaît.

LAURENCE   Merci, Madame. Et voilà mon CV[1].   15

L'EMPLOYÉE   Merci, Mademoiselle. Dès que vous aurez fini de remplir les formulaires, vous pourrez passer dans le bureau du directeur.

seat   *Le directeur offre un siège° à Laurence et examine son dossier.*

LE DIRECTEUR   Alors, comme langues étrangères vous avez indiqué anglais et espagnol — lu, écrit, parlé ; et puis allemand — lu et parlé.   20

LAURENCE   Oui, Monsieur. J'ai fait trois ans d'allemand et cinq ans d'anglais et d'espagnol au lycée. Je me spécialise en linguistique à l'université.

LE DIRECTEUR   Avez-vous de l'expérience dans ce genre de travail ?

LAURENCE   J'ai participé aux programmes de l'OTU[2] et du Club Méditerranée, mais en tant que[3] membre, pas comme organisatrice.   25

taper (à la machine) *to type*   LE DIRECTEUR   Très bien, Mademoiselle. Et vous tapez 35 mots-minute à la machine° ?

LAURENCE   Oui, Monsieur.

LE DIRECTEUR   Avez-vous jamais travaillé avec un ordinateur ?

software   LAURENCE   Ah oui, j'ai un micro-ordinateur chez moi. J'ai aussi des logiciels° pour le traitement de texte° et pour la base de données°.   30

word processing / data base   LE DIRECTEUR   Excellent...

Le lendemain matin, Laurence reçoit un coup de téléphone de l'agence. On lui offre un poste et elle pourra commencer à travailler lundi prochain. Elle téléphone à Julien ce soir-là.

JULIEN   Ça s'est bien passé, l'interview ?

LAURENCE   Oui, et ce matin on m'a offert le poste.   35

You will get along   JULIEN   Félicitations ! Tu verras que tous les employés sont sympa. Tu t'entendras° bien avec eux.

LAURENCE   J'espère que oui. Et je te remercie. Si je ne t'avais pas rencontré lundi, je n'aurais pas trouvé ce travail.

JULIEN   Et je n'aurais pas su que tu cherchais un emploi.   40

Répondez aux questions. (lignes 1–8)

1. Quelle sorte de poste Laurence espère-t-elle trouver ?
2. Qu'est-ce qu'elle lit ?
3. Où y a-t-il un poste, d'après Julien ?
4. Qu'est-ce qu'elle va faire ?

Elle apprend à utiliser un micro-ordinateur.

[1]Curriculum Vitae (en anglais, on dit souvent « *a résumé* »)
[2]Organisation du Tourisme Universitaire
[3]*as* (littéralement, *in the capacity of*)

(lignes 9–17)

5. Avec qui Laurence a-t-elle rendez-vous ?
6. Qu'est-ce que l'employée lui donne ?
7. Quand est-ce qu'elle pourra passer dans le bureau du directeur ?

(lignes 18–31)

8. Quelles langues étrangères Laurence parle-t-elle ?
9. En quelle matière se spécialise-t-elle à l'université ?
10. À quels programmes touristiques a-t-elle participé ?
11. Quelle sorte de logiciels a-t-elle ?

(lignes 32–40)

12. Quand est-ce qu'on a offert le poste à Laurence ?
13. Pourquoi téléphone-t-elle à Julien ?
14. Qu'est-ce qui serait arrivé si elle n'avait pas rencontré Julien ?

Projets[1]

1. D'abord, ajoutez quelques lignes aux conversations entre Laurence et Julien (dans un café, au téléphone), par exemple les salutations. Ensuite ajoutez d'autres questions à celles que le directeur pose à Laurence.
2. Vous êtes le directeur du personnel d'une compagnie aérienne[2]. Vous interviewez plusieurs personnes qui ont fait une demande pour le même poste.
3. Vous êtes un psychologue qui travaille pour une grande entreprise. Vous posez des questions aux personnes qui cherchent un emploi.
4. Vous êtes mère de deux enfants. En été, vous habitez dans une grande maison de campagne. Vous cherchez une jeune fille pour garder vos enfants pendant cinq heures chaque jour, sauf le week-end. Vous et votre mari, vous interviewez plusieurs jeunes filles.
5. Vous tenez une boutique à Paris et vous cherchez un vendeur ou une vendeuse bilingue qui travaillera à mi-temps[3], cinq jours par semaine. Vous interviewez plusieurs personnes.

B Expressions utiles

Métiers et professions[4]

*agent de police	dépanneur(euse)	*médecin
*agent de voyage	dessinateur(trice)	musicien(ne)
*architecte	diplomate	ouvrier(ière) (non)
artiste	*écrivain	spécialisé(e)[5]
assistant(e) social(e)	électricien(ne)	pharmacien(ne)
aviateur(trice)	employé(e) de bureau	photographe
avocat(e)	esthéticien(ne)	*professeur
bibliothécaire	fonctionnaire	psychiatre
*cadre (moyen / supérieur)	garçon (serveuse)	psychologue
chimiste	guide de tourisme / musée	savant(e) / scientifique[6]
commerçant(e)	infirmier(ière)	secrétaire (de direction)
comptable	*ingénieur	steward (hôtesse de l'air)
(sténo-)dactylo	instituteur(trice)	traducteur(trice)
décorateur(trice)	interprète	vendeur(euse)
dentiste	journaliste	vétérinaire

[1]Vous pouvez consulter l'**Application E** de cette leçon pour quelques-unes des questions que vous allez poser.

[2]*airline company*

[3]*part-time*

[4]Les noms précédés d'un astérisque n'ont pas de forme féminine.

[5]*(un)skilled*

[6]*scientist* (On dit aussi « chercheur(euse) ».)

Le travail

chercher / trouver
faire une demande pour } un { emploi
travail
poste } { à mi-temps[1]
à temps complet / à plein temps[2]

choisir
exercer
abandonner } { un job[3]
un métier
une profession

gagner { de l'argent (de poche)
sa vie
800 F par heure / par semaine / par mois
un salaire suffisant / insuffisant

changer de travail
donner sa démission
être licencié / mis à la porte
prendre sa retraite

être { au chômage / sans travail
embauché
à la retraite

(ne pas) s'entendre bien avec { son patron / sa patronne
ses supérieurs / ses collègues

C Pratique

1. Trouvez deux emplois dans la liste de métiers et de professions qui nécessitent un apprentissage relativement court.[4]
2. Quels métiers et quelles professions demandent non seulement de l'expérience mais aussi des talents artistiques ?

[4]*part-time*

[5]*full-time*

[1]expression familière, s'appliquant au travail à mi-temps

[2]Dites, par exemple : « le métier de vendeur ».

« Dans mon travail, je rencontre des clients intéressants. »

3. Lesquels exigent des diplômes universitaires et de longues études spécialisées ?
4. Si on veut gagner beaucoup d'argent, quel métier ou quelle profession est-ce qu'on choisira ?
5. Quels emplois exigent des études dans une école spécialisée, mais non pas à l'université ?
6. Expliquez la différence entre chaque paire d'expressions.

être à la retraite / être au chômage
être mis à la porte / donner sa démission
travailler à mi-temps / travailler à temps complet

7. Comment s'appellent les personnes qui travaillent :

dans une usine ?	dans un avion ?	dans un atelier ?
dans un bureau ?	dans un cabinet[1] ?	dans une bibliothèque ?
dans un restaurant ?	dans une école ?	dans un hôpital ?

D **Questions :** *Laurence Savin, une étudiante à l'université, travaille dans une agence de voyage. Lisez d'abord ce qu'elle dit, ensuite posez des questions sur les parties soulignées.*

C'est aujourd'hui (1) le 10 juillet. Je travaille ici (2) depuis 10 jours. J'avais besoin (3) d'argent et c'est (4) mon copain Julien qui m'a dit qu'il y avait un poste dans cette agence. Je travaille (5) 33 heures par semaine et gagne à peu près (6) 2.000 francs. Ce n'est pas mal comme emploi d'été. D'ailleurs, (7) le travail est intéressant — je fais des réservations, je donne des renseignements sur les voyages organisés par notre agence, je donne des conseils aux clients au sujet de (8) leurs itinéraires. Dans mon travail j'utilise souvent (9) un ordinateur. J'aime mon emploi (10) parce que j'ai l'occasion d'utiliser ma connaissance des langues étrangères. Les gens avec qui je travaille sont (11) sympathiques. Je rencontre aussi des clients (12) intéressants. J'ai l'intention de travailler (13) jusqu'au 20 septembre. Après, j'aurai presque quatre semaines de vacances avant de rentrer à l'université. Je veux aller (14) en Yougoslavie et en Grèce. (15) Le voyage ne coûtera pas cher, car mon billet d'avion sera payé (16) par notre agence de voyage. C'est chouette !

[1]A doctor's or lawyer's office is usually referred to as a **cabinet**.

E *Vous cherchez un emploi d'été dans une moyenne entreprise[1]. Vous vous présentez dans le bureau du personnel. Le directeur du personnel examine votre dossier et il va vous poser des questions. Comment allez-vous lui répondre ?*

LE DIRECTEUR	En quelle matière est-ce que vous vous spécialisez à l'université ?
VOUS	...
LE DIRECTEUR	Pour quelle raison aimeriez-vous travailler dans notre société[2] ?
VOUS	...
LE DIRECTEUR	Avez-vous de l'expérience dans ce genre de travail ?
VOUS	Oui, Monsieur. ...
LE DIRECTEUR	Excellent. Connaissez-vous quelqu'un qui travaille dans notre société ?
VOUS	...
LE DIRECTEUR	Avez-vous jamais travaillé avec un ordinateur ?
VOUS	...
LE DIRECTEUR	Seriez-vous content(e) de travailler en équipe, ou préférez-vous travailler seul(e) ?
VOUS	Cela dépend, Monsieur. ...
LE DIRECTEUR	Très bien. Si je vous promettais ce poste, à partir de quelle date seriez-vous libre ?
VOUS	...

F **Composition :** *Choisissez un des sujets suivants et écrivez une composition d'à peu près 250 mots.*

1. Faites le résumé d'un film (d'une émission à la télévision) que vous avez vu récemment. Racontez ce qui s'est passé dans le film (l'émission) en employant des temps du passé. Donnez votre opinion sur le film (l'émission).
2. Avez-vous jamais travaillé pendant l'été ? Décrivez ce que vous avez fait, ce que vous pensez de ce travail, et dites pourquoi vous voudriez ou vous ne voudriez pas le refaire.
3. Vous cherchez un travail d'été. Vous trouvez une annonce d'emploi dans un quotidien. Écrivez une lettre pour poser votre candidature à[3] ce poste. N'oubliez pas de décrire brièvement votre expérience et d'indiquer pourquoi vous pensez que vous êtes qualifié.[4]
4. À quelle profession vous préparez-vous ? Pourquoi avez-vous choisi cette profession ? Si vous n'avez pas encore choisi de profession, dites entre lesquelles vous hésitez et pourquoi.
5. Vous avez sans doute appris quelque chose sur la France en étudiant et en écoutant votre professeur. Choisissez deux ou trois aspects de la France (ou d'un pays francophone) et comparez ce que vous pensiez savoir avant d'étudier le français et ce que vous avez appris depuis.

G **Renseignements et opinions**

1. Avez-vous un job ? Cherchez-vous un emploi à mi-temps ? Quelle sorte d'emploi cherchez-vous ? Combien de temps par jour pouvez-vous travailler ?
2. En quelle matière est-ce que vous vous spécialisez ? Quelle profession voudriez-vous choisir après vos études ? Pourquoi ?

---

[1]*middle-sized company* (entre une petite entreprise et une grande entreprise)

[2]*company*

[3]**poser sa candidature à**   *to apply for* (a position)

[4]Il ne s'agit pas ici de préparer un CV, mais plutôt d'écrire une lettre qui l'accompagnera.

3. Une jeune femme qui habite seule dans un appartement a été blessée par un cambrioleur. Elle avait entendu des bruits et des cris épouvantables dans l'escalier. Elle est sortie de son appartement pour voir ce qui se passait. Qu'est-ce que vous auriez fait à sa place ?

4. Qu'est-ce que vous auriez fait si vous n'étiez pas entré à l'université ?

5. Combien de fois par semaine est-ce que nous nous voyons dans ce cours ? À quelle heure est-ce que nous nous disons « au revoir » ?

6. Qu'est-ce que vous ferez dès que ce cours sera terminé ? Et dès que vous aurez terminé vos études à l'université ?

7. Est-ce que quelqu'un éteint la lumière quand le cours est terminé ? Quand est-ce qu'on éteint la lumière ?

8. Combien de cours avez-vous suivis le semestre (trimestre) dernier ? Combien de cours suivrez-vous (en automne) ?

Compréhension auditive (*basée sur l'Application A*)

Compréhension auditive (*basée sur l'Application B*)

Compréhension auditive (*basée sur l'Application B*)

Dictée : « Une carte postale de Jacques »

H   Lecture

Ces gens qui travaillent

Comme beaucoup de pays industrialisés, la France traverse une période de crise économique dont l'inflation et le chômage sont les corollaires ; celui-ci° touche 10,7 % de la population active, et la situation est particulièrement angoissante pour les jeunes. En effet, parmi les 200.000 personnes de moins de 25 ans qui essaient, chaque année, d'entrer dans la vie professionnelle, une sur° quatre ne trouve pas d'emploi pendant environ un an. Certains se 5
recyclent, d'autres continuent leurs études en espérant qu'un diplôme plus coté° leur ouvrira les portes du marché du travail, d'autres, enfin, se contentent d'un travail provisoire, parfois mal rémunéré, en attendant de trouver mieux°.

the latter (celui-ci°)

out of (sur°)
ici, *higher* (coté°)

trouver quelque chose de meilleur (mieux°)

Nicole, 23 ans

Après mon bac[1], j'ai fait deux ans d'études dans une école de préparation aux carrières 10
touristiques qui forme° les hôtesses de l'air, les hôtesses au sol° et les guides. Après six mois
de recherches, j'ai été embauchée par une agence internationale, Jet Tours, qui organise des
voyages dans le monde entier. Pour l'instant, je suis chargée de° faire visiter° la France à des
étrangers. Je les accueille à l'aéroport et, pendant dix jours, je les promène en car° ; d'abord
à Paris pour trois jours, ensuite au Mont-Saint-Michel, puis dans la vallée de la Loire et 15
finalement sur la Côte d'Azur°. C'est un travail fatigant, car il faut donner toutes les explications
en deux ou trois langues, être toujours aimable et souriante, et disponible° 24 heures par jour.
Mais c'est aussi un travail agréable, car il me permet de beaucoup voyager, de rencontrer
des gens intéressants, et de parfaire mes connaissances en anglais, en allemand et en
espagnol. Quand j'aurai fait ce travail pendant trois ou quatre ans, j'aurai peut-être envie de 20
trouver quelque chose de plus stable, mais, pour le moment, je suis tout à fait satisfaite, et
je considère que j'ai beaucoup de chance° d'avoir trouvé du travail relativement vite. J'aurais
pu chercher pendant un an ou deux ans, comme certaines de mes camarades. Si je n'avais
pas été embauchée par Jet Tours, je serais sans doute allée à la fac° pour faire des études
de langues et me diriger vers l'enseignement. Mais finalement, pour moi, tout s'est bien passé ! 25

trains (**formation** *training*)/*ground hostesses* (forme° / hôtesses au sol°)
in charge of/showing (chargée de° / faire visiter°)
car = voiture d'excursion (car°)

French Riviera (Côte d'Azur°)
available (disponible°)

luck (chance°)

Faculté, université (fac°)

[1]baccalauréat (on dit aussi un « bachot ») ; examen national à la fin des études au lycée (qui permet à ceux qui y réussissent d'entrer à l'université)

Michel, 25 ans

mal = difficulté

Étant diplomé de l'École Supérieure de Commerce de Paris, je n'ai eu aucun mal° à trouver du travail. J'ai eu plusieurs offres intéressantes pendant ma dernière année d'études, et, après

customary / subsidiaries

les interviews d'usage°, j'ai choisi de travailler pour une des filiales° d'un groupe métallurgique

steel boilers / raw materials

qui fabrique des chaudières en acier°. Je suis responsable de l'achat des matières premières°, 30

cost prices

des approvisionnements, du contrôle des frais généraux et des prix de revient°. De plus, je

warehouses

suis chargé de la gestion des stocks et des magasins°. Il y a huit personnes dans mon équipe

get along

et nous nous entendons° bien. Évidemment, les journées sont très longues. Je rentre souvent chez moi vers 20 ou 21 heures et mes week-ends ne sont pas toujours libres ; mais c'est normal quand on débute. On a beaucoup de choses à apprendre. Pour l'instant, je vis en 35

I miss Paris

province et Paris me manque°. D'un autre côté, ce n'est pas plus mal d'être dans une petite ville pendant les deux premières années de ma carrière, car il y a peu de distractions. Si j'avais été nommé dans la banlieue parisienne, j'aurais eu beaucoup plus de mal à passer mes week-ends devant un ordinateur !

A *Indiquez si les commentaires suivants sont vrais ou faux. Corrigez ceux qui sont faux.*

1. L'inflation et le chômage constituent les corollaires de la crise économique actuelle[1].
2. Plus de 12 % des Français ne trouvent pas de travail.
3. À peu près 150.000 personnes de moins de 25 ans trouvent un emploi pendant la première année de leur recherche.
4. Certains jeunes pensent qu'un diplôme plus coté les aidera à trouver un bon poste.
5. Nicole a trouvé son emploi tout de suite après son baccalauréat.
6. Elle est fatiguée de faire visiter son pays aux étrangers.
7. Elle promène les étrangers dans des régions touristiques de la France.
8. Certaines de ses camarades n'ont pas pu trouver d'emploi pendant un ou deux ans.
9. Nicole parle quatre langues et donne des explications en deux ou trois langues.
10. Michel n'a eu qu'une seule offre intéressante après avoir reçu son diplôme.
11. Les six personnes dans l'équipe de Michel s'entendent bien.
12. Puisque Michel est débutant, il ne trouve pas que ce soit normal de travailler pendant les week-ends.

B *Trouvez dans le texte les adjectifs qui correspondent aux noms suivants.*

économie	touriste	profession
fatigue	angoisse	sourire
disponibilité	stabilité	intérêt
liberté	responsabilité	activité

C *Trouvez dans le texte les mots qui sont définis ci-dessous.*

1. examen national à la fin des études au lycée
2. action d'acheter
3. voiture d'excursion
4. commencer sa carrière
5. la zone autour d'une ville
6. engagé pour un travail
7. difficulté
8. équipé d'industries
9. état d'être sans travail
10. personne qui a obtenu un diplôme

[1]*current, present*

VOCABULAIRE

Noms

une **agence** (**de travail**/ de voyage)	(employment/ travel) agency	le dossier	résumé; dossier	OTU	Organisation du Tourisme Universitaire
une annonce	ad	un **emploi** (d'été)	(summer) job		
la base de données	data base	un **événement**	event	la **paix**	peace
la **Bible**	Bible	une expérience	experience	le personnel	personnel
le **cas**	case	le feu	fire	les petites annonces	want ads
le club	club	une interview	interview		
le Club Méditerranée	Club Med	**la Joconde**	Mona Lisa	le **portrait**	portrait
le CV	Curriculum vitae, résumé	le lendemain	next day	le **poste**	position
		la linguistique	linguistics	le siège	seat
la demande	application	le logiciel	software	le texte	text
le **diplôme**	diploma	le membre	member	le **tonnerre**	thunder
le **directeur**	director, manager	les mots-minute	words per minute	le traitement de texte	word-processing
les données f	data	le **neveu**	nephew		
		l'organisatrice f	organizer		

Verbes

allumer	to light; to turn on	**s'inscrire (à)**	to register for (a course)	se spécialiser (en)	to specialize (in); to major (in)
attraper	to catch				
avertir	to notify	**obtenir** irrég	to obtain	**suivre** irrég	to follow; to take (a course)
craindre irrég	to fear	passer dans	to go into		
éteindre irrég	to extinguish; to turn off	**peindre** irrég	to paint	taper (à la machine)	to type
		plaindre irrég	to pity	**vivre** irrég	to live
s'entendre avec	to get along with	**se plaindre (de)** irrég	to complain (about)		

Adjectif

exigeant(e)   demanding

Autres expressions

À bas + nom !	Down with + noun!	**J'espère que oui.**	I hope so.
après que	after	**Mathusalem**	Methuselah
aussitôt que	as soon as	**outre**	beyond, besides, other than
dès que	as soon as	prendre rendez-vous	to make an appointment
en tant que	as, in the capacity of	**suivre un cours**	to take a course
en tout cas	in any case	**Vive(nt)** + nom !	Long live + noun!
faire une demande	to apply, make an application		

25 Avez-vous lu le journal ?

LESSON OBJECTIVES

Theme and Culture

Printed media: newspapers and magazines

Communication Skills

1. Making generalizations (*most of...*, *some of...*, *none of...*, etc.

2. Making causative statements (*to have/get something fixed, to have someone do something*)

3. Learning to use/recognize the use of **ne** in affirmative sentences in formal speech and writing

4. Learning to recognize the use of "literary" tenses in formal writing

Structures

25.1 Use of **la plupart**, **quelques-uns**, etc.

25.2 Use of **faire faire**

25.3 Use of "redundant" **ne**

25.4 The *passé simple* and *passé antérieur*

25.5 The imperfect and pluperfect subjunctive

CONVERSATIONS

A. Il est trop conservateur.

YANNICK   Tu as lu l'article de Blancard dans *Le Figaro* ?

LAURENT   Non, la plupart des articles du *Figaro* sont trop conservateurs.

YANNICK   Tu exagères. Quelques-uns, peut-être. Mais lis celui-là, quand même. Blancard a des idées originales.

LAURENT   Mais non, aucun de ses articles ne m'intéresse.

B. Je le ferai lire à ma fille.

MME SAVIN   Vous avez lu l'article dans *Le Monde* ?

M. LEROUX   Lequel ?

MME SAVIN   Celui sur la réforme du baccalauréat. Ça pourrait intéresser Sophie.

M. LEROUX   Ah oui, sûrement. Je vais le faire lire à ma fille.

C. Il est plus tard que tu ne penses.

MME VERNIN   As-tu réparé l'antenne de télé ?

M. VERNIN   Non, mais je le ferai cet après-midi, à moins qu'il ne pleuve.

MME VERNIN   Il est plus tard que tu ne penses ; il est déjà une heure. Catherine et ses enfants vont arriver à deux heures.

M. VERNIN   D'accord, d'accord ! Je la réparerai avant qu'ils arrivent.

STRUCTURES

25.1 PRONOMS INDÉFINIS **LA PLUPART, QUELQUES-UNS, AUCUN, CHACUN**

1. **La plupart** *most, the majority* is a third-person *plural* pronoun. It is usually followed by **de** + determiner + plural noun. The **de** + determiner + plural noun can be replaced by **en** if it is the direct object.

Est-ce que ce sont des journaux français ?

— Non, **la plupart de ces journaux** sont étrangers.

Avez-vous lu ces revues[1] ?

— Oui, j'ai lu **la plupart des revues**.

— Oui, j'**en** ai lu **la plupart**.

La plupart is often followed by **d'entre** before **nous**, **vous**, and **eux/elles**.

La plupart **d'entre nous** connaissent ce journal.	*Most of us know this newspaper.*
La plupart **d'entre vous** ont écouté les actualités[2].	*Most of you have listened to the news.*
Ces étudiants ? Je connais la plupart **d'entre eux**.	*Those students? I know most of them.*

[1]*magazines* (a magazine for light reading, accompanied by illustrations, is also called **un magazine**, not to be confused with **un magasin** a *store*)

[2]*news* (ce mot est toujours employé au pluriel dans ce sens)

« *Quelques-uns de ces articles sont complètement idiots.* »

2. **Quelques-uns** and **quelques-unes** *some, a few* are also pronouns. They are used in the same way as **la plupart**. **Quelques-unes** is used only for exclusively feminine nouns and pronouns.

Est-ce que les étudiantes lisent *Le Monde* ?

— **Quelques-unes des étudiantes** (**d'entre elles**) le lisent.

Avez-vous déjà vu ces films ?

— J'ai vu **quelques-uns de ces films**.

— J'**en** ai vu **quelques-uns**.

Regardez-vous *La roue de la fortune* ?

— **Quelques-uns d'entre nous** la regardent.

Quelques *a few* is an adjective and is always followed by a noun which it modifies. It implies a somewhat limited but still indefinite quantity.

Quelques étudiants n'ont pas entendu la nouvelle[1].	*Some students have not heard the news.*
Je vais t'apporter **quelques disquettes**.	*I'm going to bring you a few diskettes.*

3. **Aucun, aucune** *none, not a single one* is a third-person *singular* pronoun, and is used in the same way as **la plupart** and **quelques-un(e)s**. Since it is a negative word, the verb is preceded by **ne**.

Achetez-vous cette revue de temps en temps ?

— **Aucun** de nous/d'entre nous **ne** l'achète.

Ces hôtesses parlent-elles russe ?

— **Aucune** d'elles/d'entre elles **ne** parle russe.

4. **Aucun, aucune** can be used as an adjective before a singular count noun; it corresponds to English *not a single* + noun.

Est-ce que ces étudiants comprennent le chinois ?

— **Aucun étudiant ne** comprend le chinois.

Savez-vous pourquoi il veut parler de cet article ?

— Moi, je **n'**ai **aucune idée** !

---

[1]En français, ce mot peut être employé au singulier ou au pluriel.

5. The opposite of **aucun**, **aucune** as a pronoun is **chacun**, **chacune** *each (one).*

Chacun de nous/d'entre nous est abonné[1] à cette revue.

Elle a écrit à **chacun** de vous/d'entre vous.

J'ai parlé à **chacune** de ces jeunes filles.

The opposite of **aucun**, **aucune** as an *adjective* is **chaque** *each.*

PRONOUN

Chacun (des lecteurs) a compris cet article.

Nous avons écrit à **chacun** (des lecteurs).

ADJECTIVE

Chaque lecteur a compris cet article.

Nous avons écrit à **chaque** lecteur.

	most	*some*	*no/none*	*each*
PRONOUN	**la plupart**	**quelques-un(e)s**	**aucun(e)**	**chacun(e)**
ADJECTIVE	——			**chaque**

Aucun des étudiants **ne** parle anglais.

Un des étudiants parle allemand.

Quelques-uns des étudiants parlent espagnol.

La plupart des étudiants parlent français.

TABLEAU 124

A *Répondez aux questions d'après ce modèle.*

Avez-vous lu toutes ces revues ?
(Jeanne) **J'ai lu la plupart de ces revues.**
(Michel) **J'ai lu quelques-unes de ces revues.**
(Claudine) **Moi, je n'ai lu aucune de ces revues.**

1. Avez-vous lu tous ces articles ?
2. Avez-vous vu toutes ces photos ?
3. Avez-vous vu toutes les émissions ?
4. Avez-vous compris toutes mes questions ?
5. Avez-vous parlé à tous mes amis ?
6. Avez-vous parlé de tous vos ennuis ?

B *Répondez aux questions en employant* **la plupart**, **quelques-un(e)s**, *ou* **aucun(e)**.

1. Comprenez-vous l'anglais ?
2. Comprenez-vous l'espagnol ?
3. Comprenez-vous le polonais ?
4. Lisez-vous le *New York Times* ?
5. Lisez-vous *Le Figaro* ?
6. Lisez-vous *Newsweek* ?
7. Buvez-vous de la bière ?
8. Êtes-vous allés en France ?
9. Avez-vous fait les devoirs ?
10. Vous êtes-vous couchés tard ?

C *Complétez les phrases suivantes avec votre partenaire.*

1. La plupart de nos cours...
2. Aucun d'entre nous...
3. Chacun de nous...
4. Quelques-uns des professeurs...
5. Aucun des étudiants dans ce cours...
6. Chaque étudiant à l'université...
7. La plupart des émissions à la télévision...
8. Chaque cours à l'université...

[1]**être abonné à** *to subscribe to, to be a subscriber of*

Exercice supplémentaire

Exercice supplémentaire

Compréhension auditive

25.2 EMPLOIS DE **FAIRE FAIRE**

A *causative* construction expresses the idea that the subject of the verb does not perform an action denoted by the infinitive but instead causes it to be performed by someone else. In English, the causative meaning is often expressed by the verbs *to have* (*I have him cut the grass; We had the car repaired*), *to get* (*I'll get Mary to do the work; We can get the machine fixed*), and *to make* (*I made them work*).

1. In French, the most typical causative construction is **faire** + infinitive. These two verbs form an inseparable unit, so that no word may come between them. In the examples below, **Monique** is the actor of the verb **lire**, even if **Monique** follows the infinitive. It can also become the *direct-object* pronoun and precede **faire**, as in the third example.

Monique lit bien.	*Monique reads well.*
Je fais lire **Monique**.	*I have Monique read.*
→ Je **la** fais lire.[1]	→ *I have her read.*

In the following examples, **le poème** is the thing acted upon by the verb **lire**. Note that it can also become the *direct-object* pronoun and precede **faire**, as in the third example.

On lit **le poème**.	*One (Someone) reads the poem.*
Je fais lire **le poème**.	*I have the poem read.*
→ Je **le** fais lire.[1]	→ *I have it read.*

2. When both the actor and the thing performed follow the infinitive, the actor is expressed by either **à** + noun or **par** + noun; the noun can be replaced by a stressed pronoun.

Monique lit **le poème**.	*Monique reads the poem.*
Je fais lire **le poème à**[2]/**par Monique**.	*I have Monique read the poem.*
→ Je **le lui** fais lire.[2] }	
→ Je **le** fais lire **par elle**. }	→ *I have it read by her.*

3. If the action expressed by the infinitive is performed *to* or *for* the subject of **faire**, then **se faire** + infinitive is used. Like any reflexive construction, **se faire** is conjugated with **être** in compound tenses, but the past participle **fait** remains invariable.

Je **me coupe** les cheveux.	*I cut my hair.*
→ Je **me** les **coupe**.	→ *I cut it.*
Je **me fais couper** les cheveux.	*I have my hair cut.*
→ Je **me** les **fais couper**.	→ *I have it cut.*
Je **me suis fait couper** les cheveux.	*I had my hair cut.*
→ Je **me** les **suis fait couper**.	→ *I had it cut.*

[1]When the direct-object pronoun alone is used, there is an ambiguity of meaning: **Je le fais chanter** can mean *I have him sing* or *I have it sung*; **Je la fais nettoyer** can mean *I have her clean* or *I have it cleaned.*

[2]The use of **à** + noun or indirect object results in ambiguity. It can be either the subject of the infinitive (*I have her read it*) or the indirect object (*I have it read to her*).

Elle **fait** la robe.	*She makes the dress.*
→ Elle **se fait faire** la robe.	→ *She has the dress made for herself.*
Elle **s'est fait faire** une robe.	*She had a dress made for herself.*
→ Elle **se** l'**est fait faire**.	→ *She had it made for herself.*

4. A few verbs are usually considered intransitive, that is, they cannot take a direct object.

bouillir	*to boil*		**frire**	*to fry*
cuire	*to cook*		**pousser**	*to grow*
fondre	*to melt*		**rôtir**	*to roast*

In order to use such verbs transitively, **faire** must be placed in front of the infinitive.

L'eau **bout**.	*The water is boiling.*
Je **fais bouillir** l'eau.	*I am boiling the water.*
Cette viande **cuit** vite.	*This meat cooks fast.*
Je **fais cuire** cette viande.	*I am cooking this meat.*
Le beurre **fond** dans la poêle. /pwal/	*The butter melts in the pan.*
Je **ferai fondre** du beurre.	*I will melt some butter.*
Les légumes **poussent**.	*The vegetables are growing.*
Vous **faites pousser** les légumes.	*You are growing the vegetables.*

TABLEAU 125

Voici un poème.
Il est beau, ce poème.
Je veux **le** faire lire.

Voilà Marie.
Elle lit bien.
Je veux **la** faire lire.

Je fais lire le poème à Marie.
Je **le lui** fais lire.

 A   *Il y a des choses que vous faites vous-même, et il y a d'autres choses que vous faites faire par quelqu'un. Répondez aux questions d'après ce modèle.*

Nettoyez-vous votre chambre ?
Oui, je la nettoie moi-même (*ou* **Non, je la fais nettoyer).**

1. Nettoyez-vous votre chambre ?
2. Lavez-vous vos chaussettes ?
3. Faites-vous votre lit ?
4. Faites-vous vos devoirs ?
5. Préparez-vous votre déjeuner ?
6. Réparez-vous votre montre ?
7. Vous coupez-vous les ongles ?
8. Vous coupez-vous les cheveux ?
9. Vous arrachez-vous les dents ?
10. Vous lavez-vous les mains ?

 B   *Modifiez les phrases suivantes d'après ce modèle.*

La dinde rôtit dans le four.
Je fais rôtir la dinde dans le four.

1. Le poulet rôtit dans le four.
2. La viande cuit dans le four.

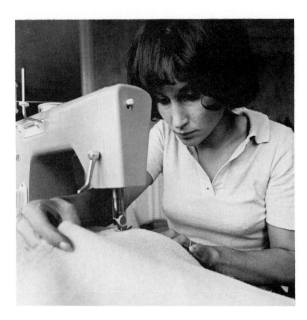

« J'aurais dû faire faire cette robe par une couturière. »

3. Le beurre fond dans la poêle.
4. L'eau va bouillir dans quelques minutes.
5. Les légumes poussent dans le jardin.
6. Les enfants mangeront à midi.
7. On a inspecté ma voiture.
8. On a vérifié les résultats.

C *Répondez aux questions.*

1. Qu'est-ce que c'est qu'un horloger ? Par qui faites-vous réparer votre montre ?
2. Qu'est-ce que c'est qu'un bijoutier ? Par qui faites-vous réparer votre bague ?
3. Qu'est-ce que c'est qu'un mécanicien ? Par qui faisons-nous réparer nos voitures ?
4. Qu'est-ce que c'est qu'un dépanneur ? Par qui faisons-nous réparer nos postes de télévision ?
5. Qu'est-ce que c'est qu'un coiffeur ? Par qui se fait-on couper les cheveux ?
6. Qu'est-ce que c'est qu'un dentiste ? Par qui vous faites-vous nettoyer et soigner les dents ?
7. Qu'est-ce que c'est qu'un garçon ? Par qui se fait-on servir un repas dans un restaurant ?
8. Qu'est-ce que c'est qu'un facteur ? Par qui la Poste fait-elle distribuer le courrier ?

📟 *Exercice supplémentaire*

📟 *Compréhension auditive*

📟 *Compréhension auditive*

25.3 EMPLOI DE **NE** EXPLÉTIF

1. In formal speech and written language, you will often find **ne** used in subordinate clauses that are *affirmative* rather than negative. Called "redundant," "expletive," or "pleonastic," this **ne** does not express a negation but reflects the speaker's wish that something *would not* happen, and there are no negative words like **pas**, **jamais**, **plus**, or **rien** after the verb. It is used, for example, after a main verb denoting fear, such as **avoir peur** and **craindre**.

J'**ai peur** qu'il **ne** pleuve.	*I'm afraid it will rain.*
Il **a peur** que vous **ne** sachiez la vérité.	*He's afraid you know the truth.*

Nous **craignons** que vous **n'**ayez tort.	*We are afraid you are wrong.*
Craignez-vous que cet article **ne** révèle la vérité ?	*Do you fear that this article reveals the truth ?*

2. The "redundant" **ne** also occurs after conjunctions such as **avant que** *before*, **à moins que** *unless*, and **de peur que** *for fear that*, *lest*.

Je veux partir **avant qu'**il **ne** pleuve à verse.	*I want to leave before it pours.*
Elle t'achètera le livre **à moins que** tu **ne** l'aies déjà lu.	*She'll buy you the book unless you have already read it.*
Il a caché le journal **de peur que** tu **ne** lises l'article.	*He hid the newspaper for fear that you might read the article.*

Examine the following sentences, which contrast the "redundant" **ne** and a true negation (with another negative word after the verb).

Je crains qu'elle **ne** l'ait lu.	*I'm afraid she read it.*
Je crains qu'elle **ne** l'ait **pas** lu.	*I'm afraid she didn't read it.*
Nous irons chez Yannick à moins qu'il **ne** fasse beau.	*We'll go to Yannick's unless the weather is nice.*
Nous irons chez Yannick à moins qu'il **ne** fasse **pas** beau.	*We'll go to Yannick's unless the weather isn't nice.*

3. You will also hear or see the "redundant" **ne** in the comparison of *inequality*, that is, in **plus ... que** and **moins ... que**, if the term of the comparison is *affirmative*.[1]

Renée est **plus** conservatrice **que** vous **ne** (le) croyez.	*Renée is more conservative than you believe/think.*
Cette revue a coûté **moins** cher **que** je **ne** (l')avais supposé.	*This magazine cost less than I had supposed/expected.*

BUT (in negative sentences)

Renée **n'**est **pas plus** âgée **que** vous (le) pensez.	*Renée isn't older than you think.*
La revue **n'**a **pas** coûté **plus** cher **qu'**elle (l')avait supposé.	*The magazine did not cost more than she had supposed/expected.*

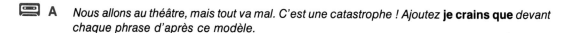 **A**   *Nous allons au théâtre, mais tout va mal. C'est une catastrophe ! Ajoutez* **je crains que** *devant chaque phrase d'après ce modèle.*

Il pleut à verse.
Je crains qu'il ne pleuve à verse.

1. Nous sommes en retard.
2. Il n'y a pas de taxi.
3. La pièce a déjà commencé.

4. Les acteurs sont médiocres.
5. Vous n'êtes pas content.

Maintenant, ajoutez **j'ai peur que** *devant chaque phrase.*

6. La représentation est mauvaise.
7. La pièce ne plaît à personne.
8. Tout le monde est mécontent.

9. On sort avant la fin de la pièce.
10. C'est une soirée perdue !

---

[1]The pronoun **le**, invariable in form, is used often to sum up an idea: **Croyez-vous qu'elle est malade ? — Oui, je le crois.** After an expression of comparison, it can be dropped, as in the examples that follow.

B *Reliez les deux phrases d'après ces modèles.*

> Nous allons partir. Il pleuvra.   (avant que)
> **Nous allons partir avant qu'il ne pleuve.**
> Je ne peux pas finir ce travail. M'aiderez-vous ?   (à moins que)
> **Je ne peux pas finir ce travail à moins que vous ne m'aidiez.**
> Il est parti. Il avait peur qu'elle ne soit fâchée.   (de peur que)
> **Il est parti de peur qu'elle ne soit fâchée.**

1. Je vais finir ce travail. Il viendra.   (avant que)
2. Il va se coucher. Avez-vous besoin de lui ?   (à moins que)
3. Nous partirons. Nous avons peur qu'il ne pleuve.   (de peur que)
4. Je ne sortirai pas. Il ne fera pas beau.   (à moins que)
5. Nettoyez votre chambre. Vos parents arriveront.   (avant que)
6. Il a appelé un taxi. Il avait peur que je ne sois en retard.   (de peur que)
7. Elle est partie. Elle avait peur que nous ne soyons pas prêts.   (de peur que)
8. Je n'irai pas au concert. M'accompagnerez-vous ?   (à moins que)

C *Répondez aux questions d'après ce modèle.*

> Êtes-vous travailleur ?
> **Je suis moins (plus) travailleur que vous ne le supposez (pensez, croyez).**

1. Êtes-vous paresseux ?
2. Êtes-vous optimiste ?
3. Est-ce que vous courez vite ?
4. Est-ce que vous lisez souvent ?
5. Travaillez-vous beaucoup ?
6. Conduisez-vous bien ?
7. (Jean) se lève-t-il tôt ?
8. (Marie) se couche-t-elle tard ?

Compréhension auditive

25.4   PASSÉ SIMPLE ET PASSÉ ANTÉRIEUR

1. The *passé simple* (also called *le passé défini*) is an equivalent of the *passé composé* and is used in written, literary French. There are three sets of endings for this tense. First-conjugation verbs (**-er**) have a set of their own endings, and the singular endings are identical with those of the future tense. Second- and third-conjugation verbs (**-ir** and **-re**) share another set of endings. The singular forms of second-conjugation verbs are identical with those of the present indicative (Lesson 4.5).

parler	finir	vendre
je **parlai**	je **finis**	je **vendis**
tu **parlas**	tu **finis**	tu **vendis**
il **parla**	elle **finit**	on **vendit**
nous **parlâmes**	nous **finîmes**	nous **vendîmes**
vous **parlâtes**	vous **finîtes**	vous **vendîtes**
ils **parlèrent**	elles **finirent**	ils **vendirent**

2. The set of *passé simple* endings required by most irregular verbs can be predicted from their past participles. Many irregular verbs whose past participle ends in **-i**, **-is**, **-it** take the same endings as second- and third-conjugation verbs.

s'asseoir	(assis)	je m'**assis**	nous nous **assîmes**
dormir	(dormi)	je **dormis**	nous **dormîmes**
partir	(parti)	je **partis**	nous **partîmes**
rire	(ri)	je **ris**	nous **rîmes**
sentir	(senti)	je **sentis**	nous **sentîmes**

suivre	(suivi)	je **suivis**	nous **suivîmes**
mettre	(mis)	je **mis**	nous **mîmes**
prendre	(pris)	je **pris**	nous **prîmes**
dire	(dit)	je **dis**	nous **dîmes**
écrire	(écrit)	j'**écrivis**	nous **écrivîmes**
faire	(fait)	je **fis**	nous **fîmes**

Verbs conjugated like **ouvrir** and **craindre** also take the same endings.

ouvrir	(ouvert)	j'**ouvris**	nous **ouvrîmes**
souffrir	(souffert)	je **souffris**	nous **souffrîmes**
craindre	(craint)	je **craignis**	nous **craignîmes**
éteindre	(éteint)	j'**éteignis**	nous **éteignîmes**

The following verbs also take the same endings as the verbs above. Note that **tenir** and **venir** retain the **n** after **i** or **î**: the spellings **in** and **în** are pronounced /ɛ̃/ throughout the conjugation.

tenir	(tenu)	je **tins**	/tɛ̃/	nous **tînmes**	/tɛ̃m/
venir	(venu)	je **vins**	/vɛ̃/	nous **vînmes**	/vɛ̃m/
voir	(vu)	je **vis**		nous **vîmes**	
naître	(né)	je **naquis**		nous **naquîmes**	

3. **Être**, **avoir**, and most irregular verbs whose past participle ends in **-u** have a third set of endings in the *passé simple*.

avoir		**être**	**boire**
j'**eus** /y/		je **fus**	je **bus**
tu **eus**		tu **fus**	tu **bus**
il **eut**		elle **fut**	on **but**
nous **eûmes**		nous **fûmes**	nous **bûmes**
vous **eûtes**		vous **fûtes**	vous **bûtes**
ils **eurent**		elles **furent**	ils **burent**

croire	(cru)	je **crus**	nous **crûmes**
devoir	(dû)	je **dus**	nous **dûmes**
lire	(lu)	je **lus**	nous **lûmes**
plaire	(plu)	je **plus**	nous **plûmes**
pouvoir	(pu)	je **pus**	nous **pûmes**
recevoir	(reçu)	je **reçus**	nous **reçûmes**
vivre	(vécu)	je **vécus**	nous **vécûmes**
vouloir	(voulu)	je **voulus**	nous **voulûmes**
falloir	(fallu)	il **fallut**	
valoir	(valu)	il **valut**	
pleuvoir	(plu)	il **plut**	

Mourir also takes the same endings as the verbs above.

mourir	(mort)	je **mourus**	nous **mourûmes**

The verb **aller** takes the same endings as first-conjugation verbs.

aller	(allé)	j'**allai**	nous **allâmes**

4. The past anterior (**le passé antérieur**) consists of an auxiliary verb in the *passé simple* and the past participle of the verb that expresses the action. It is used to

denote an action that had immediately, or almost immediately, occurred *before* (i.e., anterior to) another past action. It typically occurs in clauses that begin with **aussitôt que**, **dès que** *as soon as*, **à peine ... que** *hardly . . . when*, **après que** *after*, and **quand**, **lorsque** *when*.

Elle **sortit** de la maison **dès qu'**il **eut cessé** de pleuvoir.

À peine fut-il **rentré**[1] **que** le téléphone **sonna**.

Il **rentra** du bureau **après qu'**ils **eurent terminé** le travail.

Elle **ouvrit** la porte **quand** elle **eut trouvé** la clé.

Elle **rentra lorsqu'**elle **eut fini** ses courses.

A *Donnez la troisième personne du singulier et du pluriel et la première personne du pluriel de chaque verbe.*

Modèle : je parlai
   il parla, ils parlèrent, nous parlâmes

1. je trouvai	4. j'eus	7. je bus
2. je choisis	5. je fus	8. j'écrivis
3. j'attendis	6. je fis	9. je vins

B *Répétez chaque verbe après moi, ensuite mettez-le au passé composé.*

1. il parla	7. vous vendîtes	13. tu fis
2. nous finîmes	8. ils prirent	14. ils vinrent
3. j'entendis	9. on suivit	15. il eut
4. elle partit	10. elle s'assit	16. je dus
5. nous allâmes	11. il vécut	17. elle sourit
6. je naquis	12. ils firent	18. vous lûtes

C *Mettez au passé composé les verbes qui sont soulignés dans les passages suivants.*

On (1) vint nous chercher pour nous mettre à table, et je (2) suivis mon conducteur dans une salle magnifiquement meublée, mais où je (3) ne vis rien de préparé pour manger. Une si grande solitude[2] de viande, lorsque je périssais de faim, (4) m'obligea de lui demander où on avait mis le couvert. Je (5) n'écoutai point[3] ce qu'il (6) me répondit, car trois ou quatre jeunes garçons, enfants de l'hôte, (7) s'approchèrent de moi dans cet instant, et avec beaucoup de civilité (8) me dépouillèrent[4] jusqu'à la chemise. Cette nouvelle cérémonie (9) m'étonna si fort que je (10) n'en osai pas seulement demander la cause à mes beaux valets de chambre, et je ne sais comment mon guide, qui (11) me demanda par où je voulais commencer, (12) put tirer de moi ces deux mots : *Un potage* ; mais je (13) les eus à peine proférés, que je (14) sentis l'odeur du plus succulent mitonné[5] qui (15) frappa jamais le nez. Je (16) voulus me lever de ma place pour chercher la source de cette agréable fumée ; mais mon porteur (17) m'en empêcha : « Où voulez-vous aller ? » (18) me dit-il.

Cyrano de Bergerac, *Voyage dans la lune*

Elle (1) rencontra Candide en revenant du château, et (2) rougit : Candide (3) rougit aussi ; elle (4) lui dit bonjour d'une voix entrecoupée, et Candide (5) lui parla sans savoir ce qu'il disait. Le lendemain après le dîner, comme on sortait de table, Cunégonde et Candide (6) se trouvèrent derrière un paravent ; Cunégonde (7) laissa tomber son mouchoir. Candide (8) le ramassa, elle (9) lui prit la main, le jeune homme (10) baisa innocemment la main de la jeune

[1]Inversion is used after **à peine** when it begins a sentence.

[2]ici, absence

[3]**ne ... point** = ne ... pas du tout

[4]ici, déshabillèrent

[5]*simmering soup*

demoiselle avec une vivacité, une sensibilité[1], une grâce toute particulière ; leurs bouches (11) se rencontrèrent, leurs yeux (12) s'enflammèrent, leurs genoux (13) tremblèrent, leurs mains (14) s'égarèrent. Monsieur le baron de Thunder-ten-tronckh (15) passa auprès du paravent, et, voyant cette cause et cet effet, (16) chassa Candide du château à grands coups de pied dans le derrière ; Cunégonde (17) s'évanouit ; elle (18) fut souffletée par madame la baronne dès qu'elle (19) fut revenue à elle-même ; et tout (20) fut consterné dans le plus beau et le plus agréable des châteaux possibles.

Voltaire, *Candide*

Compréhension auditive

Compréhension auditive

25.5 IMPARFAIT ET PLUS-QUE-PARFAIT DU SUBJONCTIF

1. The imperfect subjunctive is derived from the *passé simple*. The third-person singular of the imperfect subjunctive is identical with that of the *passé simple*, except for the addition of a circumflex over the vowel in the ending and also of **-t** in the case of first-conjugation verbs ending **-a** (→ **ât**).

il **parla** → il **parlât**	elle **finit** → elle **finît**	on **eut** → on **eût**
il **aima** → il **aimât**	elle **vendit** → elle **vendît**	on **fut** → on **fût**
il **alla** → il **allât**	elle **prit** → elle **prît**	on **put** → on **pût**

The stem vowel in the rest of the conjugation remains the same as that of the **il** form. Note that the forms of the second-conjugation verbs (**-ir**) are identical with those of the present subjunctive (Lesson 19.2), except for the **il** form.

parler	finir	vendre
je **parlasse**	je **finisse**	je **vendisse**
tu **parlasses**	tu **finisses**	tu **vendisses**
elle **parlât**	il **finît**	elle **vendît**
nous **parlassions**	nous **finissions**	nous **vendissions**
vous **parlassiez**	vous **finissiez**	vous **vendissiez**
elles **parlassent**	ils **finissent**	elles **vendissent**

avoir	être	dire
j'**eusse** /ys/	je **fusse**	je **disse**
tu **eusses**	tu **fusses**	tu **disses**
il **eût**	elle **fût**	il **dît**
nous **eussions**	nous **fussions**	nous **dissions**
vous **eussiez**	vous **fussiez**	vous **dissiez**
ils **eussent**	elles **fussent**	ils **dissent**

2. The pluperfect subjunctive consists of an auxiliary verb in the imperfect subjunctive and the past participle of the verb that expresses the action.

On doutait qu'elle **eût achevé** le travail.

Il resta dans sa chambre jusqu'à ce que tous les invités **fussent partis**.

Il était impossible que tout le monde **eût écouté** le conférencier.

3. The "signals" that call for the use of the present subjunctive (summarized in Lesson 21.1) also apply to the use of the imperfect and pluperfect subjunctive. The basic

[1]sensitivity

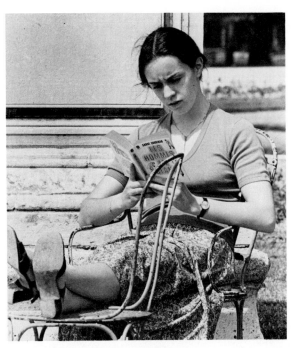

« ...et il fit tout son possible pour qu'elle fût heureuse. »

rule is that these "literary" tenses occur when the verb in the main clause is in a past tense or in the conditional mood. Compare the use of various subjunctive tenses in the examples below.

MAIN VERB IN THE PRESENT OR FUTURE

| (Colloquial) | Je **veux** que vous **partiez**. |
| (Literary) | Je **veux** que vous **partiez**. |

| (Colloquial) | Je **ne croirai jamais** qu'elle l'**ait dit**. |
| (Literary) | Je **ne croirai jamais** qu'elle l'**ait dit**. |

MAIN VERB IN THE PAST OR CONDITIONAL

| (Colloquial) | Je **voulais** que vous **partiez**. |
| (Literary) | Je **voulais** que vous **partissiez**. |

| (Colloquial) | Je **ne croyais pas** qu'elle l'**ait dit**. |
| (Literary) | Je **ne croyais pas** qu'elle l'**eût dit**. |

| (Colloquial) | Il **voudrait** que nous **ayons** de la patience. |
| (Literary) | Il **voudrait** que nous **eussions** de la patience. |

4. The pluperfect subjunctive may replace the past conditional.

Qui l'**eût cru** ? Qui l'**eût dit** ? (= Qui l'**aurait cru** ? Qui l'**aurait dit** ?)

Je ne fis rien de tout cela, qui **eût été** inutile. (= qui **aurait été** inutile)

Je n'**eusse** pas **voulu** le revoir. (= Je n'**aurais** pas **voulu**)

The imperfect and pluperfect subjunctive may also occur in the **si** clause of a contrary-to-fact statement. (For the verb tenses in such statements in colloquial French, see Lessons 17.3 and 24.5.)

Restez, ne **fût**-ce qu'un moment. (= même si ce n'**était** qu'un moment)

Le nez de Cléopâtre : s'il **eût été** plus court, toute la face de la terre aurait changé.
(= s'il **avait été** plus court)

A *Lisez chaque phrase, puis remplacez les temps de la langue écrite par ceux de la langue parlée d'après ce modèle.*

> On souhaitait qu'elle revînt.
> **On souhaitait qu'elle revienne.**

1. Il fit tout son possible pour qu'elle fût heureuse.
2. Il l'emmena chez ses parents avant qu'elle ne quittât la France.
3. Il voulait l'inviter ce week-end à moins qu'elle ne fût occupée.
4. Elle fut étonnée que ses parents l'eussent considérée comme leur fille.
5. Elle était heureuse qu'ils l'eussent accueillie chez eux.
6. Il fallait qu'elle rentrât aux États-Unis.
7. Tout le monde eût voulu qu'elle restât plus longtemps.
8. Ils étaient contents qu'elle eût pu les connaître.

B *Faites de même.*

1. Qui l'eût cru ? Qui l'eût dit ?
2. Ô toi que j'eusse aimée, ô toi qui le savais !
3. Mon amie me manquait mais je n'eusse pas voulu la revoir.
4. Nous eût-il dit la vérité, nous lui eussions pardonné.
5. *Déclaration d'un grammairien à sa mie*[1]

> Oui, dès l'instant que je vous vis,
> Beauté féroce, vous me plûtes ;
> De l'amour qu'en vos yeux je pris
> Sur-le-champ[2] vous vous aperçûtes.
>
> Ah ! fallait-il que je vous visse,
> Fallait-il que vous me plussiez,
> Qu'ingénument je vous le disse,
> Qu'avec orgueil vous vous tussiez ?
>
> Fallait-il que je vous aimasse,
> Que vous me désespérassiez,
> Et que je vous idolâtrasse
> Pour que vous m'assassinassiez ?
>
> H. Gauthier-Villars

APPLICATIONS

A **Situations**

Qu'est-ce que vous lisez ?

newsstand *Au kiosque à journaux°*

JEAN-PAUL	Bonjour, Madame. Donnez-moi *Le Monde*, s'il vous plaît.
LA VENDEUSE	Voilà, Monsieur.
JEAN-PAUL	Est-ce que vous avez *Archeologia* ? C'est une revue mensuelle.
LA VENDEUSE	Non, Monsieur. Pour ça, il faut aller à la maison de la presse, rue Victor Hugo. 5

Jean-Paul rencontre son camarade Ahmed dans la rue.

[1]à son amie, à sa petite amie
[2]Tout de suite

« *Donnez-moi* Le Monde, *s'il vous plaît.* »

	AHMED	Tu lis *Archeologia* ? Je croyais que tu étais étudiant en anglais.
issue	JEAN-PAUL	Je l'ai acheté parce qu'une de mes cousines a écrit un article qui est publié dans ce numéro°.
	AHMED	Ah oui ? C'est un article sur quoi ? 10
	JEAN-PAUL	Sur les bijoux romains. Elle est spécialiste en histoire ancienne.
Show me.	AHMED	Ah oui ? Fais voir.°
	JEAN-PAUL	Voilà. Elle a pris les photos elle-même.

Michel rencontre Ignès à la maison de la presse.

	MICHEL	Bonjour, Ignès. Tu lis *Vieilles Maisons Françaises*[1] ? On y décrit quelques-uns de 15 tes châteaux ?
manor	IGNÈS	Mes châteaux, tu plaisantes ! Non, mais il y a un article sur le manoir° d'un de mes oncles.
	MICHEL	Ah oui ? Fais voir. « Un manoir du seizième siècle... » Il est très beau, ce manoir.
	IGNÈS	Oui, il est dans la famille depuis deux cents ans. 20
	MICHEL	Tiens, il y a aussi un article sur les monuments historiques de la Dordogne. Je serai dans la région en juillet.
	IGNÈS	Je devrais m'abonner à ce magazine. Il y a pas mal d'articles intéressants.
	MICHEL	Où l'as-tu trouvé ? Je vais m'en acheter un numéro.
	IGNÈS	Dans ce rayon-là. Mais qu'est-ce que tu fais avec tous ces magazines féminins... 25 *Elle, Marie-France, Vogue* ?
sister-in-law	MICHEL	C'est ma belle-sœur° qui m'a demandé de les acheter.

Projets

1. Vous rencontrez un de vos camarades. Il porte un numéro de *Vogue* (ou d'un autre magazine) et vous lui demandez pourquoi il lit ce magazine (de mode).
2. Vous demandez à une camarade si elle a lu un certain article dans un hebdomadaire. Vous lui expliquez pourquoi vous l'avez trouvé intéressant.
3. Vous faites une liste de revues sur votre passe-temps préféré[2] (la photographie, les avions, les sports, le camping, la pêche, etc.) et vous expliquez quelle sorte d'articles on peut y trouver.

[1]revue consacrée à la préservation des vieux bâtiments en France
[2]hobby

4. Vous apportez un magazine américain peu connu (ou un magazine français) et vous décrivez la table des matières[1] et le type de lecteurs qui achètent ce magazine.

B **Expression utiles**

Les journaux et les revues

le lecteur ⎫ : ⎧ acheter / lire ⎫ une publication ⎧ quotidienne
la lectrice ⎭ ⎩ être abonné(e) à ⎭ ⎨ hebdomadaire
⎩ mensuelle

vendre ⎫ ⎧ un journal ⎫ ⎧ au kiosque (à journaux)
acheter ⎭ ⎩ une revue / un magazine[2] ⎭ ⎨ à la maison de la presse

Il y a des pages consacrées[3] ⎧ au courrier des lecteurs.
à la culture et aux spectacles.
à l'économie / à la vie économique.
à l'éditorial.
aux faits divers[4].
aux nouvelles internationales / à la vie internationale.
aux petites annonces[5].
à la politique / à la vie politique.
à la publicité[6] / aux annonces publicitaires.
aux sciences.
à la société.
⎩ aux sports.

Sur une page, il y a ⎧ une manchette / un en-tête[7].
des articles *m.*
des paragraphes avec des titres[8].
des colonnes.
⎩ des photos (avec des légendes[9] *f*).

Il y a des publications destinées ⎧ aux consommateurs.
à la famille.
au grand public.
aux jeunes.
⎩ aux sportifs.

ceux qui travaillent pour un journal : ⎧ un reporter /RpɔRtɛR/
un collaborateur régulier[10]
un rédacteur[11]
un chroniqueur sportif[12]
un correcteur
un correspondant / envoyé spécial
⎩ (à l'étranger / étranger)

[1]*table of contents*
[2]Les magazines sont en général illustrés de photos.
[3]Chacune de ces rubriques traite des sujets mentionnés dans son titre.
[4]*various minor news items*
[5]*want ads*
[6]*advertising*
[7]*headline*
[8]*small headlines*
[9]*captions*
[10]*columnist*
[11]*editor;* le mot **éditeur** signifie *publisher.*
[12]*sportswriter*

C Pratique

1. Quelle est la différence entre un rédacteur et un reporter ?
2. Qu'est-ce que c'est qu'un éditorial ?
3. Quelle est la différence entre un journal et un magazine ? Et entre un magazine et une revue ?
4. Qui a lu un journal aujourd'hui ? Lequel avez-vous lu ? Quelle manchette y avait-il à la une[1] ?
5. Quel est votre journal ou magazine préféré ? Pourquoi ? Y êtes-vous abonné ? Quel journal ou magazine ne lisez-vous pas ? Pourquoi ?
6. Choisissez un journal américain ou français (par exemple, *Newsweek* ou *Le Point*). Quelles sont les sections de ce journal ?
7. Si vous étiez un envoyé et si vous faisiez un reportage à l'étranger, dans quel pays voudriez-vous aller ?
8. Si vous étiez rédacteur d'un journal, sous quelles rubriques classeriez-vous les articles suivants ?

Sous la rubrique...

1. des faits divers.
2. des sciences.
3. de la politique.
4. des spectacles.
5. des petites annonces.
6. des sports.
7. du courrier des lecteurs.
8. de l'économie.

a) Offres ou demandes d'emplois
b) Le ministre de l'Intérieur vient de donner sa démission.
c) Il y a eu trois cambriolages dans la ville.
d) L'équipe de Lille a gagné le match de football.
e) Le taux d'intérêt a baissé de nouveau[2].
f) Une lectrice donne son opinion sur un article.
g) Un compte rendu sur le SIDA
h) Le nouveau film allemand a eu beaucoup de succès.

POUR PASSER VOTRE ANNONCE

Rien de plus facile

Appelez :
42 .33 .44 .31

D *Voici les titres de quelques articles et des extraits trouvés dans un journal. Consultez les Expressions utiles et indiquez à quelle rubrique ils appartiennent.*

a) L'équipe de Bordeaux éliminée de la finale
b) Violents incidents à l'occasion du 1er mai en Pologne
c) Le nouveau violon solo[3] du National : Maxime Tholance, un Parisien de 29 ans, a été nommé à l'unanimité premier violon solo de l'Orchestre National de France.
d) Trois militaires britanniques ont été tués aux Pays-Bas par l'IRA
e) Des laboratoires clandestins de cocaïne découverts en Italie
f) Échec pour l'OPEP[4] à Vienne : l'Arabie saoudite[5] refuse de baisser sa production
g) Les Américains maîtres du marché international des programmes de télévision
h) Quatre Prix Nobel[6] français lancent un appel antiraciste
i) Banques : la fin de l'âge d'or ?
j) Sté[7] japonaise recherche assistant commercial ; très bon niveau d'anglais et expérience dans le domaine chimie
k) Le cinéma français peut être fier d'avoir Mehdi CHAREF dans ses rangs
l) La nicotine est une drogue

[1] à la première page
[2] *again*
[3] *head violinist*
[4] Organisation des Pays Exportateurs de Pétrole
[5] *Saudi Arabia*
[6] *Nobel prize winners*
[7] Société *Company*

*« Voyons... qui a gagné le
match de tennis ? »*

m) Le Français Alain Prost a remporté sa 29ᵉ victoire en Formule 1 sur le circuit mexicain
n) Nous plaçons des secrétaires bilingues à tous niveaux
o) Deux tableaux de Monet disparaissent du musée d'Amsterdam
p) Étudiant 22 ans, bonnes connaissances anglais et espagnol, cherche emploi pour juillet
q) Vendeur(se)s bilingues français-anglais, mi-temps, 5 jours/semaine, libre dimanche et
     lundi. Bon salaire. Bonnes références exigées.
r) Un garçon de 12 ans se jette dans le Rhône pour sauver son frère

E Composition : *Vous travaillez pour un journal. Choisissez un des sujets suivants et écrivez
un « article ». (Si besoin est[1], suivez nos suggestions données entre parenthèses.)*

1. l'éditorial (votre opinion sur un événement récent)
2. l'éducation (les avantages et les inconvénients du système de notes « *pass/fail* » ; les
   critères pour choisir une université — raisons académiques, économiques, personnelles,
   etc.)
3. les sports (les résultats de quelques matchs et votre opinion sur les équipes/champions)
4. les spectacles (le résumé d'un film ou d'une émission et votre opinion)
5. les nouvelles nationales/internationales (visite du président de la France aux États-Unis ;
   otages libérés au Liban[2] ; élections)
6. le campus (le compte rendu d'un événement qui s'est passé récemment ou qui se passera
   bientôt)
7. la vie économique (la situation sur les emplois d'été ; le chômage des jeunes)
8. faits divers/événements locaux (un cambrioleur/gangster arrêté ; le gagnant d'une loterie ;
   les aventures et les mésaventures de quelqu'un qui a fait de l'auto-stop)
9. les petites annonces (vente/location[3] d'une maison ou d'un appartement ; offres/demandes
   d'emplois)

F Renseignements et opinions

1. Comment sont la plupart de vos professeurs ? Comment sont quelques-uns d'entre eux ?
2. Regardez la liste des films américains de la Leçon 23 (à la page 506). Avez-vous vu la
   plupart de ces films ? Qui n'a vu aucun de ces films ?

[1]*If need be*
[2]*Lebanon*
[3]*sale/rental*

Les intellectuels apprécient l'exactitude rigoureuse du Monde.

3. Qu'est-ce que je vous fais faire dans ce cours ? Et qu'est-ce que vous voulez me faire faire ?
4. Quand vous étiez petit, qu'est-ce que vos parents vous faisaient faire ? Le faites-vous toujours ?
5. Au début du semestre, aviez-vous peur que ce cours ne soit trop difficile ? Craigniez-vous qu'il n'y ait trop de travail ?
6. Vous voilà presque à la fin de ce livre. Vous avez beaucoup travaillé. Est-ce que le français est moins difficile que vous ne le pensiez ?

🔲 *Compréhension auditive (basée sur l'Application A)*

🔲 *Compréhension auditive (basée sur l'Application B)*

🔲 *Compréhension auditive*

G **Lecture**

Les journaux français
En 1631, le premier journal français, *La Gazette*, fit son apparition, et, depuis, le nombre des journaux n'a pas cessé de se multiplier. La plupart des Français lisent le journal tous les jours, mais, bien entendu, ils ne lisent pas tous le même ! Selon son niveau d'instruction et ses goûts politiques, chacun choisit le journal qui lui convient° le mieux et, en général, y reste fidèle. Certains sont abonnés à leur quotidien préféré, mais la plupart des gens l'achètent 5 dans des kiosques ou au bureau de tabac, et le lisent dans le métro, le bus, ou le train, en allant au travail ou en rentrant à leur domicile.

    Le plus prestigieux des journaux quotidiens est *Le Monde*, qui fut fondé en 1944. D'apparence sévère — on y voit très peu de photos et de publicité — il traite surtout de politique nationale et internationale, mais aussi d'économie, de littérature, et de théâtre. Les articles 10

convenir à *to suit*

experienced
business people
executives

sont écrits par des journalistes chevronnés° dans un style extrêmement soigné. Il s'adresse surtout aux intellectuels, aussi bien les hommes d'affaires° conservateurs que les jeunes cadres° et les étudiants « de gauche » qui apprécient son exactitude rigoureuse et ses analyses approfondies.

Le Figaro est un des plus vieux journaux de France. Il est nettement plus à droite, plus 15 conservateur, que *Le Monde*, et aussi plus facile à lire. Il traite surtout d'événements d'intérêt général, de littérature, de cinéma, de sport. On y trouve beaucoup de réclames, et les petites annonces sont pleines d'offres d'emplois.

Par opposition au *Monde* et au *Figaro*, qui s'adressent aux classes éduquées, *France-Soir* plaît au grand public. Abondamment illustré, il se consacre surtout aux drames humains : prise 20 d'otages, terrorisme, histoires d'amour de princes et princesses, accidents spectaculaires, laissant peu de place aux nouvelles politiques et économiques.

Le Canard Enchaîné tient une place spéciale dans la presse française : il attaque sans pitié les hommes politiques aussi bien de droite que de gauche, et les ridiculise dans des articles et des dessins humoristiques caustiques. Personne n'échappe à son humour mordant. 25

aficionados
voice

Le Parti Communiste est représenté par le quotidien *L'Humanité* (*L'Huma* pour les initiés°). Ce journal est le porte-parole° officiel du Parti et reflète sa position dans tous les domaines, aussi bien politiques qu'artistiques.

tenir au courant *to*
keep informed
at any rate/**que...** *whether*

En province, beaucoup de gens préfèrent lire la presse régionale qui les tient au courant° de la politique et des événements locaux, tout en mentionnant, bien sûr, les grands faits de 30 l'actualité nationale et internationale. Mais de toutes façons°, qu'on° habite à Nantes, à Lyon ou à Nancy, on peut aussi lire *Le Monde* ou *Le Figaro*, qui sont imprimés à Paris pendant la nuit, voyagent par train alors que tout le monde dort encore, et sont déposés chez le marchand de journaux du quartier avant que la plupart des lecteurs ne soient réveillés.

A *Indiquez si les commentaires suivants sont vrais ou faux. Corrigez le sens de ceux qui sont faux.*

1. C'est surtout leur niveau d'éducation et leurs goûts qui guident les Français dans leur choix d'un journal.
2. La plupart des Français préfèrent s'abonner à leur journal.
3. *Le Monde* a été fondé il y a à peu près un demi-siècle.
4. *Le Monde* est lu par beaucoup de Français éduqués qui apprécient l'exactitude des reportages et les analyses approfondies.
5. *Le Monde* est plus difficile à lire que *Le Figaro*.
6. Si on cherche un emploi, on devrait acheter *Le Figaro* plutôt que *Le Monde*.
7. Il y a plus de photos dans *France-Soir* que dans *Le Monde*.
8. Si on veut lire un journal à sensation, on achète *l'Humanité*.
9. *Le Monde* est un quotidien destiné aux classes bien éduquées.
10. Le quotidien qui plaît le plus aux gens instruits est *France-Soir*.
11. *Le Canard Enchaîné*, qui ridiculise tout, est publié par le Parti Communiste.
12. La presse régionale traite d'actualités locales plutôt que d'événements nationaux et internationaux.

B *Trouvez dans le texte les mots qui sont définis ci-dessous.*

1. publicité
2. expérimenté
3. pénétrant
4. de droite
5. extérieur
6. rendre ridicule
7. pendant que
8. personne qui lit
9. contraste
10. qui a pris un abonnement
11. ce qui arrive
12. exprimé avec humour
13. journal qui paraît tous les jours
14. personne ou publication qui prend la parole au nom d'un groupe

VOCABULAIRE[1]

Noms

Archeologia	monthly magazine	le **four**	*oven*	la **poêle**	*frying pan*
le **baccalauréat**	national examination at the end of lycée	un **horloger**	*watchmaker*	le **polonais**	*Polish language*
		le **kiosque** (à journaux)	*newsstand*	la **réforme**	*reform*
la **bague**	*ring*	le **lecteur**	*reader*	la **représentation**	*performance*
la **belle-sœur**	*sister-in-law*	le **magazine**	*magazine*	le **résultat**	*result*
le **bijoutier**	*jeweler*	le **manoir**	*manor*	le(la) **spécialiste**	*specialist*
la **chaussette**	*sock*	*Marie-France*	fashion magazine	la **table des matières**	*table of contents*
le **courrier**	*mail*	le **mécanicien**	*mechanic*		
le **dépanneur**	*repairman*	la **mode**	*fashion*	le **type**	*type*
la **dinde**	*turkey*	*Le Monde*	daily newspaper	*Vieilles Maisons Françaises*	monthly maga-zine
Elle	fashion magazine	le **numéro**	*issue*		
Le Figaro	daily newspaper	la **pêche**	*fishing*	*Vogue*	fashion magazine

Verbes

s'**abonner à**	*to subscribe to*	**fondre**	*to melt*	**soigner**	*to take care of, look after; to treat*
arracher	*to pull out*	**pousser**	*to grow*		
bouillir *irrég*	*to boil*	**réparer**	*to repair*		
cuire *irrég*	*to cook*	**rôtir**	*to roast*		

Adjectifs

mensuel(le)	*monthly*	**publié(e)**	*published*
perdu(e)	*wasted*	**romain(e)**	*Roman*

Pronoms

aucun(e)	*none*	**la plupart de** + *nom*	*most* + noun
chacun(e)	*each (one), every (one)*	**quelques-un(e)s**	*some, a few*

Autres expressions

aucun d'entre nous	*none of us*	Fais voir.	*Show me.*
de peur que	*for fear that, lest*	**ne** (pleonastic)	
faire faire qqch par qqn	*to have something done by someone*		

---

[1]The vocabulary for sections 25.4 and 25.5 is not included. It appears in the *Lexique*.

Appendices

A. COGNATES

Words in two languages having approximately the same spellings are known as cognates. Some cognates are similar only in form and not in meaning. For example, the French words **lecture**, **rester**, and **demander** do not mean *lecture*, *to rest*, and *to demand*, but *reading*, *to remain*, and *to ask (for)*. But the majority of cognates in French and English share similarities in both form and meaning. Forms can be recognized by the stem as well as the ending. Typical cognate endings are listed below.

Noun endings

-ance/-ence　　　　　　　→ **-ance/-ence (-ency)**
　　importance, élégance, tolérance, défiance, finance
　　absence, innocence, intelligence, excellence, compétence
-eur (f -euse/-trice/-drice)　→ **-er/-or**
　　danseur, voyageur, acteur, décorateur, ambassadeur
-ie　　　　　　　　　　　→ **-y**
　　géographie, industrie, académie, ironie, hiérarchie
-isme　　　　　　　　　→ **-ism**
　　nationalisme, militarisme, réalisme, optimisme, mécanisme
-ité　　　　　　　　　　→ **-ity**
　　capacité, possibilité, activité, curiosité, nécessité
-ment　　　　　　　　→ **-ment**
　　appartement, gouvernement, encouragement, segment, élément
-sion/-tion　　　　　　→ **-sion/-tion**
　　décision, occasion, possession, profession, expression
　　nation, éducation, exclamation, affirmation, négation
-ture　　　　　　　　　→ **-ture**
　　nature, culture, créature, structure, architecture

Noun and adjective endings

-ain (f -aine)　　　　　→ **-an**
　　romain, africain, américain, humain, puritain
-aire　　　　　　　　　→ **-ary/-ar**
　　dictionnaire, secrétaire, imaginaire, ordinaire, itinéraire
　　circulaire, polaire, cellulaire, populaire, insulaire
-ien (f -ienne)　　　　→ **-ian**
　　italien, algérien, canadien, musicien, technicien
-ique　　　　　　　　→ **-ic/-ical**
　　république, musique, économique, logique, dramatique
-iste　　　　　　　　→ **-ist/-istic**
　　optimiste, pessimiste, humaniste, pianiste, journaliste

Adjective endings

-able/-ible → *-able/-ible*
    capable, stable, séparable, invariable, sociable
    possible, visible, accessible, combustible
-al/-el (*f* **-ale/-elle**) → *-al*
    national, général, social, normal, littéral
    naturel, visuel, partiel, réel, professionnel
-eux (*f* **-euse**) → *-ous*
    dangereux, délicieux, curieux, fameux, religieux
-if (*f* **-ive**) → *-ive*
    positif, adjectif, actif, passif, exclusif, possessif

Verb endings

-er → (no ending)/*-e*/*-ate*
    calmer, affirmer, amuser, admirer, indiquer, célébrer, associer
-ier → *-y*
    vérifier, glorifier, terrifier, simplifier, multiplier
-ir → *-ish*
    finir, punir, accomplir, bannir, nourrir, périr
-iser/-yser → *-ize*/*-yze*
    organiser, centraliser, nationaliser, utiliser, analyser

B. NOUN GENDERS

The ending of a noun, especially when it is a suffix, often provides a clue to the gender of the noun. The list below presents general guidelines for determining the gender of nouns.

Masculine endings

-age	patinage, village, étage, courage
-al	animal, journal, hôpital, cheval
-at	chocolat, soldat, doctorat, consulat
-eau	tableau, morceau, couteau, château
-ent	parent, client, président, antécédent
-er	dîner, déjeuner, danger
	épicier, boulanger, charcutier (*occupations*)
	pommier, poirier, pêcher, bananier (*arbres*)
-et	objet, buffet, cabinet, projet
-eur	vendeur, chanteur, acteur, professeur (*occupations*)
	moteur, radiateur, indicateur (*appareils*)
-ien	technicien, mécanicien, canadien
-in	médecin, marin, cousin, voisin, coussin
-isme	optimisme, nationalisme, impérialisme
-ment	monument, gouvernement, mouvement
-oir	soir, couloir, mouchoir, rasoir, devoir

Feminine endings

-ade	façade, orangeade, salade, charade
-aine	douzaine, fontaine, américaine
-aison	terminaison, comparaison, conjugaison
-ance	enfance, tendance, correspondance

-ande	demande, commande, viande, Hollande
-ée	cuillerée, année, journée, entrée
-eille	bouteille, oreille, corbeille
-ence	différence, agence, patience, présence
-ère	boulangère, épicière, charcutière (*occupations*)
-esse	vitesse, noblesse, richesse, jeunesse (*noms abstraits*)
	hôtesse, maîtresse, princesse, tigresse
-ette	assiette, fourchette, serviette, cigarette
-eur	chaleur, horreur, terreur, honneur (*noms abstraits*)
-euse	vendeuse, chanteuse, voyageuse, danseuse
-ie	géographie, mélodie, épicerie, crémerie
-ienne	technicienne, musicienne, canadienne
-ine	usine, machine, vitrine, cuisine, voisine
-ique	musique, boutique, botanique, basilique
-ise	valise, église, cerise, surprise
-oire	baignoire, poire, victoire, histoire, gloire
-onne	personne, consonne, colonne, Sorbonne
-sion	télévision, décision, discussion, profession
-té	liberté, nationalité, vérité, beauté
-tion	nation, question, correction, addition
-trice	lectrice, directrice, actrice
-tude	étude, attitude, habitude, solitude
-ure	culture, voiture, gravure, architecture

C. CONJUGATION OF REGULAR VERBS

French verbs have moods (such as the *indicative*, the *conditional*, and the *subjunctive*). Each mood has several tenses, which are divided into *simple* and *compound*, the latter consisting of the auxiliary verb and a past participle. In the following chart, the lesson or lessons in which a particular tense is discussed are given in parentheses.

1. Infinitif (Lessons 2.1, 4.5, 5.3)

parl**er**	fin**ir**	descend**re**

2. Participe présent (Lesson 22.5)

parl**ant**	finiss**ant**	descend**ant**

3. Participe passé (Lessons 9.2, 9.4)

parl**é**	fin**i**	descend**u**

4. Indicatif

présent (Lessons 2.1, 4.5, 5.3)

je parl**e**	je fin**is**	je descend**s**
tu parl**es**	tu fin**is**	tu descend**s**
il parl**e**	il fin**it**	il descend
nous parl**ons**	nous fin**issons**	nous descend**ons**
vous parl**ez**	vous fin**issez**	vous descend**ez**
ils parl**ent**	ils fin**issent**	ils descend**ent**

passé composé (Lessons 9.2, 9.4)

j'**ai** parlé	j'**ai** fini	je **suis** descendu(e)
tu **as** parlé	tu **as** fini	tu **es** descendu(e)
il **a** parlé	il **a** fini	il **est** descendu
nous **avons** parlé	nous **avons** fini	nous **sommes** descendu(e)s
vous **avez** parlé	vous **avez** fini	vous **êtes** descendu(e)(s)
ils **ont** parlé	ils **ont** fini	ils **sont** descendus

imparfait (Lesson 10.1)

je parl**ais**	je finiss**ais**	je descend**ais**
tu parl**ais**	tu finiss**ais**	tu descend**ais**
il parl**ait**	il finiss**ait**	il descend**ait**
nous parl**ions**	nous finiss**ions**	nous descend**ions**
vous parl**iez**	vous finiss**iez**	vous descend**iez**
ils parl**aient**	ils finiss**aient**	ils descend**aient**

plus-que-parfait (Lesson 23.5)

j'**avais** parlé	j'**avais** fini	j'**étais** descendu(e)
tu **avais** parlé	tu **avais** fini	tu **étais** descendu(e)
il **avait** parlé	il **avait** fini	il **était** descendu
nous **avions** parlé	nous **avions** fini	nous **étions** descendu(e)s
vous **aviez** parlé	vous **aviez** fini	vous **étiez** descendu(e)(s)
ils **avaient** parlé	ils **avaient** fini	ils **étaient** descendus

futur (Lesson 15.2)

je parler**ai**	je finir**ai**	je descendr**ai**
tu parler**as**	tu finir**as**	tu descendr**as**
il parler**a**	il finir**a**	il descendr**a**
nous parler**ons**	nous finir**ons**	nous descendr**ons**
vous parler**ez**	vous finir**ez**	vous descendr**ez**
ils parler**ont**	ils finir**ont**	ils descendr**ont**

futur antérieur (Lesson 24.3)

j'**aurai** parlé	j'**aurai** fini	je **serai** descendu(e)
tu **auras** parlé	tu **auras** fini	tu **seras** descendu(e)
il **aura** parlé	il **aura** fini	il **sera** descendu
nous **aurons** parlé	nous **aurons** fini	nous **serons** descendu(e)s
vous **aurez** parlé	vous **aurez** fini	vous **serez** descendu(e)(s)
ils **auront** parlé	ils **auront** fini	ils **seront** descendus

passé simple (Lesson 25.4)

je parl**ai**	je fin**is**	je descend**is**
tu parl**as**	tu fin**is**	tu decend**is**
il parl**a**	il fin**it**	il descend**it**
nous parl**âmes**	nous fin**îmes**	nous descend**îmes**
vous parl**âtes**	vous fin**îtes**	vous descend**îtes**
ils parl**èrent**	ils fin**irent**	ils descend**irent**

passé antérieur (Lesson 25.4)

j'**eus** parlé	j'**eus** fini	je **fus** descendu(e)
tu **eus** parlé	tu **eus** fini	tu **fus** descendu(e)
il **eut** parlé	il **eut** fini	il **fut** descendu
nous **eûmes** parlé	nous **eûmes** fini	nous **fûmes** descendu(e)s
vous **eûtes** parlé	vous **eûtes** fini	vous **fûtes** descendu(e)(s)
ils **eurent** parlé	ils **eurent** fini	ils **furent** descendus

5. **Conditionnel**

présent (Lesson 17.3)

je parler**ais**	je finir**ais**	je descendr**ais**
tu parler**ais**	tu finir**ais**	tu decendr**ais**
il parler**ait**	il finir**ait**	il descendr**ait**
nous parler**ions**	nous finir**ions**	nous descendr**ions**
vous parler**iez**	vous finir**iez**	vous descendr**iez**
ils parler**aient**	ils finir**aient**	ils descendr**aient**

passé (Lesson 24.5)

j'**aurais** parlé	j'**aurais** fini	je **serais** descendu(e)
tu **aurais** parlé	tu **aurais** fini	tu **serais** descendu(e)
il **aurait** parlé	il **aurait** fini	il **serait** descendu
nous **aurions** parlé	nous **aurions** fini	nous **serions** descendu(e)s
vous **auriez** parlé	vous **auriez** fini	vous **seriez** descendu(e)(s)
ils **auraient** parlé	ils **auraient** fini	ils **seraient** descendus

6. **Subjonctif**

présent (Lesson 19.2)

je parl**e**	je finiss**e**	je descend**e**
tu parl**es**	tu finiss**es**	tu descend**es**
il parl**e**	il finiss**e**	il descend**e**
nous parl**ions**	nous finiss**ions**	nous descend**ions**
vous parl**iez**	vous finiss**iez**	vous descend**iez**
ils parl**ent**	ils finiss**ent**	ils descend**ent**

passé composé (Lesson 19.3)

j'**aie** parlé	j'**aie** fini	je **sois** descendu(e)
tu **aies** parlé	tu **aies** fini	tu **sois** descendu(e)
il **ait** parlé	il **ait** fini	il **soit** descendu
nous **ayons** parlé	nous **ayons** fini	nous **soyons** descendu(e)s
vous **ayez** parlé	vous **ayez** fini	vous **soyez** descendu(e)(s)
ils **aient** parlé	ils **aient** fini	ils **soient** descendus

imparfait (Lesson 25.5)

je parl**asse**	je fin**isse**	je descend**isse**
tu parl**asses**	tu fin**isses**	tu descend**isses**
il parl**ât**	il fin**ît**	il descend**ît**
nous parl**assions**	nous fin**issions**	nous descend**issions**
vous parl**assiez**	vous fin**issez**	vous descend**issiez**
ils parl**assent**	ils fin**issent**	ils descend**issent**

plus-que-parfait (Lesson 25.5)

j'**eusse** parlé	j'**eusse** fini	je **fusse** descendu(e)
tu **eusses** parlé	tu **eusses** fini	tu **fusses** descendu(e)
il **eût** parlé	il **eût** fini	il **fût** descendu
nous **eussions** parlé	nous **eussions** fini	nous **fussions** descendu(e)s
vous **eussiez** parlé	vous **eussiez** fini	vous **fussiez** descendu(e)(s)
ils **eussent** parlé	ils **eussent** fini	ils **fussent** descendus

7. **Impératif** (Lessons 3.3, 18.3)

[tu] Parl**e** !	[tu] Fin**is** !	[tu] Descend**s** !
[nous] Parl**ons** !	[nous] Fin**issons** !	[nous] Descend**ons** !
[vous] Parl**ez** !	[vous] Fin**issez** !	[vous] Descend**ez** !

D. CONJUGATION OF IRREGULAR VERBS

The following list presents the simple tenses of all main irregular verbs. In most cases, only the forms of the first-person singular (**je**) and plural (**nous**) are given, since the other forms can be derived from these two. Where this is not possible, the specific irregular form is provided in parentheses, or a reference is made to the grammar explanations in which the entire conjugation is found. If the verb normally occurs only in impersonal expressions (for example, **falloir** and **pleuvoir**), only the third-person singular form (**il**) of each tense is given. The principal parts of each verb appear in the following order. The abbreviations in parentheses are those used in the verb list.

Infinitif

participe passé (**part.pas.**) (Lesson 9.2, 9.4)	participe présent (**part.prés.**) (Lesson 22.5)
présent de l'indicatif (**prés.ind.**) (passim)	imparfait de l'indicatif (**imp.ind.**) (Lesson 10.1)
futur de l'indicatif (**fut.ind.**) (Lesson 15.2, 15.4)	présent du conditionnel (**prés.cond.**) (Lesson 17.3)
présent du subjonctif (**prés.subj.**) (Lesson 19.2, 19.3)	passé simple (**pas.simple**) (Lesson 25.4)
	imparfait du subjonctif (**imp.subj.**) (Lesson 25.5)

References in parentheses in the list below indicate the lesson in which all the forms (endings) of a given tense are presented.

accourir (*same conjugation pattern as* **courir**)
accueillir (*same conjugation pattern as* **cueillir**)
acquérir
part.pas. *j'ai* acquis **part.prés.** acquérant
prés.ind. j'acquiers, nous acquérons **imp.ind.** j'acquérais, nous acquérions
fut.ind. j'acquerrai, nous acquerrons **prés.cond.** j'acquerrais, nous acquerrions
prés.subj. j'acquière, nous acquérions **pas.simple** j'acquis, nous acquîmes
  imp.subj. j'acquisse, nous acquissons

admettre (*same conjugation pattern as* **mettre**)
aller
part.pas. *je suis* allé(e) **part.prés.** allant
prés.ind. (*see Lesson 4.3*) **imp.ind.** j'allais, nous allions
fut.ind. j'irai, nous irons **prés.cond.** j'irais, nous irions
prés.subj. j'aille, nous allions **pas.simple** j'allai, nous allâmes
  imp.subj. j'allasse, nous allassions

apparaître (*same conjugation pattern as* **paraître**)
appartenir (*same conjugation pattern as* **tenir**)
apprendre (*same conjugation pattern as* **prendre**)
s'asseoir
part.pas. *je me suis* assis(e) **part.prés.** s'asseyant
prés.ind. je m'assieds, nous nous asseyons **imp.ind.** je m'asseyais, nous nous asseyions
fut.ind. je m'assiérai, nous nous assiérons **prés.cond.** je m'assiérais, nous nous assiérions
prés.subj. je m'asseye, nous nous asseyions **pas.simple** je m'assis, nous nous assîmes
  imp.subj. je m'assisse, nous nous assissions

atteindre (*same conjugation pattern as* **éteindre**)
avoir
part.pas. *j'ai* eu **part.prés.** ayant
prés.ind. (*see Lesson 2.6*) **imp.ind.** j'avais, nous avions
fut.ind. j'aurai, nous aurons **prés.cond.** j'aurais, nous aurions
prés.subj. (*see Lesson 19.3*) **pas.simple** j'eus, nous eûmes
  imp.subj. j'eusse, nous eussions

boire

part.pas.	*j'ai* bu	**part.prés.**	buvant
prés.ind.	je bois, nous buvons	**imp.ind.**	je buvais, nous buvions
fut.ind.	je boirai, nous boirons	**prés.cond.**	je boirais, nous boirions
prés.subj.	je boive, nous buvions	**pas.simple**	je bus, nous bûmes
		imp.subj.	je busse, nous bussions

bouillir

part.pas.	*j'ai* bouilli	**part.prés.**	bouillant
prés.ind.	je bous, nous bouillons	**imp.ind.**	je bouillais, nous bouillions
fut. ind.	je bouillirai, nous bouillirons	**prés.cond.**	je bouillirais, nous bouillirions
prés.subj.	je bouille, nous bouillions	**pas.simple**	je bouillis, nous bouillîmes
		imp.subj.	je bouillisse, nous bouillissions

comprendre (*same conjugation pattern as* **prendre**)

concevoir (*same conjugation pattern as* **recevoir**)

conclure

part.pas.	*j'ai* conclu	**part.prés.**	concluant
prés.ind.	je conclus, nous concluons	**imp.ind.**	je concluais, nous concluions
fut.ind.	je conclurai, nous conclurons	**prés.cond.**	je conclurais, nous conclurions
prés.subj.	je conclue, nous concluions	**pas.simple**	je conclus, nous conclûmes
		imp.subj.	je conclusse, nous conclussions

conduire

part.pas.	*j'ai* conduit	**part.prés.**	conduisant
prés.ind.	je conduis, nous conduisons	**imp.ind.**	je conduisais, nous conduisions
fut.ind.	je conduirai, nous conduirons	**prés.cond.**	je conduirais, nous conduirions
prés.subj.	je conduise, nous conduisions	**pas.simple**	je conduisis, nous conduisîmes
		imp.subj.	je conduisisse, nous conduisissions

connaître

part.pas.	*j'ai* connu	**part.prés.**	connaissant
prés.ind.	je connais, nous connaissons (il connaît)	**imp.ind.**	je connaissais, nous connaissions
fut.ind.	je connaîtrai, nous connaîtrons	**prés.cond.**	je connaîtrais, nous connaîtrions
prés.subj.	je connaisse, nous connaissions	**pas.simple**	je connus, nous connûmes
		imp.subj.	je connusse, nous connussions

conquérir (*same conjugation pattern as* **acquérir**)

consentir (*same conjugation pattern as* **sentir**)

construire

part.pas.	*j'ai* construit	**part.prés.**	construisant
prés.ind.	je construis, nous construisons	**imp.ind.**	je construisais, nous construisions
fut.ind.	je construirai, nous construirons	**prés.cond.**	je construirais, nous construirions
prés.subj.	je construise, nous construisions	**pas.simple**	je construisis, nous construisîmes
		imp.subj.	je construisisse, nous construisissions

contredire

part.pas.	*j'ai* contredit	**part.prés.**	contredisant
prés.ind.	je contredis, nous contredisons (vous contredisez)	**imp.ind.**	je contredisais, nous contredisions
		prés.subj.	je contredirais, nous contredirions
fut.ind.	je contredirai, nous contredirons	**pas.simple**	je contredis, nous contredîmes
prés.subj.	je contredise, nous contredisions	**imp.subj.**	je contredisse, nous contredissions

coudre

part.pas.	*j'ai* cousu	**part.prés.**	cousant
prés.ind.	je couds, nous cousons	**imp.ind.**	je cousais, nous cousions
fut.ind.	je coudrai, nous coudrons	**prés.cond.**	je coudrais, nous coudrions
prés.subj.	je couse, nous cousions	**pas.simple**	je cousis, nous cousîmes
		imp.subj.	je cousisse, nous cousissions

courir

part.pas.	*j'ai* couru		part.prés.	courant
prés.ind.	je cours, nous courons		imp.ind.	je courais, nous courions
fut.ind.	je courrai, nous courrons		prés.cond.	je courrais, nous courrions
prés.subj.	je coure, nous courions		pas.simple	je courus, nous courûmes
			imp.subj.	je courusse, nous courussions

comprendre   (*same conjugation pattern as* **prendre**)
couvrir   (*same conjugation pattern as* **ouvrir**)

craindre

part.pas.	*j'ai* craint		part.prés.	craignant
prés.ind.	je crains, nous craignons		imp.ind.	je craignais, nous craignions
fut.ind.	je craindrai, nous craindrons		prés.cond.	je craindrais, nous craindrions
prés.subj.	je craigne, nous craignions		pas.simple	je craignis, nous craignîmes
			imp.subj.	je craignisse, nous craignissions

croire

part.pas.	*j'ai* cru		part.prés.	croyant
prés.ind.	je crois, nous croyons (ils croient)		imp.ind.	je croyais, nous croyions
fut.ind.	je croirai, nous croirons		prés.cond.	je croirais, nous croirions
prés.subj.	je croie, nous croyions		pas.simple	je crus, nous crûmes
			imp.subj.	je crusse, nous crussions

croître[1]

part.pas.	*j'ai* crû		part.prés.	croissant
prés.ind.	je croîs, nous croissons		imp.ind.	je croissais, nous croissions
fut.ind.	je croîtrai, nous croîtrons		prés.cond.	je croîtrais, nous croîtrions
prés.subj.	je croisse, nous croissions		pas.simple	je crûs, nous crûmes
			imp.subj.	je crûsse, nous crûssions

cueillir

part.pas.	*j'ai* cueilli		part.prés.	cueillant
prés.ind.	je cueille, nous cueillons		imp.ind.	je cueillais, nous cueillions
fut.ind.	je cueillerai, nous cueillerons		prés.cond.	je cueillerais, nous cueillerions
prés.subj.	je cueille, nous cueillions		pas.simple	je cueillis, nous cueillîmes
			imp.subj.	je cueillisse, nous cueillissions

cuire

part.pas.	*j'ai* cuit		part.prés.	cuisant
prés.ind.	je cuis, nous cuisons		imp.ind.	je cuisais, nous cuisions
fut.ind.	je cuirai, nous cuirons		prés.cond.	je cuirais, nous cuirions
prés.subj.	je cuise, nous cuisions		pas.simple	je cuisis, nous cuisîmes
			imp.subj.	je cuisisse, nous cuisissions

décevoir   (*same conjugation pattern as* **recevoir**)
découvrir   (*same conjugation pattern as* **ouvrir**)
décrire   (*same conjugation pattern as* **écrire**)
défaire   (*same conjugation pattern as* **faire**)
déplaire   (*same conjugation pattern as* **plaire**)
desservir   (*same conjugation pattern as* **servir**)
détruire   (*same conjugation pattern as* **construire**)
devenir   (*same conjugation pattern as* **venir**; *conjugated with* **être** *in compound tenses*)

devoir

part.pas.	*j'ai* dû (*f* due)		part.prés.	devant
prés.ind.	je dois, nous devons (ils doivent)		imp.ind.	je devais, nous devions
fut.ind.	je devrai, nous devrons		prés.cond.	je devrais, nous devrions
prés.subj.	je doive, nous devions		pas.simple	je dus, nous dûmes
			imp.subj.	je dusse, nous dussions

[1]Aside from the infinitive, future, and conditional, the *accent circonflexe* occurs in all forms that are otherwise identical with **croire.**

dire
part.pas.	*j'ai* dit	**part.prés.**	disant
prés.ind.	je dis, nous disons (vous dites)	**imp.ind.**	je disais, nous disions
fut.ind.	je dirai, nous dirons	**prés.cond.**	je dirais, nous dirions
prés.subj.	je dise, nous disions	**pas.simple**	je dis, nous dîmes
		imp.subj.	je disse, nous dissions

disparaître   (*same conjugation pattern as* **paraître**)

distraire
part.pas.	*j'ai* distrait	**part.prés.**	distrayant
prés.ind.	je distrais, nous distrayons (ils distraient)	**imp.ind.**	je distrais, nous distrayions
fut.ind.	je distrairai, nous distrairons	**prés.cond.**	je distrairais, nous distrairions
prés.subj.	je distraie, nous distrayions	**pas.simple**	(*none*)
		imp.subj.	(*none*)

dormir
part.pas.	*j'ai* dormi	**part.prés.**	dormant
prés.ind.	je dors, nous dormons	**imp.ind.**	je dormais, nous dormions
fut.ind.	je dormirai, nous dormirons	**prés.cond.**	je dormirais, nous dormirions
prés.subj.	je dorme, nous dormions	**pas.simple**	je dormis, nous dormîmes
		imp.subj.	je dormisse, nous dormissions

écrire
part.pas.	*j'ai* écrit	**part.prés.**	écrivant
prés.ind.	j'écris, nous écrivons	**imp.ind.**	j'écrivais, nous écrivions
fut.ind.	j'écrirai, nous écrirons	**prés.cond.**	j'écrirais, nous écririons
prés.subj.	j'écrive, nous écrivions	**pas.simple**	j'écrivis, nous écrivîmes
		imp.subj.	j'écrivisse, nous écrivissions

élire   (*same conjugation pattern as* **lire**)
émouvoir   (*same conjugation pattern as* **mouvoir**)
s'endormir   (*same conjugation pattern as* **dormir***; conjugated with* **être** *in compound tenses*)

entretenir   (*same conjugation pattern as* **tenir**)

envoyer
part.pas.	*j'ai* envoyé	**part.prés.**	envoyant
prés.ind.	j'envoie, nous envoyons (ils envoient)	**imp.ind.**	j'envoyais, nous envoyions
fut.ind.	j'enverrai, nous enverrons	**prés.cond.**	j'enverrais, nous enverrions
prés.subj.	j'envoie, nous envoyions	**pas.simple**	j'envoyai, nous envoyâmes
		imp.subj.	j'envoyasse, nous envoyassions

éteindre
part.pas.	*j'ai* éteint	**part.prés.**	éteignant
prés.ind.	j'éteins, nous éteignons	**imp.ind.**	j'éteignais, nous éteignions
fut.ind.	j'éteindrai, nous éteindrons	**prés.cond.**	j'éteindrais, nous éteindrions
prés.subj.	j'éteigne, nous éteignions	**pas.simple**	j'éteignis, nous éteignîmes
		imp.subj.	j'éteignisse, nous éteignissions

être
part.pas.	*j'ai* été	**part.prés.**	étant
prés.ind.	(*see Lesson 1.6*)	**imp.ind.**	j'étais, nous étions
fut.ind.	je serai, nous serons	**prés.cond.**	je serais, nous serions
prés.subj.	je sois, nous soyons	**pas.simple**	je fus, nous fûmes
		imp.subj.	je fusse, nous fussions

exclure   (*same conjugation pattern as* **conclure**)

faire
part.pas.	*j'ai* fait	**part.prés.**	faisant
prés.ind.	(*see Lesson 4.1*)	**imp.ind.**	je faisais, nous faisions
fut.ind.	je ferai, nous ferons	**prés.cond.**	je ferais, nous ferions
prés.subj.	je fasse, nous fassions	**pas.simple**	je fis, nous fîmes
		imp.subj.	je fisse, nous fissions

falloir

part.pas.	*il a* fallu	**part.prés.**	(*none*)
prés.ind.	il faut	**imp.ind.**	il fallait
fut.ind.	il faudra	**prés.cond.**	il faudrait
prés.subj.	il faille	**pas.simple**	il fallut
		imp.subj.	il fallût

frire

part.pas.	*j'ai* frit	**part.prés.**	(*none*)
prés.ind.	je fris (*no plural forms*)	**imp.ind.**	(*none*)
fut.ind.	je frirai, nous frirons	**prés.cond.**	je frirais, nous fririons
prés.subj.	(*none*)	**pas.simple**	(*none*)
		imp.subj.	(*none*)

fuir

part.pas.	*j'ai* fui	**part.prés.**	fuyant
prés.ind.	je fuis, nous fuyons (ils fuient)	**imp.ind.**	je fuyais, nous fuyions
fut.ind.	je fuirai, nous fuirons	**prés.cond.**	je fuirais, nous fuirions
prés.subj.	je fuie, nous fuyions	**pas.simple**	je fuis, nous fuîmes
		imp.subj.	je fuisse, nous fuissions

inscrire (*same conjugation pattern as* **écrire**)
interdire (*same conjugation pattern as* **contredire**)
joindre

part.pas.	*j'ai* joint	**part.prés.**	joignant
prés.ind.	je joins, nous joignons	**imp.ind.**	je joignais, nous joignions
fut.ind.	je joindrai, nous joindrons	**prés.cond.**	je joindrais, nous joindrions
prés.subj.	je joigne, nous joignions	**pas.simple**	je joignis, nous joignîmes
		imp.subj.	je joignisse, nous joignissions

lire

part.pas.	*j'ai* lu	**part.prés.**	lisant
prés.ind.	je lis, nous lisons	**imp.ind.**	je lisais, nous lisions
fut.ind.	je lirai, nous lirons	**prés.cond.**	je lirais, nous lirions
prés.subj.	je lise, nous lisions	**pas.simple**	je lus, nous lûmes
		imp.subj.	je lusse, nous lussions

maintenir (*same conjugation pattern as* **tenir**)
mentir

part.pas.	*j'ai* menti	**part.prés.**	mentant
prés.ind.	je mens, nous mentons	**imp.ind.**	je mentais, nous mentions
fut.ind.	je mentirai, nous mentirons	**prés.cond.**	je mentirais, nous mentirions
prés.subj.	je mente, nous mentions	**pas.simple**	je mentis, nous mentîmes
		imp.subj.	je mentisse, nous mentissions

mettre

part.pas.	*j'ai* mis	**part.prés.**	mettant
prés.ind.	je mets, nous mettons	**imp.ind.**	je mettais, nous mettions
fut.ind.	je mettrai, nous mettrons	**prés.cond.**	je mettrais, nous mettrions
prés.subj.	je mette, nous mettions	**pas.simple**	je mis, nous mîmes
		imp.subj.	je misse, nous missions

mourir

part.pas.	*je suis* mort(e)	**part.prés.**	mourant
prés.ind.	je meurs, nous mourons	**imp.ind.**	je mourais, nous mourions
fut.ind.	je mourrai, nous mourrons	**prés.cond.**	je mourrais, nous mourrions
prés.subj.	je meure, nous mourions	**pas.simple**	je mourus, nous mourûmes
		imp.subj.	je mourusse, nous mourussions

mouvoir

part.pas.	*j'ai* mû (*f* mue)	**part.prés.**	mouvant
prés.ind.	je meus, nous mouvons	**imp.ind.**	je mouvais, nous mouvions
fut.ind.	je mouvrai, nous mouvrons	**prés.cond.**	je mouvrais, nous mouvrions

prés.subj.	je meuve, nous mouvions	**pas.simple**	je mus, nous mûmes
		imp.subj.	je musse, nous mussions

naître

part.pas.	*je suis* né(e)	**part.prés.**	naissant
prés.ind.	je nais, nous naissons (il naît)	**imp.ind.**	je naissais, nous naissions
fut.ind.	je naîtrai, nous naîtrons	**prés.cond.**	je naîtrais, nous naîtrions
prés.subj.	je naisse, nous naissions	**pas.simple**	je naquis, nous naquîmes
		imp.subj.	je naquisse, nous naquissions

nuire

part.pas.	*j'ai* nui	**part.prés.**	nuisant
prés.ind.	je nuis, nous nuisons	**imp.ind.**	je nuisais, nous nuisions
fut.ind.	je nuirai, nous nuirons	**prés.cond.**	je nuirais, nous nuirions
prés.subj.	je nuise, nous nuisions	**pas.simple**	je nuisis, nous nuisîmes
		imp.subj.	je nuisisse, nous nuisissions

obtenir   (*same conjugation pattern as* **tenir**)

offrir

part.pas.	*j'ai* offert	**part.prés.**	offrant
prés.ind.	j'offre, nous offrons	**imp.ind.**	j'offrais, nous offrions
fut.ind.	j'offrirai, nous offrirons	**prés.cond.**	j'offrirais, nous offririons
prés.subj.	j'offre, nous offrions	**pas.simple**	j'offris, nous offrîmes
		imp.subj.	j'offrisse, nous offrissions

ouvrir

part.pas.	*j'ai* ouvert	**part.prés.**	ouvrant
prés.ind.	j'ouvre, nous ouvrons	**imp.ind.**	j'ouvrais, nous ouvrions
fut.ind.	j'ouvrirai, nous ouvrirons	**prés.cond.**	j'ouvrirais, nous ouvririons
prés.subj.	j'ouvre, nous ouvrions	**pas.simple**	j'ouvris, nous ouvrîmes
		imp.subj.	j'ouvrisse, nous ouvrissions

paraître

part.pas.	*j'ai* paru	**part.prés.**	paraissant
prés.ind.	je parais, nous paraissons (il paraît)	**imp.ind.**	je paraissais, nous paraissions
fut.ind.	je paraîtrai, nous paraîtrons	**prés.cond.**	je paraîtrais, nous paraîtrions
prés.subj.	je paraisse, nous paraissions	**pas.simple**	je parus, nous parûmes
		imp.subj.	je parusse, nous parussions

parcourir   (*same conjugation pattern as* **courir**)

parfaire   (*same conjugation pattern as* **faire**)

partir

part.pas.	*je suis* parti(e)	**part.prés.**	partant
prés.ind.	je pars, nous partons	**imp.ind.**	je partais, nous partions
fut.ind.	je partirai, nous partirons	**prés.cond.**	je partirais, nous partirions
prés.subj.	je parte, nous partions	**pas.simple**	je partis, nous partîmes
		imp.subj.	je partisse, nous partissions

peindre

part.pas.	*j'ai* peint	**part.prés.**	peignant
prés.ind.	je peins, nous peignons	**imp.ind.**	je peignais, nous peignions
fut.ind.	je peindrai, nous peindrons	**prés.cond.**	je peindrais, nous peindrions
prés.subj.	je peigne, nous peignions	**pas.simple**	je peignis, nous peignîmes
		imp.subj.	je peignisse, nous peignissions

permettre   (*same conjugation pattern as* **mettre**)

plaindre

part.pas.	*j'ai* plaint	**part.prés.**	plaignant
prés.ind.	je plains, nous plaignons	**imp.ind.**	je plaignais, nous plaignions
fut.ind.	je plaindrai, nous plaindrons	**prés.cond.**	je plaindrais, nous plaindrions
prés.subj.	je plaigne, nous plaignions	**pas.simple**	je plaignis, nous plaignîmes
		imp.subj.	je plaignisse, nous plaignissions

plaire

part.pas.	*j'ai* plu		**part.prés.**	plaisant
prés.ind.	je plais, nous plaisons (il plaît)		**imp.ind.**	je plaisais, nous plaisions
fut.ind.	je plairai, nous plairons		**prés.cond.**	je plairais, nous plairions
prés.subj.	je plaise, nous plaisions		**pas.simple**	je plus, nous plûmes
			imp.subj.	je plusse, nous plussions

pleuvoir

part.pas.	*il a* plu		**part.prés.**	pleuvant
prés.ind.	il pleut		**imp.ind.**	il pleuvait
fut.ind.	il pleuvra		**prés.cond.**	il pleuvrait
prés.subj.	il pleuve		**pas.simple**	il plut
			imp.subj.	il plût

pouvoir

part.pas.	*j'ai* pu		**part.prés.**	pouvant
prés.ind.	je peux, nous pouvons (ils peuvent)		**imp.ind.**	je pouvais, nous pouvions
fut.ind.	je pourrai, nous pourrons		**prés.cond.**	je pourrais, nous pourrions
prés.subj.	je puisse, nous puissions		**pas.simple**	je pus, nous pûmes
			imp.subj.	je pusse, nous pussions

prendre

part.pas.	*j'ai* pris		**part.prés.**	prenant
prés.ind.	je prends, nous prenons (ils prennent)		**imp.ind.**	je prenais, nous prenions
fut.ind.	je prendrai, nous prendrons		**prés.cond.**	je prendrais, nous prendrions
prés.subj.	je prenne, nous prenions		**pas.simple**	je pris, nous prîmes
			imp.subj.	je prisse, nous prissions

prévoir   (*same conjugation pattern as* **voir**)
produire   (*same conjugation pattern as* **conduire**)
promettre   (*same conjugation pattern as* **mettre**)
promouvoir   (*same conjugation pattern as* **mouvoir**)
recevoir

part.pas.	*j'ai* reçu		**part.prés.**	recevant
prés.ind.	je reçois, nous recevons (ils reçoivent)		**imp.ind.**	je recevais, nous recevions
fut.ind.	je recevrai, nous recevrons		**prés.cond.**	je recevrais, nous recevrions
prés.subj.	je reçoive, nous recevions		**pas.simple**	je reçus, nous reçûmes
			imp.subj.	je reçusse, nous reçussions

reconnaître   (*same conjugation pattern as* **connaître**)
recouvrir   (*same conjugation pattern as* **ouvrir**)
récrire   (*same conjugation pattern as* **écrire**)
rejoindre   (*same conjugation pattern as* **joindre**)
relire   (*same conjugation pattern as* **lire**)
repartir   (*same conjugation pattern as* **partir**; *conjugated with* **être** *in compound tenses*)
repeindre   (*same conjugation pattern as* **peindre**)
résoudre

part.pas.	*j'ai* résolu		**part.prés.**	résolvant
prés.ind.	je résouds, nous résolvons		**imp.ind.**	je résolvais, nous résolvions
fut.ind.	je résoudrai, nous résoudrons		**prés.cond.**	je résoudrais, nous résoudrions
prés.subj.	je résolve, nous résolvions		**pas.simple**	je résolus, nous résolûmes
			imp.subj.	je résolusse, nous résolussions

ressentir   (*same conjugation pattern as* **sentir**)
ressortir   (*same conjugation pattern as* **sortir**; *conjugated with* **être** *in compound tenses*)
retenir   (*same conjugation pattern as* **tenir**)
revenir   (*same conjugation pattern as* **venir**; *conjugated with* **être** *in compound tenses*)
revoir   (*same conjugation pattern as* **voir**)
rire

part.pas.	*j'ai* ri		**part.prés.**	riant
prés.ind.	je ris, nous rions		**imp.ind.**	je riais, nous riions

fut.ind.	je rirai, nous rirons		**prés.cond.**	je rirais, nous ririons
prés.subj.	je rie, nous riions		**pas.simple**	je ris, nous rîmes
			imp.subj.	je risse, nous rissions

rompre

part.pas.	*j'ai* rompu		**part.prés.**	rompant
prés.ind.	je romps, nous rompons (il rompt)		**imp.ind.**	je rompais, nous rompions
fut.ind.	je romprai, nous romprons		**prés.cond.**	je romprais, nous romprions
prés.subj.	je rompe, nous rompions		**pas.simple**	je rompis, nous rompîmes
			imp.subj.	je rompisse, nous rompissions

savoir

part.pas.	*j'ai* su		**part.prés.**	sachant
prés.ind.	je sais, nous savons		**imp.ind.**	je savais, nous savions
fut.ind.	je saurai, nous saurons		**prés.cond.**	je saurais, nous saurions
prés.subj.	je sache, nous sachions		**pas.simple**	je sus, nous sûmes
			imp.subj.	je susse, nous sussions

sentir

part.pas.	*j'ai* senti		**part.prés.**	sentant
prés.ind.	je sens, nous sentons		**imp.ind.**	je sentais, nous sentions
fut.ind.	je sentirai, nous sentirons		**prés.cond.**	je sentirais, nous sentirions
prés.subj.	je sente, nous sentions		**pas.simple**	je sentis, nous sentîmes
			imp.subj.	je sentisse, nous sentissions

servir

part.pas.	*j'ai* servi		**part.prés.**	servant
prés.ind.	je sers, nous servons		**imp.ind.**	je servais, nous servions
fut.ind.	je servirai, nous servirons		**prés.cond.**	je servirais, nous servirions
prés.subj.	je serve, nous servions		**pas.simple**	je servis, nous servîmes
			imp.subj.	je servisse, nous servissions

sortir

part.pas.	*je suis* sorti(e)		**part.prés.**	sortant
prés.ind.	je sors, nous sortons		**imp.ind.**	je sortais, nous sortions
fut.ind.	je sortirai, nous sortirons		**prés.cond.**	je sortirais, nous sortirions
prés.subj.	je sorte, nous sortions		**pas.simple**	je sortis, nous sortîmes
			imp.subj.	je sortisse, nous sortissions

souffrir	(*same conjugation pattern as* **offrir**)
soumettre	(*same conjugation pattern as* **mettre**)
sourire	(*same conjugation pattern as* **rire**)
soutenir	(*same conjugation pattern as* **tenir**)
se souvenir	(*same conjugation pattern as* **venir**; *conjugated with* **être** *in compound tenses*)

suffire

part.pas.	*j'ai* suffi		**part.prés.**	suffisant
prés.ind.	je suffis, nous suffisons		**imp.ind.**	je suffisais, nous suffisions
fut.ind.	je suffirai, nous suffirons		**prés.cond.**	je suffirais, nous suffirions
prés.subj.	je suffise, nous suffisions		**pas.simple**	je suffis, nous suffîmes
			imp.subj.	je suffisse, nous suffissions

suivre

part.pas.	*j'ai* suivi		**part.prés.**	suivant
prés.ind.	je suis, nous suivons		**imp.ind.**	je suivais, nous suivions
fut.ind.	je suivrai, nous suivrons		**prés.cond.**	je suivrais, nous suivrions
prés.subj.	je suive, nous suivions		**pas.simple**	je suivis, nous suivîmes
			imp.subj.	je suivisse, nous suivissions

surprendre	(*same conjugation pattern as* **prendre**)
survivre	(*same conjugation pattern as* **vivre**)

se taire

part.pas.	*je me suis* tu(e)		**part.prés.**	taisant
prés.ind.	je me tais, nous nous taisons		**imp.ind.**	je me taisais, nous nous taisions

fut.ind.	je me tairai, nous nous tairons	**prés.cond.**	je me tairais, nous nous tairions
prés.subj.	je me taise, nous nous taisions	**pas.simple**	je me tus, nous nous tûmes
		imp.subj.	je me tusse, nous nous tussions

teindre   (*same conjugation pattern as* **éteindre**)

tenir

part.pas.	*j'ai* tenu	**part.prés.**	tenant
prés.ind.	je tiens, nous tenons (ils tiennent)	**imp.ind.**	je tenais, nous tenions
fut.ind.	je tiendrai, nous tiendrons	**prés.cond.**	je tiendrais, nous tiendrions
prés.subj.	je tienne, nous tenions	**pas.simple**	je tins, nous tînmes
		imp.subj.	je tinsse, nous tinssions

traduire   (*same conjugation pattern as* **conduire**)

vaincre

part.pas.	*j'ai* vaincu	**part.prés.**	vainquant
prés.ind.	je vaincs, nous vainquons (il vainc)	**imp.ind.**	je vainquais, nous vainquions
fut.ind.	je vaincrai, nous vaincrons	**prés.cond.**	je vaincrais, nous vaincrions
prés.subj.	je vainque, nous vainquions	**pas.simple**	je vainquis, nous vainquîmes
		imp.subj.	je vainquisse, nous vainquissions

valoir

part.pas.	*j'ai* valu	**part.prés.**	valant
prés.ind.	je vaux, nous valons	**imp.ind.**	je valais, nous valions
fut.ind.	je vaudrai, nous vaudrons	**prés.cond.**	je vaudrais, nous vaudrions
prés.subj.	je vaille, nous valions	**pas.simple**	je valus, nous valûmes
		imp.subj.	je valusse, nous valussions

venir

part.pas.	*je suis* venu(e)	**part.prés.**	venant
prés.ind.	je viens, nous venons (ils viennent)	**imp.ind.**	je venais, nous venions
fut.ind.	je viendrai, nous viendrons	**prés.cond.**	je viendrais, nous viendrions
prés.subj.	je vienne, nous venions	**pas.simple**	je vins, nous vînmes
		imp.subj.	je vinsse, nous vinssions

vêtir

part.pas.	*j'ai* vêtu	**part.prés.**	vêtant
prés.ind.	je vêts, nous vêtons	**imp.ind.**	je vêtais, nous vêtions
fut.ind.	je vêtirai, nous vêtirons	**prés.cond.**	je vêtirais, nous vêtirions
prés.subj.	je vête, nous vêtions	**pas.simple**	je vêtis, nous vêtîmes
		imp.subj.	je vêtisse, nous vêtissions

vivre

part.pas.	*j'ai* vécu	**part.prés.**	vivant
prés.ind.	je vis, nous vivons	**imp.ind.**	je vivais, nous vivions
fut.ind.	je vivrai, nous vivrons	**prés.cond.**	je vivrais, nous vivrions
prés.subj.	je vive, nous vivions	**pas.simple**	je vécus, nous vécûmes
		imp.subj.	je vécusse, nous vécussions

voir

part.pas.	*j'ai* vu	**part.prés.**	voyant
prés.ind.	je vois, nous voyons (ils voient)	**imp.ind.**	je voyais, nous voyions
fut.ind.	je verrai, nous verrons	**prés.cond.**	je verrais, nous verrions
prés.subj.	je voie, nous voyions	**pas.simple**	je vis, nous vîmes
		imp.subj.	je visse, nous vissions

vouloir

part.pas.	*j'ai* voulu	**part.prés.**	voulant
prés.ind.	je veux, nous voulons (ils veulent)	**imp.ind.**	je voulais, nous voulions
fut.ind.	je voudrai, nous voudrons	**prés.cond.**	je voudrais, nous voudrions
prés.subj.	je veuille, nous voulions	**pas.simple**	je voulus, nous voulûmes
		imp.subj.	je voulusse, nous voulussions

Lexique Français-Anglais

The vocabulary list below includes all words occurring in the **Conversations, Structures, Applications**, and the **Cahier d'exercices**. Only numerals have been omitted. The number following the English equivalent indicates the lesson vocabulary in which a given word or expression is listed. Words and phrases *without* lesson references are those that do *not* occur in the lesson vocabularies.

1. *Nouns.* Noun gender is indicated by the article. In a few cases, however, it is shown by *m* or *f* after the noun. Irregular plural forms are listed in parentheses after the entry.

œil (yeux)	the plural form is **yeux**
bijou(oux)	the plural form is **bijoux**
cheveux *pl m*	the word normally occurs in the plural
gratte-ciel *pl invar*	the plural form is the same as the singular

2. *Adjectives.* Irregular feminine forms are indicated in parentheses. If **(e)** follows the adjective, it is regular (the feminine form is derived from the masculine by the addition of **e** in spelling). If nothing follows the masculine form, the feminine form is identical.

âgé(e)	the feminine form is **âgée**
actif(ive)	the feminine form is **active**
bref (brève)	the feminine form is **brève**
jeune	the feminine form is also **jeune**

3. *Verbs.* All irregular verbs appearing in the book are preceded by an asterisk (*) in this vocabulary. Their principal parts are listed in Appendix D.

4. *Idioms and Prepositional phrases.* Idiomatic expressions and prepositional phrases are normally listed under each word.

agent de police	listed under **agent** and **police**
bien sûr	listed under **bien** and **sûr**

5. An "aspirate" *h* at the beginning of a word blocks both liaison and elision. It is marked by a dot under the "**h**".

   ḥaut

6. "Index" refers to the grammatical index at the end of the book. Other abbreviations are listed below.

adj	adjective	*past part*	past participle
adv	adverb	*pl*	plural
f	feminine	*pres part*	present participle
fam	familiar, colloquial	*pron*	pronoun
inf	infinitive	*qqch*	**quelque chose**
invar	invariable	*qqn*	**quelqu'un**
m	masculine	*sing*	singular

A

à (*see Index*) at, to, in 2; **à la une** on the front page
abandonner to leave, abandon
À bas + *nom* ! Down with + *noun*! 24
à bicyclette on a bicycle 6
À bientôt. See you soon. 4
abondamment profusely
abonné : être abonné(e) (à) to have a subscription (to) 12
un **abonnement** subscription; **la carte d'abonnement** pass
s'abonner (à) to subscribe to 25
d'abord first of all 9; **tout d'abord** first of all
abriter to shelter; to house 16
une **absence** absence
absent(e) absent 21
absolu(e) absolute 17
absolument absolutely 17
académique academic
l'**Acadiana** *f* Louisiana Cajun country 10
l'**Acadie** *f* Acadia
acadien(ne) Acadian; **un(e) Acadien(ne)** Acadian, Cajun (*person*)
un **accent** accent 7; **accent aigu** acute accent 7; **accent circonflexe** circumflex accent; **accent grave** grave accent 7
acceptable acceptable
accepter to accept 11; **accepter de** + *inf* to accept to + *inf* 15
un **accès** access 19; **accès interdit** no entry 19; **donner accès à** to give access to
un **accessoire** accessory
un **accident** accident 10
accompagné(e) guided; accompanied
accompagner to accompany 9
un **accord** agreement; **d'accord** O.K., fine, agreed 2; **être d'accord** to agree 23
accorder : faire accorder to make agree
*****accueillir** to receive, welcome
un **achat** purchase 22; **faire des achats** to go shopping 22
acheter to buy 7; **s'acheter** to buy for oneself 22
achever to achieve, finish 16
l'**acier** *m* steel 16
à côté de next to, beside 1
acquis(e) acquired
une **acquisition** acquisition, purchase
un(e) **acrobate** acrobat
l'**Acropole** *m* Acropolis
un **acte** act

un(e) **acteur (actrice)** actor (actress) 11
actif(ive) active 8
une **action** action 14
une **activité** activity 8
l'**actualité** *f* current events; **les actualités** news (*on the radio or television*)
actuel(le) current, present
une **addition** check, bill (*café or restaurant*) 5
À demain. See you tomorrow. 1
adhésif : le ruban adhésif adhesive tape
un **adjectif** adjective
*****admettre** to admit
admirer to admire 11
adorer to love 5
une **adresse** address 3
s'addresser à to contact; to be written for
à droite on/to the right 9
un **adulte** adult
un **adverbe** adverb
adverse opposing; opponent
aérien(ne) (of) air; **la compagnie/ligne aérienne** airline
l'**aérobique** *f* aerobics 8
un **aérogramme** air letter
un **aéroport** airport
les **affaires** *pl f* belongings 11; business; **ranger ses affaires** to put away one's belongings 11
une **affiche** poster 14
affiché(e) posted
afficher to post, display (*notice, poster, etc.*)
affirmatif(ive) affirmative 17
affirmativement affirmatively 17
affirmer to affirm, assert 23
l'**Afrique** *f* Africa 9; **Afrique du Nord/Centrale/du Sud** North/Central/South Africa
agaçant(e) aggravating, irritating
agacer to irritate
à gauche on/to the left 9
un **âge** age 5; **Quel âge avez-vous ?** How old are you? 5; **l'âge d'or** the golden age
âgé(e) old 11
une **agence** agency 24; **agence de travail** employment agency 24; **agence de voyage** travel agency 24
un **agenda** appointment book
un **agent** agent; **agent (de police)** policeman 4; **agent de voyage** travel agent
une **agglomération** metropolitan area 9
s'agir (de) : il s'agit de it is a matter of, a question of 23;

de quoi il s'agit what it's about 23
un **agneau** lamb
à grand spectacle spectacular
agréable (à + *inf*) pleasant (to + *inf*) 16
Ah ! Oh! 3; **Ah bon !** Really!, I see. 1; **Ah non !** Oh, no! 1; **Ah oui ?** Really? 3; **Ah oui alors !** That's for sure! 23
une **aide** help
aider to help 9; **aider (qqn) à** + *inf* to help (somebody) + *inf* 15
Aïe ! Ouch! 13
aigu(ë) acute 7; **accent aigu** accute accent 7
une **aile** wing 16
ailleurs elsewhere, somewhere else 20; **d'ailleurs** besides 11
aimable kind, nice 18
aimer to like, love 2; **j'aimerais** I would like 12
ainsi so, thus 16; **ainsi que** as well as 16
un **air** air; looks 8; **avoir l'air** + *adj* to seem, look + *adj* 8; **de plein air** outdoor (*sport*); **en plein air** outdoors
Air France *national airline of France*
ajouté(e) added
ajouter to add 16
à la maison at home 2
à la manière de in the manner of 16
à la place de instead of 14
l'**alcool** *m* alcohol 6; alcoholic beverage
alcoolisé(e) alcoholic (*beverage*)
à l'extérieur outside 16
l'**Algérie** *f* Algeria
un **aliment** food
alimentaire alimentary, related to food
une **alimentation** grocery store
à l'intérieur inside 16
l'**Allemagne** *f* Germany 12; **Allemagne de l'Est** East Germany; **Allemagne de l'Ouest** West Germany
allemand(e) German 11; **l'allemand** *m* German language 12; **un(e) Allemand(e)** German (*person*)
un **aller (simple)** one-way ticket 19; **un aller-retour** round-trip ticket; **un aller et retour** round-trip ticket
*****aller** (*see Index*) to go; to be (*health*) 4; **aller bien à qqn** to become someone, to fit someone 11; **aller mal à qqn**

not to become someone, not to fit someone; **aller** + *destination* + **en voiture** to drive to somewhere 16

une **allergie** allergy

Allô ! Hello! (*telephone*) 4

une **allocation** allowance, aid; **les allocations de rentrée scolaire** *subsidy for back-to-school expenses*; **les allocations de salaire unique** *subsidy for single-income families*; **les allocations familiales** *subsidy for raising children*

un **allié** ally

allumer to light; to turn on 24; **s'allumer** to start up, go on

alors then 1; at that time, in that case; so; well; **alors que** while; **Ah oui alors !** That's for sure! 3

les **Alpes** *pl f* Alps

l'**alphabet** *m* alphabet

l'**alvéole** *m* ridge behind the gums

à ma montre by (according to) my watch 2

un(e) **amant(e)** lover

une **ambassade** embassy

une **ambiance** mood, atmosphere 23

une **ambulance** ambulance 13

un **aménagement** settling, arrangement

amener to bring 5

américain(e) American 1; **un(e) Américain(e)** American (*person*) 11

l'**Amérique** *f* America 9; **Amérique du Nord/Centrale/du Sud** North/Central/South America

un **ami** (*see Index*) friend (*male*) 1

amical(e) friendly

une **amie** friend (*female*) 2

à mi-temps part-time

à moins que unless 20

à mon avis in my opinion

un **amphi(théâtre)** amphitheater

une **ampoule** light bulb

amusant(e) amusing 8

un **amuse-gueule** *pl invar* appetizer, snack

amuser to amuse; **s'amuser** to have fun 13

un **an** year 5; **avoir x ans** to be x years old 5; **le Jour de l'An** New Year's Day; **tous les ans** every year; **tous les sept ans** every seven years 16

une **analyse** analysis

un(e) **ancêtre** ancestor

ancien(ne) old 8; antique; former (*before a noun*) 16

anglais(e) English 11; **l'an-**

glais *m* English language 1; **un(e) Anglais(e)** Englishman (Englishwoman) 12

l'**Angleterre** *f* England 12

angoissant(e) distressing

l'**angoisse** *f* anxiety

un **animal** animal 8

une **animation** animation; bustle

animé(e) animated 23; **un dessin animé** cartoon 23

une **année** year 3; **Bonne Année !** Happy New Year!

un **anniversaire** birthday 3; **anniversaire de mariage** wedding anniversary 21; **Bon Anniversaire !** Happy Birthday! 18

une **annonce** ad 24; **les petites annonces** *pl* want ads 24; **les annonces publicitaires** ads

annoncer to announce 17

un **annuaire** telephone directory

annuel(le) yearly, annual

annuler to cancel

anonyme anonymous 15

un **antécédent** antecedent

une **antenne** antenna 16; **Antenne 2** TV channel 2

antérieur(e) anterior

l'**anthropologie** *f* anthropology

anti-polio (le vaccin) polio vaccine

un **antiquaire** antique dealer

l'**Antiquité** *f* Antiquity 16

antiraciste antiracial, antiracist

un **antonyme** antonym

août *m* August 3

à part separate(d) 10

à peine hardly 13

*s'apercevoir de to notice; to perceive

un **apéritif** before-dinner drink 6

à peu près approximately 16

à pied on foot 6

à point medium (*meat*)

Apostrophes literary TV program

un **appareil** camera 20; apparatus; **appareil photo** camera; **Qui est à l'appareil ?** Who is speaking? 21

une **apparence** appearance

une **apparition** apparition; **faire son apparition** to appear

un **appartement** apartment 3

*appartenir (à) to belong (to) 23

un **appel** (phone) call

appeler to call 7; **s'appeler** to be called, one's name is 13; **Comment s'appelle(nt)... ?** What is (are) the name(s) of...? 3

une **appendicite** appendicitis 13

un **appétit** appetite; **Bon appétit !** Enjoy your meal. 6; **de bon appétit** heartily

applaudir to applaud 4

une **application** application

s'appliquer (à) to apply (to)

l'**appoint** *m* exact change; **faire l'appoint** to give exact change

apporter to bring 3

une **appréciation** appreciation 11

apprécier to appreciate

*apprendre to learn 6; **il apprend** he's learning 5; **apprendre à** + *inf* to learn to + *inf* 6

un **apprentissage** training period

approcher to get closer; **s'approcher de** to approach

approfondi(e) in-depth

approprié(e) appropriate

un **approvisionnement** supplies

approximatif(ive) approximate

appuyer (sur) to press, push

après after 3; **après que** after 24; **d'après** according to 10; **l'année d'après** the following year

un **après-midi** *pl invar* afternoon 2; **l'après-midi** in the afternoon; **tout l'après-midi** all afternoon 10

une **aquarelle** watercolor 11

à quelle heure at what time 2

à quelle page on what page 2

À quel nom ? What is the name? 14

à quelques minutes a few minutes (away) 9

l'**arabe** *m* Arabic language

l'**Arabie saoudite** *f* Saudi Arabia

un **arbre** tree 4

un **arc** arch 16; **l'Arc de Triomphe** Arch of Triumph 16

Archeologia monthly magazine 25

l'**archéologie** *f* archeology

un **architecte** architect 8

une **architecture** architecture

les **archives** *f* archives

l'**argent** *m* money 6; **argent de poche** spending money

une **aria** aria

aristocratique aristocratic

l'**Arkansas** *m* Arkansas River

une **arme** arm, weapon

une **armée** army 16

une **armoire** wardrobe

une **armure** armor

arracher to pull out 25

une **arrestation** arrest

un **arrêt** stop 6

arrêté(e) arrested

s'arrêter to stop 20; **s'arrêter de** + *inf* to stop + *pres part* l'**arrière** *m* back, rear 17; **à l'arrière de** in the back of 17; **en arrière** down, back

l'**arrière-pays** *m* hinterland

une **arrivée** arrival

arriver to arrive 2; to happen 10; **arriver à destination** to reach one's destination; **arriver à** + *inf* to succeed in + *pres part*

arrogant(e) arrogant

un **arrondissement** district (*in Paris*)

l'**art** *m* art 11; **les beaux-arts** fine arts

un **artichaut** artichoke

un **article** article 2; (piece of) equipment; gear; **articles en cuir** leather goods

artificiel(le) artificial

un(e) **artiste** artist

artistique artistic

un **ascenseur** elevator 9; **en ascenseur** in an elevator 9

l'**Ascension** *f* Ascension Day

à sensation sensationalistic

l'**Asie** *f* Asia

un **aspect** aspect

une **asperge** asparagus 6

aspiré(e) aspirate

une **aspirine** aspirin 7

assassiné(e) murdered

assassiner to assassinate, murder

*s'asseoir to sit down 19

un **assemblage** gathering

Asseyez-vous. (Please) sit down. 6

assez de enough 7

une **assiette** plate 6; **assiette de crudités** raw vegetables with vinaigrette

assis(e) seated, sitting 19; **être assis(e)** to be seated 19; **une place assise** seat

un(e) **assistant(e)** assistant; **assistant(e) social(e)** social worker

assister à to attend 13

l'**Assomption** *f* Assumption Day

assorti(e) assorted

s'assurer to make sure

un **astérisque** asterisk

l'**astrologie** *f* astrology 11

astucieux(euse) clever, cleverly done

À table ! Let's sit down (at the table)! 6

un **atelier** workshop, studio

à temps complet full-time

Athènes Athens 12

atlantique Atlantic; **l'océan Atlantique** Atlantic Ocean

une **atmosphère** atmosphere

À tout à l'heure. See you soon. 1

attaquer to attack

*atteindre to reach 24

atteler to harness

attendre to wait for 5

attentif(ive) attentive

une **attention** attention, care; **Attention !** Careful! 13; **faire attention (à)** to pay attention (to); **faire attention à ne pas** + *inf* to be careful not to + *inf*

attentivement attentively 19

attraper to catch 24

un **attribut** attribute

une **auberge** inn; **Auberge de Jeunesse** Youth Hostel

au bord de on the bank of, at the edge of 7

au centre de in the center of 16

au contraire on the contrary 2

au cours de in the course of 10

aucun(e) ... (ne) not any, not a single 23; *pron* none 25; **aucun d'entre nous** none of us 25

au-delà (de) beyond

au-dessous (de) underneath 10

au-dessus (de) above 10

auditif(ive) auditory

au fond (de) in the back (of), in the background

aujourd'hui today 2

au moins at least 2

au niveau de on/at the level of 14

auprès de near

auquel to which one

au revoir good-bye 1

aussi also, too 2; **aussi bien que** as well as 9; **aussi ... que** as ... as 11; **lui aussi** he (him) too 8

aussitôt que as soon as 15

l'**Australie** *f* Australia

autant que as much as, as many as 14

un **autobus** bus 5; **en autobus** by bus

un **autocar** bus (*interurban or sightseeing*) 16; **en autocar** by bus

automatique automatic

automatiquement automatically

l'**automne** *m* autumn 3; **en automne** in autumn

une **auto(mobile)** automobile, car 16; *adj* automotive

un(e) **automobiliste** car driver

autonome autonomous

un **autoportrait** self-portrait

une **autorisation** authorization

une **autoroute** highway 9

l'**auto-stop** *m* hitchhiking; **faire de l'autostop** to hitchhike

autour de around 11

Au travail ! Let's get to work! 12

autre other 3; **autre chose** something else 18; **qui d'autre** who else 18

autrefois long ago, before 10; **d'autrefois** of former times, of long ago

autrement otherwise

l'**Autriche** *f* Austria 12

un(e) **Autrichien(ne)** Austrian (*person*)

Au voleur ! Thief! 16

aux États-Unis in the United States 3

auxiliaire auxiliary

auxquel(le)s to which ones

avance : à l'avance ahead of time

avancer to advance 2; **avancer (de ... minutes)** to be ... minutes fast (*clock*) 2

avant before 9; **avant de** + *inf* before + *pres part* 14; **avant que** before 20; **en avant** forward, in front

un **avantage** advantage

avantageux(euse) advantageous

avant-hier the day before yesterday 10

avec with 2; **avec plaisir** with pleasure, gladly 4

l'**avenir** *m* future 15

une **aventure** adventure

une **avenue** avenue 3

avertir to notify 24

un(e) **aveugle** blind person 17

un(e) **aviateur(trice)** aviator, pilot

l'**aviation** *f* aviation

un **avion** airplane 15; **en avion** by plane; **par avion** by air mail 21

un **avis** opinion 11; **à votre avis** in your opinion 11

un(e) **avocat(e)** lawyer

*avoir (see *Index*) to have 2; **avoir besoin de** (+ *inf*) to need (+ *inf*) 7; **avoir bonne mine** to look well, healthy 13; **avoir chaud** to be warm 5; **avoir confiance (en)** to have confidence (in); to trust 18; **avoir de la chance** to be lucky 2; **avoir de la fièvre** to have a fever 13; **avoir de la veine** to be lucky 12; **avoir des nausées** to feel nauseous 13; **avoir du mal à** + *inf* to have trouble + *pres part* 18; **avoir envie de** + *inf* to feel like doing (something) 12; **avoir faim** to be hungry 5; **avoir froid** to be cold 5; **avoir hâte de** + *inf* to be eager to + *inf* 8; **avoir l'air** + *adj* to seem, look + *adj* 8; **avoir le mauvais numéro** to have the wrong number (*telephone*) 21; **avoir l'intention de** + *inf* to intend + *inf* 21; **avoir mal à** + *part of body* to have an ache or a pain in that part of the body 13; **avoir mauvaise mine** to look sick 14; **avoir peur (de)** to be afraid (of) 14; **avoir raison** to be right 5; **avoir rendez-vous** to have an appointment, a date 2; **avoir soif** to be thirsty 5; **avoir sommeil** to be sleepy 5; **avoir tort** to be wrong 5; **avoir x ans** to be x years old 5

à votre avis in your opinion 11

à votre santé to your health 15

À votre service. You're welcome. 9

avril *m* April 3

B

le **bac(calauréat)** *national examination at the end of lycée* 25

le **bachot** *familiar term for* **baccalauréat**

le **bacon** bacon 7

les **bagages** *pl m* baggage, luggage 19

la **bagarre** fight

la **bague** ring 25

la **baguette** long, thin loaf of bread 7

la **baie** bay

la **baignoire** bathtub 14

bâiller to yawn 4

le **bain** bath 6; **bain de boue** mud bath; **bain de soleil** sunbath; **prendre un bain de soleil** to sunbathe; **la salle de bains** bathroom 10

baiser to kiss

baisser to go down; to lower

le **bal** danse

le **balcon** balcony

la **balle** ball 10

le **ballon** ball; balloon 19

la **banane** banana 8

le **banc** bench

la **bande** : **bande dessinée** comic books, comics; **bande magnétique** recording tape

la **banlieue** suburb

la **banque** bank 14

la **banquette** seat (*in a train*)

le **baron** baron

la **baronne** baroness

la **barrière** barrier

bas(se) low; **À bas** + *nom* ! Down with + *noun*! 24; **en bas** down below 9

la **base** base; **base de données** data base 24

basé(e) sur based on

le **base-ball** baseball 4

la **basilique** basilica 16

le **basket(-ball)** basketball 4

le **bassin** basin

la **Bastille** Bastille 9

le **bateau** boat, ship 21; **en bateau** by boat; **par bateau** by surface mail 21

bâti(e) built, constructed

le **bâtiment** building 2

bavard(e) talkative

bavarder to chat 13

le **Bazar de l'Hôtel de Ville (BHV)** *large discount store in Paris* 22

beau (bel, belle) beautiful, handsome 4; **il fait beau** it's nice weather 4

beaucoup a lot 2; **beaucoup de** much, many, a lot of 7

les **beaux-arts** *pl m* fine arts

beige beige

un(e) **Belge** Belgian (*person*) 12; *adj* Belgian 22

la **Belgique** Belgium 12

La Belle et la Bête *Beauty and the Beast* 3

la **belle-mère** mother-in-law

la **belle-sœur** sister-in-law 25

bénéficier (de) to benefit (from)

Berne Bern 12

le **besoin** need, want 7; **avoir besoin de** to need 7; **on n'a pas besoin de** + *inf* it is not necessary to + *inf*; **si besoin est** if need be

bête stupid, dumb 8

la **bêtise** foolishness; stupidity 23

le **beurre** butter 6; **le sandwich jambon-beurre** ham in buttered French bread

le **BHV** = **Bazar de l'Hôtel de Ville** *large discount store in Paris* 22

le **bibelot** knickknack

la **Bible** Bible 24

la **bibliographie** bibliography 2

le(la) **bibliothécaire** librarian

la **bibliothèque** library 2; bookshelf

la **bicyclette** bicycle 6; **à bicyclette** on a bicycle 6

le **bidet** bidet 14

bien well; fine; very 1; **bien que** although 20; **bien sûr** of course 6; **aller bien à qqn**

to become someone, to fit someone 11; **aussi bien que** as well as 9; **Eh bien...** Well . . . 6; **Merci bien.** Thanks a lot. 9; **ou bien** or else 15; **si bien** so well **bientôt** soon 8; **À bientôt.** See you soon. 4

la **bière** beer 5; **bière (à la) pression** beer on tap 5

le **bifteck** steak 6

le **bijou(oux)** jewel

le **bijoutier** jeweler 25

bilingue bilingual

le **billet** ticket 19; note; **billet d'avion** plane ticket; **billet de tourisme** tourist ticket

la **biologie** biology

le **biscuit (salé)** cracker

le **bistrot** café, bar 20

bizarre strange 10

la **blague** joke; **Sans blague ?** No kidding? 23

blanc (blanche) white 8; **la nuit blanche** sleepless night 14; **un petit blanc** a glass of white wine

une **blanchisserie** laundry

blessé(e) wounded 16

bleu(e) blue 11

blond(e) blond; light 8

le **blouson** jacket, windbreaker 3

le **blue-jean** (*pl* blue-jeans) blue jeans 11

le **bœuf** beef 7

*boire to drink 7

la **boisson** drink 5

la **boîte** box; can; **boîte aux lettres** mailbox 21; **boîte de conserves** can; **boîte de nuit** nightclub 10

le **bol** bowl 6

bon(ne) good; right, correct 2; **Bon appétit !** Enjoy your meal. 6; **Bon, ben...** Oh, well . . . 22; **Bonne fête !** Happy saint's day! 3; **bon marché** *invar* cheap, inexpensive 12; **Ah bon !** Really!, I see. 1; **À la bonne vôtre !** To your health!; **le bon numéro** the right number (*telephone*)

le **bon** bond; **Bon du Trésor** Treasury Bond

les **bonbons** *pl m* candy 14

bondé(e) crowded 10

bonjour hello, good morning (afternoon) 1

bon marché *invar* cheap, inexpensive 12

Bonsoir Good evening 3

le **bord** edge, bank 7; **au bord de** on the bank of, at the edge of 7

bordé(e) (de) lined (with), bordered (by)
le **Bordeaux** Bordeaux wine 6
la **botanique** botany; *adj* botanical
la **botte** boot
la **bouche** mouth 13; **bouche de métro** subway entrance (*on the street*)
le(la) **boucher(ère)** butcher
se boucher to plug; to cover
la **boucherie** butcher shop 7
la **boue** mud; **le bain de boue** mud bath
bouger to move
*****bouillir** to boil 25; **faire bouillir qqch** to boil something 25
le(la) **boulanger(ère)** baker 7
la **boulangerie** bakery 7
la **boule** ball; **les boules** bocci; **jouer aux boules** to play bocci
le **boulevard** boulevard 3
bouleversé(e) very upset 17
le **boulot** job, work
le **bouquet** bouquet (*flowers*) 3
le **bouquin** *fam* book 17
les **bourgeois** *m* upper-middle-class people
la **Bourgogne** Burgundy; **de Bourgogne** Burgundy-style
la **bourse** scholarship; **la Bourse** Paris stock exchange
bousculer to bump 17
la **boussole** compass 22
le **bout** end; **au bout de** at the end of; **jusqu'au bout** until the end, all the way
la **bouteille** bottle 6; **demi-bouteille** half-bottle 6
la **boutique** boutique, shop 3
le **bouton** button 11
le **bracelet** bracelet
le **bras** arm 13
la **brasserie** café-restaurant
Bravo ! Bravo! 6
bref (brève) short 17
le **Brésil** Brazil
un(e) **Brésilien(ne)** Brazilian (*person*)
brièvement briefly 17
brillant(e) brilliant
briller to shine 4
la **brioche** sweet roll, bun
britannique British
le **brocanteur** antique dealer at flea market
la **broche** brooch, pin 11
la **brochette** shish kebob
la **brosse à dents** toothbrush 21
brosser to brush; **se brosser** to brush oneself (off) 13
brouillé(e) scrambled
le **bruit** noise 10; **faire du bruit** to make noise 19
brûler to burn; **brûler un feu rouge** to run a red light

brun(e) brown; dark 11
Bruxelles Brussels 12
la **bûche de Noël** Yule log, cake
le **budget** budget
le **buffet** buffet 6
le **bulletin météorologique** weather report
le(la) **buraliste** tobacco shop owner
le **bureau** office 1; study; desk; **bureau de poste** post office 7; **bureau de tabac** tobacco shop 7; **bureau d'information** information office; **Bureau des Objets Trouvés** Lost and Found; **bureau des P.E.T.** Post Office; **Bureau International des Poids et Mesures** International Bureau of Weights and Measures
le **Burkina Faso** Burkina Faso
le **buste** bust
la **butte** hill 16

C

ça that 5; **(Comment) ça va ?** How are you? 1; **Ça ne fait rien.** It doesn't matter. 17; **c'est ça** that's right, that's it 22
la **cabane** cabin 10
la **cabine** cabin 21; **cabine téléphonique** telephone booth
le **cabinet** office; **cabinet de toilette** bathroom (*without toilet*); **cabinet de travail** study
le **câble** cable
la **cacahouète** peanut 15
caché(e) hidden
cacher to hide 16; **se cacher** to hide (oneself)
le **caddy** folding shopping cart
le **cadeau** present 11; **faire un cadeau** to give a present
le **cadre** executive
le **café** café; coffee 5; **café au lait** coffee with hot milk; **café-couette** bed and breakfast
le **cahier** notebook 1; **cahier d'exercices** workbook 4
le **Caire** Cairo
la **caisse** cash register 22; **Caisse Nationale d'Épargne** National Savings Bank
la **caissière** cashier
le **calcul** figuring, computation 22; **faire des calculs** to do the figuring 22
la **calculatrice** calculator 21
calculer to calculate 21
le **calendrier** calendar 3
la **Californie** California
calme quiet, calm
la **calorie** calorie
le(la) **camarade** friend 3; **camarade de chambre** roommate 4
le **cambriolage** burglary

le **cambrioleur** burglar
le **Camembert** Camembert cheese
le **Cameroun** Cameroon
le **camion** truck 16
la **camionnette** station wagon; van
la **campagne** country, countryside; **à la campagne** in the country; **de campagne** country-style
le **camping** camping 3
le **campus** campus 2
le **Canada** Canada 7
canadien(ne) Canadian 3; **le(la) Canadien(ne)** Canadian (*person*)
le **canal** canal; channel
le **canapé** sofa; open-faced sandwich
le **canard** duck; **canard à l'orange** roast duckling in orange sauce; *Le Canard Enchaîné* satirical newspaper; **le confit de canard** preserved duck
la **candidature : poser sa candidature à** to apply for (*a position*)
le **caoutchouc** rubber 20
capable (de) capable (of) 20
la **capacité** capacity, ability
la **capitale** capital 9
car because, for 4
le **car** bus; **en car** by coach
le **caramel** caramel; **la crème au caramel** custard
cardinal(e) cardinal
le **carnet** notebook; book (*of stamps, etc.*)
la **Caroline du Nord** North Carolina
la **carotte** carrot 6; **carottes râpées** grated carrots with vinaigrette
la **carrière** career
la **carte** (playing) card 7; map 12; menu; **la Carte Bleue** Visa card 14; **carte d'abonnement** pass; **carte de crédit** credit card 9; **carte d'identité** ID card 9; **carte orange** metro pass; **carte postale** postcard 15; **carte verte** car insurance paper; **jouer aux cartes** to play cards 7
le **carton** cardboard
le **cas** case 24; **en tout cas** anyway; in any case 24; **selon le cas** as the case may be
la **case** box
le **casino** casino
la **casquette** cap
le **casse-noisette** nutcracker
casser to break; **se casser** to break 13

la **cassette** cassette, tape 1
le **cassis** black currant
le **cassoulet** beans with meat
le **catalogue** catalog
la **catastrophe** catastrophe
la **catégorie** kind, category
Le Cathare *restaurant in Toulouse*
la **cathédrale** cathedral 16
le **cauchemar** nightmare
la **cause** cause
  causer to cause
  caustique sharp; caustic
la **cave** cellar
la **cavité** cavity
  ce (cet, cette) (*see Index*) this,
    that 5; **ce ...-ci** this ... 22;
    ce ...-là that ... 22; **ce
    dont, ce que, ce qui** that
    which 18
  céder to give up
la **cédille** cedilla
la **ceinture** belt
  cela that 5; **cela ne vaut pas
    la peine** it's not worth the
    trouble 19
  célèbre famous 16
  célébrer to celebrate
  célibataire single, unmarried
  celui, celle, ceux, celles this
    (one), that (one), the one,
    these, those 22; **celui-ci** this
    one 22; **celui-là** that one
    22
  cent one hundred 3
le **centime** centime (*1/100 of one
    franc*)
le **centimètre** centimeter
  central(e) central
  centralisé(e) centralized
le **centre** center 16; **centre
    (commercial)** (shopping) cen-
    ter 16; **centre ville** down-
    town; **au centre de** in the
    center of 16
le **cèpe** wild mushroom; **la poêlée
    de cèpes** pan-fried wild
    mushrooms
  ce que what, that which 7; **ce
    que c'est (que)** what it is/
    they are 17
  (Ce) que... ! How ... ! 11
  ce qui that which
les **céréales** *pl f* cereal 7
la **cérémonie** ceremony
la **cerise** cherry 7
  certain(e) (de) certain; some
    19
  ces these, those 5
  cesser (de + *inf*) to stop, dis-
    continue + *pres part* 21
  c'est-à-dire that is (to say)
  c'est ça that's it, that's right
    22
  C'est dommage. It's a pity;
    That's too bad. 15
  c'est donné it's a bargain 22

  c'est ... que it's ... that/who
    14
  c'est ... qui it's ... that/who
    14
  c'est très gentil de votre part
    it's very nice of you 18
  chacun(e) *pron* each (one),
    every (one) 25
la **chaîne** chain; channel
la **chaise** chair 1
la **chaleur** heat 13
la **chambre** bedroom 3;
    chambre à coucher bedroom
    10; **chambre d'amis** guest
    room; **la femme de chambre**
    cleaning woman
le **champagne** champagne 7
le **champignon** mushroom
le(la) **champion(ne)** champion 4
le **championnat** championship
la **chance** luck 2; **avoir de la
    chance** to be lucky 2
le **changement** change
  changer (de) to change 17
  chanter to sing 22
la **chanteuse** singer
le **chapeau** hat 11
la **chapelle** chapel 16
le **chapitre** chapter
  chaque each, every 7
la **charcuterie** pork butcher shop
    7; cold cuts
le **charcutier** pork butcher
  chargé(e) (de) in charge of
le **chariot** rental cart
  charmant(e) charming
le **charme** charm
le **charter** charter
la **chasse** hunting
le **chasse-mouches** *pl invar*
    flyswatter
  chasser (de) to chase (from)
le **chat** cat 2
  châtain(e) brown (*for hair*)
le **château(x)** castle 9; **château
    de sable** sand castle 16
  chaud(e) warm 4; **avoir
    chaud** to be warm (*person*)
    5; **il fait chaud** it is warm
    (*weather*) 4
la **chaudière** furnace; boiler
le **chauffage** heat; heating
  chauffé(e) heated
le **chauffe-eau** hot-water heater
  chauffer to heat
le **chauffeur** chauffeur; driver 15
la **chaussée** pavement, road 9;
    street
la **chaussette** sock 25
la **chaussure** shoe 11
le **chef-d'œuvre** (*pl* **chefs-
    d'œuvre**) masterpiece
le **chemin** way, route 9; **chemin
    de fer** railroad
la **cheminée** chimney; fireplace
    10

la **chemise** shirt 11; **chemise de
    nuit** nightgown 13
le **chemisier** blouse 11
le **chèque** check 22; **chèque de
    voyage** traveler's check 22;
    toucher un chèque to cash a
    check
  cher (chère) expensive 9;
    dear (*before a noun*); **pas cher
    (chère)** inexpensive 9
  chercher to look for 2
le **chercheur** researcher; scientist
le(la) **chéri(e)** darling 14
le **cheval** horse 8
les **cheveux** *pl m* hair 11
la **cheville** ankle
  chevronné(e) experienced
  chez at (to) the house (store,
    office) of 4; with, among
  chic *invar* chic, elegant
le **chien** dog 2
le **chiffre** number 21; **le numéro
    à huit chiffres** eight-digit
    number
la **chimie** chemistry 2
  chimique chemical
le(la) **chimiste** chemist
la **Chine** China
  chinois(e) Chinese 11; **le chi-
    nois** Chinese language 5;
    le(la) Chinois(e) Chinese
    (*person*)
les **chips** *pl f* potato chips
le **chocolat** chocolate 5; **le pain
    au chocolat** round roll with
    chocolate inside
  choisir to choose 4
le **choix** choice
le **cholestérol** cholesterol
le **chômage** unemployment; **être
    au chômage** to be unem-
    ployed
la **chose** thing 11; **autre chose**
    something else 18; **quelque
    chose** something 5; **qqch
    de** + *adj* something + *adj*
    10
  chouette *fam* great
  Christophe Colomb Christo-
    pher Columbus
le **chroniqueur sportif** sports-
    writer
  chronologique chronological
  Chut ! Sh!
la **chute** (water)fall; **les chutes du
    Niagara** Niagara Falls
  -ci (*see Index*) this, these
  ci-dessous below
  ci-dessus above 17
le **ciel** sky 4
le **cigare** cigar
la **cigarette** cigarette 12
le **cinéma** movie theater; movies
    2
la **cinémathèque** film library 16
la **cinquantaine** about fifty

le **Cinzano** Cinzano
circonflexe circumflex; **un accent circonflexe** a circumflex accent
la **circonstance** circumstance
le **circuit** circuit
circulaire circular 16
la **circulation** traffic
circuler to go around; to drive around 16
la **cire** wax 9
le **cirque** circus
les **ciseaux** *pl m* scissors 6
la **citadelle** citadel; fort 9
la **cité (universitaire)** student dormitory area
citer to cite 13
le **citron** lemon 5; **citron pressé** fresh lemonade 5
la **civilité** politeness
clair(e) bright 14; clear 19
clandestin(e) clandestine
la **classe** class, classroom 1; **la salle de classe** classroom 1
classer to classify
classique classic(al)
la **clé** key 1; answer key 22; **fermer à clé** to lock 14
Cléopâtre Cleopatra
le(la) **client(e)** customer 5
le **climat** climate
le **climatisateur** air conditioner
la **climatisation** air conditioning 16
la **clinique** private hospital 13
le **clocher** steeple 16
le **clown** clown
le **club** club 24; **le Club Méditerranée** Club Med 24
le **Coca(-Cola)** Coca-Cola 5
la **cocaïne** cocaine
le **cocktail** cocktail; cocktail party 15
le **code** code number; **code postal** zip code
le **cœur** heart 10; center
le **cognac** cognac
le **coiffeur** barber, hairdresser 13
la **coiffeuse** beautician 13; dressing table
le **coin** corner 7; **le petit coin** rest room
coincé(e) squeezed 17
le **Cointreau** Cointreau
le **col** collar 11; **col roulé** turtleneck 11; **le pull à col roulé** turtleneck sweater 11
la **colère** anger 17; **être en colère** to be angry 17
le **colis** parcel 21
le **collaborateur régulier** columnist
le **collant** pantyhose
la **collection** collection 11
collectionner to collect 11

le(la) **collègue** colleague
coller to stick (on); to glue (on)
la **colline** hill
le **colon** settler
colonial(e) colonial
la **colonie** colony
la **colonne** column
le **Colorado** Colorado
coloré(e) brightly colored
combien (de) how much, how many 2; **combien de fois** how many times, how often 4; **combien de temps** how long 12; **Combien mesurez-vous ?** How tall are you? 11; **De combien de façons** In how many ways 17; **depuis combien de temps** (for) how long 13
combiner to combine
la **comédie** comedy; **comédie musicale** musical
comique comical 21
commander ìo order 5
comme how 3; as, like 4; since 11; **comme ça** that way 6; **comme ci comme ça** so-so 1
commémorer to commemorate 16
le **commencement** beginning
commencer to begin 2
comment how 1; **Comment !** What! 13; **(Comment) ça va ?** How are you? 1; **Comment allez-vous ?** How are you? 1; **Comment cela ?** How so? 2; **comment s'appelle(nt)** what is (are) the name(s) of 3
le **commentaire** comment; commentary 12
le(la) **commerçant(e)** merchant, shopkeeper
le **commerce** commerce, trade
commercial(e) commercial 16; **le centre commercial** shopping center 16
*commettre** to commit
la **commode** dresser 14
la **communication** phone call; connection
communiquer (avec) to be connected (with)
communiste communist
la **compagnie** company; **compagnie aérienne** airline
le **compagnon** companion
la **comparaison** comparison
le **comparatif** comparative
comparer to compare 17
le **compartiment** compartment 19
le **complément** complement; **complément d'objet direct**

direct object; **complément d'objet indirect** indirect object
le **complet** man's suit
complet(ète) full, complete 14; **à temps complet** full-time; **le pain complet** whole wheat bread
complètement completely
compléter to complete 7
le **compliment** compliment 11; **faire des compliments** to pay compliments 11
complimenter to compliment 11
compliqué(e) complicated 9
composé(e) mixed; composed 8; compound (*tense*); **le passé composé** present perfect; **la salade composée** mixed salad; **aux temps composés** in compound tenses
composer to dial 21
le **compositeur** composer 11
la **composition** composition; paper 16
composter to punch (*a ticket*) 19
le **composteur** ticket-punching machine 19
la **compréhension** comprehension
*comprendre** to understand 6; to include; to consist of
compris(e) included 6; **non compris** not included; **y compris** including
*compromettre** to compromise
le **compromis** compromise
le(la) **comptable** accountant
le **comptant** cash; **acheter au comptant** to buy with cash
le **compte** account; **compte d'épargne** savings account; **compte en banque** bank account; **compte rendu** report
compter to count 2; **compter sur** to count on 7
le **comte** count
concerner to concern 23; **en ce qui concerne** concerning 23
le **concert** concert 3
le(la) **concierge** building superintendent 6
la **Conciergerie** *monument in Paris*
la **conclusion** conclusion
le **concombre** cucumber
conditionnel(le) conditional
le **conditionnel** conditional 17
le **conducteur** leader; conductor
*conduire** to drive; to lead 16; **conduire** + *person* + *destination* to drive (take) somebody

somewhere; **le permis de conduire** driver's license 22
le **conférencier** lecturer
la **confiance** trust, confidence 18; **avoir confiance en** to have confidence (in); to trust 18
confidentiel(le) confidential
le **confit** duck or goose cooked in its own fat and preserved
la **confiture** jam 7
le **conflit** conflict
le **confort** comfort 11
confortable comfortable 9
confortablement comfortably 19
confus(e) embarrassed 18
le **congé** leave, day off 3
le **Congo** Congo Brazzaville
la **conjonction** conjunction
la **conjugaison** conjugation
conjugué(e) conjugated
conjuguer to conjugate 6
la **connaissance** knowledge; acquaintance 8; **faire la connaissance de qqn** to make somebody's acquaintance 8
*****connaître** to know; to be familiar with 8
connu(e) known
consacré(e) (à) devoted (to)
se **consacrer à** to be devoted to
le **conseil** advice 7
conseillé(e) advised
conseiller to advise 22; **conseiller à qqn de** + *inf* to advise somebody to + *inf* 22
consentir à (+ *inf*) to consent, agree to (+ *inf*) 21
conservateur(trice) conservative
le **conservatoire** conservatory
conservé(e) preserved
conserver to preserve
les **conserves** *pl f* canned goods
considéré(e) considered
considérer to consider 16
la **consigne** checkroom; locker 19
le **consommateur** consumer
le **consommé** broth
consommer to use up
consonantique of consonants
la **consonne** consonant
constamment constantly 17
constant(e) constant
consterné(e) in dismay
constituer to make up; to represent 16
la **construction** building; construction 16
*****construire** to build; to construct 16
construit(e) built, constructed

consulter to consult 18
contemporain(e) contemporary
*****contenir** to contain
content(e) content, glad 8; **être content(e) de** + *inf* to be satisfied/glad + *inf* 20
se **contenter (de)** to make do (with)
le **contenu** contents 6
le **contexte** context
le **continent** continent
continental(e) continental
continu(e) continuous
continuel(le) continual
continuer to continue; to go on 5; **continuer à** + *inf* to continue to + *inf* 21
la **contraction** contraction
la **contradiction** contradiction; **être en contradiction avec** to disagree with
le **contraire** contrary, opposite; **au contraire** on the contrary 2
contrairement à contrary to
le **contraste** contrast
contre against; **par contre** on the other hand
la **contrefaçon** counterfeit; counterfeiting
contribuer to contribute
le **contrôle** verification; control, supervision
contrôlé(e) controlled; checked
le **contrôleur** ticket collector, inspector
convenable appropriate, decent 23
convenir (à) to suit
la **conversation** conversation 5
le **copain** friend, pal 4
Copenhague Copenhagen
copier to copy 5
la **copine** friend, pal
le **coquillage** shellfish
la **corbeille** wastebasket 1
la **corde** : **cordes vocales** vocal cords, larynx
le **cordon-bleu** gourmet cook 11; **le Cordon-Bleu** *famous cooking school in Paris*
la **corne** horn
le **corps** body 13
le **correcteur** proofreader
la **correspondance** correspondence; connection; transfer 17
le **correspondant** party (*telephone*) 21; correspondent
correspondre (à) to correspond (to)
corriger to correct 7
le **corollaire** result, consequence
le **costume** outfit; costume
la **côte** hill 9; coast; cutlet; **la Côte d'Azur** French Riviera; **la Côte-d'Ivoire** Ivory Coast

coté(e) prestigious; **plus coté** higher (*degree*)
le **côté** side; **à côté de** next to, beside 1; **de ce côté** in that direction; **d'un autre côté** on the other hand; **mettre de côté** to save
la **côtelette** chop
le **cou** neck 13
couchage : **le sac de couchage** sleeping bag
coucher to go to bed 10; **se coucher** to go to bed 13
la **couchette** economy-class berth 19; **la voiture-couchettes** economy sleeping car 19
la **couette** comforter; **le café-couette** bed and breakfast
la **couleur** color 13; **de quelle couleur** what color 13
le **couloir** hall, hallway 1
le **coup de main** help; helping hand 18; **coup de pied** kick; **coup de téléphone** phone call 15; **donner un coup de main** to give a hand; to assist 18
la **coupe** cup; parfait glass; **la Coupe** Cup (*sports*)
coupé(e) cut
couper to cut 6; **se couper** to cut oneself 13
le **couple** couple 6
courant : **tenir au courant** to keep informed
*****courir** to run 20
le **courrier** mail 25
le **cours** course; class 1; **cours (du change)** exchange rate 22; **au cours de** in the course of 10
la **course** errand 7; race; **faire des courses** to do/run errands 7
le **court** court 4; **court de tennis** tennis court
court(e) short 8
le(la) **cousin(e)** cousin 8
le **couteau** knife 6; **couteau de poche** camping knife 22; **couteau suisse** Swiss army knife 7
coûter to cost 11; **coûter cher** to cost a lot 20
la **couture** sewing; **la haute couture** high fashion
le(la) **couturier(ière)** dressmaker; fashion designer
le **couvert** cover; cover charge; **mettre le couvert** to set the table
couvert(e) (de) covered (with) 16
la **couverture** blanket
*****couvrir (de)** to cover (with)

cracher to spit 17
***craindre** to fear 24
la **cravate** tie 11
le **crayon** pencil 1
la **création** creation
la **crèche** manger; nativity scene
le **crédit** credit 9; **à crédit** on credit; **la carte de crédit** credit card 9
créer to create
un **crème** a cup of coffee with milk
la **crème** cream 7; **crème au caramel** custard with caramel sauce
la **crémerie** cheese and milk shop 7
le **crémier** dairy merchant
créole Creole
la **crêpe** crepe 16
la **crevette** shrimp 19; **le filet à crevettes** fishing (*literally,* shrimp) net 19
le **cri** scream
le **criminel** criminal
la **crise** crisis 17; **crise cardiaque** heart attack 17
le **cristal** crystal
le **critère** criterion
le **critique** critic 23
la **critique** criticism
le **croco(dile)** alligator leather 11
***croire (à)** to believe (in); to think 11; **croire au père Noël** to believe in Santa Claus; to be naïve 11; **croire en Dieu** to believe in God; **Je crois que oui/non.** I think so/I don't think so. 11
le **croisement** crossing, crossroad
le **croissant** croissant 12
la **croix** cross
le **croque-madame** *grilled ham and cheese sandwich with an egg on top*
le **croque-monsieur** *grilled ham and cheese sandwich* 5
cru(e) raw
les **crudités** *pl f* raw vegetables with vinaigrette
la **cuillère** spoon 6
le **cuir** leather 22; **les articles en cuir** leather goods
***cuire** to cook 25; **faire cuire qqch** to cook something 25
la **cuisine** kitchen 6; cooking 10; food; **cuisine minceur** low-calorie cooking; **faire la cuisine** to do the cooking 10
cuisiné(e) prepared; **les plats cuisinés** prepared food
la **cuisinière** stove, range
la **cuisse** thigh; **cuisse de grenouille** frog leg
cuit(e) cooked 22; **bien cuit(e)** well-done; **trop cuit(e)** too well-done 22

cultivé(e) educated, knowledgeable; cultivated
cultiver to cultivate
la **culture** culture
culturel(le) cultural
la **cure** treatment in a spa
curieux(euse) curious 22
le(la) **curiste** patient in a spa
le **C.V.** curriculum vitae, résumé 24
le **cycle** cycle
le **cyclisme** cycling
le **cycliste** cyclist
le **cyclomoteur** moped

D

d'abord first of all 9
d'accord OK, fine, agreed 2; **être d'accord** to agree 23
le(la) **dactylo** secretary
d'ailleurs besides 11
le **Dakota du Sud** South Dakota 12
la **dame** lady 1
le **Danemark** Denmark
le **danger** danger
dangereux(euse) dangerous 8
le(la) **Danois(e)** Dane
dans in, inside 1
la **danse** dance
danser to dance 7
d'après according to 10
la **date** date 3; **date limite** deadline
dater (de) to date (back to) 16
de (*see Index*) of 1; **de ... à** from . . . to 2
le **débat** debate
déboucher to open into
debout standing 19; **être debout** to be standing 19
le **début** beginning 10; **au début de** at the beginning of
le **débutant** beginner
débuter to begin one's career
décembre *m* December 3
***décevoir** to disappoint
décider (de) to decide (to do) 10
la **décision** decision
la **déclaration** declaration; statement 3
déclarer to declare 16
déclencher (qqch) to get (something) started
De combien de façons In how many ways 17
le **décor** decor 23
le(la) **décorateur(trice)** interior decorator 8
décoré(e) (de) decorated (with)
découragé(e) discouraged
découvert(e) discovered
la **découverte** discovery
***découvrir** to discover; to uncover 14

***décrire** to describe 14
décrit(e) described
décrivez describe 4
décrocher to unhook, lift (*telephone receiver*)
déçu(e) disappointed
de droite (on the) right 3
le **défaut** flaw, defect; shortcoming
défendre to defend; to forbid 19; **défendre à qqn de** + *inf* to forbid somebody to + *inf* 22
défendu(e) forbidden 17
la **défense** military defense; **la Défense** *modern neighborhood in Paris*; **défense de** + *inf* it is forbidden to + *inf*
déficient(e) deficient
le **défilé de mode** fashion show
défini(e) definite; defined
définir to define
la **définition** definition
de gauche (on the) left 3
dehors outside 10
déjà already 2
déjeuner to eat lunch 2
le **déjeuner** lunch 6; **le petit déjeuner** breakfast 6
le **Delaware** Delaware
délicieux(euse) delicious 5
délivré(e) issued
demain tomorrow 2; **À demain.** See you tomorrow. 1
la **demande** application 24; **faire une demande** to apply, make an application 24; **sur demande** upon request
demander to ask (for) 2; **demander à qqn de** + *inf* to ask somebody to + *inf* 22
déménager to move 12
demeurer to live
demi(e) half 2; **la demi-bouteille** half-bottle 6; **la demi-heure** half an hour; **le demi-million** half-million; **la demi-tasse** small cup (of coffee)
la **démission** resignation; **donner sa démission** to resign
la **demoiselle** young lady
démolir to demolish 16
démonstratif(ive) demonstrative
dense dense
la **dent** tooth 13; **la brosse à dents** toothbrush 21
le(la) **dentiste** dentist 3
le(la) **dépanneur(euse)** repairman (repairwoman) 25
le **départ** departure
le **département** department
le **dépassement** passing
dépasser to exceed 9; to pass
se **dépêcher** to hurry up 13

dépendre : cela dépend that depends

la **dépense** expense

dépenser to spend

dépit : en dépit de in spite of

déplacer to move; **se déplacer** to move; to travel 17

*__déplaire (à)__ to displease 23

de plus moreover

la **déportation** deportation

déporter to deport

déposer to deposit; to drop

dépouiller to strip

déprimant(e) depressing 10

depuis since, for, from 11; **depuis combien de temps** (for) how long 13; **depuis quand** since when/how long 13

de quelle couleur what color 13

déranger to disturb 22

De rien. You're welcome. 1

dernier(ière) last 3; **le dernier à + *inf*** the last to + *inf*

derrière behind 1

le **derrière** behind

des some 1

dès from; **dès l'instant que** as soon as; **dès que** as soon as 15

désagréable unpleasant 17

descendant(e) descending, falling

descendre (de) to go down; to get off 5

la **description** description

désespérément desperately

désespérer to drive to despair

se déshabiller to get undressed 13

désigner to designate

le **désinfectant** disinfectant

désirer to desire 19

désolé(e) sorry 14

le **despotisme** despotism

desquel(le)s of which ones 22

le **dessert** dessert 6

le **dessin** drawing; **dessin animé** cartoon 23; **dessin humoristique** cartoon

le(la) **dessinateur(trice)** draftsman (draftswoman); designer

dessiné(e) : la bande dessinée comic book, comics

dessiner to draw, design

dessous : au-dessous de underneath 10; **ci-dessous** below

dessus : au-dessus de above 10; **ci-dessus** above 17; **là-dessus** concerning it 23

le(la) **destinataire** addressee

la **destination** destination; **arriver à destination** to reach one's destination

destiné(e) (à) intended (for) 23

le **détail** detail; **timbres au détail** stamps in small quantity

de ta part of you, on your part 12

de temps en temps from time to time 4

se détendre to relax 23

*__détenir__ to detain; to hold

le **déterminant** determiner

détester to hate 2

Détroit Detroit

*__détruire__ to destroy 16

la **dette** debt

le **DEUG = Diplôme d'Études Universitaires Générales**

deux points colon

devant in front of 1

le **développement** development

se développer to develop

*__devenir__ to become

deviner to guess 7

la **devise** motto

*__devoir__ (*see Index*) to owe; to have to, must 15

le **devoir** homework 4; duty

de votre part of you, on your part 20

d'habitude usually 16

le **diabolo-menthe** *mint-flavored drink*

le **dialogue** dialogue 9

le **diamant** diamond

la **diapo(sitive)** slide 16

la **dictée** dictation

le **dictionnaire** dictionary 15

le **dieu** God; **Mon Dieu !** Goodness! 6; **croire en Dieu** to believe in God

la **différence** difference 14

différent(e) different

difficile (à + *inf*) difficult (to + *inf*) 2; fussy

la **difficulté** difficulty

digestif(ive) digestive

le **digestif** after-dinner drink

la **digestion** digestion

diligemment diligently 17

diligent(e) diligent 17

le **dimanche** Sunday 3

la **dimension** dimension

le **diminutif** nickname

la **dinde** turkey 25

dîner to have dinner 4

le **dîner** dinner 6

le **diorama** diorama 9

le(la) **diplomate** diplomat

le **diplôme** diploma 24

diplômé(e) : être diplômé(e) de to hold a degree from

*__dire__ to say; to tell 10; **dire à qqn de + *inf*** to tell somebody to + *inf* 10, 22; **dire qqch à qqn** to tell somebody something; **Dis donc !** Say!, Hey! 11; **Dites donc** Say

7; **c'est-à-dire** that is (to say); **se dire** to say to oneself; **Elle a dit que oui.** She said so.; **Elle a dit que non.** She said no.

direct(e) direct; **en direct** live (*radio, television*)

directement directly 18

le **directeur** director, manager 24

la **direction** direction; management; leadership; supervision 17

se diriger vers to go toward; to prepare oneself for

la **disco(thèque)** disco 20

le **discours** speech

discret(ète) discreet 8

discrètement discreetly 17

la **discussion** discussion 23

discuter (de) to discuss 18

*__disparaître__ to disappear

disperser to disperse

la **disponibilité** availability

disponible available

la **disposition : être à la disposition de** to be available to

la **dispute** argument, fight

le **disque** record 9

la **disquette** floppy disk(ette) 7

la **distance** distance; **à distance** from afar; long-distance

la **distinction** distinction

distinguer to distinguish

la **distraction** recreation, entertainment

se distraire to entertain oneself

distribuer to distribute 17

la **distribution** distribution

divers(e) diverse, varied; **les faits divers** minor news items

divisé(e) divided

divorcé(e) divorced

la **Dixième** second grade

la **dizaine** about ten 23

d'occasion second-hand, used 22

le **docteur** doctor 13

le **doctorat** doctorate, Ph.D.

le **document** document

le **documentaire** documentary 23

le **dodo** sleep; **faire dodo** *fam* to go nighty-night

le **doigt** finger 7

on doit we must 14

le **dollar** dollar 14

le **domaine** field

le **domicile** home, residence; **domicile habituel** permanent address

la **domination** domination

dominé(e) dominated

dominer to dominate 16

Dommage ! It's a pity! 15; **C'est (Il est) dommage.** It's a pity; That's too bad. 15; **Quel dommage !** What a pity! 15

les **données** *pl f* data 24; **la base de données** data base 24

donc so, therefore; then 12; **Dis donc !** Say!, Hey! 11; **Dites donc !** Say!; Hey! 7

donner to give 3; **donner accès à** to give access to; **donner droit à** to entitle to; **donner rendez-vous à qqn** to make an arrangement to meet somebody 20; **donner sa démission** to resign; **donner sur** to open out on 14; **donner un coup de main** to give a hand 18

dont of whom, which; whose 18

la **Dordogne** Dordogne River 7

*dormir to sleep 13

le **dos** back 13; **le sac à dos** backpack 7

le **dossier** folder; résumé; dossier 24

d'où from where 7; hence

la **douane** customs 14; **passer la douane** to go through customs

le **douanier** customs official 10

le **double** twice the amount 22; *adj* double

doublé(e) dubbed

la **douche** shower 6

le **doute** doubt; **sans doute** probably

douter (de) to doubt 20

douteux(euse) doubtful 19

doux (douce) soft, gentle; mild; sweet

le **drame** drama

le **drap** sheet

le **drapeau** flag

la **drogue** drug

le **droit** law; right; **donner droit à** to entitle to

droit(e) straight 9; right (*hand, foot*) 13; **à droite** on/to the right 9; **de droite** (on the) right 3; **tout droit** straight ahead 9

drôle funny 3

le **Dubonnet** Dubonnet 15

d'une autre façon in another way 3

duquel of which one 22

dur(e) hard 6; solid, harsh; hard-boiled; **être dur(e) d'oreille** to be hard of hearing 6

durer to last 12

la **dynamite** dynamite

E

l'**eau** *f* water 5

échangé(e) switched

échanger to exchange, switch

échapper à to escape

un **échec** failure, fiasco

éclairer to light up

une **école** school 12; l'**École Supérieure de Commerce de Paris** *business school in Paris*

l'**économie** *f* economics; **les économies** savings

économique economic(al)

économiser to save (money)

écouter to listen (to) 2

un **écouteur** (telephone) receiver (*for listening only*)

écrémé(e) skimmed; **le lait écrémé** skimmed milk

une **écrevisse** crawfish

*écrire to write 12

écrit(e) written 8

une **écriture** writing 17

un **écrivain** writer 11

un **édifice** building

un **éditeur** publisher

un **éditorial** editorial

une **éducation** education

éduqué(e) educated

effacer to erase 7

un **effet** effect, result; **en effet** indeed, in fact 13

également likewise, also 16

s'égarer to wander

une **église** church 9

l'**Égypte** *f* Egypt 16

un(e) **Égyptien(ne)** Egyptian (*person*)

Eh bien... Well . . . 6

une **élection** election

un(e) **électricien(ne)** electrician

l'**électricité** *f* electricity

électrique electric(al)

l'**électro-ménager** *m* home appliances

électronique electronic

élégamment elegantly 17

l'**élégance** *f* elegance 11

élégant(e) elegant 11

un **élément** element 16

un(e) **élève** pupil, student

élevé(e) raised; high

éliminé(e) eliminated

elle she 1; **elle-même** herself 11; *disjunctive (see Index)* 12

Elle fashion magazine 25

emballé(e) carried away, enthusiastic

embauché(e) hired

une **embouchure** mouth of a river

un **embouteillage** traffic jam, bottleneck

*émettre to emit; to broadcast

une **émission** TV program 3

emmener to take, take away 16

une **émotion** emotion

émouvant(e) moving

empêcher (qqn de + *inf*) to prevent (somebody from + *pres part*) 22

emphatique emphatic

un **emploi** use; employment 24; **emploi d'été** summer job 24; **emploi du temps** schedule

un(e) **employé(e)** employee 7; **employé(e) de bureau** office worker

employer to use 7

emporter to take out

emprunter (à) to borrow (from) 18

en (*see Index*) in 1; of it 14; **en** + *pres part* while/by doing (something) 22; **en arrière** down, back; **en ascenseur** in an elevator 9; **en avant** forward, in front; **en bas** down below 10; **en ce moment** right now 7; **en dépit de** in spite of; **en direct** live (*radio, television*); **en effet** indeed, in fact 13; **en face de** opposite, across from 21; **en général** generally 6; **en haut** upstairs; above 10; **en haut de** at (to) the top of; **en même temps** at the same time 22; **en PCV** collect (call) 21; **en plein air** outdoors; **en plus** besides, in addition 22; **en recommandé** by registered mail 21; **en retard** late 1; **en route** on the way 21; **en solde** on sale 11; **en sus** extra 20; **en tant que** as, in the capacity of 24; **en tout** in all, altogether 21; **en tout cas** in any case 24; **en ville** downtown 10; **en voiture** by car 6

encercler to encircle

un **enchaînement** linking

enchanté(e) (de) delighted, thrilled (by, to do) 15

encore still; again 4; **encore de** + *definite article* some more; **encore une fois** one more time; **pas encore** not yet 18

encourager (qqn à + *inf*) to encourage (somebody to + *inf*) 22

un **endroit** place, spot 17

l'**énergie** *f* energy 7

énergique energetic 8

énergiquement energetically 17

énervé(e) nervous

une **enfance** childhood
un **enfant** child 4
  enfin finally; in short 18
  s'enflammer to burn with passion
  engagé(e) hired
  engager to engage; to start
un **engrais** fertilizer
  enlever to remove; to take off
un **ennemi** enemy
un **ennui** trouble, problem 12;
  boredom 20
  ennuyé(e) bothered, upset;
  annoyed 17
  s'ennuyer to be bored 13
  ennuyeux(euse) boring 8
  énorme enormous, huge 6
  énormément very much 23
  enregistré(e) recorded
un **enseignement** teaching,
  education
  enseigner to teach
  ensemble together 2
un **ensemble** outfit 11; group
  ensuite next, then 7
  entendre to hear 5; **entendre
  dire** to hear (somebody say);
  s'entendre avec to get along
  with 24; **bien entendu** of
  course
un **en-tête** headline
  entier(ière) entire, whole
  entouré(e) (de) surrounded (by)
  9
  entre between, among 5
  entrecoupé(e) broken
une **entrée** entrance 9; first course
une **entreprise** firm
  entrer (dans) to enter, go in
  2
  ***entretenir** to entertain; to main-
  tain, support
une **énumération** list
  envahir to invade
une **enveloppe** envelope 3
une **envie** desire, longing 12; **avoir
  envie de** + *inf* to feel like +
  pres part 12
  environ around 22
  envoyé(e) sent
un **envoyé (spécial)** (special)
  correspondent
  ***envoyer** to send 7
  épais(se) thick 14
une **épargne : la Caisse Nationale
  d'Épargne** national savings
  bank; **le compte d'épargne**
  savings account
  épargner to save (*money*)
une **épaule** shoulder 8
  épeler to spell 6
une **épicerie** grocery store 7
un(e) **épicier(ière)** grocer
les **épinards** *pl m* spinach 8
  l'**Épiphanie** *f* Epiphany
une **époque** era 16; **la Belle**

Époque turn of the century
  épouvantable dreadful
l'**épouvante** *f* horror; **le film
  d'épouvante** horror movie
  épuisé(e) exhausted
une **équipe** team 11
  équipé(e) equipped
un **équivalent** equivalent 14
une **erreur** error, mistake 14
un **escalator** escalator 16
un **escalier** staircase 10; **escalier
  roulant** escalator
une **escalope** cutlet (*veal*)
un **escargot** snail 12; **escargots
  de Bourgogne** *snails baked
  in shell with butter, garlic,
  minced parsley, and shallot*
un **espace** space 16
  l'**Espagne** *f* Spain 12
  espagnol(e) Spanish 11; **l'espagnol** *m* Spanish language
  6; **un(e) Espagnol(e)** Span-
  iard 12
  espèces *f* : **payer en espèces**
  to pay cash
  espérer to hope 6; **J'espère
  que oui.** I hope so. 24;
  J'espère que non. I hope
  not.
  l'**espionnage** *m* espionage; **le
  film d'espionnage** spy movie
  essayer to try (on) 3; **essayer
  de** + *inf* to try to + *inf*
  l'**essence** *f* gasoline
  essuyer to wipe 7
  l'**est** *m* east; **de l'est** east; **le
  nord-est** northeast
  est-ce que... ? *question marker*
  (*see Index*) 1
un(e) **esthéticien(ne)** beautician
un **estomac** stomach
  et and 1; **et toi ?** and you?,
  what about you? 1; **et vous ?**
  and you?, what about you? 1
  établir to establish
un **établissement** establishment,
  place
un **étage** floor, story 10; **au pre-
  mier/deuxième étage** on the
  second/third floor
une **étagère** bookshelf
une **étape** section
un **état** state 9; condition
les **États-Unis** *pl m* the United
  States 3; **aux États-Unis** in
  the United States 3
  l'**été** *m* summer 3; **en été** in
  the summer
  ***éteindre** to extinguish; to turn
  off 24; **s'éteindre** to go off
une **étiquette** label 21
une **étoile** star 16
  étonnant(e) astonishing 19
  étonné(e) (de) astonished, surprised 20

  étonner to astonish
  étranger(ère) foreign 5
un(e) **étranger(ère)** foreigner;
  stranger 14; **à l'étranger**
  abroad
  ***être** (*see Index*) to be 1; **être
  abonné(e) (à)** to have a subscription (to) 12; **être à la
  disposition (de)** to be available; **être à la maison** to be
  (at) home 2; **être à l'heure**
  to be on time 19; **être à la
  retraite** to be retired; **être à
  qqn** to belong to someone
  12; **être au régime** to be on
  a diet; **être content(e) de** +
  inf to be satisfied/glad + *inf*
  20; **être d'accord** to agree
  23; **être debout** to be standing 19; **être diplômé(e) (de)**
  to hold a degree (from); **être
  dur(e) d'oreille** to be hard of
  hearing 6; **être en colère** to
  be angry 17; **être en contradiction (avec)** to disagree
  (with); **être en panne** to be
  broken, not to be working 2;
  être en retard to be late 1;
  être en train de + *inf* to be
  in the process of + *pres part*
  22; **être habitué(e) à** to be
  used to 21; **être pressé(e)**
  to be in a hurry 15; **c'est ça**
  that's right, that's it 22
  étroit(e) narrow
une **étude** study 9; **faire ses
  études** to study
un **étudiant** (male) student 1
une **étudiante** (female) student 1
  étudier to study 2
  Euh... Well . . . (*hesitation*)
  l'**Europe** *f* Europe 4; **Europe
  Occidentale/Centrale/de l'Est**
  Western/Central/Eastern Europe
  eux them 12; **eux aussi** they
  also; **eux-mêmes** themselves
  s'évanouir to faint
un **événement** event 24
  l'**Évian** *m* *Évian mineral water*
  évidemment obviously; of
  course
  évident(e) obvious 19
un **évier** kitchen sink
  éviter (de) to avoid (doing)
  évoquer to evoke, conjure up
  (*in one's mind*)
  exact(e) exact
  exactement exactly 7
  l'**exactitude** *f* exactness
  exagérer to exaggerate 18
un **examen** exam, test 2; **passer
  un examen** to take an exam
  17; **réussir à un examen** to
  pass an exam 11

examiner to examine 14
excellent(e) excellent 15
excentrique eccentric
une **exception** exception
exceptionnel(le) exceptional 11
exceptionnellement exceptionally
excessif(ive) excessive
excessivement excessively
une **excursion** excursion 12
exclamatif(ive) exclamatory
une **exclusion : à l'exclusion de** excluding, except
une **excursion** excursion 12
excuse-moi excuse me 1
excuser (**qqn de** + *inf*) to excuse (somebody for + *pres part*) 22; **s'excuser** to apologize 17
excusez-moi excuse me 1
un **exemple** example 11
exercer to practice; to do; to hold (*a job*)
un **exercice** exercise 1; **le cahier d'exercices** workbook 4
exigeant(e) demanding 24
exiger to demand 19
exister to exist 16
exorbitant(e) exorbitant
expédier to send
un(e) **expéditeur(trice)** sender
une **expérience** experience; experiment 24
expérimenté(e) experienced
un **expert** expert
une **explication** explanation 9
expliquer to explain 10
un **explorateur** explorer
une **exploration** exploration 9
explorer to explore
exposé(e) exhibited 19
exposer to exhibit
une **exposition** exhibition 16
exprès on purpose 17; **faire exprès** to do on purpose 17
express express
une **expression** expression; phrase 9
exprimer to express 11
l'**extérieur** *m* outside, exterior 16; **à l'extérieur** outside 16
un **extrait** excerpt
extraordinaire extraordinary 16
extrêmement extremely
l'**extrémité** *f* outer limit

F

fabriquer to manufacture 12
fabuleux(euse) fabulous
la **façade** front (*of a building*)
la **face** face; **en face de** opposite, across from 21

fâché(e) angry; sorry 12
facile (**a** + *inf*) easy (to + *inf*) 2
facilement easily 16
faciliter to facilitate
la **façon** way 3; **d'une autre façon** in another way 3; **De combien de façons** In how many ways 17; **de toutes façons** in any case
le **facteur** mailman 17
la **facture** bill
facultatif(ive) optional
la **Fac(ulté)** college, university
faible weak
la **faim** hunger 5; **avoir faim** to be hungry 5; **mourir de faim** to starve 20
***faire** (*see Index*) to do; to make; to be (*weather*) 4; to dial; **faire attention** to pay attention; **faire attention à ne pas** + *inf* to be careful not to + *inf*; **faire bon voyage** to have a good trip 9; **faire de l'auto-stop** to hitchhike; **faire de la musique** to study music; **faire de la natation** to swim; **faire des achats** to go shopping 22; **faire des compliments** to pay compliments 11; **faire des courses** to do/run errands 7; **faire dodo** to go nighty-night; **faire du bien (à)** to do some good; **faire du bruit** to make noise 19; **faire du football** to play soccer; **faire du français** to study French; **faire du jogging** to jog; **faire du patin (à glace)** to ice-skate, go ice-skating 4; **faire du ski** to ski, go skiing 4; **faire du sport** to practice sports 4; **faire du tennis** to play tennis; **faire exprès** to do on purpose 17; **faire faire qqch par qqn** to have something done by somebody 25; **faire fonction de** to act as; **faire inspecter qqch** to have something inspected; **faire la connaissance de qqn** to make somebody's acquaintance 8; **faire la cuisine** to do the cooking 10; **faire la grasse matinée** to sleep late 23; **faire l'appoint** to give exact change; **faire la queue** to stand in line 22; **faire la sieste** to take a nap 5; **faire le pont** to take a long weekend; **faire les calculs** to add up the figures; **faire manger qqn** to feed somebody; **faire partie de** to belong to; **faire**

pipi to pee 19; **faire rire qqn** to make somebody laugh; **faire sa toilette** to wash and dress; **faire sa tournée** to make one's rounds; **faire son apparition** to appear; **faire un cadeau** to give a present; **faire un petit tour** to take a short walk; **faire un pique-nique** to have a picnic 7; **faire une demande** to apply, make an application 24; **faire vérifier qqch** to have something verified; **faire visiter** to show; **se faire mal (à)** to hurt oneself 13; **Ça ne fait rien.** It doesn't matter. 17; **Fais voir.** Show me. 25; **il fait beau, chaud, du soleil, du vent, frais, froid, mauvais** the weather is nice, warm, sunny, windy, cool, cold, bad 4; **il se fait tard** it is getting late; **se faire mal à** + *part of body* to hurt that part of the body
le **fais-dodo** Saturday-night dance (*in Acadia*)
le **fait** act, action; event; fact; **les faits divers** minor news items
***falloir** to be necessary; to require 19; **il faut (que)** it is necessary (that); one must 19; **il ne faut pas** + *inf* one must not + *inf* 19
familial(e) (of) family
familier(ière) familiar
la **famille** family 4; **famille nombreuse** large family
fatigant(e) tiring 19
la **fatigue** fatigue 20
fatigué(e) (de) tired (of) 5
le **faubourg** neighborhood; **Faubourg Saint-Honoré, Faubourg Saint-Germain** *elegant neighborhoods in Paris*
Fauchon Fauchon's (*specialty store in Paris*)
il faut it is necessary; one must 19; **il ne faut pas** one must not 19
la **faute** mistake 4
le **fauteuil** armchair; **fauteuil d'orchestre** theatre seat
faux (fausse) false, wrong
le **faux-filet** sirloin
favoriser to encourage
la **fédération** federation
Félicitations ! Congratulations! 11
féliciter to congratulate 11
le **féminin** feminine; *adj* **féminin(e)** feminine
la **femme** woman; wife 8; **femme de chambre** cleaning woman

la **fenêtre** window 4
la **fente** slot
le **fer** iron; **le chemin de fer** railroad
férié : le jour férié legal holiday
ferme ; la terre ferme terra firma, solid ground
fermé(e) closed 3; **fermé(e) à clé** locked 14
fermer to close 6; to turn off; **fermer à clé** to lock 14
féroce ferocious
ferré(e) : la voie ferrée railroad
la **fête** holiday; saint's day 3; party; **la Fête de la Victoire** Victory Day; **la Fête du Travail** May Day (Labor Day); **Bonne fête !** Happy saint's day! 3
fêter to celebrate 3
le **feu** fire 24; traffic light; **brûler un feu rouge** to run a red light
la **feuille** leaf 4; sheet of paper
le **feuilleton** serial
la **fève** bean
février m February 3
le **fiancé** fiancé 17
la **fiancée** fiancée 11
la **ficelle** string
la **fiche** slip, card 4
se **ficher de** to make fun of 22
fictif(ive) fictitious
fidèle faithful
fier (fière) (de) proud (of)
la **fièvre** fever 13; **avoir de la fièvre** to have a fever 13
Le Figaro daily newspaper 25
une **figure** figure 9; face 13
le **filet** net; mesh bag 19; **filet à bagages** luggage rack; **filet à crevettes** fishing (literally, shrimp) net 19
la **filiale** subsidiary
la **fille** daughter 8; girl; **la jeune fille** girl, young lady 2
le **film** movie, film 3
le **fils** son 8
la **fin** end 16
fin(e) thin
final(e) (pl **finals**) final
la **finale** final
finalement finally 17
financier(ière) financial
les **fines herbes** pl f herbs for seasoning or garnish
finir to finish 4; **finir de** + inf to finish + pres part; **finir par** + inf to end up + pres part 22
fixe : à prix fixe set-priced
le **flacon** bottle 14
flâner to wander leisurely 22
la **fleur** flower 3
le **fleuve** river
la **Floride** Florida 9

le **foie** liver; **foie gras** liver of specially fattened goose or duck; **le mal au foie** upset liver
la **fois** time 4; **chaque fois que** each time (when); **combien de fois** how many times 4
la **fonction** function; **faire fonction de** to work as
le(la) **fonctionnaire** civil servant, state employee
le **fond** back; bottom 19; **au fond (de)** at the bottom (of), at the end (of) 19; in the background
fonder to found 16
fondre to melt 25; **faire fondre qqch** to melt something
fondu(e) melted
la **fontaine** fountain
le **foot(ball)** soccer 3; **football américain** American football
le **footing** jogging 4
la **formation** formation
la **forme** form, shape
former to form; to train 19
formidable great 2
le **formulaire** form 18
la **Formule** Formula
fort(e) strong; loud; adv loudly 21; **plus fort** louder 21; **si fort que** so much that
le **fort** fort 9
fortifié(e) fortified
la **fortune** fortune
le **forum** forum 16; **Forum des Halles** modern, undergound shopping center in Paris
le **foulard** scarf
se **fouler** to sprain 13
le **four** oven 25; **four à micro-ondes** microwave oven; **les petits fours** m bite-sized cookies
la **fourchette** fork 6
fourni(e) provided
fournir to supply, furnish
la **fourrure** fur
le **fragment** piece, fragment
frais (fraîche) cool 4; fresh 20; **il fait frais** it is cool (weather) 4
les **frais** pl m expenses
la **fraise** strawberry 5; **le lait-fraise** cold milk with strawberry syrup
franc (franche) frank 17
le **franc (F)** franc (French monetary unit) 6
français(e) French 1; **le français** French language 1; **le(la) Français(e)** Frenchman (Frenchwoman) 4
la **France** France 1; **France 3** TV channel 3

France-Soir French newspaper
franchement frankly 17
les **Franco-Canadiens** m French Canadians
francophone French-speaking 10
frapper à to knock on (a door) 3
fréquemment frequently 17
la **fréquence** frequency
fréquent(e) frequent 17
le **frère** brother 3
la **fresque** fresco
le **frigo** refrigerator
*frire to fry; **faire frire qqch** to fry something
les **frites** pl f french fries 6; **pommes (de terre) frites** french fries
froid(e) cold 4; **avoir froid** to be cold 5; **il fait froid** it's cold (weather) 4
le **froid** cold 13
le **fromage** cheese 6; **le plateau de fromages** assorted cheeses; **une omelette au fromage** cheese omelette 6
la **frontière** border
frugal(e) frugal 17
frugalement frugally 17
le **fruit** fruit 7; **fruits de mer** seafood; shellfish; **le jus de fruit(s)** fruit juice
fumé(e) smoked
la **fumée** smoke
fumer to smoke 12
le **fumeur** smoker 19
le **funiculaire** cable car 9
furieux(euse) furious 20
le **futur** future; **futur antérieur** future perfect

G

le **Gabon** Gabon
le **gadget** gadget
le(la) **gagnant(e)** winner 14
gagner to earn; to win 14; **gagner sa vie** to earn a living
la **galerie** gallery 18; **galerie d'art** art gallery 18; **les Galeries Lafayette** large department store in Paris 17
la **galette** cake; **galette des rois** Epiphany cake
le **gallon** gallon
le **gangster** gangster
le **gant** glove 11
le **garage** garage 4
le **garçon** waiter; boy 5
la **garçonnière** boys' room 10
garder to keep; **garder des enfants** to babysit
le(la) **gardien(ne)** building manager
la **gare** station 16; **gare routière** bus station 18

garer to park 9
garni(e) garnished (with a vegetable and/or potatoes)
la **Garonne** Garonne River
gaspiller to waste
gastronomique gourmet
le **gâteau** cake 15; **les petits gâteaux** cookies 3
gauche left 6; **à gauche** on/to the left 9; **de gauche** (on the) left 3
le **gaz** gas
La Gazette *first French newspaper*
gazeux(euse) bubbly, carbonated
la **gelée** jelly; **en gelée** in aspic
gêné(e) embarrassed 9
gêner to bother 14
le **général** general 16
général(e) general; **en général** generally 6
généralement generally
la **généralisation** generalization
le **généraliste** general practitioner 13; **le médecin généraliste** general practitioner 13
généreux(euse) generous 8
la **générosité** generosity
Genève Geneva 9
le **genou(oux)** knee 13
le **genre** gender; kind 21; genre
les **gens** *pl m* people 5; **les jeunes gens** young people 5
gentil(le) nice 3; **C'est très gentil de votre part.** It's very kind of you. 18
gentiment nicely, kindly
la **géographie** geography 12
géographique geographic(al)
géométrique geometric(al)
la **Géorgie** Georgia
gérer to manage
la **gestion** management
gigantesque gigantic
la **glace** ice cream 20; ice; mirror
le **glaçon** ice cube
glissant(e) slippery 9
le **golf** golf 4; **le terrain de golf** golf course
le **golfe** gulf
la **gorge** throat
gothique Gothic 16
le **gourmet** gourmet
le **goût** taste
goûter to taste 9
le **goûter** mid-afternoon snack
le **gouvernement** government
gouverner to govern 23
le **gouverneur** governor 9
la **grâce** grace; **grâce à** thanks to
gracieusement gracefully 17
gracieux(euse) gracious, graceful 17

la **grammaire** grammar 4
le **grammairien** grammarian
le **gramme** gram
grand(e) tall; great 8; **grand magasin** department store; **Grand Prix de Longchamp** *horse race in Paris*; **à grand spectacle** spectacular
la **Grande-Bretagne** Great Britain
la **grand-mère** grandmother 8
le **grand-père** grandfather 8
les **grands-parents** *pl m* grandparents 8
gras (grasse) fat 23; **le foie gras** liver of specially fattened goose or duck
gratiné(e) au gratin, with cheese and bread crumbs
le **gratte-ciel** *pl invar* skyscraper
se **gratter** to scratch oneself
gratuit(e) free of charge
grave serious 6; grave; **un accent grave** grave accent 7
la **gravure** engraving, etching 18
le(la) **Grec (Grecque)** Greek (*person*)
la **Grèce** Greece 12
le **grenier** attic 10
la **grenouille** frog 23; **la cuisse de grenouille** frog leg
grillé(e) grilled
la **grippe** flu
gris(e) gray 11; **gris-bleu** blue-gray
gros (grosse) big, fat 11
grossir to put on weight 22
grouillant(e) teeming
grouiller to swarm
le **groupe** group; **groupe prépositionnel** prepositional phrase
groupé(e) grouped
guérir to cure; to heal
la **guerre** war
le **guichet** box office; ticket window 10
le **guide** guidebook; guide 10
guidé(e) guided
guillotiner to guillotine 16
la **Guinée** Guinea
la **gymnastique** gymnastics 4

H

s'**habiller** to get dressed 13
un **habitant** inhabitant 9
une **habitation** home; lodging
habiter to live 4
une **habitude** habit; **d'habitude** usually 16
habitué(e) (à + *inf*) used to (+ *pres part*) 21
habituel(le) permanent; **le domicile habituel** permanent address
s'**habituer à** to get used to 15
la **hache** axe

haché(e) ground
Haïti *m* Haiti
une **haleine** breath; **hors d'haleine** out of breath
Les **Halles** *pl f* *wholesale food market in Paris* 16
un **hamburger** hamburger
un **haricot** bean; **les haricots verts** *m* green beans 6
la **hâte** haste 8; **avoir hâte de + *inf*** to be eager to + *inf* 8
haut(e) high, tall 16; **à haute voix** out loud 19; **du haut de** from the top of; **en haut** upstairs; above 10; **en haut de** at (to) the top of; **la haute couture** high fashion; **Haut les mains !** Hands up!
la **Haute-Volta** Upper Volta
Hawaii *m* Hawaii
La Haye The Hague 12
hebdomadaire weekly
un **hebdomadaire** weekly magazine 12
l'**hébreu** *m* Hebrew language
Hein ? What? 10
Hélas ! Alas! 15
un **hélicoptère** helicopter 23
l'**herbe** *f* grass 17; **fines herbes** herbs for seasoning or garnish
une **hésitation** hesitation
hésiter (à + *inf*) to hesitate + *inf* 21
une **heure** hour; o'clock 2; time; **à quelle heure** (at) what time 2; **À tout à l'heure.** See you soon. 1; **être à l'heure** to be on time 19; **les heures de pointe** rush hour 17; **Les 24 Heures du Mans** *car race in Le Mans*; **Quelle heure est-il ?** What time is it? 2; **un quart d'heure** a quarter of an hour 13
heureusement fortunately 19
heureux(euse) (de) happy (about/to do) 8
se **heurter (à)** to bump (into) 17
un **hexagone** hexagon
hier yesterday 9; **avant-hier** the day before yesterday 10; **hier soir** last night, yesterday evening 9
la **hiérarchie** hierarchy
l'**histoire** *f* history 2; story
historique historical 9
l'**hiver** *m* winter 3; **en hiver** in winter
le **hockey** hockey
un(e) **Hollandais(e)** Dutchman (Dutchwoman) 12

un **homme** man 4; **homme
 d'affaires** businessman;
 homme d'état statesman;
 homme politique politician
un **honneur** honor; **en l'honneur
 de** in honor of
un **hôpital** hospital 2
un **horaire** timetable, schedule 19
une **horloge** clock; **horloge par-
 lante** correct time (*telephone*)
un **horloger** watchmaker 25
une **horreur** horror; **un film
 d'horreur** horror movie
 hors d'haleine out of breath
 le **hors-d'œuvre** *pl invar* hors
 d'oeuvre 6
 hors taxe *invar* tax-exempt,
 duty-free
un **hot dog** hot dog
un(e) **hôte (hôtesse)** host (hostess)
 11; **hôtesse au sol** ground
 hostess; **hôtesse (de l'air)**
 flight attendant 18
un **hôtel** hotel 9; **Hôtel de ville**
 City Hall 9; **hôtel particulier**
 residence
 l'**huile** *f* oil
une **huître** oyster 6
 humain(e) human 13; humane
 L'Huma(nité) *Communist newspaper*
 humoristique humorous
 l'**humour** *m* wit, humor
 l'**hygiène** *f* hygiene; **les produits
 d'hygiène** health products
un **hypermarché** large supermarket and discount store

I

 ici here 5
 l'**Idaho** *m* Idaho 12
 idéal(e) ideal
 idéaliste idealistic
une **idée** idea 2
 identifier to identify
une **identité** identity 9; **la carte
 d'identité** ID card 9
 idiot(e) stupid
 idolâtrer to idolize
 il he; it 1
 il apprend he's learning 5
une **île** island 16
 **il fait beau, chaud, du soleil, du
 vent, frais, froid, mauvais**
 the weather is nice, warm,
 sunny, windy, cool, cold, bad
 4
 l'**Illinois** *m* Illinois River
 illustré(e) illustrated
 Il n'y a pas de quoi. You're
 welcome. 9
 il pleut it's raining 4
 ils sourient they smile 11

 il y a (*see Index*) there is (are)
 2; **il y a** + *time* time + ago
 9
 imaginaire imaginary
 imaginatif(ive) imaginative 11
 l'**imagination** *f* imagination 7
 imaginer to imagine 11
 imbattable unbeatable
 imiter to imitate
une **immatriculation** title registration
 immédiatement immediately
 immense immense, huge 16
un **immeuble** building 18
 immobilisé(e) immobilized
 l'**immunité** *f* immunity
 imparfait(e) imperfect
 l'**imparfait** *m* imperfect (*tense*)
 l'**impatience** *f* impatience; **avec
 impatience** impatiently
 impatient(e) impatient 18
 l'**impératif** *m* imperative (*mood*)
 impérial(e) imperial
un **imperméable** raincoat 11
 impersonnel(le) impersonal
une **importance** importance 11
 important(e) important 8
 n'importe où anywhere
 n'importe quel(le) + *nom* any +
 noun 23
 n'importe qui anyone
 n'importe quoi anything
 imposé(e) added (*tax*)
 imposer to impose; to tax
 impossible impossible 10
un **impôt** tax
une **impression** impression
 impressionnant(e) impressive,
 imposing
un **impressionniste** Impressionist;
 adj Impressionist; impres-
 sionistic
 imprévu(e) unexpected
 imprimé(e) printed
 imprimer to print
 l'**imprimerie** *f* printing
 improviste : à l'improviste
 impromptu, on the spur of
 the moment
une **incertitude** uncertainty
un **incident** incident
 inconnu(e) unknown 16
un **inconvénient** disadvantage,
 drawback
 indéfini(e) indefinite
 l'**indépendance** *f* independence
 les **Indes occidentales** *pl f* West
 Indies
un **index** index
 l'**Indiana** *m* Indiana 12
 l'**indicatif** *m* indicative (*mood*);
 code (*phone*)
une **indication** indication
un(e) **Indien(ne)** Indian (*person*); *adj*
 Indian
une **indigestion** indigestion 11

 indiqué(e) indicated 16
 indiquer to indicate 12
 indirect(e) indirect
 indiscret(ète) indiscreet 8
 l'**indiscrétion** *f* indiscretion; nosi-
 ness
 indiscutablement unquestiona-
 bly
 indispensable indispensable
 individualiste individualistic 23
 industrialisé(e) industrialized
une **industrie** industry
 industriel(le) industrial
 inférieur(e) lower 19
un **infinitif** infinitive 21
une **infirmière** nurse 3
 l'**inflation** *f* inflation
une **information** information; **les informations** news (*radio, television*); **le bureau
 d'informations** information
 office
 l'**informatique** *f* computer science 15
 informé(e) informed 23
une **infusion** herbal tea 5
un **ingénieur** engineer 11; **ingénieur-chimiste** chemical engineer
 ingénument naively
un **ingrédient** ingredient
 inhabituel(le) unusual
 **initiative : le syndicat d'initia-
 tive** tourist information office
un(e) **initié(e)** connoisseur, aficionado
 innocemment innocently
une **innovation** innovation
 inquiet(ète) worried
 s'inquiéter to worry; to be concerned 17
 *****s'inscrire (à)** to register for (*a
 course*) 24
une **insistance** insistence
 inspecté(e) inspected 16
 inspecter to inspect 14
 installé(e) settled 19
 installer to install, set up 16
un **instant** instant; **dès l'instant
 que** as soon as; **pour
 l'instant** for the time being
un **institut** institute 5
un(e) **instituteur(trice)** schoolteacher 3
une **instruction** instruction;
 schooling
 instruit(e) educated
un **instrument** instrument 17
 instrumental(e) instrumental
 insuffisant(e) inadequate
 intellectuel(le) intellectual
un **intellectuel** intellectual
 intelligemment intelligently
 17
 intelligent(e) intelligent 6
une **intention** intention 21; **avoir**

l'**intention de** + *inf* to intend + *inf* 21

interdit(e) forbidden 17; **interdit aux moins de 13 ans** children under 13 not admitted

intéressant(e) interesting 1; advantageous (*price*)

intéresser to interest 16; **s'intéresser à** to be interested in

un **intérêt** interest 8

l'**intérieur** *m* inside, interior 16; **à l'intérieur** inside 16

interminable endless

international(e) international 8

une **interprétation** interpretation

un(e) **interprète** interpreter

interrogatif(ive) interrogative

une **interrogation** interrogation

interroger to question, ask 9

interurbain(e) intercity

*intervenir to intervene

une **interview** interview 24

interviewer to interview

intestinal(e) intestinal

intime intimate

une **intonation** intonation

intrépide fearless

une **introduction** introduction

inutile useless 18

Les Invalides *pl m former residence of war veterans* 16

invariable invariable

inventer to invent

une **invention** invention

une **inversion** inversion

une **invitation** invitation 15

un(e) **invité(e)** guest 6

inviter (à) to invite (to) 6; **inviter qqn à** + *inf* to invite somebody + *inf* 6

l'**Iowa** *m* Iowa 12

l'**IRA** IRA

un(e) **Irlandais(e)** Irishman (Irishwoman)

l'**Irlande** *f* Ireland 12

irrégulier(ière) irregular

l'**Israël** *m* Israel

un(e) **Israélien(ne)** Israeli

l'**Italie** *f* Italy 12

italien(ne) Italian 11; **l'italien** *m* Italian language 12; **un(e) Italien(ne)** Italian (*person*) 12

un **itinéraire** itinerary

J

J'aimerais I would like 12

jamais ever 10; **ne ... jamais** never 12

la **jambe** leg 13

le **jambon** ham 7; **jambon cru de campagne** very thin-sliced raw ham; **jambon de Bayonne** prosciutto-type ham; **le (sand-**

wich) jambon-beurre ham in buttered French bread

janvier *m* January 3

le **Japon** Japan 12

japonais(e) Japanese 5; **le japonais** Japanese language 2; **un(e) Japonais(e)** Japanese (*person*)

le **jardin** garden 2

jaune yellow

je I 1

le **jean** jeans

Jeanne d'Arc Joan of Arc 20

Jérusalem Jerusalem

jeter to throw (away) 7; **se jeter dans** to empty into (*river*); to jump into

le **jeu** (*pl* **jeux**) game, play; gambling; **les Jeux Olympiques** Olympic Games

le **jeudi** Thursday 3

jeune young 4; **la jeune fille** girl, young lady 2; **le jeune homme** young man; **les jeunes gens** *m* young people 5; **le nom de jeune fille** maiden name

la **jeunesse** youth; **une Auberge de Jeunesse** Youth Hostel

Je vous en prie. You're welcome. 9

le **job** (part-time) job

la **Joconde** Mona Lisa 24

le **jogging** jogging

la **joie** joy 18

joli(e) pretty; nice 5

jouer (à) to play 4; **jouer aux boules** to play bocci; **jouer aux cartes** to play cards 7

le **jouet** toy 17

le **joueur** player 19

la **joueuse** player 17

le **jour** day 2; **le Jour de l'An** New Year's Day; **jour férié** legal holiday; **tous les jours** every day 4; **un de ces jours** one of these days 12

le **journal** newspaper 8; **journal à sensation** sensationalistic newspaper

le **journalisme** journalism 2

le(la) **journaliste** journalist 1

la **journée** day 10; **toute la journée** all day

joyeux(euse) joyous, merry

le **judo** judo 11

juger to judge 23

juillet *m* July 3

juin *m* June 3

la **jungle** jungle

la **jupe** skirt 11

le **jus** juice 5; **jus de fruit(s)** fruit juice

jusqu'à until 2; **jusqu'à ce que** until 20; **jusqu'au bout** until the end, all the way; **jusqu'en**

up to, until; **jusque-là** up to there 9

juste just, right 19; *adv* just 9

justement as a matter of fact; exactly 2

la **justice** justice; **le Palais de Justice** courthouse 16

K

le **Kentucky** Kentucky 12

le **kilo** kilo 11

le **kilomètre** kilometer; **kilomètre (à l')heure** kilometer per hour

le **kiosque (à journaux)** newsstand 25

L

là there 2; **là-bas** over there 1; **là-dessus** about it 23; **jusque-là** up to there 9

-là (*see Index*) that, those

le **labo** lab 9

le **laboratoire** laboratory 2

le **lac** lake 9; **le lac Supérieur** Lake Superior; **les Grands Lacs** Great Lakes

laid(e) ugly 8

la **laine** wool

laisser to leave 9; to let; **laisser le bon temps rouler** to have a good time; **laisser passer** to let through 17; **laisser tomber** to drop

le **lait** milk 5; **lait écrémé** skimmed milk; **lait-fraise** cold milk with strawberry syrup

la **lame** blade 22

la **lampe** lamp 14

lancer un appel to call for

la **langue** language 6; tongue

le **lapin** rabbit 23

sur laquelle about/concerning which 11

large wide

latin(e) Latin; **le Quartier Latin** Latin Quarter 16

le **lavabo** bathroom sink 14

laver to wash; **se laver** to wash (oneself) 13

le **lave-vaisselle** *pl invar* dishwasher

le (la, les) the 1; *pron* him, it, her, them

la **leçon** lesson 2

le **lecteur** reader 25

la **lectrice** reader

la **lecture** reading

légal(e) legal

la **légende** caption

léger(ère) light 8; slight

légèrement lightly

le **légume** vegetable 6; **la soupe aux légumes** vegetable soup

le **lendemain** next day 24
lent(e) (à + *inf*) slow (to + *inf*)
21
lequel, laquelle, lesquels, lesquelles (*see Index*) which,
which one(s) 22
la **lettre** letter 2; **les lettres**
literature
leur(s) their 4; *pron* to them
10; **le(la) leur** theirs 22
lever to raise 7; **lever la main**
to raise one's hand 7; **se
lever** to get up 13
la **lèvre** lip
le **lexique** vocabulary list
la **liaison** liaison, linking
le **Liban** Lebanon
libéral(e) liberal 8
libéré(e) freed, liberated
la **liberté** freedom 10
le **libraire** bookstore owner
la **librairie** bookstore 17
libre free, unoccupied 4
le **libre-service** self-service; **le
restaurant libre-service** cafeteria
le **libretto** libretto
la **Licence** *French university
degree*
licencié(e) kicked out, fired
la **licorne** unicorn
le **lieu** place; **lieu de travail**
place of employment; **au lieu
de** instead of
la **ligne** line 17; figure; **ligne
aérienne** airline
la **limite** limit 22; **la date limite**
deadline
la **limonade** *soft drink somewhat
like 7-Up*
la **linguistique** linguistics 24
*lire to read 12
Lisbonne Lisbon 12
lisez read 3
lisible readable, legible 17
lisiblement legibly 17
la **liste** list 16
le **lit** bed 4
la **lithographie** lithograph
le **litre** liter 7
littéralement literally
la **littérature** literature
le **livre** book 1; **livre de poche**
paperback
la **livre** pound
livré(e) delivered; issued
livrer to deliver
le **livret** booklet
local(e) local
la **location** rental
locatif(ive) locative
la **locomotion** locomotion; **le
moyen de locomotion** means
of transportation
la **locomotive** locomotive
la **locution** locution

loger to house 16
le **logiciel** software 24
logique logical
le **logis** hotel, inn
loin (de) (far (from) 9; **loin des
yeux, loin du cœur** out of
sight, out of mind; **loin d'ici**
far from here; **plus loin** farther, beyond 10
la **Loire** Loire River 8
Londres London 8
long (longue) long 8; **le long
de** along 7
longtemps (for) a long time 16
longuement at great length
la **longueur** length
les **lorgnettes** *pl f* spectacles
lorsque when
la **loterie** lottery
louer to rent 7
la **Louisiane** Louisiana 9
Louksor Luxor 16
lourd(e) heavy 8
le **Louvre** Louvre museum 16
la **luette** uvula
lui to him (her) 10; *disjunctive*
(*see Index*) 12; **lui aussi** he
(him) too 8; **lui-même** himself
la **lumière** light 14
lumineux(euse) lighted
le **lundi** Monday 3
la **lune** moon
les **lunettes** *pl f* glasses 12;
lunettes de soleil sunglasses
lutter to fight
le **luxe** luxury; **de luxe** luxury
le **Luxembourg** Luxemburg 12;
le jardin du Luxembourg
Luxemburg garden 20
le(la) **Luxembourgeois(e)** Luxemburger 12
le **lycée** French high school 8

M

ma my 3
le **machin** gizmo, whatchamacallit
22
la **machine** machine 21; **machine à laver** washing machine 21; **taper à la machine**
to type 24
Madagascar Malagasy Republic
Madame (*pl* **Mesdames**) *f* Mrs.,
ma'am 1
Mademoiselle (*pl* **Mesdemoiselles**)
f Miss 1
le **magasin** store 7; warehouse;
le grand magasin department store; **magasin de régime** health-food store
le **magazine** magazine 25; TV
show
le **magicien** magician

la **magie** magic
magistral(e) : le cours magistral lecture course
magnétique magnetic; **la
bande magnétique** recording
tape
le **magnétophone** tape recorder
1
le **magnétoscope** VCR
magnifique magnificent, splendid 4
magnifiquement magnificently
mai *m* May 3
maigre skinny; lean
le **maillot de bain** swimsuit 11
la **main** hand 3; **à la main** in
one's hand; **donner un coup
de main** to give a hand 18;
Haut les mains ! Hands up!
le **Maine** Maine
maintenant now 1
*maintenir to maintain, keep
mais but 2; **mais enfin** well;
mais non oh, no 2
le **maïs** corn
la **maison** house 1; company; **la
Maison Blanche** The White
House; **maison de la presse**
newspaper and magazine
store; **maison de poupée**
dollhouse; **à la maison** at
home 2
le **maître** master; **maître d'hôtel** :
sauce maître d'hôtel butter
seasoned with parsley and
lemon
la **maîtresse** schoolteacher 19
la **Maîtrise** *French degree more or
less like the Master's degree*
la **majuscule** capital letter
mal badly, poorly 13; **ce n'est
pas plus mal** it's not a bad
idea; **pas mal** not bad 1;
pas mal de + *nom* quite a
few + *noun*
le **mal** pain 13; **mal au foie** upset stomach; **avoir du mal à** +
inf to have trouble + *pres
part* 18; **avoir mal à** + *part
of body* to have an ache or a
pain in that part of the body
13; **se faire mal à** + *part of
body* to hurt that part of the
body
malade sick 10; **tomber malade** to get sick
le(la) **malade** patient 13
la **maladie** illness 14; **maladie
de foie** liver ailment
malgré despite
le **malheur** unhappiness, misfortune
malheureux(euse) unhappy 8;
malheureux(euse) (de) unhappy, unfortunate (about/to
do)

malheureusement unfortunately 17

le **Mali** Mali

la **maman** mom 12

la **Manche** English Channel

la **manchette** headline

le **mandat** money order; **expédier un mandat télégraphique** to wire some money

manger to eat 4

la **manière** manner; way 16; **à la manière de** in the manner of 16

le **mannequin** fashion model

le **manoir** manor 25

manquer to miss; to lack 17; **Paris me manque.** I miss Paris.

le **manteau** coat 11

le **manuel** textbook

la **maquette** (scale) model

le **Marais** neighborhood in Paris

le **marathon** marathon 20

le(la) **marchand(e)** merchant 22; **marchand de primeurs** vegetable merchant 17

marchander to haggle, bargain

la **marchandise** merchandise; piece of merchandise

la **marche** step 16; walking; **marche à pied** walking; **se mettre en marche** to start (up)

le **marché** market 22; **Marché aux Puces** Flea market 22; **marché du travail** work force; **bon marché** invar cheap, inexpensive 12; **meilleur marché** cheaper

marcher to walk 2; to work, function, run 20; **marcher sur** to step on 17

le **mardi** Tuesday 3

le **mari** husband 3

le **mariage** wedding; marriage 17; **un anniversaire de mariage** wedding anniversary 21

marié(e) married 11

la **mariée** bride; **la robe de mariée** wedding gown

Marie-France fashion magazine 25

la **marine** marine; seascape

maritime (of) sea; maritime

les **Marlboro** f Marlboro

le **Maroc** Morocco 12

marocain(e) Moroccan 5

la **maroquinerie** fancy leather shop 22

la **marque** brand, make

marquer to mark

la **marraine** godmother

mars m March 3

la Marseillaise French national anthem

Marseille Marseilles 9

le **martini** vermouth

le **masculin** masculine; adj **masculin(e)** masculine

le **massage** massage

le **Massif Central** mountainous region in center of France

le **match** game 17

les **maths** pl f math 8

les **mathématiques** pl f mathematics

Mathusalem Methuselah 24

la **matière** subject 8; **les matières premières** raw materials

le **matin** morning 2; **le matin** in the morning

la **matinée** morning, entire morning 19; **faire la grasse matinée** to sleep late 23

la **Mauritanie** Mauritania

mauvais(e) bad 4; wrong; **avoir le mauvais numéro** to have the wrong number (telephone) 21; **avoir mauvaise mine** to look sick 14; **il fait mauvais** the weather is bad 4

maximum invar maximum

me me 9; to me 10

le **mécanicien** mechanic 25

méchant(e) bad, nasty, vicious

mécontent(e) (de) dissatisfied (with) 8

le **médecin** doctor 1; **médecin généraliste** general practitioner 13

la **médecine** (field of) medicine

médical(e) medical

le **médicament** medicine 9; pl medicine

médiéval(e) medieval

médiocre mediocre 20

la **(mer) Méditerranée** Mediterranean Sea

méditerranéen(ne) Mediterranean

meilleur(e) better 11

le **mélange** mixture 5

mélanger to mix 6

le **membre** member 24

même same (before noun) 5; itself (after noun); **en même temps** at the same time 22; **quand même** anyway 11; **elle-même** herself 11

même adv even 13

-même(s) (see Index) -self (-selves)

la **mémoire** memory; **avoir bonne mémoire** to have a good memory

le **ménage** housekeeping; **un article de ménage** household item

mener à to lead to 9; to take to; to go to

mensuel(le) monthly 25

la **menthe** mint

mentionné(e) mentioned

mentionner to mention 11

le **menu** menu 6; **menu à prix fixe** set-price menu; **menu gastronomique** gourmet menu; **menu promotionnel**, **menu touristique** special-priced menu

la **mer** sea; **à la mer** at the seaside; **la mer Méditerranée** Mediterranean Sea; **les fruits de mer** seafood; shellfish

merci thank you 1; **Merci bien.** Thanks a lot. 9

le **mercredi** Wednesday 3

la **mère** mother 3

mériter to deserve

mes my 3

la **mésaventure** misadventure 17

le **message** message 21

la **messe** Mass; **messe de minuit** midnight Mass

la **mesure** measure, measurement

mesurer to measure 11; **Combien mesurez-vous ?** How tall are you? 11

le **métal** metal 8

métallurgique related to metal, metal manufacturing

la **météo** weather report

météorologique related to weather; **le bulletin météorologique** weather report

le **métier** trade, job

le **mètre** meter 11

métrique metric

le **métro** subway 16

métropolitain(e) metropolitan

le **metteur en scène** film director 23

*****mettre** to put, place; to put on (clothes) 11; **mettre à la porte** to fire; **mettre à la poste** to mail; **mettre au point** to perfect; **mettre de côté** to save (money); **mettre ensemble** to put together; **se mettre en marche** to start (up)

le **meuble** piece of furniture 14

meublé(e) furnished

meunière sauteed in butter and parsley

le **meurtre** murder

mexicain(e) Mexican; **un(e) Mexicain(e)** Mexican (person)

Mexico Mexico City 8

le **Mexique** Mexico 12

Michel-Ange Michelangelo

le **Michigan** Michigan 12

les **micro-ondes** f microwaves; **le four à micro-ondes** microwave oven le **micro-ordinateur** microcomputer 12

midi *m* noon 2

le **Midi** *south of France* 12

la **mie** sweetheart

le **mien (la mienne)** mine 22

mieux better 8; **mieux que** better than 17; **le mieux** the best 17; **Mieux vaut tard que jamais.** Better late than never.; **il vaut mieux** + *inf* it is better + *inf* 19; **il vaudrait mieux** + *inf* it would be better + *inf* 19

mil *m* one thousand 4

le **milieu** (*pl* **milieux**) middle 19; **au milieu de** in the middle of 19

le **militaire** soldier; *adj* military

mille *m* one thousand 4

le **mille** mile

le **millier** (about a) thousand

le **million** million 9

le(la) **millionnaire** millionaire 11

mince thin

minceur : la cuisine minceur low-calorie cooking

la **mine** look 13; **avoir bonne mine** to look well, healthy 13; **avoir mauvaise mine** to look sick 14

minéral(e) mineral 6

miniature miniature 9; **en miniature** miniature

le **mini-bar** mini-refrigerator

la **mini-composition** short composition

minimiser to minimize 11

le **minimum** minimum

le **ministère** ministry, cabinet

le **ministre** minister

le **Minitel** Minitel computer

le **Minnesota** Minnesota

minuit *m* midnight 2

minuscule tiny 6; lower-case

la **minute** minute 2; **à quelques minutes** a few minutes (away) 9

la **minuterie** timed light switch

mis(e) put

la **mise en scène** directing

la **mission** mission

le **Mississippi** Mississippi River

le **Missouri** Missouri 12; Missouri River

à mi-tarif half-price

à mi-temps part-time

le **mitonné** simmering soup

mixte mixed

le **mobilier** furniture

le **mode** mood

la **mode** fashion 25; **à la mode** fashionable; **le défilé de mode** fashion show; **la présentation de mode** fashion show

le **modèle** model, example;

modèle réduit scale model

moderne modern 6

moderniser to modernize; **se moderniser** to get modernized

la **modestie** modesty 11

modifier to modify, change

moi me, to me 7; *disjunctive* (*see Index*) 12; **moi aussi** me too, I also 12; **moi-même** myself 11; **Moi non plus.** Neither do I. (Me, neither.) 12; **Moi, si.** I do. 12; **Pas moi.** Not I.

moins minus 2; less; **au moins** at least 2; **le moins** the least 14; **moins de** less than 14; **moins le quart** a quarter to (*time*); **moins que** less than 14; **moins ... que** less . . . than 11; **à moins que** unless 20

le **mois** month 3

à moitié half

le **moment** moment; time 7; **en ce moment** right now 7; **pour le moment** for the time being

mon my 3; **Mon Dieu !** Goodness! 6

Monaco *m* Monaco 12

le **monde** world; *Le Monde* *daily newspaper* 25; **tout le monde** (*see Index*) everybody 6

le **moniteur** instructor

la **monnaie** change (*money*); **une pièce de monnaie** coin 21

le **monologue** monologue

le **Monopoly** Monopoly 14

monotone monotonous

Monsieur *m* Mr., sir 1

le **monsieur** gentleman 8

monstrueux(euse) monstrous

la **montagne** mountain

montagneux(euse) mountainous

montant(e) rising

la **montée** climb

monter (dans) to go up; to get on 6

Montmartre *neighborhood in Paris*

Montparnasse *neighborhood in Paris*

la **montre** watch 1; **à ma montre** by (according to) my watch 2

Montréal Montreal 8

montrer to show 9

le **Mont-Saint-Michel** Mont-Saint-Michel

le **monument** monument 3

le **morceau** piece 7

mordant(e) biting

la **mort** death 16

mort(e) dead, deceased 3; **la nature morte** still life

Moscou Moscow

la **Moselle** Moselle River

le **mot** word 2; **les mots-minute** words per minute 24

le **moteur** motor 9

la **moto** motorcycle 23; **en moto** on a motorcycle

mou (molle) soft 22

le **mouchoir** handkerchief 14

mouillé(e) wet 20

*mourir (de) to die (from) 20; **mourir d'ennui** to die of boredom; **mourir de faim** to starve 20; **mourir de soif** to die of thirst 20

la **mousse au chocolat** chocolate mousse 6

la **moustache** mustache 8; **à moustache** with a mustache

la **moutarde** mustard

le **mouton** sheep

le **mouvement** motion; movement

le **moyen** means 17; **moyen de locomotion** means of transportation; **moyen de transport** means of transportation 17

moyen(ne) medium; mediocre; middle-sized; mid-level

le **Moyen Âge** Middle Ages 16

muet(te) mute

multiples : de multiples many; a variety of

se **multiplier** to multiply

le **mur** wall 1

la **muraille** wall; **la Grande Muraille** Great Wall

mural(e) mural

musclé(e) muscular 4

la **musculation** bodybuilding 4

le **musée** museum 3

musical(e) musical; **la comédie musicale** musical

le(la) **musicien(ne)** musician

la **musique** music 6

musqué : le rat musqué muskrat

musulman(e) Moslem 6; **un(e) musulman(e)** Moslem (*person*) 6

N

nager to swim 21

la **naissance** birth

*naître to be born 9

la **nappe** tablecloth 6

la **natation** swimming 4

la **nation** nation

national(e) national 3; **la route nationale** national highway

la **nationalité** nationality 3

la **nature** nature; **nature morte** still life; *adj* plain

naturel(le) natural 19

naturellement naturally 16

la **nausée** nausea 13; **avoir des nausées** to feel nauseous 13

le **navet** bad film 23

navré(e) very sorry 17

ne (*see Index*); **ne ... aucun(e)** not any, not a single 23; **ne ... jamais** never 12; **ne ... ni ... ni** neither . . . nor 23; **ne ... pas** not 1; **ne ... pas du tout** not at all 12; **ne ... personne** nobody 10; **ne ... plus** no longer, not anymore 12; **ne ... point** not at all; **ne ... que** only 23; **ne ... rien** nothing 10; **ne** explétif 25

né(e) born 9

nécessaire necessary 11

la **nécessité** necessity

nécessiter to necessitate, require

négatif(ive) negative 17; **au négatif** in the negative

la **négation** negation

négativement negatively 17

négliger (**de** + *inf*) to neglect (to + *inf*) 14

la **neige** snow

neiger to snow 4

n'est-ce pas ? (*see Index*) isn't it so? 5

net : le prix net price with service charge included

nettoyer to clean 7

nerveux(euse) nervous

neuf (neuve) brand-new 22

le **neurologue** neurologist 15

la **Neuvième** third grade

le **neveu** (*pl* neveux) nephew 24

le **nez** nose 23

ni ... ni neither . . . nor 23; **ni de** nor 11; **Ni moi non plus.** Neither do I. 23

niçois(e) Nice-style; **la salade niçoise** vegetable and tuna salad

la **nicotine** nicotine

la **nièce** niece

nier to deny 20

le **Niger** Niger

n'importe où anywhere; **n'importe quel(le)** + *nom* any + *noun* 23; **n'importe qui** anyone; **n'importe quoi** anything

le **niveau** level 14; **au niveau de** on/at the level of 14

Noël *m* Christmas 3

noir(e) black 11; dark

le **nom** name 3; **À quel nom ?** What is the name? 14; **au nom de** in the name of; **le nom de jeune fille** maiden name

le **nombre** number

nombreux(euse) numerous 10; **la famille nombreuse** large family

nommé(e) appointed

nommer to name; to appoint

non no; not 1; **non plus** neither 14; **Ah non !** Oh, no! 1; **mais non** oh, no 2

le **nord** north; **du Nord** North; **nord-est** northeast; **nord-ouest** northwest

normal(e) normal 20

la **Norvège** Norway

un(e) **Norvégien(ne)** Norwegian (*person*)

la **notation** notation

la **note** bill 14; grade 15; note; mark; **prendre des notes** to take notes

notre (nos) our 4

le(la) **nôtre** ours 22

Notre-Dame Notre Dame cathedral

se **nourrir** to eat

nous we 1; us 4, 9; to us 10; *disjunctive* (*see Index*); **nous-mêmes** ourselves

nouveau (nouvel, nouvelle) new 5; **de nouveau** again

le **Nouveau-Brunswick** New Brunswick

le **Nouveau-Monde** New World

le **Nouvel An** New Year's Day 3

la **nouvelle** piece of news; *pl* news

la **Nouvelle-Angleterre** New England

la **Nouvelle-Écosse** Nova Scotia

la **Nouvelle-France** New France

la **Nouvelle-Orléans** New Orleans 10

Nouvelles Frontières *f* a French charter company 12

novembre *m* November 3

le **nu** nude (*painting*)

le **nuage** cloud 4

la **nuit** night 12; **la boîte de nuit** nightclub 10; **passer une nuit blanche** to spend a sleepless night 14

nul(le) worthless

le **numéro** number 2; issue 25; **avoir le bon numéro** to have the right number (*telephone*); **avoir le mauvais numéro** to have the wrong number (*telephone*) 21

numéroté(e) numbered

O

obéir (à) to obey 4

un **obélisque** obelisk 16

un **objet** object 11; **objet d'art** objet d'art, artifact 11; **objet**
direct direct object; **objet indirect** indirect object

obligatoire mandatory, compulsory

obligé(e) (de) obligated; obliged (to) 20

obliger to oblige

*obtenir** to obtain 24

une **occasion** opportunity; **à l'occasion de** on the occasion of; **d'occasion** used, secondhand 22

occidental(e) Western

occupé(e) occupied, busy; taken 15

occuper to occupy; to take up space 16; **s'occuper** to stay busy; **s'occuper de** to take care of

un **océan** ocean; **l'océan Atlantique** Atlantic Ocean

octobre *m* October 3

une **odeur** smell

un **œil** (*pl* yeux) eye 13

une **œuvre** work; **œuvre d'art** work of art

un **œuf** egg 7; **œuf dur (en gelée)** hard-boiled egg (in aspic)

un **office** office

officiel(le) official

officiellement officially

une **offre** offer; **offre d'emploi** job offer

*offrir** to offer 14

Oh ! Oh! 6; **Oh ! là ! là !** Oh my! 2

l'**Ohio** *m* Ohio; Ohio River

une **oie** goose; **le confit d'oie** preserved goose meat

un **oignon** onion

olympique olympic; **les Jeux Olympiques** Olympic Games

une **omelette** omelette 6; **omelette au fromage** cheese omelette; **omelette nature** plain omelette

un **omnibus** slow train; commuter train

on one, they, we 7; **on doit** we must 14

un **oncle** uncle 8

un **ongle** nail 13

la **Onzième** first grade

l'**ONU** *f* = l'**Organisation des Nations Unies** United Nations

l'**OPEP** *f* = **Organisation des Pays Exportateurs de Pétrole** OPEC

l'**Opéra** *m* Opera 17; opera house

une **opinion** opinion 23

opposition : par opposition à in contrast to

optimiste optimistic 8

une **option** option

l'**or** *m* gold

oral(e) oral 8
oralement orally
une **orange** orange 7; *adj invar* orange-colored
une **orangeade** orange-flavored carbonated drink
un **Orangina** *orange-flavored soda* 7
un **orchestre** orchestra; first floor (*theater*); **l'Orchestre National de France** French National Orchestra; **le fauteuil d'orchestre** first-floor theater seat
ordinaire ordinary
ordinal(e) ordinal
un **ordinateur** computer 7
une **ordonnance** prescription
l'**ordre** *m* order 15; **l'ordre du jour** agenda
une **oreille** ear 6
un **oreiller** pillow
une **organisation** organization
une **organisatrice** organizer 24
organisé(e) organized; **le voyage organisé** tour
organiser to organize
l'**orgueil** *m* pride
oriental(e) Eastern
s'orienter to get one's bearings
un **original** original; *adj* **original(e)** original 11; **la version originale** original version
une **origine** origin
l'**O.R.T.F.** *m* = l'**Office de Radiodiffusion-Télévision Française** *state radio and TV office*
l'**orthographe** *f* spelling
oser to dare
un **otage** hostage
l'**OTU** *f* = l'**Organisation du Tourisme Universitaire** *university tourism organization* 24
ou or 1; **ou bien** or else 15; **ou ... ou** either . . . or
où (*see Index*) where 1; when; **d'où** from where 7; hence; **Où en sommes-nous ?** Where are we? 17
oublier to forget 4; **oublier (de** + *inf*) to forget (to + *inf*) 11
l'**ouest** *m* west 7; **le sud-ouest** southwest; **de l'Ouest** West
Ouf ! Whew! 23
oui yes 1; **Ah oui ?** Really? 3; **Ah oui alors !** That's for sure! 23
outre beyond, besides, other than 24
ouvert(e) open 2
(elle) ouvre (she) opens 3
Ouvrez Open 13
un(e) **ouvrier(ière)** worker 18; **ou-**

vrier(ière) (non) spécialisé(e) (un)skilled worker
une **ouvreuse** usher
*****ouvrir** to open 14; **s'ouvrir** to open up 19
oval(e) oval

P

la **page** page 2
le **pain** bread 6; **pain au chocolat** round roll with chocolate inside; **pain complet** whole wheat bread
la **paire** pair 14
la **paix** peace 24; **en paix** in peace 24
le **palais** palace; large public building 16; palate; **Palais de Justice** courthouse 16
le **pamplemousse** grapefruit
le **panaché** half beer, half **limonade**
le **Panama** Panama
la **pancarte** sign; billboard 19
le **panier** basket 19
la **panne** breakdown; **en panne** out of order; **être en panne** to be broken, not to be working 2
le **panneau** panel, board 19
le **panorama** panorama
le **pantalon** pants 11
le **papa** dad 8
la **papeterie** stationery shop 7
le **papetier** stationery shop owner
le **papier** paper 6; **papier à lettre** stationery
Pâques *pl f* Easter
le **paquet** package 6
par by 2; through; per; **par contre** on the other hand; **par semaine** per week 4; **par terre** on the ground 17
le **paragraphe** paragraph
*****paraître** to seem, appear 23; **il paraît que...** it seems that . . . 23
le **parapluie** umbrella 4
le **paratonnerre** lightning rod
le **paravent** screen
le **parc** park
parce que because 3
*****parcourir** to travel; to cover (*distance*)
parcouru(e) traveled; covered (*distance*)
pardon excuse me 1
pardonner to forgive
les **parents** *pl m* parents 3; relatives
la **parenté** kinship
la **parenthèse** parenthesis
paresseux(euse) lazy 8
*****parfaire** to perfect
parfait(e) perfect 12

parfaitement perfectly 13
parfois sometimes
le **parfum** perfume 14; flavor
parisien(ne) Parisian 8; **un(e) Parisien(ne)** Parisian (*person*)
le **parking** parking lot 9
parler to speak, talk 2
parmi among
la **parodie** parody
la **parole** (spoken) word; utterance, remark; **prendre la parole** to speak, take the floor
le **parrain** godfather
part : à part separate(d) 10; **d'autre part** on the other hand; **de ta (votre) part** of you, on your part 12 (20)
partager to share 18
le(la) **partenaire** partner 4
le **parti** party
le **participe** participle; **participe passé** past participle; **participe présent** present participle
participer (à) to participate (in) 20
particulier(ière) private 17; special; **en particulier** in particular; **un hôtel particulier** residence
particulièrement especially
la **partie** part; portion 9; game 14
*****partir** to leave; to depart 8; **partir en vacances** to leave (go) on a vacation 8; **à partir de** beginning with; based on
partitif(ive) partitive
partout everywhere 10
*****parvenir** à to succeed in
pas : ne ... pas not 1; **pas cher (chère)** inexpensive 9; **pas de** not any 2; **pas de ... ni de** no . . . nor 11; **(ne ...) pas du tout** not at all 12; **pas encore** not yet 18; **pas mal** not bad 1; **pas mal de** + *nom* quite a few + *noun* 11
passable acceptable, passable 23
le **passage** passage
le **passager** passenger 19
le(la) **passant(e)** passer-by 9
passé(e) past
le **passé** past 10; **passé antérieur** past anterior; **passé composé** present perfect; **passé défini, passé simple** past definite
le **passeport** passport 22
passer to spend 8; to give; to pass; to show (*movie*); **passer le temps à** + *inf* to spend

time + *pres part* 8; **passer dans** to go into 24; **passer la douane** to go through customs; **passer le péage** to go through the gate; **passer sur** to go onto; **passer un examen** to take an exam 17; **passer une nuit blanche** to spend a sleepless night 14; **se passer** to happen 10; **se passer bien** to go all right

le **passe-temps** pastime; **passe-temps préféré** hobby

passif(ive) passive

passionnant(e) exciting 9

se **passionner (pour)** to be very interested (in)

le **pâté** pâté 7; **pâté de campagne** country-style (liver) pâté 7

patiemment patiently 17

la **patience** patience 14

patient(e) patient 11

le **patin** skate; **patin (à glace)** (ice) skate 4; **patin à roulettes** roller skate; **faire du patin (à glace)** to ice-skate, go ice-skating 4

le **patinage** skating 8

patiner to skate 17

la **pâtisserie** pastry; pastry shop

le(la) **patron(ne)** boss 23

pauvre poor 8; unfortunate (*before noun*); poor, destitute (*after noun*); **les pauvres** poor souls 10

payant(e) pay; not for free 14

payé(e) paid

payer to pay (for) 3; **payer en espèces** to pay cash

le **pays** country 12; region

le **paysage** landscape

les **Pays-Bas** *pl m* The Netherlands 12

en **PCV** collect (call) 21

le **péage** toll; **une autoroute à péage** toll highway; **passer le péage** to go through the gate

la **peau** skin

la **pêche** fishing 25

***peindre** to paint 24

la **peine** pain; trouble 19; **à peine** hardly 13; **à peine ... que** hardly . . . when; **valoir la peine** to be worth the trouble 19; **cela ne vaut pas la peine** it's not worth the trouble 19

le **peintre** painter 11

la **peinture** paint; painting

Pékin Beijing

le **pèlerinage** pilgrimage

la **pelouse** lawn

pendant during, for 9; **pendant combien de temps** how long; **pendant que** while 10

la **penderie** closet

la **pendule** clock 2

pénétrant(e) penetrating, incisive

pénible painful; difficult 17

la **pénicilline** penicillin 14

la **Pennsylvanie** Pennsylvania

penser (à) to think (of) 7; **penser de** to have an opinion about 23; **nous pensons que oui** we think so; **nous pensons que non** we don't think so

le **penseur** thinker

le(la) **pensionnaire** boarder

la **Pentecôte** Pentecost

le **Pepsi(-Cola)** Pepsi-Cola

***percevoir** to collect

perdre to lose 17; to waste

perdu(e) wasted 25; lost

le **père** father 3; **le père Noël** Santa Claus 11; **croire au père Noël** to believe in Santa Claus; to be naïve 11

perfectionné(e) perfected

la **période** epoch, period

le **Périphérique** *freeway around Paris*

périr to perish

***permettre de** + *inf* to allow to + *inf* 15; **permettre à qqn de** + *inf* to allow somebody to + *inf*

le **permis de conduire** driver's license 22

le **Perrier** *carbonated mineral water;* **Perrier-menthe** *mixture of mint syrup and Perrier*

le **personnage** character

la **personnalité** personality

la **personne** person 3; **personne d'autre** nobody else 23; **ne ... personne** nobody 10

le **personnel** personnel 24

personnel(le) personal 23

la **perspective** perspective; panorama, view 16

la **perte** loss

peser to weigh 11; **faire peser** to have weighed

pessimiste pessimistic 8

les **PET = Postes et Télécommunications** Post Office; **le bureau des PET** Post Office

petit(e) small 6; **les petites annonces** *f* want ads 24; **un petit blanc** a glass of white wine; **le petit coin** rest room; **le petit déjeuner** breakfast 6; **la petite-fille** granddaughter; **le petit-fils** grandson; **le petit four** bite-sized cookie; **le petit gâteau** cookie 3; **les petits-enfants** *pl m* grandchildren 11; **les petits pois** *pl m* peas 6

le **pétrole** petroleum 16

peu little, few 14; **peu de** few, little 7; **à peu près** approximately 16; **un peu** a little 2; **un peu de** a little 7; **un tout petit peu** just a little bit 15; **très peu** very little

la **peur** fear 14; **avoir peur (de)** to be afraid (of) 14; **de peur que** for fear that, lest 25

peut-être perhaps 12

la **pharmacie** pharmacy 7

le(la) **pharmacien(ne)** pharmacist

la **philosophie** philosophy

phonétique phonetic

le **phonographe** phonograph

le(la) **photographe** photographer 8

la **photo(graphie)** photo(graph) 8; photography; **un appareil photo** camera

la **phrase** sentence 3

le **physique** physique

la **physique** physics 8; *adj* physical

le **piano** piano

le **pichet** pitcher

la **pièce** room 10; play 23; **pièce (de monnaie)** coin 18 (21); **pièce de théâtre** play

le **pied** foot 6; **à pied** on foot 6; **le coup de pied** kick

le **piéton** pedestrian 16

la **pile** battery

le **pilote** pilot 11

pipi : faire pipi to pee 19

le **pique-nique** picnic 7; **faire un pique-nique** to have a picnic 7

pire worse

pis worse; worst; **Tant pis !** So much the worse! Too bad!

la **piscine** swimming pool 2

la **pitié** pity, mercy

pittoresque picturesque 9

la **pizza** pizza 6

le **placard** closet 22; cupboard

la **place** seat 6; square 9; room, space; place; ticket; **à la place de** instead of 14; **place assise** seat; **Place Charles de Gaulle** Charles de Gaulle Square; **Place des Vosges** *square in the Marais;* **Place Vendôme** Vendôme Square

placé(e) placed

placer to place

le **plafond** ceiling 5

la **plage** beach 15

***plaindre** to pity 24; **se plaindre (de)** to complain (about) 24

la **plaine** plain, flat country

***plaire (à)** to please; to appeal 23; **s'il te plaît** please 3; **s'il vous plaît** please 1

plaisanter to joke 6
la **plaisanterie** joke
le **plaisir** pleasure 4; **avec plaisir** with pleasure, gladly 4; **faire plaisir à** to please 18
le **plan** map 9; plan
le **planétarium** planetarium
la **planète** planet
planter to plant
la **plaque** plate; plaque
le **plastique** plastic 7
le **plat** dish; platter 17; **plat cuisiné** prepared food; **plat de résistance** main dish
le **plateau** tray; **plateau de fromages** assorted cheeses
la **plate-forme** platform
le **plâtre** (plaster) cast; **dans le plâtre** in a cast
plein(e) (de) full (of) 18; **à plein temps** full-time; **de plein air** outdoor (sport); **en plein air** outdoors
il **pleut** it's raining 4
*pleuvoir to rain 4; **pleuvoir à verse** to be pouring (rain) 20
plier to fold
la **pluie** rain
la **plupart (de)** most (of) 25; **pour la plupart** for the most part
le **pluriel** plural; adj plural
plus more 4; **plus de** more than 9; **plus fort** louder 21; **plus loin** farther, beyond 10; **plus que** more than 14; **plus ... que** more . . . than 11; **plus tard** later 4; **de plus** moreover, besides; **de plus en plus** more and more; **en plus** besides, in addition 22; **le plus** the most 11; **ne ... plus** no longer, not anymore 12; **Moi non plus.** Neither do I. (Me, neither.) 12
plusieurs several 8
le **plus-que-parfait** pluperfect, past perfect
plutôt rather
la **poche** pocket 6; **le couteau de poche** camping knife 22; **le livre de poche** paperback
poché(e) poached
la **poêle** frying pan 25
la **poêlée de cèpes** pan-fried wild mushrooms
le **poème** poem
le **poète** poet
le **poids** weight
le **point** point; period; **point d'exclamation** exclamation point; **point d'interrogation** question mark; **point de repère** reference point; **points de suspension** suspension points;

point fort forte; **point-virgule** semicolon; **à point** medium (meat); **deux points** colon; **mettre au point** to perfect; **ne ... point** not at all
Le Point weekly magazine
la **pointe** tip; **les heures de pointe** rush hour 17
la **pointure** size (shoes, gloves)
la **poire** pear
le **poisson** fish 8; **poisson rouge** goldfish 8
le **poivre** pepper 6
poli(e) polite 17
la **police** police 4; **l'agent de police** policeman 4
policier(ière) (of) police; **le film policier** detective movie
poliment politely 17
la **polio** polio
la **politesse** politeness 11
la **politique** politics; adj political
la **Pologne** Poland
un(e) **Polonais(e)** Pole; **le polonais** Polish language 25
la **pomme** apple 4; **pomme d'Adam** Adam's apple; **pomme de terre** potato; **pommes (de terre) frites** french fries; **la tarte aux pommes** apple pie
la **ponctualité** punctuality
la **ponctuation** punctuation
ponctuel(le) punctual
le **pont** bridge; **faire le pont** to take a long weekend
la **population** population 9
le **porc** pork 6
le **port** port, harbor
le **portail** portal
la **porte** door 1; gate; **porte-fenêtre** French door; **mettre à la porte** to fire, dismiss; **la Porte de Clignancourt** section of northwest Paris
le **porte-clés** key ring
le **portefeuille** wallet 8
le **porte-parole** official voice; spokesperson
porter to wear (clothes); to carry 11
le **porteur** porter
la **portière** door (subway, car) 17
le **porto** port wine 6
le **portrait** portrait 24
un(e) **Portugais(e)** Portuguese (person) 12; **le portugais** Portuguese language 12
le **Portugal** Portugal 12
poser to put; to pose 3; **poser sa candidature à** to apply for (a position); **poser une question** to ask a question 3
la **position** position, attitude
posséder to possess, own

possessif(ive) possessive
la **possession** possession; **prendre possession de** to take hold of
la **possibilité** possibility
possible possible 8
postal(e) postal 21; **le code postal** zip code
le **poste** position 24; **poste (de télévision)** (television) set 22
la **poste** post office 21; **poste restante** general delivery; **le bureau de poste** post office 7; **le timbre-poste** postage stamp; **mettre à la poste** to mail
posté(e) posted 22
le **poster** poster
postposé(e) postposed, placed behind
le **pot** fam drink 20; cocktail party; **prendre un pot** to have a drink 20
le **potage** soup
le **potager** vegetable garden
le **pouce** inch
le **poulet** chicken 23
le **poumon** lung
la **poupée** doll 16; **la maison de poupée** dollhouse
pour for 2; **pour + inf** in order to + inf 7; **pour moi** for me 3; **pour toi** for you 3; **pour que** so that 20
le **pourboire** tip
pourquoi why 2; **Pourquoi pas ?** Why not? 5
la **poursuite** chase 23; **poursuite en voiture** car chase
pourtant however
pourvu que provided that 20
pousser to push 19; to grow 25; **faire pousser qqch** to grow something
la **poutre** beam 16
*pouvoir to be able, can 5
la **prairie** prairie
la **pratique** practice; adj practical; **les travaux pratiques** lab work
préavis : avec préavis person to person 21
précédé(e) preceded
précédent(e) preceding; previous
précéder to precede
précieux(euse) precious 8
précis(e) precise
précisément precisely
*prédire to predict, foretell
préféré(e) favorite 3; **le passe-temps préféré** hobby
la **préférence** preference
préférer to prefer 7
premier(ière) first 3; **en pre-**

mier at first, first; **la Première** next-to-the-last year in lycée; **le(la) premier(ière) à** + *inf* the first to + *inf*; **la tête la première** headfirst

*prendre to take; to eat; to drink 6; **prendre des notes** to take notes; **prendre la parole** to speak, take the floor; **prendre possession de** to take hold of; **prendre rendez-vous** to make an appointment 24; **prendre sa retraite** to retire; **prendre un pot** to have a drink 20

le **prénom** first name

la **préparation** preparation

préparé(e) prepared

préparer to prepare 6; **préparer un examen** to study for an exam 17; **se préparer (à)** to get ready (for)

préposé(e) preposed, placed before

la **préposition** preposition 21

prépositionnel(le) prepositional

près de near, next to 5; nearly; **près d'ici** nearby; **tout près (de)** very close (to) 16; **à peu près** approximately 16

la **présence** presence

le **présent** present

la **présentation** introduction; presentation 15; **présentation de mode** fashion show

présenter (à) to introduce 5; **se présenter** to arrive

la **préservation** preservation

le **président** president 5

presque almost 2

la **presse** press; **la maison de la presse** newspaper and magazine store

pressé(e) squeezed 5; in a hurry 15; **un citron pressé** fresh lemonade 5

la **(bière) pression** beer on tap 5

le **prestige** prestige

prestigieux(euse) prestigious

prêt(e) ready 6; **prêt(e) à** + *inf* ready to + *inf*

prêter to lend 10

*prévenir to warn

*prévoir to foresee

prier (de) to ask, beg 22; **Je vous en prie.** You're welcome. 9

la **prière** prayer 22; **Prière de ne pas** + *inf* Please do not + *verb* 22; **prière de faire suivre** please forward

primaire primary

les **primeurs** *pl f* spring vegetables;

le **marchand de primeurs** vegetable merchant 17

le **prince** prince

la **princesse** princess

principal(e) principal, main

la **principale** main clause

le **printemps** spring 3; **au printemps** in the spring

le **Printemps** Printemps department store 11

la **priorité** right of way

la **prise** storming, taking 9

la **prison** jail, prison 16; **en prison** in jail

privé(e) private 10

le **privilège** privilege

privilégié(e) privileged

le **prix** price 14; prize; **prix de revient** cost price; **prix net** service charge included; **Prix Nobel** Nobel Prize winner; **à prix fixe** set-priced

probable probable 19

probablement probably 5

le **problème** problem 8

prochain(e) next 4

proche near 17

la **production** production

*produire to produce; to give 16

le **produit** product; **produits surgelés** frozen foods; **produits d'hygiène** health products

proférer to proffer

le **professeur** professor 1

la **profession** profession 3

professionnel(le) professional

profond(e) deep

le **programme** program 10

le **progrès** progress 17; **faire des progrès** to make progress 17

le **projet** project 16

projeter to project, show (*movie*)

la **promenade** walk 17; **faire une promenade** to take a walk 17

promener qqn to take somebody around; **se promener** to take a walk 13

la **promesse** promise 6

*promettre to promise 17; **promettre de** + *inf* to promise to + *inf*; **promettre à qqn de** + *inf* to promise somebody to + *inf*

promotionnel(le) special-priced

le **pronom** pronoun

prononcer to pronounce

la **prononciation** pronunciation

proposer to propose 16

la **proposition** clause

propre clean; proper (*after a noun*) 22

le(la) **propriétaire** owner

protester to protest

provençal(e) from Provence; **à la provençale** cooked with olive oil, garlic, tomatoes, and herbs

le **proverbe** proverb 6

la **province** province; **en province** out of Paris

provisoire temporary

prudemment prudently, carefully 16

le **Pschitt** *fruit-flavored soda* 19

le(la) **psychiatre** psychiatrist

la **psychologie** psychology

psychologique psychological

le(la) **psychologue** psychologist

public (publique) public 20

le **public** public 23; **le grand public** the general public 23

la **publication** publication

publicitaire : les annonces publicitaires ads

la **publicité** advertisement; advertising; commercials

publié(e) published 25

publier to publish

la **puce** flea 22; **le Marché aux Puces** Flea market 22

puis then 3

puisque since 20

la **puissance** power

le **pull(-over)** sweater 11; **pull à col roulé** turtleneck sweater 11

le **punch** punch

puriste purist

la **pyramide** pyramid

les **Pyrénées** *pl f* Pyrenees mountains

Q

qqch = quelque chose something

qqn = quelqu'un someone

le **quai** platform (*railroad*); pier 18; street (*along a river or a canal*)

qualifié(e) qualified

la **qualité** quality

quand when 4; **quand même** anyway 11

la **quantité** quantity 12; **des quantités de** lots of

le **quart** quarter 2; $\frac{1}{4}$ liter; **un quart d'heure** a quarter of an hour 13

le **quartier** neighborhood, area in a city 9; **le Quartier Latin** Latin Quarter 16; **le vieux quartier** Old Town 9

que (*see Index*) what 6; **(Ce) que... !** how . . . ! 11

Québec Quebec City 9

le **Québec** Quebec province 9
un(e) **Québécois(e)** Québécois, Quebecer (*person from Quebec*); *adj* **québécois(e)** of Quebec 9

quel(le) what, which 3; **quelle... ?** what . . . ? 2; **Quel(le)... !** What (a) . . . ! 9; **Quel âge avez-vous ?** How old are you? 5; **Quel dommage !** What a pity! 15; **Quelle heure est-il ?** What time is it? 2; **quelle sorte de** what kind of 7; **Quel temps fait-il ?** What's the weather like? 4; **à quelle heure** (at) what time 2; **à quelle page** on what page 2; **À quel nom ?** What is the name? 14
quelque(s) a, some, a few 7; **à quelques minutes** a few minutes (away) 9
quelque chose something 5; **quelque chose de** + *adj* something + *adj* 10
quelquefois sometimes
quelques-un(e)s *pron* some, a few 15, 25
quelqu'un someone 6; **quelqu'un de** + *adj* someone + *adj* 10
qu'est-ce que what 2; **Qu'est-ce que c'est ?** What is it?, What are they? 1; **Qu'est-ce que c'est que... ?** What is . . . ? 17; **Qu'est-ce qu'elle a ?** What's the matter with her? 13
qu'est-ce qui what 6; **Qu'est-ce qui ne va pas ?** What's wrong? 13
la **question** question 3; **être question de** to be a matter of; **poser une question** to ask a question 3
la **queue** line 10; **faire la queue** to stand in line 22
qui (*see Index*) who 1; whom 6, 16, 18; who; what 16; **qui d'autre** who else 18; **Qui est à l'appareil ?** Who is speaking? 21; **Qui est-ce ?** Who is it?, Who are they? 1; **qui est-ce que** who(m) 6; **qui est-ce qui** who
la **quiche** quiche 15
la **quinzaine** about fifteen 15
quitter to leave 2; **Ne quittez pas.** Hold the line, Just a minute. 21
quoi what 7; **Il n'y a pas de quoi.** You're welcome. 9
le **quotidien** daily newspaper 12; *adj* **quotidien(ne)** daily

R

raccrocher to hang up (*telephone receiver*)
la **racine** stem; root
raconter to tell 12
la **radio** radio 16
la **radiodiffusion** broadcasting
rafraîchissant(e) refreshing 5
le **rafraîchissement** refreshment; cold drinks
le **raisin** grapes
la **raison** reason 15; **avoir raison** to be right 5
raisonnable reasonable 22
le **rallye** rallye; **le Rallye de Monte-Carlo** car race in Monte-Carlo
ramasser to pick up 17
le **rang** row; rank
ranger to put in order 11; **ranger ses affaires** to put away one's belongings 11
râpé(e) grated; **les carottes râpées** grated carrots with vinaigrette
rapide fast
rapidement fast, quickly 17
la **rapidité** speed
le **rappel** reminder
rappeler to call back; to remind
rapporter to bring back 18
la **raquette** racket 4
rarement rarely 4
le **rat** rat; **rat musqué** muskrat
la **RATP** = **Régie Autonome des Transports Parisiens** Paris Transit Authority
rattacher to join
le **rayon** department (*in a large store*) 22
*****réadmettre** to readmit
le **réalisateur** film producer 23
réaliste realistic
récemment recently 18
récent(e) recent
le **récepteur** receiver
la **réception** front desk 14; formal party 15
le(la) **réceptionniste** front desk clerk (*hotel*) 14
la **recette** recipe 6
*****recevoir** to receive; to entertain (*at home*) 15
le **réchaud de camping** camping stove
la **recherche** search; research
rechercher to look for
la **réciprocité** reciprocity
le **récit** story
la **réclame** advertisement, ad 22
récolter to harvest
recommandé(e) registered 21; **en recommandé** by registered mail 21

recommander to recommend 16
*****reconnaître** to recognize
la **reconstitution** reconstruction; replica
se **recoucher** to go back to bed
recours : avoir recours à to resort to; to have recourse to
recréer to recreate
*****récrire** to rewrite
le **reçu** receipt
récupérer to pick up
se **recycler** to retrain
le **rédacteur** editor
la **rediffusion** rerun (*on TV*)
*****redire** to say again
redites say again 3
la **réduction** discount
*****réduire** to reduce
réduit(e) reduced; smaller than life; **le modèle réduit** scale model; **le tarif réduit** reduced rate
réel(le) real
la **réémission** rerun
*****refaire** to do again
la **référence** reference
réfléchi(e) reflexive
refléter to reflect
la **réforme** reform 25
le **réfrigérateur** refrigerator
le **refus** refusal 20
refuser de + *inf* to refuse to + *inf* 15
regarder to look at; to watch 2
regardez look (at) 1
la **régie** bureau, office
le **régime** diet; **être au régime** to be on a diet; **le magasin de régime** health-food store
la **région** region 4
régional(e) regional 8
la **règle** rule 15
regretter (**de** + *inf*) to be sorry, regret (to + *inf*) 20
régulier(ière) regular; **le collaborateur régulier** columnist
régulièrement regularly
la **reine** queen
relatif(ive) relative
relativement relatively
se **relever** to get up again
relié(e) linked
le **relief** topography
relier to link, put together
religieux(euse) religious 16
la **religion** religion
remarquable remarkable 19
remarquablement remarkably
remarquer to notice 10
le **remboursement** reimbursement
rembourser to reimburse
le **remerciement** thanks
remercier (de) to thank (for)

9; **remercier qqn de** + *inf* to thank somebody for + *pres part*

*remettre to postpone; to put back on

remonter to go back up

le **rempart** rampart 9

remplacé(e) replaced

remplacer to replace 8

remplir to fill out 4

remporter une victoire to carry off a victory

rémunéré(e) paid

la **Renault** Renault (*car*)

la **rencontre** meeting, encounter

rencontrer to meet 10; **se rencontrer** to meet

le **rendez-vous** appointment, date 2; **avoir rendez-vous** to have an appointment, a date 2; **donner rendez-vous à qqn** to make an arrangement to meet someone 20; **prendre rendez-vous** to make an appointment 24

rendre to give back 18; **rendre** + *adj* to make + *adj*; **rendre service à qqn** to do somebody a favor 18; **rendre visite à qqn** to visit someone 12; **se rendre (à)** to go/come 13

le **renom** fame

renommé(e) famous

renseigné(e) informed

le **renseignement** information 9

se renseigner to inform oneself

la **rentrée** return to school (*after summer vacation*) 3

rentrer to go (come) home 2; **rentrer dans qqch** to hit something

renverser to spill 17

la **réorganisation** reorganization

réparer to repair 25

*repartir to leave again 9

le **repas** meal 6

*repeindre to repaint

on repeint they repaint 16

répéter to repeat 5

la **réplique** reply, response

le **répondeur** answering machine

répondre (à) to answer 5

la **réponse** answer 5

le **reportage** documentary; reporting; **faire un reportage** to report

le **reporter** reporter

se reposer to rest 13

la **représentation** performance 25

représenté(e) represented

représenter to represent

la **reproduction** reproduction

*reproduire to reproduce

la **république** republic; **la République Centrafricaine** Central African Republic

la **réputation** reputation

le **R.E.R.** = **Réseau Express Régional** *express subway lines*

le **réseau** network

la **réservation** reservation 14

réserver to reserve 14

la **résidence** dormitory 2; residence; home

résidentiel(le) residential

résistance : le plat de résistance main course

résister to resist

la **résolution** resolution

*résoudre to solve

la **respiration** breathing

respiratoire respiratory

responsable (de) responsible (for)

ressembler (à) to resemble 8

*ressortir to go out again 9

les **ressources** *f* resources

restante : la poste restante general delivery

le **restaurant** restaurant 1; **restaurant libre-service** self-service restaurant; **restaurant universitaire** student cafeteria; **la voiture-restaurant** dining car 19

restauré(e) restored

restaurer to restore 16

le **reste** rest, remainder 23

rester to stay, remain 6

le **resto-U** university cafeteria 5

le **résultat** result 25

le **résumé** summary

retard : en retard late 1; **être en retard** to be late 1

*retenir to retain

le **retour** return

retourner to go back, return 6

le **retrait** withdrawal

la **retraite** retirement; **être à la retraite** to be retired; **prendre sa retraite** to retire

rétréci(e) shrunk; narrow(ed)

retrouver to find again; to meet (*by arrangement*)

la **réunion** meeting; gathering, get-together

se réunir to meet, get together 23

réussi(e) successful 15

réussir (à + *inf*) to succeed (in + *pres part*) 19; **réussir à un examen** to pass an exam 11

le **rêve** dream

le **réveil** alarm clock 13

réveillé(e) awake

le **réveille-matin** alarm clock 14

réveiller qqn to wake somebody up; **se réveiller** to wake up 13

réveille-toi wake up 10

le **réveillon** *Christmas dinner after Midnight Mass*

révéler to reveal

*revenir to come back 9; **revenir à soi-même** to come back to one's senses

la **révision** review 17

*revoir to see again 15; **au revoir** good-bye 1

la **révolution** revolution 16

révolutionner to revolutionize

la **revue** magazine, journal 12

le **rez-de-chaussée** ground floor 10

le **Rhône** Rhône River

le **rhumatisme** rheumatism

le **rhume** cold

riche rich 8

le **rideau** curtain 14

ridicule ridiculous

ridiculiser to ridicule

rien nothing; **De rien.** You're welcome. 1; **ne ... rien** nothing 10

rigoureux(euse) rigorous

*rire (de) to laugh (at) 23; **faire rire qqn** to make somebody laugh

la **rive** bank; shore

la **rivière** river 7

le **riz** rice

la **robe** dress 11; **robe de mariée** wedding gown

le **robinet** faucet 14

le **roi** king 16

le **rôle** role, part

romain(e) Roman 25

les **Romains** *m* the Romans

le **roman** novel 12

roman(e) Romanesque 16

romano-byzantin(e) Romanesque-Byzantine 16

rond : tourner en rond to go around and around

le **Roquefort** Roquefort cheese

le **rosbif** roast beef 7

rose pink 5

la **rose** rose 13

le **rosé** rosé (*wine*)

le **rôti** roast

rôti(e) roasted

rôtir to roast 25; **faire rôtir qqch** to roast something

la **roue** wheel

rouge red 8; **le poisson rouge** goldfish 8

rougir to blush

roulant : un escalier roulant escalator; **un tapis roulant** moving ramp

roulé(e) rolled 11; **un pull à col roulé** turtleneck sweater 11

rouler to drive; to run (*car*) 11; to roll up

roulette : le patin à roulettes roller skate
la **route** road 21; **route nationale** national highway; **en route** on the way 21
routier(ière) of the road; **la gare routière** bus station 18
roux (rousse) red (*hair*)
royal(e) royal 9
le **ruban adhésif** adhesive tape
la **rubrique** rubric, column, section
la **rue** street 3
la **ruelle** narrow street 22
un(e) **Russe** Russian (*person*); **le russe** Russian language 12
la **Russie** Russia
le **rythme** rhythm
rythmique rhythmic(al)

S

sa his, her, its
le **sable** sand 16
le **sac** purse 11; **sac à dos** backpack 11; **sac de couchage** sleeping bag
sacré(e) sacred 16; **le Sacré-Cœur** *basilica in Paris* 16
saignant(e) rare (*meat*)
la **Saint(e) ...** Saint . . .'s Day 3
Saint-Germain-des-Prés *neighborhood on left bank*
le **Saint-Laurent** St. Lawrence River 9
la **Saint-Sylvestre** New Year's Eve 12
la **Saint-Valentin** Valentine's Day 3
la **saison** season 4
la **salade** salad 6; **salade composée** mixed salad; **salade niçoise** Nice-style salad (*vegetables and tuna*)
le **salaire** salary
le **salami** salami
sale dirty 11
salé(e) salted; **le biscuit salé** cracker
la **salle (de classe)** (class)room 1; **salle à manger** dining room 6; **salle de bains** bathroom 10; **salle d'expériences** experiment room; **salle de séjour** living room 10
le **salon** drawing room 17
Salut ! Hi! 1
la **salutation** greeting
le **samedi** Saturday 3
la **sandale** sandal
le **sandwich** sandwich 7; **sandwich jambon-beurre** ham in buttered French bread
la **sangria** sangria
sans without 23; **Sans**

blague ? No kidding? 23; **sans doute** probably
la **santé** health 8; **à votre santé** to your health 15
le **santon** tiny clay figure
la **sardine** sardine
satisfait(e) (de) satisfied (with) 18
saturé(e) saturated
la **sauce** sauce, dressing 20; gravy
la **saucisse** sausage 6
le **saucisson** hard sausage; salami
sauf except
le **saumon** salmon; **saumon fumé** smoked salmon
sauvegardé(e) saved
sauver to save
le(la) **savant(e)** scientist 11
savoir to know (how to) 8
le **savon** soap 14
le **scandale** scandal
la **scène** scene 4; **le metteur en scène** film director 23
le **Schweppes** *tonic water*
la **science** science; **science-fiction** science fiction 23; **les sciences humaines** humanities; **les sciences naturelles** natural science; **les sciences physiques** physical sciences; **les sciences politiques** political science
le(la) **scientifique** scientist; researcher
scolaire academic; for school
le **scotch** Scotch whiskey; Scotch tape
la **sculpture** sculpture 16
se oneself 13
la **séance** show (*at the movies*)
sec (sèche) dry; harsh; hard
sécher un cours to cut a class
second(e) second
secondaire secondary 12
la **seconde** second 2
la **Seconde** fifth year in lycée 8
le(la) **secrétaire** secretary; **secrétaire de direction** administrative secretary
le **secrétariat** secretary's office
la **section** section
la **Seine** Seine River 16
le **séjour** stay; living room 10; **la salle de séjour** living room 10
séjourner to stay, spend some time
le **sel** salt 6
selon according to; **selon le cas** as the case may be
la **semaine** week 2; **par semaine** per week 4
sembler to seem
le **semestre** semester 10

la **semi-consonne** semiconsonant
le **sénateur** senator 8
le **Sénégal** Senegal
sénégalais(e) Senegalese
le **sens** direction; sense; meaning
la **sensation** sensation; **à sensation** sensational
sensationnel(le) sensational 11
la **sensibilité** sensitivity
sentimental(e) sentimental
sentir to feel; to smell; to smell like 13; **se sentir** to feel (*sick, tired*) 13; **se sentir chez soi** to feel at home
séparé(e) separated
séparément separately
séparer (de) to separate (from)
septembre *m* September 3
la **série** series 23
sérieusement seriously 17
sérieux(euse) serious 17
serré(e) squeezed 23
la **serrurerie** keys and locks
le **serveur** waiter
la **serveuse** waitress 6
le **service** service; service charge 6; **À votre service.** You're welcome. 9; **rendre service (à)** to do a favor (for) 18
la **serviette** napkin 6; **serviette de bain** bath towel 14
servir to serve 13; **servir à + *inf*** to be used for, useful for + *pres part* 21; **se servir de** to use 21
ses his, her, its 4
seul(e) alone 19; only; lonely; **(pas) un seul** (not) a single; **le(la) seul(e) à + *inf*** the only one + *inf*
seulement only 2; **non seulement ... mais aussi** not only . . . but also
sévère severe, strict; rigid
le **short** shorts
si (*see Index*) if 2; yes 3; so 11; **si besoin est** if need be; **si ... que** so (such) . . . that 11; **si + *imparfait*** suppose one + *verb*; **Moi, si.** I do. 12
le **SIDA** AIDS 23
le **siècle** century 10
le **siège** seat 24
le sien (la sienne) his, hers, its 22
la **sieste** nap 5; **faire la sieste** to take a nap
siffler to whistle; to boo
signalé(e) signaled
signaler to signal
le **signe** sign; signal
la **signification** meaning
signifier to mean; to signify 19

la **silhouette** silhouette, outline 16

s'll te plaît please 3

s'll vous plaît please 1

simple simple 6; mere (before a noun)

simplement simply 20; **tout simplement** quite simply

la **sincérité** sincerity

le **singulier** singular; adj singular

le **site** site 16

SITU computer terminal for users of Paris transit system

la **situation** situation 11

situé(e) placed, located 16

le **ski** ski 4; **ski nautique** waterskiing; **faire du ski** to ski, go skiing 4

la **SNCF = Société Nationale des Chemins de Fer** National Railroad Corporation

sociable sociable

social(e) social 8

la **société** society; company

la **sociologie** sociology

la **sœur** sister 3

soi(-même) oneself

la **soie** silk

la **soif** thirst 5; **avoir soif** to be thirsty 5; **mourir de soif** to die of thirst 20

soigné(e) polished

soigner to take care of, look after; to cure; to treat 25; **se soigner** to get cured, treated

le **soin** care; **les soins** treatment

le **soir** evening 2; **ce soir** tonight; **hier soir** last night, yesterday evening 9; **le soir** in the evening

la **soirée** evening; evening party 12

le **sol** ground; **une hôtesse au sol** ground hostess

solaire solar

le **soldat** soldier 16

la **solde** sale 11; **en solde** on sale 11

la **sole** sole; **sole meunière** sole sauteed in butter and parsley

le **soleil** sun 4; **il fait du soleil** it is sunny 4; **le bain de soleil** sunbath; **prendre un bain de soleil** to sunbathe

solide strong 22

la **solitude** absence, lack

la **solution** solution

la **Somalie** Somalia

sombre dark 10

la **somme** sum

le **sommeil** sleep 5; **avoir sommeil** to be sleepy 5

le **sommet** top; summit

somptueux(euse) magnificent

son his, her, its

sonner to ring 4

la **sonnette** doorbell 5

sophistiqué(e) sophisticated

le **sorbet** sherbet

la **Sorbonne** Sorbonne

la **sorte** kind 7; **quelle sorte de** what kind of 7; **toutes sortes de** all kinds of

la **sortie** exit 19; going out 23; **sortie de secours** emergency exit 19

*__sortir__ to go (come) out 8; **sortir de table** to leave the table

soudain suddenly 19

souffleter to slap

*__souffrir (de)__ to suffer (from) 14

souhaiter to wish 20

souligné(e) underlined

*__soumettre__ to submit

la **soupe** soup 6; **soupe aux légumes** vegetable soup

le **souper** late dinner

la **source** spring; origin; **source thermale** hot spring

le **sourd** deaf man 17

souriant(e) smiling

(ils) sourient (they) smile 11

le **sourire** smile

*__sourire (à)__ to smile (at) 23

la **souris** mouse 8

sous under 1

le **sous-sol** basement 10

le **sous-titre** subtitle

les **sous-vêtements** pl m underwear 14

*__soutenir__ to support

souterrain(e) underground 16

le **souvenir** souvenir 9

*__se souvenir (de)__ to remember

souvent often 4

spacieux(euse) spacious

spécial(e) special

spécialement especially

spécialisé(e) specialized

se spécialiser (en) to specialize (in); to major (in) 24

le(la) **spécialiste** specialist 25

la **spécialité** specialty 9

spécifiquement specifically

le **spectacle** show 20; **à grand spectacle** spectacular; **les sports-spectacle** spectator sports

spectaculaire spectacular, dramatic

le **spectateur** spectator; pl audience

splendide magnificent

le **sport** sport; sports 3; **faire du sport** to practice sports 4; **les sports d'hiver** winter sports; **les sports-spectacle** spectator sports

le **sportif** athlete; sports-minded person; adj **sportif(ive)** athletic, fond of sports 8

le **spot** spotlight

la **stabilité** stability

stable stable

le **stade** stadium 2

le **stand** booth 22

la **station** station 17; **station de métro** subway station; **station thermale** spa

le **stationnement** parking 17

stationner to park 17

la **statue** statue 18

la **statuette** statuette 18

le **steak** steak 6; **steak-frites** steak and french fries

le(la) **sténo-dactylo** secretary

la **stéréo** stereo 3

le **steward** steward

le **stock** stockroom

le **store vénitien** Venetian blind 14

la **structure** structure

le **studio** studio

le **style** style 16; **style de vie** lifestyle

le **stylo** pen 1

subitement suddenly 17

le **subjonctif** subjunctive (mood)

subordonné(e) subordinate; dependent

la **subordonnée** dependent clause

le **succès** success

succulent(e) delicious

le **sucre** sugar 6

sucré(e) sweet 5

le **sud** south; **le sud-ouest** southwest 7; **du Sud** South

la **Suède** Sweden

suédois(e) Swedish 23; **un(e) Suédois(e)** Swede

suffisant(e) sufficient, adequate

il suffit de + inf it suffices; it is enough + inf

le **suffixe** ending

suggérer à qqn de + inf to suggest to somebody + inf 22

la **suggestion** suggestion

la **Suisse** Switzerland 12

les **Suisses** the Swiss (people) 12; adj **suisse** Swiss 7; **les Trois-Suisses** large mail order house in France

suivant(e) following 3; next

suite : tout de suite right away 5

suivi(e) de followed by 21

*__suivre__ to follow; to take (a course) 24

le **sujet** subject 23; topic; **au sujet de** concerning

super invar great

superficiel(le) superficial 23

supérieur(e) superior; upper 9; high-level; **le lac Supérieur** Lake Superior

le **supérieur** superior

le **superlatif** superlative
le **supermarché** supermarket 7
supersonique supersonic
le **supplément** additional charge
supplémentaire extra; supplementary
supposer to suppose 10
sur on, on top of 1; out of; **sur laquelle** about/concerning which 11
sûr(e) (de) sure (of/to do) 14; **bien sûr** of course 6
la **surboum** party
surchauffé(e) overheated
sûrement certainly, surely 3
la **surface** surface 16; **en surface** on the street level 16; **grande surface** large supermarket and discount store
surgelé(e) frozen
les **surgelés** *m* frozen foods
sur-le-champ right away
la **surpatte** party
surpris(e) (de) surprised (to do) 20
la **surprise** surprise 18; **la surprise-party** party 15
surtout especially, above all 23
surveillé(e) watched 10
surveiller to watch
sus : en sus extra 20
suspendu(e) delayed
le **suspens** suspense; **à suspens** (of) suspense
la **syllabation** syllabification
le **symbole** symbol 16
sympa *invar* nice, likeable 8
la **sympathie** attraction; friendship
sympathique nice, likeable 5
le **symptôme** symptom 12
le **syndicat d'initiative** tourist information office
le **syndrome** syndrome
le **synonyme** synonym
le **système** system

T

ta your 3
le **tabac** tobacco 7; **le bureau de tabac** tobacco shop 7
la **table** table 1; **table de nuit** nightstand 4; **table des matières** table of contents 25; **À table!** Let's sit down (at the table)! 6
le **tableau** blackboard 1; picture; chart
le **TAC = Train-Autos-Couchettes** *train carrying passengers and their cars*
taché(e) stained
la **taille** size; height
le **tailleur** suit (*for women*) 11
*se **taire*** to be silent, become silent 23

le **talent** talent
Tanger Tangiers
tant so much, so many; **tant de** so much, so many 19; **Tant pis!** So much the worse!, Too bad!; **en tant que** as, in the capacity of 24
la **tante** aunt 8
taper (à la machine) to type 24
le **tapis** rug, carpet 17; **tapis roulant** moving ramp
la **tapisserie** tapestry
tard late 4; **plus tard** later 4; **il se fait tard** it is getting late
le **tarif** price, rate 21; **tarif réduit** reduced rate; **tarif unique** single fare; **à mi-tarif** half price
tartare : le steak tartare *chopped raw steak with condiments*
la **tarte** open-faced pie; **tarte aux pommes** apple pie
la **tartine** slice of bread
le **tas** heap 17; **un (des) tas de** lots of 17
la **tasse** cup 7
le **taudis** slum
le **taux** rate
la **taxe** tax; **hors taxe** duty-free
le **taxi** taxi 5
le **Tchad** Chad
te you 9; to you 10
la **technique** technique
le **TEE = Trans-Europ-Express** *first-class international train*
un(e) **tel(le) + nom** such a + *noun*; **tel(le) que** such as
la **télé** TV 4
la **télécarte** telephone card
la **télécommunication** telecommunication
le **télégramme** telegram
le **télégraphe** telegraph
télégraphique : expédier un mandat télégraphique to wire money
le **téléphone** telephone 4
téléphoner (à) to telephone 4
téléphonique (of) telephone
le(la) **téléspectateur(trice)** TV viewer
télévisé(e) televised
la **télévision** television 3; **le poste de télévision** television set 22
le **témoin** witness
la **température** temperature; fever 13
le **temps** weather 4; time 6; verb tense; **à mi-temps** part-time; **à plein temps** full-time; **à temps** on time; **à temps complet** full-time; **de temps en temps** from time to time

4; **en même temps** at the same time 22; **il est temps** it is time 19; **Quel temps fait-il?** What's the weather like? 4; **tout le temps** all the time 4
Tenez! Here!; Look here!; Listen!
*__tenir__ to hold; to keep 6; to manage (*a store*); **tenir au courant** to keep informed
le **tennis** tennis 3; **le court (de tennis)** tennis court
tentant(e) tempting, attractive
le **terme** term
la **terminaison** ending
la **(classe) Terminale** last year in lycée
terminé(e) finished 1
terminer to finish 9
le **terminus** end of the line
le **terrain de golf** golf course
la **terrasse** sidewalk (*of a café*) 5
la **terre** earth; land; ground 17; **par terre** on the ground 17; **terre ferme** terra firma, solid ground; **la pomme de terre** potato
terrible terrible
le **territoire** territory
le **terrorisme** terrorism
tes your 3
le **test** test 12
la **tête** head 13; **la tête la première** headfirst; **avoir mal à la tête** to have a headache 13
le **Texas** Texas 12
le **texte** text 24; **le traitement de texte** word-processing 24
TF1 TV channel 1
le **TGV = Train à Grande Vitesse** *high-speed train*
le **thé** tea 5
le **théâtre** theater 16
thérapeutique therapeutic
thermal(e) thermal; **la source thermale** hot spring; **la station thermale** spa
le **ticket** ticket
le **tien (la tienne)** yours 22
Tiens! Well! 1; Here!
le **timbre** stamp 11; **timbre-poste** (*pl* timbres-poste) postage stamp
timide timid, shy 18
le **tire-bouchon** corkscrew 22
tirer to pull 19; to draw
le **tiret** dash
le **tiroir** drawer 14
le **titre** title; small headline
le **toast** toast 7
le **Togo** Togo
toi you 1; disjunctive (*see Index*) 12; **toi-même** yourself

la **toile** canvas
la **toilette : faire sa toilette** to wash and dress; **le cabinet de toilette** bathroom (without toilet)
les **toilettes** *pl f* rest room 19
le **toit** roof 10
la **tomate** tomato 6
le **tombeau** tomb, grave 16
tomber to fall; **tomber malade** to get sick; **laisser tomber** to drop 17
ton your 3
la **tonalité** dial tone 21
la **tondeuse** lawn mower
tonique stressed, disjunctive
la **tonne** ton 16
le **tonnerre** thunder 24
tort : avoir tort to be wrong 5
le **torticolis** stiff neck
tortueux(euse) tortuous, twisted
tôt early 13
total(e) total
la **touche** (computer) key
toucher to touch 5; **toucher un chèque** to cash a check
toujours always; still 4
le **tour** walk 20; turn 22; tour; **tour de cou** neck size; **Tour de France** *bicycle race*; **faire un petit tour** to take a short walk 20
la **tour** tower 16; **la Tour d'Argent** *famous restaurant in Paris*; **la Tour Eiffel** Eiffel Tower 16; **la Tour Maine-Montparnasse** *tallest building in Europe*
le **tourisme** tourism 9
le(la) **touriste** tourist 5
touristique (of) tourist, tourism 16
le **tourne-disque** record player
la **tournée** round; **faire sa tournée** to make one's rounds
tourner to turn 9; to shoot (*film*); **tourner en rond** to go around and around
le **tournoi** tournament
la **Toussaint** All Saints' Day 3
tout *pron* everything, all 10; **pas du tout** not at all 12
tout (toute, tous, toutes) (see *Index*) all, whole, entire, every 14; **tous les deux** both; **tous les jours** every day 4; **tous les sept ans** every seven years 16; **tout l'après-midi** all afternoon 10; **tout le monde** everybody 6; **tout le temps** all the time 4; **toute la journée** all day; **toutes sortes de** all kinds of
tout quite 5; **À tout à l'heure.**

See you soon. 1; **tout à fait** quite 15; **tout d'abord** first of all; **tout de suite** right away 5; **tout droit** straight ahead 9; **tout près (de)** very close (to) 16; **en tout** in all, altogether 21; **en tout cas** in any case 24; **un tout petit peu** just a little bit 15
tracer to trace
traditionnel(le) traditional
le(la) **traducteur(trice)** translator
la **traduction** translation 14
*traduire** to translate 16
la **tragédie** tragedy
le **train** train 3; **en train** by train; **être en train de** + *inf* to be in the process of + *pres part* 22; **par le train** by train
le **trait d'union** hyphen
le **traité** treaty
le **traitement de texte** word-processing 24
traiter (de) to deal with
le **trajet** trip, ride
la **tranche** slice 7
tranquille quiet, peaceful
tranquillement peacefully 10
*transmettre** to transmit
la **transmission** transmission
transparent(e) transparent; thin 14
le **transport** transportation 17; **le moyen de transport** means of transportation
transporter to carry
le **travail** (*pl* **travaux**) work, labor 3; **Au travail !** Let's get to work! 12; **une agence de travail** employment agency 24; **la Fête du Travail** May Day (Labor Day); **les travaux pratiques** lab work
travailler to work; to study 2
travailleur(euse) hardworking, industrious 8
travers : à travers across; through
traverser to cross 6
le **tréma** diaeresis
trembler to shake, tremble
la **trentaine** about thirty
très very 1
le **trésor** treasury; treasure 9; **le Bon du Trésor** Treasury Bond
le **trimestre** quarter, trimester 10
triomphal(e) triumphant 16
le **triomphe** triumph 16
triste sad 17
les **Trois-Suisses** *large mail-order house in France*
se tromper (de) to be mistaken (about) 23

trop too, too much 5; **trop de** too much, too many 7
tropical(e) tropical
le **trouble** ailment
trouver to find 2; to think; **se trouver** to be located 15; to find oneself; **trouver mieux** to find something better; **comment trouves-tu... ?** how do you like. . . ?
le **truc** gizmo 22
la **truffe** truffle
la **truite** trout; **truite meunière** *trout sauteed in butter and parsley*
le **T-shirt** T-shirt
tu you 1; **Tu viens ?** Are you coming? 4
tuer to kill; **tuer le temps** to kill time
la **Tunisie** Tunisia
le **tuyau** pipe 16
la **TVA = Taxe à la Valeur Ajoutée** value-added tax
le **type** type 25
typique typical
typiquement typically

U

ultramoderne ultramodern 9
un (une, des) a, an, some 1
l'**unanimité : à l'unanimité** unanimously
l'**un(e) l'autre (les un(e)s les autres)** each other, one another 24
un **uniforme** uniform
une **union** union
l'**Union Soviétique** *f* Soviet Union
unique unique; only; single
uniquement exclusively
une **unité** unity; unit; **unité de valeur** credit hour
universitaire (of) university 2
une **université** university 2
un peu a little 2; **un peu de** a little 7
urbain(e) urban
l'**URSS** *f* USSR
un **usage** use; **d'usage** customary, usual
une **usine** factory
UTA = Union des Transports Aériens *French domestic airline*
utile useful 8
utilisé(e) used
utiliser to use 4

V

les **vacances** *pl f* vacation 3; **partir en vacances** to leave (go) on a vacation 8

le **vaccin** vaccine
le **valet de chambre** valet
la **valeur** value; **une unité de valeur** credit hour
valider to validate
la **valise** suitcase 14
la **vallée** valley 7
*valoir to be worth 19; **valoir la peine** to be worth the trouble 19; **cela ne vaut pas la peine** it's not worth the trouble 19; **il vaut mieux** + *inf* it is better + *inf* 19; **il vaudrait mieux** + *inf* it would be better + *inf* 19; **Mieux vaut tard que jamais.** Better late than never.
la **vanille** vanilla
la **vapeur** steam; **les pommes vapeur** *f* steamed potatoes
varié(e) varied
varier to vary
la **variété** variety 20; **spectacle de variétés** variety show
Varsovie Warsaw
le **vase** vase 18
vaste vast 16
Vas-y. Go ahead. 14
le **veau** veal 7
la **vedette (de cinéma)** (movie) star
le(la) **végétarien(ne)** vegetarian 6
le **véhicule** vehicle
la **veille** day before; eve
la **veine** luck 12; **avoir de la veine** to be lucky 12
le **vélo** bike
le **vélomoteur** moped 2
la **vendange** grape harvest
le(la) **vendeur(euse)** salesman (saleslady) 2
vendre to sell 5
le **vendredi** Friday 3
*venir to come 6; **venir de** + *inf* to have just + *past part* 6
le **vent** wind 4; **il fait du vent** it's windy 4
la **vente** sale
la **ventilation** ventilation 16
le **ventre** stomach, belly 13
Vénus *f* Venus
la **véranda** porch 10
le **verbe** verb 6
verdoyant(e) verdant
vérifier to check 14
véritable true, real
la **vérité** truth 9
le **vermicelle** vermicelli
le **vernissage** private viewing before an exhibition
le **verre** glass 6
vers around; about 10; toward
le **vers** verse

verse : pleuvoir à verse to be pouring (rain) 20
la **version originale** original version
le **verso** other side of a page
vert(e) green 6
la **vertu** virtue
la **veste** jacket 11
le **vestiaire** cloakroom
le **vestibule** vestibule
le **veston** jacket (of a man's suit)
les **vêtements** *pl m* clothes, clothing 11
le(la) **vétérinaire** veterinarian
veuf (veuve) widowed
la **viande** meat 6
le **vice-président** vice president 12
le **vice-roi** viceroy 16
le **Vichy** *Vichy mineral water*
la **victime** victim
la **victoire** victory 16; **la Fête de la Victoire** Armistice Day; **Victoire de Samothrace** Winged Victory; **remporter une victoire** to carry off a victory
vide empty 16
la **vie** life; living 15; **gagner sa vie** to earn a living
Vieilles Maisons Françaises magazine for preservation of old buildings 25
Vienne Vienna 12
tu viens ? are you coming? 4
vietnamien(ne) Vietnamese 23
vieux (vieil, vieille) old 6; **la vieille ville** Old Town; **le Vieux Carré** French Quarter (*in New Orleans*) 10; **le vieux quartier** Old Town 9
le **village** village 7
la **ville** city, town 6; **le centre ville** downtown; **en ville** downtown 10; **un Hôtel de ville** City Hall; **la vieille ville** Old Town
le **vin** wine 7
la **vinaigrette** vinegar and oil salad dressing
la **vingtaine** about twenty
violent(e) violent
violet(te) violet; purple
le **violon solo** head violinist
le **virage** turn, bend
la **Virginie de l'Ouest** West Virginia
la **virgule** comma
le **visage** face
visible visible
la **visite** visit 12; **visite guidée**, **visite accompagnée** guided tour; **rendre visite à** to visit (*people*) 12
visiter to visit 7
vite quickly 2

la **vitesse** speed
la **vitrine** window (*of a shop*)
le **Vittel** *Vittel mineral water*
la **vivacité** intensity, liveliness
vivant(e) alive; living; **les langues vivantes** *f* modern languages
Vive(nt) + *nom* ! Long live + *noun!* 24
*vivre to live 24
le **vocabulaire** vocabulary
le **vœu** (*pl* **vœux**) wish; **Meilleurs vœux** Best wishes
Vogue fashion magazine 25
voici here is, here are 2
la **voie** way 16; track (*railroad*); **voie ferrée** railroad
voilà there is, there are 1
*voir to see 11
le(la) **voisin(e)** neighbor 3; *adj* neighboring 12
la **voiture** car 4; **voiture-bar** snack car (*on a train*); **voiture-couchettes** economy sleeping car 19; **voiture-lits** sleeping car; **voiture-restaurant** dining car 19; **en voiture** by car; **aller** + *destination* + **en voiture** to drive to somewhere 16
la **voix** voice 13; **à haute voix** out loud 19
le **vol** flight 12; theft
la **volaille** fowl
le **volant** steering wheel 9
le **volcan** volcano
volcanique volcanic
voler to steal 16
le **volet** shutter 14
le **voleur** thief 16; **Au voleur !** Thief! 16
la **volonté** will
volontiers gladly 15
votre (vos) your 3
le(la) **vôtre** yours 22; **À la bonne vôtre.** To your health.
*vouloir to want, wish 5; **vouloir bien** to be willing 15; **vouloir dire** to mean 5
vous you 1, 9; to you 10; *disjunctive* (*see Index*) 12; **vous-même(s)** yourself (yourselves)
le **voyage** trip 9; **une agence de voyage** travel agency 24; **un chèque de voyage** traveler's check 22; **faire bon voyage** to have a good trip 9
voyager to travel 7
le **voyageur** traveler 12
le **voyant** panel (*computer*)
la **voyelle** vowel
Voyons... Let's see . . . 6
vrai(e) true 3
vraiment really 12

vu(e) seen
la **vue** view, sight 16

W

le **wagon** wagon; coach; **wagon-bar** snack car (*on a train*); **wagon-lits** sleeping car; **wagon-restaurant** dining car
les **w.-c.** *pl m* toilet 14
le **week-end** weekend 5

le **western** western (*film*)
le **whisky** whiskey
le **Wisconsin** Wisconsin (*state*) 12; Wisconsin River

Y

y (*see Index*) there 15; **y compris** including
le **yachting** sailing (yachting)
les **yeux** *m* eyes (*sing* **œil**) 12

un(e) **Yougoslave** Yugoslavian (*person*)
la **Yougoslavie** Yugoslavia

Z

le **Zaïre** Zaire
le **zéro** zero
la **zone** zone
la **zoologie** zoology
Zut (alors) ! Shucks! 2

PHOTO CREDITS

Chapter 1 Page 15: Peter Menzel/Stock, Boston. Page 17: Will McIntyre/Photo Researchers. Page 23: Richard Kalvar/Magnum Photos. Page 25: Stuart Cohen/Comstock. Page 26: Owen Franken. Page 30: Stuart Cohen/Comstock.

Chapter 2 Page 36: Owen Franken. Page 37: Stuart Cohen/Comstock. Page 41: Mark Antman/The Image Works. Page 42: Peter Menzel. Page 48: M. P. Hagiwara. Page 49: (left) Peter Menzel, (center) Stuart Cohen/Comstock, (right) The Bettmann Archive. Pages 50 and 51: Peter Menzel/Stock, Boston. Page 52: Ulrike Welsch/Photo Researchers.

Chapter 3 Page 58: Mike Mazzaschi/Stock, Boston. Page 59: De Sazo/Rapho/Photo Researchers. Page 65: Mark Antman/The Image Works. Page 69: Peter Menzel/Stock, Boston. Page 72: M. P. Hagiwara. Page 73: Mark Antman/The Image Works. Page 74: The Bettmann Archive. Page 77: Mike Mazzaschi/Stock, Boston.

Chapter 4 Page 81: Rancinan/Sygma. Pages 82 and 84: Stuart Cohen/Comstock. Page 86: (left) Mark Antman/The Image Works, (right) Peter Menzel. Page 89: Peter Menzel. Page 93: Beryl Goldberg. Page 95: Mark Antman/The Image Works. Page 96: Beryl Goldberg.

Chapter 5 Page 102: Judy Poe/Photo Researchers. Page 106: Owen Franken/Stock, Boston. Page 108: Mark Antman/The Image Works. Page 112: (left) Mark Antman/The Image Works, (center) Owen Franken/Stock, Boston, (right) Peter Menzel. Page 114: (top) Stuart Cohen/Comstock, (bottom) Beryl Goldberg.

Chapter 6 Pages 121 and 122: Peter Menzel. Page 124: Beryl Goldberg. Page 130: Peter Menzel. Page 134: Monique Manceau/Photo Researchers. Page 137: Helena Kolda/Photo Researchers.

Chapter 7 Page 143: (left) Judy Poe/Photo Researchers, (right) Stuart Cohen/Comstock. Page 144: Owen Franken. Page 147: Peter Menzel. Page 150: Helena Kolda/Photo Researchers. Page 152: Stuart Cohen/Comstock. Page 153: Monique Manceau/Photo Researchers. Page 155: Rémi Berli/Rapho/Photo Researchers. Page 157: (left) Peter Menzel, (right) Mark Antman/The Image Works. Page 159: (top and center right) Stuart Cohen/Comstock, (center left) Adecio de Andrade/Magnum Photos, (bottom left) Peter Arnold, (bottom right) Mike Mazzaschi/Stock, Boston. Page 160: Stuart Cohen/Comstock.

Chapter 8 Page 166: (left) Peter Menzel, (right) Owen Franken/Stock, Boston. Page 167: Mark Antman/The Image Works. Page 171: (left) Peter Menzel, (right) Stuart Cohen/Comstock. Pages 177 and 178: Peter Menzel/Stock, Boston. Page 182: Stuart Cohen/Comstock.

Chapter 9 Page 187: Mark Antman/The Image Works. Page 188: (left) Owen Franken, (right) Stuart Cohen/Comstock. Page 192: Stuart Cohen/Comstock. Page 196: J. P. Laffont/Sygma. Page 202: (left) Stuart Cohen/Comstock, (right) Mike Mazzaschi/Stock, Boston. Page 204: Stuart Cohen/Comstock. Page 206: The Bettmann Archive.

Chapter 10 Page 211: (left) Richard Kalvar/Magnum Photos, (right) Helena Kolda/Photo Researchers. Pages 216 and 220: Owen Franken/Stock, Boston. Page 223: Owen Franken. Pages 225 and 229: M. P. Hagiwara.

Chapter 11 Page 234: (top) Peter Menzel/Stock, Boston, (bottom) Mark Antman/The Image Works. Page 236: Jean-Euck Pasquier/B. D. Picture Service. Page 242: (left) Monique Manceau/Photo Researchers, (right) Mark Antman/The Image Works. Page 247: HALARY/Photo Researchers. Page 249: Stuart Cohen/Comstock. Page 251: (left) Mark Antman/The Image Works, (right) Peter Menzel. Page 253: Abbas/Magnum Photos.

Chapter 12 Page 258: (left) Beryl Goldberg, (center) Mark Antman/The Image Works, (right) Danny Lyon/Magnum Photos. Page 260: Marc Riboud/Magnum Photos. Page 265: Stuart Cohen/Comstock. Page 267: (left) Lehmann/Peter Arnold, (right) Stuart Cohen/Comstock. Page 270: Peter Menzel/Stock, Boston. Page 272: M. P. Hagiwara. Page 273: Mark Antman/The Image Works.

Chapter 13 Page 278: Stuart Cohen/Comstock. Page 280: Mark Antman/The Image Works. Page 283: Helena Kolda/Photo Researchers. Page 286: Monique Manceau/Photo Researchers. Page 291: Stuart Cohen/Comstock. Page 293: Martine Franck/Magnum Photos.

Topical and thematic index

Numbers refer to pages in the text in which pertinent vocabulary and phrases, or discussions, are found. The *n* following a page number refers to a footnote appearing on that page. The listening comprehension and writing activities in the **Cahier d'exercices** are not included.

Grammatical index

Numbers refer to pages in the text. The *n* following a page number refers to a footnote appearing on that page. The following abbreviations are used to indicate the tenses and moods of verbs. All tenses listed in the index are in the indicative mood, unless marked as *cond.* or *subj.*

cond.	conditional	*part.*	participle
fut.	future	*p.c.*	passé composé
imp.	imperfect	*p.s.*	passé simple
ind.	indicative	*pres.*	present
inf.	infinitive	*subj.*	subjunctive

à: contraction with **le, les**, 40, 478; with **lequel, lesquels, lesquelles**, 391, 471; no contraction with **le, les**, 458; à + inf., 452–453, 458, 476; used with geographical names, 259; meaning *to, in, at*, 40, 87, 259; meaning *with*, 445

Accent marks, 149–150, 172, 492–493
  exercice de prononciation #3 (p. 2)

Active voice, 350

Adjective, *see* Demonstrative adjective; Descriptive adjective; Interrogative adjective (**quel**), Possessive adjective

Adverb: adverbs/adverbial expressions of frequency, 83; of quantity, 151–152, 168, 306–307; of past, 198; of manner, 368–369; of place/time, 395–396; formation, 368–369; position, 395–396; comparative and superlative, 370–371; *see also* Interrogative adverb

Agreement: of demonstrative adjective, 105; descriptive adjective, 27–28, 169–170; interrogative adjective, 68–69; possessive adjective, 66–67, 89–90; of past part. with preceding direct object, 194–195, 268, 304, 349; with subject, 197–198, 350–351; of demonstrative pronoun, 473; interrogative pronoun, 471; possessive pronoun, 477–478

Aller: pres., 87; p.c., 196; imp., 212; fut., 330; pres. cond., 373; pres. subj., 416; pres. part., 480; p.s., 540; *see also Appendix D*; meaning *to become*, 248*n*, 484; referring to health, 14–16, 87

Alphabet, exercice de prononciation #3 (p. 2)

Ami *vs.* **camarade** *vs.* **copain**, 113*n*

An *vs.* **année**, 497

Antecedent (of relative clause), 347, 397

Apprendre: pres., 122–123; p.c., 193; *see also Appendix D*

Après que, 516–517

Articles, *see* Definite article; Indefinite article; Partitive article
  exercice de prononciation #14 (p. 8)

Aspirate **h**, 44–45

S'asseoir: pres., p.c., fut., 419; p.s. 539; *see also Appendix D*

Aucun, aucune, 533–534

Auquel, à laquelle, auxquels, auxquelles: as a relative pronoun, 391–392; as an interrogative pronoun, 471

Aussi, used in comparison: of adjectives, 241–242; of adverbs, 370–371

Auxiliary verbs (in compound tenses): p.c. 191–192, 196–197, 287–288; past subj., 416; pluperfect, 500; fut. perfect, 516; cond. perfect, 519; passé antérieur, 540–541; pluperfect subj., 543; verbs conjugated with **avoir**, 191–193; with **être**, 196–197, 287–288; *see also Appendix C*

Avant que *vs.* **avant de**, 517

Avoir: pres., 49; p.c., 192; imp., 212; fut., 330; pres. cond., 373; imperative, 394; pres. subj., 416; pres. part., 480; p.s., 540; imp. subj., 542, *see also Appendix D*; idioms with **avoir**, 111–112, 179*n*, 270–271; **avoir besoin de**, 155–156, *see also* **Il y a**

Boire: pres., 154; p.c., 192; imp., 212; fut., 326; pres. cond., 373; pres. subj., 413; pres. part., 480; p.s., 540; *see also Appendix D*

Causative construction, 535–536

Ce (pronoun): to summarize an idea, 376, 397; as antecedent, 397–398; **c'est/ce sont**, 17, 50; **c'est ... que/qui**, 308–309; **il est** *vs.* **c'est**, 62, 239, 376; **ce que** in exclamatory sentences, 246; **ce que c'est**, 378

Ce, cet, cette, ces (demonstrative adjective), 105

Cela, ça, 104*n*, 498–499

Celui, celle, ceux, celles (demonstrative pronoun), 473–474

Chacun, chacune, chaque, 534

Chez, 95*n*, 158*n*

-ci, -là, 471–472, 473

Cognates, 69–70, 135*n*, 170, 235*n*; *see also Appendix A*

Combien (de), 45, 145, 151

Combined subject, 25, 262

Comment, 145

Le Canada

le Québec

Saint-Pierre-
et-Miquelon, D.O.M.

Les États-Unis

la Louisiane

Saint-Martin,
T.O.M.

La Guadeloupe,
D.O.M.

Haïti

La Martinique,
D.O.M.

La Guyane française,
D.O.M.

Tahiti

La France

La Co

Le Maroc

L'Algé

La Mauritanie

Le Sénégal

Le Mali

La Guinée

Le Burkina Faso

La Côte-d'Ivoire

Le Togo

Le Bénin

Le Cameroun

Le Gabo

Le Con